D0891492

GROUP THERAPY

A PRACTICAL APPROACH

By

JAMES A. JOHNSON, JR., M.D.
Assistant Professor of Psychiatry
Emory University School of Medicine
Atlanta, Georgia

The Blakiston Division
McGRAW-HILL BOOK COMPANY, INC.
New York   Toronto   London

To my own family "group"
my wife Mary Martha
my sons Jimmy, Buddy, Carsh, and Steve
my inspiration

Foreword

The author's practical approach to the dynamics of human group behavior and the simplicity of his style of writing make this volume an extremely absorbing source of tested theories for the professional as well as for the interested layman.

Group Therapy: A Practical Approach is a book that will be useful to the medical student, the resident in psychiatry, the psychiatrist, the social worker, and other professionals in the mental health field; and it is a book based on the soundest possible foundation, the author's own rich experience gained through hours of group therapy with hundreds of patients and through teaching medical students, psychiatric residents, nurses, social workers, and psychologists.

Dr. Johnson clearly defines the criteria to use in selecting patients and delineates the limitations, the advantages, and the goals of group therapy. He also traces the development of group behavior and its relation to everyday behavior in all types of groups. From the material presented it will be clear to the reader that the group dynamics learned in the therapeutic group are applicable to any group, whether it be a family or church group, or a political caucus. The extensive index will facilitate the locating of the many references to the various types of group behavior and the technical problems so frequently found in group therapy.

Careful attention is given to a much-neglected subject: group therapy training for psychiatric residents. An experience in group therapy sharpens the resident's awareness of group dynamics in other contexts, as in dealing with the patient's family, with the resident's peers, as a member of a psychiatric team, and in group relationships in general hospitals.

Chapter 7 is the heart of the book. The valuable data presented in that chapter will give the reader an opportunity to formulate his own interpretation of the data. In an unmistakably frank manner the author discusses the dynamics of each session and then, from a technical point of view, discusses what was done and what errors were made. The author is at his best when he writes about the actual therapy of a group. He speaks authoritatively: "This is how I see the problem; this is the technique I use; these are the results I get." However, the author is keenly aware that much research is still needed in the field of group therapy, and while he states his views strongly, it is not in a spirit of dogmatism. It is based on personal experience and observation.

BERNARD HOLLAND, M.D.
Professor and Chairman
Department of Psychiatry
Emory University

Preface

Twenty-five years ago *group therapy* was a little-known term. Today the professions of psychiatry, psychology, and social work are using group therapeutic methods extensively in the treatment of emotional illnesses. The growth of group therapy has not, however, been systematic. No one has ever clearly defined what group therapy is and what it should attempt. As a result, the models and techniques used range from merely supportive treatment to group psychoanalysis.

The purpose of this book is to present the theory, dynamics, and technique of one model of group therapy—a model based on the psychodynamic understanding of human group behavior. This model is not, of course, the first to employ psychodynamic methodology. An examination of the literature on group therapy reveals many theories and techniques that purport to be psychodynamic. Unfortunately, few studies explain in detail just how psychodynamic methodology may be therapeutically used in a group situation. This book proposes to do just that. The author recognizes that there are still many unanswered questions about group therapy in general and even about this model in particular, and that a great need exists for properly controlled research. However, instead of attempting to resolve all the conflicting claims or to offer a definitive analysis of group therapy—a task clearly beyond the scope of one book or study—the present work is offered merely as a primer on the subject. Professional personnel interested in group therapy can profit from the understanding of the dynamics of group relationships and their application to the model of group therapy here presented. The principles outlined in these pages may be adapted to psychology or social work studies as well as psychiatry.

The group-therapy trainee with little or no prior experience is frequently beset with anxiety in attempting therapy with a group of people. At the Department of Psychiatry of the Emory University School of Medicine, residents who received prior instruction in group therapy were more interested in starting groups themselves. In their instruction they found it useful to review a group that had been in treatment for a number of months. Individual meetings were discussed with the residents from the standpoint of dynamics and therapist's technique. Many of the recurrent problems in technique were reviewed. Approximately 20 hours of instruction were devoted to this group review. Didactic lectures were given on the dynamics of group therapy, the group therapist's technique, and the everyday details of organizing and orienting a group. In addition, the residents attended regular group supervisory conferences already in progress until their own groups were organized. Our residents unanimously felt that some prior understanding of dynamics and techniques was extremely helpful in starting group therapy. They particularly liked the format we have adopted because the discussions helped to diminish anxiety in themselves as well as in their patients.

It is hoped that this book can be of a similar service to others interested in treating patients by the group method. The author wishes to emphasize, however, that the art and skill required to be a group therapist cannot be developed from books alone. As in any of the medical specialities, training in group therapy proceeds best under the watchful eye of a professional colleague who provides adequate instruction and supervision.

Finally, a word of caution is necessary. Group therapy has its limitations and cannot be considered as a therapeutic panacea in the treatment of persons with emotional illnesses. Group therapy programs for patients with emotional illnesses should be part of an overall treatment program that is based on the patient's specific needs, such as individual therapy, group therapy, supportive therapy, family therapy, drugs, hospitalization, vocational and occupational therapies, and physical therapies. In other words, a good treatment program should consider the patient's psychological, biological, and sociocultural needs. Group therapy can play an important role in this treatment program. Adequate research studies in future years will more correctly assess its proper role among the therapies at our disposal today.

ACKNOWLEDGMENTS

Few technical books are written without assistance, and the author of this one is indebted to many people. The largest debt is owed Dr. Bernard C. Holland, Chairman and Professor of the Department of Psychiatry, Emory University School of Medicine, Atlanta, Ga. Without him this book might never have been written. Dr. Holland provided the initial encouragement and followed the writing with close attention, frequently offering advice and criticism. Others of the author's colleagues in the Department of Psychiatry were also of great assistance. Drs. Richard S. Ward and Morris Perkins reviewed the book and were particularly helpful on the subject of group anxiety (Chap. 2). Drs. McRae Temples, William Maden, Anita Adams, and Martha McAnulty also reviewed the book and made various suggestions. Other colleagues in this department, Mr. Robert A. Porter and Mr. Thomas M. Parham, Jr., both Assistant

Professors of Psychiatry (Social Work), were equally helpful. Formerly in the department and now in Boston, Mass., Dr. Susan Homans made contributions to the material on hospital ward meetings (Chap. 9), including the complete transcript of one meeting. Many of the residents, nurses, and psychiatric assistants in the department conducted or recorded group meetings and freely gave the author invaluable examples and suggestions from their own experience.

Further, the author is pleased to acknowledge the help he received beyond his own department. Drs. William Rottersman of Atlanta, Nathan Ackerman of New York City, and James Mann of Boston graciously consented to review the manuscript critically and to offer suggestions for its improvement. Mrs. Dorothy Bier and her associates of the Family Service Society, Atlanta, read portions of the book and provided valuable assistance. Dr. Irville H. MacKinnon, Superintendent of the Milledgeville State Hospital, Milledgeville, Ga., offered encouragement and practical suggestions. The author is also grateful to the publisher's consultants, Dr. Jack Ewalt, Professor of Psychiatry at Harvard and Dr. Leonard Cammer, Associate Clinical Professor, Department of Psychiatry, New York Medical College.

To Mrs. William Hale, a graduate student in the Emory University English Department, is due the major credit for editing and organizing almost all the material in the book. Others who helped in this task were Mr. James M. Wood, Jr., Miss Margaret Giddings, Mrs. Ray Antley and Miss Anne Serfling. Lastly the author gratefully acknowledges the help of his secretaries—Mrs. Beatrice Vega, Mrs. Julianne Waters, Mrs. Helen Brazee, Mrs. Louise Hanna, Mrs. Mary Miller, Miss Sarah Kelso, Mrs. Sue Jefferson and Miss Lucy Forrester—who typed the original manuscript and revisions.

JAMES A. JOHNSON, JR.

Contents

I

Introduction

The model of group therapy presented in this book recognizes that group therapy is a form of psychotherapy aimed at improving the function of the participants. Psychotherapy has many meanings. In a very broad sense psychotherapy refers to any mechanism, either scientific or nonscientific, that modifies human behavior. Its methods are based on human relationships—the relationship of one person with another, whether the approach is skilled or nonskilled. Dr. Lawrence S. Kubie expresses the meaning and role of psychotherapy from two points of view: "Thus, the term psychotherapy is used in two senses: (1) as a name for all homely common-sense aids to wise and peaceful living, i.e., nontechnical psychotherapy; and (2) as a technical term for certain specific methods of altering the neurotic process, methods which take up where the simpler remedies fail." Dr. Kubie subdivides nontechnical psychotherapy into three categories: (1) practical support (advice, counsel, and other measures of help for environmental situations), (2) emotional support (sympathy, encouragement, companionship, recreation), and (3) educational reorientation of the patient's emotions so that he becomes consciously aware of their effect on his behavior.[1]

CHARACTERISTICS OF THE MODEL

It is beyond the scope of this book to offer a clear and concise definition of psychotherapy. However, the terms *psychotherapy* and *group psychotherapy* in this book refer to specific psychological methods that are employed in group therapy to alter neurotic and psychotic illnesses. The model of group therapy presented here recognizes the limitations in altering neurotic and psychotic illnesses. Group therapy does not attempt to uncover deep-seated conflicts and problems. Group therapy is primarily a social and psychological process in which an emotional reeducational and relearning experience can occur. Group therapy is concerned with both conscious and unconscious conflicts of patients. Group therapy also employs a professional person who utilizes special skills to accomplish his goals. Thus the various group programs described in this book are designed to help relieve patients of disturbing symptoms of emotional illnesses; they employ, in Dr. Kubie's classification, both nontechnical and technical psychotherapy.

Goals

In general, the goals for people in this model of group therapy are: (1) to improve their reality testing, (2) to aid in their socialization, (3) to foster the development of psychological aptitude—that is, the awareness of the relationship of emotional reactions to anxiety and defensive patterns of behavior, and (4) to provide motivation for continued improvement in function through additional therapy on an individual or group basis. More specifically, our kind of group therapy can provide the person with new identifications, mutual support, diminished feelings of isolation, the release of impounded anger, and improved self-esteem and self-assertion. It helps modify the rigid conscience and diminishes feelings of guilt; it increases ability to abstract (to see things from several points of view rather than in one concrete manner), decreases unrealistic dependency needs, diminishes taboos, fears, and guilt associated with sexual feelings, identifies feelings and reactions to authority figures, and provides greater objectivity in social relationships. Finally, it offers an opportunity for the group members to see that their reactions and feelings in a therapeutic group are similar to their reactions and feelings in other groups and that whatever emotional reeducation and relearning they may achieve in group therapy can also be applied to their outside relationships.

Role of Anxiety

Our model of group therapy focuses on the anxiety that develops in human group behavior. The defense mechanisms that develop in various forms of behavior can be seen as efforts to defend against, prevent, or alleviate anxiety. Such anxiety occurs in all group relationships in our culture. It has its origins or explanations in the history of the individual and his family experiences as a result of the interaction between the individual and his parents, siblings, and other significant adults. The experiences in family relationships are the most intense group experiences in the history of the individual, and they are the origin of anxiety in interpersonal relationships. In other groups—social, religious, recreational, occupational, professional, and educational—the experiences of individuals are usually less intense than in the family group. Anxiety may occur, its degree being proportional to the intensity of the group experience.

The type of group therapy discussed in this book recognizes that anxiety occurs among people in group relationships as a defense and protection against the dangers of close relationships, and it exploits the emotional responses among a group of patients and a leader (group therapist). The act of bringing patients together in a group and promoting closeness between them and the therapist usually creates additional anxiety. With the development of additional anxiety, the group members' characteristic patterns of behavior become apparent. Their patterns of behavior are lifelong defenses that have been utilized as protection against the dangers of closeness. Over the period of group therapy the therapist encourages the members to discuss, examine, and identify patterns of behavior that occur during the group meetings. However, as anxiety and tensions arise among a group of people, problems that tend to promote group disorganization are created. Intellectual reasons for keeping the group together become overshadowed by emotional reactions among the members of the group. These problems include destructive and sexual acting out, hostility, silence, tardiness at meetings, absences, scapegoating, competitiveness with the group therapist, and forming of subgroups within and without the group. In this model of group therapy the dynamics of the group process identify these problems as manifestations created by group anxiety. Failure to resolve such anxiety accounts for group losses or drop-outs—a persistent problem for all group therapists. A successful resolution of group anxiety must be accomplished before effective group work can be done, but it cannot be achieved quickly. In groups of neurotic patients 25–40 meetings may be necessary, or possibly a period of 6–9 months in groups that meet once a week. Our model of group therapy, therefore, suggests that satisfactory group-therapy programs cannot be accomplished in short periods of time. In general, group-therapy programs for neurotic patients who meet on a weekly basis should be of a minimum duration of 18 months.

Opportunity for Emotional Reeducation

For adult neurotic patients, group therapy helps to bring about behavioral change by affording the members an opportunity for emotional reeducation and relearning. The structure of the group constantly brings the members face-to-face. The technique employed by the therapist decreases dependency gratifications and urges the members to be more assertive and independent. Psychological aptitude, or awareness of the relationship of emotional reactions to anxiety and defense mechanisms, gradually develops over the months of group therapy. The members are encouraged to identify and isolate the emotional defenses against anxiety that characterize their patterns of behavior. For instance, the defenses against the anxiety of closeness are continually identified during many months of group therapy. The members learn to recognize that their own hostile feelings lead them to expect hostility in others. They find that they use hostility as a defense against closeness, and that laughter, sarcasm, teasing, silence, sleep, humor, intellectualizing, and tardiness or absences from meetings are reactions against group tension and anxiety. The therapist, who symbolically represents parents and other authority figures of previous life experiences, can through the proper technique help the members to identify their emotional reactions to authority figures. Self-assertion with each other and with the therapist occurs. The release of impounded anger and the increased ability for self-assertion raises the members' self-esteem and diminishes feelings of guilt and depression.

Repeated exposure to group-reality events gives the members an opportunity to examine their faulty emotional responses to cancelled meetings, therapist's vacation, and other disappointments. Termination of the group affords an understanding of the anxieties about separation. They have the opportunity to reexperience and identify emotional reactions associated with separation. The members learn that the separation from each other brings up feelings associated with separations and losses in prior life experiences. They discover that their reactions to separation are emotional in origin. At the end of group therapy the members, having developed psychological aptitude, are aware that emotional problems are diminished in some areas of behavior and identified intellectually in other areas, but are for the most part still present. Their ability to recognize that other people also have problems increases their objectivity in interpersonal relationships. They progress from a state of magical dependency strivings to the recognition that solutions to their conflicts and problems can come only from their own efforts. A modification takes place in the overstrict, punitive conscience of the group members. Feelings, attitudes, and reactions previously associated with guilt and depression are less evident. The members also experience interest in further therapy on an individual or group basis. Improved reality testing and socialization—two important goals of group therapy—appear both within and without the group.

The model of group therapy is based on a psychodynamic understanding of human group behavior. The dynamics of the group process are centered around the group as a separate unit—a functioning structured unit within itself. A group approach to therapy is emphasized—not individual therapy in a group. The mutual analysis of problems and interactions within the group members is encouraged. The members are taught by the therapist's technique to identify their own patterns of behavior and make interpretations to each other. The therapist's responses in every facet of the group process are made on a group level.

Three Stages of Therapy

Three stages of group therapy have been recognized in this model. Although the stages are not delineated into three clear-cut periods, there is a series of events during the life of an adult group of neurotic patients which assume recurrent patterns; these events can be classified as stage I, stage II, and stage III. Stage I is the period when the therapist forms a working relationship with group members. Its length ranges from 25–

40 meetings. Stage II, which is primarily concerned with the recognition of authority hostility and the development of the group identity, may occupy 10–15 meetings. Stage III may be called the period of mutual analysis; its length consists of the remaining meetings from stage II until the termination of therapy.

Role of Group Therapist

The therapist plays an important role in group therapy. Transference and countertransference reactions become important factors in the dynamics of group therapy as the members come to identify the therapist with parental figures. Accordingly the therapist must be willing to examine his emotional impact in a group of people and be able to recognize that his own conscious and unconscious mechanisms can markedly influence the behavior of a group of people. In order to promote his self-awareness, regular discussions with a group recorder or observer and supervisory conferences with a group therapy supervisor are necessary.

Use of Group Contract

A group contract is utilized in our mode of group therapy whereby its physical structure (number of members, time and place of meetings, length of meetings, length of group therapy, loss and addition of members, therapist's role, recorder's role, attendance of members, fees, cancelled meetings, or termination of the group, etc.) is integrated into the dynamics of the group process. These events (group-reality events) enter into the dynamics of group therapy and afford members an understanding of the feelings of rejection, anger, separation anxiety, and other emotional responses to such events.

USE AND LIMITATIONS OF GROUP THERAPY

The theory and process of our model of group therapy and the techniques of the group therapist can be modified and adapted to the type of group in treatment—psychotic, neurotic, psychosomatic, adolescent groups, or other types. Patients are thoroughly evaluated and screened before being placed in a group. The goals for the patients and the technique of the therapist are then formulated on the basis of the type of patients making up the group. For example, in groups of psychotic patients the fear of close relationships induces marked anxiety. The therapist must therefore be more supportive, patient, outgoing, and understanding. He pursues group interaction very slowly. In groups of neurotic patients, anxiety associated with close relationships can be more easily tolerated than in groups of psychotic patients. The therapist can pursue group interaction at a faster pace. Similarly, the neurotic's better ego integration means that treatment goals can be more extensive. In adolescent delinquent groups the fear of close relationships creates tremendous anxiety and motivates acting-out behavior. The therapist must modify his technique to include more social structuring, shorter meetings, and other measures that lessen the anxiety level.

Moreover, in addition to its adaptability to different types of mental illness, our model of group therapy can also be applied to a variety of therapeutic and nontherapeutic group activities such as hospital ward meetings with patients, staff conferences, occupational and recreational activities, and leadership-training conferences.

Throughout this book group therapy is represented by the model described above. The theory, dynamics, and techniques of group therapy are presented. Particular attention is devoted to the group contract and the role of the therapist. One chapter discusses the special problems of silence and acting out in group therapy. An out-patient group is presented in its entirety in order to illustrate theoretical concepts and the therapist's technique in detail. A separate section reviews the special problems encountered by the therapist in groups composed entirely of psychotic patients. The final chapter is devoted to the adaptation of this model of group therapy in hospital ward meetings.

The reader will notice throughout the text humorous references made to the manifestation of close relationships, emotional closeness, and closeness of people in their everyday group relationships as well as in therapeutic group relationships. In this context of closeness, the author identifies the emotions of love, warmth, tenderness, pleasure, happiness, joy, sharing, trusting, and gaiety.

REFERENCE

1. Kubie, L. S.: *Practical and Theoretical Aspects of Psychoanalysis,* International Universities Press, Inc., New York, 1950, chap. 4.

2

The Development, Structure, and Therapeutic Use of Group Behavior

DEVELOPMENT OF GROUP BEHAVIOR

All groups have a similar structure and are based on two units: a leader and a set of people willing to be led. The success of the great empires and dynasties of world history can be ascribed to the working relationships between the leaders and their followers. The most meaningful and influential group in our culture is the family group. The leaders of this group are the parents; the followers, the children.

The role of the leader of the group and the type of effect he exerts on the group were pointed out by Freud. Freud was aware of the two separate and well-defined features of group structure when he wrote of the church and the army and the relationship of their constituents to the central authority figure or leader.[1] The leader has great influence on the feelings and reactions of the group. The violent, destructive actions of mobs demonstrate group action without a leader; impulses fly rampant, unchecked and uncontrolled. The authoritative leadership needed to hold such a group in control is lacking. Even in the present-day struggle between freedom and communism we see a similar relationship between the group and its leaders. The leaders of these different ideologies are dependent on their groups for support, guidance, and success in their endeavors.

In religious history small groups were employed as an aid for man to understand himself in his relationship with others. Trappist and Benedictine monks have followed a procedure, dictated by Saint Benedict in the year 1000, that brings them together in a group at a structured time and date (one or more times weekly). At this meeting the monks are asked to criticize themselves in order to strive for a spirit of perfection of one's own ways as well as to call attention to unrecognized traits in the other's presence. This meeting is known as the Chapter of Faults. The superior of the order acts as leader. He discusses each fault, one by one, admonishing, advising, encouraging, and supporting as the condition indicates.

Religious class societies were popular in England during the seven-

7

teenth century. In 1739 John Wesley, a member of the Church of England, felt that religious values were influenced and attained in the relationship between people as well as with the Deity. He organized small groups, called *class meetings,* composed of twelve people and a leader that met at a regular time and day each week. The purpose of the meetings was similar to the Chapter of Faults of the monks. Wesley came to America in the eighteenth century and promoted the class meetings. From his efforts emerged the Methodist Church in this country.

The cathartic effect of public disclosure of forbidden thoughts and guilty feelings, followed by acceptance in the group, has been recognized as a beneficial device for hundreds of years. Today we are aware that mentally ill people benefit greatly from sharing their feelings and responsibilities with others. These mechanisms are utilized in our present group therapeutic procedures.

Group methods were employed by Anton Mesmer of France in his hypnotic sessions during the latter part of the nineteenth century.[2] Pratt has been recognized for his group work with tubercular patients in Boston, Mass. during the early part of the twentieth century.[3,4] Collective counseling of patients with alcohol problems, stammering difficulties, and sexual disorders was popular in Europe between 1900 and 1930. Simmel made use of group methods in German hospitals during World War I with soldiers who had experienced traumatic neuroses of war.[5] A pioneer psychiatrist in group therapeutic procedures was Dr. Alfred Adler, who applied group methods in child guidance clinics.[6]

Various models of group therapy have been popular in the United States during the past twenty-five years; Moreno,[7] Klapman,[8] Frank,[9] Schilder,[10] Foulkes,[11] Mann,[12–14] Semrad,[15,16] and Slavson [17–19] have made significant contributions during this time. An upswing in the use of group methods for psychotherapy followed World War II. In state mental institutions with large patient populations and few doctors, group therapy offered a means of treating a larger number of patients despite personnel shortages.

Presently more than half the state mental institutions in this country employ group therapy and group activities in their treatment programs. The therapeutic value of group therapy and related group activities has been found to be more than merely an expedient method of providing treatment for more patients. Child guidance clinic staffs are enthusiastic proponents of group therapy and group activities. Training schools with the task of attempting rehabilitation of adolescents, as well as federal prisons, employ group techniques and find therapy groups advantageous. A wide range of neurotic problems (Chap. 4) are being treated throughout the country. These groups have variable compositions. Their members may be formed from husbands and wives, parents of patients, mothers of children with psychosomatic and other disorders, alcoholics, drug addicts, mental defectives, epileptics, elderly people, and stroke victims.

Public-health officials have found group work with expectant mothers advantageous. Professional personnel utilize this form of therapy in teaching groups to gain insight and understanding. A number of psychiatric-resident training programs include a year of group therapy with the residents as members of the group.

METHODS OF GROUP THERAPY

Frank and Powdermaker describe five general methods of group psychotherapy that are currently in practice: (1) didactic groups, (2) therapeutic social groups, (3) repressive-inspirational groups, (4) psychodrama, and (5) free-interaction groups.[20]

Didactic Groups

Didactic methods of group therapy use many methods but primarily consist of lectures by the leader to the group members. Emphasis is directed toward intellectual insight for the group members.

Therapeutic Social Groups

Therapeutic social groups are beneficial in affording identification, encouragement, acceptance, understanding, and reassurance to people with physical and emotional illnesses. Alcoholics Anonymous and Addicts Anonymous can be placed in this category. Many alcoholic clinics have group therapy programs with limited goals. For some participants the only benefit is a group to be dependent on, but they may receive enough help to abstain from alcohol and readjust their livelihoods. Clubs composed of discharged patients from psychiatric hospitals are frequently formed in large cities. In such clubs mutual support and encouragement may be helpful in their posthospital adjustment. A statewide program in Georgia to rehabilitate victims of cerebral accidents has been very successful. This is a therapeutic group activity outside the psychiatric field that utilizes group methods.

Repressive-inspirational Groups

Repressive-inspirational groups cover a wide field, but generally speaking are dependent on a strong, authoritative leader who, by providing a structured situation, evokes group feelings and group responses. Different formats, such as group singing, testimonials, and recreational or occupational programs, are employed. At times the group therapist as leader gives talks similar to the didactic method of group therapy. Repressive-inspirational groups have been very popular in state hospitals. Such types of group experiences are helpful in that patients are able to ventilate their feelings and discuss their problems with others. Many people who are mentally ill have no awareness that others have similar feelings. To be able to talk about their illnesses in a group diminishes their feelings of isolation. An important factor in this type of group therapy is the interest and enthusiasm of the group leader. His conduct in group meetings can create an atmosphere of acceptance and understanding, and indicate to the patients that someone is interested in their welfare. One might question the therapeutic value of repressive-inspirational groups alone but they can be a helpful adjunct to an overall treatment program.

Psychodrama

Moreno employed group methods in his development of psychodrama. He began his work in Europe and established an institute in New York State in 1936. Psychodrama utilizes a trained group of people on a stage to act out significant events of an individual's life. The audience was a patient or group of patients.[7]

Free-interaction Groups

Free-interaction groups also encompass a variety of forms, referred to as analytical group therapy, group analysis, and psychoanalytic group therapy. Schilder was a pioneer (1930–1940) of the free-association method of group therapy and made interpretations in group sessions along the line of psychoanalytic theory.[10] Group analysis and psychoanalytic group therapy depend mainly on the orientation of the therapist. Wolf and Schwartz are proponents of group analysis that utilizes individual sessions with each group member, group sessions with the same group therapist, and alternate sessions without the group therapist (leaderless). Interpretations are made to members of the group. The reporting of dreams is encouraged and dream material is utilized extensively in the therapy sessions. The groups are open-ended—that is, members may be added at varying times throughout the life of the group.[21]

Mann [12-14] and Semrad,[15,16] working with psychotic, neurotic, and teaching groups for the past fifteen to twenty years, have developed a model of group therapy based on a psychodynamic understanding of human group behavior—the concept that an individual develops defensive patterns of behavior to protect himself against the anxiety that is present in all groups. During group therapy the therapist's role is to exploit this anxiety therapeutically. Group dynamics are centered around the group as a whole—a functioning structured unit within itself. Mann defines group therapy as "a method of psychotherapy in which the emotional reactions of members of the group to each other and to the leader are understood as being reflections of interpersonal conflicts of the individuals comprising the group. The collection of individuals into a group provides a setting in which these conflicts are intensified and even exaggerated because of the number and variety of pressures exerted by the presence of a group of people. The leader of the group exploits the setting and the emotional reactions for the direct general benefit of the group as a whole, indirectly for the individual members of the group." Emphasis is placed on the emotional interaction and behavior within the group at the moment. Individual therapy within the group, didactic lectures, anamnestic material, historical data, and dream analysis are avoided.[14] The model of group therapy adhered to in the present work is generally based on the dynamics of the group process as described by Semrad, Mann, and associates. Full credit should be given to these men for their valuable research and development in this type of group therapy.

In view of the numerous and varied approaches, the reader may wonder whether all of these group techniques are effective and therapeutic. More research and study are needed before an adequate assessment of group techniques can be formulated. Generally speaking, however, many types of group therapy can be beneficial and therapeutic if the therapist carefully evaluates the anxiety level of the patient and the group. Groups of psychotic, neurotic, and adolescent patients as well as related groups (obese people, patients with psychosomatic disease, parents of children and adolescents with emotional disorders, husbands and wives, etc.) do not produce the same levels of anxiety. The dynamics of the group interaction are similar but the psychodynamics of the individual group members produce unique characteristics of anxiety. Such anxiety created is a key factor in the goals of treatment and has a direct bearing on the technique employed by the therapist during group therapy.

Thus, before turning our attention to a discussion of the different types of group therapy, activities, and goals, it is necessary to discuss anxiety, personality development, and the general structure of all groups. We shall observe that the effect of anxiety on group members, the technique of the therapist during group therapy, and the goals of a group therapy program are interrelated and together form the basis for the model of group therapy presented in this book.

ANXIETY

The study of anxiety is basic to dynamic psychiatry. Feelings and reactions that are associated with anxiety are part of the experience of every person. Anxiety can be a constructive force, setting in motion changes that can lead to improved adaptation and maturity. Most important for psychiatry, however, is the fact that when anxiety is not being used constructively it can have certain damaging effects on personality functioning. This phenomenon plays a major role in all mental illnesses.

There is incomplete agreement on the role of anxiety, but most psychiatrists and investigators believe that it can be understood as a normal response to the threat of danger. Henry Laughlin defines anxiety as the "apprehensive tension or uneasiness which stems from the anticipation of imminent danger, in which the source is largely unknown or unrecognized." [22] The concept of anxiety is not clearly differentiated from the concept of fear. Although *The Psychiatric Glossary* distinguishes between the two by saying that "anxiety is primarily of intrapsychic origin, in distinction to fear which is the emotional response to a consciously recognized and usually external threat or danger," [23] many other writers do not sharply differentiate the two. Sandor Rado, for example, equates fear with anxiety and speaks of fear as a response to danger.[24] For a discussion of the many factors that contribute to anxiety, the reader is referred to Laughlin's work.[22]

Origins

From the standpoint of our discussion of group therapy, the most important anxieties are those that stem from interpersonal relationships. These can be understood in terms of their occurrence in the family, the basic group of our society. The individual experiences anxiety initially in the interpersonal relationships of his family setting.

The anxiety that develops in group interaction is the key to our model of group therapy. It can be observed that a certain kind of anxiety is an almost inevitable accompaniment to group interaction. Anxiety can be seen from the start of group therapy; its level fluctuates from session to session, being high at times and low at others, but always present in some form or other. Although tending to be minimized in structured group situations, it is more pronounced when the interaction in groups is less structured. In the evolution of the group process this anxiety seems to be highest when the group members are struggling toward greater emotional closeness with each other.

In this instance a structured group situation refers to those everyday groups in our culture that have minimal emotional interaction among its members, such as a group attending a lecture. Actually, some types of group therapy have an organization similar to everyday rigidly structured groups. James Mann has called attention to the rigid design of some types of therapy groups in which the therapist, either consciously or unconsciously, utilizes a technique that minimizes the emotional stimulation among the members. In these types of group therapy the therapist and the patients are more comfortable and less anxious when the group meetings consist of didactic lectures or when preplanned subjects are discussed.[14]

Theory

It is basic to our discussion of group therapy that we understand why anxiety develops in the close relationships of people's interactions in groups. It should be recognized that the group situation is emotionally stimulating to each member of a group. As a response to the stimulation, there is a stirring into action of a level of behavior which is characterized by a high degree of spontaneity and lessened conscious control—that is, a level which we call *emotional behavior*. From the point of view of control, this level of behavior can be classified as semivoluntary. Subjectively the members experience an impulse to "let go," to act or speak with less reserve or restraint—a sense of temptation or an impelling urge to some kind of emotional behavior.

It is this spontaneity in group interaction, of course, which is the main source of pleasure in group relationships. It is also the source of anxiety. Some of the impulses that arise are acceptable; others are not. Generally, people in our culture have different degrees of comfort and discomfort in relation to the various kinds of emotional behavior that can be stimulated in groups, depending upon the history of their personal development. Some people can freely relax their behavior in some areas, while in others, they feel a need for varying degrees of control. Because these areas of behavior, once stirred into action, are under only partial or semivoluntary control, anxiety occurs when the individual is tempted to let go in an area that normally makes him uncomfortable.

In most of the everyday groups of our culture, interaction is somewhat structured. It is the function of this structuring to control the range of emotional stimulation and response of the members. In this way members can relax and engage in group behavior while impulses that are unacceptable or discomforting to them can be held in abeyance. In groups where a great deal of security from this danger is desired, behavior may be almost completely ritualized. Ritualizing eliminates surprises, and the danger of spontaneous behavior.

It is a feature of our model of group therapy that interaction in the group is deliberately kept unstructured. Free interaction among the members is encouraged so as not to shunt off any part of the full range of emotional behavior. Being unstructured, the group therapy situation encourages unacceptable impulses to come to the surface and allows the group therapist to observe them. Thus the crucial factor of the emotional behavior of people in groups of our culture—and, too, in group therapy—is the anxiety experienced by the members of these groups as a result of their relationships and interactions with each other.

Each person in the group must understand the particular anxieties experienced in the area of emotional behavior in terms of his early developmental experiences as a child. It is during these years that the child makes his first explorations of emotional behavior in close personal relationships. The period from 1½ to 6 years of age is crucial in the development of his emotional patterns. At this same time the child is subject to the disciplinary demand of his parents. His impulses are bent toward self-gratification but his behavior is under partial or fragmentary control.

Thus he is often caught in the conflict between the impulse to do something and the need to avoid behavior that will bring displeasure and disapproval from his parents.

The child's impulses (also called instinctual impulses, id impulses, and drives) are inherent parts of his behavior equipment. At this stage of development the child explores the realm of his emotional behavior governed by two main considerations: (1) the need to gratify his impulses as naturally as possible, and (2) the need to maintain his approval relationship with his parents. For the sake of clarification, impulses refer to such things as the urge to climb on the furniture, to play with mother's sewing paraphernalia, to twist the television control knobs, to fondle his genitals, to bang on the piano keys, to play with feces, to splash in the toilet bowl, to climb into daddy's lap, or to hold the cat and examine it. Many of these would seem to be so minor as never to require inhibiting, yet it is the parent's function to inhibit those which are dangerous. The process by which parents help or hinder the child in the development of his emotional behavior is strongly influenced by their own personality and by certain factors (accidents, illnesses) in the child's growth. The freedom with which he can gratify impulses is determined by what he perceives as the limit of the security relationship with his parents. The child looks to the parents for cues to inhibit his behavior or let himself go naturally. Some children can inhibit certain impulses without any impairment of their general freedom. Other children may react with guarded emotional behavior after inhibiting more than a few impulses. Still others may inhibit a great number of impulses and be greatly impaired or over-inhibited in their general freedom. They may actually feel that they have less freedom than their parents allow. They begin to distrust all of their impulses and cannot be "natural" in their behavior.

When parents are relatively clear about what is allowed and forbidden, yet patient and consistent in their discipline, the child develops a certain degree of comfort with his instinctual impulses. He screens out the less acceptable impulses and lets the better ones come through to action naturally. Rarely if ever in our culture does this learning proceed without difficulty. Most people grow into adulthood with some areas of natural behavior about which they are not sure and do not feel comfortable. This uncertainty always results in some loss of pleasure for them—pleasure that would accompany natural behavior in these areas. With the loss of pleasure comes a sense of frustration and anger. There may even be anger toward parents or other people who are perceived as people who will not let them behave as freely as they might wish. If, as usually happens in our culture, the expression of anger toward parents is one of the natural areas of behavior in which one is uncomfortable, the situation is further complicated and adds to one's emotional constriction.

In the course of development most people have learned ways of protecting themselves against the anxiety aroused in them by the stimulating of their "uncomfortable areas" of behavior. They have developed *defense mechanisms*—habitual and automatic maneuvers designed to prevent the arousal or completion of these behavior patterns and the anxiety associated with them. The defense mechanisms are also called *dynamisms* and *mental mechanisms*. There are many kinds of defense mechanisms, the more prominent ones being repression, projection, denial, displacement, rationalization, reaction formation, sublimation, and identification.

Defense mechanisms do not usually occur singly. Each person employs several of them as a protection against the anxiety of unconscious emotional conflicts. Defense mechanisms are employed unconsciously to aid the process of repression. They give a characteristic stamp to one's personality; the particular patterns of rigidity that a person exhibits in his everyday group relationships are manifestations of his defense mechanisms in action.

The group interaction in our model of group therapy is emotionally stimulating and inevitably touches on areas of behavior about which the members have conflict and anxiety. The group situation, in the person of the leader of the group, also provides a present-day representative of the parent figures who played such an important role in the original development of these conflicts and anxieties. Thus the group process both stirs up old problems in terms of the unhealthy functioning of emotional behavior and provides a setting in which there is a new opportunity to view current behavior in the light of previous emotional associations. The leader of the group usually becomes the recipient of the hostility and anger which the group members have held toward their parents. At the same time, however, the group members wish to protect themselves against the anxiety aroused in them by the stimulation of their uncomfortable areas of behavior. In the course of this struggle by group members with their own anxieties the defense mechanisms stand out in bold relief and can be clearly recognized by the therapist.

The model of group therapy presented in this book exploits the emotional behavior between the group members and the therapist in an organized structured situation—the group meetings. The organized structured situation refers to the physical aspects, i.e., the arrangements and regulations of group therapy (Chap. 4). Our model of group therapy is tightly structured in regard to its physical aspects, but the content of the group meetings is not preplanned and structured. The therapist neither gives lectures nor assigns subjects for general discussion. Actually the members set their own structure from the emotional interaction with each other and with the therapist. Those areas of each group member's behavior that produce discomfort and symptoms are stimulated into action. This stimulation of the emotional behavior of the members always produces anxiety. As a result of the group's anxiety the defense patterns of behavior (defense mechanisms) of the members are more prominently displayed in the meetings. The therapist focuses on this anxiety of the group members and on their defensive patterns of behavior. In this way, by means of the group interaction, he works through the barriers to promote the identification, modification, and changing of their faulty behavior patterns. This reeducation should ultimately result in more pleasure and comfort for them in their everyday relationships.

ANXIETY: DEFENSE MECHANISMS AND PERSONALITY TYPES

The behavior patterns which the person employs in order to prevent or alleviate anxiety constitute his personality structure. In the course of growth and development the behavior patterns of each personality structure become deeply ingrained and fixed within the individual. Consequently they enter automatically and unconsciously into the emotional interaction of day-to-day group relationships. The behavior patterns are not the same in different people, although different behavior patterns may be utilized for the same dynamic reason (such as protection against expressing angry feelings).

There is no satisfactory agreement in professional circles regarding the classification of personality structures. In the literature, personality structures are referred to as personality types, character types, characterological illnesses, personality disorders, personality pattern disorders, and personality trait disturbances. In this book we chiefly follow the standard classification of the personality types listed in the *Diagnostic and Statistical Manual of the American Psychiatric Association.*[25]

Patterns of behavior in people do not follow any prescribed model. There may be one type of behavior in one person, another type of behavior in a second person, and a mixture of the two in a third. The presence of several behavior patterns in a person indicates a special type of personality. These types are: passive-nonassertive (also called depressive), passive-dependent, passive-aggressive, obsessive-compulsive (also called the obsessive personality, the obsessive character, and the compulsive personality), hysterical, schizoid, paranoid, cyclothymic, inadequate, emotionally unstable, and sociopathic (also called the psychopathic personality and the antisocial character type).

Each of the above-named personality types consists of a constellation of several behavior patterns or personality traits that are utilized in their day-to-day group relationships. For example, the person with a passive, nonassertive personality is fearful of authority figures and reacts to them in his everyday group relationships by denial, ingratiation, and fear. He maintains this role as a defense against unconscious (rage) impulses and the subsequent expectation of retaliation from others. His passive, nonassertive personality assures him that he will not express his rage and thus he avoids the fear of retaliation that would be aroused.

The passive-dependent personality is very similar in many respects to the passive nonassertive personality, except that the dependency needs of the former are more prominent. Like the dependent and helpless child, the person with a passive-dependent personality expects others to look after his every need. There is no mutual sharing of feelings and needs with the passive-dependent person. He expects everything and gives nothing in return. The dependency is so ingrained in his personality structure that he considers it normal. In his group relationships he relates to other people as parental figures and expects them to gratify his dependency needs.

The passive-aggressive personality utilizes a series of passive patterns of behavior to reveal underlying aggressiveness. The patient with such a personality is childish, immature, stubborn, and obstinate. He does not openly rebel against people but utilizes a series of delaying tactics to show his defiance and resentment. When he is given a job to do there is no open expression of resentment about it. However, he goes about the task so slowly and with so many excuses that he reveals his aggressiveness by his passive obstructionism.

The obsessive-compulsive personality is characterized by patterns of behavior that consist of competitiveness, intellectualizations, religiosity, meticulousness, perfectionism, and other measures that avoid expression of angry feelings. The conscience of a person with an obsessive-compulsive personality is very rigid and punitive. In group relationships he protects himself against the expression of angry feelings by intensifying or exaggerating his patterns of behavior. Like the person with a passive, nonassertive personality, he maintains his role (patterns of behavior) to avoid expressing his rage or betraying his fear that retaliation would be aroused by the expression of rageful feelings.

The hysterical personality * consists of a constellation of patterns of behavior that include, among others, changing emotional moods, childlike behavior, shallow emotional relationships, dramaticism, exhibitionism, seductiveness, suggestibility, and an uninhibited conscience. Dependency needs may be very pronounced. The hysterical personality is most commonly seen in the female. Seemingly without a care in the world, she can charm others in group relationships to secure her dependency gratifications. The hysterical personality may also be passive and nonassertive; failure to obtain dependency needs may result in helplessness and depression.

The schizoid personality has patterns of behavior that reveal passivity, nonassertiveness, withdrawal, and emotional detachment from people.

* The author is aware that the diagnosis of hysterical personality is questioned in some professional circles.

The schizoid person does not form close relationships with other people but lives a life of emotional detachment. He is extremely sensitive, and in group relationships he pushes people away to avoid being hurt or rejected. He is colloquially referred to as odd or eccentric. He does poorly in educational and occupational pursuits, being content to live in a fantasy world of his own. When forced into close relationships the schizoid personality may become psychotic and exhibit symptoms of acute schizophrenic psychosis.

A person with a paranoid personality is one who has developed patterns of behavior that protect him from anxiety by projecting his own impulses onto others. Recognizing no difficulties or problems within himself, he accuses others of a variety of sins. Basically he does not like himself but he projects his self-hatred on imaginary enemies. He is suspicious, envious, jealous, and oversensitive in his group relationships. He questions the motives of everyone and complains loudly about the injustices done to him. The person with paranoid personality functions well in superficial relationships, but jealousy, resentfulness, suspiciousness, and extreme sensitivity are present in those relationships where he has to be close to people. He can be very shrewd, clever, and calculating in group relationships. Nevertheless he is the one who is against everything and may even try to lead a reform movement to correct what he considers to be wrong. Attempts to deal with such an individual on a reality basis are usually met with resentfulness and defiance.

The cyclothymic personality is characterized by cyclic mood swings from depression to hypomania. The person with a cyclothymic personality is basically a depressed person who in his periods of hypomania uses a pattern of behavior that denies the depression. In his group relationships he may, during periods of hypomania, be overtalkative, overactive, outgoing, and humorous, and may relate to others in a warm and friendly manner. He performs exceptionally well in occupational roles. The hypomanic is well known for his success in "salesmanship" roles. In group relationships he is the center of attention, being frequently referred to as "the life of the party." During the depressive phase the patterns of behavior are approximately opposite to those of the hypomanic phase. The person is sad and gloomy. He has difficulty relating to other people. He does poorly in his occupational role. He sees every task as a severe difficulty. In contrast to the hypomanic's bright outlook, the depressed person sees only the dark and gloomy side of life.

The mood swings of the cyclothymic personality are variable. The periods of hypomania and depression may be alternately brief or long. The behavior patterns are influenced by the degree of anxiety encountered in group relationships. If the anxiety cannot be contained by the defensive patterns of behavior, the person with a cyclothymic personality may become psychotic. In such cases the illness resembles a manic-depressive psychosis.

The inadequate personality is characterized by behavior patterns that give general inadequate response in all areas. Dependency, immaturity, withdrawal, poor intellectual and occupational abilities, and a lack of emotional responsiveness are typical traits. The dependency features of the inadequate personality are outstanding. There is no drive or ambition to accomplish any type of task; such people are content merely to exist and let someone else assume responsibility for them. In many respects the inadequate personality resembles the schizoid personality and the chronic schizophrenic reaction. The hobo, drifter, barfly, and wino are slang epithets for people who demonstrate an inadequate personality.

The emotionally unstable personality is one with ineffectual defensive patterns of behavior for protection against anxiety. The emotionally unstable person does not have sufficient control to perform adequately in group relationships. Minor provocations are characterized by defiance, resentment, and anger. The emotionally unstable person is also childlike and dependent and has difficulty in all of his group relationships. Depression, drug and alcohol addiction, and antisocial behavior occur frequently among this group of people.

The person with a sociopathic personality is one who has developed behavior patterns that protect him from anxiety but, in so doing, has created much anxiety in other people. His patterns of behavior are frequently antisocial and keep him in conflict with authorities. In group relationships he does not consider the feelings or rights of others. Interested only in self-gratification, he uses numerous methods and maneuvers to accomplish his goal. He views the world with bitterness and feels that all people are against him. He may be very clever, shrewd, and calculating. He may also have behavior patterns similar to those of the emotionally unstable personality. Extreme anger and defiance are common in the psychopathic personality.

Persons with a sociopathic personality may have varying degrees of anxiety. Often the level of anxiety is kept low through alloplastic behavior, but if they are confined to jail or an institution they may develop symptoms of a somatic nature.

Schizophrenia and Personality Types

Although schizophrenia is a type of mental illness and is not, strictly speaking, a personality type, it deserves special consideration here because of the role anxiety plays in it. The schizophrenic's anxiety in group relationships is more massive and threatening than the neurotic's. Difficulties in perception, marked ambivalence, and deficient reality testing all add to the increased anxiety experienced by the schizophrenic in interpersonal relationships. Intensified patterns of behavior are necessary for the schizophrenic when group relationships are pursued. Withdrawal, suspiciousness, obsessive and hysterical mechanisms, psychosomatic symptoms, depression, and hostility, are frequently observed. With overwhelming anxiety these behavior patterns give way and unconscious feelings, previously held in abeyance by defensive mechanisms, erupt into consciousness and a psychosis becomes clearly evident. In the family group the schizophrenic may have been withdrawn, timid, and shy. If so, he will repeat this pattern in other group relationships. Close relationships are avoided for protection against anxiety. Social, intellectual, and occupational pursuits may be lacking. The defensive patterns of behavior of the schizophrenic, regardless of the type, are exaggerated responses in group relationships.

Each of the personality types exhibits behavior patterns in his group relationships peculiar to his personality structure. Later we shall observe that each of the personality types brings his lifelong patterns of behavior into group therapy. The therapy group will simulate the patient's other group relationships, particularly those of his family group. A complete description of all the personality types and their reactions in group therapy is given in Chap. 4.

PATTERNS OF BEHAVIOR COMMON TO ALL PEOPLE

In an earlier paragraph it was pointed out that one's personality structure is not determined by a specific group of behavior patterns but by the preponderance of several patterns that, taken collectively, indicate the type of personality. The behavior patterns that a person uses vary considerably. Many of the behavior patterns described in the personality types occur to some extent in all people.* Most of us at some time in our lives get depressed or feel better than normal. On occasion, suspicious thoughts occur about others. A common behavior pattern present in many people is a tendency to blame others for their own weaknesses. Passive-aggressive behavior patterns are not confined merely to the person who has a passive-aggressive personality. The attractive female who demonstrates hysterical behavior patterns is not exceptional. Daydreams are commonly present in all people. Phobias, obsessions, or various compulsive traits are common among most people. It is a rare person who comes through childhood and adolescence without exposure and participation in one or more acts of delinquent or antisocial behavior.

Whether or not behavior patterns are of serious import to the person and affect his function in group relationships depends on factors such as the type of behavior patterns, their degree of severity and intensity, the

* This discussion does not concern itself with what specifically is normal or abnormal behavior but merely illustrates common behavior patterns of all people.

anxiety tolerance, and the amount of stress incurred in group relationships. The intensity of one's behavior patterns in group relationships may indicate either healthy, mature functioning or unhealthy, abnormal functioning. There are healthy, mature, independent and well-adjusted people with the behavior patterns of the hysterical personality. On the other hand, there are immature, dependent, poorly adjusted people with the intensified and exaggerated behavior patterns of the hysterical personality. Similarly, there are people with obsessive-compulsive personalities who lead happy and well-adjusted lives, and others whose behavior patterns are so intensified and exaggerated that depression and anxiety lead to unhappiness and poor life adjustments.

BEHAVIOR PATTERNS: PERSONALITY TYPES AND EMOTIONAL ILLNESS

Behavior patterns are important in the classification of personality types. *The Statistical and Diagnostic Manual of the American Psychiatric Association* classifies many of the personality types described here as personality disorders and classifies them into three main groups. The types of behavior patterns and the variations in their intensity and severity are the basis for the classification. The three groups are (1) personality pattern disturbances (inadequate, schizoid, cyclothymic, and paranoid personalities); (2) personality trait disturbances (emotionally unstable, passive-aggressive and compulsive personalities); and (3) sociopathic personality disturbance (antisocial and dyssocial reactions, sexual deviations and addictions).[25]

The stress that a person encounters from his relationships with other people will naturally increase his anxiety and intensify his defensive behavior patterns in order to protect him from experiencing anxiety. For example, the school student will encounter more anxiety with a school teacher who is angry, rigid, and controlling than with one who is understanding and flexible. In such a situation a student might, if he is of the passive-dependent personality type, intensify his behavior patterns by becoming more ingratiating and more passive in an effort to prevent the overt expression of his anger. Similarly, the person who has an angry, dictatorial, and dominating boss will experience more anxiety in his relationships with him than with one who is understanding and tolerant.

There are also a series of behavior patterns utilized by people in their day-to-day group relationships that are not specifically related to their types of personality structure. The most common behavior patterns that occur in day-to-day group relationships are overtalkativeness, intellectualizations, humor, laughter, superficial conversation, hostility, silence, rapid changing of subject material, ingratiation, competitiveness, scapegoating, absences, tardiness, leaving the group, nonpayment of bills, sleeping, gifts, formation of subgroups within and outside the group, excessive smoking, restlessness, pouting, scowling, and frowning.

RELATIONSHIP OF ANXIETY TO THE STRUCTURE OF GROUPS

Let us now turn our attention to the relationship of anxiety to the structure of groups. First of all it should be reemphasized that the human animal does not live in isolation. Man has always existed in group relationships. He begins life in the family group. During childhood, adolescence, and adulthood he participates in educational, recreational, social, religious, professional and occupational groups. In many groups he is a member and in some he may be the leader. Throughout one's life one is always subjected to the pressures of group behavior.

Family Group

Anxiety initially occurs in a person in his family group. Here in the family group a person develops personality traits or behavior patterns from the interaction with his parents, the leaders or authority figures of the family group, and with his siblings (the other members of the family group). He uses these behavior patterns in his group relationships with his family. As the person begins to take part in other group relationships he continues to use the same behavior patterns with the authority figures and members of other groups.

At this point it would perhaps be useful to emphasize the basic structure of groups. All groups are composed of the members of the group and the leaders or authority figures of the group. People may react to any group in the same way as they react in their original family group, because they symbolically perceive the new group as identical to their original family group. The persons in a group unconsciously and automatically project on the leader or authority figure their childhood thoughts and feelings about their fathers and mothers and the thoughts and feelings they shared with their siblings. Therefore as the person moves about from group to group he reacts to the authority figure as he reacted to his parents. Similarly, he will react to the peers in other groups in the same way that he reacted to his siblings in the family group. In this respect, the different types of groups in which the person participates throughout life are symbolic of the original family unit.

Groups may be simply structured in their make-up (for example, one leader and several members) or they may be intricate and complicated. Depending on their size and function, some groups may have a leader plus several members in leadership roles. The basic group of our culture— the family—has two persons in leadership roles, the father and mother. In the average normal family group the roles and duties of each parent are defined. Normally the father is the leader and the mother his assistant.

The children in such families learn to respect and relate to each parent according to his role, thus making a healthy identification with them. Even parental differences of opinion afford the children opportunities to look at the issues from more than one point of view. This healthy type of dual leadership within the family group is, however, not always present. A mother or father may not have the physical or psychological skill to fulfill his or her role. There are many factors that may interfere with or change the leadership role of the family—the death of a parent, chronic disabling physical and emotional illnesses, or personality conflicts between parents. In such situations the mother, an older son, or a daughter may replace the father as the leader of the family group.

There are other types of group structure that are intricate and complicated. As a general rule they have a leader or supreme authority figure, plus a series of assistant or subordinate leaders who play an important role in the functions and goals of the group.

Governmental, educational, and political groups also may have a complicated structure with multiple and diversified roles and goals. They maintain subordinate leaders, each with his own specific role and goal, whose group membership may be only a part of the larger group. The U.S. House of Representatives is an example of a large, heterogeneous group with a speaker as the supreme authority figure and numerous other persons in positions of leadership—the majority whip and his opposite, the minority whip. Then there are many small committees, each with a chairman who enjoys prestige and can wield strong influence and power. All of these leaders and members are necessary for the proper function of the legislative body. At times there are controversial issues before the House which create great tension and stress among its leaders and members. The leadership may be divided and the members may or may not cross over party lines. Throughout all such events, regardless of their magnitude, the speaker of the house is the overall authority figure who—depending upon his skill as the leader of the entire group—can be the ultimate leader in resolving issues. In this body there are many examples of the dynamics of human group behavior—anger, defiance, competition, subgroups, superficial conversations, tardiness at meetings, and absenteeism. However, the members of the House of Representatives, the United States Senate and many state legislative bodies exhibit at least two rewarding traits from which many other groups can profit: (1) their ability to express themselves fully on issues, and (2) their ability to differ and argue among themselves. Significantly these actions usually take place without impairing the working relationships among the members.

In some groups the leader's role and authority may exist with a subordinate leader or some other member of the group. An examination of the social system of organizations such as hospitals, business organizations, unions, or political bodies may reveal that power and authority do not rest with the person delegated as the head but with someone else in the organization. Usually extenuating circumstances create such situations. The delegated leader may be disabled, unauthoritative, or have lost the respect of his group members. The real leader emerges from the chaos and confusion created by the difficulties of the delegated leader. In such cases the latter is bypassed and the other leader makes all major decisions and influences the rank and file of the group members.

Groups may also be structured along homogeneous and heterogeneous lines, depending upon their goals and composition. They may be homogeneous in the sense that the leader and members have one common purpose—for example, a group supporting a political candidate, or participating in social, educational, or recreational activities. However, these same groups are heterogeneous in the sense that their membership is made up of people with different personality types. The degree of their heterogeneity will be subject to the factors that influence the structure and function of all groups.

Groups are thus of a simple or complicated structure. The leadership can vary—one leader in some, two leaders in others (such as the family group), or a number of leaders in various roles (as in an army or religious group). However, most of these groups, regardless of their structure, have one person who is the supreme authority figure. In general, all groups are a prototype of basic group structure—the leader and the members of the group.

A discussion of groups would be incomplete without a word on the influence of unconscious mechanisms on group action and group behavior. Freud points out the influence of a person's unconscious impulses in group behavior.[1] He describes a group as impulsive, changeable, irritable, and dominated by the instinctual impulses of the unconscious. He says that group function may be heroic and generous or cruel and cowardly, depending on the structure and function of the group; that a person may be civilized and cultivated in an isolated situation but in a group situation may become a barbarian. In effect, Freud is saying that when people come together in a group, the emotional reactions that occur may change their ordinary behavior.

Fenichel has also described an unconscious mechanism in group behavior that influences the actions of its members. People may seek group associations that afford them pleasurable relief from guilt feelings because the action comes from the group rather than from the individual. Such people unconsciously desire to do forbidden things but are individually inhibited by their own guilt feelings. In a group the thing forbidden to the individual is made permissible by the participation of all. Fenichel states that "the relief of guilt feeling through becoming aware that others dare to do that about which one has felt guilt is one of the cornerstones of mob psychology."[36]

There are also other factors that operate on a conscious level and influence group behavior. Some people may participate in certain group actions that are entirely foreign to their principles so as not to be labeled an outsider or someone who is "different." They fear reprisals and rejection if they are not part of the crowd. Such people may later experience severe guilt for their actions. In this respect the influences of suggestion and contagion are present. Like children who get caught up in a neighborhood form of recreation, group members are strongly influenced by the majority opinion. Members who remain doubtful despite the contagion of group spirit are sometimes exhorted or even coerced into following the others in their endeavors.

Probably the most aggressive and destructive behavior that occurs in groups results from mob action. Mobs are composed of rageful and defiant people who demand immediate gratification of their impulses. Both conscious and unconscious emotional reactions are present in mob behavior. There is another extremely important factor, however, that influences mob behavior—the absence of an effective leader or authority figure. Characteristically mobs do not have responsible leaders. As we have pointed out many times, the leader is the most important person in any group. He is needed to hold the group together. Groups without good leaders are subject to a breakthrough of emotional reactions that are ordinarily held in check by the leaders. Thus, although both conscious and unconscious mechanisms influence all groups, these mechanisms are primarily destructive with ineffective or no leadership.

FACTORS THAT INFLUENCE THE STRUCTURE AND FUNCTION OF GROUPS

There are a number of factors that influence the structure and function of a group and the person's anxiety and behavior patterns in the group. Some of the chief ones are: (1) degree of closeness within the group, (2) size of the group, (3) goals and purposes of the group, (4) personality structure and patterns of behavior of the group leader, and (5) social and cultural factors.

Degree of Closeness within the Group

Whenever any group of people come together for a period of time emotional reactions come to the surface. The closer people are in a group and the more time they spend with each other, the greater will be the emotional interaction among them. Where there is more closeness among the members of a group there is more anxiety. Increased anxiety results in the members utilizing their characteristic behavior patterns as a protection against anxiety. The family group (father, mother, and children) is the closest-knit of all group relationships, and it is within this basic group of our culture that the damaging effects created by anxiety are most apparent. Next in importance to the family group is one's occupational group. The effects of anxiety in occupational groups account for behavior patterns among its members such as depression, physical symptoms, tardiness, absenteeism, accident-proneness, and conflicts between members. There is less emotional interaction and anxiety in religious, social, and recreational groups, since there is less closeness among the members.

The specific meaning of *closeness* to a person varies, of course, depending on his personality type and his psychodynamics. A close relationship between two or more people is accompanied by an emotional reaction that may be of minor or major proportions. James Mann, in discussing the meaning of close relationships, states: "In every relationship there are hidden fears ranging from the schizophrenic dilemma that love equals mutual destruction to the neurotic conflict wherein love threatens to make real what were castration fantasies." [14] Thus, closeness between people brings out many of the fears of mankind. People avoid closeness because of the fear of exposure. If they reveal themselves to others, the self-knowledge of their personal weaknesses, idiosyncrasies, and thoughts generates fears of disapproval and rejection. Fears of exposure encompass such thoughts as badness, worthlessness, helplessness, abandonment, profligacy, inferiority, unlovableness, detection of rage, and sexual inadequacies. A person's lack of sexual identity—inability to separate warm and tender feelings from sexual and angry feelings—may induce a variety of fears. Close relationships to those with a lack of sexual identity may cause fears of a homosexual "pass" or a heterosexual attack. Sexual feelings may be either accompanied by or disguised as angry feelings. Fears of anger or rage may range all the way from an undefined, uncomfortable sensation when people exhibit anger to the dread of hurting someone's feelings or getting hurt, and ultimately, to the terror of the schizophrenic that someone will discover his murderous rage and turn it against himself.

Superficial conversation as contrasted to the expression of true feelings has a relationship to closeness, emotional interaction, and the anxiety level of the members of a group. In close-knit groups such as family groups and occupational groups the denial of true feelings by the use of superficial conversation increases anxiety and the behavior patterns of its members. The child who can express true feelings to his parents in an understanding and accepting atmosphere has less anxiety than the child who has to deny true feelings and use superficial conversation because of parental fear. Similarly, the worker who can express true feelings to an understanding boss (authority figure) has less anxiety than one whose boss is hard and unsympathetic. In some people, however, the opportunity to speak freely may serve to arouse fears of disclosing their repressed rage. The schizophrenic, for example, would be expected to be more comfortable where there is more structure and less freedom in expressing feelings.

In other groups (social and recreational) superficial conversation is common and is actually a satisfactory method of communication. It is not necessary to express true feelings to everyone. However, superficial conversation is a handicap when used to repress feelings and can lead to anxiety and emotional conflict.

Size of the Group

The size of the group influences the emotional interaction of its members. In general, the larger the group the less emotional interaction and the less closeness among its members. For example, twelve students and a teacher in a classroom will emotionally interact with each other to a greater degree than forty students and a teacher. In large religious groups of several thousand people the members come and go with hardly any notice from the others. In the small religious group of several hundred people the members know each other well and are aware of the loss or addition of a single member.

Goals and Purposes of the Group

The goals of the group contribute significantly to the emotional interaction and anxiety of its members. Each type of group in our society has its own specifically defined goals. The diversified and numerous goals of the family group include (among others) economic, social, religious, biological, educational, and recreational satisfactions. Educational, professional, religious, social, recreational, and occupational groups have goals that are specifically defined. An important goal is the mutual satisfaction of needs, nowhere more important than in the family group. The successful and understanding relationship between the members of a family is based on their capacity for mutual love and respect, sharing, and sacrifice of individual desires for the good of the family. Such a family relationship demonstrates the mutual satisfaction of needs. Each family member is dependent on the others. The wife depends on her husband to work and provide for the family's economic security. The husband depends on his wife to maintain the home, prepare meals, and care for the children. The children depend on their parents for love, food, security, and other growth needs. Each family member receives satisfaction from the others. The mutual satisfaction of needs that occurs between a child and his parents is closely related to the feelings of warmth and love that each one has for the other. The more satisfactions the child receives from his parents the greater will be his feelings of love for them. Of course the child will become frustrated when the parents institute disciplinary measures; his frustrations are related to feelings of anger and guilt. Similarly, the more frustrations the child receives from his parents the more anger and guilt will be present. In later group relationships the presence of either the welfare emotions (warmth, love, pleasure) or the emergency emotions (anger, hate, fear, guilt) toward authority figures or group members will depend on the degree of satisfactions or frustrations that occurred in the family group. Satisfactory relationships with parents and siblings in the family group will be the forerunner of satisfactory relationships with authority figures and peers in other group relationships.

The Leader of the Group

The most important and influential member of all types of groups is the leader or authority figure of the group. The leader has more influence on the group members than any other person. In the family group the leaders (parents) are the prototypes for their children. The family leaders' conduct, attitudes, and reactions with each other and with their children contribute more to the presence or absence of anxiety in the family than any other factor. In the school group the teacher assumes the role of the authority figure. The Sunday School teacher, Scoutmaster, basketball coach, baseball club manager, platoon sergeant, straw boss of a work gang, board chairman or hospital superintendent are a few examples of the leaders of their respective groups. In each instance the leaders of these groups, like the leaders of the family group, contribute more to the presence or absence of anxiety in the groups than any other member. Leaders who are angry, rigid, dominating, and controlling, who demand complete allegiance of the members at all costs, and who do not understand the effect of their emotional interaction with people cause a high anxiety level among members of their groups. Similarly, leaders of groups who are understanding, flexible, tolerant, and sensitive produce a lower level of anxiety among the members of their groups.

The leader has one other important position in society—to hold the group together. A group without a leader is like a ship without a rudder. In the family the parents, as leaders, hold the group together. Without the parents, the family disintegrates. The civic club, basketball team, religious group, professional organization, and political party depend on leadership for successful operation. Leadership implies the concept of authority. All of us have been subjected to numerous brushes with authority and discipline in childhood and adolescence. Restrictive discipline is necessary in order to bring our impulses into conformity with the demands of society. We associate authority figures or leaders of groups with restrictive discipline on either a conscious or unconscious level. In discussing the function of authority, Abram Kardiner says that a social organization cannot exist without restrictive discipline.[26] All cohesive groups have a leader who has the ability to exert the necessary restrictive discipline and at the same time inspire the members toward efficient operation. There is, however, an additional factor that holds groups together—the willingness of the members of groups to be dependent on their leaders. One positive sign of emotional maturity is our ability to be interdependent by helping one another and sharing our mutual responsibilities. In successful groups the members are dependent on the leaders and the leaders are dependent on the members. Here again we see that the mutual satisfaction of needs is necessary.

A series of situations occur in group relationships that require authoritative, aggressive leadership and cooperation regardless of individual feelings and wishes. Such situations arise in emergencies of one kind or another, either in the small family group or in larger groups of varied composition. If one member of a family group becomes seriously ill, the family may have to forego other wishes and pleasures. Decisions have to be made quickly and authoritatively regardless of personal desires—there is no time to weigh individual feelings and wishes of other family members. In such instances the parents (usually the father) assumes complete command and makes the decisions necessary for the care and treatment of the ill member. A fire in a hospital immediately sets in operation the emergency measures necessary to remove patients to safety and to bring the fire under control. Authoritative and aggressive leadership is necessary and cooperation by employees and patients is imperative. In army units during wartime, the leadership of the commanding general carries the same import. His decisions are final and must be carried out by officers and enlisted men.

It is apparent that emergency situations in group relationships are dependent on strong, authoritative leadership. People in such positions who are not able to provide adequate command subject the group to loss, disorganization, or deterioration.

A most important role of the leaders of groups—a role associated with the necessary restrictive discipline of group organization and the dependency of the group members on each other and the leader—is that of utilizing the principle of reward and punishment. In all groups, leaders employ various tactics to reward the members for their performances, or to institute disciplinary measures against those who do not conform to rules and policies. The principle of reward and punishment actually denotes approval or disapproval. Parents use this principle with their children. The child, from his interaction with parents, other significant adults, and siblings forms concepts about approval and disapproval. He is extremely sensitive to these parental indications. Approval from parents means that he is loved, respected, and cared for. Disapproval indicates loss of love and dependency and arouses fears of abandonment. The child's feelings are related not only to the parent's verbal statements but also to the parent's nonverbal behavior—facial expression, mannerisms, attitudes, and actions.

As the person moves from the family group to educational, religious, social, recreational, and occupational groups, approval or disapproval influences his level of anxiety and function in the group. In these groups the leaders, like the parents in the family group, utilize verbal and non-verbal responses to indicate approval or disapproval. Depending on the individual's interpretations, the group member's responses will vary; since, however, the leader is the authority figure of the group the member's anxiety and behavior patterns will be more influenced by the leader's indications than by those of the other members of the group.

In order to indicate reward and punishment, the leader of the group may utilize material things as well as verbal expressions of approval. In our culture great emphasis is placed on giving material gifts (approval) or withholding them (disapproval). More importantly, though, the leaders of all groups indicate approval or disapproval through their nonverbal communication to their group members. In therapeutic and nontherapeutic groups the author has repeatedly observed that the members of these groups feel the group therapist's or group leader's nonverbal behavior is a more important indication of approval or disapproval than are his verbal statements. In group therapy, members have stated on numerous occasions that the therapist's attitudes and mannerisms were more significant to them in terms of acceptance and approval than his verbal statements. Similar reactions have been experienced with psychiatric residents and their supervisor in group supervisory conferences and with staff members (residents, nurses, and aides) and their ward administrator.

Social and Cultural Factors

Social and cultural factors are influences that may lead to tension and conflict in groups and thus predispose people to anxiety. The social adaptation of people is influenced by occupational, educational, religious, social, recreational, and other similar motivational groups. Overlapping and permeating institutional groups are such factors as social class and ethnic origin.

Social Class. Perhaps the most influential and most persuasive factor in social and cultural patterns of behavior is the social class. One cannot deny the existence of social class, social position, and status in the United States, although their determining criteria vary to some extent in different sections. Regardless of the geographic location, social class, standards, and status affect the behavior patterns of people.

A community study by Hollingshead and Redlich, described in *Social Class and Mental Illness,* illustrates how social and cultural factors operating within society affect the anxiety and behavior patterns of families in five social classes. Class I and class II families were those commonly referred to as the upper classes. They were economically secure. Their education was college-level or above. The families in the lower social classes (class IV and class V) were low on the economic and educational scale. The basic family group was less intact. Family homes were substandard and neighborhood facilities for play and recreation were limited. Thus community and school group relationships for adults and children were lacking. The anxiety level of the families in class IV and class V was greater than that in the class I and class II family, and the behavior patterns of families in class IV and class V revealed that more patients were treated for mental illness; sexual, aggressive, and dependent impulses were more pronounced and primitive; the family members revealed more defective superegos; and there were higher percentages of acting-out behavior, delinquency, and crime.[27]

Race. Other factors that have always contributed to tension, conflict, and anxiety of many social groups are race and ethnic origin. The introduction of any new group of people into an existing society has always been accompanied by tension and conflict in both the new and old populations. Minority racial groups, like minority religious groups, have frequently been the recipients of group tensions (i.e., "scapegoated") from the majority groups.

Occupational Group. In conjunction with the factors of race and social class are the institutional groups in which people interact. Educational groups play a major role during childhood, adolescence, and possibly early adulthood. The child's relationships with his fellow students and with such authority figures as his teachers and school principals afford him a variety of group interactions. Later, when an individual begins to work his occupational group comes to the fore as second only to his family in the degree of closeness produced. Here an individual's tension and conflict are geared to (1) his typical behavior patterns with his peers and authority figures, (2) the personality and behavior of his superiors, (3) the stress that may be endemic to the profession itself, and (4) the goals of both the individual and the group. Generally the most successful workers chose the profession that best suits their personality. A hypomanic person will become a salesman, or an obsessive will choose bookkeeping or research. Much conflict and tension can result when an individual's personality type is unsuited to the type of work demanded of him in his occupational group.

Religious and Social Groups. Less important although still significant social and cultural factors are religious and social groups. An individual's religious group may influence his feelings (and thus his anxiety) about many things, ranging from anger and sex to his role in society. Social and recreational groups usually have less closeness (and thus less anxiety) than most group relationships. Physically strenuous recreations are one of the most satisfactory outlets for tension, especially in adolescence. Often in our society religious and social groups overlap, particularly in smaller communities, with religious organizations providing social activities for their members. Although this combination is sometimes satisfactory, it can occasionally lead to further tension and conflict as when groups or even individuals cannot agree on whether the church basement is a satisfactory place for dances or bingo parties.

Relationship of Group Structure and Function to Group Therapy

In general, the primary factors that determine a person's interpersonal relationships in any group relate to his *psychodynamics*—his personality type and defensive behavior patterns that have developed out of earlier child-parent interactions in his family. Naturally, factors that influence all groups—size, degree of closeness, and leadership—have a profound influence in group therapy. Because the therapy group of this model is of relatively small size, having only eight group members, a group therapist, and a recorder, the emotional interactions of the group's constituents are increased. Another important feature of our model of group therapy results from the active promotion of closeness and mutual satisfaction of needs. The therapy group has authority figures—the group therapist and the recorder. In the therapy groups, as in others, the therapist is the most important and influential person. The group's size, degree of emotional interaction, closeness, relationships between its members, and the role of its leader (therapist) are all analogous to the family, the basic group of society. During group therapy a group identity develops that is symbolic of the identity that occurs in the family group.

We have previously stated that the person's everyday group relationships can be influenced to some degree by such social and cultural factors as social class, education, and occupation. In this respect social and cultural institutions may predispose the person to tension, conflict, and anxiety. In group therapy we observe that group members, as they develop psychological aptitude, recognize how their distorted and faulty patterns of behavior have affected their relationships in all groups. The group members recognize that their behavior with each other and with the group therapist has many similarities to their behavior in everyday groups. Problems in prior group relationships, such as educational difficulties and occupational conflicts, are better understood. New insights gained from group therapy can then be applied to occupational, educational, social, and other pursuits. The results that occur have a multiple effect. The ability to perform educationally, to be gainfully employed, and to socialize in other groups raises the person's self-esteem and improves his social and cultural position among his peers.

RELATIONSHIP OF ANXIETY TOLERANCE OF PATIENTS TO PSYCHOTHERAPY

Before we discuss the different types of group therapy and their goals, there are several basic facts that should be reiterated concerning the patient with emotional conflicts and problems. The patient who seeks therapy has a personality structure of deeply ingrained personality traits or behavior patterns and the symptoms of a personality pattern disorder or emotional illness. The patient's emotional conflicts and problems are a result of an inability to tolerate anxiety in his day-to-day group relationships. The patient's anxiety tolerance depends on his personality structure, his type of emotional illness, and the degree of stress from his group relationships. His anxiety tolerance can also be looked upon as a gauge of his ego strength, his ability to test reality, and his reactions in group relationships. In general, these factors are stronger in the patient with a neurosis than in the patient with a psychosis; that is, the former can tolerate more anxiety than the latter. Adolescents normally experience more anxiety than adults; the adolescent with a neurosis is expected to have more anxiety in his group relationships than the adult with a neurosis. Juvenile delinquents notoriously experience excessive anxiety in their group relationships. Similarly, the individual with alcohol or drug addiction experiences excessive anxiety, becoming quickly frustrated in his group relationships and resorting to the use of alcohol or drugs.

Technique in Individual Therapy

The fact that anxiety has different manifestations in patients has an important relationship to the type of treatment programs best suited for the patient, regardless of whether the treatment is on an individual or group basis. The treatment of the patient on an individual basis involves a group of two people—the patient and the therapist. The treatment of an individual on a group basis involves a larger group of people and the group therapist. Both are group relationships. In either type of therapy, anxiety is experienced by the patient. The therapy situation becomes another group relationship for the patient. He reacts with anxiety in the therapy situation as he reacts with anxiety in other group relationships. In individual therapy, the therapist utilizes techniques with the patient that may be probing, investigative, directive, or supportive, depending on the psychodynamics and anxiety tolerance of the patient. For example, the therapist can be probing and investigative of the neurotic patient's symptoms and patterns of behavior. The patient who has a psychosis may not tolerate the therapist's using probing and investigative techniques. He becomes too anxious and uncomfortable, and his symptoms and illness may recur. Thus when treating a patient with a psychosis the therapist's technique should be less probing and investigative, more directive and supporting. The point to be emphasized is that the therapist gauges his technique by the anxiety of the patient. Children, adolescents, and juvenile delinquents should also be treated according to their ability to tolerate anxiety.

Technique in Group Therapy

The model of group therapy presented in this book recognizes that anxiety occurring in the therapeutic group is a basic factor in the dynamics of the group process, in the technique of the group therapist during group meetings, and in the therapist's goals for the group members. Our model of group therapy is a type of psychotherapy designed like all basic group structures. It has members and an authority figure as leader. The therapist is the authority figure and the patients are the members of the group. In group therapy the group members are forced by the technique of the therapist to interact emotionally with each other and with the therapist. Thus the therapist promotes closeness between the members of the group and himself. In all types of groups in society the more closeness and emotional interaction between the members of a group, the more anxiety is present. Since the emotional interaction and closeness among the members of a therapy group are similar in many respects to the emotional interaction and closeness of the members of a family group, the anxiety level of the members of a therapy group will be high. In group therapy the therapist encounters problems with anxiety similar to those of the therapist with individual patients, except that the group therapist's problems are magnified by the presence of more people. As in individual therapy, the neurotic patient in group therapy can tolerate more anxiety than the psychotic patient. The group therapist, like the individual therapist, can employ a technique during group therapy that is more probing and investigative of the patterns of behavior of the neurotic patient and a technique during group therapy with psychotic patients that is less probing and investigative and more directive and supportive. Similarly, groups of adolescent behavior disorders (personality disorders, neuroses, psychoses, and juvenile delinquency) should be treated according to their ability to tolerate anxiety.

For all, however, anxiety is a necessary part of the psychotherapeutic process. The aim of both individual and group therapist is to maintain the anxiety of the patient at the optimum level for constructive therapeutic work. If the anxiety level is too low, the therapeutic process can slow down to a point where it becomes noneffective. If, on the other hand, his technique produces prolonged, excessive anxiety, the group members become too uncomfortable and frightened. When the group therapist's technique produces high anxiety levels, the group members react with exaggerated behavior patterns and illness symptoms. Tardiness and absences of the group members at meetings is common. Acting-out behavior is more prominent. Group members begin to leave the group. In other words, the group begins to fall apart or disintegrate. Instead of being a helpful experience, group therapy has produced so much anxiety in the group members that to avoid the group is more comfortable to them.

RELATIONSHIP OF GROUP THERAPIST'S TECHNIQUE
TO HIS GOALS

One of the most important and perhaps unique characteristics of our model of group therapy is that the goals of each new group are defined in advance by the group therapist, his technique throughout therapy being geared to these goals. His definition of goals depends on the type of patients he will treat in the group.

We have stated that the group member who has a better ego integration and tolerance for anxiety (that is, the group member with a neurosis) can tolerate a more probing and investigative therapy technique than the group member with less ego integration and less tolerance for anxiety—in other words, the group member with psychosis. Let us now examine how the anxiety tolerance of the group members and the technique of group therapy are related to the therapist's goals. His goal for the group members is to help them overcome uncomfortable and distressing manifestations of their emotional illnesses. In order to accomplish this goal he must use a technique that protects each member against excessive, prolonged anxiety in the group meetings. Since group members with neuroses can tolerate more anxiety than group members with psychoses, the therapist can afford to be more probing and investigative of neurotic patterns of behavior. Because the psychotherapy of group members can be pursued more intensely, the goals of the therapist will be more extensive. Group members with neuroses will have the opportunity to examine their relationship to the therapist, to recognize unrealistic dependency wishes, to identify in themselves and others faulty emotional responses that have resulted in their behavior patterns, and to recognize and possibly modify behavior patterns so that they can lead a more comfortable life in their everyday group relationships. For group members with psychoses, however, there is a minimum tolerance for anxiety; the therapist's technique has to be more directive and supporting. His goals are thus less extensive. In groups of psychotic people the therapist allows the patients to become dependent on him and on the group, to discuss realistic problems, and to support one another. The therapist encourages the ventilation of feelings and employs a technique that reestablishes their behavior patterns and increases repression. In adolescent groups the therapist should follow the same general pattern in establishing his goals.

GOALS IN GROUP THERAPY

In considering the overall goals of group therapy programs, the author would like to stress that our model of group therapy does not attempt to remove deep-seated emotional conflicts or to change the basic personality structure of people. As in individual therapy, group therapy programs with patients may be a psychotherapeutic experience in some instances and a supportive form of therapy in others. In general, our goals for people in group therapy are: (1) to improve reality testing, (2) to aid socialization, (3) to foster the development of psychological aptitude— i.e., the awareness of the relationship of feelings to anxiety and patterns of behavior—and (4) to provide motivation for additional therapy on an individual or group basis.

To some extent these four general goals apply to all types of group therapy programs. There are, however, other factors: the age, sex, and intelligence level of the patient; the degree of ego strength; the diagnosis, personality structure, and overall needs of the patient; the physical location of the group therapy program; and the availability of professional personnel. By taking into consideration these influencing factors, the therapist should be able more accurately to ascertain his goals.

TYPES OF GROUP PROGRAMS

Because the goals and technique of the therapist are flexible, many aspects of our model of group therapy can be adapted to various forms of mental illness. Sometimes the goals and technique are so flexible and unstructured that the process cannot really be considered group therapy, but rather *group activity*. Nevertheless, the same basic group dynamics take place, and the therapist or group leader tries to utilize the immediate interaction of the group members in order to accomplish his goals.

The principal aim of this book is to show how our model of group therapy can be a useful tool in the treatment of neuroses and psychoses. At this point in the general discussion of group behavior, however, we wish to give a general survey of the ways in which group dynamics can be successfully exploited in a variety of group programs.

Group Therapy for Neuroses

Group therapy can be an extremely useful tool in the treatment of neuroses; indeed, a large part of this book is devoted to the use of our model of group therapy with neurotic patients. With neurotic patients the goals of the group therapist can be moderately extensive. The motivation, ego strength, and anxiety tolerance of neurotic patients allow for a more intensive psychotherapeutic program. In groups of neurotic patients the members' relationship to the therapist can be worked through. Transference reactions occur and become the tool with which many of the faulty emotional responses of the group members can be recognized and corrected. The group members learn to talk and express their feelings. With the release of impounded anger, improved self-esteem and self-assertion occur. The group members learn that others have similar problems, and feelings of isolation are diminished. Behavior patterns that result from anxiety are identified within the therapy group and are recognized as similar to those used in other group relationships. Difficulties in being close to people, trusting people, and sharing with people are recognized as emotional reactions coming from within. An awareness of separation anxiety is fostered through understanding of their emotional reactions to the reality events of group therapy—the cancelled group meetings, changes in the time and day of meetings, losses, additions, absences and vacations of group members, absences and vacations of the therapist and recorder, termination of the group, and similar delays and frustrations. (These reality events are discussed in detail throughout Chap. 4.) The therapist's goals for his group members are thus an emotional reeducation and relearning process that fosters a recognition and understanding of behavior patterns, improves reality testing, aids socialization, and develops psychological aptitude.

To accomplish these goals in groups of neurotic patients that meet once a week for 1½ hours, a minimum period of 18 months is necessary. Short-term group programs for neurotic patients where 12, 24, or 32 meetings are planned should have limited goals. In such groups the goals are primarily for the ventilation of feelings and mutual support. Changes in behavior patterns do not occur in these short-term group programs. Sometimes the short-term programs are organized around didactic lectures, movies, and demonstrations, in which case they are basically a group activity, not group therapy.

On several occasions other group therapists have questioned the author's view on the length of group therapy—that is, a specific period such as 18 months. They ask, "Why stop a treatment program that can be of additional benefit to the group members if it can be continued?" The answer is that group members can profit from a continuation of group therapy over a period of possibly several years. In those situations where it is feasible, group therapy should continue. In fact, one important goal of our model of group therapy is to aid in the patient's motivation for future treatment on either an individual or group basis. However, group therapy should not continue endlessly—as with one patient who was a member of a therapy group for nine years! In this instance the group became the patient's substitute family and took the place of all the patient's social contacts in the everyday world.[87]

Group therapy programs and psychiatric training programs are generally designed for specific periods—a necessity because of the format of resident programs. One great advantage of resident's ending groups during their period of training is the knowledge and understanding they receive of separation anxiety in groups (see Chap. 5).

From the basic neurotic outpatient group the group therapist can also develop other group programs with parents of children or mates of adults with emotional disorders, with patients with psychophysiological or psychosomatic complaints. In each his technique of group therapy will be the same and his general goals will remain similar to those of an outpatient group of neurotic patients. However, he must pay attention to the type of group and adjust his specific goals accordingly. For example, in a parents' group his goal will be to help the parents recognize how their feelings and reactions affect the behavior of the child. In a psychophysiological group the therapist's goals will be to help the group members understand the relationship of physical symptoms to their emotional responses.

Group Therapy for Psychoses

Group therapy is also a popular form of treatment for psychotic patients, in both hospital inpatient and outpatient groups. Our model of group therapy recognizes that the goals of the group therapist are different in groups of psychotic patients and in groups of neurotic patients. The lack of ego strength and poor anxiety tolerance of psychotic patients necessitate that the group therapist use a more supportive technique and plan for limited goals. Here again the four general goals of group therapy apply, but in a more restrictive manner. Long-term group therapy ($1\frac{1}{2}$ years or longer) with psychotic patients allows them to become dependent on the therapist and the group. Current reality problems the group members have in their home and at work can be discussed in the group. The group members learn to express some of their feelings in the group atmosphere. The goals of the therapist are to strengthen defensive patterns of behavior, provide support and dependency, and increase repression. By so doing, future attacks of overt psychotic behavior necessitating hospitalization may be curtailed. In general, for psychotic patients to achieve the same goals as neurotic patients several years (3–5) of group therapy are necessary. There are, of course, exceptions to this statement. Some psychotic patients will make tremendous gains in group therapy, while some neurotic patients will show few if any gains.

Long-term group therapy programs are popular in state hospitals, veterans' hospitals, and other institutions where patients are hospitalized for extended periods of time. Some hospitals have inpatient-outpatient groups. In these groups the goals of the therapist are oriented towards discharging the patient from the hospital and continuing group therapy on an outpatient basis. Since rehospitalization of the chronically ill psychotic patient is a frequent necessity, the group therapy program will continue regardless of whether the patient is in or out of the hospital.

Short-term group programs for recently hospitalized psychotic patients are popular in state and private psychiatric hospitals. In this type of group activity the patient remains in the group only during his period of hospitalization. The group is not composed of a stable membership; new members are added as others leave the hospital. The goals of the group leader are oriented towards those methods that will resolve the psychosis by reestablishing defensive patterns of behavior and increasing repression. Two important goals of the group leader are to help the patient recognize his illness and to motivate ventilation of feelings and the discussion of conflicts with other patients and staff personnel, as well as other conflicts that existed before hospitalization. The leader does not encourage the group members to explore intragroup feelings. To do so would raise their anxiety level too high. In this type of group activity his primary goal is to help resolve the psychosis of the patient.

The structured hospital ward meeting is a modification of the short-term type of group therapy. A detailed account of hospital ward meetings is given in Chap. 9. Group activities, though similar in many respects to group therapy, are classified differently from group therapy. A separate section at the end of the present chapter discusses group activities in detail.

A popular form of group therapy in state-hospitals is the repressive-inspirational type described earlier. In this form the goals of the therapist are to increase socialization of the group members, provide mutual support, encourage the ventilation of feelings, and demonstrate interest in the welfare of the members. The various techniques used by therapists in repressive-inspirational therapy are actually those of a supportive type. As with other types of group therapy for psychotic patients, the general goals of the therapist are limited.

Geriatric Group Therapy

Group programs with geriatric patients are of several types. A group activity that utilizes social, recreational, and occupational measures conceived along psychotherapeutic principles would more correctly describe the group programs for geriatric patients. The elderly depressed person, the chronic schizophrenic, and persons with organic brain diseases may be placed in geriatric groups. The goals of the group leader are to improve patient behavior for the hospitalized patient, encourage ventilation of feelings, provide support in the hospital, increase self-esteem by the performance of various tasks, and offer support for the patient who is able to leave the hospital. Dr. Maurice E. Linden worked with 51 senile women patients in groups for over a period of two years. These women, whose average age was 70 years, were patients in a state hospital for an average period of 21 months. The group program did not follow the technique of formal group therapy but consisted of a variety of methods to induce group interaction such as educational talks, recitations by group members, and dual leadership. The results of this group activity program were that 30 per cent of the women were able to leave the hospital and resume their former roles in society, and an additional 15 per cent were discharged as soon as placements could be made for them.[28] Dr. Matthew Ross surveyed the literature of group programs with elderly patients in 1959 and concluded that a variety of group activities improved the morale and general behavior of geriatric patients.[29] With these patients the goals of the therapist or leader are necessarily limited, but, as shown in studies by Linden and Ross, the group can be worthwhile and helpful for the elderly patient.

Group Programs for the Mentally Retarded

Group programs are now being employed in institutions for the mentally retarded. Staff personnel in these institutions are becoming more aware of the emotional problems involved; Dr. Rudolph Kaldeck, for example, has found that a large percentage of the mentally retarded are incapacitated more by emotional difficulties than by intellectual deficit. Dr. Kaldeck started group programs in a state school and employed techniques of group therapy according to the specific needs of the mental defectives. The results revealed an improvement in the interpersonal relationships.[30]

Group programs for mentally retarded people should have two goals: (1) improvement of emotional difficulties for the mildly retarded, and (2) training programs for the mildly, moderately, and severely retarded. The mildly retarded person can be trained for a satisfactory vocation within the limits of his intellectual ability. Group programs with the moderately and severely retarded require skilled leaders with special training. With the latter group of patients the goals of these programs are elementary and consist of training in how to dress, eat, and control body functions.

Group programs with mentally retarded people should be classified as a group activity and not formal group therapy. The goals and type of the group activity for the mentally retarded will depend on their specific needs.

Adolescent Group Therapy

Group therapy programs with adolescents and children require modifications of goals and technique of the therapist depending upon the age, diagnosis, patterns of behavior, tolerance for anxiety, and physical setting of the group program. Group therapy programs and group activity programs are employed for the adolescent neurotic patient, the adolescent psychotic patient, the juvenile delinquent, and children in the latency period of development.

Neurotic Patients. Adolescent groups of neurotic patients can be treated satisfactorily on an outpatient basis. There are several factors the therapist must be aware of in treating adolescent neurotic patients. The psychological and physiological changes at puberty account for the activation of intense feelings within the normal adolescent. Infantile conflicts are reactivated. The ego undergoes changes and reorientation. Adolescents are ambivalent about their dependency needs. Adult sexual feelings become apparent in the adolescent. There are marked mood swings, increased hostility, and explosive outbursts over minor provocations.[31] The adolescent experiences increased anxiety in all his group relationships. In the adolescent patient with a neurosis, anxiety is even more pronounced. A group therapy program for adolescent neurotic patients should therefore be designed so that the anxiety of the patients can be properly controlled. The therapist must be more supportive, directive, and active in adolescent groups of neurotic patients. He must utilize methods for relieving anxiety, such as serving food and drink or providing social and recreational activities. There are other factors that influence the technique of the therapist. The adolescent is primarily peer-oriented,[32] and if he is allowed to discuss his feelings among his peers he may better understand them than if obliged to discuss them with an adult. Thus the therapist should not make interpretations to the group members.

Adolescents often have hostile feelings to authority figures. In group therapy they should be encouraged to ventilate their hostile feelings to the authority figure (group therapist) of the group. Usually sexual feelings should not be discussed in adolescent groups of neurotic patients.[33] As with adult groups of neurotic patients, the discussion of sexual material in group meetings raises the anxiety level and leads to group problems of withdrawal and absences. The adolescent may protest against it, but he secretly likes structure and control. The therapist should set limits with his group members and provide the necessary controls. At the same time he should be aware that physical activity (sports and recreation) is one of the best ways for the adolescent to relieve tension. The therapist may need to incorporate physical activities in the structure of the group therapy. Adolescent groups of neurotic patients should be structured according to the age of the patients. There should not be a wide age range between the group members. Groups are composed of group members aged 12–14 years, 14–16 years, 16–18 years, or close within these age groupings. The maturation of the ego, physical size, intellectual ability, and social interests of the 16–18-year-old adolescent are different from those of the 12–14-year-old youngster. Adolescent groups of neurotics may be all boys, all girls, or both sexes. Dr. Nathan Ackerman states that the mixed group is the more realistic.[33]

Group therapy programs for adolescent patients with neuroses may be similar to group programs for children in that the group therapy is a part of an overall treatment program. The adolescent may also be treated with individual therapy. His parents, too, may be actively involved in the treatment program. With the younger adolescent (12–14 years) therapeutic work with parents is frequently a necessity. The specific goals of the program will depend on the needs of the patient. Group therapy can help the resocialization of the silent and withdrawn adolescent who has difficulties with his peer relationships. The passive, nonassertive, and depressed adolescent who has conflicts with authority figures can benefit from group therapy through the development of self-assertion and the ventilation of angry feelings.

Psychotic Patients. Group therapy programs for psychotic adolescents will naturally have more limited goals than programs with neurotic adolescents. From the standpoint of treatment by group therapy, the psychotic adolescent can be compared to the psychotic adult. The illness is more severe; there is less ego integration, and the tolerance for anxiety is limited. The therapist's technique should be supportive and flexible. As with adult groups of psychotic patients, his technique with groups of psychotic adolescents should be such that the group members' anxiety does not reach disintegrative levels. The therapist usually finds it helpful to use social, recreational and occupational activities within the framework of the group program.

Juvenile Delinquent Patients. Group therapy with the juvenile delinquent differs from that for the adolescent neurotic youngster. The personality structure of the delinquent reveals an intense need for acting-out behavior as a protection against his inner anxieties. The delinquent's tolerance for anxiety is at such a minimum that any attempt to form a relationship with another person results in acting-out behavior. Then, too, the delinquent is not motivated for any type of psychotherapy. For these reasons the delinquent can be treated in group therapy in the institutional setting where there are sufficient controls against acting-out behavior. The therapist's goals for the juvenile delinquent is directly related to the overall treatment program of the entire institution. An isolated program for the delinquent would be of questionable value. The more successful programs now employ a series of group structures centered around their dormitory life as well as their educational, recreational, and occupational duties. The therapist's technique is closely related to the psychodynamics of the delinquent. Their anxiety tolerance is at such a minimum that the technique has to be considerably more active, supportive, and directive. The anxiety tolerance of the juvenile delinquent is less than that of the psychotic patient. In group therapy the juvenile delinquent fights against forming relationships with peers and opposes all authority with his entire resources. His most common method of protection against anxiety is acting-out behavior. In the controlled environment of an institution the increased anxiety of the delinquent in group therapy requires careful coordination by the therapist and institution staff. Within the group the anxiety level can quickly reach a disintegrative level. The therapist should furnish food and drink to the delinquents as an anxiety-relieving device, and he should also incorporate social, recreational, and athletic activities in the program. Moreover, the therapist has to be firm and authoritative with the delinquent group members and exert the necessary controls to prevent acting-out behavior in the meetings.

The specific goal of the therapist in a program for juvenile delinquents is to work towards establishing a relationship with the members by encouraging them to talk about their problems, by helping them recognize the self-destructive results of acting out, and to modify their impulsive patterns of behavior.

Group Therapy for Children

Group therapy and group activity programs for children are becoming popular in many child guidance clinics, hospitals, and schools. The type of group program depends on the age of the child, diagnosis, and type of behavior exhibited by the child. Group programs for the older child (7–11 years) are often referred to as *activity group therapy*.[17] Group programs for the younger child (4–6 years) are spoken of as *play therapy*.

Group programs for children differ from group programs for adults, and are only one part of the overall treatment program. Each child in the group is usually seen in individual therapy, and the parents are seen by a social worker or caseworker. A team approach is used that consists of the child psychiatrist, psychologist, psychiatric social worker, and others. The focus is on the individual child. In contrast to adult group therapy which emphasizes a group approach with group goals and group unity, children's groups focus on the individual child at the expense of group goals and group unity.[34]

In general, the goal of group programs with children is to supplement the overall therapeutic program by providing an opportunity for peer relationships. More specifically, group programs for children encourage the ventilation of feelings, aid the child in his socialization with others, and allow him an outlet for aggression in a structured setting. Group programs for children also help the individual child's therapist to understand how the child functions in group relationships. In addition, the child's group behavior can be pointed out to the parents so that they can be given specific knowledge of how their child reacts to peers and authority figures. Thus group programs for children not only benefit the child but afford the psychiatric team additional valuable information on the child's behavior in groups.[35]

Family Therapy

The development of family therapy during the past few years has raised the question in professional circles of the relationship between group therapy and this new psychotherapeutic procedure. Both family therapy and group therapy utilize a therapeutic relationship that involves a group of people. However, each person in group therapy is suffering from some form of emotional illness. Family therapy differs in that the group is composed of the emotionally ill person plus his immediate family. Thus the emotionally ill family member is more or less isolated among the remaining family members who are not primarily emotionally ill. As with group therapy, however, one of the primary purposes of family therapy is to provide a setting whereby faulty behavior patterns can be recognized and treated. Like the goals in group therapy, the recognition and modification of the family behavior patterns should result in less anxiety in the family and improvement in the family members who are emotionally ill. Dr. Nathan Ackerman, a pioneer in the study of the psychodynamics of family life, points out that family therapy is complex and involves a clinical team which, at appropriate times depending on the status of the family, utilizes individual therapy with the emotionally ill family member or other family members, joint sessions with parents or siblings, and, of course, therapy with the entire family group. Dr. Ackerman speaks of family therapy procedures as a flexible combination of individual therapy and group therapy.[38]

A comparative study of family therapy and group therapy by Dr. Joseph H. Handlon and Dr. Morris B. Parloff, both of whom have had experience in treating patients in family therapy and group therapy, describes four conditions that contrast the two types of therapy:

1. Group therapy is composed of people who are all experiencing emotional difficulties. Group members are not alone or isolated with their emotional conflicts and profit from sharing their feelings with each other. In family therapy, the "sick one" is alone and isolated. Other family members usually do not recognize the need of treatment for themselves. The sick family member is not on an equal footing with the other family members. In group therapy the group members are not together except in actual group meetings, but the family members are together constantly. Family pressures outside of meetings result in treatment difficulties.

2. Group therapy offers the group members the opportunities to recognize their faulty patterns of behavior in a new setting and to experiment with new ways of modifying or changing them. In family therapy the patterns of behavior of its members can be seen only in a setting that is rigid and of long standing. The patterns of behavior of the family unit preserve its way of life and the chances of recognizing faulty patterns of behavior and changing them may be seen by the family as a threat to its integrity and function.

3. Distortions of reality due to faulty patterns of behavior are recognized by the group members in group therapy. In family therapy distortions of reality are shared and supported by the family. Each family member has a specific role structure which, taken collectively by all the family members, produces an equilibrium in the family. This equilibrium, regardless of its unrealistic components, is very resistant to change.

4. In group therapy the group members recognize and utilize transference reactions to understand reality distortions of their everyday group relationships.

In family therapy transference distortions may occur between the emotionally ill family member, his parents, and the therapist. The transference distortions of the emotionally ill family member are usually supported by the family structure which again is highly resistant to change. Then, too, multilevel transference distortions may occur in the interpersonal relationships of the various members of the family. In group therapy the group members can examine transference reactions with one authority figure. In family therapy the situation is much more complicated because family groups may have a variety of authority figures, the therapist, the parents, and possibly even the grandparents.[39]

There is one additional aspect of family therapy that poses a problem in treatment of the entire family—scapegoating. The emotionally ill family member is usually the scapegoat of the family. Anxiety experienced by other family members is displaced onto the sick family member. A family equilibrium is thus established in which the other family members remain anxiety-free by displacing their anxiety on the scapegoat. Thus if treatment changes this pattern of family behavior, other family members become anxious and uncomfortable, developing negative feelings for the treatment procedure that make them feel thus. Such situations do not occur only in family therapy. The patient in individual therapy and group therapy may describe similar situations in his own family. Family therapy involves a special problem in that other family members are also encouraged to change their behavior patterns, and this complication produces the uncomfortable symptoms associated with anxiety. In the final analysis the specific needs of the patients should at all times determine the type of treatment.

GROUP ACTIVITIES

Much of the confusion and misunderstanding about group therapy is caused by the large number of diversified group programs called *group therapy* and *group psychotherapy*. According to our definition given earlier, many of these group programs are not group therapy, but *group activities*. Group therapy is tightly structured (see Chap. 4), and is chiefly concerned with therapeutic goals. Group activities, on the other hand, can be quite easily structured; the members often come and go at will, and their number is not prescribed; the technique of the leader can vary from meeting to meeting and include such widely diverse things as lectures, movies, and physical games; and the goals of the group can be nontherapeutic as well as therapeutic.

Therapeutic Group Activities

In many respects therapeutic group activities can be termed a type of psychotherapy, since the members of these groups may receive help in understanding their emotional problems. The hospital ward meeting for psychiatric patients (Chap. 9) is an excellent example of a beneficial therapeutic group activity. These therapeutic group activities can serve a variety of purposes, as are recreational and occupational therapy programs, short-term group programs for hospitalized patients, social activities, specially designed group programs in schools with students and teachers, social clubs for discharged patients from mental hospitals, Addicts Anonymous, Alcoholic Anonymous, and similar groups. A group program in an institution for patients with mental retardation may have as its goal training patients to eat, dress, and care for themselves. A group program for elderly people may have as its goal improved patient behavior on a ward. A group recreational program on an intensive-treatment ward encourages patients to become more active and develop new talents. A group social program on an intensive-treatment ward helps the patient to interact and relate to others in a social atmosphere. A group program in a school with latency-age children who have behavior problems has as its goal improved behavior of the children and utilizes social and recreational activities to accomplish it. A social club for discharged patients from mental hospitals is a group program that offers the discharged hospital patient a place where he can feel accepted and understood. These are a few of many kinds of group programs that have various composition, structure and goals. Even though they are called group therapy by some people and are helpful to patients in understanding their emotional problems, for purposes of definition in this book they are classified as therapeutic group activities.

These therapeutic group activities have many positive features and rewards. Group discussions can provide a method for identifying personal feelings and promote an understanding of conscious differences, feelings of belonging or acceptance, education, support, socialization and desires to help one another. Also our population contains a large segment of people who experience feelings of inferiority, inadequacy, low self-esteem, and guilt. Group activities prove to be supportive for these people as they come to realize that others have feelings similar to theirs. A mother is often relieved to find that other mothers experience troubled feelings about their children. Students in college find nightly "bull sessions" in the dormitory rewarding. Group programs (often loosely called "group therapy") that employ didactic material, lectures, movies, and discussion topics fall in the category of group activities. They benefit their members by allowing the ventilation of feelings and thoughts and by providing the realization that others have feelings similar to theirs. The success of Alcoholics Anonymous throughout the world testifies to the value of an activity that utilizes techniques similar to those in group therapy.

The use of therapeutic group activities in treating patient with emotional illness is just as important as the more formal types of therapy (individual therapy and group therapy). Milieu therapy in psychiatric hospital wards emphasizes the therapeutic value of informal group relationships between the staff and personnel and the patients. The groups of patients who participate with a staff leader in social, recreational, and occupational therapy programs are examples of the informal group relationships on a psychiatric ward. The regular structured hospital ward meeting for the patients typifies a large informal group, while the conversation between a psychiatric aide and a patient is an example of a small informal group relationship. In each of these group relationships, patterns of behavioral interaction can be observed between the members of the group and its leader—that is, the dynamics of the group relationship come into play. The patient on the psychiatric ward reacts with other patients and the staff in behavior patterns that he has used throughout his life. His behavior patterns in the informal group relationships of the psychiatric ward are similar to those of his group relationships on the outside, and can be utilized therapeutically during his period of hospitalization. With the staff's help the patient has the opportunity to observe his reactions and faulty emotional responses to other patients and to staff personnel.

Therapeutic group activities with children are becoming more popular in public schools and institutions for the care and treatment of mental retardation, epilepsy, cerebral palsy, poliomyelitis, and juvenile delinquency. There is also an increasing awareness among psychiatrists, psychologists, psychiatric social workers, and educators that group support for school teachers and institution staffs should be accomplished concurrently with the group program for the student or patient. Treatment goals are enhanced when staff members participate in staff conferences, in-service training programs and other groups where self-expression is encouraged.

Nontherapeutic Group Activities

Nontherapeutic group activities include a wide field of programs in professional, business, social, public health, religious, and other circles. Group programs that are being employed for training purposes, education, social reform, and civic improvement can be classified as nontherapeutic group activities.

In psychiatry, nontherapeutic group activities may consist of staff conferences, supervisory conferences, ward rounds, journal clubs, and other such structured programs where staff personnel meet together on a regular basis. Actually structured staff group activities associated with the care of hospital patients are therapeutic in the sense that the patients benefit from the feedback of such activities.

It is important to emphasize, though, that regardless of whether the group program is formal group therapy with outpatients, an informal recreational therapeutic group activity with patients on a psychiatric ward, or a nontherapeutic group activity such as a staff conference, the interactions among the members of each group have many similar characteristics. The same basic group dynamics occur as in group therapy. The emotional interaction among the members of a group activity may completely overshadow its intellectual purpose or goal. The anxiety of the members is further increased by the leader who does not recognize or understand the behavior patterns of the members of the group activity; for example, the silent group member, the group member who arrives late at meetings, the absentee, the group member who is competitive with the group leader, the group members who get angry with each other, the group members who get together independently of the others (forming subgroups), and the group member who is overtly hostile and defiant to the leader. The inept leader who does not know the dynamics of the group interaction reacts with anxiety and hostility himself, and attempts to force and coerce the members into action. The leader who is frightened of the anxiety created within a group of people, who cannot resolve issues related to the group interaction, and who has difficulty separating intellectualizations from genuine insight will have problems in operating a group activity program satisfactorily. The result may be bedlam. Even if the group activity does not disintegrate, its goals are not accomplished and meeting after meeting is held with no constructive work accomplished.

The group activity leader who has a knowledge of the dynamics of group relationships recognizes when anxiety occurs among the members of the group activity. He should make every attempt to reduce this anxiety before proceeding with the intellectual purpose of the group. Effective leadership of group activities depends on an awareness and understanding of the dynamics of group relationships.

Description of a Nontherapeutic Group Activity. The author has been a member of a staff group activity that has repeatedly demonstrated the dynamics of group relationships. The staff group was composed of staff psychiatrists, psychiatric residents, a psychologist, a psychiatric social worker, nurses, occupational therapist, and psychiatric aides. One of the psychiatrists was the ward administrator and staff leader. The goal of the staff group was the diagnosis and treatment of patients on a 20-bed psychiatric ward. The emphasis was on milieu therapy. Formal methods of treatment included individual therapy, group therapy, drugs, and electroconvulsive treatments. Informal group relationships were an important part of the ward structure. Patient ward meetings were held twice weekly at a regularly structured time and place. Social, recreational, and occupational therapy groups were part of the daily activities of the patients. The staff group activities consisted of a daily one-hour conference with the staff psychiatrists, residents, nurses, and psychiatric aides and a once-weekly staff meeting.

Many of the behavior patterns exhibited by the staff personnel were similar to those of group members in group therapy or of patients who are members of a group activity. Invariably there was hostility to the staff psychiatrist (who, we have seen, was the ward administrator and staff leader). On one occasion the anxiety and hostility to the staff leader reached a very high level. The chairman of the department of psychiatry, although not the titular head of the ward, attended the daily staff conferences several times a week. He supervised residents, gave regular lectures, and held weekly teaching conferences for the residents. Because of other commitments, the chairman was absent from the ward and from his other duties for a month. The reaction to his leaving occurred immediately after his departure. The residents became very hostile and angrily attacked the staff leader in the daily staff conferences. Prior conflicts with the staff group leader that had seemed minor now reached major proportions. The increased anxiety of the residents spread to the other members of the staff and the patients. Several of the patients became more disturbed during this period. The staff leader encouraged the residents to ventilate their feelings. Within a week's time the anxiety had subsided and the ward was back to normal operation. In this instance, separation anxiety (absence of the chairman of the department) precipitated the hostile reactions of the residents. Their anger with the chairman for cancelling supervision, lectures, and conferences was displaced to the staff leader. Following the ventilation and recognition of their angry feelings, the residents' anxiety subsided.

On other occasions residents and nurses became angry with the staff psychiatrist for admitting patients at night or for admitting acutely disturbed patients that required extra attention. The residents and nurses would "subgroup" with one another and angrily denounce the staff psychiatrist. However, they would not talk to the staff psychiatrist—the staff group leader. In his presence they denied the existence of any problems.

Nurses on occasions would be extremely competitive with each other and with residents. The nurse who had a conflict with a resident might attempt to perform additional therapeutic work with the resident's patient. The nurse might also go to the staff group leader and report a difficulty the resident was having rather than discuss the difficulty with the resident.

An unresolved conflict between the chief nurse and the psychiatric aides later found expression in the repeated lateness of the aides. On another occasion, the staff leader had to reprimand a resident. The resident became angry but could not discuss the incident with the staff leader. Instead, the resident scapegoated a female psychiatric aide. His anger at the staff leader was displaced to a subordinate.

These behavior patterns of the staff personnel illustrate their reactions to the anxiety resulting from the emotional interaction with each other and with the staff leader. The behavior patterns in this staff group are no different from those of people in many other groups of society.

SUMMARY

Man has always lived in a society of group relationships. He starts life in the family group. Over the years of history he has moved from tribal, hunting, religious, warlike and other such groups to the varied groups of modern culture (professional, occupational, social, religious, or recreational). All of these groups, however, are basically the same, each being structured around a leader and a set of members, with behavior determined by the degree of anxiety produced in the group, the anxiety in turn being influenced by the amount of closeness in the group and the personality patterns of its members and leader.

Because they reproduce the basic dynamics of everyday group relationships, group methods of treating people with emotional illnesses have been found to have therapeutic value, and have progressed from the separate use of group activities in the early years of this century to the present status of group therapy as an accepted form of psychotherapy. The interest in group dynamics and the numerous methods and techniques of group therapy and group activities utilized at the present time account for its rapid growth and expansion in hospitals and related institutions, guidance clinics, and private practice. The author feels that the model of group therapy described here is based on a theory of group dynamics that can be universally applied to all forms of group relationships—family, social, occupational, professional, recreational, and religious groups—and, of course, the more formal types of therapeutic groups. Although differing from group therapy, a wide range of group activities (group counseling, recreational groups, occupational therapy groups, activity groups, and social clubs) can be understood by means of this theory of group dynamics and utilized therapeutically with people who have either emotional or physical illnesses. The difference between group therapy and group activities can be clarified and the goals of a total group program can be placed in the proper prospective.

REFERENCES

1. Freud, S.: *Group Psychology and the Analysis of the Ego,* Liveright Publishing Corporation, New York, 1949.
2. Mesmer, A.: *Hypnotism,* Walter Scott Publishers, London, 1908 (translated by A. F. Hoplink).
3. Pratt, J. H.: "The Principles of Class Treatment and Their Application to Various Chronic Diseases," *Hosp. Social Serv.,* 6:404, 1922.
4. Pratt, J. H.: "The Home Sanatarium Treatment of Consumption," *Johns Hopkins Hosp. Bull.,* XVII:140, 1906.

5. Simmel, E.: *Psychoanalysis and War Neuroses*, International Psychoanalytic Press, Vienna, 1921, pp. 30–44.
6. Adler, A.: *Guiding the Child*, Greenberg: Publisher, Inc., New York, 1931.
7. Moreno, J. L.: *The First Book of Group Psychotherapy*, 3d ed., Beacon House, Inc., New York, 1958.
8. Klapman, J. W.: *Group Psychotherapy Theory and Practice*, Grune & Stratton, Inc., New York, 1946.
9. Frank, J. D.: "Group Therapy in the Mental Hospital," Monograph Series No. 1, American Psychotherapy Association, Mental Hospital Service, Washington, D.C., 1955.
10. Schilder, P.: *Psychotherapy*, W. W. Norton & Company, Inc., New York, 1938.
11. Foulkes, S. H.: *Introduction to Group-Analytic Psycho-Therapy*, William Heinemann, Ltd., London, 1948.
12. Mann, J., and E. V. Semrad: "The Use of Group Therapy in Psychotics," *J. Social Casework*, 29:176–181, 1948.
13. Mann, J.: "Group Therapy with Adults—General Observations," *Am. J. Orthopsychiat.*, 23:332–337, 1953.
14. Mann, J.: "Some Theoretic Concepts of the Group Process," *Internat. J. Group Psychotherapy*, 5:235–241, 1955.
15. Semrad, E. V.: "Psychotherapy of the Psychoses in a State Hospital," *Dis. Nerv. System*, 9:105–111, 1948.
16. Semrad, E. V., and J. Arsenian: "The Use of Group Processes in Teaching Group Dynamics," *Am. J. Psychiat.*, 108:358–363, 1951.
17. Slavson, S. R.: *An Introduction to Group Therapy*, The Commonwealth Fund, New York, 1943.
18. Slavson, S. R.: *The Practice of Group Psychotherapy*, International Universities Press, Inc., New York, 1947.
19. Slavson, S. R. (ed.): *The Fields of Group Psychotherapy*, International Universities Press, Inc., New York, 1956.
20. Arieti, S. (ed.): *American Handbook of Psychiatry*, Basic Books, Inc., New York, 1959, pp. 1362–1374.
21. Wolf, A., and E. K. Schwartz: "The Psychoanalysis of Groups: Implications for Education," *Internat. J. Social Psychol.*, 1:9–17, 1955.
22. Laughlin, H.: *The Neuroses in Clinical Practice*, W. B. Saunders Company, Philadelphia, 1956.
23. American Psychiatric Association Committee on Public Information: *A Psychiatric Glossary*, Washington, D.C., 1957.
24. Rado, S.: *Collected Papers in the Psychoanalysis of Behavior*, Grune & Stratton, Inc., New York, 1956, p. 214.
25. American Psychiatric Association: *Diagnostic and Statistical Manual: Mental Disorders*, Washington, D.C., 1952, pp. 34–39.
26. Kardiner, A.: *The Individual and His Society*, Columbia University Press, New York, 1939, p. 69.
27. Hollingshead, A. B., and F. C. Redlich: *Social Class and Mental Illness*, John Wiley & Sons, Inc., New York, 1958.
28. Linden, M. E.: "Group Psychotherapy with Institutionalized Senile Women: Study in Gerontological Human Relations," *Internat. J. Group Psychotherapy*, 3:150–170, 1953.
29. Ross, M.: "Recent Contributions to Gerontological Group Psychotherapy," *Internat. J. Group Psychotherapy*, 9:442–450, 1959.
30. Kaldeck, R.: "Group Psychotherapy with Mentally Defective Adolescents and Adults," *Internat. J. Group Psychotherapy*, 8:185–192, 1958.

31. Josselyn, I. M.: *The Adolescent and His World,* Family Association of America, New York, 1952.
32. Schulman, I.: "Transference, Resistance and Communication Problems in Adolescent Psychotherapy Groups," *Internat. J. Group Psychotherapy,* 9:496–503, 1959.
33. Ackerman, N. W.: "Group Psychotherapy with a Mixed Group of Adolescents," *Internat. J. Group Psychotherapy,* 5:249–260, 1955.
34. Ginott, Haim, G.: *Group Psychotherapy with Children,* McGraw-Hill Book Company, Inc., New York, 1961.
35. Lippman, H. S.: *Treatment of the Child in Emotional Conflict,* McGraw-Hill Book Company, Inc., New York, 1962, pp. 71–85.
36. Fenichel, O.: *The Psychoanalytic Theory of Neurosis,* W. W. Norton & Company, Inc., New York, 1945, pp. 498–499.
37. Personal communication from Dr. William Rottersman, Atlanta, Ga.
38. Ackerman, N. W.: *Psychodynamics of Family Life,* Basic Books, Inc., New York, 1958, pp. 304–315.
39. Handlon, J. H., and M. B. Parloff: "The Treatment of Patient and Family as a Group: Is It Group Psychotherapy?" *Internat. J. Group Psychotherapy,* 12:132–141, 1962.

3

The Dynamics of Group Therapy

In many ways this chapter on the dynamics of group therapy is the pivotal one in the book. Heretofore the concern has been chiefly with the general phenomena of group behavior. We can now discuss group therapy itself and examine the mechanisms involved in the process of a specific model of group therapy. It is necessary, however, to distinguish our model of group therapy from other forms of group therapy, psychotherapy, and psychoanalysis in order to show how the basic technique is related to the adaptational frame of reference, to examine the group's similarity to the family, and, finally, to show how the total group process falls into three general stages.

THE MODELS OF GROUP THERAPEUTIC PROGRAMS

The types of group therapeutic programs in practice today are described in a recent study.[8] Winick, Kadis, and Krasner sent out questionnaires in 1960 to the entire membership of the American Group Psychotherapy Association. They received replies from 64 per cent of the membership (643 out of 1,003 recipients in the United States). The type of group therapeutic programs reported revealed that 48 per cent were psychotherapy groups, 28 per cent psychoanalytic groups, 14 per cent counseling groups, 2 per cent guidance groups, 1 per cent supportive groups, and less than 1 per cent psychodrama groups.

In the literature the treatment of emotionally ill patients in groups is variously referred to as *group therapy, group psychotherapy, analytic group therapy, group analysis,* and *group psychoanalysis.* Generally, most of the terms for group therapy can be used interchangeably. Group psychoanalysis differs from group therapy in claiming that patients with emotional illnesses can be psychoanalyzed in the group setting. Both group therapy and group psychoanalysis are based on psychoanalytic theory—the encouragement of ventilation of material, an understanding of transference reactions, overcoming resistances, development of insight, and changes in behavior. There are basic differences, however, in procedures and goals in the various group therapeutic programs. Since the different models and techniques of group therapeutic programs (both group therapy and group psychoanalysis) cut across each other in theory and practice, a discussion of these basic practices or issues seems the best approach to understanding how they differ from each other and how they compare with our model of group therapy. The major issues are:

1. Cohesiveness versus noncohesiveness in groups.
2. Treatment approaches to the individual in the group versus treatment approaches to the group as a complete unit.
3. A therapist's technique that focuses on the behavior of the group members during group meetings versus techniques that focus on anamnestic material, dreams, fantasies, and free association.
4. The therapist as an authority figure to the group versus his assuming multiple roles in the group.
5. Extensive versus moderate goals for the patient in group therapy.
6. Cotherapists versus one therapist.
7. The selection of patients for group therapy.
8. Alternate meetings without the therapist versus no meetings without the therapist.

Cohesiveness in Therapeutic Groups. The issue of whether or not there is cohesiveness in therapeutic groups is often debated. Some therapists feel that the structure of a therapy group cannot develop cohesiveness. Each member should remain aloof from the group so that he can have the freedom to discuss his conflicts and problems. The group is not viewed as having a common aim.[9] Most therapists, however, feel that the therapeutic results of the group come from the common bonds of interest, cohesiveness, and group spirit that develop among the members; that the freedom to express both positive and negative feelings is based on the mutual respect the members develop for each other.[3,10-13] The model of group therapy presented in this book adheres to this latter principle.

Individualized Treatment. There are group therapists who feel that each member of the group should be treated as an individual. A variety of techniques are utilized; the group therapist can ask or direct questions of individual members, make interpretations to individual members, or see the patient in both individual interviews and group meetings.[9,12,14-16] Other therapists employ a group approach in their questions, their observations being directed to the entire group rather than to a single member.[3,10,11,13,17] Our model of group therapy is *group-oriented* throughout. During group meetings, the therapist elicits only group responses. Interpretations are not made to individual members; in fact, each group member is encouraged to make his own interpretation (mutual analysis).

Individual contacts between the group members and the therapist are discouraged; if they do occur, the subjects raised are brought to the group. The therapist does not practice individual therapy with any one member of the group.

Type of Material. The third issue is concerned with whether the technique of group programs should deal primarily with the here-and-now of the group meetings—the behavior of the group members during the meetings—or with anamnestic material, dreams, fantasies, and free associations. Those group therapists whose goals are more oriented towards modifying behavior patterns through improved reality testing and increased socialization generally employ a technique that deals with the behavior of the group members during group meetings.[3,10,13,17] Those therapists who adhere to the principle that psychoanalysis can be accomplished in groups also focus on the behavior of the group members during group meetings, but in addition they place a strong emphasis on anamnestic material, dreams, fantasies, and free associations in the group process.[12,14–16,18] Our model of group therapy deals primarily with the *behavior of the group members during the group meetings*. Through observations of this behavior the group members learn to recognize, modify, and hopefully change faulty behavior patterns. Dream analysis, free associations, and anamnestic material from the group members are discouraged.

The Therapist as an Authority Figure. There are group therapists who feel their roles are multiple—that is, they are a leader or authority figure, a participant as a group member, and an observer. Thus they employ techniques that are very flexible. Group meetings without the group therapist may occur (the alternate meeting).[12,14–16] Other therapists recognize that the leader is the authority figure of the group and that he occupies a position different from that of the group members.[3,10,11,13,17] Our model of group therapy recognizes that *the therapist is an authority figure at all times*. He thus becomes the most important person in the group and influences the behavior of the group members more than anyone else. In the therapist's role as an authority figure, transference reactions develop and form the basis of his working relationship with the group members.

Extensive versus Moderate Goals for Patients. The proponents of group psychoanalysis state that the goals of patients can be extensive; that psychoanalysis can be accomplished in the group setting; and that a reconstruction of the personality is possible.[12,14,16] Other therapists have more moderate goals. They see group therapy as a form of psychotherapy that primarily promotes a reeducational and relearning process for patients in a group setting.[3,10,11,13,19] Our model of group therapy has *moderate goals* for patients.

Cotherapists versus One Therapist. A few group therapists favor the use of cotherapists in group therapy. Cotherapists are said to create a more normal family setting and provide two authority figures for the therapy group. Cotherapists aid the group process by increasing the group interaction and strengthening interpretations.[21-24] Those therapists who question the value of cotherapists point out such hazards as competition for each therapist by the group members, competition between the therapists themselves, and differences the therapists may have about group members and themselves.[3,13,25-27] Our model of group therapy adheres to the principle of *one group therapist.* Group members have a difficult enough time forming a relationship with one therapist. Cotherapists in one group would only add to the group members' confusion and difficulties. Our model of group therapy places considerable emphasis on the employment of a recorder or observer during group meetings. The recorder is a nonparticipating member of the group who takes written notes and makes observations of the verbal and nonverbal behavior of the group therapist and the group members. By discussions with the recorder after group meetings, the group therapist can evaluate his own behavior in the group, but since the recorder does not actively participate during group meetings the hazard of the recorder's being considered a cotherapist is avoided.

Selection of Patients. Some therapists treat a wide variety of diagnostic categories in groups and make claims that personality disorders, neuroses, psychophysiological illnesses, and psychoses are amenable to group therapy. The proponents of group psychoanalysis include a wide variety of emotional illnesses in their group programs and plan extensive treatment goals.[12,14,16] Most therapists now recognize that patients to be treated in groups should be carefully selected.[3,13,19] Our model of group therapy recommends that *patients for treatment in group therapy should be carefully selected.* The limitations of group therapy are recognized. For many patients, group therapy can be a satisfactory treatment procedure; for others, group therapy is contra-indicated. The reader is referred to Chap. 4 for a detailed discussion of the selection of patients for group therapy.

Alternate Meetings without Therapist. Much controversy has developed among group therapists regarding alternate meetings. Those group therapists who advise alternate meetings without the group therapist's being present feel that the value of these meetings is that they increase ego strengths, develop peer relationships, dilute the transference relationship to the group therapist, help group members to recognize their relationship to the group therapist, increase communication and serve as a means of testing the group members' acting-out behavior.[12,14-16,18] Group therapists who oppose alternate meetings feel that the group members are encouraged to act out, that leaderless groups are nonstructured, nonfunctioning and nontherapeutic.[3,13,17,20] Our model of group therapy *does not employ alternate meetings.* Psychotherapy is dependent on the trained skills of a professional person who employs these skills in a therapeutic atmosphere to help patients to understand, recognize and hopefully change their faulty patterns of behavior. Group therapy should employ the same principles. Then, too, treating a group of people makes it imperative that the therapist insist on the necessary safeguards and structure for the group members. An extremely important factor in group therapy is the group members' establishing a working relationship with the therapist. The series of events that occur with the group members in the development of a working relationship with the therapist are discussed in detail in this chapter. The point to be made here is that a satisfactory group therapy cannot be accomplished in the absence of the therapist.

GROUP THERAPY, PSYCHOTHERAPY, AND PSYCHOANALYSIS

Claims have been made in the literature as to the vast benefits and limitations of group therapy. Group therapy has been hailed as the successor to individual therapy. The proponents of group psychoanalysis consider a personal analysis incomplete without group psychoanalysis. However, the author does not feel that group therapy should be looked upon as a therapeutic panacea. It can be a beneficial treatment procedure, but there are definite limitations in its use. Group therapy does not resolve deep-seated conflicts or change the characterological structure of people. The same is true in individual psychotherapy. Intensive, individual psychoanalysis in a one-to-one relationship is the only tool available for resolving deep-seated problems and conflicts. A comparison of psychoanalysis, psychotherapy, and our model of group therapy is shown in the table and summarized below.

Psychoanalysis is characterized by a very intense relationship between the analysand and the analyst. The patient is seen four to five times a week for several years. The method is rigid and the couch is commonly used. The goals of psychoanalysis are extensive, for it tries to correct early disturbances of the child-parent relationship. Free associations, dreams, and regressive behavior are extensively utilized and the transference is analyzed carefully. Through this very close and intense relationship with the analyst, the patient's relationships with his mother and father are traced. Distortions of the patient's relationship with his parents are examined and compared to the reality of the analytic situation. The key to analysis is the long, intense, close relationship between the patient and the analyst.

Psychotherapy has a less intense relationship than does psychoanalysis. The frequency of visits may vary from one to three times a week. The length of psychotherapy is shorter than psychoanalysis. The couch is seldom used. The goals are limited and are directed towards current problems and conflicts of the patient, such as occupational problems, family difficulty, or sexual conflicts. The transference may or may not be utilized; if it is used, the emphasis is on the reality of the present. Dreams and free associations are also employed with emphasis on the current difficulties of the patient. Early child-parent relationships are not extensively pursued as in psychoanalysis.

In our model, group therapy differs qualitatively and quantitatively from psychoanalysis and psychotherapy. In contrast to the one-to-one relationship of psychoanalysis and psychotherapy, group therapy employs a "one-to-group" relationship—a patient and his relationship to the group. In psychoanalysis and psychotherapy the patient reacts with the analyst or therapist on a one-to-one basis and to the people in his home and social environment. Group therapy thus offers an extra dimension in terms of the emotional interaction between the patient and members of the group. Dreams, free associations, and historical information are not employed in this model of group therapy. The current situation is utilized at the moment of the group meeting. The focus is on the interaction within the group at the time of the meeting. This socialization process is an important goal of group therapy. The depth of group therapy is less when compared to psychoanalysis and psychotherapy. The length may be one year, two years or longer. The frequency of meetings is usually once a week for a period of 1 to 1½ hours. The intense, close relationship fostered in psychoanalysis is much less intense in group therapy. The deep unconscious meanings of free associations and dreams that are utilized extensively in psychoanalysis and to some extent in psychotherapy are not utilized in group therapy. The relationship of a patient with his parents is surveyed in group therapy. Transference phenomena are present; the group therapist is recognized as an authority figure and compared with parents and other authority figures. Members of the group may be seen as brothers or sisters, and the group may be compared to a family. The social interaction within the group is often similar to their early family interaction.

In all forms of psychotherapy the therapist is vitally concerned with the patient's anxiety. Nathan W. Ackerman feels there are common denominators in all forms of psychotherapy. The effect of anxiety is manifest in different ways in individual therapy, psychoanalysis, and group therapy. Anxiety is activated by the patient's inability to perceive and understand the discrepancies between real and unreal experiences. These perceptions of the patient are affected by his inner needs and the inner state of his psyche. In individual psychotherapy the patient is protected by the acceptance of the therapist. The understanding and acceptance of the patient by the therapist in his nonauthoritative role encourage free association.[1] In individual therapy the patient may be able to win the acceptance of a therapist. In group therapy the anxiety of the patient is greatly increased. It may be far more difficult to win the acceptance of the thera-

Table 3.1 *Comparison of Psychoanalysis, Psychotherapy, and Group Therapy*

	Psychoanalysis	Psychotherapy	Group therapy
Goals	Extensive relearning, reeducation, and readaptation of the personality	To reduce anxiety in specific areas related to current conflicts and problems	Improve reality testing Socialization Development of psychological aptitude Prepare for later therapy
Method	Rigid; usually couch; concentration on relationship of past experiences to present personality patterns	Less rigid; no couch; concentration on aspects pertinent to present situation	Concentration on group interaction "at moment" between group, therapist, and individual members during group meeting
Relationship	One-to-one; intense; intimate	One-to-one; less intense than psychoanalysis	One-to-group
Interaction	Patient interacts with analyst and outside world	Patient interacts with therapist and outside world	Patient interacts with therapist, a group of people, and outside world
Length	3–5 years	Variable, several months to 1 or 2 years	1–1½ years or longer
Frequency	4–5 times a week	1–3 times a week	Once a week
Depth	Extensive	Less extensive	Superficial
Transference	Very intense; analyzed carefully in terms of past and present	Less intense, related to current situation; may or may not be utilized	Still less intense, related to group situations utilized as group transference
Dreams	Extensively used	Used less; related to current situation	Not used
Free associations	Extensively used	Used less; related to current situation	Not used
Anamnesis (past history)	Extensively used	Partially used	Not extensively used
Interpretations	By analyst	By psychotherapist	By group members, not group therapist

pist and the group members at the same time. The anxietal manifestations are greatly increased in a group situation. The reality directly confronts the members in group therapy, and the patient's perception of the here-and-now of the group situation mobilizes intense feelings that play a significant part in his future attitude toward the group.

GROUP THERAPY AND THE ADAPTATIONAL FRAME OF REFERENCE

Our model of group therapy has a relationship to the adaptational frame of reference. The behavior of the members during the group meetings is utilized by the therapist so that they can examine and identify their failures in adaptation. They learn that these failures are due to their faulty emergency responses to fear, anger, and guilt. Once the failures in adaptation have been recognized by the group members, new methods of adaptation can be attempted either by modifying or changing their maladaptive patterns. Over the many months of group therapy the group members examine and practice new methods of adaptation, first within the group with each other and with the therapist and later in their daily group relationships. Ovesey and Jameson, in discussing the adaptational technique of psychoanalytic therapy, make the following observations: *

Freud placed his reliance upon the uncovering of unconscious memories. Insight into these memories achieved through the emotional experience of the transference was held to be the curative agent. The classical technique, therefore, emphasized the developmental past and all efforts were bent at a meticulous reconstruction of the infantile neurosis. Little if any attention was paid to the reality present. In fact, the patient often was forbidden to make any important alterations in his current life situation until the analysis of the infantile neurosis was completed. The present, it was believed, would care for itself once the patient had sufficient insight into the past. The transference was managed in the same context. It was viewed by Freud as the product of an innate force, the repetition-compulsion, and was interpreted to the patient in terms of infantile experience without reference to adult needs.

The adaptational technique does not neglect the past, but its emphasis is on the immediate present. The therapist is primarily concerned with failures in adaptation today, how they arose, and what the patient must do to overcome them. To these ends, he keeps in constant touch with the patient's faulty emergency responses of fear, rage, guilty fear, and guilty rage. He tracks them down to their origins from influences in a developmental path and demonstrates to the patient their inhibitory action on behavior in the present. He then analyzes the patient's attempts at magical repair, cuts them down and directs the patient's efforts toward realistic solutions. At all times the patient's adaptation here and now is kept in the foreground. Interpretations always begin and

---

* Lionel Ovesey and Jean Jameson, "The Adaptational Technique of Psychoanalytic Therapy," in S. Rado and G. E. Daniels (eds.), *Changing Concepts of Psychoanalytic Medicine,* Grune & Stratton, Inc., New York, 1956. Used by permission.

end with the present. The principle applies to all behavior, including the transference, which, in an adaptational contact, always reflects a failure in current adaptation. The patient is not permitted to engage in an endless preoccupation with the past. It is not held necessary for him to recover every minute detail of his infantile neurosis before he undertakes corrective steps toward a healthier adaptation.

To the contrary, insight, even partial, as quickly as it is achieved, is used as leverage to encourage him to make the required attempts. The adaptational technique is based on the conviction that insight alone is not enough. It is only the beginning. The patient must then enter into his realized situation, again and again, until, through practice, he undergoes a process of emotional reeducation, brings his faulty emergency responses under control and automizes new patterns of healthy behavior. It is this process of automatization, rooted in Pavlovian principles, that is ultimately curative, not the achievement of insight, and it takes place in the real world, not in the doctor's office.[2]

The author does not wish to give the impression that this model of group therapy singles out the adaptational frame of reference for acceptance and preference over the other psychoanalytic schools. Ovesey's description of the technique of the adaptational frame of reference is given here because it is an excellent description of the therapeutic use of the behavior occurring during the therapy hour. Many analysts, both Freudian and non-Freudian, take issue with Ovesey's statement that the classical technique of psychoanalysis emphasizes primarily the developmental past. Ruth L. Munroe points out that many analysts of all schools deal with present-day reality adaptations of their patients.[28]

Group therapy is also concerned with the present—in this case the reality within the group and the feelings and reactions that occur. As these reality events happen, the group members' faulty emergency responses of fear, anger, and guilt become apparent. Each member exhibits maladaptive patterns of behavior that have been used by them in previous group relationships. These maladaptations began in the early life of the group members and were habitually used in the early social environment of the family. The maladaptations have continued to occur in day-to-day relationships with family, occupational, social, recreational, and religious groups. The group members' behavior and relationships to each other in the group meetings are a repetition of previous behavior and relationships with siblings, peers, and others from their early family and childhood experience. Similar maladaptive behavior patterns have occurred in their daily adult group relationships.

Group therapy thus becomes an experience in social relationships whereby the group members' habitual maladaptations or behavior patterns occur in the here-and-now of the group meetings. The therapist should therefore employ a technique that explores with the group members their behavior patterns as they occur. In this way the members should be able to see similarities between their behavior in the formal therapeutic group and their behavior in day-to-day groups. This is essentially one of the major goals in the model of group therapy.

In this respect the goal of the therapist is to confront the members with their faulty emergency responses and maladaptations in the current here-and-now relationship with other members and with the therapist. During group therapy the members enter the here-and-now of the meetings again and again. They become aware that anxiety occurs in group meetings. The group recognize and interpret to each other their recurrent behavior patterns that have resulted in maladaptations. They develop psychological aptitude or an awareness of their emotional interaction with others. They recognize that the same behavior patterns that occur in group therapy also occur in their day-to-day relationships on the outside. As the group members practice and learn new methods of communicating and relating in the group, they utilize these new methods in their group relationships on the outside. New adaptations of behavior learned in group therapy become new adaptations of behavior in other outside groups. Essentially the group members have undergone a learning and reeducational experience in group therapy.

Group therapy thus can be defined as a structured, reeducational experience involving a group of people and a therapist. The reeducational experience comes, as we have seen, from a specific therapeutic procedure which sets in motion an emotional process. A behavior pattern evolves from this emotional process which fosters both the growth and development of the group as a whole and of the individuals in the group. The term *structure* is concerned with both the physical requirements and the formalized social structure of group therapy. The physical structure and the formalized social structure of group therapy together become the group contract. Inclusion of the group contract into the dynamics of this model of group therapy is one of the most important aspects of the group therapist's technique. This area has been seriously neglected by group therapists in the past. The physical structure of the group (time and day of meetings, attendance or lack of attendance of group members, loss of group members, cancelled meetings, therapist's absences, fees and other rules and regulations pertaining to group therapy) constitutes the important reality events of group therapy. The group members experience intense emotional reactions to any changes in the structure of the group. A cancelled meeting by the therapist implies separation. After a cancelled meeting feelings of rejection, low self-esteem, loss of dependency, and fears of group dissolution may be present. The group members' anxiety increases. They become angry with the therapist for cancelling the meeting and then feel guilty for their anger. The loss of a member from the group has several meanings to the other members. They fear that expressing feelings may dissolve the group. They are also angry at the therapist for not keeping the lost member in the group. From the reality events that occur during group therapy, the members, with the help of the therapist, are able to recognize and identify many of their faulty emergency responses and maladaptive behavior patterns. Chapters 2, 5, and 7 discuss in detail the therapist's technique in integrating the group contract into the dynamics of group therapy.

To the therapist is also delegated the responsibility of teaching the members how to cooperate with him and with each other. The social reality of a group of people being together evokes behavior patterns and feelings. The therapist encourages the members to say what they think and feel. In time the members express feelings of mutual acceptance and interest for each other and for the therapist. With these positive feelings other feelings are created that produce complications. The original goals of the patients are opposite to those of the therapist. Although each member is part of the group, he hopes that the group therapist will like him and cure him without his having to become a real part of the group. Most of the members desire a magical solution to their disturbing problems through some form of treatment such as individual attention from the therapist, hypnosis, or drugs. The goal of the therapist is to help the members understand, through interaction with one another, the behavioral reactions that have been so disturbing to them. The failure of the group members to receive a magical solution to their problems combined with the necessity of being close to others sets the stage for a variety of patterns of behavior on both verbal and nonverbal levels. Absences, lateness, nonpayment of fees, overtalkativeness, intellectualizations, humor, laughter, ingratiation, competition with the therapist, peripheral involvement, overt hostility to a member or members, subgroups within and outside the group, silence and nonverbal attitudes of restlessness, scowling, frowning, tenseness, excessive smoking, and the like are anxietal phenomena that occur in the emotional interaction of the group process. The therapist has the specific role of treating the group as a whole rather than as individuals. At his disposal are a series of maneuvers (techniques) that follow the framework of the group contract (see Chap. 4), or agreement between the therapist and the group members. As soon as the patient begins to react to the stress of the group he wants to change the contract. Then, by attracting attention to the patient's incessant violation of the contract, the therapist can show him how he wants to twist the reality of the group contract to suit his own neurotic maladaptive patterns. The group contract thus becomes the instrument for carrying out the process of emotional interaction; the physical structure of the group, technique of the therapist, and anxietal manifestations of the members are utilized in specific ways throughout the life of the group as a part of the mechanics of the group contract.

The role of the therapist is important in the here-and-now of the group situation. He promotes group interaction by asking the group members how they feel toward each other and toward him. The therapist does not make interpretations nor point out to an individual member transference phenomena, anxiety, acting-out behavior, or behavior patterns. Instead he asks the group members to discuss the thoughts and feelings that each member expresses and then to make the interpretations. An atmosphere of mutual analysis can thus begin early in group therapy and rise to a high, constructive pitch when the members have worked through the anxiety of the group process.

To say that the technique employed by the therapist calls the group's attention to the manifestations of group interaction, both verbal and nonverbal, may give the impression that the therapist sets up interpretations for the group. A more nearly correct view is to see the therapist's role as that of a catalyst. He utilizes expressed thoughts and feelings from the group meetings. He organizes verbal conversation and content as well as nonverbal attitudes and behavior into proper perspective for the group, and comments on the various manifestations of group dynamics that occur. He points out silence, overtalkativeness, restlessness, and the other behavioral characteristics among the members. They, in turn, pick up his cues and begin to develop an awareness of what these things mean from a standpoint of group behavior. As the group members give up their individual wishes and desires and become a part of the group itself, recognition, analysis, and interpretation of group behavior reach a constructive level. A comment or observation from the group therapist about the group behavior will usually elicit a variety of responses and interpretations.

Another important duty of the therapist is to encourage the ventilation and recognition of the defensive hostility of the members. James Mann, in discussing group dynamics, states: "Hostility takes precedence as a means of dealing with all the other people present. The more mature the group, the more covert and subtle will this hostility be and, by the same token, the less mature, or, the more disorganized the group, so will the hostility be more overt and less subtle." [3]

This defensive hostility is manifest in a variety of ways: silence, apathy, boredom, lateness, absences, intellectualization, humor, laughter, ingratiation, overtalkativeness, and competition with the therapist. As previously noted, these manifestations of fear tend to lead to disintegration of the group in order to avoid its closeness.

Working through the group hostility requires patience and understanding leadership from the therapist. Member-to-therapist hostility and member-to-member hostility must be cleared away before constructive mutual analysis of group conflicts and problems can be accomplished. When the group hostility has been resolved, group cohesion and unity are apparent. The members are now willing to be closer to one another and are interested in the common exploration of problems within the group. The use of here-and-now experiences in the group are similar to the here-and-now technique utilized in the adaptational frame of reference.

There is an extra dimension in group therapy. In individual psycho-therapy there is the one-to-one relationship to the therapist and the ex-amination of the patient's behavior with people on the outside. Group therapy has an examination of the members' relationship to the group therapist, an examination of their relationships to people on the outside, and an extra dimension—the examination of the relationship of the group members to each other in the here-and-now situation of the group. From the group interaction in the here-and-now situation springs a therapeutic tool—the group identity, which is actually the security and structure of the group. This group identity emerges from the individual identities of all its members. Ackerman has proposed a theory of family identity that is similar to group identity.[4] He states: *

Family identity is not, and cannot be, a fixed pure thing. It is crystallized out of fluid, on-going processes of multiple competing and partial identity rep-resentations. When two people marry and set themselves to create a new family group with offsprings of their own, they bring with them as individuals a per-sonal identity linked to the identities of their original families. At some levels, these identities representations conflict; at others they collaborate and they may even merge. Therefore, family identity represents a fluid, continuously evolving psychosocial process. It pertains to a dominant identity pattern composed of joined goals, values, and strivings in a life context where there is perpetual competition of partial identities and values. In this sense family entity cannot be a clear, single, unadulterated entity. It is the result of a dynamic evolution of ever-new integrations of shared identity created out of competing components of identity. It is in the very nature of the family phenomenon that each in-dividual member must reconcile his personal identity and values with the shifting representations of family identity. This is deeply influenced by the ongoing processes of integration of the individual's personality into changing family roles. In this context one can readily understand the significance of family in molding the individual success or failure in coping with conflict, either new or old.

Similarly, people in group therapy bring together their personal identi-ties, which are linked to the identity of their original families. From the group interaction emerges the group identity, which forms a structure and a means of relative security for the group members. Each group member forgoes individual wishes and desires for those of the common good of the group. Conflicts and problems are approached not by "What should I do?" but "What does the group feel should be done?" Each individual member would like to pursue his own wishes. At the onset of therapy each member also wants the approval of the therapist and forgoes all personal wishes to have this approval.

One of the therapist's wishes is for the group members to express their

* Nathan W. Ackerman, "Emotional Forces in the Family," Chapter V, p. 79, J. B. Lippincott Co., 1959. Used by permission.

thoughts and feelings. The members begin to do so in order to get the approval of the therapist, with whom they have identified. After a period of time the group members begin to identify each other's behavior and undertake a process of mutual analysis. These new insights are sufficiently rewarding because the members are no longer dependent on the approval of the therapist. When the individual patients are able to analyze their own behavior, the need for approval by the therapist fades as a central issue. Soon the members begin to analyze the group itself, to recognize and discuss the similarities of the group to a family. Members are compared to siblings, relatives, and other influential figures from their past experiences. Reactions to the therapist are seen and experienced as being similar to those with their parents.

The security and structure of the group identity are also similar to the security and structure of the family atmosphere or family identity, in that group members receive support, understanding, and guidance from the therapist and from each other in the same way that normal family members receive these things from parents and siblings. In group therapy the therapist exerts the authoritative control over the members as a father does over his children. He holds the members together. A family without parents falls apart. Similarly, without the group therapist there would be no group. The emotionally ill person is frequently lacking in the love, understanding, respect, and authoritative guidance that is present in the normal family atmosphere. For them the group atmosphere symbolically becomes the family atmosphere longed for in the past but never attained.

THE STAGES OF GROUP THERAPY

It is difficult to delineate with any degree of sharpness the various phases of group therapy. However, there are a series of events or recurrent patterns during the natural history of an adult neurotic group that can be classified as stage I, stage II, and stage III. During stage I there is the formation of a working relationship with the group therapist. Stage II is a transition period between stage I and stage III characterized by the recognition and ventilation of hostile feelings to the group therapist and the development of the group identity. Stage III may be termed the period of mutual analysis or mutual cooperation.

Stage I—Formation of a Working Relationship

In the beginning the group members are totally unaware of the dynamics of group therapy. They have agreed to try group therapy in the hope that they will receive help for disturbing manifestations of anxiety. Many members have doubts about being able to talk before a group of people. Some will question how other people who are ill can help them. Nearly every member enters the group with the hope that the therapist will like him (or her) best and provide some type of magical solution for his problems. He is not particularly concerned with the other members of the group. The goals of the therapist are different. His tasks are to keep the group together, to develop a working relationship with the group members, to promote closeness among the group members and to encourage mutual analysis and mutual cooperation.

The author is aware that some people enter group therapy with excellent motivation for treatment, good psychological aptitude, and minimal expectations of magic from the therapist. Training groups composed of psychiatric residents, psychologists, social workers, or teachers might fall into this category. In patient groups the members' expectations of magic from the group therapist may vary from one extreme to the other, depending on such things as their psychodynamics, previous psychiatric therapy, cultural level, and intellectual abilities. In the author's experience with low-cost clinic groups, most of the members look to the therapist for an easy solution to their problems. In private-practice groups, the membership is usually made up of patients with economic security, higher cultural levels, and greater intellectual ability. Their expectations of magic from the group therapist are less than with patients from low-cost clinic groups.

During the initial group meetings the members are polite and try to impress each other and the therapist. Superficial matters are commonplace topics for discussion and the subjects are rapidly changed. The silent people encourage the talkative people to dominate the conversation. Denial, projection, and rationalization are the most common defense mechanisms used. Each group member exhibits a screen or protective shell against exposure, embarrassment, or rejection which socially isolates him from the others. He employs every maneuver possible to obtain the approval of the other members and particularly of the therapist. Politeness and superficiality are used as a defense against exposure of his real feelings. He is afraid to expose himself because he is fearful of rejection. With each successive meeting each group member becomes more afraid of closeness because closeness means exposure. Most of the group members wish for individual gratifications (dependency, individual love and attention) from the therapist. The structure of group therapy forces each member to interact with the others and this creates frustration. Since the goals of the therapist and those of the group members are different, the members find themselves frustrated, angry and in conflict with the therapist.

It is to be expected that the first few meetings of the group will create some confusion and frustration for the members. In this respect the members experience feelings similar to those that many students experience in their relationship with teachers. In any teacher-student relationship the process of learning is dependent on mutual understanding—freedom to express feelings, desire of the student to learn, and the teacher's skill in imparting knowledge. Normally a teacher-student relationship requires a period of adjustment. If both teacher and student can express their feelings and thoughts with comfort and ease, this mutual adjustment occurs quickly. Nevertheless, there are many occasions for students to be angry with the authority figure or teacher, depending upon the expectation of the students, the cultural factors involved, and the skill of the teacher. Psychotherapy and group therapy resemble the teacher-student relationship in that many of the same ingredients go into the psychotherapeutic process. Thus members beginning group therapy would be expected to experience the frustrations that would ordinarily occur in nontherapeutic groups during their period of adjustment. However, the situation with the members in group therapy is further complicated by the difficulties in expressing feelings, greater dependency needs, fears of rejection, and needs for approval. Then, too, the group therapist's technique of encouraging the group members to provide their own structure rather than obtaining it from the group therapist is at first vague and confusing to the group members. They seek guidance that the therapist does not provide. They ask questions that go unanswered. The members want a guarantee that after each meeting their fears and conflicts will diminish. All these factors create frustration and hostility which are directed against the therapist. Then, too, the role of the therapist may contribute to the confusion and frustration of the members. Naturally his experience and skill in the dynamics and techniques of group therapy will influence the degree of their confusion and frustration.

In the group the member uses the same day-to-day behavior patterns that he used previously outside the group. If gratifications were not obtained from an authority figure (parent, boss, supervisor), the group member either acted out by overt hostility, silence, or competition for the imaginary positions of others, or else quit the group. When their wishes are frustrated by their new authority figure (the therapist), the group members become anxious. Ordinarily, without vigorous leadership and control by the therapist, the members would leave the group. Even with vigorous leadership and control by the therapist, some members do leave the group at this time. They cannot bear the frustration brought about by the therapist and so repeat the behavior patterns which they have used many times on the outside.

At this time the members want to avoid discussing their relationships with each other. The therapist encourages them to do so. There are many techniques the members use to avoid discussing their relationships in the group. They frequently demand that the therapist assign subjects for group discussion, books to read and other activities that would provide structure for the meetings. Early group issues discussed in meetings are the therapists' refusal to answer questions from the members, his technique of exploring group feelings and his encouraging the group to set its own structure. As the anxiety level rises, the group members' defenses against anxiety and behavior patterns become more prominent, and tardiness at meetings, absences, intellectualizations, competitiveness, overtalkativeness, laughter, or hostility occur frequently.

Hostility to the therapist may sometimes be expressed in the first few meetings (one to five). There are several factors that apparently influence the expression of hostility at that time. Some members may have been previously hospitalized in settings where patient ward meetings and other aspects of milieu therapy are employed. During their hospitalization they may have been encouraged to express their feelings. In early meetings these members may express hostility to the therapist because they have learned that expressing feelings is one way to win approval. Other members who commonly express overt hostility in their day-to-day group relationships may start off with similar behavior in group therapy. It is interesting to note that when transference reactions develop, the hostility of the group members (whether or not they have been previously hospitalized) diminishes and they become more passive and compliant.

Probably the most overtly hostile type of group member that a therapist encounters in early group meetings is the juvenile delinquent. The author's experiences in group therapy with juvenile delinquents in a controlled environment (a state training school) have been characterized by the expressions of extreme verbal hostility to the group therapist. Generally the anxiety level of juvenile delinquents is extremely high and it is necessary for the therapist to set limits to prevent acting-out behavior.

Severely ill psychotic patients in early group meetings tend to exhibit more fear, silence, passivity, and compliance than neurotic patients. Even though their rage is present and constitutes more of a problem than for neurotic patients, they are generally afraid to express it verbally.

Gradually the members become less fearful of each other and begin to comply with the wishes of the therapist. They begin to break down superficial barriers by reciting anamnestic material about themselves and their families. As one member tells of his conflicts and problems, others receive encouragement to do likewise. An early positive value of group therapy occurs as the members begin to realize that other people have similar feelings and problems and that they can now talk freely without being rejected or misunderstood. This discussion in the group meetings of reality events that have occurred outside of the group (in the family, in occupations, and in society) serves a useful purpose. The other members and the therapist are asked for advice. Once more the therapist refers all such questions back to the group for their suggestions and recommendations. The members begin to help each other and point out ways to handle reality problems. This helping each other with their problems and conflicts is the beginning of mutual analysis. Meanwhile, the therapist continues to promote group emotional interaction and uses every opportunity to focus on their relationships with each other in the group here-and-now. But this is not an easy matter. The members fear rejection by the therapist if true and real feelings are expressed. Scapegoating, or the displacing of hostility meant for the therapist onto other members, occurs. The members' feelings about group reality events are denied and dismissed as nonexistent. Individual wishes and desires of the members for the therapist's undivided attention still prevail. Attempts may be made to secure individual attention from the therapist by requests for interviews before or after group meetings and telephone calls between group meetings.

During the middle part of stage I (10th to 20th meetings) the members become more passive and feel obligated and even coerced to do whatever the therapist wishes. Transference relationships develop. These are repetitions of early, infantile, inappropriate relationships to parental figures or authority figures. Hostility that may have been expressed to the therapist in earlier meetings is now denied. The members' anxiety has increased manyfold since the onset of group therapy; they recognize that it is directly related to the group meetings; they are now intensely involved in the emotional interaction with the therapist. The original reasons of the group members for undertaking therapy seem overshadowed by their relationships to the therapist. The members become overly concerned with tardiness at meetings, absenteeism, and cancelled meetings. Fears of group dissolution are magnified by absenteeism, loss of group members, cancelled meetings or any reality events that affect the group and the therapist. The anxiety of the group members is primarily due to their fear of the therapist and, to a lesser extent, of the member-to-member relationships. The central theme of the group meetings revolves around their relationship to the therapist. The defense mechanisms of denial and projection are prominent. Hostility between the members increases and they attempt to pick out a scapegoat who can become the target of their hostile feelings. Competition, jealousy, and rivalry between the group members are keen. The members' feelings about the therapist are denied—because expressing their hostile feelings toward him will, they feel, lead to retaliation. Their emotional reactions underneath this cloak of passive resistance are rebellious, rageful, and defiant. Unless their hostility is removed, the group remains in this stage of passive resistance; hence the therapist's need to recognize its presence and encourage its ventilation.

The remainder of stage I consists of working through the group members' transference feelings and reactions. The therapist keeps the relationship to him active by repeatedly asking the members to examine their feelings and attitudes about him. The result of this technique is that the members gradually recognize the similarity between their feelings and reactions to him and those to parents and other authority figures. Hostility experienced toward parents is also experienced toward the therapist. When the expected retaliation from the therapist does not occur, the members are slowly able to ventilate hostility to the therapist. Not all of the members can express their angry feelings in this way. There are those who react with fear, silence, or an urge to defend the therapist. But in later meetings they see that nothing disastrous happens; no one has been destroyed or rejected. The therapist does not retaliate. For the members this is a corrective emotional experience. Thus they receive encouragement to express their feelings as the end of stage I blends into the beginning of stage II.

Other features of stage I that are directly related to the dynamics of group therapy are the dependency wishes of the members, the identification of the group members with the therapist, and the transference reactions. These group entities are closely related to one another but for purposes of explanation they are given here in separate paragraphs.

At the beginning of group therapy the members become dependent on the therapist and the group. Each member has problems of one kind or another and needs help with them. By becoming dependent on the therapist and the group, the member grows more comfortable and feelings of loneliness and helplessness are diminished. The therapist and the group offer each member security and protection. He feels that now he is going to be liked and cared for and to receive help for his problems. However, as the therapist encourages him to be more assertive and independent, frustration occurs. Naturally the degree of dependency varies with the individual members and, accordingly, affects their behavior during group therapy.

Sandor Rado, in describing the adaptational technique of psychoanalytic therapy, lists four levels of cooperation of the patient in his treatment behavior: the aspiring level, the self-reliant level, the parentifying level, and the magic-craving level. The aspiring and self-reliant levels are those of adult, mature people and are based on common sense. With the parentifying and magic-craving levels the treatment behavior of the patient is of emotional dependence on the doctor and is childlike in character.[5] The dependency wishes and expectations (group-treatment behavior) of the members during early group meetings are those of the magic-craving level. The group members wish for the favored treatment of the therapist as children wish favored treatment from their parents. Following the development of transference reactions (group meetings 10–20) the members parentify the therapist and assume the roles of obedient or disobedient children in their treatment behavior. This is the parentifying level. Those members who are fearful of the parentified therapist become obedient or compliant in their group treatment behavior. Behavior patterns that the obedient or compliant group members use in group meetings are complete agreement with the therapist, ingratiatory techniques to please the therapist, and seductive maneuvers to obtain the therapist's love. Those members who become resentful and antagonistic to the parentified therapist become disobedient or defiant in their group treatment behavior. Behavior patterns that the disobedient or defiant group members use in group meetings are tardiness and absence at group meetings, scapegoating other group members, competitiveness with the therapist and resentful and coercive techniques.

The members' identification with the therapist begins at the initial group meetings, becomes intensified after 10–20 group meetings with the development of transference feelings and, over the entire course of group therapy, serves as a significant therapeutic tool in the dynamics of the group process. During early group meetings the members' identification with the therapist resembles in some respects the identification of children with their parents and other significant adults. Just as a son or daughter copies the traits and mannerisms of his parents, so do group members copy the therapist. They may switch to the brand of cigarettes smoked by the therapist. If the latter smokes cigars, some of the men may take up cigar smoking. Members may also change their style in clothing to be more like the group therapist. Female group members may begin using cosmetics similar to those of a female therapist. The mannerisms, gait, and language of the group therapist may also be copied. In other non-therapeutic groups, such as a group composed of surgical resident physicians and the chief surgeon, similar identifications can be observed. The resident physicians may copy the words, phrases, voice inflections, and mannerisms of the chief surgeon. Physicians develop the traits and mannerisms of their teacher out of respect and admiration.

The physical characteristics of the members' identification with the therapist occur on both conscious and unconscious levels and have several motivational meanings. The identification indicates positive feelings when the members take on traits and mannerisms of the therapist out of warmth, respect, approval, and admiration. There is also an element of ingratiation present, since the goal is to secure the therapist's love and attention by pleasing him through imitation. However, underneath the ingratiatory defenses there exists a considerable degree of hostility and anger. James Mann, in describing this stage of group therapy, states that the process of identification with the aggressor is present and accounts for resemblances between the physical and verbal attitudes of the members and those of the therapist. Mann points out that the process of identification with the aggressor is a developmental step of the group wherein group anxiety is covered over by a passive and pseudoconforming identification with the therapist.[6] The anxiety level of the members is very high. However, the passive identification with the therapist leaves the group members feeling powerless to act. In discussing identification with the aggressor, Anna Freud refers to this mechanism as one of the ego's most potent weapons for protection against anxiety.[7]

The group members' identification with the therapist is a basic part of their transference relationship. They bring into the group feelings present since childhood and transfer them to the therapist. Through projection the therapist is given their parents' traits and attitudes. The significance of the transference in group therapy is illustrated by the fact that the entire emotional climate of group meetings is keyed to the group therapist's verbal and nonverbal responses.

During stage I the transference is more individualized among the group members. Each member exhibits patterns of behavior and defenses against anxiety peculiar to his character structure. With development of the group atmosphere or group identity in stages II and III the individual attitudes, wishes, and desires of members blend into those of the group. Through the group cohesion of stages II and III, the transference of the members assumes more of a group pattern.

Estimates of the length of stage I vary widely, but the majority of adult, neurotic groups may require 25–40 meetings. Groups that meet on a weekly basis usually require 6–9 months of group therapy to complete stage I. The length of stage I of group therapy may be influenced by the type of patient and the experience of group therapist. Patients who are members of a profession (medicine, law, dentistry, engineers, lawyers, educators) and others whose education is of college level have higher motivational levels for psychotherapy than those with less education. College graduates tend to move faster in group therapy and to reach stage II and stage III sooner than others. Then, too, the experienced therapist who is comfortable in a group of people and is familiar with the dynamics of group therapy will naturally be able to reach stage II and stage III sooner than the inexperienced group therapist.

Stage II—Authority Hostility and Group Identity

Stage II can be considered a transitional period between stage I and stage III that is characterized by the group member's ventilation and recognition of hostile feelings to the group therapist and the development of the group identity. This expression of hostility begins toward the end of stage I and continues during stage III. Stage II incorporates a period of 5–15 group meetings in which authority (therapist) hostility may be more pronounced. Its expression does not follow any set pattern. A comparison of the first 20 to 25 meetings with the last 20 to 25 meetings of a group of neurotic outpatients of 1½ to 2 years' duration reveals clearly the firm features of stage I and stage III. Stage II is usually much less clearly defined. Group members may openly ventilate their feelings and then withdraw for one or more meetings, only to start over again. In general they inform the therapist of their feelings about not receiving dependency gratifications, his failure to answer questions or provide a group structure, and his passivity during the meetings. He may be accused of being a hard-boiled boss, strict schoolteacher, or censor. Group members may charge the therapist with not being human, or compare him unfavorably with other doctors who are more supportive, who tell the patient about their families and personal life, talk to them and give help— including various drugs. The members project their own feelings on the therapist and complain that he is bored, irritated, or angry at them.

With the ventilation and (importantly) the recognition of these feelings, the anxiety level of the group diminishes and increasing signs of group identity appear. There are further indications of group cohesion and group unity. As the group members approach stage III there is a decrease in dependency needs that parallels the working-through of their hostility to the therapist. The members are now much more comfortable with each other. Their unrealistic demands from the therapist are recognized. They have progressed from their original wishes for the therapist's undivided attention to their present state of wanting to share and help one another. Competitiveness, rivalry, and jealousy between members diminish. They have increased interest and respect for each other. Their group treatment behavior is now more on the self-reliant level.

Stage III—Mutual Analysis

Stage III is defined as the period of group mutual analysis. Its length varies and depends on the entire period of group therapy. For example, in a group that met once a week for 18 months and required 40 meetings to work through stage I and stage II, stage III would consist of the remaining 38 meetings. In stage III the group atmosphere has changed to one of cohesiveness, unity, and self-reliance. The goals of the members now approach those of the therapist. There is an atmosphere in the group of wanting to help one another because the members see the advantage of mutual aid. The therapist is viewed in a new light. He is understanding, receptive, and interested in helping them solve their mutual problems. Instead of denying or projecting their feelings on others, the members are now more willing to examine basic problems relating to themselves within the group. Other behavior patterns and manifestations of anxiety are less prominent. Hostility to the therapist continues to be present, its level rising or falling with the reality events of group therapy. The most common reality events that affect the hostility level of groups are meetings cancelled by the therapist, change of meeting time or day, absence of the recorder, substitute recorder, group observers, attendance problems of group members, loss of group members, addition of new group members and termination of the group. Even though the group members have reached the self-reliant level, when they become angry at the group therapist they may revert to the parentifying and magic-craving levels of treatment behavior. Thus the group members may vacillate from the self-reliant to the parentifying and magic-craving levels, depending on the reality events of group therapy and the dynamics of the group process. Even in this advanced stage of group therapy the prospect of increased closeness to one another continues to be fraught with fears of rejection by other members or by the therapist. The members' response to this fear is hostility, but the hostility is more readily identified and dissipated than in earlier stages of group therapy.

Mutual analysis is at a high level. The members identify character traits and patterns of behavior in each other and the therapist with important figures of their past—fathers, mothers, brothers, and sisters. They project previous family patterns of behavior and interaction onto the group. The group is recognized as having many characteristics of their original family. The members recognize likes and dislikes in each other. They attack, defend, support, and encourage one another in a constructive atmosphere. They do not expect the therapist to perform their work. His remarks are viewed with deliberation and thought. There is a genuine interest in understanding their mutual relationships. Frequent comparisons are made between their therapy group and their group relationships on the outside. As the group ends, separation anxiety and its numerous manifestations receive attention and understanding.

It is important to emphasize that the members of the group never completely work through their authority relationship with the therapist. The ambivalence exhibited here is reflected in the group function. Positive identification with the therapist is manifested in an increase in group feelings and work. The members cooperate in their treatment at the self-reliant level. They want to help themselves and the others. The negative identification with the therapist that is brought about when members become angry with the therapist is characterized by the group members' treatment behavior regressing to the parentifying and magic-craving levels. The group becomes less productive. This pattern of ambivalence is present throughout the life of the group. It weighs heavily on the negative side during stage I and stage II. During stage III the positive identification or self-reliant level is more evident, although the negative identification (parentifying and magic-craving levels) persists to a degree, depending on group issues and group reality events. This group pattern of treatment behavior is repeatedly used for protection against closeness, expected retaliation, and rejection.

Once the therapist is recognized as an authority figure the group members have numerous opportunities to observe and evaluate their reactions to him. As reality issues are presented to the group on numerous occasions and as the members have the opportunity to observe their faulty emergency responses, recognition and isolation of their emotional reactions toward the therapist occur. This ability to isolate their reactions to authority figures is a very healthy sign of psychological growth. The conscious awareness of this feeling plays a significant part in the group member's self-understanding. Behavior patterns utilized with authority figures can now be modified or changed. Self-assertion and self-esteem rise with the release of impounded anger. Behavior patterns toward authority figures outside the group are recognized. Having practiced self-assertion in the group, the member can make similar attempts outside the group in family, social, and occupational roles. A further boost in self-esteem occurs when these attempts are successful.

Patients manifest different psychodynamic patterns and varying degrees of anxiety tolerance. In group therapy some members advance faster than others. The reader is referred to the group reported in Chap. 7. At the end of 55 meetings (14 months of group therapy), three members had advanced farther than the others. Mrs. Kitch, Mr. Smith, and Miss French had worked through the second stage of the group and had given up their individual desires and magical wishes. They were now devoting their interest to the mutual needs of the group. The others, Mr. Boler, Mr. Foy, and Mr. Holt, continued to express strong dependency needs by asking for more help from the therapist in the form of drugs, hypnosis, and magic.

Other factors that influence the growth of the group are the transference and countertransference feelings of the therapist. The therapist who cannot accept hostility and who projects his own unconscious wishes on the members may not be able to face the authority-figure relationship of the first and second stage of group therapy. The therapist who does not understand the dynamics of group process and who cannot maintain control of the group meetings will delay the growth of his group.

Groups of patients with psychoses proceed extremely slowly from stage I to stage II. The anxiety of the group is so massive and threatening to the members that many months of diligent work are required before the members can begin to look at any of their feelings. Very often the therapist's goal for patients with shattered ego structures who suffer from episodic psychotic behavior is primarily supportive.

Groups of neurotic patients, of course, proceed at a faster pace. Here the goal of the therapist is to reach the third stage where group unity is present and mutual analysis can proceed at a high constructive level. This does not mean that mutual analysis occurs only during the third stage. Actually, there are meaningful interpretations made to one another during the early part of stage I. These interpretations (or mutual analysis) increase during stage II and reach their highest level during stage III.

Mutual analysis means the members' recognition and discussion of the various behavior patterns they exhibit in the structured group therapy meeting. These patterns occur on a conscious and unconscious level. Once the members have recognized behavior patterns with the therapist it is easier for them to recognize them with each other. The members can correctly identify each other's characteristic behavior patterns. As these are subjected to repeated analysis they come to be identified either by the group member or others. When a member recognizes that verbal or nonverbal behavior is the result of group anxiety and tension, he becomes aware of unconscious motives of behavior. When a member notices that his reaction to an authority figure is the same as his reaction to authority figures in the past, he sees that this reaction is due to his own feelings and not the feelings of the authority figure. The members must repeatedly identify the stress and anxiety that follow in reaction to the stress and the psychodynamic pattern of behavior accompanying the anxiety. The group member enters this reality situation (group meetings) over and over again—learning, practicing and reeducating himself to his behavior patterns. In group therapy, as in any form of psychotherapy, the thoughts, feelings, and reactions of members are not confined to the actual therapeutic session. For example, a member recognizes that he reacts with fear and hostility to the therapist. In the group meeting the therapist asks about reactions to authority figures in other group relationships. The member goes home and thinks about his reaction to his father, boss, and therapist. Frequently during the subsequent days he thinks about the therapist's observations and reactions. Many constructive hours are spent between meetings thinking and dwelling over the interaction of previous meetings. The therapy thus goes on every day of the week. Group reality events (group therapist's absence and cancelled meetings, a recorder's absence, the absences of group members, a change in group structure, etc.) are, as we have seen, distorted by the group members during the early stages of group therapy. Group reality events that they have viewed as rejection are repeatedly analyzed by the members during group meetings. They learn that although the group therapist may occasionally miss a meeting, he shows up the following week. He has not rejected anyone, nor has he been driven away. Members, too, may miss meetings but when they return they are not chastised or reprimanded. Through this process of emotional reeducation over many months of group therapy the members recognize that their faulty responses of fear, guilt, anger, rejection, and separation to group reality events are not realistic. They see that reality events of group therapy are similar to reality events of day-to-day living. They recognize that their previous reactions have been inappropriate and distorted; they speak of the need to be "more objective" and "more tolerant of other people." New patterns of behavior emerge from the repetition of practicing and learning new responses within the reality of the group.

THE GROUP IDENTITY

From analyzing their reactions to each other the group members learn to recognize their difficulties in being close to other people, of sharing with one another, and of trusting others. They repeatedly react with anxiety when they are faced with having to get close to each other and to the therapist. Again by this constant analysis of behavior patterns over months of group therapy the members come to recognize and identify many of their defense patterns. They observe that they project their own feelings of hostility on others; that closeness can be avoided by getting angry at people and driving them away; that laughter, sleep, silence, overtalkativeness, humor, intellectualizations, tardiness, or absences are used by people as behavior patterns to avoid tension and anxiety. They also see that sex is related to closeness. When the group members discuss closeness they often experience sexual feelings which may make them feel inadequate as a male or female. Fears of sexual attack as well as fears of homosexuality may occur even in the most casual friendship. They recognize motives for likes and dislikes in each other. By recognizing and identifying these emotions the members gain a better understanding of themselves in interpersonal relationships. Improved socialization and reality testing—two very important goals in group therapy—become apparent both within and outside the group.

From these experiences in reality testing and socialization the group members develop the ability to abstract—that is, to examine situations from several points of view. They learn through repeated practice of observing, examining, and accepting other methods of behavioral interaction.

Mutual analysis thus emphasizes the behavior "at the moment" in the group. Faulty emergency responses by members are focused on time and time again. Some are brought under control and new responses substituted. Others are only recognized intellectually, but members profit from the knowledge that emotions are the etiological agent. They have developed psychological aptitude. Mutual analysis contributes significantly to the group members' understanding that other people also have problems. It also helps to diminish the sense of isolation in people who feel that they are the only ones in the world who have conflicts and problems. Increased objectivity toward other people's feelings occurs.

In the long run, group therapy offers the group members an opportunity to understand and experience a very basic necessity of all human group relationships—the mutual satisfaction of needs. All human beings are dependent on others for love, security, support, guidance, and material possessions. Those people who are crippled by emotional disorders seek their needs through unrealistic demands on others. One of the greatest rewards of group therapy comes when group members give up their un-realistic demands for love, security, magic, dependency, and other grati-fications from the group therapist and mutually share themselves with others. In this respect the members are now able to obtain some of their long-wished-for gratifications on a more emotionally mature level; they can feel closer and warmer to other people without suffering the tortures from previously distorted emotional reactions. They can now approach relationships with other people that involve sharing, trusting, giving, and taking. The members, like all people in our culture, basically want to love and be loved by their fellow man. This is the desire of every member who enters group therapy. For those members who have a satisfactory group therapeutic experience some of these gratifications are made pos-sible.

Emotional maturity in everyday group relationships is dependent on a clear concept of the group's goals, the mutual satisfaction of needs ob-tained from the group, and the objectivity, adaptability, and flexibility of the individuals within the group to the vicissitudes of environmental and cultural demands. Those group members who have profited from their group therapeutic experience should be able to fulfill more com-fortably and satisfactorily these criteria for emotional maturity in their future relationships in society.

Finally, however, there are some factors independent of the group member's period of therapy that influence his improvement or lack of improvement. It is wise to remember that the relationships within the therapy group are only a small segment of the group member's entire group relationships. Family, social, and occupational roles continue for the member on either a healthy or unhealthy basis. For example, a woman who is neurotic and has a paranoid husband does not reveal any essential improvement from 12 months of group therapy. Her husband changes jobs every few months. His financial state is near bankruptcy. Their children suffer for lack of proper clothing and other necessities of life. The family eases by one crisis only to face a new one. In another instance a successful white-collar male experiences a psychosis requiring a brief period of hospitalization. In 18 months of group therapy he exhibits transient improvement at times but with recurrent psychotic episodes. A dominat-ing, controlling, rigid, obsessive wife has relegated him to the role of a small boy in the family. Under her periodic outbursts of aggressive be-havior he succumbs periodically to various illnesses. The wife has refused psychiatric treatment, and at the end of group therapy the husband is un-improved. These unhealthy outside group relationships have been detri-mental to the treatment of the patient in group therapy. Other people are able to profit sufficiently from group therapy alone to overcome obstacles and move toward more mature relationships. Still others have achieved healthier relationships through the willingness of other family members to accept psychiatric treatment.

In concluding this chapter on the dynamics of group therapy the author wishes to stress that the emotional interaction that occurs during group therapy continues every day on a much larger scale in the lives of the group members. The successful therapist recognizes that more than one member of a family may need psychiatric treatment. He is aware that failures result not only from the dynamics of the group process but also from the unhealthy emotional climate of the group member's day-to-day living.

REFERENCES

1. Ackerman, N. W.: *Psychodynamics of Family Life*, Basic Books, Inc., New York, 1958.
2. Rado, S., and G. E. Daniels (eds.): *Changing Concepts of Psychoanalytic Medicine*, Grune & Stratton, Inc., New York, 1956, pp. 145–146.
3. Mann, J.: "Some Theoretic Concepts of the Group Process," *Internat. J. Group Psychotherapy*, 1:236, 1955.
4. Ackerman, N. W.: *Emotional Forces in the Family*, J. B. Lippincott Company, Philadelphia, 1959, p. 79.
5. Rado, S., and G. E. Daniels (eds.): *Changing Concepts of Psychoanalytic Medicine*, Grune & Stratton, Inc., New York, 1956, pp. 92–94.
6. Mann, J.: "Psychoanalytic Observations Regarding Conformity in Groups," *Internat. J. Group Psychotherapy*, 12:7, 1962.
7. Freud, A.: *The Ego and the Mechanisms of Defense*, International Universities Press, Inc., New York, 1946, p. 117.
8. Winick, C., A. L. Kadis, and J. D. Krasner: "The Training and Practice of American Group Psychotherapists," *Internat. J. Group Psychotherapy*, 7:131–154, 1961.
9. Slavson, S. R.: "Are There Group Dynamics in Therapy Groups?", *Internat. J. Group Psychotherapy*, 7:131–154, 1957.
10. Foulkes, S. H.: "Group Analytic Dynamics with Specific Reference to Psychoanalytic Concepts," *Internat. J. Group Psychotherapy*, 7:40–52, 1957.
11. Frank, J. D.: "Some Determinants, Manifestations, and Effects of Cohesiveness in Therapy Groups," *Internat. J. Group Psychotherapy*, 7:53–63, 1957.
12. Mullan, H., and M. Rosenbaum: *Group Psychotherapy*, The Macmillan Company (Free Press of Glencoe), New York, 1962.
13. Semrad, E. V.: "The Middle Phase in Group Psychotherapy: Some Considerations of the Dynamic Process," paper presented at the New England Society of Group Psychotherapy, April 25, 1958.
14. Locke, N.: *Group Psychoanalysis*, New York University Press, New York, 1961.
15. Kadis, A. L.: "The Alternate Meeting in Group Psychotherapy," *Am. J. Psychotherapy*, 10:275–291, 1956.
16. Wolf, A.: "A Psychoanalysis of Groups," *Am. J. Psychotherapy*, 3:525–558, and 4:16–50, 1950.
17. Lindt, H.: "The Nature of Therapeutic Interaction of Patients in Groups," *Internat. J. Group Psychotherapy*, 8:55–69, 1958.

18. Locke, N.: "The Use of Dreams in Group Psychoanalysis," *Am. J. Psychotherapy*, 11:98, 1957.
19. Slavson, S. R.: "Criteria for Selection and Rejection of Patients for Various Types of Group Psychotherapy," *Internat. J. Group Psychotherapy*, 5:3, 1955.
20. Bieber, T.: "The Emphasis on the Individual in the Psychoanalytic Group," *Internat. J. Social Psychiat.*, 2:275, 1957.
21. Lundin, W. H., and B. M. Aronod: "The Use of Co-therapists in Group Psychotherapy," *J. Consult. Psychol.*, 16:76–81, 1952.
22. Hulse, W. C., W. V. Lulow, B. K. Rindsberg, and N. D. Epstein: "Transference Reactions in a Group of Female Patients to Male and Female Co-leaders," *Internat. J. Group Psychotherapy*, 6:430–435, 1955.
23. Solomon, A., F. J. Loeffler, and G. H. Frank: "An Analysis of Co-therapists' Interaction in Group Psychotherapy," *Internat. J. Group Psychotherapy*, 3:171–180, 1954.
24. Mullan, H.: "Transference and Counter-transference: New Horizons," *Internat. J. Group Psychotherapy*, 5:169–180, 1955.
25. Gans, R. W.: "Group Co-therapists and the Therapeutic Situation: A Critical Evaluation," *Internat. J. Group Psychotherapy*, 12:82–88, 1962.
26. Powdermaker, F. B., and J. D. Frank: *Group Psychotherapy*, Harvard University Press, Cambridge, Mass., 1953, pp. 10–12.
27. Cameron, J. L., and R. A. Y. Stewart: "Observations of Group Psychotherapy with Chronic Psychoneurotic Patients in a Mental Hospital," *Internat. J. Group Psychotherapy*, 5:346–360, 1955.
28. Munroe, R. L.: *Schools of Psychoanalytic Thought*, The Dryden Press, Inc., New York, 1955.

4

The Group Contract

When a treatment program is outlined for a patient in individual therapy, there are many aspects that one might call a contract. Plans and goals of treatment are discussed to some extent. The patient is seen at a regularly scheduled hour, and consideration is given to the proposed length of therapy. Fees, handling of cancelled hours, changes in appointments, vacations, and similar aspects that involve both the patient and the therapist are a part of the contract. Similarly, there are a series of factors in group therapy that can be called the group contract. Many unnecessary conflicts and problems within the group may be avoided if the members and the therapist clearly understand all the components that enter into the arrangements for group therapy. These components, which establish certain criteria for both the group and the therapist, are termed the group contract. The author feels that it is necessary to fully clarify the contract with the group members by referring to it, or to parts applicable, at the outset and at intervals throughout the course of group therapy.

The following factors are integral parts of the group contract: (1) purpose of group therapy, (2) composition of the group, (3) role of the group therapist, (4) recorder, substitute recorder, and mechanical reproduction of meetings, (5) physical arrangements, (6) period of group therapy, (7) loss and addition of group members, (8) attendance of members, (9) fees, (10) drugs, physical illnesses, hospitalization and other therapies, (11) conversations, telephone calls, personal contacts, and meetings by group members outside of the regular structured group therapy session, and (12) modifications of the group contract.

PURPOSE OF GROUP THERAPY

After a patient has been interviewed and selected for group therapy, the therapist should explain its purpose. The patient should be told that through the group therapy experience he and other members of the group may be able to acquire an increasing understanding of the relationships among themselves and with people in the outside world. By helping each other with their problems they will be learning to help themselves. Others can help them to look at what they cannot see themselves, since objectivity is frequently lost when people live close to their problems. The patient is informed that all members of the group are experiencing areas of emotional tension and stress, and that many of their problems have occurred in their relationships with other people. The patients are told that everyone participates in group relationships throughout their lives; that many of their problems and difficulties have occurred in their day-to-day group relationships; that they will discover that the therapy group is similar in many respects to their everyday group relationships; and that they can learn about the feelings and reactions which have contributed to their illnesses from the therapy group, thus gaining knowledge and understanding about themselves that can be applied to their other group relationships in the future.

The purpose of group therapy will also be governed by and closely correlated to the specific type of patients in the group. For example, in a group of parents having children with emotional disorders, the therapist should focus on parent-child interaction and the possible benefits from group therapy in fostering the understanding of the parents' relationship to their children. In a psychosomatic group the therapist should emphasize the relationship of anxiety to their physical complaints. In general, the therapist should clarify the purpose of group therapy with the patients in relation to the particular type of group therapy planned.

Patients exhibit more reticence for group therapy than for individual therapy. Most patients for whom group therapy has been recommended express doubts as to how a group of people can benefit from a discussion of their problems; fears of talking to a group of strangers; fears that other members of the group may know them; dread of exposure; doubts about the group's ability to keep confidential the discussions of each meeting; fears that group therapy will not help their particular problem; fears of association with other people; excessive shyness and timidity with other people; and preferences for individual therapy over group therapy. Because of such fears and doubts some patients refuse to accept group therapy. If group therapy is instituted while the patient is hospitalized or immediately following his hospitalization, he is usually receptive to the new form of treatment. Hospital ward meetings that employ a modified technique of group therapy afford the patient an introduction to group feelings. Other patients whose motivations for group therapy are good are those who are already in individual treatment with a therapist.

Most patients fear any form of treatment that involves a group of people. In the initial interviews with the prospective group member, the therapist should encourage the ventilation of these fears. He can support the prospective group member by pointing out that such fears are common to all prospective group members. He should emphasize that these fears and feelings should be an early subject for group discussion.

Printed instructions and leaflets describing group therapy and the role of the group member are not encouraged. These devices are no better than giving a patient in therapy a list of books to read. Emotional insight is not gained and confusion may occur. Group therapy's educational and learning process takes place most effectively through the medium of the group itself.

COMPOSITION OF A GROUP

There appears to be rather general agreement among group therapists that the membership of a group should not exceed eight people.[1] Smaller groups are also advantageous. Foeser lists a number of properties that characterize the advantages of a small number of people (4–8) for a therapeutic group. Such a group is large enough to dilute the transference feelings of its members and provide heterogeneity. At the same time, it is small enough for effective leadership, operation and control. Foeser feels that a smaller group cannot be destroyed by one or two people.[2] Slavson began working with small groups of disturbed children and adults in 1934. He feels that a true therapy group should not exceed eight persons and that interpersonal reactions and interactions occur best in a group this size.[3] Geller in 1951 related the size of groups to the goals of the therapeutic procedure, saying that the more intensive therapy takes place in the smaller group (less than 10 patients).[4] Group activities with less therapeutic orientation (social, recreational, etc.) are composed of a larger membership. Naturally with a larger group the interaction among its members is curtailed and the goals of the group activity are more limited than those of a therapeutic group.

Group membership may be all male, all female, or mixed. In state hospital group therapy, groups of the same sex are more common. Many outpatient clinics and private patient groups are composed of an equal number of men and women. A well-balanced medium for group therapy is provided in groups composed of four male members, four female members, a male therapist, and a female recorder. Patients who have difficulty in relating to the opposite sex can profit by the opportunity to explore and understand their behavior in a group of this composition.

The age span of the members in adult groups ranges from 21 to 50 years. With adolescents, the age span would be markedly narrowed. Groups composed of members from 12 to 14, or 14 to 16, or 15 to 18 years of age will function better. The changing interests, rapidly enlarging ego capacities, intellectual endowments, social patterns, and physical growth of adolescents are factors of importance and must be taken into consideration where group therapy is undertaken with them.

Intellectual endowment plays the same important role in group therapy patients as it does with those in individual therapy. People with an IQ of 100 and above are satisfactory for group therapy. Those people who are mentally deficient or of limited intellectual capacity should not be placed in regular groups. (This does not preclude the possibility of group activities where persons with mental deficency and epilepsy are treated in institutions.)

Indications and Contraindications of Patients for Group Therapy

The indications and contraindications of patients for group therapy are complex, because this form of therapy is now employed in a wide variety of illnesses and settings, and for a wide variety of goals. There are a number of factors to be considered, such as age, sex, intellectual endowment, psychodynamics, diagnosis, goals and purposes of the treatment program, and physical location of the patient (state or private hospitals, service hospitals, mental health clinics, child guidance clinics, training schools, or private practice). Thus groups can be composed of patients with neuroses, psychoses, psychophysiological illnesses, personality disorders, juvenile behavior disorders, epilepsy, mental deficiency, or geriatric diseases.

The selection of many patients for group therapy is predetermined by the specific purpose of the treatment program. For example, group therapy in state hospitals is made up of patients who have experienced psychotic illnesses; in training schools, of juvenile delinquents; in institutions, of people with epilepsy and mental deficiency, where group treatment programs are organized around their specific needs.

The most popular form of group therapy in practice today is the outpatient group. Outpatient groups operate in settings such as mental health clinics, family service organizations, child guidance clinics, state mental hospitals, outpatient departments of psychiatry and private practice. Here again the selection of members for such groups is predetermined by the goals and purposes of the treatment program. Many of the members of these groups are people who have sought help for disturbing manifestations of emotional illness. An outpatient department of a general hospital may have group programs for patients with peptic ulcer, dermatoses, obesity, hypertension, arthritis, or other psychophysiological conditions. Group programs may also be designed to involve the family of an emotionally ill person. For example, a child guidance clinic may have a group program with the parents of emotionally disturbed children, or a mental health clinic group may be composed of the husbands or wives of sick mates.

Inpatient groups are popular in hospitals and other institutions. Groups in hospitals may also be designed for inpatients and outpatients. Many hospitals have outpatient facilities for discharged patients. Inpatient and outpatient groups allow the group members to continue group therapy even if a hospital readmission is necessary.

Selection of Members for Outpatient and Inpatient Groups. The selection of patients for outpatient groups and inpatient groups should be evaluated from the standpoint of motivation for treatment, ego strength, anxiety tolerance, diagnosis, and needs of the patient.

Motivation for Treatment. As with other forms of psychotherapy, group therapy patients must be motivated for treatment. People who are experiencing pain, anxiety, guilt, depression, and the other manifestations of suffering from emotional conflicts are seeking relief. If they themselves seek treatment, their motivation is sincere. There are other people, however, whose motivations should be questioned. Individuals who come to the psychiatrist under court order are poorly motivated. Coercion of an individual by his family, husband, or wife, accompanied by threats, does not necessarily instill motivation. In the author's experience sociopaths are very poorly motivated and are not good risks for treatment. They enjoy their way of life and exhibit minimal anxiety. They frequently want treatment only when in trouble with authorities and thus their motivation for treatment is questionable.

Psychiatrists are becoming increasingly aware of people who emotionally influence others with no conscious insight of their behavior. These people come from all walks of life. A father or mother may be completely unaware of destructive behavior towards a son or daughter which has contributed to an emotional disturbance in the child. Similar situations may exist with husbands and wives and others who interact with each other in close relationships. When psychiatric treatment is suggested for these people several responses may occur, such as denial of conflict, projection of blame on others, anger, indecision, or doubt at the psychiatrist's recommendation—or sometimes agreement and acceptance. For those people who are indecisive and doubtful, group therapy may be an acceptable form of treatment and should be considered as an excellent method of involving them in a treatment program. In many instances people with doubtful motivations may be converted to sincere efforts at correcting behavior problems.

Ego Strength. Prospective patients for group therapy should be able to function or have the capacity for future function in one or more of the following areas: the work area, the family area, or the social area. There should be a certain amount of fluidity in the life situations, such as financial, educational, social, or family matters. The patients should also have some capacity for combating obstacles (ego strength) and some desire to work at solving conflicts and problems.

It is advisable to evaluate the ego strengths and attitudes of the members of the prospective group member's family. In some cases a hostile spouse or an uncooperative parent creates problems for the group member that may interfere with group therapy.

Anxiety Tolerance. Patients in group therapy should have some tolerance for anxiety. The emotional interaction between the group members and the group therapist creates anxiety and, in group therapy, this anxiety is utilized therapeutically by the group therapist. The anxiety level of the group can be considered a gauge of group function. In the author's experience, patients who cannot tolerate this anxiety are not good risks for treatment. Patients who notoriously fall into this category are alcoholics, drug addicts, persons with certain personality disorders (paranoid personality, emotionally unstable personality, sociopathic personality disturbance) and juvenile delinquents. The latter respond better to treatment in institutions; the delinquent in outpatient groups too often acts out and runs away from the group.

Diagnosis. The diagnosis, whether it is neurosis, psychosis, psychophysiological or psychosomatic disorder, or personality disorder, is an important factor in choosing the proper patient for the proper group.

The Neuroses. In our experience, neurotic patients with diagnoses of depressive reaction, obsessive-compulsive neurosis, anxiety reactions, conversion hysteria, dissociative reactions, and phobic reactions may be considered candidates for group therapy. None of these emotional disorders occurs in a pure state whereby one person is phobic, another is depressed, and still another has a conversion hysteria. The personality structure of the person may show traits of other personality structures; for example, the obsessive personality may have some traits characteristic of the hysterical personality. Difficulties in managing the emotions of fear, rage, and guilt result in the development of different patterns of behavior. From the individual's family interaction during childhood, defenses against anxiety become learned behavior patterns that are incorporated within the personality or character structure of the patient. Just as families vary in their interaction and behavior, so do behavior patterns. Personality traits or behavior patterns determine the type of personality structure; the preponderance of a group of emotional symptoms determines the type of emotional illness.

Personality disorders are discussed in more detail in a later section in this chapter. Since the depressive personality, hysterical personality, and obsessive personality are closely allied with neurotic illness, they are discussed with the neuroses. The personality structure predisposes to some extent the type of illness that may occur; for example, the hysterical personality subjected to an environmental stress may develop a conversion hysteria or a dissociative reaction. The obsessive personality or obsessive-compulsive personality may develop an obsessive-compulsive neurosis.

Regardless of the diagnostic label placed on patients, many of their basic emotional conflicts are similar. In general, neurotic patients who request treatment have the following conditions present:

1. Chronic, repressed anger
2. Passivity and nonassertiveness
3. Chronic guilt
4. Low self-esteem
5. Difficulties in interpersonal relationships
6. Disturbing manifestations of anxiety
7. Distortions of reality
8. Conflicts with authority figures
9. Sexual conflicts

It is wise, therefore, to remember that beneath the individual behavioral patterns are many similar emotional reactions and thoughts. Phobic, depressed, and obsessive-compulsive patients, for example, have a basic conflict in handling their angry feelings. The phobic patient displaces fear of angry feelings on another object and becomes afraid of it; the depressed patient turns his anger inward, and the obsessive-compulsive patient utilizes a series of behavioral maneuvers to stifle the expression of angry feelings. Actually, group therapy offers an advantage over individual therapy by taking into account the variety of personality structures and behavior patterns shown by the group members. The group members not only learn about their own feelings and reactions but acquire an understanding of how other people handle similar problems, such as angry feelings. Insight on the part of the group members allows for greater objectivity and understanding in future group relationships.

As far as overt symptoms are concerned, depressive reactions account for the largest group of illnesses treated in group therapy. During group therapy the depressed person improves from the recognition and ventilation of repressed anger or rage. Self-assertion develops first in the therapy group and is then carried over into day-to-day group relationships. With the ventilation of anger and improved self-assertion there is a rise in self-esteem and a lessening of guilt. Other neurotic symptoms which may be present, such as a psychophysiological (migraine) headache, also tend to diminish as the impounded anger is released. Along the same lines, there are many people who, although not overtly depressed, exhibit personality traits that suggest a depressive personality. These people are usually passive, nonassertive, and dependent, and are somewhat withdrawn and quiet in their relationships with other people. They cannot talk and verbalize their feelings. Some are able to talk to one or two people comfortably, but when placed in a group of people they become quiet, withdrawn, and frightened. In many instances they are comfortable with their peers but "freeze up" or "go blank" in their relationships with authority figures. Similar difficulties were encountered in childhood and adolescence with their parents. During school years they were not able to talk to their teachers. Many of the misunderstandings that occur in everyday group relationships are due to the fear and anxiety that accompany such reactions to authority figures (boss, parent, and others in superior roles). Though the authority may give clear and explicit directions, the recipient may be so overwhelmed with fear and anxiety that the communication is either not heard or distorted.

We feel that group therapy is an advantageous type of treatment for the depressive personality. They can learn to socialize and talk with the other members of the group. They learn to recognize the group therapist as an authority figure and can practice self-assertion in the group. As they profit from the educational and relearning experience of group therapy, they can begin to carry these new techniques out into their day-to-day group relationships.

In planning treatment for the obsessive-compulsive neuroses the group therapist should be aware of the underlying personality structure, the degree of illness, and the associated neurotic manifestations. The basic personality structure of these people is organized around a series of personality traits that collectively constitute the obsessive personality (also called the obsessive character, the obsessive-compulsive personality, or the compulsive personality). The development of the obsessive-compulsive neurosis follows environmental stress and conflict in such a personality structure. The obsessive-compulsive personality is organized around a strict and rigid conscience, meticulousness, perfectionism, competitiveness, intellectualization, and other personality traits that make up a character armor designed to avoid and prevent the expression of angry feelings. The personality traits or behavior patterns vary in intensity and type but are all utilized for the same dynamic purpose. The most common type of patient seen by psychiatrists exhibits the character armor of the obsessive-compulsive personality, and because of environmental stress have developed anxiety. This increased anxiety results in an exaggeration of one or more of their patterns of behavior. With one the symptoms may be increased compulsiveness (increased housework, longer working hours); with another, obsessive thoughts or ritualistic behavior. Internalization of angry feelings may occur and result in depression.

A large group of people who come to the attention of the psychiatrist are not experiencing anxiety per se but exhibit destructive behavior to other people in their group relationships. Although these people may fall into a number of different diagnostic categories (neuroses, psychoses, personality disorders) the obsessive-compulsive personality makes up the larger number. Being void of psychological aptitude, they have no awareness of their relationships to husbands, wives, children, and others. They are cold, aloof, dogmatic, dictatorial, rigid, and controlling in their behavior, and do not recognize that other people have emotional problems. Often, they become anxious and angry with no conscious awareness. In their group relationships they cannot recognize their part in the depression of a wife, the acting-out behavior of a son, the poor school record of a daughter, or the alcoholism of a husband. Psychiatrists are increasingly aware of the damaging effect these people have on the emotional health of families and of the need to involve the families in treatment programs. Attempts should be made to motivate these people for treatment. Individual therapy, family conferences, family therapy, and group therapy are beneficial methods of treatment. Group therapy is often rewarding and useful because it develops an awareness of relationships to families and other groups.

From the standpoint of treatment the obsessive-compulsive personality and the obsessive-compulsive neuroses do not appear to be far removed from each other. Some are motivated for treatment; others are not. If treatment by group therapy is accepted, the behavior patterns come into play immediately. Competitiveness, intellectualizations, humorous and witty behavior, and denial of emotional problems are common behavior patterns in group meetings. During the course of group therapy there are many obsessive-compulsive patients who show improvement. The development of psychological aptitude (awareness of how one interacts with other people) improves interpersonal relationships. Probably one of the most important stages of improvement occurs when the obsessive-compulsive patient recognizes the various ways he shows his anger. The recognition and ventilation of angry feelings diminishes anxiety and guilt and raises self-esteem. Concurrently, the conscience becomes less rigid. In general, the obsessive and compulsive defenses of the patient should be supported and maintained. The obsessive-compulsive personality disorder, like other personality disorders, is not basically changed by group therapy.

The anxiety reactions are a diffuse group of emotional and physical symptoms that may occur on an acute, subacute, or chronic basis. The emotional symptoms may be described by the patient as fear, anxiety, tension, apprehension, irritability, depression, poor attention span, and difficulty in concentration. Physical symptoms may be expressed in vertigo, headache, chest pain, palpitation, increased awareness of heart action, nausea, abdominal discomfort, diarrhea, or frequency of urination. Acute anxiety reactions may occur in all types of emotional illness. These have not been treated by group methods except as an accompaniment of another illness; for example, an acute anxiety state in a depressive reaction. Patients in group therapy experience anxiety from the emotional interaction within the group. With the active cooperation of the patient, some with chronic anxiety states may receive help in group therapy. Their response resembles the response of those with a depressive reaction. In general, though, we feel that persons with chronic anxiety states are poor candidates for long-term group therapy. Many are passive, nonassertive, dependent people who cannot tolerate the anxiety of group therapy.

People with conversion hysterias and dissociative reactions have not been treated to any extent in group therapy. Conversion hysteria is seldom seen and is usually treated by individual therapy. Persons with dissociative reactions are more commonly encountered. They may present a clinical picture of acute psychosis. Frequently the illness is of short duration. The dissociative reactions indicate a more severe disorder than conversion hysteria. The chronic dissociative reaction closely resembles a chronic psychotic state and is often called a psychosis. Somnambulism, amnesias and fugue states are also classified as dissociative reactions. They are not common and have not been treated by group methods.

Group therapy is not indicated for the acute dissociative reaction per se but may be beneficial in preventing future attacks by working through emotional conflicts that have caused the illness. Patients with chronic dissociative reactions can be treated in group therapy, but the therapist should be aware of low anxiety tolerance in these patients. In general we have found that the chronic dissociative reactions will do better in groups of psychotic patients than in groups of neurotic patients.

The diagnosis of hysterical personality is questioned in some professional circles. Where accepted, it is felt to consist of a constellation of personality traits that include (among others) changing emotional moods, immaturity, shallow emotional relationships, strong dependency needs, dramaticism, exhibitionism, seductive behavior, suggestibility, and an easy, nonstrict conscience. The hysterical personality is often the predominate personality in those people who experience conversion hysteria and dissociative reaction. Probably the most common neurotic illness that occurs in the hysterical personality, however, is depression. The hysterical personality is more prevalent in women than in men.

The hysterical personality in group therapy is characterized by strong dependency needs, exhibitionism, dramaticism, and ingratiating behavior, together with passivity and nonassertiveness in group relationships. Projection, denial, and rationalization are the most common defense mechanisms. Yet beneath the passivity, nonassertiveness, and ingratiating behavior lies a massive degree of rage or anger. The dependency needs of the hysterical personality are revealed in requests for special attention, such as individual interviews and approved tranquilizing drugs between group meetings. During the course of group therapy a gradual awareness of the underlying rage develops. The recognition and ventilation of angry feelings are followed by improved self-assertion and self-esteem, decreased dependency needs, and lessened depression. It should be again emphasized that in our model of group therapy the basic patterns of behavior of the hysterical personality are not changed.

Phobic reactions, which have not been treated to any large degree in group therapy, occur most often in association with other neuroses—i.e., depression, obsessive-compulsive neurosis, and chronic anxiety reactions. At times patients exhibit phobic difficulties prior to the beginning of group therapy, or develop phobias as the anxiety of the group process increases during stage I of group therapy. Like the depressive personality and the hysterical personality, phobic patients are passive, nonassertive and dependent, their reaction and progress during group therapy being similar to those of patients with depressive and hysterical personalities. They can receive help from group therapy if the anxiety of the group process can be tolerated. The successful treatment of phobic reactions is dependent on the patient reentering the phobic situation over and over again. Frequently relationships with people are at the basis of the phobia. The interaction between the group members during group therapy meetings creates for the phobic patient a weekly confrontation and examination of the anxiety underlying his fears. Because difficulties in interpersonal relationships in day-to-day groups contributes to the patients' phobic difficulties, group therapy offers the patient an opportunity to recognize such difficulties. As the patient develops self-assertion and independence in group therapy, his phobic manifestations decrease.

The therapist should be aware that there are neurotic patients who do not respond to group therapy. These include people whose only desire is to have their dependency needs met, whose fears of retaliation so inhibit the expression of rageful feelings that a rigid control has to be maintained at all times, and whose tolerance for anxiety is too low for the requirements of group therapy. Frequently the therapist cannot determine whether such patients can benefit from group therapy until they have attended group sessions.

The Psychoses. Psychotic patients who can be considered for group therapy are those with schizophrenic reactions, manic-depressive reactions, psychotic depressive reactions, and involutional psychotic reactions. Chapter 8 discusses group therapy for the psychotic patient.

We have found that group therapy is an advantageous type of treatment for psychotic patients in both the outpatient and inpatient setting. However, the group therapist usually encounters more problems with psychotic patients than with neurotic patients. These problems are created by the anxiety of the psychotic patient. In general, psychotic patients in group therapy exhibit much more anxiety than do neurotic patients.

Psychotic patients may have different degrees of illness and variable behavior characteristics. For example, one schizophrenic person may have had only a brief period of overt psychotic behavior, while another may have periodic psychotic attacks. Schizophrenia is by definition a psychotic illness. There are, however, many people with schizophrenia who have never had overt psychotic illnesses with hallucinations, delusions, loose thought associations, and regressive behavior. Their contact with reality is adequate, but disturbing conflicts and problems are encountered in day-to-day group relationships.

The different degrees of illness of psychotic patients are reflected by their anxiety tolerance in group therapy. The ambulatory schizophrenic patient who has not suffered recurrent psychotic episodes can tolerate more anxiety in group therapy than the schizophrenic patient who has had repeated psychotic attacks or a prolonged period of psychosis. Group therapy programs should take into consideration the anxiety of the patient. The anxiety level of the psychotic patient requires the group therapist to modify his goals with the patient and influences his technique of group therapy. For these reasons we have found it advisable to divide the selection of psychotic patients for group therapy into two general types.

Type I includes ambulatory patients who have not experienced recurrent or prolonged psychotic episodes with regressive behavior, hallucinations, and delusions. There may have been one or more acute episodic psychotic illnesses over a period of time but the psychosis has not been a recurrent or severely damaging condition. Difficulties in interpersonal relationships are manifested by withdrawal, autism, depression suspiciousness, disturbed thought processes, ambivalence, hyperactivity, confusion, aggressive outbursts, and sexual conflicts. Many of these patients are able to function in one or more areas of their family, occupational, or social life. In our experience, patients who are classified as type I can be treated satisfactorily along with neurotic patients in the outpatient neurotic group. In fact, group therapy offers a certain degree of protection and security for these patients, many of whom can tolerate anxiety in a group of people, which seemingly dilutes their transference feelings. Frightening and disturbing thoughts are reduced. Difficulties in talking and verbalizing material, which to the schizophrenic may be very painful and threatening in a one-to-one situation, are counteracted by the presence of the other group members.

Type II patients have severe ego psychopathology. Their illness is characterized by recurrent or prolonged psychoses. Repeated admission to hospitals or prolonged periods of hospitalization may be present. Because of their severe psychopathology and reactions to anxiety, type II patients should not be placed in outpatient neurotic groups. Group therapy programs for these patients differ from group therapy programs with neurotic patients in a number of respects. Chapter 8 discusses the type of group therapy program, goals in treatment, technique of the group therapist, indications and contraindications for group therapy, and other required modifications of the group contract for type II patients.

The Psychophysiological Disorders. Physicians in medical and surgical specialities and in psychiatry are becoming increasingly aware of the influence of the emotions in the physical symptoms of people. For many years the "hypochondriac" has been well known in every doctor's office. The dermatologist recognizes the emotional conflict in the chronic dermatoses, the pediatrician in asthmatic children, the gastroenterologist in peptic ulcers, and the orthopedist in backaches. To this list can be added migraine headaches, pruritus, some cardiovascular reactions, obesity, diarrheas, ulcerative colitis, and genitourinary disturbances. Physicians are referring more and more of these people to the psychiatrist for treatment of their illnesses.

There are only a few reports in the literature of patients with psychophysiological disorders being treated by group methods. Group therapy for patients with psychophysiological disorders is a rather recent development in the field of psychotherapy. For this reason the following reports from the literature are included here. Milberg reported a 4½ years' observation of 54 private patients with various neurodermatoses.[5] The patients were in both individual and group therapy. He felt the results were inconclusive but warranted further study. Cooper and Katz treated 35 patients with migraine headaches in groups.[6] Results were good in approximately 50 per cent of the patients completing more than 50 sessions of group therapy. Fortin and Abse treated nine college students who had developed peptic ulcers during their years at college.[7] The onset of symptoms was correlated with leaving home and attending college. The group met twice a week for 1½ hours for a period of one year. The authors concluded that group therapy for peptic ulcer patients was helpful. The patient's ulcer symptoms diminished during the latter months of group therapy but would recur with anxiety and stress. Clapham and Sclare attempted to treat 12 asthmatic patients in group therapy.[8] Six of the patients stopped treatment during the early period of treatment. The other six members remained in the group for one year. The dependency features of the patients were striking. In fact, their reaction to the termination of group therapy was so alarming the group had to be continued. The authors concluded that group therapy led to better reality adaptation and fewer attacks of asthma for the patients. Igersheimer analyzed extensively and thoroughly the results of two therapy groups of psychosomatic illnesses.[9] The two groups were composed of four patients with asthma and four patients with migraine headaches and rheumatoid arthritis. The groups met twice a week for 1½ hours for one year. These patients had chronic somatic diseases with more-or-less severe organic changes. Igersheimer felt that the patients became more aware of the psychological component of their symptoms. Anxiety became less diffuse and more specifically related to emotional situations. At the follow-up evaluation one year following termination of group therapy, two of the four asthma patients had had severe relapses. The other two asthmatics had less asthma but showed signs of substitute symptom formation. In the mixed psychosomatic group (migraine, arthritis), three of the patients were improved and one patient had had a mild relapse.

Patients who have psychophysiological disorders should be evaluated very carefully before planning treatment by group therapy. Psychophysiological disorders may be acute or chronic in character. In general, the psychiatrist sees these problems after several years of medical treatment by other doctors and by this time they have reached a stage of chronicity. The psychophysiological disorders may be present in association with any of the neuroses, psychoses, and personality disorders and as such are subject to the same criteria in their selection for group therapy. The therapist should be aware of the dependency features of patients with psychophysiological disorders, especially in those patients with asthma, peptic ulcer, hyperventilation, and hypochondriacal symptoms. He should weigh several factors before selecting a patient with a psychophysiological disorder for group therapy—type of illness, length of illness (acute or chronic), personality structure, psychodynamics, and degree of dependency present. The patient with whom successful treatment might be possible should have an illness of recent origin, a good motivation for treatment, some ego strength, a tolerance for anxiety, and an absence of pronounced dependency needs. Patients with chronic psychophysiological disorders can be treated in groups, but the therapist should be reconciled to obtaining only limited results. Group therapy will not change personality structures or behavior patterns that have been present for a number of years. Hopefully, the patient will have an amelioration of symptoms. In many respects the chronic asthma patient or the hypochondriacal patient can be compared to the chronic paranoid person. The disease process is of long duration, ingrained, and rigidly fixed.

The goals in group therapy with patients who have psychophysiological disorders should be directed toward the development of an awareness of the influence and effect of the emotions on the physical organs of the body. For example, a passive, nonassertive wife has conflicts with her husband. She becomes angry with him. She is unable to assert herself with him, represses her anger, and develops a headache or backache. In group therapy the wife should be able to ventilate anger, develop areas of self-assertion with the other group members and the therapist, and recognize the emotional component of the psychophysiological disorder. Future relationships with her husband should be more comfortable if the wife can be self-assertive and express her feelings adequately. Usually the group therapist's goals are limited to an amelioration of symptoms in people who have chronic psychophysiological disorders. Here again the development of psychological aptitude may make it possible for the patient with asthma, hypochondriasis or colitis to experience fewer symptoms and to be more comfortable.

The group therapist should be very cautious in establishing treatment goals in patients with psychophysiological disorders and should thoroughly evaluate the patient both from a medical and psychiatric point of view before planning group therapy. At the present time group therapy's role in psychophysiological disorders should be considered as one method of treatment that may or may not be beneficial.

*The Personality Disorders.** The personality disorders are described by the Diagnostic and Statistical Manual of the American Psychiatric Association as being developmental defects in the personality of persons who exhibit little or no anxiety or discomfort. The disorders are characterized by behavior patterns of lifelong duration.[10]

Personality disorders include the inadequate personality, the schizoid personality, the cyclothymic personality, the paranoid personality, the passive-aggressive personality, the passive-dependent personality, the compulsive personality, the sociopathic personality, homosexuality and other sexual deviations, and alcohol and drug addiction.

From the standpoint of anxiety, people with personality disorders have developed defenses against anxiety or patterns of behavior that are deeply embedded and ingrained in the personality make-up. In their everyday group relationships they exhibit little or no anxiety and no overt symptoms of emotional illness unless repeated stress or an acute stress occurs. Following stress, the patterns of behavior automatically and unconsciously attempt to protect the individual from anxiety by becoming intensified and exaggerated. At this time the individual may become aware of changes or interferences with his defensive structure or behavioral patterns. For example, the obsessive-compulsive personality may notice that increased ritualistic behavior is present. When the defense mechanisms are taxed beyond their capacity, anxiety is experienced by the individual either by: (1) direct expression (acute anxiety reactions, panic and tension); (2) neurotic illnesses (depression, phobias, obsessive-compulsive neuroses, conversion reactions, and dissociative reactions); (3) psychophysiological or psychosomatic illnesses (migraine headaches, asthma, peptic

---

* The personality disorders are described in Chap. 2 as personality types. The classification of personality types in the literature is confusing. The passive, nonassertive personality, the hysterical personality and the obsessive-compulsive personality described earlier in this chapter and also in Chap. 2 are not classified as personality disorders. In fact, the diagnosis of one of them, the hysterical personality, is questioned in some professional circles. The author feels that the person with an obsessive-compulsive personality may be just as much of a personality disorder as the person with a passive-aggressive personality or a cyclothymic personality. However, to avoid confusion, the classification of the Diagnostic and Statistical Manual of the American Psychiatric Association is followed in this book.

ulcer, and ulcerative colitis); and (4) psychotic reactions. For example, a man with a passive-aggressive personality encounters conflicts with his wife. He becomes anxious and depressed. He resorts to alcohol for the relief of anxiety and depression. Over a period of years of repeated conflict with his wife he becomes addicted to alcohol. Or a person with a schizoid personality may develop symptoms of anxiety upon moving from a farm to an urban community. On the farm he was comfortable. Relationships with other people could be successfully avoided. The urban community is different. He cannot avoid people. He becomes anxious, depressed, and suffers from headaches and stomach disorders from the stress encountered in group relationships of the new surroundings.

The therapist, in his evaluation of patients for group therapy, should recognize that neurotic, psychotic, or psychophysiological illnesses may be superimposed in people who have personality disorders. A group therapy program should attempt to treat the manifestations of the neurosis, psychosis, or psychophysiological disorder and not the personality disorder. Group therapy does not change the basic patterns of behavior of personality disorders. With the proper motivation for treatment, ego strength, and minimal acting-out behavior, people with some of the personality disorders—schizoid personality, cyclothymic personality, passive-aggressive personality, and compulsive personality—can develop psychological aptitude and become aware of their emotional interaction and relationships with others. In these instances the socialization process and educational and relearning aspects of group therapy are most important.

The patient with a schizoid personality in group therapy exhibits patterns of behavior that are similar in many respects to the patterns of behavior of the type I schizophrenic patient. He is passive, nonassertive, and withdrawn in his group relationships. During group therapy he can learn to talk, express some feelings, and improve his relationships with others. Once he has achieved these gains he can apply them in other group relationships. Group therapy does not remove the patterns of behavior of the schizoid personality but can make the patient less schizoid in day-to-day group relationships. His silence in group meetings may be very troublesome and continue for many meetings. But, like the silent schizophrenic patient in group meetings, the silent schizoid patient profits from the interaction of the other group members and the group therapist.

The cyclothymic personality in group therapy exhibits behavior patterns characteristic of the particular mood swing that is present. When the patient is depressed, his behavior patterns are like those described in the discussion of depressions. When he becomes hypomanic, he frequently quits group therapy. If he remains in this state, overtalkativeness, humorous behavior, competitiveness with the group therapist, and denial of illness are common patterns of behavior. In group therapy he may go from a depressed state to one of hypomania, or vice versa. The cyclothymic personality is very difficult to treat in group therapy. The author is not familiar with any patients with cyclothymic personalities who have completed group therapy.

The passive-aggressive personality in group therapy exhibits behavior patterns like those exhibited in day-to-day group relationships. A patient with this type of personality will passively avoid group decisions and group issues by delaying tactics, silence, and other methods of obstruction. He never, in so many words, refuses to do something but employs various excuses to justify his actions. He can become intellectually aware of the passive manner in which he exhibits anger from the interaction with other group members and the therapist. He learns to express feelings, particularly angry feelings, thereby reducing the necessity of having to use his passive-aggressive patterns of behavior. In day-to-day group relationships he can make a better adjustment by decreasing his passive-aggressive maneuvers and thus avoid having people react to his controlling behavior of anger.

The compulsive patient in group therapy exhibits patterns of behavior similar to the obsessive-compulsive personality described in this chapter.

In the author's experience the other types of personality disorders—the paranoid personality, the inadequate personality, the emotionally unstable personality disturbance, and the sociopathic personality disturbance—are contraindicated for this model of group therapy. To this list should be added the passive-dependent personality, especially if the dependency wishes of the individual are pronounced.

The patient with a paranoid personality does not usually present himself for psychiatric treatment. He does not recognize any conflicts or problems related to himself. He feels that other people do not like him and are attempting to harm him in some manner. Suspiciousness, jealousy, and envy are usually present. Family members, business associates, or anyone with whom the paranoid personality has close relationships become the target for numerous complaints. The projective mechanism of placing blame on others is rigid and well ingrained within the personality structure. In a group, the same type of behavior occurs. For this reason the paranoid personality disorder should not be considered for group therapy.

The inadequate personality does not have the ego strength or the motivation for any type of psychotherapy. Such people are dull, uninteresting, and seemingly do not find any pleasure in life. Inadequacy correctly characterizes their entire existence.

The emotionally unstable personality is characterized by an inability to tolerate anxiety. The patient with such a personality is a very dependent person who, in group relationships, becomes irrationally angry at the least provocation. In our experience the anxiety of group therapy cannot be tolerated by the emotionally unstable personality.

These people with sociopathic personality disturbances are contraindicated for this model of group therapy. As a general rule they are not sincerely interested in any form of therapy. They may ask for or be coerced into obtaining therapy after problems with their family, employer, or local authorities have occurred. However, such motives are usually manipulatory on their part and are attempted for their own gain. The sociopathic personality disturbance characteristically exhibits no anxiety or symptoms of emotional illness. Psychiatrists are aware of the numerous treatment problems, lack of sincere motivation, and manipulatory tactics of these patients.

In the author's experience, homosexuality and other sexual deviations cannot be treated in group therapy. The homosexual can, however, profit from group therapy in other ways. The homosexual is frequently filled with low self-esteem and guilt feelings. He is not accepted by people in other groups and is stigmatized by society. The homosexual is often quite afraid of the opposite sex. Passivity, nonassertiveness, chronically impounded anger, and infantile behavior are frequent findings in the effeminate homosexual. For these reasons the homosexual can receive help from group therapy by being accepted and understood by other people and through the development of psychological aptitude. He can become more self-assertive and aggressive in group relationships. Group therapy can help the homosexual to understand his sexual nature—not to change it.

In planning group therapy for the homosexual the group therapist should be emphatic in telling the patient that the homosexuality is not being treated. He should point out that other conflicts and problems that may be associated with homosexuality can be helped.

Patients addicted to alcohol and drugs fall into many diagnostic categories. Addictions are not confined to the personality disorders. In seeking relief for disturbing manifestations of anxiety, these people complicate their problems by superimposing an addiction to alcohol or drugs upon their basic illnesses. For example, the schizophrenic patient may drink for the relief or the removal of disturbing thoughts and feelings. The depressed patient either drinks or takes drugs to elevate his mood. The phobic patient finds that alcohol or drugs relieve anxiety and fears. The passive, nonassertive person may drink or take drugs in order to be more assertive and comfortable in group relationships. Alcohol and drug addiction can occur in any type of mental illness.

Patients addicted to alcohol and drugs are rarely good candidates for psychotherapy. The same holds true for the model of group therapy presented in this book. These people do not profit from group therapy although they may profit from a group activity such as Alcoholics Anonymous. Their tolerance for anxiety is minimal, and the anxiety of group therapy cannot be tolerated. Where anxiety occurs they resort to their previous patterns for relief—alcohol or drugs.

The author has observed several characteristic features that alcohol and drug addicts exhibit in group therapy. They are easily frustrated by the anxiety in group therapy and utilize alcohol or drugs for relief. They refuse to recognize the therapist as an authority figure even though other group members do. They refer to the therapist as a moderator or arbitrator. They encounter marked difficulty in expressing feelings of anger and have to maintain a rigid control over their angry feelings by denial, projection, and rationalization. Patients addicted to alcohol and drugs are usually very dependent people. They expect a magical solution to their problems from the therapist. They become excessively dependent on both group and therapist, remaining at this level throughout the course of group therapy. Repeated episodes of alcoholism and the excessive use of drugs result in absences from group meetings for varying periods of time. However, their dependency wishes from the group and therapist bring them back, always hoping for the desired magical solution. The manner in which they handle anxiety resembles that of the juvenile delinquent in group therapy. The latter if placed in an outpatient group becomes anxious and repeats his acting-out behavior in antisocial acts. The usual result is that he stops group therapy. The alcoholic or drug addict does the same thing in a different way. He becomes anxious in group therapy and repeats his former patterns of alcoholism or takes an excessive amount of drugs. He may quit the group or continue attending while resorting to alcohol or drugs for dependency gratification.

The chances of success with delinquents in group therapy are greatly enhanced when it is part of an overall therapeutic milieu program in a controlled environment, such as a training school. Group anxiety and acting-out behavior occur in a controlled setting. The therapist, being aware of the anxiety of the delinquent, modifies his technique toward shorter sessions, less probing maneuvers (identification of defenses against anxiety), and increased support. Perhaps similar types of programs for the alcohol or drug addict would also be successful; their anxiety tolerance suggests that group programs for such patients should be modified in several ways from the more formal model of group therapy. The therapist's technique should be directed toward increased support and dependency. Probing maneuvers (identification of defenses against anxiety) that increase group anxiety should be avoided. Larger groups (10–25 people) would tend to decrease group anxiety. Didactic lectures, movies, and intellectual discussions are other measures that provide support and dependency and lessen group anxiety. Although patient beds in institutions are few and expensive, treatment programs for the patient with alcohol or drug addiction would probably be more successful if carried out in a controlled environment during the initial period of treatment. At a later time, outpatient treatment can be undertaken if the patient's condition warrants it.

The entire field of alcoholism and drug addiction is very complex. There are many unanswered questions and unknown factors. Further research is needed before the value in these disorders can be ascertained.

The Group Therapist's Feelings and Attitude Concerning Patients. In general the selection of patients for group therapy should be governed by the criteria discussed above. There is, however, an additional factor that plays a part in the selection of patients—the feelings and attitude of the therapist toward patients. The therapist's feeling that he can help patients provides a rapport and bond for them that may contribute significantly to the progress of the group. The therapist's investment in the group members is a part of the group therapy process that cannot be defined in concrete terms.

The literature on group therapy suggests that improvement occurs with different disciplines, various therapist's techniques, and difference in the composition and structure of groups. Dreikurs and Corsini reviewed approximately 500 papers on group therapy in 1954 in order to study purposes, methods and mechanisms. They made reference to the numerous models of group therapy in practice.[11] Their observation that all divergent theories and techniques employed in group therapy seemed to be beneficial to some degree raises the question in the author's mind if there may be some mechanisms of the group process that are similar in all of the divergent theories. Professional personnel engaged in any form of psychotherapy are aware of the importance of the therapist-patient relationship. Liking and accepting the group members and letting them know that you are interested in their welfare and can help them may be an important factor in any type of group therapy.

The Role of Group Therapy in an Overall Treatment Program. The humanistic approach to the treatment of people with mental illness has received tremendous impetus during the past 10–15 years. In 1953 the Expert Committee on Mental Health of the World Health Organization reported that the therapeutic atmosphere in mental hospitals was the most important single factor in the efficacy of treatment.[12] Greenblatt, in reviewing the treatment program of the 160-bed Massachusetts Mental Health Center in Boston, confirms the report of the Expert Committee on Mental Health of the World Health Organization and adds further that the informal relationships that make up the therapeutic atmosphere (group activities, ward meetings, social-recreational activities, therapy groups with relatives, and industrial therapy groups) may be more important than all other forms of formal therapy.[13] Psychiatrists who have followed the progress of patients in hospitals are well aware of the therapeutic value of the relationships of patients to nurses, social workers, occupational therapists, or aides.

There are many therapies and other therapeutic measures available for the patient with a mental illness. The question is often asked whether a patient should receive individual therapy, group therapy, both, or some other type of treatment. Actually there are a number of factors that influence the treatment of patients. The location and extent of facilities (hospital or outpatient clinic), the availability of therapists, and the patient's finances are several of the major factors that influence the type of treatment program for patients. For the group therapist the following general observations apply to patients and group therapy:

1. Group therapy is not a form of psychotherapy for the acutely ill patient. In such cases hospitalization, individual treatment, drugs and other therapies should be carried out as indicated. For example, severely depressed, suicidal patients should be hospitalized. Group therapy may be considered at a later time when the acute manifestations of the illness have subsided.

2. Group therapy may be indicated for the patient already in individual therapy and individual therapy may be desired for the patient already in group therapy. In any event the therapist should not attempt individual therapy with the members of his group. The therapist does have certain obligations to the group members regarding illnesses, drugs and hospitalization, as discussed in detail elsewhere in this chapter.

3. The therapist in selecting group members should pay some attention to the anticipated role (behavior) of each member at the onset and during the early meetings of group therapy. He should have a general idea of this role from the psychiatric history, mental status, and psychodynamics of the prospective group member. A careful history of the members' behavior pattern in day-to-day groups (family, business, social, and recreational) affords the therapist an idea of the prospective member's anticipated pattern of behavior in group therapy. For example, the silent, withdrawn person who has difficulty relating and talking to others can be expected to be silent and withdrawn in group therapy. The controlling and competitive person in day-to-day group relationships can be expected to be controlling and competitive in group therapy. The group therapist should try to include members in the group who have different anticipated behavior roles. The group should not be composed entirely of one type of patient—either silent, withdrawn, depressed patients or hyperactive patients; variety in the types of behavior will promote group interaction.

4. Finances are not a major problem for patients in state hospital groups, low-cost clinic groups and the like. In the private practice of psychiatry, finances are quite important both to the patient and the group therapist. Many patients cannot afford a $20 to $25 fee for one hour of psychotherapy per week. They can, however, afford the $5 to $10 weekly fee for group therapy. In such cases, if group therapy is at all indicated, a treatment program can be arranged that will benefit the patient and not be a financial hardship.

5. The attitude and training of the therapist will influence to some degree the type of therapy for his patients. The therapist who has a

knowledge of group dynamics and the techniques of group therapy and group activities will recognize their usefulness in his practice. Group treatment programs will become an important adjunct in the overall treatment programs of his patients, whether he practices in an institution, in a child guidance clinic, or in private practice.

In general, many of the patients who are treated successfully in groups can also be treated successfully in individual therapy. It is not possible to divide patients categorically into those suited for individual therapy and those suited for group therapy. Individual therapy, group therapy, and other therapeutic measures should complement one another. An overall therapeutic program for patients should include individual therapy, group therapy, family therapy, supportive therapy, occupational therapy, hospitalization, and therapeutic group activities.

When the therapist does consider group therapy in treatment plans for a patient he should be aware of its helpfulness as well as its limitations. The indications and contraindications for group therapy discussed in this section should be helpful to the group therapist in selecting patients for group therapy. An absolute, rigid structure regarding the selection of patients for group therapy is not advised. The therapist should be flexible and take into account his own feelings about prospective group members, the specific needs of the group members, and the goals of the group therapy program.

THE ROLE OF THE GROUP THERAPIST

In all groups, whether therapeutic or nontherapeutic, the leader or authority figure is the most important person in the group. The leaders of groups influence the anxiety level and patterns of behavior more than any of the members of groups. In group therapy the therapist is the leader or authority figure of the group. He influences the anxiety level and patterns of behavior of the group members more than anyone else. The therapist's role is therefore one of extreme importance and requires professional training and skill.

The requirements and qualifications for a group therapist are similar to those described for the psychotherapist by Dr. Kenneth Mark Colby. Dr. Colby lists five qualifications: *

1. A body of knowledge concerning normal and pathological thoughts and behavior in our culture.
2. A logically cohesive group of theoretical concepts which are convenient in understanding this thought and behavior.
3. Technical experience in therapeutically integrating observations with concepts through clinical work with patients.
4. Intuition as a practiced and controlled ability to read between the lines

* Kenneth Mark Colby, *A Primer for Psychotherapists,* The Ronald Press Co., 1951. Used by permission.

and empathically grasp what the patient means and feels beyond the face
value of what he says.

5. Awareness of his own inner-wishes, anxieties, and defenses and their influence on his therapeutic technique.[14]

In addition, the group therapist must have an awareness and understanding of the dynamics of group relationships. Psychotherapy, whether
it is individual therapy in a one-to-one relationship or group therapy in
a one-to-eight relationship, has as its primary goal the relief of distressing
and uncomfortable symptoms of anxiety for the patient. The therapist,
with the unique role of treating a group of people at one time, will work
toward this goal through the employment of a technique of group therapy
that promotes an understanding of the basic relationships between the
group members and himself. The therapist's knowledge of group dynamics will reinforce his awareness that he has a specific, all-important
position in the group. He is the therapist, group therapist, doctor, leader,
central figure, or authority figure—the name does not matter. He is an
authority figure to the members who ultimately view him as a father,
husband, older brother, supervisor, school teacher or boss. Mann feels
the therapist cannot become a member of the group even if he so desires.[15] The members see him as a parent and a possessor of power and
strength. This was demonstrated in the following group meeting. An outpatient group of neurotic patients had worked through most of their
hostility toward the group therapist. At the 35th meeting the group members were discussing some of their conflicts with each other in an angry
manner. One member compared the arguments in the group to family
arguments. This was focused on by the group therapist in the following
manner: "Mr. F. speaks of the group's being like a family. What are your
thoughts about this?" The group agreed that their quarreling had many
analogues in the family. The group therapist was not directly referred
to as a parent, but one member referred to him as definitely not being a
part of the group and said he was in a different position.

Keeping the group intact is a very important goal of the group therapist.
This must be kept clearly in mind at every meeting. During the initial
six to nine months in groups of neurotic patients, and for much longer
periods of time in groups of psychotic patients, solidifying the members
into a group requires careful leadership. The therapist must have a constant awareness of doing group therapy—*not individual therapy within
the group.* His technique during group therapy should emphasize group
rather than individual responses. He keeps a close eye on the anxiety
level within the group. He should have at his disposal a series of techniques for reducing the level of anxiety when it is too high, as well as
for raising it when required. He must have the ability to retreat when
the group is moving ahead too fast, and to advance when it is too slow.

As he gauges the level of anxiety, he should recognize when it is at the proper level for constructive work and mutual analysis.

The therapist must recognize his position in the group. He has brought a group of people together to help one another, to become close to one another, and to facilitate an understanding of how they relate to one another. An important function of the therapist's role is to clear away the hostility in the group. Rather than allow the members to displace their hostility on each other the therapist must, in essence, become the group's scapegoat.

The period of time required for this hostility to the therapist to be recognized and ventilated constitutes stage I and stage II of group therapy. Mann feels that this process takes between 25 and 35 meetings in nonpsychotic groups.[16] In groups of neurotic patients the author has observed that hostility begins to be expressed guardedly to the therapist by the 8th–10th meeting. Then, with the development of transference reactions (10th–20th meetings), hostility is denied to the therapist but is expressed covertly and overtly to other group members. In later meetings (25th–40th meetings) the group members reexpress hostility to the therapist much more forcefully than in earlier meetings. By the 40th–55th meeting, groups of neurotic patients will have recognized and ventilated their hostile feelings to the therapist. Although this is the general pattern of hostility in the group, various factors, such as the reality events of group therapy, the degree of closeness within the group, and the skill of the therapist can affect the hostility of the patients. Moreover, the group members never work through all of their hostility toward the therapist, and the hostility level vacillates up and down throughout the life of the group.

It is extremely important—in fact a necessity—for the therapist to be cognizant of the dynamics of the group meeting. To fulfill his proper role in developing close relationships within the group he should be in control of the group. The therapist does not accomplish this by taking over the group and discussing a subject or providing a lecture. He listens and observes. He notes the nonverbal methods of communication. He assimilates the content of the material, keeping in mind that group patients are like individual patients; that the content may be of extraneous matters but the true meaning has to do with the here-and-now of the group meeting. His ability to follow the conversation between the members and to assess its true meaning gives him control of the group. This control is not necessarily concerned with activity or passivity on the therapist's part. Some group meetings require the active participation of the therapist, while others need very little intervention; both situations can be under his control. The stage of the group, the anxiety level, the manner of the defenses, and the behavior patterns of the members all indicate to the therapist, through the group's verbal communication and nonverbal attitudes, what is going on in his group.

Every group meeting has a theme; one of the tasks of the therapist is to recognize this theme and to explore it with the group members, knowing that it is affected by the reality events of group therapy. Absences of group members and the loss of one or more group members will bring about fears of group dissolution. In such instances the theme of the group meeting will be related to the group members' feelings about the absences or the loss of members.

When the therapist is not aware of the group dynamics, the group flounders. He does not know the theme of the meeting. The conversation jumps from one subject to another. Both the therapist and the group members become anxious. The group senses the therapist's anxiety and a vicious circle develops, the underlying theme being, "Who is confusing whom?" At times the therapist is aware that he not in control and debates his next move. In this situation he is somewhat like the fisherman with an empty creel who remains quiet and waits for a nibble. Similarly, the therapist assimilates the material being discussed by the group members and then makes pertinent observations to them. His control or lack of control of the group meetings is determined by his assessment of the verbal and nonverbal communications of the group members. The following examples of group meetings illustrate control and lack of control by the therapist:

A group began the 14th meeting with a discussion of personal problems. They spoke of starting to discuss their feelings and then turning to generalizations, admitting that it was painful and difficult to face problems. There was a short silence, followed by a change to subject matter which was not related to their feelings in the group. The therapist asked the group members about several statements that had been made about their feelings in the group. One member spoke of being confused whenever the therapist said anything. They talked of the need to be tactful, and admitted frustrations and confusion. The therapist continued to refer general statements back to the members. He was not in control of the group. He did not recognize the theme of the meeting. The members were experiencing feelings toward him. They talked of anxiety and frustrations in the group meeting. Had the therapist been in control, proper attention would have been directed toward an exploration of their feelings toward him.

Lack of control of the group can bring about scapegoating of a member. In the 18th meeting of an outpatient group, the therapist was in control at the beginning of the session but lost control during the meeting. The resulting hostility, primarily meant for the therapist, was displaced to a member. The hour began with irrelevant subject material followed by a request that the therapist become more active during the meeting. Two members asked him direct questions. He did not answer and asked the group how they felt when he did not answer questions. There were several hostile remarks directed to the therapist.

The subject was changed several times. The group was active during this interval. One male member had exhibited defiant behavior for a number of meetings. Following a recurrence of his hostile and sarcastic remarks at this meeting the group turned on him violently and rebuffed him with a series of angry retorts until the end of the meeting. The therapist should have asked about their feelings toward him when the subject was changed. He should have done this several times if necessary. He should have stopped the group attack on one member, reviewed pertinent material that had taken place, and asked the group to examine their reasons for attacking one member.

At the second meeting of an outpatient group there was rapid-fire conversation between the members. Numerous subjects were discussed—jobs, automobiles, families, husbands and wives. At group supervision the therapist spoke of being pleased with his group. He felt they were very active. He didn't have to interfere with their conversation. The recorder remarked there was no way to keep up with the rapid conversation between the members. The therapist was not aware that the members were handling their anxiety in the group meeting by overtalkativeness. He was not in control of the group. He should have focused on the rapid, changing conversation. Usually within 10 to 15 minutes after the hour begins the therapist should attempt to identify the theme of the meeting. As soon as he is aware of such behavior during a session, he can make the following observation: "You have talked about a number of things today. Any ideas about what you are doing as far as this meeting is concerned?" The members may or may not deal with the significance of his remarks in an early meeting. He may find it necessary to make this observation several times. Sooner or later the group members become aware of the meaning of the therapist's remarks and begin to look at their feelings and actions more closely in the group meetings.

The anxiety level was high at the third meeting of an outpatient group. At the beginning, one member was twisting beads with her hands and another was continually kicking her foot. A reference to their behavior was made by the therapist. The subject was dealt with superficially and explained by the members in terms of tension and nervousness. One spoke of problems with her husband, a religious fanatic. Another member stated that religion doesn't solve problems. Still another member discussed conflicts between herself and her mother. This group member became so uncomfortable during the session that she left the room for approximately 10 minutes. After she returned, the therapist said to the group: "Mrs. Brown found it necessary to leave the room for a short period. Do you have any ideas about her need to do this?" The member who had left the room immediately broke down, began crying, and verbalized extensive material about problems with her mother. The group gave her support. As a result, she appeared less anxious for the remainder of the session. The group then entered into a discussion of doctors in terms of failing to receive help from them. The therapist focused on this statement by saying: "You have been talking about doctors today. I'm a doctor here in group therapy with you. Any thoughts about it?" In this group meeting the therapist was in control. The material discussed was related to their feelings in the group meeting; for example, the anxious behavior of two members, the member leaving the meeting and returning, and statements concerning doctors.

The following events occurred at the first meeting of an outpatient group. The group members were introduced to each other and to the recorder by the therapist, who discussed the contractual agreements: purpose of group therapy, the recorder, the selection of new members, the use of an observer at infrequent intervals and tape recording of meetings, the time and place of the meetings, the duration of the group, the attendance, fees, drugs, outside contacts between group members, and vacations. Following the completion of the therapist's remarks there was a period of silence. Then the group members spoke of a reluctance to talk: they had never seen each other before, they were strangers; what were they supposed to do; and what does a psychiatrist do? Several questions directed to the therapist were reflected back to the group. Two members spoke of their difficulties with doctors. One said that she had been in the hospital for a period of weeks, but that the doctor had not done anything for her. Another member said that doctors don't believe her, that she could never get any satisfaction from them, and that only her minister seemed to understand. The therapist asked the group for their feelings about hospitals and doctors. In a somewhat hostile tone, the members continued the discussion of doctors and hospitals. The therapist appeared to be in control of this initial session. Fears of closeness were discussed with the group. The theme of hostility to doctors was quite evident during the latter part of the meeting. The members were somewhat puzzled and bewildered at this point because the therapist was not active and they were supposed to do the talking. Their feelings of fear to meet and know new people were very evident. By correctly calling attention to the events occurring in the meeting which involved silence, direct questions, and hostility to doctors and hospitals, the therapist demonstrated an awareness of the content and context of the meeting. He was in control of the group.

An interesting sequela has been observed at group supervisory conferences when group meetings are being reported where the reporting group therapist experienced problems of control. During the presentation of the material the personnel at the supervisory conference frequently become bored and restless. This can be first noted by nonverbal behavior during the presentation, and later by verbal expressions during the discussion period. On the other hand, if the group being reported is well controlled the supervisory conference reflects feelings of warmth and interest. The mood of the supervisory conference often parallels that of the group meeting under study.

On rare occasions the group therapist may be confronted with more difficult situations in exercising control of group meetings. Group members are encouraged to talk about their feelings rather than to act them out in a motor or physical fashion. Infrequently group members will resort to various devices during group meetings, such as lying on the floor, raising and lowering windows repetitively, pacing back and forth in the room, leaving and returning to the meeting, and making threatening remarks to other group members or the therapist. Such physical behavior during group meetings results from the anxiety of the group members. A common concern among group members is whether or not control of their angry feelings can be maintained. Group members look to the therapist for personal reassurance yet expect him to maintain control of the entire group. The therapist's task is to assess the physical or motor activity of the members during group meetings and to keep it within bounds. In every instance the group's attention should be directed towards exploring why a group member has to leave the room, pace the floor, raise and lower windows, etc. If the group members' motor activity becomes disruptive to the group meeting, the therapist should immediately exercise the necessary restraining measures and then explore the meaning of this behavior with the other group members.

The following examples of motor activity in group meetings illustrate the need for control by the group therapist.

At the 12th meeting of a mixed, outpatient group of neurotic patients a female member (Miss R.), who had displayed seductive behavior in prior group meetings, got up from her chair, removed her shoes and lay down on the floor directly in front of the group therapist. The group therapist ignored Miss R. and continued a discussion already in progress. Miss R.'s behavior disrupted the group during the length of time she was recumbent on the floor but she finally got up and returned to her former seat. In this instance the therapist should have asked and if necessary directed Miss R. to return to her seat at the outset of her dramatic exhibit and immediately explored the meaning of her behavior with the other group members.

At the 13th meeting of a mixed, outpatient group of neurotic patients the group therapist was confronted with an angry tirade by a male group member (Mr. L.) who became incensed at the therapist for focusing on their relationships with each other and with him. In prior group meetings Mr. L. had been exhibiting increasing evidences of defiance and rage. At this meeting Mr. L. accused the therapist of interrupting him. Mr. L. got up from his chair, dashed over to where the therapist was sitting and in a defiant and rageful manner shook his fist within inches of the therapist's face and shouted, "Shut up!" Immediately the therapist got up from his chair and in a very firm and authoritative manner directed Mr. L. to return to his chair. Mr. L. returned to his seat and remained quiet and sullen thereafter. The therapist asked about this incident during the remainder of the meeting and at several later meetings. Observations from the group members in later meetings supported the therapist's strong and forceful intervention at the 13th meeting. Even Mr. L. said he was glad the therapist had controlled him.

Some therapists advise their group members at the outset that no physical attacks on each other will be allowed. We have not found it necessary to make such statements. The group member who is told about the possibility of physical attacks or fighting entertains uncomfortable thoughts about a type of psychotherapy that requires such regulations. We are aware that during group therapy meetings the group members become uncomfortable and fear they will lose control of their angry feelings. However, by his technique the therapist can impart to the group members the assurance that their physical and motor activity will not get out of hand. The therapist does not do it by making statements to the group members about its possible occurrence, but by maintaining the proper control during the group meetings.

There is a period during the first stage of group therapy with neurotic patients when the therapist should carefully evaluate the dynamics of the group process so that proper control and progress of the group can be maintained. During this period the therapist may feel that his group has settled down and started to work. The group members attend meetings fairly regularly. They respond to the therapist's wishes and discuss topics during group meetings that suggest improved group interaction. However, a close examination of the group dynamics reveals that intragroup issues are being avoided. The group members discuss conflicts and problems in an intellectual and superficial manner in terms of their day-to-day group relationships, not their own feelings and reactions within the therapy group. Any mention of the relationships between each other and the group therapist creates anxiety. Silences are more pronounced. Defensive patterns of behavior of the group members are more prominently displayed. Subjects are changed quickly. Angry feelings are expressed about parents, husbands, wives, and other authority figures such as bosses. Trivial differences between members may lead to overt outbursts of hostility. Tardiness and absences of group members often bring about violent indignations from the others. It seems as if the group members are filled with anger and minor provocations release an escape valve. The group will usually try to pick out a scapegoat. If they are successful the scapegoat will be the recipient of their angry feelings. Competition, jealousy, and rivalry among the members becomes very keen.

There is one person who seems to be set apart from the group at this point—the therapist. The group members defensively deny any feelings about his role. In earlier meetings they may have expressed hostility to him for his failure to answer questions, his passivity and lack of group structure. Now these feelings are denied. For example, if the therapist is late or cancels a meeting the members may say nothing, whereas the tardiness or absence of a group member may be greeted by overt hostility. The therapist's remarks are intellectualized or treated superficially. The group members may make attempts to deal with group issues but there is a surprising lack of emotional content to their verbalizations.

From the standpoint of group dynamics it is extremely important for the therapist to be aware of this period of pseudoconformity in the group. The therapist may feel that the group is making progress and allow them to continue in this direction. Group therapists have been known to continue in this particular period for many group meetings, feeling that the group is making progress. In actuality the therapist is allowing the group members to defend themselves against the expression of feelings and is not, therefore, in control. By comparing this period to earlier ones the therapist can see that the group members now feel obligated and even coerced to attend meetings and to follow the directions of the therapist. It is as if they are afraid to disagree or challenge him. Group reality events are dismissed as unimportant. The therapist is treated as an all-powerful, omnipotent figure whose good graces are necessary for survival. James Mann has called attention to this period in group therapy with professional people (didactic or training groups). Mann states that the role of the therapist has allowed the development of transference reactions. The therapist is now seen as an omnipotent person who can either love them or (more importantly) retaliate against them. Concurrently with the development of transference reactions the group members identify with the therapist as an aggressor.[16] Thus, the group members, out of fear of the therapist's omnipotence, become passive, defensive, or ingratiatory. The cooperativeness, conformity, and impression of group unity are merely a false front. Underdeath this façade of group unity the members may experience a massive degree of anger, rebellion, and defiance. Afraid to defend themselves, they can only comply with the therapist's wishes.

Once the members have developed transference reactions they tend to react to the therapist's observations about intragroup relationships with silence. This silence reaction may spread to the entire group, particularly at the outset of group meetings. The therapist notes this change in behavior. In earlier meetings he did not encounter any difficulties in getting the meetings under way; the members were usually talkative and seemingly anxious to get the meeting started. Now the anxiety level has gone up. Invariably the therapist himself becomes anxious at this particular time because of inexperience with this problem. He is quite concerned by their change in behavior. The therapist sometimes is so eager for the group members to begin talking that he frequently forgets to deal with the primary problem—the silence of the group members. Because of his anxiety, control of the group may become a problem. The therapist may find himself asking irrelevant questions or making unnecessary observations to the group members. His anxiety actually forces him to get the meeting under way. He thus experiences some of the same feelings as the group members. The latter have grown anxious over the development of transference reactions; they are not as comfortable as in earlier meetings. The therapist is also more anxious. His group is not functioning as well as in the earlier meetings. He begins to feel insecure and inadequate in his role as a group therapist.

With psychotic patients the transference reactions are much more intense than with neurotic patients. The psychotic patient is much more fearful and frightened of what he recognizes to be the retaliatory powers of the therapist. Anxiety levels in groups of psychotic patients are much higher than with neurotic patients. For psychotic groups the therapist's technique has to be modified in order to delay dealing with the group members' relationship to him. This means that the time required for psychotic groups to examine their relationship with the therapist is very prolonged. In fact, psychotic groups may require several years to reach stage II of group therapy.

Sandor Rado has described four levels of cooperation of the patient in his treatment behavior: the aspiring level, the self-reliant level, the parentifying level, and the magic-craving level.[17] The stage of pseudoconformity in group therapy is identical to Rado's description of the patient whose treatment behavior is at the parentifying level. After transference reactions develop, the group members parentify the therapist and behave like obedient or disobedient children. Group members who thus become obedient or compliant are actually fearful of the parentified therapist. They exhibit behavior patterns of subservience, ingratiation, and outright seduction in order to obtain the therapist's approval or love. Group members who become disobedient or defiant in their group treatment behavior exhibit resentful and antagonist attitudes to the parentified therapist. They may arrive late at meetings, but absences are even more common. They may be competitive with the therapist or show overt hostility to him and to other group members. The disobedient or defiant group member displays resentful and coercive behavior patterns toward the therapist whenever possible. Group losses during this period are often due to this sort of defiant behavior.

The author has repeatedly observed this period of pseudoconformity during the first stage of therapy in outpatient neurotic groups. It begins between the 10th and 15th meetings and is usually clearly evident by the 15th to 20th meeting. Its length will depend on the therapist's awareness of the group dynamics and his ability to tolerate hostility from the group members. The group therapist's technique thus becomes an extremely important procedure. Before cohesiveness and unity can be obtained (stage III of Group Therapy) the underlying hostility and rebellion of the group members must be cleared away.

The following example of an outpatient neurotic group illustrates this period of group therapy. The group was composed of four males, four females, a male therapist, and a female recorder. During the first 15 meetings the members verbalized hostility to the therapist for not answering questions, failing to provide a group stucture, and making them aware of their behavior in group meetings. Some of their initial fears of group therapy were verbalized and cleared away. Sporadic absenteeism occurred with several members. At times only four or five members were present for meetings. Two members quit the group prior to the 10th meeting and one new member was added at the 12th meeting. At group supervision the therapist announced that he wanted to discuss three meetings: the 16th, 17th, and 18th. He commented that attendance was excellent, that group issues were being discussed, and that he was pleased with the group's progress. A closer look at the group during these three meetings revealed that group issues were discussed in terms of husband, wives, children, and parents. One member who was tardy for two of the meetings was angrily attacked by the group. Another member who missed one meeting was treated in a similar fashion. The therapist cancelled one meeting between the 17th and 18th meetings. The members denied any feelings about the cancelled meeting or the therapist's absence. A third member was subjected to continuous hostility from the others. During earlier group meetings this member had been extremely competitive with the therapist, who had repeatedly focused on her behavior during the earlier meetings. Now her competitiveness was less, but the members began attacking her again as if they felt the therapist wished them to do so. The members' anxiety level was high in all three meetings. They talked of being angry with others outside of the group and angry with other group members. One member said self-assertion led to retaliation and thus caused guilt and fear. Several members said that assertion caused parents to get sick or husbands to leave home. They spoke of their fears of displeasing people. On several occasions the therapist asked about the feelings in the group but was ignored or sidetracked by the substitution of group issues for similar situations outside the group. Rather than refocusing on the relationships within the group, the therapist continued the discussion underway. In the 17th and 18th meetings the members discussed sexual feelings in a superficial manner and in terms of their family situations. One member of the group was a homosexual. He revealed his sexual problem at the 17th meeting. During supervision the therapist was asked why the group members spent so much time discussing sexual feelings in two consecutive meetings. The therapist answered that he had encouraged them to do so because he mistakenly felt that sexual feelings were the central issue at this point.

The 16th, 17th, and 18th group meetings illustrate quite clearly the dynamics of this particular period of group therapy. In these meetings the therapist was not in control of the group, nor was he aware of the theme of the meeting. The members seemingly cooperative and ingratiatory behavior was interpreted as satisfactory group progress. Moreover, the subject discussed—sexual feelings—pleased the therapist. Another influence on his technique was the fact that this was his first group; he admitted fear and anxiety over possible hostility from the group members. However, following group supervision, the therapist began to explore in more detail their relationships with each other and himself.

At the 19th, 20th, and 21st group meetings (following group supervision session) sexual feelings were not mentioned. The group members spoke of being annoyed with the therapist for creating competition and rivalry among them. Fear of authority and the need for compliance were discussed. One group member spoke of putting the therapist on a pedestal, another felt he was omnipotent, and a third wanted the therapist to be perfect. Resentment of authority, as well as the need to challenge and test anyone in authority, was also discussed. Angry outbursts continued to occur between the group members. At the 21st meeting the members admitted that irritations and anger were building up and were being displaced on the most susceptible group member (scapegoating). Then, too, the group members guardedly admitted their increasing anger toward the therapist. The latter continued to maintain control of the meetings. The content of the 19th, 20th, and 21st meetings points out the members' feelings about authority figures.

The therapist should be aware of this period during the first stage of group therapy. He should remember at all times that the central theme of these meetings will be the members' relationship to him. At every opportunity he should encourage the members to examine and express their feelings about him. He should also be aware that these feelings will not be fully expressed in one or two meetings. This exploratory period is a necessary part of the group's development and growth, requiring a certain period of time. It may take a number of meetings before the group members can deal with their relationship to the group therapist. However, the therapists' constant and consistent observations to the members to explore their feelings about him encourages group participation. As the expected retaliation from the therapist fails to materialize and their unrealistic demands (dependency gratifications) are recognized, the members can move forward with the expression of their feelings.

The therapist should not let this period lull him into feeling that true group unity and cohesiveness have occurred. Hostility feelings towards the therapist must be ventilated. Then, and only then, can the group get down to a constructive analysis of their relationships with each other and with the therapist. The latter's technique, awareness of the theme of the meetings, control of the group, and ability to accept the members' hostility are important factors in this period of therapy.

Another series of problems posed for the therapist concerns the expression of sexual feelings by the members. Many people feel that sex should not be discussed in any group. Sexual taboos have often led to misunderstandings and distorted concepts about sexual feelings, including guilt feelings, low self-esteem, worthlessness, and rejection. Most of the people who enter group therapy have sexual conflicts of one kind or another—inadequate or demanding spouse; extramarital and premarital sexual affairs; promiscuity; frigidity; impotence; homosexuality; homosexual feelings in the dependent, heterosexual person; anger associated with sexual feelings; fears of heterosexual or homosexual attack from others; guilt feelings for the presence of sexual thoughts and feelings; guilt feelings when discussing sexual subjects; and inability to separate and understand sexual feelings as they occur in close relationships with others.

As we have already seen, the structure of group therapy forces the members to come close to each other and to the therapist. The reactions that are generated by this closeness include sexual feelings. An important goal of the therapist is for the members to discuss and understand their sexual feelings. However, the therapist must be aware of the anxiety in group members when sexual discussions take place. Sexual conversations during group meetings create even more anxiety among the group members than do discussions about angry feelings. Group members experience more difficulty in discussing sexual subjects than they experience with any others.

The feelings of group members about discussing sexual matters in group meetings is illustrated in the brief summaries of 10 outpatient groups of neurotic patients.

Group No. 1. Mixed composition, male group therapist, female recorder. At the 5th group meeting a male group member who had had previous psychiatric treatment (individual therapy for one year) discussed sexual conflicts. He asked other group members about sexual problems. The group anxiety level rose sharply during this discussion. The group therapist did not divert the conversation. A female group member became extremely anxious over the sexual material that was discussed. She stopped group therapy. Later she told the group therapist that she was not interested in attending a group where sexual material was discussed.

Group No. 2. Mixed composition, male group therapist, female recorder. At the 17th and 18th meetings sexual conflicts were discussed in terms of day-to-day group relationships. One group member admitted homosexuality and received support from the others. The group therapist admitted later that he encouraged the group members to discuss sexual feelings. The homosexual group member will usually tell the group of his sexual role early in group therapy (5–15th meeting). His motivation for discussing it is not sexual. The homosexual group member primarily wants to receive support, acceptance, and approval from the other group members and the group therapist. The homosexual person is not accepted in society. At the beginning of group therapy he has the same feelings of nonacceptance in the group meeting.

Group No. 3. Mixed composition, male group therapist, female recorder. At the 12th, 15th, 18th, 32nd, and 38th group meetings there were brief discussions of sexual conflicts in day-to-day group relationships. Sexual feelings within the group were avoided both by the group members and the group therapist.

Group No. 4. Mixed composition, male group therapist, female recorder. Sexual feelings were initially discussed at the 52nd group meeting. In later meetings (61st, 67th, 68th) sexual feelings within the group were explored.

Group No. 5. Mixed composition, male group therapist, female recorder. The group completed its contract of 60 meetings without any discussion of sexual feelings in any meetings.

Group No. 6. Female group, female group therapist, female recorder. The group discussed sexual feelings on three occasions over a period of 60 meetings. At the 13th meeting one group member admitted homosexuality. At the 35th and 50th meetings sexual feelings were discussed superficially in terms of marital situations. Sexual feelings within the group were not discussed.

Group No. 7. Male group, female group therapist, female recorder. Sexual feelings were discussed at the 29th and 40th meetings of the group. The discussions were in terms of other group relationships, not their intragroup sexual feelings.

Group No. 8. Mixed composition, male group therapist, female recorder. After 56 group meetings sexual feelings had only been discussed once superficially at the 35th meeting.

Group No. 9. Mixed composition, female group therapist, female recorder. In 45 group meetings sexual feelings had not been discussed.

Group No. 10. Mixed composition, male group therapist, female recorder. The group completed its contract of 65 meetings. Sexual feelings were discussed superficially at the 21st and 35th meetings. At the 49th, 57th, 60th, 61st, and 62nd meetings sexual feelings within the group were explored.

The anxiety that arises from discussing sexual feelings in group meetings of neurotic patients makes it necessary for the therapist to vary his technique. During the early meetings of the group (meetings 1–10) the therapist should avoid discussing sexual feelings. If a group member brings up this subject, the group therapist should direct the conversation in another channel, utilizing previous material discussed in group meetings. He does not have to state that sexual feelings will not be discussed; all that is necessary is to change the subject. The members are keenly sensitive to the therapist's observations. In this period of group therapy they will be greatly relieved if the subject of sexual feelings is avoided.

In later meetings (10–35) as the group members become more comfortable with each other and with the therapist, sexual difficulties in their day-to-day group relationships may be discussed. Even at this time the members discuss these sexual problems with caution. Increased group anxiety usually occurs. Each member is quite concerned as to how the therapist and the other members will react to his statements. Fears of rejection, guilt feelings, and low self-esteem continue to be present. The therapist should use extreme caution in exploring sexual feelings. The anxiety level of the group will serve as a gauge for his technique. A safe procedure for the therapist is to explore sexual feelings in terms of their other group relationships (family and social) and to avoid discussing sexual feelings of the group itself.

When the members have reached the final stage (stage III) of group therapy the therapist can gradually begin to explore the sexual feelings within the group. As with other areas of behavior, the members cautiously approach the sexual area, become anxious, fearful, and guilty, withdraw for several meetings and then proceed again. At first they discuss their sexual feelings for each other. The group members find it very difficult to discuss their sexual feelings for the therapist. At this time the therapist must be patient and understanding. He should gradually work towards the ventilation and recognition of the group members' sexual feelings towards him. An example of how group members handle sexual feelings with each other and with the therapist during stage III of group therapy is given in Chap. 8.

Sexual feelings in group therapy also occur on an unconscious level. Group members make many sexual inferences during group meetings by symbolic language. In general, their symbolic references to sexuality does not increase the anxiety of the group. The perceptive therapist will recognize this type of behavior of the group members. In general he will let it pass unless the group is in the final stage (stage III) of therapy. Then he can assess its meaning and determine whether or not to call its attention to the members.

The therapist's own unconscious feelings may create problems in the sexual area. He can have unconscious sexual conflicts that encourage the members to discuss sexual material during meetings and promote sexual acting out between group meetings. The therapist with unconscious homosexual conflicts may encourage a member with similar conflicts to act out his homosexual feelings. The therapist who is frightened of his own sexual feelings may become anxious when sexual material is discussed by the group members. They, in turn, will pick up the therapist's anxiety and become more anxious. The therapist with severe, unconscious sexual conflicts may be very destructive to the group. One may question whether or not a person with such conflicts should attempt to be a group therapist at all. Group therapist-recorder discussions and group supervision, however, can be valuable to the therapist in fostering an awareness of minor unconscious sexual conflicts and their effect on the group members. The therapist who recognizes such difficulties can modify his techniques in order to correct any group problems that may be present.

Finally, the therapist may encounter particular difficulties with members who are lonely, sexually frustrated, and prone to sexual acting out. In mixed groups many male and female group members have encountered sexual conflicts with their wives or husbands. Once group therapy starts, these members may become attracted to other members of the group. Sexual fantasies toward each other can occasionally lead to conversations and meetings between group meetings. In rare instances a sexual affair may occur between two group members. The group contract provides safeguards against such acting-out behavior. Communications and contacts with each other outside of the group meeting are not allowed.

If by chance meetings do occur, the group members are directed to report such at the next group meeting. Careful attention to the group contract by the therapist will help curtail these types of problems.

The Advantages of Training in Group Therapy

A discussion of the therapist's role would be incomplete without emphasizing the training it requires. Adequate supervision is just as important for the beginning group therapist as for the therapist with individual patients. The importance attached to the training of group therapists is illustrated in the program employed in the residency training at the Department of Psychiatry, Emory University School of Medicine. The goals are twofold: (1) to develop an understanding of group dynamics, and (2) to train residents to be group therapists.

It is important for every therapist, whether or not he ever uses group therapeutic procedures, to understand the dynamics of group relationships. No one will deny the influence of group relationships to the patient in individual therapy. The patient's progress may be directly related to these group relationships (family, occupational, or social). At times the therapist employs a type of group approach when he sees the family together with his patient. He may wish to see the family regularly—using a procedure referred to as *family therapy*.

The therapist himself enters into numerous group relationships. During his period of professional training he participates in conferences, supervisory sessions, hospital rounds, and other group activities. An awareness of his own behavior in group relationships points the way to self-understanding of his personality structure. The staff relationships on hospital floors also comes into clearer focus. When attending meetings of various types (professional, educational, or social), a knowledge of group dynamics will afford the therapist an ability to read between the lines of the verbal communications and grasp the underlying theme. An awareness of the dynamics of group relationships in the treatment of his patients and in his association with colleagues will broaden the therapist's understanding of human behavior.

The format of psychiatric residency programs throughout the United States varies as to when the resident receives training in group therapy. Some group therapy programs begin in the first or second year, while others only offer training in the third year. The author feels that it is advantageous to begin training in group dynamics and group therapy during the first year of residency. Preparing the resident for group therapy requires 5–6 months. The actual period of supervision of the resident's group is 18 months. During the first year of training the resident has the opportunity to apply his knowledge of group dynamics and group therapy in other areas of his training. In authoritative roles such as the administrator of a ward the resident can better understand the relationships within the staff. He will find himself more relaxed and comfortable in dealing with staff problems. Staff relationships to authority can be recognized in their proper perspective and not be made personal issues. In staff conferences, patient ward meetings, family conferences, and other group activities the resident's knowledge of group dynamics will make him a better psychiatrist.

During the resident's initial year of training approximately 20 hours of didactic material and discussion periods over a period of 3 months should be devoted to the dynamics of group reationships and the dynamics of group therapy. The features of the group contract should be stressed. Many of the common, recurrent problems in technique of group therapy can be pointed out. Recorded tapes of group meetings and group supervisory conferences are recommended for specific types of group therapy problems. A selected bibliography should be assigned for extra reading. The residents can also attend group supervisory conferences for the second- and third-year residents for 6–8 weeks in order to become acquainted with its format. In 5–6 months the new residents can select patients for their groups, secure a recorder, and begin group therapy. The initial didactic conference then becomes group supervision. It should be held for a period of 2 hours once a week. In attendance are the residents, recorders, and supervisor. The residents can rotate in the presentation of their groups. The recorders should take an active part in the supervisory conference by reading or summarizing the notes of the therapist's group meetings. Since several group meetings elapse between each group therapist's presentation, short summaries of each meeting can be presented so that continuity of each group can be maintained with the supervisory group. At least one meeting, however, should be reported in detail so that the group therapist's technique can be more critically evaluated.

Group supervisory conferences continue throughout the three years of the residency program. Attempts should be made to limit each conference to six group therapists and their recorders so that each group therapist can present his group fairly often.

The first group therapy experience for the first-year resident will probably be with clinic outpatients. The clinic outpatient groups are composed of neurotic patients and schizophrenic patients who are not severely disabled. During his second and third year the resident may also attempt group therapy with adolescents, juvenile delinquents, and psychotic patients. With these people group therapy is a more difficult procedure and prior group therapy experience with a group of neurotic patients is recommended.

The successful group therapist becomes cognizant of a series of events during his period of training. He has a front-row seat in the arena of his group and feels the impact of the members' emotional interaction with each other and with him. He develops an awareness of his own anxiety in a group of people and recognizes its constructive and destructive components. Through his relationship with the recorder and the group supervisory conference the group therapist senses the importance of "looking at himself" and develops the abilities to recognize mistakes, to accept criticism in a constructive manner, and to modify or change his behavior. Transference and countertransference feelings are viewed from a group level, a process that is similar in many respects to that encountered with the individual person in therapy.

The group supervisory conference plays as important a role for the group therapist as individual supervision does to the therapist with individual patients. This second group is actually group supervision within a group, and many of the same feelings come into play that are seen in the patient's group. Such an arrangement serves a double purpose—besides the instruction afforded the group therapist with his patient group, patterns of behavior among the members of the supervisory group offer an experience in the dynamics of group relationships. This was demonstrated in a recent group supervisory session when a first-year resident was to report his group meeting. He arrived late, slouched down in a chair, and announced his presence. The supervisor asked him to give a brief description of each patient in his group. He did this in a haphazard, wryly humorous fashion, omitting many pertinent details. Others present began to chuckle and talk among themselves. The supervisor stopped the resident and asked about the behavior in the conference. Hostility toward the resident for his tardiness and poorly prepared presentation was expressed by the other residents and the recorders. Their method of dealing with it by derisive laughter and extraneous conversation was also discussed.

The group supervisory experience also affords a means whereby the group therapist can learn to express himself and receive understanding and support during his period of training. The anxiety of the group therapist is at a much higher level than with other forms of therapy. Feelings of inadequacy, inferiority, and low self-esteem are not uncommon. Learning that other group therapists experience similar problems is very supportive to the training resident and is analogous to the reward that patient group members experience when they find that others have feelings and problems like theirs. Then, too, the residents recognize their own patterns of behavior in each other and find that they are similar to the behavior patterns of their group members. Also, as in regular group therapy, competitiveness, hostility, and ingratiatory techniques are employed with the supervisor.

The recorder's role in group therapy is discussed in detail in the present chapter. It is important at this point to note the influence played by the recorder in group therapy, particularly in implementing the dynamics of the group process through the relationship of the recorder to the therapist and the group members. The adage that we live so close to ourselves that it is impossible to recognize our own behavioral patterns is brought into awareness in group therapy. The group therapist's anxiety and nonverbal behavior in a group meeting may be completely foreign (unconscious) to him. The recorder can recognize and evaluate verbal and nonverbal attitudes of the group therapist and his group members. His observations can be a helpful gauge of how the anxiety is flowing in the group.

As a learning experience, the group therapist and recorder can become aware of their relationships to one another and to the group. Differences of opinion and conflicts do occur between them, but this is not necessarily an unhealthy development unless there are unresolved problems. The technique of the group therapist may be questioned. The recorder may side (identify) with the group members against the group therapist. There may be differences of opinion regarding certain group issues. On occasion, the recorder may become competitive with the therapist and communicate this feeling to the members. Anxiety created by unresolved conflicts between the therapist and the recorder is reflected in the meetings and interferes with the group's progress. Limentani, Geller, and Day have pointed out that many of the difficulties between the group therapist and the recorder stem from the fact that conscious motivations, goals, and respective roles of the group therapist and recorder are at variance with their unconscious ones. This condition is further intensified by the stress of the group situation.[18] If the therapist-recorder discussions and group supervisory conferences can be assimilated in a healthy, mature manner, the variables in their conscious and unconscious motivations and goals will be diminished, self-awareness will be enhanced, and the patient group will reflect this improvement in terms of constructive work.

Moreover, the training of the therapist can be further advanced by a personal analysis. The feelings, attitudes, and reactions of the therapist during group meetings are by far the single most important factor in group therapy. The reactions of the group members are influenced not only by conscious communications from the group therapist but also by the unconscious (nonverbal) communications from the therapist. If the therapist feels lethargic or depressed, the members may become depressed. If he is anxious, the members sense this and become anxious themselves. Group members have said that the most important factor that determines their feelings about the therapist is his attitude. Thus it stands to reason that if the group therapist is more aware of his own conscious and unconscious motivations, reactions to anxiety, and behavior patterns, his own anxiety and the anxiety that occurs among the members of a group can be more successfully and comfortably managed.

The duties of the group therapist cannot be called a simple task. His training milieu is an anxiety-provoking situation filled with the ups and downs of many therapeutic experiences. Once his technique is mastered, however, the therapist usually becomes filled with enthusiasm. The fascinating subject of the dynamics of group relationships unfolds before him. He recognizes that the group is under his control. He knows what they are doing, for their behavior has a meaning and significance. Not only do the group members learn from each other but the therapist also shares in the learning experience.

A discussion of the therapist's role would not be complete without an assessment of his investment in the group members. Psychotherapy is a two-way street. The patients have an investment in the group therapist, and the therapist has an investment in his patients. The attitude of the therapist is all-important. The sincerity, understanding, and honesty of his feelings in relation to the group members, as well as his ability to submerge his individual likes and dislikes in treating the group as a unit, can create a group spirit that will reward his efforts. The ability of the therapist to accept his members becomes an extremely important factor in group therapy. One can speculate that the therapist's verbal and non-verbal communication to his members that "I want to help you, I feel that I can help you," is perhaps his most effective therapeutic tool.

Psychiatrists, psychologists, psychiatric social workers, occupational therapists, and nurses comprise the majority of professional personnel who are group therapists. By far the larger number of therapists are in the first three categories. A frequent question arises as to who is qualified to be a group therapist. Although it is sometimes held that only psychiatrists have the proper medical background, there are many who feel that the field of group therapy can be best performed by psychologists and psychiatric social workers. Actually, there is a role in group therapy for all persons with training in psychology and a knowledge of psychiatry. With the proper qualifications, a knowledge of group dynamics and adequate control and instruction by a group therapy supervisor, personnel in the related fields of psychiatry can perform satisfactorily as group therapists in specific areas of their ability.

RECORDER, SUBSTITUTE RECORDER, MECHANICAL REPRODUCTION OF GROUP MEETINGS

A recorder or note-taker is a necessary adjunct in the training period of the group therapist. The recorder's value in the assessment of the group has been previously discussed. The recorder is not an absolute necessity once the therapist has achieved awareness of the dynamics of group therapy and has developed his knowledge of technique to a degree that he is comfortable with groups. But even to the well-trained therapist a recorder can be an asset. Treating a group of people that have a multiplicity of anxietal phenomena and transference-countertransference manifestations is not an easy task. The recorder can be a valuable and supportive ally.

Some group therapists frown on the use of any recorder, observer, or mechanical means of reproduction of group meetings (such as a tape recorder). They feel that any form of recording slows up and prevents the flow of material from the group members. Generally, however, the advantage of using a recorder far outweighs the slight risk of checking the flow of material. The recorder does not necessarily have to be a doctor. Nurses, social workers, occupational therapists, ward secretaries, and psychiatric aides can be utilized in this role. Recorders may or may not be paid for their services. A fellow resident may serve as recorder for another resident's group. However, time schedules may prevent a resident from serving as group therapist in one group and recorder in another. When other than resident personnel are used (which is usually the case) we have found it advantageous to pay recorders on a scale depending on the type of group. The recorder's pay varies from $3 to $5 per week, depending on whether the group is from the low-cost clinic or composed of private patients.

During his initial interviews with the group members the therapist should explain the role of the recorder as part of the group contract. He should emphasize that the recorder will attend all meetings, take written notes, and be a silent, nonparticipating member of the group. The therapist should stress the confidential nature of the material and emphasize that none of the recorded information ever goes beyond the therapist-recorder relationship and the department files of which they are a part. The therapist may wish to use a substitute recorder during the absence of a regular recorder. If so, he should inform the group of his plans at the time he explains the role of the recorder. The use of tape recorders should be explained in the same manner. It is well to point out to the group members that the therapist and group can profit from the recorded material because frequent discussion between the therapist and recorder occurs which affords the therapist a better way of keeping in touch with the progress of the group.

The technique of the recorder may vary according to the therapist's wishes. Some generalizations, however, can be made. It is usually best for the recorder to enter the group therapy meeting in the company of the therapist. If the recorder enters alone or before the therapist, the members may make repeated efforts to engage him in conversation. If such conversation remained on a superficial level, there would be no problems. Invariably, though, the group members want to discuss group business.

Recorders are advised to seat themselves comfortably in a part of the room where the therapist and the entire group can be observed. The recorder should sit apart from the therapist; when he is too close, some of the therapist's conscious and unconscious attitudes and reactions may be missed. The position of the therapist with respect to the group usually remains the same at every meeting. The recorder may or may not sit in the same place at every session.

Once the meeting begins, the recorder's chief duty is to take notes. It is impossible for the recorder to take down all of the material discussed during a session unless he is specifically trained in shorthand techniques. Recorders should set their own pace. A recorder who is wholly absorbed in note taking may miss the nonverbal communication of the group members and therapist. Frequent observation of the members' attitudes is extremely important. Excessive smoking, restlessness and its various forms of activity, silence, overtalkativeness, changes in seating arrangement, late arrivals, the reactions of the therapist, and the recorder's own feelings are all excellent gauges of anxiety in the group and should be noted by the recorder. All observations and statements by the therapist to the group should, however, be recorded verbatim. The timing, content, and nonverbal manifestations of the therapist are valuable indicators of his effectiveness. Does he recognize the theme of the meeting? Is he in control of the group? What is his state of self-awareness? Such questions as these are of concern to the recorder. In his silent, nonparticipating role within the group the recorder's anxiety does not rise as high as that of the members or therapist; he can, accordingly, render a more objective opinion on these issues.

The recorder should note the seating arrangement of each group meeting by making a small diagram showing each member's place in the room. Over a long period of group therapy an analysis of the seating arrangement may be informative. Members who sit near the group therapist may be dependent, ingratiatory, or need protection from the therapist; others who sit at a distance from the group therapist may do so because of hostility. For example, in a group of psychotic females one member was comfortable only sitting next to the therapist. She insisted on this seating position and when asked about it spoke of her dependency on the therapist. She verbalized that sitting near him meant he would take care of her. In the 11th meeting of a group composed of the husbands of schizophrenic wives, one member who had been treated with hostility by the others in previous meetings was again subjected to hostility. Even though the therapist recognized the displacement of hostility (scapegoating) to this member and attempted to deal with the group concerning it, this member moved to a chair immediately to the left of the therapist—obviously to be under his protecting "wing." In other groups of neurotic patients, members who repeatedly occupied positions near the therapist were alleged by other members to be "hiding behind the therapist," "the teacher's pet," "wishing a magical cure," or "wanting the therapist's approval."

Generally, however, a majority of the group members retain their same seating position throughout the length of group therapy. If a member does move, he usually shifts during the initial six months of group therapy. Extremely anxious members in groups of neurotic patients sometimes move about uncomfortably from seat to seat. In groups of psychotic patients a member may move his chair away from others, or speak of being "more comfortable" when not too close to others; a position in the corner of the room was often used by one member who kept trying to withdraw from the group. The observation that this place was the "seat of isolation" was not the therapist's deduction but resulted from discussion and analysis by the group members. Group members who attempt to occupy the group therapist's chair are usually greeted with hostility from the other members. In a program of 11 months' duration for a group of psychotic male patients, an angry, competitive male member had created group problems at a number of meetings. Repeated attempts by the therapist to have the members deal with his behavior were unsuccessful; they were angry but refused to interfere. Finally the therapist offered the unruly member his own chair and suggested that he take over the meeting. The member was quite agreeable to the therapist's suggestion and changed places with him. Immediately there was a hostile reaction from the other members of such intensity that the unruly member promptly vacated the therapist's place and resumed his regular chair.

Observations of the seating arrangement in biweekly ward meetings of a private (20-bed) psychiatric hospital over a period of 7 months revealed several interesting features. At each meeting the ward leader sat in the same seat. Those patients who had assumed the role of assistant ward leader (active, supportive, and ingratiatory to the ward leader) usually sat in a chair immediately to the right of the ward leader. Three male patients occupied this position for fairly long periods of time. The chair on the ward leader's left was rarely occupied. The ward leader felt this chair represented an unstable seating position. Occasionally, a recent admission or a disorganized psychotic patient would sit in it, but not for long. The ward leader also observed that when the patients entered the room for the meeting the actual seating proceeded from the back of the room toward the front. The ward leader sat in the front of the room. When the patients seated themselves from front to back the ward leader could anticipate acting-out behavior.

In addition to taking notes and diagraming the seating arrangement, the recorder fills an important relationship with the therapist. The recorder has, of course, a personality structure and a specific set of behavioral patterns. Ideally, the group therapist and recorder should be able to express feelings openly in their weekly discussion periods and profit from the interchange. But experience has shown that problems and conflicts between the therapist and the recorder frequently are recognized by the group members. Another valuable service of the group supervisory conference comes from the confrontation, exploration, and resolution of the situation, which generate self-awareness for the therapist and the recorder. Examples of the importance of therapist-recorder relationships have occurred in the following situations:

Prior to a meeting the therapist was aware of a mild physical disorder and felt depressed, dull, and lethargic. The meeting, reflecting the same feeling tone, was dull, uninteresting, and depressing. The recorder sensed this feeling early in the meeting and reported it at the therapist-recorder discussion and group supervision. The therapist was able to see the effect his feelings had on the recorder and the group members.

At another meeting the therapist had no control over his group. He did not perceive the feeling and emotions behind the verbal statements of group members. The subject matter was irrelevant and superficial, with frequent changes in topics of conversation. The anxiety level of the group was quite high. The group members said that the therapist was a stranger, that he had no faith in them and that he did not understand them. Early in the meeting the recorder noticed this lack of control and became concerned. Later she became irritated at the therapist because he was not controlling the group. When this group was presented at supervision the recorder openly discussed her feelings about the therapist. The supervisory group agreed with the recorder and the therapist admitted his anxiety and his loss of control during this session.

In another group, the therapist had selected a female recorder of whom he was extremely fond and towards whom he had experienced warm and positive feelings. This warmth was manifested by many conscious acts before, during, and after group meetings. His group members were aware that he was married. Several members of the group made reference to the situation at the completion of a meeting and one said to the therapist, "Doctor, aren't you married?" At group supervision this relationship was discussed openly, with the therapist admitting warm and friendly feelings for the recorder.

Conflict between the therapist and the recorder can cause serious problems in the group. In two state hospital groups, the therapist-recorder relationships were as follows: resident A was the therapist, resident B was the recorder for one group, while resident B was the therapist and resident A was the recorder for the other group. Resident A was a defensive individual who refused to discuss his feelings and utilized denial constantly. Naturally he was exhibiting the same patterns with his group members. Resident B was introspective, discussed feelings openly, and admitted conflicts with resident A. Discussions held between the two residents and at group supervision did not resolve the situation. Acting out occurred with their being late at meetings, changing the hours of group meetings, disagreeing over recorded material, etc. Finally, resident A changed the hour of his group meeting to conflict with resident B's schedule so that he could not serve as his recorder. At group supervision, resident A continued his defensive attitude and denied his acting out role. Both obtained new recorders from the nursing staff. Resident A continued his former role but was less threatened by a nurse as recorder. Six meetings later, during one of resident A's meetings, a member made reference to the recorder and the notes being written down. As this subject was developed another group member said to the group therapist, "Doctor, you didn't like your other recorder, did you?" The therapist changed the subject quickly. His group continued to function poorly. Resident B, with his ability to examine his own feelings, admitted mistakes and corrected them, and his group made good progress.

Group members at times contact the recorder between meetings with various types of requests. For example, an eleven-months-old group of neurotic outpatients had worked through many of their authority conflicts with their therapist. There was one member, however, whose dependency needs were not being met. This group member acted out by telephoning and attempting to manipulate the recorder into helping with a problem with his daughter. He felt the recorder was sympathetic and understanding, but that the group therapist would never understand. When the group therapist and recorder discussed this development both were aware that this group member's behavior was a manifestation of hostility to the therapist and was directly related to the group dynamics. When events such as this occur the underlying feelings of the member should be examined. We recommend that the recorder refer all such requests to the therapist who will, in turn, request that this member bring the problem to the group. Emergency problems of necessity should be handled as the situation demands. In an outpatient group of neurotics at the 10th meeting the following situation developed:

The group therapist had cancelled the 9th meeting because of an illness. Several days later the recorder was contacted by a group member who requested advice concerning a traffic violation and fears of appearing in court. The recorder referred him to the therapist who, in turn, asked the member to bring the matter to the group. During the discussion in the next meeting the member revealed that in his distress at the therapist cancelling the meeting, he had become inebriated, and subsequently had been involved in an accident with another man's wife. His passivity, nonassertiveness, and the dynamics behind his desire for the therapist to write a letter to the court so that he could avoid this situation was recognized by the group. He was advised to go to court himself, to stand up and work out his own problems.

Even though the recorder is formally not an active participant in the group, the members have a strong emotional investment in him. Quite often his feelings are ambivalent and seem to parallel the member-therapist relationship. The members identify the recorder with the therapist. This is easily understandable from the structure of the group. During early meetings the members deny their feelings about a recorder and note taking. Frequently, superficial comments will be made about the notes, but denial occurs when the group therapist pursues the subject. Actually there are many feelings of suspicion, lack of trust, and fears of various sorts, depending on the dynamics of the individual member. As the group matures the members feel more secure with each other and the therapist and can ventilate their feelings more easily. In the 20th meeting of a group of neurotic patients the subject of the recorder and notes came up and was pursued by the therapist. The group members, who were becoming more aware of hostile feelings toward the therapist, reacted with hostility in their remarks about the recorder. At the 48th meeting of the same group this subject again came up. The members spoke of their earlier fears of the recorder, and of whether or not the material would be used against them. One group member felt the notes would be published. At this time the feeling was on a more positive level for the recorder and paralleled to a degree their relationship with the therapist. They spoke of the recorder as being a part of the group, but again separated her from the category of being a member.

Absences of the recorder evoke a series of feelings in the group. Again, early in therapy, the members handle recorder absences by denial and evasion. If a substitute recorder appears they frequently accept him as the equivalent of the regular recorder. As the group matures, the feelings expressed are quite different. This factor was very clearly illustrated at the 15th meeting of an outpatient group of neurotics. The recorder (female) was on vacation and a substitute recorder (male) was present. Because the group members did not make any reference to the new recorder, the therapist brought this to their attention before the meeting was over and asked their feelings about it. The group said they could see no difference. He was taking notes just like the regular recorder did. The recorder's absence did not concern them. They denied any effect on the group whatsoever. Actually the group therapist felt this meeting was quite stilted with the theme being centered around the absence of the recorder and the presence of the substitute recorder. At the 49th meeting of the same group the same substitute recorder was present. This meeting began with extremely hostile remarks about the regular recorder's absence. The therapist explored their feelings on the matter. Another spoke of not liking to change the composition of the group under any circumstances. He said any change affected him and produced tension and frustration. They recalled that when the substitute recorder had been present before they had referred to him as "that bird." They asked a series of questions about the regular recorder and asked if her absence was temporary. They spoke of missing her cheery smile and greeting. One member spoke of her feelings of hopelessness and guilt when other members are absent and said she had noted this feeling at this meeting. By openly bringing out their feelings for approximately the first 7 to 10 minutes of the meeting, the way was cleared for the more constructive work and mutual analysis that took place during the rest of the meeting. The therapist was aware of the anxiety. By discussing the issue with the group members until it was dissolved, he prevented a loss of group functioning. The maturity of the group, too, played a part. They were closer to one another and to the therapist, and felt freer to express their feelings.

The therapist's investment in the group also has its parallel in the recorder. The positive feeling of the recorder for the group and for the therapist is readily detected by the group members and provides an atmosphere of acceptance and understanding of their mistrust, anger, fears, and guilt as they begin to explore their feelings toward each other and toward the therapist.

Therapist-recorder discussions of each group meeting are advised. A policy suggested is for the therapist and recorder to review the meeting together immediately after its completion while the material is still fresh in their minds.

PHYSICAL ARRANGEMENTS

Time, Place, and Length of Group Meetings

The physical arrangements of time and place for group therapy meetings should be discussed and settled during the interviews prior to the formation of the group. A room comfortably furnished and spacious enough to accommodate members, therapist, and recorder is of course necessary. It is best, however, to avoid seating the group around a large table, since the latter tends to create a barrier in the group.

The day and time of the meeting is set up by the group therapist after having arranged the services of a recorder. From the standpoint of the group contract, the group therapist's wishes are respected at this stage. At a later time conflicts may develop in the therapist's schedule. A necessary change in either day or time of group therapy then becomes a group issue. The group contract and the dynamics of the group process are involved. While it is not difficult for a therapist to rearrange hours or days for an individual patient, the situation is more complex with a group of people (including a recorder). Some members of the group may have arranged their week around the original schedule. A change made from afternoon to evening hours may create domestic conflicts. If the therapist wishes to make a change, plans for it should be presented to the group for discussion and approval, since, as previously noted, patients are extremely sensitive to his wishes. Many times they will agree to changes which greatly inconvenience them. The group therapist should be aware of these feelings and foster their ventilation for a number of meetings before changing the group structure. He should respect the reality factors of his group members and work out the best possible solution from the standpoint of the group as a whole. If he loses a member or members, every effort should be made to place them in another group or some other form of therapy.

The therapist should also be aware of the emotional meaning of changes to a patient. Group members have spoken of tension and frustration as the results of changes. To the schizophrenic patient, changes are associated with feelings of loss, rejection, rage, destruction, retaliation, and guilt.

Groups that operate in state hospitals and other institutions are not faced with the same problems as private-patient and outpatient clinic groups. Structural changes can be more easily accomplished. The feelings behind changes in state hospital groups, however, are usually intense because these patients are generally psychotics.

Groups normally meet for a period of 1 or 1½ hours. Groups of psychotic patients, adolescent groups of neurotic and psychotic patients, and groups of juvenile delinquents usually meet for periods of 1 hour because the anxiety tolerance of the members of these groups is lower than that of groups of adult neurotic patients. Group meetings of 1½ hours' length seem to be a satisfactory period of time for neurotic patients. Group members have said that group meetings require 20 to 30 minutes for them to get settled down to work. Neurotic patients who have attended meetings of 1 or 1½ hours' duration like the longer meetings best. They have stated that they are not left dangling at the end of the group meeting with unresolved issues as often in the longer meetings. We recommend that group meetings be 1½ hours in length for groups of neurotic patients, but this figure can be adjusted to suit the wishes of the therapist.

Occasionally a therapist may wish to change the group structure by increasing the length of his meetings. As with changes in time and day of meetings, the same contractual factors and procedures are present in changes to length of meetings.

The therapist should give careful consideration and thought to his original plans for the group structure. He sets up the original contract and is in charge of its structure. The group members agree to the conditions of the original group contract. If he wishes a change in the group contract the complexity of the problem increases manyfold. The contract change becomes a matter between the group members and the therapist. Working out the change becomes a part of the dynamics of the group process.

PERIOD OF GROUP THERAPY

There is no established pattern as to how often groups should meet or for what length of time. There are group therapists who hold meetings from one to three times per week, 1 to 1½ hours in length. In our experience, the best plan seems to be for groups of neurotic patients to meet once a week for sessions of 1½ hours over a minimum period of 1½ years. Over this length of time the group members will be able to work through their relationship to the therapist and reach the stage of mutual analysis (stage III). Groups of psychotic patients may meet for longer or shorter periods of time depending on the location of the group and the goals of the therapist. The average group will meet approximately 45 times during a year. Allowance is made for the group therapist's vacation and other factors such as holidays, medical meetings, and personal factors.

Group therapy does not have to be limited to any specific period. Groups may be designed for 1, 1½, 2 years or longer. The group therapist specifies the period of group therapy for the members in the group contract at the beginning of treatment. He may later decide that the members can profit from an additional treatment period of 6 to 12 months or longer. The therapist can then suggest to the members that the contract be modified and give his reasons for the proposed modification. Modification of the contract requires agreement of both parties—the therapist and the members. The following events occurred in an outpatient group of neurotic patients: The original contract with the group was for a period of 12 months. At the end of 9 months the therapist felt the group could profit from an additional 6 months. Extension of the length of therapy was presented to the group. There was immediate acceptance by all the members. Numerous statements of positive feelings were expressed, and the original group contract was amended by both the therapist and the members. In later meetings, however, the members voiced their suspicions of needing more help than they originally supposed. They felt the therapist must be genuinely concerned about them to recommend an additional period of treatment, or that the group must not be making the expected progress. Lying hidden in their feelings was also the awareness that the therapist was asking them to get closer to one another.

Group Therapist's Absence

Some therapists allow their groups to meet in his absence. Others prescribe semiweekly meetings—one with the group therapist, the other without. There are still others who employ the recorder as "therapist" when the group therapist is away. However, the dynamics of the group process involves a tremendous investment on the part of the group members in the group therapist. Transference reactions develop rapidly as group involvement is fostered. The relationship of the group members to the group therapist is an ambivalent one; as stated previously, many meetings pass before the members' hostility to the therapist is understood and dissolved. Accordingly we do not recommend alternate meetings without the regular group therapist, nor do we recommend using a substitute therapist in the absence of the regular therapist, except during the first 2 months of therapy, when the recorder may meet with the group, not so much as a therapist, but primarily to hold the group together. When the therapist feels he must use the recorder or some other individual as a substitute therapist it is extremely important for him to examine his reasons, keeping in mind his countertransference problems in the group. The author feels as strongly about this as others do about switching therapists among individual patients. Using a substitute therapist for one or several meetings is not a profitable procedure after the first 2 months of therapy. Instead, we recommend that meetings be cancelled when the regular group therapist cannot be present.

Cancelled Meetings

In many ways the group therapist's relationship with his group is similar to the individual therapist's relationship to his patient. When a therapist doing individual therapy goes on a vacation or cancels an hour, he advises the patient in advance and discusses in later meetings the patient's reaction to the missed session. These feelings are explored in detail, since separation anxiety enters into the patient's emotional problems. A similar probing should be done in group therapy. At a group meeting after an absence of the group therapist, the group therapist should ask about his absence, its meaning to the members, and how this affects them. It is extremely important to explore the feelings members have about absences. Planned absences should be discussed for several meetings before their occurrence and again afterwards. Sudden cancellations should be a topic for the group therapist following such events. The timing of this discussion is also important. The group therapist doesn't have to start the meeting by bringing this to their attention. He can wait for 30–45 minutes to see if the members mention the absence. Then if it is not brought up he can remind them of the absence and explore their feelings.

Substitute Group Therapist

There is one exception to the rule regarding cancelled meetings of a group. During the first two months of group therapy (4–8 meetings) an unexpected cancellation of a group meeting may have a disastrous effect on the group. Group losses and exacerbations of members' symptoms are common occurrences. In groups of psychotic patients reactions to a sudden loss of the therapist for only one meeting may precipitate psychotic behavior. Hospitalization may be necessary. In order to protect the group during the early meetings, the therapist should plan the beginning of therapy at a time when he does not anticipate being absent. If, however, the therapist simply cannot attend, the meeting should not be cancelled. The recorder, in this instance, should serve as the group therapist. The recorder's role during the meeting should be to encourage group interaction. Problems with technique may occur. However, the most important factor for the group members at this time is the meeting of the group.

Meetings without the therapist occur on an unofficial basis in many groups. The members may congregate for a social hour over coffee or other refreshments. One group planned luncheon meetings on a weekly basis. Another group, at the insistence of one member who was very competitive with the group therapist, drove home together in a station wagon after each meeting. Recalling the contractual arrangements that conversations and meetings between members outside of the group should be brought to the group therapy session, the group therapist explored the meaning and reason for this outside meeting. The competitive group member discussed the fact that he was going to be forced to get a larger station wagon in order to carry everyone home. He brought this out in the meeting to promote his competitiveness with the therapist. The latter immediately realized what was transpiring in the group and asked about the outside meetings. Feeling of guilt for not following the therapist's previous instructions were mentioned. They talked of being more comfortable and less inhibited in the absence of the therapist and said he was somewhat like a strict schoolteacher. When the therapist referred to this behavior and asked for their thoughts, they began to see and talk about their feelings toward an authority figure.

As previously stated, many of the feelings involving absences of the group therapist and cancellation of hours are the same in group therapy as they are in individual therapy. The manner by which their behavior is exhibited will depend on a number of factors:

1. *Degree of Psychopathology.* Schizophrenic patients and neurotics may react to separation with feelings of rejection, low self-esteem, and guilt. They frequently become angry with the group therapist when the hour is cancelled. Patients with strong dependency features also may feel that their crutch is gone; patients with alcohol problems may turn to the bottle as a substitute; others may view the therapist's absences as an expression of his disinterest in the group.

2. *Degree of Group Involvement (Maturity of the Group).* Here again the situation is analogous to the one with individual patients. Once a patient has formed a relationship with the therapist, he can ventilate many of his angry feelings about absences and cancellation of meetings. The same is true in group therapy. Early in the group process the relationship of member to therapist and member to member is tenuous. The protective shell against exposing themselves is still there and patients use denial, displacement, and other means to avoid revealing themselves to each other and to the therapist. After they have worked through many of their feelings toward the therapist and are more secure in the group, they will ventilate feelings of rage, anger, and loss of dependency. Patients with dependency needs will talk of their wish for the group to meet, the security offered by the therapist and the group members, and their resentment toward the therapist for not fulfilling their needs.

Change of Group Therapist

Sometimes, realistic factors may necessitate a change of therapist. A lengthy illness, moving to another location, or other reality events may make it necessary for a therapist to relinquish his group. Needless to say, the group members will react strongly to his loss. The exact effect on them will be conditional on the terms of the group contract, the maturity of the group, the psychodynamics of the group members, and the status of the therapist at the particular time of relinquishing his work.

A therapist may plan to do group therapy for only a certain period of time, say 12 to 18 months. He may specify in the original group contract that therapy may be continued with another therapist if the members so desire and that a new therapist can be secured at that time. He may also provide for placing members in other groups if such openings are available. There are several possibilities, all of which become a matter for the therapist and the members to resolve during the group therapy sessions. The original group contract can be modified by both parties (therapist and members) as desired.

The maturity of the members plays a very important part in determining the effect on the group of a change in therapist. Very closely associated with the group's maturity is the status of the therapist and the conditions requiring the change. A therapist may be taken away suddenly from his group or he may have a period of time to discuss his leaving with the members. The group may have been functioning for a long or short period of time. A group of psychotic patients will demonstrate considerably more anxiety than a group of neurotic patients when faced with the loss of their therapist. Each group has to be treated as a separate and distinct entity.

The sudden loss of a therapist from his group during stages I and II may produce a disastrous reaction among the members. During stages I and II the group members have not worked through their relationship to the therapist. His leaving a group at this time would unleash a powerful array of feelings—anger, guilt, depression, rejection, low self-esteem, frustration, and confusion. If the therapist has a number of meetings to work through the members' feelings regarding separation, and if a new therapist is available to take over, the group's chances of survival are enhanced.

If the members have worked through stages I and II, the sudden loss of the therapist creates similar feelings of anger, guilt, and depression, but their depth and intensity are less. The group is more mature. With proper support, understanding, and guidance from the new group therapist, the group can be salvaged. Here again the anxiety of separation can be cushioned considerably if the therapist has a number of meetings to work through the group members' feelings regarding separation.

In groups of psychotic patients the anxiety associated with separation is overwhelming. The sudden loss of the therapist may trigger the unleashing of feelings so strong and intense that overt psychotic behavior results. Such behavior may even occur with a gradual changeover to another therapist.

There are several important points about the therapist's technique in a change of therapist. Once a new therapist has been secured he should attend a group meeting shortly thereafter and be introduced to the group members. It is not necessary for the new therapist to remain at this meeting nor attend any future meetings until he takes over the group. The original recorder, if qualified, may take over as acting therapist. In such a case the recorder will continue in his same role until the former therapist departs. The therapist who is relinquishing the group should spend the remaining meetings working through the group members' feelings about separation from him. In general, groups of neurotic patients need 10–12 meetings to understand their feelings about separation. Needless to say, the new therapist will spend many meetings before the group members become comfortable with him. Like any new stepfather in a family, the new therapist is usually greeted with hostility from the group members. He must clear away their hostile feelings as his first order of business.

Putting the members in new groups poses the same set of problems as changing therapists, and the success of the move also depends on the psychodynamics of the members and the maturity of the group. If at all possible, group members should be placed in other groups of similar maturity. If a group member has worked through stage I and stage II of group therapy, less difficulty is encountered in his integration into a new group. From a practical standpoint the choice of a new therapist and the placement of group members in other groups depends chiefly on their availability.

LOSS AND ADDITION OF MEMBERS

A constant problem in group therapy is the loss of members and the need to add new members as replacements. Various estimates have been made that group losses average somewhere between 30 and 50 per cent of the original members. Certainly the possible odds for group losses are greater by 8 to 1 (if the group has eight members) than with the individual patient in therapy. Often this mathematical factor is not given proper consideration by group therapists. The average outpatient group will experience losses—it practically never fails to happen. The therapist should know about group losses and the wise one will give thought to replacement members very early in group therapy. However, we have observed an interesting phenomena that occurs with the therapist, the members, and to some extent the recorder: Group losses cause concern for all. The group members have many feelings about other members who drop out of the group. Feelings of guilt, rejection, and inadequacy are common. They are usually angry at the therapist for group losses. They fear that the group will break up and there will be no more group therapy. The therapist shares feelings similar to those of the members. Even though he is aware, intellectually, that losses do occur, his feelings for the group itself enter into the picture. This is especially true if a member or members have been in the group for a long period of time and then leave. To the therapist the group does not seem the same. He wonders if it can function adequately in its altered state. He may notice feelings of depression during meetings. Frequently he may have feelings of inadequacy and guilt. On other occasions he may become angry at the departed group member, his attitude being, in effect, "Why are you doing this to the other members and to me?"

The following incident occurred at the 36th meeting of a mixed group of neurotic patients. Three members had dropped out very early in group therapy; one new member had been added. For 20 or more meetings the remaining six members had been very regular in attendance. At the previous meeting (35th) a male member, Mr. G., stated that he might leave the group in the next few weeks. He was thinking about moving to another community. Mr. G., a minister, had made good progress in group therapy. The other members had encouraged him to stay, stating that he needed more therapy and that the group would not be the same if he left. Humor and laughter occurred during the meeting in which the therapist also participated. At supervision the latter remarked about the humor and his involvement in it. He said: "I laughed with the patients; there were a number of amusing incidents."

Very early in the 36th meeting another active male member, Mr. L., announced that he was considering dropping out of the group. Mr. L. said that evening work was necessary to raise his income. (At the onset of group therapy Mr. L. had been depressed and unemployed. He had returned to work during the early months of group therapy.) The therapist attempted to explore with the other group members the reasons for this turn of events. He was unsuccessful. Humor was interjected into the meeting and followed by recurrent episodes of laughter. The therapist once more participated in the laughter. He lost control of the meeting and became involved in secondary group issues. The generalized laughter persisted. During the meeting a perceptive female group member, Mrs. D., made two significant statements. She said, "There are other reasons besides work that cause people to wish to quit group therapy. Sometimes people feel they are being laughed at by the others." The therapist, embroiled in the humor and laughter of the meeting, did not explore the meaning of Mrs. D.'s observations.

At supervision it was apparent that the therapist's previously good technique had changed during the 35th and 36th meetings. He was not aware of the dynamics of the meetings, lost control of the group, and became involved in the humor and laughter himself. The therapist's remarks of enjoying the laughter with the group members were related to his own anxiety. He admitted laughter was a tension-relieving device. When confronted with his feelings regarding the threatened losses from his group (Mr. G. and Mr. L.) the therapist admitted a feeling of depression and irritation. The therapist admitted he was quite upset when Mr. L. spoke of leaving the group. The following questions were raised during supervision: Was the laughter at the 36th meeting by the members and the therapist interpreted by Mr. L. as a hostile act? Are the possible group losses related to the dynamics of the group process? Why did the therapist become so anxious and lose control of the group? The conclusions that were reached were that the therapist had become angry at the two members. He had wondered if his group was falling apart or becoming disorganized. He had then become anxious and had lost control of the two group meetings. He had failed to clarify the reasons for Mr. G.'s and Mr. L.'s wanting to stop group therapy. He had not dealt with group issues. Instead of seeking out the cause of the group laughter he had joined in it.

Group therapy offers an extra dimension that is not present in other forms of psychotherapy—the group itself. Any change in the structure of the group produces feelings of disorganization. Emotional ties and investments in the group become apparent. It is this emotional investment by the therapist in the group that produces undue alarm and concern when the group structure is threatened or changed by a loss of members. The recorder may entertain feelings similar to the therapist's. In therapist-recorder discussions and group supervisory conferences, ventilation and understanding of these feelings is conducive to the future work and growth of the group.

Reasons for Losses

Group losses occur because of physical and psychological causes. There are a variety of physical causes. Family events may interfere with attendance—e.g., a husband's transfer to another city results in his wife's dropping out of a group. In other instances, maid problems or the lack of a baby sitter may pose severely realistic problems in getting to group meetings. Sudden financial reverses may necessitate a cessation of treatment because fees cannot be paid. Changes in occupational status may conflict with the time or day of the meeting. Physical disease may develop of such severity that group therapy cannot be continued.

The therapist may play a part in the physical losses of group members. Modifications of the group contract that involve changing the hour or day of group meetings may make it impossible for a group member to attend. The group member who has arranged work or family duties around the original time and day for the meeting may not be able to comfortably change over to a new schedule.

Psychological causes for group losses encompass a variety of elements. The age, sex, race, cultural background, education, motivation, and psychodynamics of the group members must be considered. The psychodynamics, the degree of training, and the technique of the therapist can also influence group losses. Other factors are the model of group therapy employed and goals of the therapist. Very importantly, the use of a recorder in the group, therapist-recorder discussions and group supervisory conferences have a relationship to the psychological causes of group losses.

The psychological causes of group losses are directly related to the anxiety of the members.

The therapist should therefore employ every cue available to ascertain the anxiety level of the group and to encourage the members to cope with the feelings that create anxiety within the group. The untrained therapist will find this to be one of the most difficult problems of technique. If he does not recognize the group members' anxiety and, particularly, the intermember hostility that results from their anxiety, losses from the group will occur. The group members are angry with the group therapist; however, they are unable to express their true feelings to him. Instead they displace their hostility to other group members. If the therapist recognizes the dynamics of the group members' anxiety and handles it properly, he can alleviate a certain percentage of these situations. Here, therapist-recorder discussions and group supervisory conferences can help him recognize the events taking place within the group and the effect his anxiety has on the group function, and suggest methods of correction.

The following examples of patients who stopped group therapy illustrate problems that occur throughout the period of group therapy:

A very dependent patient made a series of demands on the therapist, asking for drugs, performance of miracles, and hypnosis. He became extremely angry when the therapist refused to answer his questions, and quit the group after four meetings, stating that "a bunch of patients" could not help him.

A moderately depressed patient had a fear of large men. His father was a large individual who had subjected him to cruel treatment in childhood and adolescence. For ten years he had changed jobs and moved from one city to another, but this fear of large men had forever plagued him. In the group there were several large men, including the therapist. The patient's anxiety became increasingly uncomfortable and manifested itself by lateness, silence, restlessness, and absences. He attended only eight meetings. He spoke of his fear of big men, and once outside the group, spoke of how large the therapist was. The latter was aware of this patient's dynamics, but persistent support, prescribing of drugs, and contacts following absences were of no avail. Usually, frequent absences precede dropping out. The therapist should, therefore, pay close attention to the attendance record of each member.

An inability to give up individual desires and become involved with the group interaction occurred with a 36-year-old depressed female. Group therapy was of no help to her. She "could never tell others in the group how she felt," "saw no point in this kind of therapy," and left the group after six meetings, hoping to find a doctor who would cure her.

A passive-dependent female experienced phobic difficulties when in crowds; her manifestations of group anxiety occurred in an outpatient group of neurotic patients. She was subject to periodic anxiety associated with muscular twitching in the legs and abdomen, hyperventilation, and constriction in the throat. She initially came to the clinic following a discussion during which her husband told her there would be no children until her symptoms were cured. During the initial meetings of group therapy she was prompt and regular in attendance. Soon, however, she began to be tardy and her attendance became irregular. She experienced increased discomfort with phobic and hypochondriacal symptoms. She saw that more anxiety occurred in the group than in any other situation, was less uncomfortable when talking to other members before and after the meeting. The therapist recognized the authority problem and the massive rage hidden under the cloak of somatic symptoms and phobias. He supported her at times, not from an individual standpoint but from observations and statements made to the group. At the end of six months her anxiety became severe and the meetings were very difficult to her. She had recognized that the therapist's statements made her "freeze" and that she couldn't "grasp their meaning." She expressed anger when her questions were not answered. On a number of occasions she said that the group could profit if subjects were assigned for discussion. As a Sunday School teacher she experienced no difficulty in presenting planned material. She stopped group therapy after seven months, being unable to resolve her uncomfortable manifestations. Her method of stopping indicates how group members support one another: she asked the group's permission to drop out. The group members, while admitting their irritation at her recent absences, expressed an understanding of why it was so difficult for her to attend and gave the desired permission. After an observation by the therapist as to whether or not the group had been responsible in any way for her decision, the members talked of failing to encourage and support her sufficiently in the past. They pointed out to her that she was not well and that they would welcome her back to the group at any time.

Group anxiety occurred in a 45-year-old obsessive-compulsive male who was hospitalized with a psychotic depression following a series of conflicts with his mother and brother. The immediate treatment was electroconvulsive treatment. He improved, but later became extremely dependent, was unable to work, and was a patient in the hospital intermittently for over a year before he began group therapy. He developed hypochondriacal complaints. This patient and seven other state hospital patients (who had been psychotic at the time of their admission) comprised the group. At the end of nine months of group therapy (one meeting of $1\frac{1}{2}$ hours a week) all but one of the group were discharged or furloughed from the hospital. The patient in question was placed on furlough approximately 7 months after the formation of the group. Since the anxiety level of this group could easily reach an intolerable and frightening level, the group therapist had to explore, support, and retreat, depending on the tempo of the group. Absences after discharge had to be closely followed and proper support given. By the end of 14 months the group was working on authority problems. At times this patient would get angry and then become depressed. He would miss one or two meetings; threaten to quit the group and then return after a telephone call from the therapist. As he became involved in the emotional interaction, the same thing would happen again. Eventually he stopped group therapy altogether. He had, however, profited from the amount of group therapy he had been able to endure, for his depression had lifted, he had given up some of his somatic symptoms, and he was able to return to part-time work.

So far we have been discussing the prevalence of group losses in general terms. In order to give a clearer picture of when group losses can occur, however, we have analyzed the loss of members in eight groups that had been functioning for a period of 12 months or longer. These groups are not random selections but consist of all the groups in supervision at the Department of Psychiatry, Emory University, during the period from July 1959 to December 1961. They consist of clinic outpatient groups of neurotic patients, outpatient groups of psychotic patients, private inpatient-outpatient groups of psychotic patients, and state hospital inpatient-outpatient groups of psychotic patients. The inpatient-outpatient groups are those in which group therapy began while the members were patients in the hospital. Group therapy continued after the group members were discharged from the hospital and upon some members' readmission to the hospital.

Each group was initially composed of eight members, a group therapist and a recorder. Meetings were held weekly for either 1 or 1½ hours. Therapist-recorded discussions and group supervisory conferences were regularly employed. The therapists were resident staff psychiatrists associated with the department. The model and technique of group therapy utilized is discussed in the present chapter as well as in Chaps. 3, 4, and 8.

An analysis of each group reveals the following:

Group I. The group was composed of eight females, a male group therapist and a female recorder. Their ages ranged from 30 to 50 years. All had been hospitalized one or more times for psychoses. The cultural level was middle-to-upper class. The group was classified as an inpatient-outpatient private group. Fees were $10 per meeting. The group therapist's goals were limited. The initial group loss occurred at the 24th meeting. The cause was psychological. The patient stayed out of the group 8 months, then returned to the meetings, stating that conflicts with other group members caused her to stop. The second loss occurred at the 30th meeting. The cause was psychological. Her attendance had been sporadic, and she appeared to be frightened and anxious during group meetings. The third group loss occurred at the 36th meeting; again the cause was psychological. Two new members were added at the 40th meeting. At the end of one year of group therapy three members were considered group losses. The initial loss returned to the group during the second year of group therapy.

Table 4.1 Summary of Losses in Eight Groups from July 1959 to December 1961

Group number	Type of patient	Classification of the group	Sex	Age	Fee per meeting	Social class	Group losses									
							Psychologic					Physical				
							Group meetings					Group meetings				
							1–10	10–20	20–30	30–40	40–50	1–10	10–20	20–30	30–40	40–50
1	Psychotic	Inpatient-outpatient	Female	30–50	10	Middle-to-upper-class			1	2						
2	Psychotic	Inpatient-outpatient	Female	22–46	None	Middle-to-lower-class	1	1								
3	Psychotic	Inpatient-outpatient	Male	22–48	None	Middle-to-lower-class			1			1	1			
4	Psychotic	Inpatient-outpatient	Female	25–54	10	Middle-to-upper-class				1			1	1		
5	Neurotic	Clinic outpatient	Mixed	24–50	1 to 3	Middle-to-lower-class	1			1			2			
6	Neurotic	Clinic outpatient	Mixed	23–47	1 to 3	Middle-to-lower-class				1	1		1	1		
7	Psychotic	Clinic outpatient	Female	26–44	1 to 4	Middle-to-lower-class						5				
8	Neurotic	Clinic outpatient	Mixed	31–54	1 to 3	Middle-to-lower-class	3									

Group II. The group was composed of eight females, male group therapist and female recorder. The members' ages ranged from 22 to 46 years. All had been hospitalized one or more times for psychoses and were patients in a state hospital at the onset of group therapy. The cultural level was predominantly lower-class. The group was classified as an inpatient-outpatient group. No fees were charged. The group therapist's goals were limited. Group losses occurred at the 4th and 10th meetings and were considered psychological in origin. At the outset of group therapy both of the patients who dropped out of the group had been enthusiastic about treatment. At that time they were on an inpatient status. After discharge from the hospital they did not return to any future meetings. In each case, the distance from the patient's home to the hospital was not a realistic problem that would have interfered with attendance. At the end of one year of group therapy, six members of the original group remained. No new members were added.

Group III. The group was composed of eight males, male group therapist and male recorder. The age range was 22 to 48 years. All members had been hospitalized one or more times for psychoses and were patients in a state hospital at the onset of group therapy. The cultural level was lower-to-middle-class. The group was classified as an inpatient-outpatient group. No fees were charged. The group therapist's goals were limited. Group losses occurred at the 8th, 10th, and 26th meetings. Since the meetings were held a long distance (100+ miles) from two of the group members' homes, their losses have to be considered as physical in origin. (The distinction between "physical" and "psychological" reasons is given earlier in this chapter.) One member dropped out for psychological reasons; he showed marked anxiety during group meetings. Three new members were added to the group. At the end of one year of group therapy no additional losses occurred. Two of the group losses were considered to be due to physical reasons, one loss to psychological.

Group IV. The group was composed of eight females, male group therapist and female recorder. Age of the members ranged from 25 to 54 years. All had been hospitalized one or more times for psychoses; group was classified as an inpatient-outpatient private group. Cultural level, middle-to-upper-class. Fees were $10 per meeting. The therapist's goals were limited. Initial group loss occurred at the 20th meeting; the therapist had to change the day of the meeting and the patient could not attend because of realistic, physical reasons. Second group loss occurred at the 30th meeting, the cause being psychological. Third loss occurred at the 34th meeting when financial problems forced a patient to withdraw from the group. At the end of one year of group therapy, five group members remained.

Group V. The group was composed of four females, four males, male group therapist and female recorder. Ages ranged from 24 to 50 years. Group members had applied to the outpatient clinic for treatment; their illnesses were primarily neuroses. Group was classified as an outpatient group of neurotic patients. Cultural level, lower-to-middle-class. Fees ranged from $1 to $3 per meeting, depending on annual income and number of dependents. The therapist's goals were to improve reality testing and socialization and to develop psychological aptitude. The initial group loss occurred at the 9th meeting. The cause was psychological in origin; the patient, a free-lance unemployed artist who had decided to move to another state. Initially he had been enthusiastic about group therapy and was aware the program would last for one year. The second loss occurred at the 24th meeting when a male member had to forego group therapy because the therapist changed the time and day of the meeting; the patient's occupational duties could not be rearranged. The third loss occurred at the 28th meeting when a female member had to drop out because her husband, a minister, was assigned to a church in another location. The fourth loss occurred at the 32nd meeting, when a female member left the group to get an unnecessary job. This was her way of handling anxiety. Her loss was psychological in origin. Of the four losses, two were classified as physical and two as psychological in origin.

Group VI. The group was composed of four females, four males, male group therapist and female recorder. Ages ranged from 23 to 47 years. The members had directly or indirectly applied to the outpatient clinic for treatment; their illnesses were primarily neuroses. The group was classified as an outpatient group of neurotic patients. Cultural level was predominantly middle-class. Fees ranged from $1 to $3 per meeting, depending on annual income and number of dependents. The therapist's goals were to improve reality testing and socialization and to develop psychological aptitude. The initial group loss occurred at the 32nd meeting when a female member, whose attendance at prior group meetings had not been satisfactory, left the state and returned to her former home even though she had originally planned to remain for the entire program of group therapy. Her loss was psychological in origin. The second loss occurred at the 39th meeting. A male member had neurological surgery for an inoperable brain tumor. He was unable to participate in group therapy thereafter. The third loss occurred at the 42nd meeting when a very anxious, phobic patient withdrew from the group. Her loss was considered psychological in origin. Two new members were added to the group at the 42nd meeting. At the end of one year five of the original members remained in group therapy.

Group VII. The group was composed of eight females, female group therapist and male recorder. Ages ranged from 26 to 44 years. Six of the eight members had been previously hospitalized for psychoses. The cultural level was predominantly lower-class. The group was classified as a clinic outpatient group of psychotic patients. Fees ranged from $1 to $4 per meeting. The group therapist's goals were limited. By the 8th meeting five of the original patients had withdrawn from group therapy. The initial loss occurred before the first meeting, when one member had to be sent to the state hospital in a distant city. The second loss occurred at the 6th meeting. Realistic financial problems prevented her from attending. The third loss occurred at the 7th meeting when a group member's husband was transferred to another city. The fourth and fifth losses both occurred at the 8th meeting. The second member of the original eight had to be hospitalized at a state institution. The fifth had to drop out because of pressure from her husband who was hostile to psychiatry and group therapy. Each of the five losses was classified as physical in origin. Two were due to rehospitalization in a distant city where they could not attend group meetings. Five new members were added to the group between the 8th and 20th meetings. At the completion of the first year of group therapy no additional losses had been sustained. A significant factor relative to the group losses should be noted in this group. Four of the group members who dropped out were selected for group therapy rather hastily. The therapist felt that if careful evaluation had been done in the selection of the group members, losses might have been curtailed.

Group VIII. The group was composed of four males, four females, male group therapist and female recorder. Age range was 31 to 54 years. Six of the eight members were selected from outpatient clinic files. Two of the members had been hospitalized on one occasion at a state hospital. The cultural level was lower-to-middle-class. The group was classified as a clinic outpatient group of neurotic patients. Fees ranged from $1 to $3 per meeting. The group therapist's goals were to improve reality testing and socialization and develop psychological aptitude. The initial group loss occurred at the second meeting when one male member left town unexpectedly and did not return. The therapist had been doubtful about taking this member into the group because of a psychopathic element in his behavior; subsequent events indicated these suspicions were well founded. The second and third losses occurred at the 3rd and 4th meetings respectively. One new member was added at the 6th meeting. At the end of one year of therapy the group consisted of six members. The three losses from the group were considered psychological in origin.

The eight groups studied differed in composition, diagnoses, goals, cultural background and fees paid but the model of group therapy, theory of group dynamics, technique of the group therapist, selection of group members, and employment of a recorder in the group were similar. Therapist-recorder discussions were utilized. All eight therapists participated in weekly group supervisory conferences. The statistical results of the losses in these eight groups (64 patients) are:

1. Total losses encountered during one year of group therapy were 26 patients (40.6 per cent).
2. Psychological losses occurred in 14 group members (21.8 per cent).
3. Physical losses occurred in 12 group members (18.8 per cent).
4. Psychological losses were as prevalent in meetings 1–10 as in meetings 30–40.
5. Psychological losses for all eight groups from meetings 1–20 were five group members (7.8 per cent); from meetings 20–50 there were nine losses (14.0 per cent).
6. The total psychological and physical losses for meetings 1–20 were sixteen group members (25 per cent).

Group therapists are inclined to feel that the majority of group losses are psychological in origin. A careful study of group losses often reveals that physical reasons for group losses are more prevalent than generally known; the physical losses in these eight groups occurred in nearly equal proportions to psychological losses.

Group losses can be curtailed if the group therapist's attention is focused on the following factors:

1. Selection of patients.
2. Composition of the group.
3. Goals of group therapy.
4. Understanding of the dynamics of group relationships.
5. Group therapist's technique of group therapy.
6. Awareness that the therapist influences group behavior more than any one of the group members.
7. Recorder's role in the regular structure of group therapy.
8. Discussions between the therapist and the recorder after each group meeting.
9. Participation in regular group supervisory conferences with other therapists and a supervisor.

The 25 per cent loss (physical and psychological) of group members over the first five months of group therapy (1–20 meetings) is a very satisfactory result and supports the recommendations listed above.

Adding Members

The therapist frequently finds it necessary to add members to the group. IIe should mention to the prospective group member in the initial interviews that new members may or may not be added at later intervals depending on the status of the group. He can accomplish this with a general statement. At that time the members are not acquainted with each other or with the therapist and do not attach any great significance to his remarks. After the group has been functioning for a period of time, members who drop out create anxiety in the other group members. If losses from the group are very heavy, both the members and the therapist entertain a series of fantasies about the group's dissolving. The addition of members should be discussed with the group, and their feelings concerning new members should be explored. Usually the remaining group members greet the proposal with joy—the group will not be "destroyed." The group therapist has their interest in mind and the group will continue to function. Once the new members are in the group, however, the older members mobilize their anxiety along patterns of behavior similar to those of earlier group meetings.

An example of the anxiety created by the addition of members occurred in an outpatient group when two new members were added at the 42nd meeting. The two new members had been in another group with the same therapist for a corresponding period of time. The group had talked in several meetings of their fears of the unknown and dissolution of the group. They greeted the proposal of new members with many positive statements. Only one patient admitted ambivalent feelings. During the initial meeting in which the new patients were present, one male patient, who when anxious talked rapidly with frequent changes of subject, reacted the same way he had in the early days of the group. Two of the members immediately recognized his anxiety, pointed it out to him, and reminded him that he was acting just as he did in the beginning of group therapy. This patient had also been competitive with the therapist and had utilized intellectual defenses and denial quite frequently. One of the new members had many of the same features. Soon frequent arguments occurred between these two members. As the therapist explored this development, they spoke of their competitiveness with the therapist and their anger at him for bringing them together in this "new group." Fears of rejection in the new situation were verbalized. They said that they were comfortable before, but that now it would take time to work these things out. Within four weeks their hostility toward the therapist had been ventilated and more constructive work was being accomplished in the group.

The therapist should add new members according to the needs of the group. In the event that new members are considered for a group that has been functioning beyond a period of 6 to 8 months, he should weigh several factors—length of group therapy, stage or maturity of the group, and the remaining size of the group. If the therapist planned to do group therapy only for 12 months and if he has a remaining nucleus of four to six members, he may not wish to add any new members for the few remaining months. Constructive therapy can proceed without difficulty with the remaining members. New members who have previously had group therapy can be integrated into an already functioning group easier than those who have not. Their awareness of group dynamics, previously experienced, becomes an asset in the new group. Above all, the therapist should recognize that, regardless of the conditions, bringing new members into a group creates much anxiety and tension; as group members have said, it forms a "new group." The loss or the addition of group members is a group reality event that needs complete exploration by the therapist in the group meetings.

There is one aspect of adding new members to a group that needs careful consideration and exploration. The decision of adding new members to the group lies with the therapist, not with the group members. Occasionally when the therapist is exploring their feelings, one or more of the group may voice objections to new members. They may attempt to enlist the support of others to oppose the therapist or force him to let them make the decision themselves. At times the group members can make the therapist feel guilty for wanting to add new members. Then, too, therapists have fallen into the trap set by the members and left the decision of new group members with them. The therapist should remember that this type of defiant and competitive behavior is a result of the dynamics of the group process. Once this type of behavior is recognized the therapist should attempt to explore its meaning with the group members. In the meantime, he should decide to add new members to the group according to the needs of the group.

ATTENDANCE OF GROUP MEMBERS

At the outset of group therapy the therapist should stress the need for the members to attend meetings regularly. He should emphasize that, just as he agrees to meet with them at a structured time and place, they must agree to meet with him. Attendance thus becomes a part of the group contract. Throughout the length of group therapy the therapist will have many opportunities to refer to this part of the group contract, for the attendance or lack of attendance of group members is a reality event that enters into the dynamics and technique of group therapy.

Members are usually absent from meetings for physical (reality issues) and psychological reasons. Physical reasons for absences may be due to an illness of the group member or others in the group members' families, or to occupational duties, transportation difficulties, vacations, and similar breaks in routine schedules. Over the courses of group therapy most members miss a certain number of group meetings because of reality situations. The psychological reasons for absences from group meetings are directly related to the anxiety of group therapy and have several different meanings, depending on the psychodynamics of the group member. In outpatient groups of neurotic and psychotic patients of 1 to 1½ years' duration the average attendance at group meetings is approximately 75 per cent.

An examination of the members' reactions to absences, as well as the reaction of the absent member himself, points out the important relationship to the dynamics of group therapy.

Members who are absent from meetings may provoke several different feelings among the others. First, there are usually fears and guilty feelings for possibly having "hurt his feelings" and caused a group member to be absent. Then the absence of several group members may bring out fears of group dissolution. They may feel that if some of the group members do not attend meetings the therapist will dissolve the group. With the development of increased group anxiety during the middle part of stage I (10th–20th group meetings), the members' feelings about absences become very apparent. Their intense emotional reaction is out of proportion to the reality of the individual member's absence. They angrily attack absentees even to the point of scapegoating them.

The members' feelings and responses to absentees are distorted, unrealistic, and immature. The reactions are repetitions of their feelings and responses to similar situations in previous day-to-day group relationships. The primary emotion behind their anxiety is anger. They become angry with the absent members, but the principal person for whom their anger is intended is the therapist. He is the one central figure who should hold the group together and make the group members attend all the meetings. His failure to do so elicits angry feelings among the group members.

It is just as important to understand the feelings and reactions of the group member who is absent from group meetings. The physical reasons for missing group meetings have been discussed earlier. The psychogical reasons for absences may be due to the following factors: failure to receive dependency gratifications from the other members and from the therapist; inability to obtain the desired individual attention from the therapist; fear of rejection from the other group members and from the therapist; uncomfortable feelings in the group meetings, such as "hurt" feelings or feelings of offending others; development of unrecognized and uncomfortable anxiety during group meetings; awareness of angry feelings against other group members and the therapist, with accompanying guilt. Absences from group meetings for these reasons may occur during stage I, but may also be present in stage II and stage III.

The therapist himself can be a contributory cause of group members' absences. He may consciously or (more likely) unconsciously react to a group member in such a manner that absences and even losses from the group may result. The therapist with conflicts in the aggressive or the sexual area may unconsciously enourage acting out of group members. The therapist who is frightened of hostility may defensively become hostile with one or more group members. He may identify a group member with some important figure in his past and react either positively or negatively. Here again the value of therapist-recorder discussions and group supervision is borne out.

A most important goal of the therapist during the early meetings is to keep the group intact. He should pay careful attention to the group members who are absent from meetings. He should be aware of the numerous distortions that members make of conversations in the meetings. He should be aware of the differences between the goals of the members and his own. He should be sensitive to the members' feelings and reactions to him, and constantly remember that he is the most important person in the group from the first to the final meeting. The therapist should be aware of the members' constant fear of rejection by him and by the other members. Many members have had repeated rejections in previous group relationships and expect to be again rejected in the therapy group. The therapist should be able to recognize and understand the effects of anxiety on the group members. Anxiety can be a most uncomfortable state for them.

The therapist's technique for dealing with absences involves an exploration of the group members' feelings about the absent members and absences in general. Beginning with the early group meetings, the therapist should ask the group members for their feelings about those who are absent. He can make such statements as "How do you feel when others are absent?" and "How does it affect the group when there are absences?" Other observations that encourage the group members to express their feelings should be made. During the early group meetings the members tend to deny any feelings or reactions about absences. Even in the face of repeated denial the therapist should continue to call their attention to absences. An important aspect of his technique is teaching the group members how to examine and talk about their feelings. As the members become more comfortable with each other and with the therapist, their feelings about absences will be ventilated.

The therapist should be aware that after the development of transference reactions the group members' reactions to an absent member may be quite hostile. This is particularly true if one or more members have had a series of absences. Such situations require careful management by the therapist. It is understandable that the attending members would be angry at the absentees for avoiding the group and not contributing to its growth. On the other hand, the absentees may be experiencing very uncomfortable anxiety. They find it difficult to attend group meetings and may waver between staying in the group or dropping out. The therapist must clear away the group's feelings about the absentees and at the same time offer the absentee support. He can provide support by focusing on the factors that may have caused the absences—uncomfortable symptoms from anxiety, family conflict, and the like. The group therapist can say such things as: "I wonder if you have any ideas as to why they were not able to attend meetings," or "Why do people react so strongly to absences?" or "Do you suppose they have wanted to attend the meetings but fear becoming too uncomfortable here? Have your own reactions to them contributed to their absences? What would you suggest they do to improve their attendance?" The therapist should also focus on himself and, hopefully, clear away some of the group members' hostility that is primarily meant for him but may be displaced to others, particularly absentees.

When absences do occur, the therapist himself can play an important role in helping the absentee return to the group—a role that is somewhat different from that of the individual therapist. When one or more group members are absent, the therapist should either telephone them or drop them a short note by mail within 24–48 hours. He should let the absent members know they were missed at the group meeting and encourage them to return for the next meeting. By being sensitive to the absences of group members and by consistent follow-ups, the therapist can curtail absenteeism as well as group losses. Regardless of whether the group member's absence is due to physical or psychological reasons, a telephone call or letter from the therapist can be a strong expression of interest and reassurance. Then, too, the therapist is not always sure of the member's reasons for being absent. The anxious member may tell the therapist of difficulties encountered in attending group meetings. At such time the therapist can suggest that such feelings should be talked about in group meetings so that a better understanding may be possible. The member who fears rejection from the therapist is particularly buoyed up by a contact from him.

The policy of contacting group members who have been absent is particularly important during stage I of group therapy. Later, when the group has matured, a more relaxed policy can be employed.

The presence or absence of the therapist creates more emotional re-action with the group members than any other person. Of course if he is absent the group meeting normally is cancelled. The group members fear separation, rejection, loss of dependency, and group dissolution when the therapist cancels a meeting. They react with anxiety and hostility to him. Since he is feared more than anyone else, the group members have much more difficulty in expressing their feelings about his absences than they do about the absences of group members. For example, the members may angrily attack a cohort for an absence and then completely deny any feelings about an absence of the therapist. From the standpoint of technique the therapist should repeatedly focus on their feelings and reactions about his absences. He can call to their attention their angry reaction to absences of group members and their placid reaction to his absences. Planned absences by the group therapist should be brought to their attention several meetings before and after the absence. Emergency absences naturally can only be dealt with in later meetings.

Ultimately, as the group matures the group members will be able to discuss their emotional responses to absences. Over the course of group therapy they will learn that absences can result from realistic situations; that the absence of group members does not mean the group will fall apart; and that the absence of the therapist does not mean separation and rejection. With the recognition of their faulty emotional responses, the anger associated with their prior reactions diminishes and a more ob-jective appraisal can be made. It is for these reasons that attendance prob-lems are an important reality event of group therapy.

FEES

An understanding of fees is extremely important in any form of psy-chotherapy, and group therapy is no exception. In private-practice groups, outpatient clinics, guidance clinics, and other related types of groups the subject of fees, including their collection and management, enters into the dynamics of each member of the group and of the group ther-apist. A contractual arrangement at the outset of group therapy is of extreme importance. Patients in individual therapy are informed of the fees at the beginning of treatment. They are told that bills are payable on the 10th of each month. Nonpayment of bills is an important matter for discussion with the patient. Many psychiatrists charge for the therapy hour unless they are notified of a cancellation by a specific time. In this way the schedule can be rearranged and the hour put to other use. In the group situation, eight patients are involved. Regardless of the number absent the amount of time involved for the group therapist remains the same, as do other expenditures such as office space and the services of the recorder. How then should fees be affected by the absences of group members? Members may be absent because of the tension and anxiety of the group process. Others may have to miss meetings because of realistic factors such as a physical illness, vacations, or business conflicts. Probably the therapist will handle the problem of fees according to his individual personality, professionalism, and business sense. If he has no specific contractual arrangements with his group in reference to payment of fees and handling of absences, he will probably be faced with unpaid bills. When this happens he will become angry with his group. He may, either consciously or unconsciously, demonstrate his angry feelings during the therapy hour. One therapist may bill only those members who come to group meetings, not charging for absences, while another may be very strict and bill all patients monthly regardless of absences. In this respect, the author recommends that members be charged for absences, unless there are extenuating circumstances.

Whatever method the therapist employs should be stated clearly to the group members at the beginning of group therapy. Setting a fee for each patient has its value and is recommended. The therapist should explain in detail the realistic factors about fees, pointing out that the group goes on with its work even when there are absences. The amount of the fees should be determined on the basis of several factors—the time involved, the services of the recorder (which includes time for therapist-recorder discussion), and the number of group members. In private practice fees vary from $5 to $20 per meeting. Many clinics employ a scale based on family income and number of dependents. Fees may range from $1 to $4 per session.

No one will question the role that money, with all its conflictual manifestations, plays in the average American household. Analysts have said that when people in analysis have worked through their problems and conflicts with money, substantial progress has been made. The therapist should be aware of financial problems and, when they occur, make them a group issue. For example, if there are several patients who are negligent with their accounts, the therapist can bring this fact to the attention of the group by stating that several members are not paying their bills and asking what thoughts the group has about this, and how the group is affected when some members pay and others do not. When nonpayment of bills was brought to the attention of a group of neurotic patients at the 26th meeting, the members admitted a lackadaisical attitude about payment and compared the nonpayment of fees to a lack of involvement in group therapy. Two members talked about their past patterns of not paying bills and the problems this entailed. In another outpatient clinic group that was set up with extremely small fees based on income and number of dependents, the entire group was negligent in paying bills. Here, however, the primary problem was not the group members but the passivity and tardiness of the therapist in bringing this matter to the members and exploring it as a group issue.

Other reasons why members may be lax about paying fees are related to their dependency wishes and hostility to the therapist. The member may wish the therapist to be the ever-loving father who will care for their every need—free of charge. If the therapist fails to bring unpaid bills to their attention, no payments may be forthcoming for months. Failure to obtain magical solutions to their problems increases their rage against the therapist; one manifestation of this may be defiant behavior about fees. In general, the progress of the group member in group therapy can be predicted by his attitude about the payment of fees.

Bringing fee problems to the group for discussion is often helpful but does not always solve the problem. Direct intervention by the therapist may be necessary. In the first place, the therapist should place a limit on the group member who does not pay fees; if a member cannot explain his nonpayment of fees he should be dropped. This can be done more easily if a clear, concise, and authoritative policy about fees has been pointed out to the group at the beginning of therapy. The resident in psychiatry and other salaried professional personnel who are group therapists are prone to pay less attention to the payment of fees by the group members than the psychiatrist in private practice. However, the author wishes to stress that the group therapist, whether he is in private practice or in a salaried position, should pay close attention to the payment of fees. He should examine his books monthly and take appropriate action with those who are negligent. If after discussion with the group members in a group meeting the issue is not settled, individual attention by the therapist is necessary.

Prolonged absences incurred by reality factors such as physical illness may need a fee readjustment. From his initial contacts and interviews with group members the therapist can form a tentative opinion about their ability to handle financial obligations. Flexibility is recommended when catastrophic events affect a member or members of the group. Here again the group is an excellent gauge and sounding board to solve such problems. For example, when a member has not been able to attend for four to eight meetings because of a physical illness, the therapist can discuss whether he should be charged during his absence. Such problems are, in reality, group issues and can be decided by the group members and the therapist.

DRUGS, PHYSICAL ILLNESSES, HOSPITALIZATIONS, OTHER THERAPIES

The therapist is frequently confronted with problems having to do with drugs, telephone calls, personal contacts, hospitalizations, physical illnesses, and similar matters of concern within the group. A number of variables have to be considered, such as the dynamics of the group member, the group process at the moment, and the maturity of the group itself. Although the therapist should display a certain degree of flexibility in these matters, he must not fail to take positive action whenever possible. For example, many telephone calls and personal contacts can be referred to the group for discussion. The therapist should listen attentively on the phone, then point out to the member that such matters should be referred to the group for discussion. If physical illnesses exist, they should be discussed in the initial interviews and the patient advised to consult his family physician. Each patient should have a thorough physical examination by his own physician prior to beginning group therapy and at yearly intervals thereafter.

The patient's request for drugs should be evaluated from the dynamics of the patient and the group as a whole. The schizophrenic patient, as he becomes involved in the group process, occasionally may be overwhelmed with anxiety. Phenothiazines or other medication may be very helpful in relieving this anxiety. The therapist may either prescribe such drugs or refer the patient to a colleague, depending on his evaluation of the problem. If hospitalization is indicated, either the therapist himself or a colleague should see that the patient is properly referred and cared for. In all instances these problems are group problems and should be discussed in the group meeting. The therapist will find it necessary at times to take care of an emergency illness of a group member. In such cases he should make all necessary arrangements, then discuss the member's illness at the next meeting. While the members should feel free to contact the therapist at any time, they should be told that all contacts with the therapist must be discussed at the next group meeting.

A patient may be in group therapy and individual therapy simultaneously. The important thing here is the clearly defined role of the therapist. The group therapist should not attempt individual therapy with any members of his group.

The following examples will illustrate how these problems can be handled in group therapy:

In an outpatient group a young schizophrenic female, who had initially sought help for lack of control of rage feelings, began to feel extremely uncomfortable and anxious at the 8th group meeting. She was not able to ventilate her feelings to any degree at that time. She consulted the group therapist after this meeting. Thorazine was prescribed for two weeks. The patient was asked by the therapist to discuss her feelings, her contact with him, and the prescription for drugs at the next meeting. She made two references to this in later meetings. At the next (9th) meeting she discussed the matter only superficially. At a much later meeting (38th) she discussed a number of her earlier uncomfortable feelings, such as fears of loss of control, the contact with the therapist, and the need for drugs. She did not require any additional medication.

In an outpatient group a very dependent patient made repeated requests for drugs. The therapist refused to prescribe medication and felt the patient should discuss this request with the group. The patient did this and expressed, among other things, his irritation with the therapist for not granting the request. The group pointed out his unreasonable demands and dependency on drugs. They suggested he should help himself. Several references were made to the role of the therapist. The group correctly deduced that the therapist did not answer questions because he wanted the group to look at themselves and to help one another. The patient compared the therapist to his mother, saying he had the same kind of battles with her about drugs. At a later meeting, the therapist asked if there were any ideas as to why this patient continued to bring the problem of drugs to the group. Several opinions were voiced. One member felt he wanted the doctor to do everything for him. Another said he was bringing the same problems as he had with his mother to the group meeting and had started a battle that was a repetition of his battles with his mother. They felt he should not take drugs under any circumstances.

In an outpatient group of one year's duration a group member was hospitalized for depression and acting-out behavior complicated by alcoholism. Events leading up to the hospital admission were unknown to the therapist or to the other group members. The patient always attended meetings regularly, so his absence at the 45th meeting troubled the group. The therapist notified the group that this specific member had been hospitalized. The feelings expressed by the group concerned their lack of support of him at previous meetings. One member felt guilty and expressed the fear that he might have said something at a prior meeting that contributed to the member's illness. The general mood of the group was depression. The patient's hospitalization was a loss to the group, particularly since it was sudden and unexpected.

In a group of psychotic patients of approximately eight months' duration, a female schizophrenic patient who had earlier been discharged from the hospital became quite bizarre and delusional, and refused to consider going back to the hospital. Her husband called the therapist on the day of the meeting. The therapist advised him to bring her to group therapy. At the session the therapist informed the group of the husband's call, the behavior of his wife, and his wish for her to return to the hospital. Group feelings about this turn of events were explored. The other members noted the illness of the patient during the meeting and advised her to return to the hospital. She was supported very warmly by the group, even though the circumstances were depressing to them. She reentered the hospital without difficulty. Here the therapist was able to bring a prior contact (the telephone call) and a suggested hospitalization of a member for the consideration of the group. The group's solution to the problem was the correct one. In fact, the solution of this problem by the members points out one significant factor in the response of patients to suggestions and advice: a patient will often listen to and accept suggestions and advice from other patients much more readily than from a doctor or relative.

CONVERSATIONS, TELEPHONE CALLS, PERSONAL CONTACTS AND MEETINGS BY GROUP MEMBERS OUTSIDE THE REGULAR STRUCTURED MEETING

The therapist should emphatically stress to the members prior to the outset of therapy that conversations, telephone calls, personal contacts and meetings by members outside of the regular structured meeting should be avoided; that such occurrences are destructive to group therapy; and that if by chance a conversation or telephone call does take place, it should be reported immediately at the next meeting. The therapist should be quite direct and unequivocal in explaining this issue of outside contacts. Initially, the members agree to this provision of the group contract. Later, as they become more involved in therapy, they develop attitudes quite different from those held at the beginning. Their hostile feelings toward the therapist encourages acting-out behavior— a common type being communication with one another between meetings. The lonely and sexually frustrated group member who has conflicts with his wife may become sexually attracted to a female member and attempt to contact her between meetings. At times several members will hold an informal group meeting without the therapist's knowledge. Invariably, such outside communications are acknowledged in the group meeting in deference to the therapist's prior instructions and in expiation of guilt feelings for thus displeasing him. The therapist will thus have the opportunity to explore the meaning of outside contacts as well as to re-emphasize the primacy of the group contract. The therapist must keep a watchful eye on the possible formation of subgroups, discourage them, and repeatedly focus the group's attention on the dangers implicit in their occurrence.

Outside communication between group members occurs frequently during the first stage of group therapy. If the therapist is aware that this form of group behavior has a relationship to the members' transference reactions, his technique of handling such problems will be simplified.

MODIFICATIONS OF THE GROUP CONTRACT

References have been made throughout this chapter to the various conditions that may require a change in the group contract. Therapist, recorder, and members are all a part of the group contract. One might call the therapist the "party of the first part" and the group members the "party of the second part." Agreement between the two parties is necessary for a change in the contract. Thus the need of the members to be consulted on changes in the contract is not only of great importance but appears to be the only honest, understanding approach to group therapy. Changes in the contract are reality events and as such enter into the dynamics of group therapy. The therapist should be aware of the ambivalence of the members' feelings—that while they seek and readily accede to his wishes, underneath this ingratiating attitude are feelings of quite a different character. In stage I of group therapy the members tend to deny their feelings about changes in the contract. They are so desirous of obtaining approval from the group therapist that his wishes are readily granted. In stage III of therapy the members express their real feelings about changes in the contract, their statements being conditioned by the group's maturity. The therapist should proceed slowly, deliberately, and carefully in planning all phases of the contract so that changes will be as few as possible.

In the final analysis, the group contract described here offers the members an experience in reality testing in everyday life derived from the reality testing implicit in the group contract, and it emphasizes the responsibilities of the members for their treatment program.

REFERENCES

1. Winick, C., A. L. Kadis, and J. D. Krasner: "The Training and Practice of American Group Psychotherapists," *Internat. J. Group Psychotherapy*, 11:426, 1961.
2. Foeser, L. H.: "Some Aspects of Group Dynamics," *Internat. J. Group Psychotherapy*, 7:5–19, 1957.
3. Slavson, S. R.: "Parallelisms in Development of Group Therapy," *Internat. J. Group Psychotherapy*, 9:451–462, 1959.
4. Geller, J. J.: "Concerning the Size of Therapy Groups," *Internat. J. Group Psychotherapy*, 1:118–120, 1951.
5. Milberg, I. L.: "Group Psychotherapy in the Treatment of Some Neurodermatoses," *Internat. J. Group Psychotherapy*, 6:53–59, 1956.
6. Cooper, M., and J. Katz: "The Treatment of Migraine and Tension Headache with Group Psychotherapy," *Internat. J. Group Psychotherapy*, 6:266–271, 1956.
7. Fortin, J. N., and D. W. Abse: "Group Psychotherapy with Peptic Ulcer," *Internat. J. Group Psychotherapy*, 8:44–54, 1958.
8. Clapman, H. I., and A. B. Sclare: "Group Psychotherapy with Asthmatic Patients," *Internat. J. Group Psychotherapy*, 6:383–391, 1956.
9. Igersheimer, W. W.: "Analytically Oriented Group Psychotherapy for Patients with Psychosomatic Illness," *Internat. J. Group Psychotherapy*, 9:225–238, 359–375, 1959.
10. American Psychiatric Association, *Diagnostic and Statistical Manual: Mental Disorders*, Washington, D.C., 1952, pp. 34–42.
11. Dreikurs, R., and R. Corsini: "Twenty Years of Group Psychotherapy," *Am. J. Psychiat.*, 110:567–575, 1954.

12. Expert Committee on Mental Health: *Third Report of World Health Organization,* Technical Report Series 73, Geneva, 1953, pp. 17–18.
13. Greenblatt, M.: "Formal and Informal Groups in a Therapeutic Community," *Internat. J. Group Psychotherapy,* 11:404–406, 1961.
14. Colby, K. M.: *A Primer for Psychotherapists,* The Ronald Press Company, New York, 1951, p. 19.
15. Mann, J.: "Some Theoretic Concepts of the Group Process," *Internat. J. Group Psychotherapy,* 5:238, 1955.
16. Mann, J.: "Psychoanalytic Observations Regarding Conformity in Groups," *Internat. J. Group Psychotherapy,* 12:7–9, 1962.
17. Rado, S., and G. E. Daniels (eds.): *Changing Concepts of Psychoanalytic Medicine,* Grune & Stratton, Inc., New York, 1956, pp. 92–94.
18. Limentani, D., M. Geller, and M. Day: "Group Leader-Recorder Relationship in a State Hospital: A Learning Tool," *Internat. J. Group Psychotherapy,* 10:335–336, 1960.

5

The Psychodynamics of Separation: Its Relationship to Group Therapy Reality Events and the Termination of Group Therapy

In group therapy, as in any form of psychotherapy, the members experience a series of emotional reactions that may be grouped together under the general heading of separation anxiety. The reality events that occur in group therapy from the initial meeting to the final one may be interpreted by the members in a distorted and irrational manner to mean rejection and a loss of dependency. The reality events of group therapy associated with imagined or real separation have been previously mentioned—meetings cancelled by the group therapist, a change of group therapists, absence of the recorder, a change of recorders, tardiness of the group therapist and recorder, absence of group members, loss of group members, change of meeting time, change of day of group meeting, and termination of group therapy. As we have seen, their faulty emergency responses to these reality events include feelings of anger, guilt, depression, and low self-esteem. Anxietal defenses are increased. An implied threat of separation exists.

What are the psychodynamics of separation? Where do the anxiety and the numerous emotional reactions associated with separation arise? Actually, separation and the anxiety associated with it have a broad spectrum of meanings. As a result of real or imaginary separation, people experience a gamut of emotions ranging from a subtle, obscure, and barely realized sense of loss in normal individuals to overt psychotic behavior in the schizophrenic. Examination of the child-mother relationship reveals the child's complete dependency from birth through childhood, with a steady growth of independence during latency, puberty, and adolescence. In many individuals, however, this normal transition may not occur.

158

Chronic frustration may be present in both the parent and the child, leading to fear, hostility, guilt, and a sense of inability to survive without the parent. Frequently this "survival dependency" is so strong that children will remain with their parents although their basic needs are barely being met. The relationship is a hostile, dependent one, chronically frustrating and charged with hostility. Many of these people have experienced traumatic separations in past life. With the death of a parent who never satisfied the needs of the child, a mixture of frightening and uncomfortable feelings may be present. The loss may trigger uncontrollable feelings of aggression. Earlier death wishes for a deceased parent may release strong guilt feelings.

Even a healthy person may have feelings of lassitude, apathy, boredom, irritability, mild depression, insomnia, anorexia, and variable psychosomatic symptoms that occur for a transient period when he is separated from his usual environment and placed in a new one. The husband who leaves his wife and children for an extended time, the family that moves from one city to another, the high school graduate who leaves home for college, the young adult who enters a branch of the Armed Services, and the executive or professional man who is promoted or transferred to another area are all people threatened by separation. Emotional investments in the old surroundings are given up and new ones must be undertaken.

An enlightening picture of the dynamics created by separation is clearly exemplified within the family group when the father announces to his wife and children that they are moving to another city. The children may express their anger and resentment to him in no uncertain terms. They may not want to leave friends and associates. A new home may not be as satisfactory as the one in which they live. They may have difficulty making new friends. Schools will be strange, with different people and teachers. Such feelings of separation are usually transient. Once in the new situation, the healthy ego marshals its forces. Occupational tasks are accomplished with little difficulty. Business and social contacts proceed as formerly. Children form friendships quickly, and within a few weeks happily announce to all the glories of their new environment.

A grief reaction may be placed in the same category. For example, after many years of a happy marriage a woman loses her husband by death. At first, she is quite depressed. She feels that survival is quite impossible. Her needs for him seem unsurmountable. Later, she will find other ways of meeting her needs. Emotional investments that were formerly with her husband are transferred to others. The depression lifts and she faces life realistically. Her reaction to separation is a healthy one. It is as if she is saying: "I can cope with this loss. I miss him, but I can go ahead."

To the person with an unhealthy ego, however, separation may be associated with a series of distorted ideas, feelings, and thoughts. Repetition of all defenses against anxiety, such as low self-esteem, guilt, depression, increased dependency, and paranoia, may be present. The particular pattern and distortion will vary, depending on the degree of ego strength and the defenses commonly used by the individual when threatened by the loss of an object relationship. Separation to the very dependent person creates a mixture of feelings. Panic may occur with the realization that the dependency on someone has been taken away.

The relationship to the loved object is an ambivalent one with the negative identification to the aggressor coming to the forefront, characterized by massive anger, guilt, and depression. The injured person is rejected and downcast. Feelings of low self-esteem become magnified. The patient with a paranoid integration will reveal an increase in paranoid trends and delusions. The phobic and obsessive-compulsive individuals will exhibit an increase of their defenses. Depression is a common result in the passive, nonassertive, dependent individual. To the schizophrenic, separation is a traumatic emotional experience. The ever-feared rejection by another has now happened. It was doomed to occur. The distorted situation produces extreme anger, followed by guilt and depression. The anxiety may be so overwhelming that overt psychotic behavior results.

THE GROUP'S REACTION TO SEPARATION

In group therapy, the emotionally ill person reexperiences the same feelings and thoughts as in day-to-day living. Many of the reality events of group therapy create imagined threats of rejection and result in fears of loss of dependency. A meeting cancelled by the therapist implies rejection, dependency loss, and separation. A variety of feelings, ideas, and thoughts may occur to the group members. The most common are:

1. We are angry at the group therapist for the cancellation. He has no right to cancel the meeting. He should do more for us, and not do less by being absent.

2. The group therapist is aware of our feelings. We don't like him and he doesn't like us. He wants to get rid of us. No one has ever liked us; he doesn't either.

3. The group therapist is going to reject us, so maybe we should reject him first.

4. We'll pay him back—he missed a meeting, so we'll miss the next one.

Recurrent absenteeism and the loss of one or more members bring about fears of group dissolution. Again there is anger at the therapist whom the members hold responsible for absenteeism and group losses. The members fear the therapist will discontinue group therapy because of poor attendance, and therefore the members that attend meetings will suffer because of the others. Hostility develops between members and adds to the anxiety level in group meetings.

Probably the severest blow that can be dealt to a group is the sudden loss of the therapist. The members' reactions may be catastrophic and demoralizing. The particular effect on such a group will be dependent on several factors, such as the psychodynamics of the group members, the maturity of the group, the factors that entered into the loss of the therapist and the contract. The members' fears of rejection, retaliation, loss of dependency, and separation have, it seems, all been realized.

The absence, loss, or change in the recorder involve many of the same feelings experienced toward the group therapist but the members do not have the intensity and depth of feeling for the recorder as they do for the therapist. The therapist occupies a position in the group that cannot be approached by anyone else.

In those people with more pronounced ego pathology, group-reality events may produce psychotic or episodic psychotic behavior. Several cancelled meetings, even if the therapist's other work demands them, can result in overt psychotic behavior. Any change in the group therapy structure, such as holding the meeting in a different room or a change in the time or day of the meeting, carries with it the imagined threat of rejection and separation. Group members have spoken of the uncomfortable reactions to any structural changes.

The reality events that occur during group therapy offer the therapist repeated opportunities to explore the members' feelings and thoughts of separation. From a standpoint of technique, it is essential that the members' feelings about cancelled meetings, change in the recorder's status, group members' absences, group contract modifications, etc., be brought to the group's attention time and again until their faulty and distorted emotional responses are recognized and understood.

THE TERMINATION OF GROUP THERAPY

The members, having experienced anxiety from the implied threat of separation in group-reality events, come face to face with the anxiety of actual separation when the termination of group therapy approaches. The termination will be influenced by the particular model of group therapy employed, the therapist's goals of treatment, and the psychodynamics of the group members. For example, a hospital group may have as its goal supportive treatment with patients participating as group members only during the period of their hospitalization. Some outpatient clinic groups and private patient groups are "open-ended." No termination date for the group itself is set. New members are added to the group as others drop out. Similar groups exist in hospitals, guidance clinics, and training schools. Feelings about separation are present and influence the group interaction, but due to the group therapy structure the anxietal manifestations are more individualized. The group itself does not end; only an individual in the group is involved. The model of group therapy presented in this book is structured somewhat differently. A specific period of group therapy, usually 18 months, may be designated for the group members in the group contract. New members may or may not be added, depending on the status of the group. Generally speaking, new members are not emphasized as in open-ended groups except during the initial stage (5–25 meetings) of group therapy, when group losses are replaced to keep the membership as near the original number as possible. The therapist should be hesitant to add new members if only a short period of time remains before the end of therapy.

The termination of therapy for the members of such a group, who have been together at weekly meetings for 18 months, brings into clearer focus the dynamics of separation anxiety. The members, the recorder, the therapist and the group itself are involved in a chain of events as the end of therapy approaches. Significantly, the therapist can utilize this group pattern of behavior constructively in promoting an awareness of the meaning of separation.

A more detailed explanatory account of the anxiety associated with separation is given in Chap. 7. The varied emotions exhibited by group members are illustrated in the summarized content of the meetings. The technique employed by the therapist is pointed out in the content of each meeting and discussed under the heading entitled "Technique." The index at the end of Chap. 7 lists specific manifestations of separation anxiety and the meeting in which they occurred.

In order to understand the reaction of the group members to the ending of treatment it is necessary to be constantly aware of the goals and purpose of group therapy. They are:

1. To improve reality testing.
2. To aid socialization.
3. To foster the development of psychological aptitude.
4. To provide motivation for additional therapy.

Thus when group members approach the end of treatment, symptoms of anxiety are less but conflicts and other emotional problems still remain. Facing the end of therapy adds to the group members' apprehensions about future emotional problems. They fear that anxietal manifestations, which have improved as a result of group therapy, may recur when the group ends. Here again the therapist can constructively use such verbalized material to explore the limitations of therapy and to compare the members' goals at that time with their goals at the outset of therapy.

The group spirit, the cohesiveness, and the common bonds of warm feelings that develop between the members, the recorder, and the therapist are also extremely important factors in the dynamics of terminating group therapy. The members have shared their feelings with one another and helped unravel their confusing and distorted behavioral patterns. They have learned through practice to express both positive and negative feelings. In the group, they feel they have found many of the positive values of family life they longed for during their early years. The members' feelings for the group can be described as a kind of invisible force, separate from themselves, that is protective and comforting in nature— somewhat similar to the feelings that members of a family have for the atmosphere of their home. Their identification with the group therapist, although an ambivalent one, has resulted in the development of warm feelings for him through his interest, understanding, support, and guidance. The group places him in the singular position of one who holds them together, keeps them on the right track, and cares for them. In other words, he assumes the role of father and leader. The recorder, too, shares in these feelings. If the recorder is a woman she may assume the role of mother to the group members. She is identified with the therapist and is subject to the same ambivalent feelings. (The author has never heard group members refer to the recorder in this manner, but it may be deduced from the recorder's identification as an authority figure and the members' comparison of the group to a family.)

These features of the "group family" (also called the group identity), are stressed because they enter into the dynamics of separation anxiety and need careful evaluation and handling (technique) by the therapist. The situation is somewhat different from the ending of therapy with an individual patient. In group therapy the members have developed positive feelings not only for the therapist but also for other individual members, the recorder and, very significantly, for the group itself.

At the termination of therapy the therapist's technique should be directed toward giving the members as thorough an understanding as possible of the anxiety associated with separation. If this technique is correctly employed, the members should profit therapeutically from the group experience. In prior meetings the members experienced feelings of rejection and separation from repeated group-reality events. They recognized faulty, distorted, and irrational emotional responses, and through reentering the situation (group meetings) again and again they made attempts to correct them. The therapist should announce the termination date at least 10–12 meetings before the last meeting. As with any important group-reality event, he should announce it during the early or middle part of a meeting—never at the end—so that the members will have an opportunity to express some of their feelings during the meeting.

The theme of the remaining group meetings will center around the end of therapy. The initial group reaction is depression. The members view the end of therapy as a tremendous loss. All the positive and self-rewarding investments they have developed within the group will be taken away. They will have no comfortable place to talk and to examine their reactions to others. The atmosphere created within the group will disappear. They feel rejected by the therapist. The therapist and recorder also share in the depressed mood. One cannot work with a group of people over a period of 18 months without investing in them, sharing with them, and learning from them. The emotional investment of the therapist is an important aspect in the therapeutic process of group therapy.

Group-reality events are characterized by tipping the identification with the therapist over to the negative side. The group depression enters into the psychodynamics of the reality event of terminating group therapy and is followed by increased group anxiety and hostility to the therapist. The members become angry at the therapist for terminating therapy. Defensive patterns of behavior, seen throughout the life of the group, are prominently displayed in the meetings. The therapist should use every possible opportunity to promote among the members an awareness and recognition of their hostility to him and its relationship to previous reality events and to the ending of therapy. He should, therefore, begin an exploration of their feelings about separation. The therapist will have formed an opinion of the psychodynamics of each member from previous meetings and should now use this information as a helpful guide in anticipating as well as evaluating behavior associated with the anxiety of separation. The group members will not react to separation in the same manner. For example, the passive dependent member, who has not worked through his transference feelings for the therapist, may become rageful and defiant and quit the group. He will reject the therapist before the therapist rejects him. The member with alcohol or drug problems, whose dependency strivings are well known, may become quite frustrated by the loss of dependency and resort to the bottle or drugs. Another member, who may have been slow in group interaction and participation, may make a concerted effort during the remaining meetings to become actively involved in therapy. It is as if this group member says to the therapist: "Look, I am taking part now, do you have to stop group therapy?" The schizophrenic member, who reacts to any change in group structure, greets the threat of separation with a mixture of feelings, rejection, loss of dependency, anger, guilt, depression, and other forms of anxietal manifestations.

Those members who have reached the third stage and are actively functioning in group therapy will proceed with the therapist's guidance to analyze accurately their feelings regarding separation and the termination of therapy. The traumatic effect of previous family separations may be discussed and compared to group therapy. Anger at the therapist is recognized, along with the associated feelings of guilt and depression. Ventilation of these feelings lowers the group anxiety level and raises the level of constructive group work (mutual analysis).

In the remaining meetings the therapist should be careful to explore the members' feelings about being separated from him, from the recorder, and from each other. The therapist should also attempt to promote the idea that separation can be a more pleasant experience than it may have been formerly, and that traumatic feelings regarding separation are the result of faulty emotional responses and have been exhibited in their reactions to other reality events during group therapy.

In these final meetings the therapist should also direct the members' attention to the gains they have made during therapy, their present status, and their future plans. An individual interview with each member is suggested at this time, although in the past this would have been discouraged. Those members who have developed psychological awareness of emotional problems and feel the need of additional help may wish to continue therapy on an individual basis or become the member of another group. It will be quite meaningful to the member for the therapist to advise and assist in making future plans for additional treatment.

The final meetings will also be characterized by frequent expressions of the positive values of group therapy. These positive feelings have been present throughout the life of the group but come to the forefront as the end approaches. The members usually become more objective and abstract in their feelings and attitudes for themselves and for others. They should begin to understand that the benefits of group therapy are limited; that the member's reality-facing and socialization have improved somewhat, but that emotional problems with themselves and with others will still be present. In this respect the author would like to again emphasize that the basic personality structure and behavior patterns of the group member have not been changed; it is merely that the member understands his own emotions better as well as their effect on other people. In addition, he has a clearer understanding of other people's emotional reactions.

Separation anxiety, then, is a common occurrence in human group relationships. In healthy people the manifestations of separation anxiety are quite vague and transient. In people with emotional disorders the effects of separation anxiety are more powerful and disturbing. In the model of group therapy presented in this book, group members can be given the opportunity to explore and examine the emotional reactions associated with separation anxiety as well as the relationship of separation anxiety to the reality events of group therapy and day-to-day group relationships.

As they experience and come to understand the emotional reactions associated with group-reality events, they can begin the emotional re-learning and reeducation that is, in essence, a major goal of group therapy.

6

Silence and Acting Out in Group Therapy

Of the numerous problems of technique facing the therapist, silence and acting-out behavior can be among the more troublesome. Occurring to some extent in all groups, silence and acting out in group therapy are both due to the anxiety that the members experience in the meetings, and occur most often during stage I. Perhaps the most important factor that contributes to silence and acting out is the members' hostility toward the therapist. The members react as they have to authority figures in previous day-to-day group relationships.

SILENCE

The therapist will have to deal with two different kinds of silence—silence of the entire group and silence of one or more individuals. Often, very early in groups, there may be one or more members who are not participating. The therapist should be aware of such members. After the meeting has progressed for approximately twenty to thirty minutes he can make a comment to the group as follows: "We have a couple of members who are not participating in the meeting. Do you have any thoughts as to why they are quiet?" He does not ask individuals to talk by specifically calling their names. He makes his observation in such a way that the matter addresses itself to the group. He avoids individual therapy. He is doing group therapy. Frequently such a statement may be reassuring to a silent member, who may immediately begin to take part in the meeting. Other members may encourage their participation. Some patients, however, will remain silent even though they have received encouragement. The withdrawn schizophrenic patient may go for a number of meetings without being a participant, even though he is quite aware of the group experience. A group member may receive tremendous support from another member and from the therapist through methods other than verbal communication. This factor points out the value and meaning of nonverbal communication in group therapy.

167

If individual silence persists over a number of meetings, the therapist should continue to support the member by asking the others to look at this behavior. He may also ask: "Any thoughts why it is difficult for Mr. A. to take part in the meeting? He comes regularly to every meeting but doesn't talk." A further statement can be made: "How does it affect you when someone does not participate?" Again the anxiety level of the group and its relationship to the silent member or members must be assayed and pursued by the therapist at a comfortable pace.

An early problem is the hostility felt by participating group members toward those who are silent, who are not "carrying their load." They also hold the therapist responsible for keeping nonparticipating people in the group. It becomes extremely important for the therapist to identify the feelings of the participating members as well as to support the silent ones.

Groups that have been functioning for a number of meetings will point out these silent members and examine their etiology. The therapist can supplement such interchanges with appropriate remarks where necessary. However, there are some silent members who will drop out of group therapy. Those group members who come to meetings regularly but have difficulty talking raise the anxiety level of the other members. This is particularly true when the therapist and the group members have made repeated attempts to help the one who is silent. The members become angry at the silent group member and the therapist. Actually the members hold the therapist responsible for the silent group member. If the silent member becomes aware of the hostility felt toward him by the others, the difficulties in talking before a group of people become more intensified. One solution for the silent group member is to stop group therapy.

Silence can be a troublesome problem when it occurs in the whole group. The group members, as well as the therapist and the recorder, become uncomfortable during a silence. The technique employed by the therapist will be conditioned by the anxiety level of the members, and by the psychodynamics and maturity of the group. All groups at times exhibit group silence. In groups of psychotic patients the anxiety level may reach extremely high levels and require careful management. The behavior of a group of psychotic males in a state hospital described below illustrates a series of problems associated with group silences as well as the countertransference feelings of the therapist:

The group met for one hour per week. At the 10th meeting the theme concerned dominating and controlling parents. No significant group issues were discussed. At the 11th meeting the members discussed superficially their outlets for anxiety and touched briefly on their feelings for the group therapist, but would not explore them. The subject was changed to extraneous matters. A realistic situation in the ward schedule necessitated a change in the hour of the group meeting. When the therapist discussed this change with the members, they denied any feelings about the change and readily agreed to a new time. At the 12th meeting only two members were present. The theme of this meeting was confusion and fear of groups. Those present defended the members who were absent. Hostility toward the physical aspects of the ward was expressed. The 13th meeting was cancelled by the therapist in order to allow the members to attend a dance. At the 14th meeting all members were present. The first half of the meeting was taken up with conversation about family problems, conflicts with parents, and conflicts with people in general. The importance of getting along with others was mentioned. The therapist made a statement that the conversation was about conflicts at home, getting along with others, and the importance they attach to it, adding "How do these things apply here?" There was an immediate silence. The therapist allowed this silence for four minutes. Later there were remarks concerning guilty feelings. A second long period of silence occurred with restlessness, clearing of throats, sighing, etc. Two members acted sleepy. Following a third period of silence one member suggested to the therapist that maybe he should change the subject. The therapist focused on this statement. The members changed the subject, discussing material matters until the meeting was over.

At the therapist recorder discussion, the recorder brought out that she was uneasy during the meeting. The therapist remarked that he felt the group was angry at him. At group supervision, the supervisory personnel admonished the group therapist for allowing the long silences and for attempting to force his members to deal with group feelings when they had indicated a marked degree of anxiety by silences and other nonverbal behavior. They felt the members were concerned about their feelings toward the therapist and, to some extent, toward each other. He was bringing them closer together. Their fears of exposure, retaliation, and guilt, along with accompanying hostility, must have been threatening to the group members. The therapist was angry at his group. He "paid" them back for missing the 12th meeting by cancelling the next one. He continued his anger toward them at the 14th meeting by allowing a four-minute silence, by further focusing on group feelings even though this produced more silences and anxiety, and by failing to recognize the severe degree of discomfort present. The statement by the group member requesting the subject be changed was quite significant in that a patient recognized the correct technique even though the therapist did not. The group therapist's countertransference feelings, which were apparent to him at supervision but not during the meeting, served as an efficient block to the group process. He was not in control of the group. He was not aware of the underlying group feeling. The members, too, picked up the anger of the therapist, and their anxiety level increased even more.

A group should not be allowed to remain silent for a period longer than one or two minutes. There are several techniques the therapist can employ. Proper assessment of the anxiety level is all-important. In the group of psychotic patients just described, the anxiety level was extremely high. The therapist gave them the opportunity to examine group feelings. They were not ready to do so. This was indicated by their behavior throughout the remainder of the meeting. The therapist can ask the group what their thoughts are about the silence. They may or may not deal with it. He might also ask what thoughts are being experienced during the silence. The therapist can change the subject to one that is more comfortable. He can talk in another area for a minute or so, thereby reducing the anxiety level of the group. By talking himself, or by changing the subject, the therapist lowers the level of anxiety. The members will deal with group feelings when they feel comfortable to do so.

In groups of neurotic patients the same problems with silence occur and require the same remedial technique. However, the process is not as prolonged as with groups of psychotic patients. As the group proceeds from week to week, the therapist should continue to explore group feelings and act accordingly as he gauges the anxiety level. He may push forward with vigor if the group is ready. He may need to retreat and support when the situation demands, trying again at a later time. Thus the therapist does not attempt to do their work; he merely provides the atmosphere and waits patiently and understandingly for the group to move ahead. As the group matures, the members will discuss silence. The anxiety associated with their relationship to the therapist and to one another will be brought out into the open. They learn to understand how silence is handled in the group meetings, how it can be handled outside the group, the uncomfortable aspects of silence, and the rewards that come when their feelings about silence can be expressed and understood.

In groups of neurotic patients, group silence may occur initially after transference reactions have developed. The members may be quite verbal for the initial 10 to 20 meetings but thereafter may become silent. The members' anxiety has increased markedly since the outset of group therapy. Now they are more frightened and uncomfortable in the therapist's presence. The members feel an intense need to please the therapist. Their silence may be partly due to fears of discussing matters that may be displeasing to him and partly to other feelings that have become apparent from increased group anxiety. In such situations the therapist, unless he is aware of the dynamics of the group process, becomes confused and frustrated. His once active and verbal group is now less active, nonverbal, and more anxious. In these situations the therapist's technique should be gauged by the anxiety level of the members.

One of the most persistently silent group members in the author's experience was a young, adult female who remained mostly silent, meeting after meeting, for 9 months (36 meetings). Repeated attempts by the therapist and the other members to involve her in the verbal group discussions were to no avail. On several occasions the members attempted to scapegoat her, and the therapist had to repeatedly support her. Even though this patient was not able to talk in the meetings, she attended regularly. Her nonverbal communication was phenomenal. She would reveal appropriate anger, defiance, warmth, pleasure, and sadness from the group interaction. Sometimes she would very briefly answer questions from the other members. During the 11th and 12th months of group therapy she became much more verbally active in the meetings. In the long period of her silence the therapist never abandoned or neglected her, but instead encouraged her with repeated support and interest. Improvement occurred despite her verbal silence in meetings. Her nonverbal communication, attendance, and interest in the group were quite noticeable and impressive.

This patient's situation and the author's observation of silent patients in hospital ward meetings point out that patients can improve from both group therapy and hospital meetings even though their verbal participation is practically nil or absent. In a number of instances, patients previously hospitalized in our psychiatric facilities where biweekly hospital ward meetings are employed have related after their discharge how much help they obtained from the ward meetings even though they were not able to participate verbally. Several have commented that the ward meetings made them realize the extent of their difficulties and their need for additional treatment. Thus the silent patient may be making much more progress than the extent of his participation indicates. In these patients the alert therapist or ward meeting leader can observe the extent of their nonverbal communication in group meetings.

ACTING OUT

Acting out and the problems connected with it are of particular concern to the group therapist. It is generally known that psychotherapy encourages acting-out behavior. As we have seen, psychotherapy also produces anxiety in the patient, who reacts to it with patterns of behavior derived from previous group relationships. Acting out is therefore one of his behavior patterns. Fenichel initially defined acting out as "an acting which unconsciously relieves inner tension and brings partial discharge to warded off impulses." He recognized that acting out was unconscious in origin, and that it resulted in behavior which appeared plausible and appropriate to the individual but not to others in the environment.

The social realities of group therapy very quickly mobilize the anxietal phenomena and behavior patterns of the group members. The stage is set for the emergence of repetitive-compulsive behavior, of which acting out is a component. Freud called attention to this phenomenon in discussing the psychology of groups. He said: "When an individual becomes part of a group his unconscious mental processes tend to dominate his conscious processes."

Acting-out behavior in group therapy can be observed in the members' behavior patterns such as lateness, absences, periodic alcoholic indulgence, subtle and overt forms of hostility between members, and formation of subgroups both within and outside the group. Acting out in the sexual area may range all the way from casual outside meetings to assignations and sexual intercourse, although the latter is usually a very rare occurrence. Acting out may have a constructive (therapeutic) as well as destructive aspect—constructive from the standpoint that behavior patterns can be brought to the attention of the group and analyzed. A member will often gain an awareness of his behavior when it is pointed out by other members. Repeated tardiness, absences, and meetings between members on an unofficial basis are examples of acting out that can be dealt with to advantage within the group. Because acting out of a severe nature can be destructive to the group it requires the immediate attention of the therapist. Here again the matter is a concern of the group. For example, a male and female member of the group have experienced conflicts with their mates. They strike up a relationship that leads to "dating" outside of the regular structured meeting. Immediately the therapist should ask the group for their feelings and opinion of this relationship and its effect on the group. Groups, as a rule, will deal constructively with all such problems. However, some members continue their acting-out behavior and either quit therapy or are dropped from the group by the therapist. In the latter instance the members have refused to abide by the provisions of the group contract.

It is extremely important for the therapist to be aware of the dynamics of the group process in acting-out behavior so that he can understand the causes of acting out in group members. Frequently, this and similar behavioral patterns occur when angry feelings about the therapist are present but cannot be expressed. In this respect the therapist who reacts defensively to the hostility of the group members encourages acting out of the group members.

There is no way to prevent acting out in group therapy. Acting out almost always occurs in groups and can be a very troublesome problem for any therapist. A satisfactory solution is not always possible. But, if the therapist recognizes that the problems that do occur are invariably related to the dynamics of the group process, he can set certain limits. The design and structure of the group contract incorporate safeguards, limitations, and prohibitions against acting-out behavior. Promoting self-awareness of the group therapist through the use of a recorder, therapist-recorder discussions, and group supervisory conferences is extremely helpful in recognizing conscious and unconscious mechanisms of the therapist that influence group behavior. The techniques employed by the therapist in encouraging the group to look at and work through their hostile feelings toward him play a very significant part in the degree of acting out that occurs in the group. Attention to the group as a whole, avoidance of individual therapy in the group, and a constant vigilance of group behavior at all times will curtail acting out.

REFERENCES

1. Fenichel, O.: *The Psychoanalytic Theory of Neuroses*, W. W. Norton & Company, Inc., New York, 1945.
2. Freud, S.: *Group Psychology and the Analysis of the Ego*, Liveright Publishing Corporation, New York, 1949.

7

An Illustrative Analysis of an Outpatient Group

The following pages present the course of an outpatient group from the start to completion of group therapy. The model and theoretical dynamics involved in the group therapeutic experience, outlined in previous chapters, are illustrated. The three stages of group therapy can be visualized, although the transition between each is not clearly defined. The innumerable defenses against anxiety or behavior patterns of the group members are depicted over and over again in the member-to-member, member-to-therapist, and therapist-to-member relationships. The transference relationship to the therapist becomes the key to the *modus operandi* of the group. Identification with the aggressor, or the authority relationship of the members to the therapist, is exhibited in the positive and negative aspects of the transference. This authority relationship remains an ambivalent one throughout the life of the group. The negative aspects of the transference during stage I and stage II are prominent, and even in stage III the ambivalence is easily tipped over to the negative side by group realities such as absences, loss and addition of members, cancelled meetings (absences of the therapist), recorder's absences, and a substitute recorder. In fact, when any modification of the group's structure takes place, the negative aspect of the transference relationship to the therapist is exhibited.

The transference reactions of the group members can also be described in another manner. The treatment behavior of the group members during group therapy may be on one of four levels: the magic-craving level, the parentifying level, the self-reliant level, and the aspiring level. At the outset of group therapy the members' treatment behavior is at the magic-craving level. With the development of transference reactions in stage I of group therapy the members parentify (parentifying level of treatment behavior) the therapist and react to him as either obedient or disobedient children. In stage III the members reach the self-reliant level in their treatment behavior. In group therapy the members' treatment behavior is not stable. The same events that tip the transference reactions of the members over to the negative side affect their treatment behavior by a change from the self-reliant to the parentifying and magic-craving levels. Thus the members will switch back and forth from the self-reliant levels to the parentifying and magic-craving levels, depending on the reality events of group therapy.

The need for a group contract with its important relationship to the structure and dynamics of group therapy is illustrated. The social reality of the group and its identification with, comparison to, and relationship to, the original family group are clearly shown. Projections from family relationships are identified in the therapy group as well as in other groups.

The meetings of this outpatient group have been summarized throughout the group's entire length of 1½ years. Seventy meetings were held during this interval. Each meeting is presented from the standpoint of content, theme and dynamics, and technique. Space does not permit a complete detailed analysis of the individual sessions, but the salient features are embodied in the section listed as "Content." Under "Theme and Dynamics" a brief analysis of the dynamics of each meeting is given. The technique employed by the therapist is illustrated from a critical viewpoint. Many of the problems involving the therapist's technique occur in this group. This method emphasizes the group as one unit and incorporates the group contract with both its physical and dynamic aspects into the emotional interaction that takes place during group therapy.

The similarity of behavior patterns used in group meetings to those of everyday group relationships is described in a series of discussions throughout the chapter.

Four meetings of this group are presented in greater detail so that the theme and dynamics of each meeting and the therapist's technique in this model of group therapy can be better understood. The detailed meetings presented are the first, 12th, 35th and 68th. Since no tape recordings were made, the content of these meetings is not presented verbatim but consists of notes made by the recorder. Each presentation is so organized that the theme and dynamics of the meeting and the technique of the therapist are shown and discussed concurrently with the members' verbalizations and behavior.

These four meetings are representative of several different aspects of group therapy: the outset, development of group anxiety, manifestations of transference reactions, and the period of mutual analysis. The first, 12th and 35th group meetings are in stage I of group therapy. The 68th meeting is representative of stage III of group therapy. A question often asked by the group therapist trainee is: "How does one start off with a group?" The first meeting of this group describes this situation and illustrates several important aspects of the therapist's technique. Prior to the 10th meeting, members of the group began to refer to each other on a first-name basis. However, for the sake of clarity, the author has retained the last names in the final three meetings as in the present chapter. The 12th meeting illustrates the increase of the members' anxiety and its effect on their group behavior. The 35th meeting finds the transference reactions of the members fully developed, and illustrates several common patterns of behavior that the members use to avoid expressing their feelings: intermember hostility, scapegoating, changing the subject being discussed, and denial. The 68th meeting is an excellent description of a meeting during stage III. Verbal productions and group behavior of the members in the 68th meeting is in sharp contrast to the verbalizations and group behavior in the first, 12th and 35th meetings.

The reader will note that the content of the meetings mainly concerns intragroup behavior and the group process. Naturally, the members brought up many of the problems that they had encountered in their normal group relationships. These outside problems received attention, analysis, and suggestions from the group. Many of these problems are included in the text; however, the summarized meetings primarily deal with the behavior that occurred in the here-and-now of the group meetings.

The index at the end of this chapter lists alphabetically the numerous manifestations of the group's behavior throughout its life of seventy meetings. Group-reality events, anxietal defenses, patterns of behavior and their identification (mutual analysis), group therapist's and recorder's role, scapegoating, acting-out behavior, silence, group absences, sexual feelings, separation anxiety, etc., are tabulated with reference to the specific group meetings at which such behavior occurred. Each group meeting is so organized that the reader may, by consulting the index, refer to a specific type of group behavior, its psychodynamic meaning, and the technique employed by the group therapist.

This outpatient group consisted of four males, four females, a male group therapist and a female recorder. The members were selected from the outpatient clinic of the Emory University Department of Psychiatry. They had applied to the clinic for treatment; five directly (Miss French, Mr. Foy, Mrs. Webster, Mrs. Jacobs, and Mr. Cain) and three indirectly (Mr. Holt's daughter, Mr. Darcy's wife and Mrs. Kitch's husband being already in treatment with other therapists). Each of the latter was recommended for therapy as an adjunct in the overall treatment program for the family members. Two patients (Mr. Smith and Mr. Boler) were added to the group as replacement members at the 42nd meeting. Initially the therapist considered several other people as prospective group members. He was aware that group losses can be expected during the early stages of group therapy and replacements often are necessary. Later they were placed in groups with other therapists, since no group losses occurred during the first 6 months of therapy.

A psychodynamic formulation of each member was accomplished after 2–3 interviews with the group therapist.

DESCRIPTION OF GROUP MEMBERS

Mr. Darcy is a 34-year-old married accountant. He has exhibited passive, dependent traits for a number of years. Intermittent periods of depression and paranoid trends have been evident. He and his wife have had a series of conflicts which centered around finances and sexual matters. Numerous problems have occurred with the disciplining of his children. Mr. Darcy's wife, a schizophrenic, was the initial member of the family seen at the clinic. Mr. Darcy was considered for group therapy at the request of Mrs. Darcy's therapist.

Diagnosis. Passive, dependent personality.

Therapist's Expectations. Improved marital relationships, development of psychological aptitude, improved socialization, decreased dependency needs and improved self-assertion and self-esteem.

Mr. Cain is a 44-year-old separated, unemployed male who has experienced numerous problems involving low self-esteem, inadequacy, and failure of masculine performance. Alcoholic behavior resulted in repeated losses of occupational positions. A series of conflicts have occurred with his wife. His current problems center around low self-esteem, poor sexual response, a power struggle with his wife and his wife's family, and inadequacy as a husband and father.

Diagnosis. Depressive reaction: chronic, moderately severe. Alcohol addiction: chronic, moderately severe.

Therapist's Expectations. Improved marital relationship (group therapy was also advised for wife and accepted by her), development of psychologic aptitude, improved self-assertion and self-esteem, and decreased dependency on alcohol.

Mr. Foy is a 44-year-old married male, a store clerk by occupation. He has had numerous conflicts with his father, brother, and wife over a period of years. Authority problems are pronounced, and numerous fears and inhibitions are present. Depression frequently occurs. His wife is obese, and her numerous hypochondriacal complaints have resulted in a series of surgical procedures. Patient has consulted psychiatrists in the past 10 years without benefit, and he frequently resorts to alcohol.

Diagnosis. Passive, dependent personality. Depressive reaction: chronic, moderately severe. Phobic reaction: chronic, mild.

Therapist's Expectations. Improved marital relationship, development of psychologic aptitude, decreased dependency needs, and improved self-assertion and self-esteem.

Mr. Holt is a 47-year-old widower who runs a small restaurant. He gives a history of chronic alcoholism for approximately 15 years, with abstinence for the past three years. His current problems were precipitated by the death of his wife in July, 1958, from injuries received in an automobile accident. He has three children. He initially came to the clinic at the request of a social worker who was seeing his daughter. He denied problems, but agreed to come to group therapy since his daughter might receive some help from it. He has been quite demanding, overbearing, and extremely strict in his relationship with his 14-year-old daughter. He exhibits pompous and dictatorial mannerisms.

Diagnosis. Obsessive personality. Depressive reaction: chronic, moderately severe. Alcohol addiction: chronic, moderately severe.

Therapist's Expectations. Improved relationship with his daughter, development of psychological aptitude—i.e., an awareness of destructive behavior to his daughter, relief of depression, and decreased dependency on alcohol.

Mrs. Jacobs is a 26-year-old married female who came to the clinic primarily because of numerous phobias. She becomes extremely uncomfortable around people. Anxietal manifestations such as a tightness in the throat, muscular contractions of the stomach, shortness of breath, and generalized body movements occur during these periods of tension and stress. Her recent outbreak of phobic difficulties followed her husband's insistence that they could have no children until her emotional problems had cleared up. The patient's anger and resentment toward her husband, which apparently are repressed and unconscious, have accentuated her phobic manifestations and anxiety.

Diagnosis. Passive, dependent personality. Phobic reaction: chronic, moderately severe.

Therapist's Expectations. Development of psychological aptitude, improved socialization, increased self-assertion and self-esteem, decreased dependency needs and relief of phobic symptoms.

Miss French is a 23-year-old single female. Her occupation is that of library clerk. She initially came to the clinic with complaints of aggressive feelings toward others, marked anger, guilt, suspiciousness, and difficulty in relationships with people. The onset of her illness occurred after the death of her mother four years ago. The present symptomatology became exaggerated and more pronounced after her sister came to visit a few weeks before the initial visit to the clinic. Low self-esteem and feelings of worthlessness were quite evident.

Diagnosis. Schizophrenic reaction, undifferentiated type, chronic, moderately severe.

Therapist's Expectations. Improved reality testing, development of psychological aptitude, socialization, release of impounded rage, improved self-assertion and self-esteem.

Mrs. Webster is a 45-year-old separated female who has complained of depression, phobias, and hypochondriacal symptoms over the past two years. She has had two unsuccessful marriages. Her second husband is an alcoholic. This patient had a severe conflict with her father during childhood. He was extremely dictatorial, strict, and cruel to the patient. Low self-esteem, dependency, phobic manifestations, and depression were outstanding symptoms.

Diagnosis. Obsessive personality. Depressive reaction: chronic, moderately severe. Phobic reaction: chronic, moderately severe.

Therapist's Expectations. Development of psychological aptitude, improved self-assertion and self-esteem, relief from depression and phobic symptoms.

Mrs. Kitch is a 26-year-old married female. Her husband has been classified as a schizophrenic reaction and was in treatment at the clinic. This patient was seen at the request of Mr. Kitch's therapist who felt that group therapy would be beneficial. Innumerable behavior problems have occurred with her and her husband. Recently she experienced phobias in relationship to crowds and people. She always feels insignificant in a group. Problems with low self-esteem, inadequacy, and inferior feelings were quite pronounced.

Diagnosis. Passive dependent personality. Phobic reaction: chronic, mild. Depressive reaction: chronic, mild.

Therapist's Expectations. Development of psychological aptitude, improved marital relationship, improved self-assertion and self-esteem, diminished phobic symptoms and depression.

Mr. Smith and Mr. Boler became members of the group at the 42nd meeting. Both had been members of a group with the group therapist at a state institution.

Mr. Smith is a 30-year-old married machinist who has always felt inadequate and inferior. He had numerous conflicts in childhood with his parents. His father was an unstable individual who never showed any particular interest in him. He married a girl whose family felt Mr. Smith to be below their standards. Feelings of low self-esteem plagued him from the first weeks of his marriage. Repeated authority conflicts resulted in changing occupational patterns. He became overtly psychotic in 1959. He was hospitalized in a private institution, receiving approximately sixty electroconvulsive treatments with minimal improvement. He was subsequently committed to the state hospital in November, 1959, where three months later he was placed in group therapy.

He became an active member of the hospital group and discussed many of his problems including his fears in a group, low self-esteem, inadequacy as a man, and authority conflicts. He was quite perceptive to group processes and, for the degree of illness present, made tremendous gains from the group experience. He became a member of this group after eight months of group therapy at the state hospital.

Diagnosis. Schizophrenic reaction, chronic, undifferentiated type.

Therapist's Expectations. Development of psychological aptitude, improved reality testing, improved socialization, release of impounded rage, and improved self-assertion and self-esteem.

Mr. Boler is a 37-year-old unmarried male newspaper writer who was hospitalized early in 1960 as the result of a year-long depression and two suicide attempts. He has been a homosexual since the age of fourteen, the guilt for which makes him feel despised and rejected by society. Addiction to drugs and alcohol have been present for two years. He has had numerous conflicts with his mother—a fanatical, obsessive-compulsive woman who makes repeated demands on Mr. Boler and who is, at the same time, dependent on him and his brother.

Mr. Boler was placed in the state hospital group six months before entering the present outpatient group. He was extremely active and verbal in the group situation. He discussed many of his conflicts and his need to do something about them. He spoke openly about his sexual problems. Authority problems have always been of concern to him and he began to recognize this to some degree in the group.

Diagnosis. Passive dependent personality. Drug (barbiturates) and alcohol addiction: chronic, moderately severe. Depressive reaction: chronic, moderately severe. Homosexuality.

Therapist's Expectations. Development of psychological aptitude, improved reality testing, improved socialization in group relationships, diminished depression, improved self-assertion and self-esteem, and decreased dependency on drugs and alcohol.

The group therapy program was discussed with each member in the following manner. The therapist outlined the structure of group therapy, its composition, and number of members. He pointed out that all of the members were experiencing emotional problems of one kind or another and that they might benefit from getting together each week at a regular time and place for the next 12 months and helping each other with their problems. He emphasized that many people live so close to their own problems that no awareness of the problems is present; that group therapy can help people develop an awareness of conflicts and problems. The therapist further stated to each member that in a period of time they would see their relationships with each other as similar to those among people in everyday living, and that an understanding of their group relationships could be very helpful in promoting an awareness of, as well as relieving discomfort from, emotional problems that were present.

After the prospective group members indicated interest in group therapy, the therapist explained the group structure and contract in more detail. With each one he pointed out the following features:

1. Goals and purpose of group therapy.
2. Composition of the group; four males and four females.
3. Time, place, and day of group meetings.
4. Length of each group meeting (one hour).
5. Duration of group therapy (12 months).

6. Need for regular attendance.
7. Loss and addition of group members. (If for any reason a group member has to drop out, a new member may be added at the discretion of the therapist.)
8. Absences of the group therapist. (No meetings to be held in the absence of the therapist. Ample notice to be given of planned absences or vacations, etc. In the event of sudden cancellation of a meeting, each member to be notified by letter or telephone. Meetings that fall on holidays will be cancelled.)
9. Recorder's role. (Written notes to be taken of each meeting by an observer or recorder, who would be a member of the department and attend all meetings in a silent, nonparticipating role. The written notes to be utilized for the member's and group therapist's benefit in affording to both a clearer understanding of meetings.)
10. Role of a substitute recorder. (Also a member of the department, to be present at those meetings when the regular recorder cannot be present.)
11. Confidentiality of the group meetings and recorder's written notes within the department.
12. Fees. (To be set for each member in accordance with clinic regulations, the individual fees ranging from $1 to $3 per meeting based on annual income and number of dependents of the members. Monthly statements would be sent out by the clinic secretarial staff.) The therapist did not stress the payment of fees nor did he clarify whether fees were to be charged in certain instances for absences. Later he developed a policy of only charging fees for the meetings attended.
13. Routine yearly physical examinations by family physicians encouraged. (Physical illnesses, etc., should be handled also by their family physician.)
14. Conversations, telephone calls, personal contacts and meetings of group members outside of the regular group meetings to be avoided. (If they occur, their substance should be reported at the next group meeting.)
15. Importance reemphasized of observing and discussing their feelings in the group and helping one another with their emotional problems.

The therapist for this group is a 43-year-old male. He has had 1½ years of experience with groups and was a member of a resident group during his initial year of psychiatric training.

The recorder is a 25-year-old female psychiatric occupational therapist who has had previous experience with groups as a recorder. Reality events forced her to give up recording after the 52nd meeting. During the remaining 18 sessions a 21-year-old female college student and part-time psychiatric aide served as recorder. On three occasions when the regular recorder was absent Dr. N., a male psychiatric resident in the department, served as substitute recorder.

Therapist-recorder discussions were held weekly. The content of the meetings, transference, and countertransference feelings of the members and the therapist, therapist-recorder differences, and group problems were evaluated. Group supervision with the departmental staff was held weekly. This particular group was presented to the staff approximately once a month for discussion, criticism, and evaluation. Material from these meetings (therapist-recorder conferences and group supervisory conferences) are incorporated in each of the seventy sessions under the headings "Theme and Dynamics" and "Technique."

FIRST MEETING

Seven of the eight members were present. Mrs. Webster was out of the city.

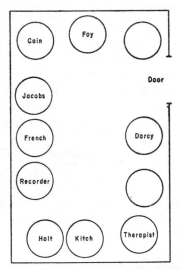

(The members were seated in the room at the time the meeting was due to start. The therapist had arrived fifteen minutes early so that the members would be sure of the meeting place. On arrival the members began introducing themselves. As the therapist and recorder entered the room the members became silent.)

> *Theme and Dynamics. The initial group silence occurs as the therapist and recorder enter the room and sit down.*

Therapist (Greets the members, asks about introductions and then introduces the recorder): I would like to take a few minutes now and review with you all of the arrangements for group therapy. I have discussed these with each one of you individually in the past several weeks. However, I would like to go back over them with you now. (The therapist restates the physical arrangements and structure of the group. He adds:) These arrangements about group therapy are called the group contract. You will hear me refer to it from time to time in future meetings. One other matter for your information. Mrs. Webster was not able to get to this meeting. She will join the group next week.

> *Therapist's Technique. Even though the therapist had discussed the group contract with each member during their individual interviews, he brings it to their attention again as the initial group issue and reviews the salient features embodied in it.*

Mr. Darcy: One more to come.

Mr. Holt (agreeably): That's what he said.

Miss French (anxious): Can we talk about anything—the carpet and the curtains!

Mr. Cain: This is a nice room.

Mr. Holt: I wonder who picked out the curtains.

Miss French: They sure are loud.

> *Theme and Dynamics. Miss French expresses her hostility in metaphorical language. She criticizes the furnishings instead of the group itself.*

Group: (Silence occurs.)

Therapist: You feel the curtains are loud.

> *Therapist's Technique. After a brief silence, the therapist encourages more conversation by repeating the last observation by a member prior to the silence. This is good technique for the first meeting of the group.*

Miss French: I don't like loud colors. Even the carpet here has too much color in it.

Mrs. Jacobs: I'm very interested in painting and decorating.

Mr. Darcy: I'm painting my house now.

Miss French (to Mr. Darcy): Inside or outside. Are you using a brush or a roller?

Mr. Darcy: Both.

Miss French: Did you and your wife have any trouble picking out colors?

Mr. Darcy: No.

> *Theme and Dynamics. The members' conversation with each other is superficial, rapid and polite.*

Mrs. Jacobs (to Miss French): You must like interior decorating. I like this room.

Miss French: I wonder if this furniture is Danish.

Mrs. Jacobs: I've been teaching school up until this year. Now I'm making artificial flowers. (She describes process of making them.)

Miss French: I like artificial roses.

> *Theme and Dynamics. The conversation between the members continues superficial, rapid and pleasant. This is their method of reducing anxiety.*

Mrs. Jacobs: They do look real. I made some of them and others when I was in college in Texas. (Mrs. Jacobs is notably anxious when she is not talking.)

Mrs. Kitch (to Mrs. Jacobs): Did you ever try chrysanthemums?

Mrs. Jacobs: You might have trouble with mums.

Therapist: Well, we've had a lot of conversation about the room, its furnishings and flowers.

> *Theme and Dynamics. The members actually do not know what to do. Some confusion and frustration is to be expected in this new situation.*
>
> *Therapist's Technique. In a general statement the therapist calls to their attention the topics of conversation during the meeting.*

Mr. Holt: It's not the things we're here for.

Mr. Cain: I'm puzzled.

Mrs. Jacobs: I don't know what I'm to do.

Therapist: Well, that's understandable since this is your first meeting. We might talk about how you feel here at this first meeting and your thoughts about group therapy.

> *Theme and Dynamics. The members are concerned about the therapist's role.*
>
> *Therapist's Technique. Therapist supports the members and makes suggestions to them. He is encouraging the members to talk about their feelings in the meeting.*

Mr. Holt: Looks like you [the doctor] will guide us as little as possible.

Mr. Darcy: Group therapy is to get people to express themselves.

Mr. Cain: I have read in the funny papers [comics] about psychiatrists.

Mr. Darcy: That would be something to start with.

Mrs. Kitch: We would have something to laugh at.

Mr. Foy (artificially): Ha! Ha! Ha! Maybe this will interest you. (He passes around a comic joke about a psychiatrist.)

> *Themes and Dynamics. Hostility to psychiatrists is expressed by humor, sarcasm, laughter and the passing around of a comic joke about psychiatrists.*
>
> *Therapist's Technique. The therapist does not focus on Mr. Cain's statement or Mr. Foy's behavior. At this first meeting his technique should primarily be flexible and supportive.*

> *However, he could have said: "You seem concerned about psychiatrists. I'm a psychiatrist. I wonder if you have any thoughts about me in the meeting today." Usual answers from the members in the first few meetings of the group are characterized by denial and ingratiation. Importantly, though, the members are encouraged to think about their feelings toward the therapist. This is one aspect of teaching the members how to do group therapy.*

Mr. Cain: That's an unusual laugh.

Mr. Foy: I haven't felt like laughing for eight years.

Mr. Cain: Laugh clown laugh—laughing on the outside.

Mr. Holt: When I laugh I often feel differently inside.

Mr. Cain: I pretend, too.

Mr. Foy: I always pretend.

Mr. Cain: I could tell a story as sad as anyone.

Mr. Holt: I strongly suspect you are not by yourself.

Miss French: You haven't laughed for eight years. That's all I do is laugh. Even when I get upset I laugh and feel as bad as anybody.

> *Theme and Dynamics. There is general agreement that laughter can be artificial and cover up depression. Miss French discusses her inappropriate laughter.*
> *Therapist's Technique. The therapist could have said, "Several of you indicate that there are different ways to cover up your feelings such as laughter and pretending. As we go along here in the group meetings from week to week I would like to encourage all of you to think about, examine and try to recognize your feelings in yourself and in the others."*

Mrs. Kitch: I did that one time. My mother-in-law fell down and broke her hip. I really laughed.

Miss French: I've laughed at everything everywhere.

Mrs. Kitch (to Miss French): Can you laugh at a joke?

Mr. Holt: Some of us are sad sacks. The public expects you to always be gay and happy.

Miss French: What I want is for people to understand me. Then I can relax and feel more at ease. If I can get one person to understand my day is brighter.

> *Theme and Dynamics. Miss French is really asking for help and understanding from the therapist and the other members.*

Mr. Holt: I guess we are all looking for understanding.

Mrs. Kitch: It's easy to find someone else a miracle.

Mr. Cain (to Mrs. Kitch): Maybe you are looking for a miracle.

Mr. Foy (humorously): I'll take several.

Mr. Cain: As for myself I'd like to get rid of my problem or learn to live with it.

Mr. Foy: So would I, then I could be happy.

Mr. Darcy: Same here.

Mrs. Kitch (to Mr. Foy): You've been sick eight years?

Mr. Foy: Yes, this is my third nervous breakdown. It seems hopeless. This is my last chance—group therapy.

Mr. Holt: Nothing is hopeless.

Miss French (to Mr. Foy): Is your trouble with the past or present?

Mr. Foy: Everything.

Group: (Asks Mr. Foy a series of questions about his illness.)

Mr. Foy: It's nothing physical but related to love and affection. It's a struggle to live. I wish I could start life over, have a new environment.

> ***Theme and Dynamics.*** *Mr. Foy seems anxious to talk about his illness. The members respond to Mr. Foy by asking him many questions about himself and his problems.*
>
> ***Therapist's Technique.*** *A common method that group members employ to relieve anxiety is to enter into long discussions with one member. Their own involvement in the group can be curtailed by involving primarily one person. Then, too, many groups have one or more members that enjoy this kind of role. The therapist should be alert for this kind of group behavior and call it to the attention of the group when it occurs.*

Mr. Holt (to Mr. Foy): I don't know you but it seems to me like you're trying too hard. You're fighting for a state of mind.

Mr. Cain: All of us are looking for something to help us. I know I am.

Miss French: Mr. Foy, what kind of work do you do?

Mr. Foy: I work for my father and brother in a store. (At this point the members began asking each other about their occupations. Mr. Cain said he is unemployed. Miss French is a secretary, Mr. Holt operates a restaurant, Mrs. Kitch and Mrs. Jacobs are housewives, and Mr. Darcy is an accountant. Families are described.)

> ***Theme and Dynamics.*** *The members exhibit interest in each other by enquiring about each other's occupational duties.*

Miss French: I feel different. I'm the only single person in the group."

> ***Theme and Dynamics.*** *Miss French feels isolated and questions the make-up of the group.*

Mr. Holt: I wouldn't think that would make any difference.

Mrs. Kitch: Neither would I.

Mr. Foy: You don't know how lucky you are.

> ***Theme and Dynamics.*** *Mr. Foy indicates marital conflicts.*

Mrs. Jacobs: Marriage is a wonderful thing. My husband and I are so happy. We never have any problems.

Miss French (to Mrs. Jacobs): I'd like to hear more about flowers, how you make artificial flowers.

> *Theme and Dynamics. The subject is changed by Miss French. Therapist's Technique. Changing the subject is a very common way of relieving anxiety in group therapy. The therapist will have numerous opportunities in later meetings to call this type of behavior to their attention.*
>
> *Mrs. Jacobs, who became very uncomfortable, could have been supported if attention had been directed to her by the therapist. He could have accomplished it in the following manner:* "Mrs. Jacobs has been becoming increasingly uncomfortable during the meeting. Do you have any ideas or thoughts about how she feels?" *He might also add:* "Any thoughts that the way she feels is related to this meeting?" *If the patient is very uncomfortable and panicky, the therapist may need to see the member after the meeting is over.*

Mrs. Jacobs (*extremely anxious*): (Describes at length and in considerable detail the process of making flowers. Miss French and Mrs. Kitch ask questions as she talks. The men remain silent. They appear disinterested.)

Therapist: Several of you have mentioned not knowing what to do here in the meeting. You mentioned that group therapy exists in order for you to express how you feel. Maybe we could talk about how you feel here in this first meeting.

Miss French: I don't know how I feel.

> *Theme and Dynamics. Miss French's observation is very true. Many patients do not know what their feelings are.*
>
> *Therapist's Technique. The therapist, aware that the subject has been changed, makes a general supportive statement that encourages them to talk about their feelings in the meeting. The therapist also points out the members' behavior during the group meeting. This is an aspect of his technique that will be employed in the future. In this respect he is teaching them how to respond in the group meetings.*

Mrs. Jacobs: (Looks at the therapist constantly. Her anxiety increases. Muscular contraction of her neck and abdomen are noticeable. She remains silent.)

Mrs. Kitch: I feel alright. I've enjoyed meeting everyone and talking about flowers.

Mr. Holt: This group should be good for me.

> *Theme and Dynamics. The group members continue to be superficial and polite. They deny their feelings in order to have each other's and the therapist's approval.*

Mr. Foy (*resigned*): It's my last chance.

Mr. Cain: I'm looking forward to the group. I want to feel better tomorrow.

Mr. Darcy: We don't know each other yet. The longer we are together the more comfortable we will be. Then it will be easier to talk here.

> *Theme and Dynamics. Mr. Darcy's observation indicates their reservations about talking.*

Mrs. Jacobs (continues to be anxious): If only we had a specific problem to talk about. Can we talk about anything we want to?

Miss French: Maybe we could pick out something to talk about?

> *Theme and Dynamics. The members are requesting a structure for the meeting.*

Mr. Foy: I don't care how I can get help but I need it right now. I'm panicky for help. The curtain is up but I don't know the plot.

Therapist: I wonder if you have any other thoughts about how you feel here today. Mr. Darcy mentioned that when you are more comfortable with each other it will be easier to talk. What about this?

> *Therapist's Technique. The therapist continues his supportive but investigative technique.*

Mrs. Kitch: I haven't found it hard to talk here. I like this group.

> *Theme and Dynamics. Mrs. Kitch, like the other members, denies her real feelings and superficially remains polite and agreeable.*

Therapist: (A silence occurs after Mrs. Kitch's remarks. The therapist then asks the other members directly about their feelings in the meeting.) Mr. Holt, how do you feel?

Mr. Holt: I like this group.

Therapist: Mr. Darcy, any comments?

> *Therapist's Technique. The therapist should not direct or ask a member a question on an individual basis. This technique is group destructive and is comparable to attempting individual therapy in the group. The proper technique is to ask the group, not an individual in the group. In this session he asks each member his feelings about group therapy. He should have said: "What are your feelings about group therapy?" or "How do you feel about this group therapy program?" or "How do you feel here in this initial meeting together?"*

Mr. Darcy: I've enjoyed today.

Therapist: Mrs. Jacobs, any thoughts about today?

Mrs. Jacobs (very anxious, uncomfortable): No.

> *Theme and Dynamics. The members' feelings about the therapist are already evident in the first meeting. Their expressions of denial to the therapist are more pronounced than their expressions to each other. By denying their anxiety and hostile feelings, they are hoping to get approval and acceptance from the therapist.*

Therapist: Miss French?

Miss French: I agree with Mr. Darcy. Later on we can talk better.

Therapist: Mr. Cain?

Mr. Cain: I'm looking forward to the next meeting.

Therapist: Mr. Foy?

Mr. Foy: Group therapy is my last hope.

Therapist: Well, time's up for today. May I take a minute and point out several things to you. You are a new group of people together. I'm sure you've had many thoughts and feelings in this first meeting about each other and about me. May I remind you of an earlier statement by one of you. Group therapy is for the expression of feelings. (As the members begin to leave the therapist says to Mrs. Jacobs:) I would like to see you for a few minutes.

> *Therapist's Technique. The therapist supports the members and makes a brief summary. Generally, a summary at the end of a group meeting is not necessary. However, in this instance the therapist's closing remarks are in order. For several meetings he should encourage the members' acceptance of each other and himself. His technique should continue to be group oriented and gradually more investigative of patterns of behavior exhibited in the group meetings.*
>
> *The therapist is concerned about Mrs. Jacobs' anxiety. He talks with her after the meeting. She is advised to report this conference at the next group meeting. Individual interviews with patients are sometimes necessary. However, in all instances, the therapist's contact with a member should be brought to the others at the next meeting for discussion.*

SUMMARY

Theme and Dynamics

This meeting shows a group of people together for the first time. They were preoccupied with their expectations from each other and from the therapist. They had fears of many kinds and they utilized individual defenses to isolate themselves. A common reaction was to become hostile, as the schizophrenic patient (Miss French) did when she attacked the therapist by criticizing the rug and other fixtures. Another defensive attitude was exhibited by the patient who circulated the joke about psychiatrists. The phobic patient became quite anxious and tense. Others handled their anxiety by talking rapidly, discussing superficial topics, and changing the subject.

Technique

The therapist was aware that because this was a group of people together for the first time, their behavior would be superficial, polite, and pleasant. The therapist's observations to the members were supportive, general, and group-oriented, except in one instance near the end of the meeting, when he directed questions to individuals in the group rather than to the group as a whole.

During the early meetings the therapist should emphasize at every opportunity his expectations of the members. In this respect the therapist's technique helps to teach the members how to interact with each other and with himself. He can expect the members to experience confusion and frustration as they come to realize that their expectations from group therapy differ from the therapist's. In this initial meeting the members talked about being puzzled and confused. The therapist's observations were appropriate and helpful for the members. However, in future meetings, the member's emotional reactions to the therapist's role will require careful management, for the members' confusion, frustration, and unrealistic expectations from group therapy and the therapist account for much of their initial hostility toward him.

In the author's experience with groups of neurotic patients, rapid conversation, superficiality, and the discussion of numerous and variable topics in the initial group meetings (1–5) is much more common than group silence. Often the members' conversation in meetings is so rapid that therapists say they cannot break into the discussions, and recorders complain that they cannot get the conversation written down.

Discussion

Several references have been already made to the superficial conversation in this group meeting. Superficial conversation is extremely common among people in their everyday group relationships. Our society and culture is not based on the frank expression of feelings. People do not go about telling everyone their real thoughts and feelings. The inclination to express true feelings depends on the degree of closeness in the group. Superficial conversation in casual relationships (social, recreational, and similar groups) is accepted behavior, reaching its ultimate in the cocktail party. Superficial conversation among members of the family, with fellow employees on the job, and with others who are frequently in close relationship with us can be a definite handicap. Superficial conversation in such situations creates anxiety and tension that may result in emotional conflict, physical symptoms, or other disturbed behavior. The wife who cannot get beyond superficial conversation with her husband may develop a migraine headache or other symptoms. The industrial worker who cannot talk about serious matters to his boss may develop fatigue and lassitude; his productivity may fall off and he may become accident-prone. The high-school basketball team that cannot get beyond superficial conversation with its coach may turn in poor performances.

From the standpoint of psychodynamics, superficial conversation may stem from many causes. A dominating, controlling, and angry husband may so overpower his wife and children that fear and dread of him inhibit discussing any subject that is likely to cause controversy. A passive, nonassertive husband may react to his wife with resignation, submission, and ingratiating behavior because he is afraid to release his pent-up feelings of rage. The leader of an industrial or professional group may not tolerate frank expression of opinion or ideas from his subordinates, demanding instead their complete allegiance. A member of such a group may be so fearful of authority figures that he is unable to relate to them except on a superficial level.

In other instances superficial conversation is used by people to avoid guilt and rejection. People are afraid to express their true thoughts because they might "hurt the feelings" of others. Friendships are based primarily on positive attitudes. Disagreements are avoided, for when they occur the friendship is impaired.

The early meetings of groups are characterized by superficial conversation between the group members. Politeness and friendliness are very noticeable. Each group member will appear at his best and try to impress and gain the approval of the therapist and the other group members.

SECOND MEETING

Seven members were present. Mrs. Webster remained out of town. Mr. Foy dominated the initial half of the meeting by discussing his own problems, seeming to enjoy the attention from the others. Mrs. Jacobs spoke of her phobic difficulties. Mr. Holt related details of his wife's death, conflicts with his children, and his alcoholic problems. Once when members mentioned group therapy the therapist asked about feelings in the meeting. Mr. Foy again spoke of needing magic and stated that he would never be able to discuss his real problems before a group of people. Mr. Holt said group therapy meant the development of more friends. Mrs. Kitch enumerated positive feelings about the group. She felt it helped to know that others had similar problems. Toward the end of the hour the therapist called the group's attention to the absent member. No significant feelings were expressed.

Theme and Dynamics

The members appeared more relaxed and comfortable with each other. Several spoke in more detail of their emotional problems. They immediately recognized Mr. Foy's wish for a magical solution. Fears of discussing problems before other people were voiced.

Technique

Therapist correctly asked about group feelings after a reference to group therapy. Group feelings and group relationships mean the feelings and reactions occurring in the group meeting between the group members and the therapist.

Therapist appeared to be inactive. This was not necessarily in error. He allowed the members to become better acquainted with one another at this early meeting.

He properly focused upon the absence of a member. Even though she had not been present at any meeting he asked for the group's feelings about her. He focused on the group. (He will continue to utilize this method in a number of different ways. He is promoting group feeling and interaction; during these early meetings, of course, he is teaching the members to look at and examine their feelings with one another.)

Absences were very diligently pursued by the therapist throughout the life of the group. A telephone call to the absentee was made within forty-eight hours after the meeting, advising him that the group missed him and hoped he would come to the next meeting.

All the group members have fears of talking about themselves in a group of people. They often express these fears as early as their interviews with the therapist before starting group therapy. During the early meetings of the group the therapist should utilize every opportunity to encourage ventilation of these fears. When Mr. Foy stated that he would never be able to discuss his problems before others, the therapist might have made the following observation: "Mr. Foy mentions fears of talking in front of a group of people. I wonder if others of you have experienced similar fears?" The therapist could also say: "What are you fearful of?" "Have you ever experienced these fears of talking before others in other groups—for example, at home or at work?" Ventilation of their fears provides an early common bond of interest among the group members.

THIRD MEETING

There were six members present. Mr. Cain and Mrs. Webster were absent. The members seemed more comfortable with one another and spoke of their conflicts and illnesses in greater detail. Mr. Holt, who had been somewhat pompous and intellectual in the previous sessions, sat immediately to the left of the therapist and acted the part of the therapist by directing statements to the other members, making interpretations, and intellectualizing. He asked for longer meetings. Mr. Foy experienced a severe headache that he felt was connected with his illness. He held his head in his hands most of the hour. Once he left the room, returning after a five-minute absence. Mrs. Jacobs spoke of her discomfort in the meeting. Mr. Darcy mentioned a feeling of numbness in his arm associated with the tension that had occurred in the meeting. The therapist made the following observation after the elaboration of physical symptoms by the above group members: "Mr. Foy speaks of a headache, Mr. Darcy of a numbness in his arm, Mrs. Jacobs of increasing discomfort. All of these symptoms are taking place here in the meeting. What are your thoughts about these symptoms occurring during the meeting?" No comment of any significance was made.

Theme and Dynamics

The relationship of the members to one another had improved and a certain number of them spoke in more detail of problems with families and others. This is a testing procedure that group members employ; in this group it began at the second meeting. When one member speaks of various aspects of his illness without being censured, others receive encouragement to do likewise. The anxiety of the group was clearly illustrated by the physical symptoms of the three members and by Mr. Holt, who tried to usurp the role of therapist.

Relating experiences in this new group relationship that have occurred within their other group relationships serves a useful purpose in the early group meetings. Even though these experiences are superficial ones, the group members find some common bonds of interest with each other. Their fears of being exposed and embarrassed before the other members and the therapist are thus diminished.

Technique

The therapist should have dealt directly with Mr. Holt, who was assuming the role of substitute therapist, thereby competing with the group therapist. This role is his defense against the anxiety created by the group process. One of the purposes of group therapy is for the group members to identify these defenses. The therapist should utilize every opportunity to do so. After Mr. Holt's behavior was clearly understood the therapist could have said: "Mr. Holt has been making a number of observations and questions, and has also suggested longer meetings—as though he were running the meeting himself today. Do you have any thoughts about this?" Besides bringing his behavior to their attention, the therapist can also support the individual member by saying: "Do you have any idea why it is necessary for him to exhibit this role here in the meeting?" At the third meeting one might question whether Mr. Holt was ready for the observations suggested above. The psychodynamics of the group member must be considered. In an extremely sick group, where psychoses have been prominent, the therapist has to play the situation "by ear." However, pointing out reality to a psychotic person is generally advantageous.

The therapist correctly correlated the physical symptoms of the three members to the group process. Even though the therapist's question was not dealt with at this meeting, the members were aware of his statement and would give it additional thought.

The therapist should have called their attention to Mr. Foy's behavior. He could have done this in the following manner: "Mr. Foy has spoken of a severe headache, he has held his head in his hands and been rather quiet during the hour, finally having to leave the room for a short period of time. What are your thoughts about this?" The therapist might also add: "Any ideas that this behavior of Mr. Foy's is related to the meeting in any way?"

Discussion

Mr. Holt's competition with the therapist in the meeting focuses on a common behavior pattern utilized in everyday groups. Competitive types encountered in groups range from the dull, apathetic, unmotivated person with no competitive drive to the obsessively competitive, highly motivated person. Healthy, mature people compete with others in an understanding atmosphere. The athlete who competes against others in sports events and the member of a debating team who competes against his opponent are working in an accepted structure. Competitiveness can also be destructive in group relationships. For example, two nurses competing for the role of assistant chief nurse of a ward become very competitive, find fault with each other, and attempt to divide the ward staff into two camps. Similar situations may occur in corporations, the business and professional worlds, and other groups in all cultural levels.

In our society, women are developing competitiveness and masculine strivings as they assume increasing prominence in the business and professional worlds. The cultural and economic factors in the changing role of women are very apparent. The employment of women in defense jobs during World War II served as an impetus to the further emancipation of women from the home. Economic stress during the past ten years has increased the number of working wives. Today there are more women in political, business, and professional roles than at any time in the history of this country.

Competitiveness may also be utilized as a defense against anxiety, or as overcompensation for feelings of inadequacy, low self-esteem, insecurity, and dependency. The individual who constantly interrupts during conversations, the professional man who engages in endless maneuvers to outwit his superior, and the person who meets social or business defeat with anger and defiance are examples of competitiveness in our society.

Competition, rivalry, and jealousy occur among children of all families. The competitive child is a healthy child. He will need competitive drives when he grows into adulthood and seeks his place in society. However, competition to the child may have other meanings. Parents may place their entire emphasis on competitiveness, showing love and approval only for the child who "succeeds" through competition. When there are several children in the family, competitiveness and sibling rivalry may be very intense. Such children in adult life may feel adequate, secure, and accepted by others only when they are successful in attaining competitive goals. Failure to obtain these goals may bring on anxiety and depression. The specific meaning of competition, rivalry, and jealousy to each person will depend on parental attitudes, family interaction, other authority influences in schools and churches, and on the economic, social, and broad cultural factors of later life.

FOURTH MEETING

All eight members were present. The essential material from this session was a statement early in the hour about the relative freedom of conversation experienced by four of the members when they rode to town together after each meeting. This statement was made by Mr. Holt, who had been exhibiting increasing hostility to the therapist at each meeting. The therapist immediately recognized the significance of his remarks and said: "You have made a comparison between this meeting and another meeting which you find more comfortable than this one. What thoughts do you have about this?" Several members immediately recognized the difference between the two meetings and discouraged such happening again. Miss French felt the therapist was a stabilizer. Mrs. Kitch and Mr. Darcy referred to the therapist as a strict school teacher. Mr. Foy said: "There is no doctor in the car, like there is here." The therapist then said: "Apparently you have some feelings about me here if you have mentioned a freedom of conversation without me and made a reference to my being a strict school teacher and a stabilizer." They responded by saying they needed a doctor and needed to be warm to each other even though they felt strange in the meeting. Mr. Holt, who made the initial statement, replied in a hostile tone that he guessed a larger station wagon would be in order. Mrs. Webster, who was attending the group for the first time, felt this problem could be solved if the doctor would provide an outline for each meeting. Mrs. Webster was treated with silence during most of the meeting. She had been introduced to the others by the therapist at the outset of the meeting. Only a few superficial questions were asked of her. She did not participate in the discussion to any degree. At the end of the hour the therapist reminded the members of that part of the group contract concerning outside contracts between the members.

Theme and Dynamics

The theme of this meeting revolved around feelings about the therapist. Intragroup and group-to-therapist anxiety is increasing. One member wanted a set of directions. Others saw the therapist as a stabilizer and a strict school teacher. They are wondering what the doctor will do and how he will act. The recognition of the therapist as an authority figure is more apparent from the outside meeting. The group picked up the fact that this outside meeting was disruptive. The riding together as a subgroup stopped following this session.

Technique

The therapist correctly handled the outside group meeting by immediately making it a group issue. He is encouraging them to examine their feelings about him.

At intervals throughout the length of group therapy the therapist makes similar references to the group contract. By so doing, he recalls to the group members the contractual arrangements of group therapy. The group contract was discussed with each member before the beginning of group therapy and reviewed with them at the first meeting. The group contract is an integral part of the dynamics of the group process. The therapist should utilize every opportunity to explore the various parts of the group contract with the group members and relate it to the dynamics of the group process.

The formation of subgroups outside of the regular meeting should be discouraged by the therapist at every opportunity. It is not unusual for these meetings to occur early in group therapy. The members want to have meetings without the therapist because they are more comfortable and at ease in his absence. On rare occasions a man and woman will meet clandestinely, if one or the other has conflicts with his mate, and engage in sexual acting out. All such happenings are group-destructive and have to be dealt with by the group. The therapist has to be alert for such occurrences and make group issues of them immediately. He has at his disposal the contractual arrangements with reference to outside contacts between members.

The therapist's phrasing of his statement with reference to the difference of feelings in the meeting and on the outside points out an important feature in his technique. The primary goals of group therapy are to promote group interaction, to encourage the examination and understanding of emotional reactions in the meeting, and to develop mutual cooperation among the members. The emotional interchange between the members and the therapist will be enhanced if the therapist makes his observations or questions to the members in words, phrases, or sentences that are more personal in context. For example, such statements as: "What's going on in the group?", "How does the group feel?", "What are the group's reactions?", etc., can be phrased in a different way that still imparts the same meaning but has an increased emotional content for the members. "How do you feel?" versus "How does the group feel?," "How does this affect you?" versus "How does this affect the group?", "What is your feeling?" versus "What is the feeling of the group?", and "What are your reactions?" versus "What are the group's reactions?" illustrate how the personal pronouns "you" and "your" indicate a more intense emotional feeling than the noun "group." Similarly, the therapist, when referring to himself, indicates to the group members' more personal feeling by saying: "I" and "me" rather than "group leader" or "group therapist."

Another cue the therapist could have used to advantage was the reference to needing a structure (outline or plan). He could have said: "Now, Mrs. Webster feels that this problem could be solved by having an outline to go by during the meeting." He might also have added: "How would an outline solve the problems here?" The therapist should have made other observations that would have kept the members looking at their feelings about him. He could have repeated earlier statements and asked for additional feelings. The members might or might not deal with them at this stage of group therapy. However, the members were aware that the therapist was asking them to do so. In later meetings, as they become more comfortable with the therapist, they will talk more freely and openly if the therapist continues to ask them to look at their feelings toward him. Accurate appraisal of the group anxiety level is extremely important. It is not uncommon during the early stages for the anxiety level to rise to a threatening height when feelings about the therapist are explored. Group silence and other nonverbal manifestations may occur. Here the therapist must determine whether to go forward or retreat. If the anxiety level is extremely high, he can change the subject to a less threatening one, or talk to the group for a minute or so; in later meetings he will again pursue this important area with the members.

The therapist should have supported Mrs. Webster. They exhibited a kind of silent hostility toward her. He could have pointed out to them that Mrs. Webster had not been able to attend previous meetings. Now that she had come, their thoughts about her feelings at her first meeting contrasted with their own present feelings could have been a focal point. He might have said: "How do you think Mrs. Webster feels here at her first meeting?" By encouraging the members to examine and verbalize their feelings the problem of her acceptance and understanding would be more easily accomplished.

FIFTH MEETING

Only seven members were present, Mr. Darcy being absent. As the meeting got under way, the members began learning each others' first names and used them during the remainder of the hour. Mrs. Jacobs again discussed her uncomfortable feelings in the meeting and received warm support. The therapist asked about group feelings by saying: "Mrs. Jacobs has talked about her uneasiness here. I wonder how the rest of you feel here in this meeting?" Mr. Foy disclosed how suspicious he was of everyone in the room. Mrs. Kitch was sure one of the patients was really an instructor, "planted" in the meeting to observe the others. Several members then began airing their trepidation about going to a psychiatrist because he might ridicule or belittle them. The therapist focused on their feelings by reflecting this subject back to them. He asked for other reactions on going to a psychiatrist. Mrs. Jacobs said that people in her age group "looked down" on anyone who consulted a psychiatrist. Mrs. Kitch referred to her mother-in-law's belligerent attitude toward anyone who visited a psychiatrist.

Theme and Dynamics

The using of first names by the group members is an increasingly positive sign of closeness. The theme of the meeting continues to relate to the members' attitudes toward the therapist. They discussed the stigma of visiting a psychiatrist. Several members mentioned some of their suspicions in the group meeting.

Technique

The therapist correctly asked about their feelings toward one another following the members' admission of being "uncomfortable."

The therapist encouraged the group to discuss their feelings about consulting a psychiatrist. This reaction is a universal phenomenon and assumes the same importance in group therapy as with the patient in individual therapy.

The author has observed a number of interesting features about the group members' feelings about the use of first and last names. Names that group members use for each other have a relationship to the dynamics of group therapy.

Generally, during group therapy meetings the members eventually begin to use first names with each other. This may occur during the initial meetings of the group (5–15 meetings) or at a later time (30–45 meetings). If it occurs during early meetings, there are no appreciable issues raised by the members. They usually find out each other's first names and relate to each other in this manner thereafter. However, if the issue of names comes up after transference reactions have developed, the members react quite differently. At this point the members want the therapist's approval at all costs. Since the therapist repeatedly addresses the members as "Mr. Smith," "Miss Jones," or "Mrs. Rogers," the members often feel that the therapist wants them to address each other in a similar manner.

Another factor influences their feelings if this issue of names comes up after transference reactions have developed—closeness. Members have said that the use of first names means getting closer to each other, getting to know each other better, and finding out other things about each other. The members will recognize that closeness can be avoided by the use of last names.

Members will often debate this point and will frequently ask the therapist to make the decision for them. Since they want his approval, his decision would reduce their anxiety and solve the matter. The therapist should not, however, make the decision for them. In fact, if he does make the decision, he finds later that while some group members have agreed with him, others have not, so that actually his decision was of no benefit. The therapist should explore the issue with the members and work towards the recognition of their needs for his approval; the relationship of names to closeness; the members' feelings towards him for promoting closeness within the group; and the members' inability to make decisions.

Discussion

The member who spoke of being suspicious of others illustrates a personality characteristic that is much more prevalent throughout our society than is generally known. Suspiciousness ranges from occasional thoughts that others are talking about you to the constant suspiciousness of the paranoid personality. Minimal suspiciousness is rather widespread in the population. Often an individual is suspicious when he sees several people talking together. He wonders if he is the subject of their conversation. Similar thoughts may be entertained in many other areas of group behavior. The person who is mildly depressed has more suspicious thoughts. As the depression recedes, so does the suspiciousness. With normal people there is no endless preoccupation with suspicious thoughts —they are fleeting and soon forgotten.

Group members usually discuss the stigma of mental illness early in group therapy. The sense of shame, fear and guilt associated with mental illness can be traced far back in our history. Early settlers in America believed that people with mental illness were possessed by demons or witches, hence evil and to be avoided at all costs. The witch trials in Salem, Mass., in the seventeenth century were an example of distorted public feeling about emotionally disturbed people. Down through the centuries to the present day this attitude toward mental illness has continued, although considerably modified by knowledge and experience. However, patients who visit psychiatrists still speak of the stigma of emotional illness. Many are secretive with their friends and neighbors about their trips to the psychiatrist's office. Psychiatrists cannot avoid the fact that their patients experience this sense of shame in seeking treatment.

Patients committed to a state hospital suffer more than others from the undeserved opprobrium of mental illness. The generally poor condition of the state hospitals in this country as compared to other hospitals (medical and surgical) is a testimony to public apathy and ignorance about mental illness and its treatment.

Moreover, some religious groups believe that emotional illness is due to sin and guilt and can be relieved only by religious experience, faithful church attendance, and prayer. It is not unusual for patients to seek help for disturbing problems through religion. Religious groups with such attitudes unintentionally reinforce the stigma attached to emotional illness.

Besides religious groups there are others who consider emotional conflict and illness a sign of personal weakness. Such groups feel that people who are emotionally ill can "pull themselves up by their bootstraps" or solve their difficulties if they really care to do so. Their lack of knowledge of the causes of mental illness also helps perpetuate the stigma.

SIXTH MEETING

Two members were absent, Mrs. Jacobs and Mr. Cain. The meeting began with several members discussing employers, bosses, husbands, and other authority figures who are dominating, unsympathetic, and strict. The therapist then said: "You have been talking about employers, bosses, and husbands who you feel are dominating and strict. I wonder if you have any thoughts about your discussion and its relationship to this meeting?" Two members replied that they didn't know what the group was. Mrs. Kitch couldn't separate individuals from the group. Mr. Holt couldn't see any correlation between the therapist's statement and the group. The subject was changed quickly. Even though the therapist referred to this statement later in the meeting, the group would not deal with it to any degree. Mrs. Webster had become more active and often asked questions of others but had never revealed anything about herself. She was directly questioned about this by Miss French, who stated that Mrs. Webster was always interested in others, but that she "had a barrier in front of herself." The group encouraged Mrs. Webster to talk. She verbalized a number of her problems following a separation from her husband. The two absent members were discussed by the group. The therapist asked for their feelings on the absences and the effect they had on the meeting. Mr. Darcy wondered if Mr. Cain's feelings were hurt at the last meeting. The other absence (Mrs. Jacobs) was held to be due to reality issues and not her discomfort in the group. Approximately half way through the meeting the therapist made this observation: "Mr. Holt seems to be depressed and has not participated in the meeting." The group began asking Mr. Holt questions. He began to talk more freely and discussed a recent problem which had resulted in some depression. Mrs. Kitch reminded him that the group was the place to talk about such things.

Theme and Dynamics

The theme of this meeting continued to center around the group's feelings about the therapist. The members feel he is dominating and strict, yet at the same time they want him to tell them what to do. The members denied any group feelings and spoke about being unable to separate individuals from the group. In a sense they are correct, since the group is only six weeks old. As yet they have not sacrificed individual wishes and desires for the group. Each member would like to have individual attention and treatment from the therapist if at all possible. A female member recognized and focused upon the stand-off attitude of another member by commenting that she had "a barrier in front of herself." This is a good example of how members will recognize and deal with the defenses of others. It is not necessary for the therapist to do it. They will make their own interpretations. This is mutual analysis.

Technique

The therapist could have been more direct in his statement to the group regarding employers, bosses, etc., by also reminding the group that in a previous meeting they had referred to him as a "strict school teacher." Any material that has been brought out in previous meetings can be utilized by the therapist to promote and foster the group process.

The therapist correctly dealt with group absences by asking for the members' feelings about them. He should have called these to their attention if not mentioned by a group member.

The individual behavior of a quiet and depressed member was recognized and pointed out to the group. The therapist needs to assess all behavior within the group, and, in his role, ask the group to examine it.

SEVENTH MEETING

There were only six members present, Mrs. Webster and Mrs. Jacobs being absent. The therapist and group members have noticed that the absence of these two members is assuming a somewhat regular pattern. The meeting of the previous week had been cancelled by the therapist on short notice because of illness in his family that necessitated an out-of-town trip. The meeting began with reference to this illness. The therapist dealt with the cancelled meeting by making the following observation: "Regardless of the reason for not meeting, how do you feel about my cancelling the meeting?" General disappointment was voiced; the cancelled meeting slowed up the group and retarded the "getting acquainted" process. Mr. Foy, who often demands magic, felt that the group was all he had to hang on to and wanted to double the time of the meeting. Miss French expressed ambivalent feelings. Mr. Holt wanted the meetings to go on without the therapist. He suggested the recorder could take charge. Mrs. Kitch wondered if another doctor couldn't be there when the therapist was absent. Others rejected her statement. Mr. Darcy wanted the doctor to do more in the meetings. Miss French retorted by asking Mr. Darcy how he would ever get anything out of the group if he didn't do it himself. The subject of absent members was brought up by Mr. Cain, who had not been present at the previous meeting. He wondered why the therapist asked for group feelings relating to absences. He couldn't understand it; his own feelings were individual ones. He asked the group how they felt about absences. Mrs. Kitch was very emphatic in stating that she had definite feelings about people who were absent. Four of the group members expressed disappointment in his absence and spoke of it being the group's loss. They really missed him.

Theme and Dynamics

Not only does this group have absences among the members, but it must also contend with the absence of the therapist. They had many angry feelings about his cancelling the meeting, regardless of the reason. Their dependence on the group was expressed in wanting longer meetings and a substitute therapist. The group's analysis of one member's absence demonstrated a certain degree of intragroup unity and interest in the members' attendance at the meetings. The interpretation by one member to the effect that "you have to help yourself rather than use an outline" was quite accurate.

Technique

The therapist correctly asked about cancelled meetings, but could have brought it to the group's attention again for exploration of additional feelings.

By relating absences to the group for examination, a group response was received and evidences of group feelings expressed.

Mrs. Kitch's anger over absences could have been explored in more detail. The therapist could have said: "Mrs. Kitch seems to have quite strong feelings about people who are absent. Any ideas why she feels this way?"

The group therapist should be very cautious about cancelling meetings during the first two months of group therapy. As we have previously pointed out, a cancelled meeting during this interval may have a disastrous effect on the group members; in outpatient groups of psychotic patients, disintegration may take place and many of the group members may stop group therapy. Although in this instance the therapist's absence was unavoidable, it is very important at this particular period of group therapy for the group to hold its meeting. The therapist should have contacted his recorder and allowed her to meet with the group. Problems with technique may be encountered by the recorder, but it is more important that the group meeting occurs. After two months of group therapy, cancelled meetings do not carry the serious import of group dissolution and can be managed without great difficulty.

Discussion

Although the main discussion of group structure and behavior is in Chap. 2, several features of group phenomena are reemphasized here to compare the behavior of patients in group therapy with the everyday behavior of people in our culture. For example, absences from group meetings occur because of reality situations, physical illness and emotional reactions due to increased group anxiety. Absences from group meetings can be compared to absenteeism in industry and other related institutions. Reality situations and physical illness account for many absences from work. However, a staggering amount of lost time from work is due to psychogenic factors. Conflicts in day-to-day group relationships (family group and occupational groups) may lead to difficulties and problems. Close relationships between people in a group increases the anxiety of its members. There is more closeness in the family group than any other group. However, industrial, professional, and other occupational groups have more closeness than social, recreational, and religious groups. Industrial and occupational groups rank second to the family group in the amount of closeness among its members. The industrial leader of a group of workers is an authority figure to them. The workers react to him as they have to authority figures in their previous life experience. Each worker has a personality structure and behavior patterns that determine how he will react to his peers and authority figures. Similar in some respects to the members in group therapy, an industrial group spends hours together with their leader or boss performing certain tasks. Their mutual relationships grow more personal with the passage of time. As is true in all groups that are together for many months or years, emotional feelings and reactions become apparent between the members of the group and the leader or authority figure. The industrial leader's personality structure and behavior patterns are the most important factors in the degree of anxiety of the workers, as are those of parents in the family group, and those of the therapist in group therapy. The dominating, controlling, and angry industrial leader who runs rough-shod over his workers, demands complete submission from them, and doesn't allow them to express their feelings can expect to have a high anxiety level among the workers. With one worker tardiness and absenteeism may occur, another may develop weakness and lassitude, and a third may get angry and quit. Since the emotional tension has not been relieved and cannot be expressed to the leader, bickering and irritation between the workers occur. The workers may choose a scapegoat and unleash their feelings on him. It is not unusual for the workers to carry their feelings home and unload them on their wives and children.

A different situation occurs with the industrial leader who is firm and authoritative, but at the same time understanding. He has a ready ear for their complaints and allows the workers to express their feelings. He accepts hostility, criticism, and advice in a constructive atmosphere. Needless to say, the anxiety of his workers will be markedly less than in the previous group. The entire group will be happier. There will be greater production and less tardiness and absenteeism.

The industrial groups described above are representative of all types of groups throughout this country. Similar situations exist with the Board of Directors and their Chairman in a large bank, corporation, etc., as well as with the straw boss and his work crew on a highway construction project.

EIGHTH MEETING

All members were present. The therapist felt that the anxiety level was quite high at the outset of the meeting. Mrs. Jacobs and Mrs. Webster arrived a few minutes late. Group feelings about their previous absences and lateness were focused on by the therapist but no significant discussion resulted. Mrs. Jacobs brought along a knitting bag and began knitting during the early part of the hour. This was brought to the group's attention by the therapist, who said: "Mrs. Jacobs feels the need to knit during the meeting. Any thoughts about this?" The group was supportive to her. During the first thirty minutes of the meeting there were four topics brought up, as well as two short periods of silence. The therapist brought this to their attention by saying: "You have talked about four different matters today and you have had two periods of silence. Any thoughts about what is going on here in the meeting?" Several members replied that they didn't know what to say. Miss French felt that everyone was fumbling. Mrs. Webster made a second request for the doctor to provide an outline for the meetings. Mr. Foy changed the subject and talked about his feelings of defeat. There followed a group attack on Mr. Foy for his role of being sicker and having more problems than anyone else. The cancelled meeting was mentioned by two members. The therapist explored their feelings again. Several members still wanted meetings without the doctor when he was absent, but the others disagreed. Mr. Darcy wondered if group therapy was some kind of experiment. Mrs. Jacobs and Mr. Holt made the observation that the doctor did not say anything. The anxiety level remained high throughout the meeting. The therapist remarked to the recorder following the completion of the hour that it was a difficult meeting for him. He was aware of the anxiety and hostility directed toward him.

Theme and Dynamics

The group is becoming increasingly hostile to the therapist. Even though there are definite evidences of intramember hostility about absences and tardiness, they exhibited a united front toward the therapist by ignoring his remarks. For example, they refused to deal with feelings about absences and Mrs. Jacobs' knitting. They would not look at group relationships, but would only say they didn't know or that they were fumbling. Mr. Foy was scapegoated to a degree. The group displaced hostility intended primarily for the therapist on a member (Mr. Foy) when he gave them an opportunity. They called group therapy some kind of experiment. Several were concerned about the inactivity of the therapist.

When any group of people are confined together for a period of time, feelings come to the surface. These group members have now been together for eight meetings or a period of two months. The members' original goals of group therapy have been thrust aside by their involvement in the emotional interaction within the group. Intragroup tension is increasing. Already there are many evidences of the group members' avoiding close relationships with each other. Their fears of expressing themselves too freely have been verbalized. The anxiety level is increasing and hostility is being used as a defense against closeness within the group.

The increase in the group members' anxiety illustrates some characteristics of their emotional behavior in a group. The group interaction has stimulated their reactions in old areas of conflict and anxiety which have in the past produced discomfort and disturbances in their everyday group relationships. In the meetings to date we have observed that the group interaction has stimulated emotional behavior that is only under partial or semivoluntary control. Mrs. Jacobs' conduct in the meetings is an excellent example of such behavior. She has spoken several times of being much more uncomfortable in the meetings than in the situations outside of group therapy. Then, too, Mrs. Jacobs' numerous body movements in other meetings are beyond her conscious control. She is not able to hold back unacceptable and uncomfortable impulses. The therapist has purposely created this situation by his technique, and over the coming months of group therapy he will gradually work toward an identification and understanding of the group members' anxieties.

Technique

It is well to remember that as the group process goes forward, hostility serves as the primary defense against closeness and group involvement. The therapist is the authority figure bringing these feelings to the surface. The group process is anxiety-provoking. It is a touchy situation and probably one of the most difficult periods for the therapist.

From the standpoint of technique, the therapist must encourage the ventilation and understanding of their feelings toward him. At the same time he has to assess his own defenses and methods of handling anxiety from the group. Here again the recorder can be of valuable service.

In the eighth meeting the therapist was aware of the increased anxiety at the beginning of the hour.

He properly asked about absences and latenesses but was ignored by the members.

He remarked on the knitting done by one member but found her supported by the group. The therapist's observation concerning changing the subject and silences could have been spelled out to the members in clearer language. He could have said: "Now let me make an observation. First, let me remind you of our contract. You are here to look at your feelings with one another and with me, and to examine how you react with others. Today you have talked about four different matters and two periods of silence have occurred. I wonder if you have any ideas as to why the subject was changed so much and why silences occurred during the meeting."

He should have prevented the group attack (scapegoating) on Mr. Foy. He could have done this in the following manner: "Now, hold up a minute. Most of you are giving Mr. Foy a rather rough time. Any ideas why you are doing this?" He might also have pointed out again the silences and variety of subjects discussed, adding that the attack on Mr. Foy occurred soon after the therapist's statement. He could have focused on himself more directly by exploring again their feelings about: (1) cancellation of a previous meeting, (2) group therapy being some sort of experimental procedure and (3) inactivity of the therapist during the meeting.

Mrs. Webster's request that the therapist provide an outline or structure for the group meeting is one that is frequently made by group members in early meetings. An outline or a structure of the group meeting would limit the emotional interaction between the members and decrease their anxiety. The anxiety in the meetings is increasing. If the therapist would take over and deliver a lecture on mental health, or suggest to the group members that they prepare outside material for discussion during the group meetings, their anxiety would be lessened.

In our model of group therapy there is no outline or structure provided by the therapist. The group members actually set their own structure from the emotional interaction with each other and the group therapist. There are models of group therapy that employ lectures by the group therapist (diadactic groups) and topics for discussion by the group members (repressive-inspirational groups). In didactic and repressive-inspirational groups the emotional interaction between the group members and the group therapist is limited by the structure of the group. Some types of group therapy (psychotic, juvenile delinquent, adolescent) need structure to limit the anxiety of the group members in meetings.

Discussion

This group is experiencing increased anxiety and tension in the group. One extremely common and well-known method for relieving anxiety and tension in any group is to place the blame for the anxiety and tension on someone else. In this group, Mr. Foy is becoming the recipient of the other group members' anxiety and tension. Rather than face up to their feelings about each other or the leader of the group (group therapist), the members find it much easier to pick on someone who is helpless and to vent their feelings on him. In other words, the group members are attempting to make Mr. Foy the scapegoat of the group. Sandor Rado has described scapegoating comprehensively and accurately. He states that, "to vent one's rage safely on a scapegoat is one of mankind's oldest ills and pervades every phase of social life. The evidence ranges from the despot who slays the bearer of bad news on the spot, to the husband who unloads his pent-up anger at the boss onto his wife, to the unscrupulous statesman who diverts the people's ire from his regime to an alleged enemy, either foreign or native." [1]

This method that people use of relieving anxiety and tension is age old. The term apparently was invented in 1530 A.D. by Tindale, a scholar who translated the Bible from the Hebrew. In Lev. 16:8–26, the original statement was, "the goote on which the loote fell to scape." Leviticus describes a solemn ceremonial of the ancient Hebrews. On the Day of Atonement, a priest transferred all the sins of his people to a live white goat. The animal was then driven away to die alone. The goat was called Azazel, or scapegoat. From this Biblical story the term *scapegoat* resulted. Christ, of course, is the divine scapegoat, taking upon Himself the sins of the world. Different cultures have used different means to carry out the principle of scapegoating. In some, humans were offered up for sacrifice in order to cleanse the tribe or cult of sins, sorrows, and disease. The ancient Greeks and Aztecs, among others, employed human sacrifices. Some say that this custom is still followed in certain African tribes.

Minority groups have always been subjected to scapegoating. Throughout religious history there are incidents of Protestants persecuting Jews and Catholics and Catholics persecuting Protestants and Jews, the persecutor always being of the religious majority. The Jews have been scapegoated throughout history more than any other religious group. In most countries they have been and still are a minority group. They have been wrongly blamed for many evils and disasters—the epidemic of bubonic plague in Europe in the fourteenth century, the alleged treason in the Dreyfus case in France, the economic disintegration of Czarist Russia, and, most notoriously, the postwar debacle in Hitler's Germany.

In the United States different racial groups have repeatedly been the targets of aggressive feelings—the Irish in the early nineteenth century and the Jews and the Negroes in the twentieth. At the beginning of World War II, when anxiety and tension of the populace increased, loyal citizens of German and Japanese descent in this country were also subjected to scapegoating.

Scapegoating is a common mechanism that is utilized in many day-to-day group relationships of people. In all groups of people, emotional reactions and anxiety occur among the members. The more closeness there is in the group the more anxiety is present, and where there is more anxiety, more scapegoating occurs. In the family group—the closest of all groups—scapegoating occurs with regularity. Parents scapegoat their children, older siblings scapegoat younger ones, and the younger children scapegoat the family pets. For example, a five-year-old child gets angry at his mother. He would like to scream at her or attack her. Unable to do either with impunity, he strikes or shouts at his dog. In the absence of a dog he may vent his anger on a younger member of the family, particularly if mother is not looking. This is the simple form of scapegoating. However, some scapegoating within the family group may have serious consequences. The family member who is emotionally ill is often the one who has been scapegoated by the parents and other siblings. Many teenagers with delinquent patterns of behavior are the scapegoats of their family. One parent may scapegoat the other parent. The wife who has a depression or the husband who is an alcoholic may be the scapegoats of their spouses.

Scapegoating commonly occurs in educational, occupational, social and recreational groups. Children pick out a scapegoat among their peers. The passive, nonassertive boy who does not fight back and who frequently is called a "sissy" may be treated cruelly by his peers. In occupational groups with a high level of anxiety, the scapegoating of fellow workers occurs regularly. Even in social and recreational groups the members usually pick out one of their number who becomes the victim of their jokes and humorous barbs.

Some people seemingly seek out the role of the scapegoat. These people are usually filled with low self-esteem and chronic guilt. They consider themselves worthless, and invite punishment from others in their group relationships. In this group Mr. Foy has many of these traits in his personality make-up and is seeking out this role of the scapegoat in the therapy group. As we shall see in later meetings of the group, the members' anxiety and tension is due to hostility to the therapist, a hostility they fear to express either verbally or nonverbally. Thus, since Mr. Foy is the group member who is seeking the role of scapegoat, he becomes the target for their hostile feelings.

NINTH MEETING

Seven members were present, Miss French being absent for the first time. As the meeting began, Mrs. Kitch remarked that she could remember names of everyone when she was at home, but she could not do so in the meeting. Mrs. Jacobs had noticed that she could not remember matters she thought of at home and wished to talk about in the meeting. The therapist asked about this, saying: "Now you indicate different feelings here in the meeting than at home or on the outside. What is it about the meeting that concerns you?" Two other members agreed with the earlier statements and one said it might be anxiety that caused it. The subject was changed. There were several periods of silences, interspersed with mention of extraneous topics. The therapist focused on the silences and on the changing subjects. Mr. Cain felt that he (Cain) was talking too much and dominating the meeting. Two members felt they were selfish. Mrs. Kitch discussed feelings of insignificance which she experienced in group therapy, as well as in outside groups, that prevented her from participating. Mr. Foy repeated his plea for magic; the group was his only crutch. Again at the end of the meeting someone made a plea for the doctor to use an outline for each meeting. Miss French's absence was discussed by the members. Mr. Foy was smoking a cigar, constantly producing an enormous volume of smoke that was quite irritating to several of the members, the therapist, and the recorder.

Theme and Dynamics

The members are recognizing the anxiety of the group process by forgetting names and events. They verbalize some of their feelings in more detail. These include feelings of insignificance, selfishness, and domination of the meeting by conversation. A continued reference to wishing for a structured situation is a manifestation of anxiety in this unstructured group situation.

Technique

The therapist dealt with the anxiety factors relating to the group. He should, however, have referred back to his original statement and asked for additional feelings. After one member mentioned anxiety, the therapist had an excellent opportunity to explore the feelings of the members. He could have said: "What about the anxiety here in the meeting?" Again he could have used material about himself that had been discussed at previous meetings and focused on himself in relation to the anxiety being experienced.

The therapist should have explored feelings in the group by reflecting back to the members that they had talked about feeling selfish and insignificant, and expressed fears of talking too much. He could have asked for group feelings about this.

Inasmuch as one member said her feelings in the group were identical with those encountered in outside groups, the therapist could have said: "Now she speaks of experiencing similar feelings here and with outside groups. How do you feel about this observation that she has made?" He might also say: "Now you are here to learn about yourselves, to see how you get along with others here. You make comparisons of this group to outside groups. I wonder if you have any ideas or thoughts about this?"

Mr. Foy's behavior with excessive cigar smoke could have been brought to the attention of the members. The therapist could say: "Mr. Foy seems to be creating a smoke screen with his cigar. How do you feel about it? Any ideas why he does this?" At every opportunity the therapist should ask the members to identify the behavior going on in the meeting. This is part of the learning process of group therapy.

TENTH MEETING

Seven members were present; Miss French continued absent. The members were laughing and talking as the therapist and recorder entered the room, whereupon the group became very quiet and reserved. Mr. Cain made a reference to this change in behavior. The therapist immediately said: "Well, what about this change after I came in?" The members ignored the therapist and changed the subject. A few minutes later the therapist again brought this to their attention. Mr. Holt replied that the therapist's presence meant he (Holt) had to become a patient, and maybe he "didn't want to deal with it." Mrs. Kitch said she was not as comfortable as in the initial meetings. Several of the members spoke of feeling an increased group atmosphere. Mr. Foy continued to fear inescapable doom. They reacted to his statement by asking a series of questions about his home and work. Mr. Foy replied that he couldn't get along with his father or brothers, but was working for them and felt dependent upon them. The members wondered why he always had to be the sickest member, why he had to be dependent on his family, and why couldn't he be independent of them. They discussed roles in their families and some of their present conflicts. Mrs. Kitch discussed her home situation. Her husband is emotionally ill and in individual treatment. Mr. Cain's alcoholism and separation from his wife and children were brought out. Mrs. Webster discussed her marital conflicts in more detail. Mr. Cain and Mr. Holt talked of their emotional problems and of feeling immature and inadequate around others. Mrs. Jacobs again brought her knitting, but she did not use it. She became increasingly uncomfortable and talked of being self-conscious of her mannerisms, but denied any emotional problems. She spoke in glowing terms of her husband and their happy marriage. The therapist asked about her phobic manifestations in the meeting. Mrs. Jacobs seemed irritated (nonverbally) with the therapist, but made no reply. Mr. Cain remarked that she didn't need her crutch (knitting) at this meeting.

Theme and Dynamics

The members are now accepting the fact that they are patients with problems, even though they would like to avoid it. Increased group consciousness is apparent. They are expressing more freely their sense of dependency, immaturity, and inadequacy. Many of the manifestations of individual therapy are also encountered in group therapy where, however, the group identifies and interprets behavior. An example of this took place with Mr. Foy. The members asked him to point out why he has to be the sickest member. They asked him why he needs these symptoms. Mrs. Jacobs was reminded that her knitting was a crutch. One of the fascinating aspects of group therapy is illustrated by the manner in which members will identify defense mechanisms and behavioral characteristics of each other. This is mutual analysis. If these interpretations came from the therapist the reaction would be entirely different and not nearly as effective.

Technique

The therapist correctly asked about the reactions in the group at the start of the meeting. Initially they would not deal with their feelings, but after emphasis was placed on this matter there was effective verbalization by the members.

When Mr. Cain and Mr. Holt spoke of their feelings of inadequacy and immaturity around other people, the therapist could have related this to the meeting and explored this issue by making the following observation: "Now two of you have spoken of feeling immature and inadequate around others. I wonder if you experience any of these reactions here?" Again the therapist would be directing the members' attention and feelings to exploring the group situation at the moment.

Discussion

The group members are now beginning to talk about their conflicts and problems. To some extent their barriers against exposure and rejection have diminished. The group members, like many people of our society, have many thoughts and reactions about themselves and others that are confusing, distorted, and vague. These thoughts and feelings remain hidden, for in general people do not tell others, not even close friends, their real and true feelings. There are many people, quite guilt-laden from either real or imagined reasons, who are too afraid of exposure and rejection to express themselves. They remain isolated with these thoughts and often have the conviction that they are the only ones with disturbing feelings, thoughts, conflicts, and difficulties. In our group the members are beginning to establish some of the early common bonds between each other through descriptions of their illnesses. They are finding out that other people do have similar feelings and conflicts. The group members profit immensely from this discovery. Feelings of isolation are diminished. This positive feature of group therapy gives them encouragement and hope, even though their anxiety and discomfort in the group meetings is much more noticeable than at the outset of group therapy.

ELEVENTH MEETING

Seven members were present. Mr. Darcy was absent. The hour began
with conversation concerning routines on the outside, at work, and at
home. Immediately the therapist asked about the routine in the meeting.
Mr. Holt, in a hostile tone, replied that he could see no relationship between the group routine and outside routines. Later he changed his
mind and said that group relationships were similar to all relationships.
Miss French spoke of having noticed increased irritability with people
and remarked that she had been depressed during her absence. She felt
that she could speak about anyone in the group, both those she liked
and those she disliked. Mr. Holt expressed the opinion that people were
unhappy with their jobs. The therapist asked about Mr. Holt's statement.
The members discussed how hard it was to please a boss. The competitiveness created in job situations was also discussed. Miss French mentioned
that people in the Army didn't like their commanding officers and stated
that this relationship would continue to exist until the end of time. Miss
French also mentioned that she had been to see a doctor while she was
ill. He gave her some medicine which had helped. He seemed like a
human being to her. She understood that he was married and had three
children. The group began discussing doctors. The therapist pointed out
their conversation in the meeting. They had spoken of being unhappy
with jobs, bosses, commanding officers, and had mentioned conversation
as related to the group meeting. They spoke of leaning on doctors for
medicine. One member said that doctors gave you "emotional trauma,"
and that they "didn't understand." Mrs. Jacobs was somewhat uncomfortable during the meeting and discussed several of her physical symptoms. Mr. Cain was active, and frequently made humorous observations
on the material being discussed. Towards the end of the hour the members asked for longer meetings. Mr. Cain felt it took half an hour to get
relaxed and comfortable. He said the meeting was just getting interesting
when the time was up. Mr. Holt even suggested they should meet two
or three times a week.

Theme and Dynamics

The content of this meeting illustrates the way in which group members use casual conversation to express their feelings. Their hostility to
the therapist is expressed in terms of unhappy jobs, bosses, commanding
officers, and doctors who do not understand. This is the underlying theme
of the meeting. Then, too, the job in group therapy concerns them. Irritation with people as well as likes and dislikes in the group were expressed.
There is a need to please the boss (therapist).

Their feelings with reference to the group process are those of coercion.

Many people in their occupational and other roles feel coerced; they go to work but hate it, motivated mainly by fear of authority. Here, they feel the therapist is using coercion in promoting interaction. Toward the end of the meeting they were demanding more from the therapist in the form of longer and more frequent meetings.

Technique

The therapist correctly focused on the feelings of the members by asking about the routine in the group.

The therapist should have been more active in this hour. He could have focused on Miss French's statement about becoming irritable with people, as well as her likes and dislikes in the group. He could have said: "Now Miss French speaks of becoming irritable with people. You are here to examine and explore your feelings with one another. What about the feelings of irritation present here?" He could also ask: "You have spoken of me before in terms of being strict, like a schoolteacher, and you have made references to freedom of conversation outside of the meeting as compared to the meeting. I wonder how you see me in terms of irritable feelings, likes, and dislikes here in the meeting?"

When unhappy job situations were discussed, the therapist could have said: "I wonder if you think our job here compares in any way to this reference to unhappy jobs?"

When bosses, commanding officers, and doctors were discussed, the therapist could have referred to the fact that he is their doctor and asked for their feelings.

When Miss French referred to consulting a doctor who acted like a human being and gave her medicine, the therapist could have repeated her observation and added: "What kind of a person do you think I am?" He might also have asked, "How do you feel about me? I don't answer your questions, don't give you medicine—how does this really make you feel?"

These observations are group-centered and they direct the members to explore feelings about the therapist. It is recalled that the underlying theme of this meeting is their hostility toward him. Clearing away this hostility by encouraging the group members to express their feelings toward him is the primary issue facing the therapist at this particular stage of group therapy.

The alert group therapist should recognize that many members will avoid the use of the word *anger*. Anger has many meanings among people. Dictionaries define anger in such terms as rage, fury, indignation, violence, vindictive passion, sudden and strong displeasure, wrath, ire, hatred, offense, etc. Different sections of the United States impart various meanings to angry feelings or anger. For example, the culture of the deep South avoids the emotion of anger. Children are taught that it is improper to be angry or to express anger. Southern adults equate anger with massive rage and the loss of control of feelings. Angry people are referred to in some circles as being mad or insane. The Southern Negro for many generations has exhibited a massive denial of anger and has been considered in his proper role when completely submissive, passive, and compliant. Northern and Eastern cultures are more tolerant and understanding of the meaning of anger and, correspondingly, are more aggressive in interpersonal relationships than Southern people. The identification and understanding of anger or rage in emotional illness is a frequent task of the group therapist. Rather than use the specific words *anger* or *angry* in his observations to his group members—particularly during the initial months of group therapy, such words as irritated, miffed, upset, and resentful (or their associated nouns) should be used. The therapist can say: "I notice that you are upset (or irritated) with me today," rather than "I notice that you are angry with me." Such words impart the same meaning to the group members as anger does to the group therapist but avoid the implication of the loss of control of feelings. Later in therapy, when the group members have worked through their relationship to the therapist and are more comfortable in the group situation, these feelings can be explored in more detail.

TWELFTH MEETING

There were seven members present. Mrs. Jacobs was absent.

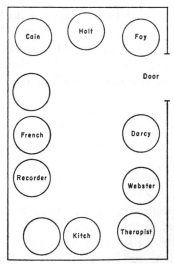

Mr. Cain (to therapist): You seem cheerful. Did something good happen to you?

Mrs. Kitch: He is smiling. Isn't that nice.

Theme and Dynamics. The theme of the meeting is suggested at the onset: their feelings about the therapist. A smile from the therapist means being liked and approved.

Therapist: You seem concerned about my facial expressions.

Therapist's Technique. Therapist recognizes theme and begins to explore it.

Mr. Holt: I think he usually hides his human side in the meetings. I like to see him smile and laugh.

Mr. Darcy: (Enters room and sits down; no one speaks to him.)

Mr. Cain: The men are against the women tonight. (The men and women are sitting on opposite sides of the room.)

Theme and Dynamics. The subject is changed by the members.

Miss French (to Mr. Darcy): Were you sick?

Mr. Darcy (to Miss French): Yes! Were you?

Theme and Dynamics. Two members made hostile comments to each other.

Miss French: No.

Mr. Cain: We're getting to be more of a group. Now we are challenging each other.

Therapist: You talked about my smiling. I wonder if you have any other thoughts about my facial expressions here in the meetings.

Therapist's Technique. The therapist is aware that the subject has been changed. He makes an observation that brings the members back to exploring their relationship to him. Therapist is in control of meeting.

Mr. Holt: Maybe the doctor has changed.

Mrs. Webster: (Enters room and sits down.)

Miss French: I would like to know the doctor better. I'm glad he's smiling. It makes me feel better.

Mr. Cain: I don't know how to say it but up until the last meeting I've had problems determining what is a fact and what is the feeling about it, especially now the doctor is smiling.

Mrs. Kitch: I've had trouble knowing what the doctor wants us to think about.

Theme and Dynamics. The members are experiencing more anxiety. They are confused about the therapist's observations. The members block and actually do have difficulty in understanding the therapist.

Therapist's Technique. The therapist's technique should be one of patience and understanding during this period. The members are anxious and do have great difficulty understanding group behavior. The therapist who has experienced anxiety himself will understand.

Mr. Holt: I think he wants us to talk about the way we feel.

> *Theme and Dynamics. The theme of the meeting—the members' feelings about the therapist—is now clear.*

Therapist: Do you have any thoughts about Mr. Cain's observations?

Mr. Holt (angrily): I don't know what you're talking about!

> *Theme and Dynamics. Anxiety causes misunderstanding.*
> *Therapist's Technique. The therapist continues to be in control of the meeting. His observation focuses on himself. He is directing the flow of conversation toward a ventilation of their feelings about him.*

Mr. Foy: I think he (Holt) is just confused. It is cold, hard therapeutic procedure, trying to get us to talk. I feel the same way.

> *Theme and Dynamics. Anxiety causes confusion.*

Miss French: The doctor's questions make me hesitate. I usually don't know how I feel.

> *Theme and Dynamics. Anxiety causes blocking.*

Mr. Darcy: I don't believe many people know how they think and feel.

Mr. Holt (to therapist): I've had a hard time knowing what thoughts you want. Sometimes we don't answer you at all.

Therapist: Have others here felt like Mr. Holt?

Group: (Verbally and nonverbally indicate they have feelings similar to Mr. Holt's.)

Miss French: At least we are thinking.

Mr. Cain: Often I get a futile feeling.

Miss French: We are not definite enough. I think it's a matter of being more definite.

Mr. Holt: The doctor's statements are too vague. I don't understand so I don't respond.

> *Theme and Dynamics. The members are ventilating well their reactions to the therapist. Such material is supportive to the members from the standpoint of their ability to assert themselves in the group. Feelings of isolation are also diminished since others have feelings similar to theirs.*
> *Therapist's Technique. Additional observations the therapist could have made so that the members could recognize their reaction to him better are: "Do you notice that you react to me differently than you do to the others here?" "Have you ever experienced reactions to other people outside of this group similar to those you have to me?" "Do your reactions to me have any connection to your illnesses?"*

Miss French: I used to become blank when he (therapist) said anything. Now I am trying to be more definite about his questions. I'm even trying to do that at work.

Mr. Cain: You mean you haven't been sarcastic? (Miss French has previously admitted being sarcastic with others.)

Miss French: No, but I'm trying.

Mr. Foy: Everyone is improving but me.

> ***Theme and Dynamics.*** *Mr. Foy is setting himself up to be the group's scapegoat by suggesting that he is the sickest member.*

Mr. Holt: Yeah, we're all sober but you.

Mr. Foy: You're right.

Mr. Darcy (to Mrs. Webster and Mrs. Kitch): Why are you two so quiet?

Mr. Holt (somewhat angrily): Have you noticed where Mrs. Webster is sitting? Some people have to get behind the doctor to hide. (Mrs. Webster was sitting adjacent to and slightly behind the therapist.)

> ***Theme and Dynamics.*** *The group expresses concern over Mrs. Webster's seating position near the therapist and her silence.*

Mrs. Webster (to Mr. Holt): I don't like you.

Mr. Foy: Let's not forget we're all neurotic!

Mr. Holt: I'm not concentrating on it.

Miss French: I wonder why Mrs. Jacobs is absent.

> ***Theme and Dynamics.*** *The members have changed the subject; concern is now being expressed over the absence of one member.*
>
> ***Therapist's Technique.*** *The therapist should have focused on members' reactions to Mrs. Jacobs' absence.*

Mr. Cain: She did not tell us either.

Mrs. Kitch: I wish she were here.

Miss French: So do I.

Therapist: Most of you have spoken today about me—wondering about my facial expression, saying that you don't understand what I say here. I wonder if you have any other thoughts about me.

> ***Therapist's Technique.*** *Therapist again attempts to get the members to explore their feelings about him. Note that therapist's observation is group oriented and invites the entire group to answer.*

Mr. Cain: We are now more of a group.

Mr. Holt (angrily): We've stopped being polite. We are no longer a group of people meeting under the fishlike eyes of the doctor.

> ***Theme and Dynamics.*** *Hostility to the therapist is expressed verbally by Mr. Holt. The protective screen of politeness and superficiality has slightly diminished.*
>
> ***Therapist's Technique.*** *Therapist errs in not refocusing on Mr. Holt's statement. He could say: "So I'm an old fish-eye.*

What's this about?" "Do you feel that I'm watching you or judging you?"

Miss French: We need to get closer to each other. I maintain a world of my own. I exclude everyone.

Mr. Cain: I know I'm too selfish about myself.

Mr. Foy: I'm the most selfish person in the whole world.

Mr. Holt (*concerned over Mrs. Webster's and Mrs. Kitch's silence*): Let's give the other ladies equal time. How do you feel?

Mrs. Kitch: I wonder if Mr. Foy is bragging or complaining.

Miss French: As usual he's punishing himself.

> *Theme and Dynamics. Mrs. Kitch's observation suggests that Mr. Foy may be the scapegoat. She is aware of Mr. Foy's masochistic role.*
>
> *Therapist's Technique. The therapist allows the members to talk about their feelings in outside group relationships. He could have said: "You've been thinking about yourselves here. How does it make you feel here in the meeting?" One goal of the therapist is for the members to recognize that their behavior in outside group relationships is similar in many respects to their behavior in this group.*

Group: (All of the members take part in a discussion of their roles outside of the group—things they can do to keep from thinking about themselves and getting depressed. The group then begins attacking Mr. Foy.)

Mr. Holt: He (Mr. Foy) acts this way for attention.

Mr. Holt: Yes, you are demanding attention when you insist on being different.

Mr. Foy: What I said could be an expression of utter defeat. That's the way I feel.

> *Theme and Dynamics. Group continues to focus on Mr. Foy's role. He is becoming the recipient of the group's tensions.*

Mr. Darcy (*to Mr. Foy*): I think your main trouble is that you need more praise. You don't get it anywhere else.

Therapist (*aware that Mrs. Webster is anxious and quiet*): We have someone today who is not participating.

> *Therapist's Technique. Therapist draws attention to the member (Mrs. Webster) who has been silent in the meeting. In this way he interrupts the members' discussion about Mr. Foy.*

Mr. Holt: We have tried to get her in the act.

Mr. Darcy (*to Mr. Holt*): When you sat by the doctor you didn't say much.

Miss French: I have tried to get her to talk. You can ask her questions, but she doesn't say much.

Mrs. Webster: I don't feel like talking.

> *Theme and Dynamics. The group members, at the therapist's bidding, ask Mrs. Webster a series of questions.*

Miss French (to Mrs. Webster): Don't you think we're doing better? Here we do it ourselves. If you take things slow and study them, you can reap better results.

> **Theme and Dynamics.** *Miss French is a very perceptive group member. Her observations are astute.*

Mr. Holt: Once you cure a disease it's gone. I don't feel we can do it ourselves. We can't put enough into it. I'm impatient like my father. I'm afraid I'll reach a saturation point and not even be close to getting well.

> **Theme and Dynamics.** *Mr. Holt discusses his expectations from group therapy; he questions how other people can help.*

Miss French: You feel if there were only four people here it would be better?
Mr. Holt: No, I didn't mean that.
Therapist (supporting Mrs. Webster): Miss French said that Mrs. Webster doesn't talk much. Why do you suppose it's hard for her to talk here?

> **Therapist's Technique.** *Therapist continues to support Mrs. Webster by refocusing on her group behavior.*

Miss French: She's shy.
Mr. Darcy: She's not aggressive.
Mr. Holt: She was late starting in the group. She's behind—she has to catch up.

> **Theme and Dynamics.** *The group members support Mrs. Webster.*

Miss French: Mrs. Kitch doesn't talk much either.
Mrs. Kitch: I'm just taking it all in.
Miss French (to Mrs. Webster): Do you feel left out?
Mr. Darcy (in a low voice): Do you feel more at ease?
Mr. Holt (interrupts, speaks angrily to Mr. Darcy): Darcy, will you please talk louder?
Mrs. Webster (sobbing, anxious): I just don't feel like talking about my problems. I feel like I'm in a vise. I'm not feeling better, I'm getting worse.

> **Theme and Dynamics.** *One manifestation of the increased anxiety level of the group is increased hostility between the members—e.g., Mr. Holt's response to Mr. Darcy, Mrs. Webster and Mr. Foy; the interplay between Miss French and Mr. Darcy; and other members' responses to Mr. Foy.*
> **Therapist's Technique.** *No intervention or observation from the therapist is necessary. Even though the present discussion is away from the central theme of the meeting, it is most important for silent, anxious members like Mrs. Webster to receive support from the therapist and the members.*

Miss French (sympathetically to Mrs. Webster): Do you feel like we should let you alone?
Mrs. Webster (cries openly, sobbing): No, no.

Miss French: I'll help you in any way I can.

Mr. Holt (to Mrs. Webster): The way you feel—well, it comes to all of us sometimes.

> **Theme and Dynamics.** *The members continue to support Mrs. Webster.*

Miss French: I wish I could cry.

Mr. Holt: It helps.

Miss French: I don't think so.

Mr. Darcy: It must be uncomfortable to cry in a group.

Mr. Cain: I have a friend who sees a psychiatrist in private sessions. When he got worse the doctor saw him more often.

> **Theme and Dynamics.** *The support for Mrs. Webster has resulted in the members' acceptance of her, whereas formerly they had been angry at her for starting group therapy late (4th meeting), attending irregularly, and not participating in the meetings. Mrs. Webster feels this acceptance from the others. She is now more verbal and comfortable.*

Mrs. Webster: I'm getting worse faster than I want to.

Therapist: Do you have any other thoughts about helping Mrs. Webster?

Miss French: At least it's out in the open now.

Mr. Cain: I think she is more comfortable now.

Mr. Darcy (to Mrs. Webster): Has anything happened to you that is upsetting?

Mr. Foy: I think she derives more out of receiving than being aggressive. Everything she has talked about has been important.

Mr. Holt: A psychiatrist can't change unpleasant living conditions. (Mrs. Webster is separated from her husband and living with her daughter.)

Mrs. Webster (much more comfortable): Mrs. Jacobs speaks of having such a happy marriage, no problems. (Mrs. Jacobs has made repeated references to her perfect, happy marriage, which the others doubt.)

Mr. Cain (to Mrs. Webster): I envy your ability of displaying emotions.

> **Theme and Dynamics.** *Mr. Cain's statement, and Miss French's earlier remark that she wished she could cry, indicate some of the group members' inability to recognize or express their emotions.*

Mrs. Webster: No you wouldn't. You would feel foolish.

Therapist: What does Mr. Cain mean when he says that he envies Mrs. Webster's display of emotions?

Miss French: I don't think I show my emotions. I wish I could. I wish I could laugh and really feel happy.

Mr. Foy: Laughing has to come from the heart.

Mr. Holt: Society frowns on crying so we cover it with laughter. But here in the group and our family we should be able to do so.

Mr. Foy: I feel if I laughed I'd be hysterical.

Therapist: Time's up for today.

Therapist's Technique. If time had permitted, the therapist might have followed his observation about displaying emotions by saying: "You talked earlier in this meeting about reactions to me. I wonder what emotions you are experiencing about me?" "Are you having any difficulty displaying your emotions about me?" At every opportunity the therapist should encourage the members to explore their feelings and reactions to him. It is not necessary for the therapist to summarize the content of the meeting at the end of the hour. When the hour is over, the therapist should so signify to the members. If important group material is being discussed he can make reference to it in the following manner: "Now you have been discussing some of your feelings. If you wish to explore them further, you may bring them up at a later meeting. Time's up for today."

SUMMARY

Theme and Dynamics

The theme of this meeting is overtly demonstrated by the hostility expressed towards the therapist. He is an old fish-eye; he is not a human being. It would be interesting to know at what level the group wants him. If he were a human being and came close to them they would be extremely frightened. Some want him to smile and be a Santa Claus, while others speak of wanting more structure. But in group therapy there is no structure until the group puts it there. This lack of structure makes the members anxious. This is the group process in action.

The attitude toward Mrs. Webster was an excellent demonstration of how members will rescue and support someone in distress. It was the group's loss if she did not participate. To be able to cry and express feelings was something to encourage in the group and in the family; as Mr. Holt aptly observes, "Society frowns on crying so we cover it with laughter."

Technique

In the author's experience the members will usually begin meetings with statements that are suggestive of the central theme of the meeting. Sometimes the members talk in symbolic language. For example, when the members are angry with the therapist the meeting may begin with heated statements about bosses, parents and other authority figures. In this meeting the members began the meeting with direct statements about the therapist.

Once the therapist is aware of the meeting's theme he should pursue it. In this meeting he correctly did so. The therapist recognized the hostility. He knew it was there and kept refocusing on himself until it was expressed.

The technique that the therapist employed to support Mrs. Webster is extremely important in group therapy. The silent, anxious member needs patient and understanding attention from the therapist. Such people may need support for many meetings. They should never be neglected.

The therapist was in control of the meeting. In control means that the therapist was able to direct the meeting so as to derive the greatest therapeutic benefit from it. In order to maintain control, the therapist must be able to assess correctly: (1) the basic theme of the meeting, and (2) the anxiety level of the group. If he can correctly assess these factors he can use them as goals to direct the meetings. If, however, he fails to understand the theme or assess the anxiety level, he will lose contact with the driving forces of the meeting and will therefore be unable either to direct or control it therapeutically. Admittedly these factors are difficult to assess correctly because of the many variables that may interfere. Discussions with the recorder after each meeting can be quite useful to the therapist, since the recorder as an observer may be able to note indications of failure to maintain control that the therapist himself has missed.

The anxiety level of the group represents the therapist's assessment of the verbal and nonverbal communication occurring during the group meeting from member to member, member to therapist, and therapist to member. The group process creates emotional reactions among the members. Anxiety occurs as the therapist promotes closeness among the members. Each member tends to repeat behavior patterns in the meetings that have been used throughout his life. There may be considerable variance with group members in both the verbal and nonverbal manifestations of communication and anxiety. Under the stress of anxiety, one member may become overtalkative, another may become competitive with the therapist, while still another may show his reaction by silence. A common verbal manifestation of anxiety in group meetings is the rapid changing of subjects and the discussion of superficial topics. The nonverbal manifestations of anxiety in group therapy account for a major part of the total group anxiety. Restlessness, scowling, frowning, smiling, pensiveness, facial movements, extrinsic body movements, laughter and excessive smoking are a few of the nonverbal methods of communicating anxiety. The group anxiety level can gradate from a low level of almost complete apathy to a high point that threatens imminent group disintegration. The therapist's correct evaluation of the combined effects of the group members' anxiety determines his ability as a group therapist. When the group anxiety level is too low, the therapist should take steps to raise it; when it becomes too high he should institute measures to lower it.

The therapist should strive to keep the group anxiety level moderately high so that constructive group work can be accomplished.

The importance of the flexibility of the therapist's technique is illustrated in this meeting when the therapist directed the group's attention away from the central theme of the meeting to Mrs. Webster. On occasion members may talk about several important group issues during the course of one meeting. Frequently therapists will ponder which group issue should be discussed, because all of those mentioned by the members are important and group-oriented. Each group issue could occupy considerable time in a meeting. It would be impossible for the therapist to deal adequately with all the group issues the members have brought up in the meeting. However, in such situations the therapist should focus on those group issues that he feels are the most important ones to the group at that particular time. Material the members bring up in meetings can be discussed in later meetings. Thus the therapist can plan to raise important group issues at an appropriate time in later meetings.

THIRTEENTH MEETING

Seven members were present, Mrs. Webster being absent. Mr. Holt brought a container of flowers for all the members and placed it on the center table. Early in the hour Mrs. Jacobs said she felt better but that it hurt her feelings for anyone to ask about her difficulties. Mrs. Kitch agreed with her, adding that she often wished she could "fade away" when someone inquired about her personal life. The subject was changed to psychiatrists. Again they talked of people being downgraded and belittled by visiting a psychiatrist. The therapist asked about their feelings in a general statement. His remarks were not dealt with by the members to any degree. Mr. Cain discussed again the therapist's being inactive during the meeting, whereupon the therapist immediately asked for feelings about his role. Miss French thought that he kept everyone from getting off the track; the group agreed somewhat humorously that he was not going to change. The therapist focused on Holt's bringing flowers to the members, asking if the members had any thoughts as to why flowers were brought to the meeting. Several of the female members voiced pleasure at his thoughtfulness; Cain felt that maybe this was Holt's way of getting attention from the therapist.

Theme and Dynamics

The theme of the meeting continues to revolve around attitudes toward the therapist. Mrs. Jacobs' and Mrs. Kitch's feelings of being hurt and wanting to fade away are related to their fear of the authority figure—

the therapist. Again they discussed people's reactions about visiting a psychiatrist. The therapist's inactivity was mentioned.

The motivation for bringing gifts to the meeting was explored and this attention-seeking mechanism was verbalized.

Technique

The therapist could have explored Mrs. Jacobs' and Mrs. Kitch's attitudes in more detail by making the following statement: "Mrs. Jacobs says that it hurts her feelings to be asked about her difficulty. Mrs. Kitch wants to 'fade away' if someone asks her about herself. What thoughts do you have about these statements?" He could pursue this further by adding: "Just how do these feelings relate to this meeting? What about getting hurt here? Where do you fit me into this picture of getting hurt or feeling insignificant?" The therapist should recognize that the feelings the members are experiencing in their relationship to him are basic ones. They are saying, "Stay away from me, don't ask me any questions. It's too uncomfortable." The need to explore these feelings is self-evident.

The therapist should have been quick to sense this need with reference to his inactivity in the meeting. When they laughingly agreed that he was not going to change, he could have said: "You seemed amused about this, but I have heard you make several statements in recent meetings about my inactivity. Now, I wonder just what *are* your feelings about me?"

The therapist correctly asked about the meaning of bringing flowers to the group. Gifts of this kind become a group issue and should be handled accordingly.

Discussion

The flowers that Mr. Holt brought to the meeting constituted an attempt to ingratiate himself with the therapist and the other group members. Ingratiation is a common technique utilized by people in their day-to-day group relationships. It may have several different meanings. Abram Kardiner has defined ingratiation as follows: "Ingratiation is the name of a technique, the object of which is to make oneself loved or favored by another individual in such a way as to gain some end or advantage. It is a technique; which means it is an activity, which can be established on the basis of several ego attitudes. The most noteworthy attitude is that of dependency; but it may also proceed from the wish to be like the other person or out of hatred of the other person." [2]

The technique of ingratiation has also been influenced by cultural factors. Our society places great emphasis on giving material things. An example is the image being created by manufacturers and advertisers during the Christmas season. The number of Christmas cards mailed each year has reached such mammoth proportions that post offices are taxed to their limits during December. The major motivating factor in mailing Christmas cards seems to be "keeping up with the Joneses" rather than any desire for warm and friendly greetings between friends. Christmas gifts, too, are given out of proportion to their meaning. For example, a child is expected to give a gift for Christmas to his schoolteacher, to his Sunday school teacher, and to others with whom he has group relationships. Adults are expected on various occasions to give gifts to a wide range of business and social acquaintances. The exchange of gifts at Christmas is a good example of the use of material things to express love, but Christmas gifts are only one form of ingratiation. Invitations to birthday parties involve the tacit requirement of bringing a gift. Many children are more interested in the type and number of gifts received than in the relationship with their peers. Similarly, high school and college graduations, weddings, and other functions require the giving of gifts. Manufacturers and salesmen rely on various kinds of gifts to customers to further their business interests. Banks and savings and loan associations offer gifts for new accounts. Insurance companies do the same for the prospective policyholder. Gifts are employed so widely in all group relationships that the individual has no way of escaping society's demand for their use.

Material gifts may have several psychodynamic implications in the family group. They serve as an expression of warmth and friendship, as an attempt to secure acceptance, as a method of controlling behavior, and as a means by which others become obligated to the giver. Parents who are unable to demonstrate love and affection for their children may indulge them with excessive gifts and try to "buy" their love. Children may develop the feeling that the only way to be accepted and loved is through the giving or receiving of material gifts. In later life they may attempt to obtain love and acceptance by giving a gift rather than giving themselves. Instead of sharing a gift with a close friend, they may use it merely to acquire acceptance and security. Parents who have difficulty with disciplining their children may resort to gifts in an effort to control acting-out behavior.

FOURTEENTH MEETING

Again, seven members present; this time the absent member was Mr. Cain. The preceding week's meeting had been cancelled due to the brief illness of the therapist. A secretary in the clinic notified the members by telephone and told each member why the meeting was cancelled.

At the outset the members were extremely concerned about the therapist's health. Missing one meeting was a severe loss. This intense feeling was quite evident from their nonverbal attitude. The entire group acted as if it were pleading for the therapist not to leave them—to take care of them. Mrs. Jacobs said she was more serious about group therapy now than at the outset. It was a joke then, but not any longer. She really felt the absence of the group last week for the first time. Mr. Foy had asked to see the therapist prior to the meeting. He related a problem for which advice was needed. The therapist advised him to discuss this problem with the group. During the meeting he told them that he had come to the clinic last week and found the door locked. Mr. Holt, who had also come to the clinic, met Mr. Foy and as they left the building Foy remarked that he was going to get drunk. He went to his mother's home and had dinner. A female friend of the family came by. She had a bottle of whiskey with her and they had a number of drinks together. He accepted her offer to drive him home, but she was drunk and they had an automobile accident. Foy has been subpoenaed as a state's witness. He feels extremely guilty. He doesn't know what to do. He is unable to tell his wife, who was in Florida at the time of the accident. The lady's husband understands, but his wife, he says, never will. He spoke of this being a platonic relationship. The members, except Mr. Darcy, were extremely supportive to Mr. Foy. Mr. Darcy felt that Foy should go to church and pray to God for help. Miss French retorted angrily to Mr. Darcy that "God helps those who help themselves." The members stated that Mr. Foy should assert himself with his wife; he should tell her the facts as well as go to court, admit the truth, and speak up for himself. All the group members participated in the discussion with Foy, who wanted the therapist to give him a statement that, because of his emotional problems, it would be best for him not to go to court. The therapist made an issue of this and asked what they thought Foy should do. The response was that he shouldn't be given a statement, but should go to court, tell the truth, and assert himself with his wife.

After the meeting was over, Mr. Foy inquired of the therapist what he should do. The therapist replied that the group members' recommendations were quite clear.

Theme and Dynamics

The theme of this meeting began with an entirely different tone from prior ones. The stage was set by the cancelled meeting and illness of the therapist. The members appeared to be pleading for him not to go away— to take care of them. They were afraid of his absence. One also must consider the hostile tone of the prior meeting and the guilt feelings that members may have had as a result of driving the therapist away. The behavior of Mr. Foy was precipitated by the cancelled meeting. His problem was very adequately handled by the group. This is mutual analysis in action. The instance involving Foy clearly illustrates the bluntness that members can display in a group—they told him he was not a man, that he should face his wife in court, and that he should not seek out the therapist to solve his problem.

Technique

The therapist could have been more active in exploring how the members reacted to his absence. He could have said: "You seem very concerned over last week's cancellation. I wondered how you felt when notified by the secretary that no meeting would take place." He might also add: "You say it was a severe loss for you not to meet. Any ideas of what was happening to you?" or "Regardless of my reasons for cancelling the meeting, how do you feel toward me for not being here?"

He correctly handled the request of Mr. Foy, who consulted the therapist prior to the meeting. Any conflicts or problems experienced by the group members become group issues. The group interpreted Foy's behavior and problem in a constructive way, and their advice to him was clear, concise, and to the point. By making this problem a group issue, Foy's psychodynamics became a matter for the members to analyze and advise. This was accomplished.

FIFTEENTH MEETING

This meeting had to be held in another room of the department because a new secretary had failed to leave the door of the regular room unlocked. The recorder was on vacation. A resident in the department served in her place.

All eight members were present. The group was introduced to the substitute recorder. Mr. Holt began the hour by remarking that the therapist was not high enough in the department to have a key. Mr. Foy referred to the substitute recorder as a new secretary. The major part of the meeting was taken up with a discussion of Foy's problem which was brought to the group at the 14th meeting. He stated that he did not go to court. The lawyer handled all the details. He was unable to face his wife. He could not tell her the truth. The therapist asked about Foy's inability to cope with his problem. Miss French and Mr. Holt were quite disappointed in him; since he asked them for advice, they felt ignored. Mrs. Kitch felt that Foy was at least talking about his problems rather than keeping them to himself. Others said he had to grow up and be a man; that you can't function in life by telling falsehoods and being dishonest. Miss French identified her mother with Foy's wife. The entire group was quite active. Several times during the meeting the members would begin talking about their own feelings in the group and then switch back to questioning Mr. Foy. When this had occurred the third time, the therapist asked why they were spending so much time discussing Foy's problems.

They replied in a somewhat hostile manner that it was necessary. They continued to talk to Foy as the hour ended.

Theme and Dynamics

The group was in a strange room with a strange recorder. Any change in the group structure is a disturbing factor and creates a certain amount of anxiety and tension. Frequent references were made to these changes by two members. There was continued analysis of Mr. Foy's situation, the members expressing disappointment that he could not follow through with their suggestions. The most threatening factor, however, relates to the similar problems of each group member. The fact that they cannot assert themselves is becoming apparent. Another factor is related to the tremendous unhappiness of the members. Probably many of the fantasies (not verbalized) about Foy and his lady friend are sexual, and they secretly wish for a similar affair of their own. Foy's situation also points to a loaded area for all of the group members—closeness in human relationships.

The inability of the members to look at their own problems was demonstrated by their repeatedly going back to Mr. Foy. They reacted with hostility when this was pointed out to them.

Technique

The therapist could have explored their feelings about the change in group structure. Following Holt's hostile remark about the room, he could have asked, "How does it affect you to meet in another room?" or, "What thoughts do you experience by a change like we have today?" Regarding the recorder, he could have reflected Mr. Foy's observation about the new secretary to them and then added: "Now, our regular recorder is not here. Dr. M. is serving in her place. What do you think about having a new person here?" He might make other pertinent observations about their attitude toward him for securing a substitute recorder, their feelings toward the regular recorder, and her relationship to them.

The therapist was aware that the members continued to discuss Mr. Foy's problem in order to avoid their group feelings. He brought this to their attention but appeared to be somewhat vague in his statement. He could have been more direct in making his point, as well as supportive to Foy. The following statement may have been clearer to the members: "Now you have been very concerned about this problem with Foy. You have discussed it in detail with him. Several times you have talked about group problems and then immediately gone back to Foy. I wonder if you have any ideas or thoughts as to why you are spending so much time on Mr. Foy and his problem?"

Discussion

Experience in group therapy has clearly revealed the effects on the group members of changing a meeting room, altering the seating arrangement in a room, or similar departures from custom. The group members react more strongly to changes in the therapist's position than in others. Sometimes a group member may sit in the therapist's chair, but the hostility that this act arouses in the others makes him return to his usual seat. No doubt each group member secretly wants to sit in the therapist's chair, and for this reason the group as a whole condemns any one member's usurpation of it.

The degree of psychopathology of the group members influences their feelings and reactions to changes. The sicker the group member, the more anxiety he experiences. To the patient who is psychotic, changes imply separation, rejection, and loss of dependency. With patients who are neurotic there is less anxiety but definite reactions to changes.

Changes affect most people in one way or another. Often the subjective experience is subtle and not clearly defined. The manifestations of changes are very striking in the family. Feelings associated with people and families moving to new locations have been discussed in Chap. 5. There are also reactions to changes in the more intimate interaction of family life. Children in a home profit from a well-defined and organized structure regarding meals, bedtime, chores, homework and the like. The adolescent may react with hostility to specific rules regarding dates or bedtime schedules, but actually he enjoys the security from the family structure. Frequent changes and indecisive structure by parents contribute to feelings of insecurity and inadequacy. The reaction of children to changes in regular seating arrangements within the family structure has several interesting features. Mealtime is actually one of the most meaningful and important periods of the day in the life of a family. For many families it is the only time that the entire family is together. Then, too, the evening meal is more significant than the other two. Breakfast is served at different times because of the different departure times of father and the children. At lunch, father is usually away and the children are in school. Thus the dinner meal becomes the one time when the whole family is together. It is customary for father, mother, and each of the children to take the same places at the table. Father's position, at the head of the table, signifies his authority position. Changes in their seating arrangement can create hostility among children, since their respective places at table can denote structure and security and may assume great status significance to them. There can, of course, be different meanings about seating arrangements depending on the psychodynamics of the family—a child may show defiance by sitting as far away from his parents as possible; another may do the same out of fear of one parent or the other; still others will sit near a parent to seek approval, love, etc. In the den or living room father's regular chair denotes something special to children; they like to sit in it when he is away from home. One patient, in describing his early family environment, remarked that his father's chair always felt more comfortable than other chairs. He was fearful of his father and always jumped up from father's chair when father caught him sitting in it.

Families that move about frequently during the childhood and adolescence of their children may affect their social role among their peers. They are never able to establish themselves in their school, social, and recreational groups before moving to a new community. They tend to be "followers" rather than "leaders" and may become passive and non-assertive from their "back seat" or "outside" roles. Changes have a very intense effect on elderly people. A home that has been lived in for many years represents a greater emotional investment to its occupants than its physical worth. Even though the children have married and moved away, that time-honored statement "There's no place like home" remains quite appropriate. Relatives, physicians, and lawyers often advise elderly people to give up their home for smaller apartments without considering the emotional effect on them. Elderly people may become depressed when they have to give up a home and its emotional investments for another place.

SIXTEENTH MEETING

All eight members were present. Mrs. Jacobs and Mrs. Webster were ten minutes late. A certain amount of intermember hostility has begun to develop in regard to these two members, who have established a pattern of being 10 to 15 minutes late at the meetings. Mr. Darcy began the hour by discussing in detail many of his own feelings, irritations, and conflicts with his wife and children. He spoke of the need to take a vacation and to be alone. Mr. Foy agreed, saying that vacations were nice when you were able to get away from everyone. He mentioned how happy he was when his wife was away from home; the house was entirely different. Mr. Holt remarked that running away from problems did not solve anything.

Theme and Dynamics

There was a significant trend in the group: a person could talk about his problems and feel accepted, as was the case with Mr. Foy. Mr. Darcy appeared more at ease and talked more freely.

The need to be alone, to take vacations relates to the anxiety of the meeting.

Technique

The group has a problem with the tardiness of two members. The therapist should have called this to their attention. He could have said: "Mrs. Jacobs and Mrs. Webster have been arriving late rather regularly during the past several meetings. Do you have any thoughts about their inability to get here on time?" or, "Any ideas as to whether their tardiness is related to the group meeting?" or, "How do you feel about people not being on time for the meetings?"

The therapist could have related the need to be alone and take vacations by saying: "Now you speak of needing to be alone and the pleasure of vacations away from people. You are a group of people. How does wanting to be alone and away from others compare to coming here, and your feelings with one another and with me?"

SEVENTEENTH MEETING

All eight members were present; Mrs. Jacobs and Mrs. Webster were again 10 minutes late. Mr. Foy began the meeting by relating numerous complaints: the need for magic, drugs, and hypnosis. The members asked him a series of questions but frequently laughed at his remarks. The humorous atmosphere was focused on by the therapist. The members admitted laughing at Foy and being amused by his pattern of always being sicker than anyone else. He had a habit of complaining and seemed to enjoy it. When Mrs. Jacobs and Mrs. Webster arrived, the members talked of their pattern of tardiness. The therapist asked for their feelings about the late members. They only dealt with it superficially and returned to asking Foy a series of questions. The therapist pointed out that they were discussing Foy as in the last meeting. They made no response and changed the subject. Later, when there was a silence, Mr. Holt remarked that he guessed they would have to discuss Mr. Foy again. However, Mrs. Jacobs spoke of incurring increased phobic difficulties with others and wished to discuss the matter. When she had completed her discussion, Mr. Holt remarked that probably her phobic problem was related to being with people. The therapist asked about Mrs. Jacob's situation, and its relationship to people. He asked for comparisons with the people in the meeting. The members would not deal with his statement. Mr. Cain, Mr. Holt, and Miss French denied any comparison to the group from the discussion. When the hour was over, Holt came up to the therapist and related a problem of going blank and freezing when the therapist made an observation. The therapist suggested that Holt bring this up for discussion at the next meeting.

Theme and Dynamics

The trend in the group continued to be related to mutual acceptance in discussing problems. Anamnestic material was not directly related to the group process, but the members have been becoming better acquainted with one another. They were using this method as part of the process of revealing themselves and coming closer to one another. Mr. Holt's observation that Mrs. Jacobs' phobic difficulties occurred when she was around people was quite accurate. They appeared to be digging a little deeper into their own problems. Their group feelings appeared to be a loaded and threatening area for them. Their repeated questioning of Mr. Foy, their failure to deal with issues brought to their attention by the therapist, and their refusal to compare the group to Mrs. Jacobs' phobic problem with people were all methods of avoiding group anxiety.

Technique

This group meeting was handled well. First, the therapist asked about their feelings for Mr. Foy, which created laughter in the meeting. Then he pointed out and directed the members toward their feelings with each other. He recognized the tension of the group process and did not attempt to raise the anxiety level too high.

He also properly referred Mr. Holt's postmeeting remarks to the group. He avoided individual interpretation and suggested that the members deal with this problem.

Discussion

The observation that the group members' phobic difficulties are due to relationships with people is a very significant and important statement. *Phobic manifestations in most patients arise from conflicts in interpersonal relationships.* There are two patients in this group with phobic symptoms. Both have conflicts with their fathers, husbands, and other authority figures. They are passive, dependent and nonassertive in their interpersonal relationships. Along with their phobic manifestations they suffer from depression and psychosomatic symptoms. Moreover, their phobic symptoms are being increased by the anxiety of the group process.

Phobic symptoms may occur in different personality types and different emotional illnesses. Phobias are common in obsessive-compulsive neurosis. Probably the outstanding personality trait of people with phobias is their dependency need. If the patient can become dependent on the group rather than expecting the therapist to fulfill his dependency need, his chances of securing help are good. Since the group is made up of people, the patient can help overcome phobic difficulties by being confronted with people every week at the group meetings. In this way the patient reenters the phobic situation time and time again, and this repeated reentrance is a necessary factor in the treatment of patients with phobic difficulties.

EIGHTEENTH MEETING

There were only six members present, Mrs. Jacobs and Mrs. Webster remaining absent. Mrs. Jacobs called the clinic to report that her absence was caused by the death of her grandmother.

The hour began with Miss French relating conflicts with her family. She spoke of the reasons for leaving home. The members interacted well with her. At a lull in the meeting, the therapist asked about their relationships with each other in the meeting. Mr. Holt reacted in a very hostile manner, saying that the doctor brought up questions he could not understand. He could see no connection with Miss French's conversation and the doctor's statement. Miss French and Mr. Darcy spoke of understanding the therapist. Mr. Cain wanted the therapist to open up and become a member of the group. Others felt he should not be a member; it was up to them to run the meeting. They all agreed that questions from the therapist related to the group. The therapist again pointed out the inability of some members to grasp his questions. Mrs. Kitch felt confused and dazed by the therapist's statements. Mr. Cain agreed with Holt and Mrs. Kitch. Mr. Darcy felt that Holt and Cain would get an idea of what was going on if they would only listen to other members. Mrs. Kitch wondered if the members were eight individuals or a group. Mr. Cain replied the group was like a deck of cards; each member was a card, but together they were the deck. Mr. Holt wondered if the doctor was the joker. The therapist reminded them at the end of the hour that important group material was being discussed that could be pursued further in later meetings if they so desired.

Mrs. Jacobs' and Mrs. Webster's absence was discussed. Mrs. Kitch felt the group was better off without them. Mr. Holt admitted it affected the group to have only six-eighths of the members present.

Theme and Dynamics

The members' hostile reaction to the therapist was quite apparent when he asked about group relationships. Their fears of the therapist—the authority figure—have become more apparent in terms of interruptions, confusion, remarks about being unable to understand him, and lack of comprehension on the part of the members. Subjects other than group relationships are more comfortable and understandable. The group has begun to develop a considerable amount of intergroup tension and hostility toward Mrs. Jacobs and Mrs. Webster for their absences and tardiness at meetings.

Mrs. Kitch's confused and dazed reaction to the group therapist's statements is due to anxiety induced by her fear of authority figures. Other group members are also experiencing anxiety in the group meetings. The anxiety level of the group is higher than during the early group meetings.

Technique

The therapist demonstrated excellent control of the meeting. He was aware of the theme of hostility and the numerous maneuvers designed to avoid group interaction. He allowed Miss French to ventilate material concerning herself, and then focused on group issues. Essential exploration of feelings toward the group and the therapist occupied the remainder of the hour.

It is important for the therapist to understand the meanings and feelings of the anxious group member. In this respect the therapist who has been a member of a training or didactic group, or who has undergone a personal analysis, can better understand the anxiety of the group member. Many of the group members at this stage of the group cannot identify their anxiety. They can only describe its subjective component. They are uncomfortable and tense. There may be dryness of the mouth, perspiration, tachycardia, headaches, gastrointestinal symptoms, etc. They actually do "freeze" or "go blank" following the therapist's comments. The group members' anxiety may interfere with their thought processes so that they become unable to talk. They are seemingly overwhelmed by the anxiety. One physician, a member of a group, described the effects of anxiety very clearly. He said, "You can't talk; you do not know what to say; you are lost in trying to figure out where the anxiety comes from." Later the same physician made another meaningful statement: "Trying to figure out why I'm anxious is a hundred times harder than going to college, medical school, and residency training. In school you can find the answer from a professor or a book. With anxiety there are so many unknowns."

The therapist should be aware that the causes of anxiety experienced by the group members are not in their conscious awareness. One of his goals is to help the group members identify how anxiety is related to their faulty emergency responses. Identifying the causes of their anxiety takes patience, understanding, and careful leadership by the therapist. The inexperienced group therapist often wants his group to move faster than is possible. He may become angry with the group for not dealing with group issues, and may attempt to make them do so. The therapist who is prone to push his group too fast to get at the source of their anxiety may cause his group to disintegrate because of persistently high anxiety levels. The importance of gauging his technique by the anxiety of the group members cannot be overemphasized.

NINETEENTH MEETING

All members were present. Mrs. Webster was 25 minutes late, and Mrs. Jacobs was 30 minutes late.

The central issue at this meeting revolved around Mrs. Jacobs and Mrs. Webster, their absences and tardiness. The hour began with a discussion of the group's feelings toward them. The group ventilated hostility, as well as concern, for this behavior. When Mrs. Jacobs and Mrs. Webster arrived they were treated with silent hostility. The tension was extremely pronounced. Mr. Darcy soon made a reference to late members. Mrs. Jacobs apologized for being late. The group's response was a continuation of the nonverbal hostility. Mrs. Jacobs began talking about the death of her grandmother. Mrs. Webster participated in this discussion with her, the other members remaining quiet. At one point Mrs. Jacobs cried. The therapist was aware of the intense feeling present and asked the members to describe what was going on. There was no response. The therapist then reminded the members of earlier statements in regard to Mrs. Webster's and Mrs. Jacobs' being late and absent and asked for additional feelings. Mrs. Webster and Mrs. Jacobs again apologized. Mr. Foy said it was "like part of him not being there" when they missed meetings. Miss French quizzed Mrs. Jacobs as to why she was always late. Mrs. Webster admitted that group therapy was getting harder for her and stated that she didn't feel like "ever bringing up any of her problems." At the end of the hour the therapist remarked to the recorder after the meeting that the intragroup tension and hostility were quite intense at first, but dissipated somewhat at the end of the hour. The therapist also felt the one-hour sessions were too brief and that a longer period, probably 1½ hours, would be better.

Theme and Dynamics

This session was an excellent example of the intense feeling and hostility that can be generated by group problems. The nonverbal manifestations of anxiety were pronounced. The therapist recognized the group problem and was able to resolve it to an extent. Mrs. Jacobs and Mrs. Webster picked up the group tension when they arrived at the meeting. The discussion of Mrs. Jacobs' grandmother's death was probably protective and defensive on her part. Mrs. Webster admitted difficulties in the group situation.

Technique

The therapist was in control and aware of the theme of the meeting. He correctly dealt with the major problems, group absences, and lateness. He felt, however, uncertain as to what was the proper technique when Mrs. Jacobs discussed the recent family death. Should he encourage the ventilation of her feelings or deal with the group problems? In this meeting he attempted to deal with each, but time did not allow sufficient discussion and ventilation of feelings.

The therapist should have considered whether or not the other members have contributed to the behavior of Mrs. Jacobs and Mrs. Webster. From a standpoint of dynamics, the other members might want to push them out of the group. The group has become blocked by the anxiety and tension of the group difficulties. As the therapist encouraged the members to ventilate their feelings toward Mrs. Jacobs and Mrs. Webster he should also have asked them to look at the reasons for exhibiting this behavior. Mrs. Jacobs' repeated phobic difficulties and discomfort are well known to all. Mrs. Webster joined late (fourth meeting) and has not integrated into the group. The therapist could have reminded them of the problems of Mrs. Jacobs and Mrs. Webster and asked if they (the other members) had contributed in any way to the fact that Mrs. Jacobs and Mrs. Webster had not been regular in attendance and were frequently late at meetings. Thus he can investigate and clarify group problems. When necessary, he should enlist support. At all times he must remember that he is involved in group therapy, not administering individual therapy.

Discussion

The hostile remarks about the two absent members made before their arrival at the meeting, and the silence following their arrival, both illustrate a very common pattern of behavior in everyday group relationships. Many people can be quite voluble in expressing their feelings about an absent person, yet cannot express these to the person himself. A small, close group has a large amount of this kind of verbal acting out. In small communities of a few thousand people, "gossip" and talking about others seem to be "standard operating procedure" and characteristic of our culture. Yet this type of behavior is not limited to small communities. It occurs to some extent in all kinds of groups. For example, a doctor admits a difficult patient to a hospital; the nurse becomes angry and tells everyone but the doctor. A college professor makes a class routine harder; the students tell everyone but the professor. An industrial worker has a conflict with a fellow employee; he criticizes him to others but shuns a direct confrontation. Even the person who is in difficulty and needs corrective counseling will be avoided by his friends. They hesitate to tell him of unacceptable behavior and delay talking with him just as long as possible. There are numerous examples in all types of groups on every cultural level. People seem to be afraid to talk not only to their superiors, but to each other. There are a number of reasons why people cannot talk to others. In a family where the expression of feelings is censored by the parents, learned behavior may dictate that others can be talked to more easily because there is less fear of reprisal or retaliation than from parents. Inability to express angry feelings to an authority figure may be displaced to other people. The authority figure who does not allow the expression of feelings encourages others to talk among themselves. Many religious groups place a premium on never disagreeing with a person in his presence, for to do so would "hurt his feelings." Such feelings find their release on others.

Many people are jealous and envious of the position, wealth, or status of others. Since they cannot have this position or status themselves, the most acceptable solution is to become angry and attack those who do have it. Some people seemingly relieve themselves of anxiety by excessive talking. They cannot retain a confidence. They enjoy hearing of people's conflicts and problems and keep the telephone lines busy telling others distorted and exaggerated versions of the problems. In small communities these people are referred to as "gossips." Their verbal acting-out behavior can, on occasion, be very detrimental. The old adage that "people can damage a person more with their tongue than with guns" illustrates the effectiveness of verbal acting out in expressing anger or rage.

TWENTIETH MEETING

All members were present and on time, but the recorder was absent. The therapist began the hour by informing the group of the recorder's absence and requested permission to record the meeting with the use of a tape recorder. There were no objections. At the onset the mood was more cheerful and relaxed. The hour began with Mr. Holt's discussing emotional problems within his family, particularly with his daughter. When the opportunity presented itself, the therapist asked about group relationships and was ignored. A discussion with Mr. Foy followed. The therapist again focused on group relationships with no response. The therapist then made the following observation: "On two occasions today I have asked you to look at your behavior here, and you pay no attention to me. Let me remind you again of the group contract and the purpose of group therapy. Why are you ignoring my observations?" They then spoke of being more cheerful. They felt closer together and did not have to be so careful now to break in and say something. The topic of understanding the therapist was discussed again by Holt, Cain, and Mrs. Kitch.

Mrs. Webster stated that financial problems necessitated going to work, and that this would interfere with her attendance. The therapist asked for their thoughts about Mrs. Webster's problems and the possibility that her plans were influenced to some degree by the meetings. Mrs. Kitch reminded Mrs. Webster that she had come to this city from a neighboring state primarily for group therapy. Mr. Holt felt she should put first things first. Mr. Cain wondered if she was running from her own problems by getting a job so that she could not attend. The members, however, were very warm and supportive in wanting Mrs. Webster to continue. They suggested that she arrange work which would not interfere with attendance at the meetings.

Theme and Dynamics

The last five meetings illustrate an important feature of group dynamics. The anxiety level of the group members is higher than in earlier meetings. The group members are becoming more hostile to each other. They have made an attempt to scapegoat Mr. Foy. Those members who have been absent from meetings have been subjected to hostility from the others. However, the members' reaction to the therapist has not been overtly hostile. They only say that they do not understand his observations and that they are confused by his remarks. They deny their hostility feelings for the therapist and react to him with ingratiation. Transference reactions have developed. Now they view the therapist as a powerful, omnipotent person who can both magically love and care for them, or, more significantly, retaliate against them. The members are angry with the therapist for not providing dependency gratifications and for promoting closeness within the group. However, their anger is covered over by their fear of him, and, as we have shown, react with passivity, denial, and ingratiation.

Technique

The therapist substituted a tape recording machine for the female recorder during the group therapy session. The use of mechanical instruments can be clarified when the group contract is initially discussed with the individual members at the onset of the group therapy program. In this instance, the therapist had not discussed this matter with his group. The group contract was thus amended for this meeting by the agreement of both parties: the therapist and the group members.

The therapist was aware of the use of anamnestic material and other matters to avoid group issues. He brought this to their attention by directing the members to group relationships.

The therapist related Mrs. Webster's problem to the members for identification and support.

TWENTY–FIRST MEETING

Only four members were present, the absentees being Mrs. Webster, Mrs. Jacobs, Mr. Holt, and Mr. Cain.

The session began with numerous questions about the absent members.

Mrs. Kitch was hostile to Mrs. Jacobs. She had problems at home and could not believe Mrs. Jacobs' repeated statements concerning her "perfect" husband and her "perfect" marriage. Miss French and Mrs. Kitch were antagonistic toward Holt and Cain for their intellectualization or "educated answers." They were sympathetic to Mrs. Webster, even bringing out that the members could be responsible for her plans since she was late joining the group and was ignored frequently when she came in to meetings. The therapist made the following observations: "Apparently you have many feelings between each other, but you are only discussing those who are not here." They agreed that it was easier to talk about people who were not present and that the comments should be made when they were in attendance. Mrs. Kitch said she felt inferior around Holt, Cain, and Mrs. Jacobs. She could talk more freely at this meeting. Once during the hour, when the therapist asked about group behavior, Miss French replied that she had to be very careful and concise with her emotions. Mr. Foy spoke of the group as being a means of unscrambling his feelings. The therapist asked about the four members who were absent. They voiced concern but felt those present were like a team who could talk better to each other.

Theme and Dynamics

The large number of absences was the central problem but group feelings were explored in more detail. The members have been becoming more aware of their relationship to each other. Mrs. Webster received additional support even though she was absent.

Technique

The therapist pointed out their ability to discuss the members who were not present, but he could have explored this important area in more detail by saying: "Let us recall that you are here to explore your feelings with one another and to understand and look at why you feel certain ways toward others. Now, Mrs. Kitch speaks of feeling inferior to certain members and has difficulty expressing herself when they are present. What are your thoughts about having such feelings?" The therapist was also quite involved in the feelings of the group members. He could have asked about himself by saying: "Several times in recent meetings you have referred to not understanding statements I make to you. What about these feelings of inferiority in regard to me?" From the response, he could have explored in more detail their relationship to him.

When Miss French spoke of having to control and be concise with her emotions, the therapist could have reflected this back for group discussion. He might say: "Now, Miss French speaks of the need to be concise with her emotions. How do you feel that you have to handle your emotions and reactions here?" Again he might ask the members to look at their relationship to him, saying: "Any thoughts as to how you have to handle your emotions with me?"

Discussion

The group member's reference to her "perfect" marriage will not be accepted by the group members. There is no such thing as a perfect marriage. In every marriage there are differences of opinions and conflicts that vary from major to minor. There is no closer relationship than that of husband and wife. The premarital courtship has some elements of closeness but does not approach the closeness of marriage partners. A general practitioner in a small southern town described courtship and marriage in the following words: "Courtship is the ice cream and cake; marriage is when you get down to turnip greens and corn bread." The closeness of marriage produces many emotional reactions in each partner. Other factors that enter into a marriage are economic, occupational, social and religious values. A successful marriage means that the self-gratification of both the husband and wife must be compromised along acceptable terms. The husband and wife must be able to talk to each other and express their feelings, both positive and negative, in a mutually understanding atmosphere. A major problem among married people is their inability to talk and communicate with each other. Silence between marital partners breeds defiance, acting-out behavior, and emotional illness.

TWENTY–SECOND MEETING

All members were present. The hour began with a discussion of how members become quiet and reticent when the therapist entered the room. The therapist asked them to explore this area in more detail. They compared him to an Army top sergeant, a bank president, a boss, and an outside authority figure of any type. Mr. Holt could see the therapist as the leader of the group, but not a member. He felt that his job related to getting the members to talk about their problems. Mrs. Kitch felt he censored the group. Mr. Darcy disagreed. He felt it was only her feelings she needed to examine. The members agreed that they were still tense, but could accept the therapist better. Mr. Holt stated he would be tense even if he completely liked him. Mrs. Kitch changed the subject and asked Mrs. Webster a series of questions. Others joined in, seeming quite interested. She asked questions about Mrs. Jacobs' present situation, saying she had noticed her increased anxiety during the meeting. Mrs. Jacobs admitted she was more uncomfortable in the meeting than anywhere else.

She said that in situations under her control (teaching elementary school and Sunday school, etc.) no major problems were present, but where she has to listen, tension occurs. (Mrs. Jacobs is really saying that she is comfortable in groups that are rigidly structured with minimal emotional interaction—i.e., didactic lectures and preplanned subject material. The emotional interaction in this group causes her to have tension and anxiety.) The therapist asked about Mrs. Jacobs' feelings in the meeting. Mr. Cain replied that her problem could be related to the top sergeant. The therapist explored the authority figure relationship. Mrs. Jacobs agreed this might be true; however, she was reluctant to discuss this matter in any detail.

Theme and Dynamics

The therapist's relationship to the members has been identified and accepted as one of an authority figure. The anxiety of examining their relationship to him is still quite threatening. He creates tension and is a censor. His job of getting the group to talk about their problems is not a comfortable one. Mrs. Jacobs' relationship to the group and the therapist was discussed and identified to a degree. Mrs. Webster continued to receive support and encouragement to remain in therapy.

Technique

The therapist pointed out his relationship to the group, but he could have been more direct in his statements. For example, when Mr. Darcy told Mrs. Kitch the censor was related primarily to her feelings, the therapist could have said: "Now, I have been called a censor by Mrs. Kitch. Mr. Darcy disagrees and says it's only her feelings. What thoughts do you have about such thoughts and differences among you here?" He could also have said: "Why do you feel I am a censor?" or, "Why should I censor you here in the meeting?" When Mr. Holt stated the therapist's job was to get them to talk about their problems, the therapist could have made the following observation: "You have compared me to a top sergeant, a boss, and other authority figures, and have said that my job here is to get you to talk about your problem. What feelings do you experience in recognizing me as an authority figure with a job to get you to talk about your problems?"

The therapist correctly focused on Mrs. Jacobs' group problem; its relationship to him was identified.

The therapist was aware of the conversation shifting from himself to Mrs. Webster. To encourage support for her was beneficial to the group. The shifting patterns of relationship between the group members and the therapist necessitated maneuvers like this. The other members have probably felt guilty for their past attitudes toward Mrs. Webster. They have become more aware of their behavior, and this awareness probably accounts for the increase in support she has begun to receive in the meeting.

One important goal of the therapist is to help the members recognize that the therapy group has many similarities to everyday groups. He made this point clear to them at the onset of group therapy. In this meeting he could have asked the members if they are reacting to him as they have to bosses and other authority figures in everyday groups. Such observations will help the members associate the social realities of the therapy group with other groups. When the opportunity presents itself, the therapist should always focus on the therapy group's comparison to everyday groups.

TWENTY–THIRD MEETING

All members were present. They continued to exhibit positive interest in Mrs. Webster's marital problems and present family situation. A detailed discussion of Mrs. Webster's problems followed. The relationship to Mrs. Jacobs showed a decided improvement. Mrs. Kitch discussed a series of conflicts with her mother-in-law. She asked for advice. They encouraged her to use assertion at every opportunity. The therapist asked about their group feelings by saying: "Several of you have talked about difficulties and problems in your families. I wonder if you find any comparison here?" There were statements of having to face their own problems and not the problems of others. Mr. Holt felt they had spent too much time talking about other people. He said that families would not change; the question was whether they can change to be more happy and comfortable with them. The subject was switched back to Mrs. Kitch and Mrs. Webster as the hour ended.

Theme and Dynamics

The acceptance of Mrs. Webster and Mrs. Jacobs by the members, as well as their increased positive feelings for the group, was quite apparent. Mrs. Kitch's relationship to her mother-in-law received attention and analysis. It was significant that she wanted advice from the others. Group problems were discussed superficially. The observation by Mr. Holt that others do not change, that this was a job for the group members, was very pertinent.

Group meetings do not necessarily follow a prescribed pattern. At the 22nd meeting, analysis of group behavior and the relationship to the therapist were explored in considerable detail. At this 23rd session, specific group problems occupied a minor part of the hour. However, bringing up the group's specific conflicts and asking for advice ties in with the group atmosphere of looking at the dynamics of the member and giving corrective emotional suggestions. Interpretations and advice to Mrs. Kitch came from the members, not the therapist.

Technique

The therapist continued to allow the members to support and encourage Mrs. Webster and Mrs. Jacobs.

Group problems were dealt with by comparing family behavior patterns with group behavior patterns. From the standpoint of technique the therapist should be flexible in dealing with reality issues of the group members. Our model of group therapy recognizes that the group members profit chiefly from the exploitation of their behavior with each other and with the therapist during group meetings. However, as the group members become more aware of their conflicts and problems inside the group, they also begin to understand their personal problems outside the group. These new insights will be brought to the group for discussion and advice. The therapist should allow pertinent issues with the group members to be discussed in group meetings. The group members, as they recognize and learn about behavior in group meetings, will usually be able to correlate and compare behavior in the therapy group with their behavior in outside groups. By his observations, the therapist should help the group members recognize the similarity between family and other patterns of behavior with their patterns of behavior in group meetings. At the same time, the therapist should be aware that the group members may try to avoid looking at their relationships in the group by discussing anamnestic material or current personal issues. Then, too, the group members may discuss their intragroup conflicts in symbolic or metaphorical language— they may talk about conflicts outside of the group that are analogous to their conflicts in the group. The group members are fearful of disapproval and rejection if they discuss intragroup conflicts directly. In this meeting the therapist was flexible. He allowed Mrs. Webster and Mrs. Kitch to discuss personal problems. Then he asked the group members to compare their extragroup relationships with their intragroup relationships.

TWENTY–FOURTH MEETING

Seven members were present, Mrs. Jacobs being absent. The hour began with Mr. Cain's discussing a recent conflict in his family. Mr. Foy followed with a restatement of his gloomy outlook on life. The members began to ask him a series of questions. The therapist attempted on three different occasions to bring them back to group relationships. The members would side-step him and proceed again with Foy. The therapist then made the following statement: "On three occasions today I have asked you to look at group relationships. Each time you ignore me and go back to asking Foy a number of questions. I wonder if you have any thoughts or ideas as to what you are doing?" Miss French said she was afraid of the future. Mr. Cain recognized a number of his own problems in Mr. Foy, and this didn't make him feel very good. Mrs. Kitch said we could all have some of his traits. Several of the members spoke of their unhappy lives in the past. Cain felt they were concerned with the present; the past could not be changed. Miss French made a comparison between the group and a baseball player who had been batting 350 and had now dropped to 250. You didn't work with his past, but the here and now—his stance, grip, etc. The therapist asked the members about their own batting average. They replied that it was up and down, but improving. Mrs. Kitch added that she was now able to express herself in the group and on the outside. She felt the members were closer to one another. Mrs. Jacobs' absence was discussed. Miss French said she had recognized one reason for disliking Mrs. Jacobs. She reminded her of a supervisor with whom she had conflicts in her work. She had disliked Holt, because of his resemblance to her father, and Cain, who had traits similar to her brother. Now she likes all three of these members better than she did before.

Theme and Dynamics

The members attempted to avoid their own problems with the diversionary tactic of discussing and quizzing Mr. Foy. He did not appear to be scapegoated. They used him primarily to avoid group involvement. The therapist was in control of the meeting and successfully brought them back to group issues. There followed an interesting series of events: (1) group identification with Foy, (2) group problems concerning the present, not the past, and (3) Miss French's verbalization of identifications with three members and her feelings within the group.

Technique

The therapist diligently pursued the tactic employed by the members to avoid the group issue. When someone relates a long, involved personal story, he does it primarily to keep away from his problems, even though the story may be revealing so far as his behavior is concerned. Such an event has to be recognized by the therapist, then brought to the attention of the group and analyzed. Emphasis should be made that the tactic employed by the members on Mr. Foy should be handled by the group members. You do not employ an individual approach. You are dealing with group reactions. Actually, it would be different for you to ask him as an individual, "Mr. Foy, how do you feel about the other members ganging up on you and repeatedly asking you questions?" When you make a group issue of the problem you ask all the members their feelings about it. After all, Mr. Foy is in the group; so he has the right to comment like anyone else.

The therapist should have explained in more detail the meaning and behavior associated with the member's refusal to pursue group relationships. On three occasions they have ignored the therapist's statements. This pattern of behavior (ignoring someone's remarks) is laden with hostility. The therapist should attempt to get the anger identified. He could say: "What does it mean when you ignore someone's observations?" "What is the feeling associated with ignoring comments from others?" "Why are you ignoring me in this meeting?"

TWENTY–FIFTH MEETING

Only six members were present, Mrs. Webster and Mr. Cain being the absentees.

The initial part of the hour was taken up with a discussion by Miss French of conflicts within her family. She described her relationship toward her father. He is now going with a lady who irritates Miss French. The members pointed out to Miss French that she is prejudiced against her father. Mr. Holt felt that she should leave him alone and concentrate on improving her local relationships. He added that many teen-age girls fall in love with their father for a period of time and later begin going with boys. Some try to stay in love with their father throughout their lives. Mr. Holt asked the therapist a direct question concerning this father-daughter relationship and followed it up by saying he knew the therapist would not answer the question, that he probably would have to get a book and look up the answer. The therapist immediately asked for their feelings toward him for not answering questions. Mr. Holt and Mrs. Jacobs admitted anger and irritation at the therapist. Miss French and Mr. Darcy felt they should work out their own problems. A discussion of group therapy followed. Mrs. Kitch wished she could feel as free on the outside in groups as on the inside with this group. Several of the members agreed with her. Others spoke of feeling like guinea pigs and wondering whether or not group therapy was part of an experiment. The recorder and her notes were discussed. They referred to her material as Chinese language. They wondered if she wrote down mannerisms and attitudes. Mrs. Jacobs was concerned as to whether or not the notes would be published in some journal. The therapist focused on feelings about the recorder and the fate of the notes. Mr. Holt referred to the therapist as an expert; there was no doubt as to how he would run this group. Mr. Foy again spoke of his problems. Mr. Darcy replied to him very aggressively that he needed more optimism and less pessimism. Toward the end of the meeting, the therapist announced he was going on a two-week vacation one month hence. He asked for group discussion. There were no comments of any significance.

Theme and Dynamics

Again the relationship of the group members to the therapist has come to the fore. Following a discussion with Miss French, which they analyzed quite well, the members explored their feelings about the therapist with particular reference to his role. They admitted anger and hostility toward him for his failure to answer questions (dependency gratifications). Several recognized the need to help themselves. Hostility was diverted from the therapist to the department with statements of being guinea pigs and part of an experiment. The recorder was included with their fears of exposure from the written notes. Mr. Darcy, usually quite passive and nonassertive, demonstrated aggressiveness and assertiveness for the initial time during his interplay with Foy.

Examination of the context of this meeting revealed a recurrent theme. The hour began with Miss French's bringing out problems with her father. Next, the members took up the therapist and followed this by talking about experimenting with doctors, the recorder, and the notes. One might postulate that they were really saying: "Look, we still have problems with our fathers; they are unresolved." Actually, the real issue was not whether the recorder's notes would be published. It was, "I still don't trust my father." It also meant "I don't trust men." It was paranoid distrust which was related to their problems with the therapist and their old problems with their fathers.

Technique

The therapist correctly exploited the group into an expression of their feelings as to his role. When Mr. Holt and Mrs. Jacobs admitted anger and irritations, he could have added: "Mr. Holt and Mrs. Jacobs admit irritations with me. What about the ability to express your feelings here, with me and with each other?"

When the members diverted their hostility from the therapist over to the department, he could have said: "You were angry at me for not answering your questions. Then you changed the subject. You started working over the department, calling group therapy an experiment and yourselves guinea pigs. What about this?"

The therapist could have asked them to look at the relationship between fathers and the therapist. He could have done so by making the following observation toward the end of the hour: "You began this session with Miss French's discussing problems with her father. You followed this by discussing some of your problems with me. I wonder if you have any ideas about this sequence of conversation here in the meeting?" The members might or might not pick up the association. Sooner or later this relationship would come out in the open for discussion.

TWENTY–SIXTH MEETING

There were seven members present. Mrs. Webster, the only member absent, called and explained that occupational duties would prevent her attendance.

The initial issue discussed was Mr. Cain's absence from the previous meeting. Mr. Cain related some of his marital conflicts and talked about the very belligerent attitude of his wife's family. He denied any feelings toward them. The therapist focused on Mr. Cain's statement of denial. Mr. Holt and Mr. Darcy felt he did have feelings about the problem. Mrs. Kitch felt that being in the group had helped Mr. Cain through this marital strife. Mrs. Kitch spoke angrily of her mother-in-law. Mrs. Jacobs discussed conflicts with her husband's mother. At this point the therapist made the following observation: "You have been talking of others outside the group; what about the feelings and attitudes here?" Mr. Holt said they had not been able to deal with the likes and dislikes among the members. Miss French was ready to discuss them if someone else would start. Mr. Darcy, Mr. Cain, Mr. Foy, and Mrs. Jacobs gave testimonials of positive feelings for the group. Miss French and Mrs. Kitch were conspicuously silent. The subject was changed by Foy, who discussed a clinic bill he had received. The therapist, at this point, dealt with the nonpayment of the bills by the group members. After an initial severely hostile blast at the department for laxity in sending out statements, they admitted nonpayment of bills was related to the group process. Miss French felt it could be just like their own problems: not paying bills is like not facing problems in the group. They admitted, finally, that the charges were quite lenient. Mr. Cain felt that paying for therapy was really part of therapy. Mr. Holt wondered if the department could not do other things to make payment easier, such as provide a box in the room for payment. The hour ended with a discussion of Mrs. Webster's absence.

Theme and Dynamics

There was a continuation of the theme from the 25th meeting. The main stream of the group process was their relationship to the therapist. Mr. Cain, Mrs. Kitch, and Mrs. Jacobs spoke of conflicts with family authority figures. After payment of fees was mentioned there was hostility toward the department followed by the analysis that the problems raised by nonpayment of fees are similar to other emotional problems.

Dependency strivings were evident by their laxity of payment and request for increased conveniences. They wanted the therapist to love and care for them and make no demands. It was as if they were saying: "We want what we want when we want it; we want treatment free." Actually, the bills were not the issue at all. True, the members were angry about money, but they were also angry with the therapist for promoting group interaction. They were having to get closer and closer to each other, and react with anger and hostility, rather than face their own feelings.

Technique

The therapist asked about group feelings by comparing outside figures to the group. He could have explored the group area more explicitly by reflecting back to them Mr. Holt's statement about members' not being able to deal with likes and dislikes in the meeting. He could have said: "Why haven't you been able to deal with the likes and dislikes here?" "What role do I play in your likes and dislikes?" "What keeps you from talking about your likes and dislikes here?"

When Miss French spoke of being ready to talk about group feelings, the therapist could have said: "What about Miss French's wanting to talk about the likes and dislikes here among you?"

The therapist correctly dealt with the nonpayment of bills and its relationship to group therapy, but he should have brought the subject of unpaid bills to their attention at a much earlier meeting. Money problems are directly related to their individual and group dynamics and should be pursued diligently by the therapist. The passivity of the therapist was quite evident in this case and related to his dynamics in regard to financial matters.

TWENTY–SEVENTH MEETING

Again, only six members were present, Mrs. Webster and Mrs. Jacobs being absent.

The initial issue concerned the absent members. Hostility was voiced for their inability to attend. Mr. Holt remarked that there was not as much friendliness as he had felt there might be. He compared the group to a civic or social club where people become friendly in a short period of time. Mr. Cain said the therapist was a moderator. The therapist asked about Mr. Holt's comparison of the group to social clubs and referred again to the group contract in his remarks. Mrs. Kitch and Mr. Darcy wondered again what the group contract said. Mr. Holt, Mr. Cain, and Miss French correctly restated it. For the second time the therapist asked about Holt's earlier remarks on the lack of friendly feelings. Mrs. Kitch, Mr. Cain, and Mr. Darcy felt the group was friendly. Miss French agreed with Holt's adverse statements. Mr. Foy observed that no one had been able to bring up real problems. A discussion of Holt followed. He admitted that his daughter was not really the problem; it was himself. One of his feelings was that no one liked him. They supported Holt strongly and discussed the dictatorial manner in which he talks. Mr. Holt was aware of his speech mannerism and wanted to correct it. Doctors were discussed in the ensuing remarks. The therapist asked about their relationship to him and again made reference to an earlier statement about the unfriendly feelings present. Miss French admitted irritability with people who stay quiet and referred, in a hostile manner, to an official of the company where she was employed. She again discussed the recorder's notes, showing less concern than at previous instances. The hour ended with Foy feeling he was insane and Holt remarking that Foy would continue this way until he was committed to the state hospital, where he would have the same problems as now.

Theme and Dynamics

The theme continued to center around their relationship with the therapist and with each other. The members were more aware of the lack of closeness in the group and their hostility to the therapist. They knew of the lack of interaction. However, they appeared to be moving gradually into these two areas. There is the concern that if they get close to each other, the group will dissolve. The individual mannerisms of Mr. Holt, which have been of concern to the members in past meetings, were brought up and analyzed.

Technique

The therapist dealt with feelings following remarks of unfriendliness in the group and comparison to social clubs. He has continued to ask the members to take a closer look at their relationship to him and to each other.

The therapist announced at the 25th meeting the impending period of two weeks without meetings. He should have called this to their attention. He could have done so as follows: "Two weeks ago I announced the cancellation of two meetings. I wonder what thoughts you have about not meeting for two weeks?" He could also have explored their feelings as to the effect of cancellation of meetings, as well as their reactions toward him for cancelling the meetings. Group members usually have strong feelings about cancelled meetings, but these feelings have not been discussed in any detail since his announcement two weeks ago.

Discussion

Mr. Holt's reference to the group's being different from (less friendly than) a civic or social group illustrates how the degree of closeness between people influences the feelings of the people in the group. Group therapy promotes closeness among its members. Civic clubs such as the Kiwanis, Rotary, Civitans, and Lions, and service organizations such as the American Legion and Veterans of Foreign Wars, Masons and Shrine organizations, and others demonstrate very clearly the reactions to the lack of closeness among its membership. The average civic club meets once a week. The program is designed for good fellowship. A meal is usually served. There are songs and jokes and an entertaining speaker adds to the hour of good fellowship, relaxation and fun. The members of the club interact with each other in a pleasant and cordial manner. Often, they do not meet each other except during this hour of the weekly meeting. Since each member puts his best foot forward, superficial friendships are commonplace. The members speak well of each other. They are not forced to be close to each other. By such relationships civic clubs and other similar organizations are an important contribution to our society. People need such outlets as a part of their day-to-day group relationships. They provide new associations and friendships and can be a source of security.

TWENTY–EIGHTH MEETING

There were six members present. Mr. Cain, who had been drinking, came early, created a scene, and left before the meeting began. A reality issue prevented Mrs. Kitch from attending.

The hour began with a discussion of Holt's feelings of not being liked and his dictatorial manner of talking to others. Again he received support and understanding. Mr. Darcy discussed a series of problems that he was experiencing and announced a planned hospitalization in the near future. Mr. Darcy's situation was focused upon by the therapist. Mr. Foy spoke of the wonderful feeling of being in a hospital and being cared for. Mr. Darcy was supported by the other members. The therapist asked about the cancelled meetings and reminded them that the next two weeks would be cancelled due to the therapist's vacation. The remarks from the members were primarily superficial in nature. They spoke of missing the group. The subject was changed several times. The therapist attempted to bring them back to group issues, finally pointing out that when group issues were mentioned the subject was frequently changed. Mrs. Webster admitted that this was a problem with her. Mrs. Jacobs said the therapist's remarks made her freeze. Miss French and Mr. Holt admitted avoiding their own feelings. They were not concentrating on the business of the group. At the end of the hour, the members very warmly wished the therapist a pleasant vacation. Mr. Holt wondered if he should leave his telephone number handy.

The therapist remarked to the recorder at the end of the session that the meeting was not handled well. Several patients in individual therapy had deteriorated rapidly and had produced a certain amount of anxiety and tension in him. He felt these factors might have influenced his management of the group.

Theme and Dynamics

The theme of this meeting is related to the vacation of the therapist and the two weeks the group will not meet. Only superficial comments were made by the members. The members avoided group problems, finally admitting the inability to concentrate and get down to the business at hand.

Technique

The therapist correctly focused on their feelings in regard to his upcoming absence, but he did not pursue the subject in sufficient detail. He should have recalled this important matter to them in more explicit and direct terms. After his initial remarks, which produced only superficial feelings, he could have asked if there were any other feelings about their not meeting. He could have explored their feelings toward him for cancelling the meetings, as well as the effect that cancelling meetings had on the group. The central issue at this meeting concerned the cancellations. They had verbalized extremely strong feelings in past meetings about absent members. Now the therapist was taking an absence. Moreover, he would not allow the group to meet. The need for extensive exploration of their feelings concerning this issue should be apparent.

TWENTY–NINTH MEETING

Four members were present. Miss French and Mr. Darcy had contacted the therapist. Mr. Darcy has been hospitalized, and there is some question as to the possibility of a brain tumor. There was no prior communication from the other absent members, Mrs. Webster or Mrs. Jacobs.

The hour began with greetings for the therapist and expressions of their hopes that he had an enjoyable vacation. Mr. Foy and Mrs. Kitch spoke of being confused as to whether or not a meeting would be held today. The therapist asked about their feelings regarding the cancelled meetings. Mrs. Kitch replied, in a somewhat hostile tone, that she enjoyed not meeting the last two weeks. Her routine was not interrupted by the necessary provisions required for attendance. Mr. Holt very angrily stated: "If you think I resented not having been at the meeting the past two weeks you are wrong. I had a glorious time." The other group members were aware of Holt's hostility. Mr. Cain made reference to Holt's behavior. The therapist made the following observation: "Apparently you have some rather strong feelings about not meeting for the past two weeks. What about this?" Mr. Holt and Mrs. Kitch admitted irritability and anger regarding the meetings. Mr. Cain spoke of feeling resentful and equated this with anger. They spoke of a lack of group feelings and of the group's being hurt. Mrs. Kitch said the group was damaged by the two cancelled meetings. They implied the therapist had destroyed the group by his vacation. Mr. Holt discussed the therapist. He mentioned that doctors were different from what they should be, but refused to go into any detail. He didn't feel the doctor was taking part in the group. Mr. Cain agreed with him. Mrs. Kitch also was in agreement and added that there is a doctor who lives near her who is human. Mr. Cain and Mr. Holt asked the therapist a group of direct questions. They were aware that the therapist would not answer their questions, but kept hoping he would slip up and do so.

The therapist interrupted the meeting approximately 20 minutes before the session was over to discuss with the members a scheduled conflict that necessitated a change in the day of the group meeting. The therapist presented the proposal to the group members and asked for their feelings, approval or disapproval of the schedule change. The members agreed to the change, saying in effect that they would fall in line if the therapist wished. Mr. Holt demonstrated slight resentment, finally saying he could make it on the new meeting day.

Theme and Dynamics

As predicted, the members were very angry at the therapist for cancelling the two meetings. However, there was a sign of group maturity in that they were able to ventilate hostile and angry feelings toward him and feel accepted. There were statements of group damage and destruction. Even though there was anger at the absent members, the therapist was blamed for the present group problems. They spoke of half a group being present, vacation from therapy, and absence of group feelings.

A number of feelings about the change in day of the meeting were also present. Only superficial comments were made, with some resentment being expressed by one member. An intense need existed to please the therapist as evidenced by the remarks of falling in line with the wishes of the therapist. The members also feared group dissolution because of the cancelled meetings and absent members.

Technique

The therapist, by repeatedly dealing with their feelings regarding the cancelled meetings, afforded the members an opportunity to express their resentments and hostility.

The therapist correctly handled the modification of the group contract regarding the change in meeting day. He allowed a period of time (four weeks) before planning the change. Additional exploration of feelings and notification to the other members could be accomplished satisfactorily during this interval.

THIRTIETH MEETING

There were only four members present, Mrs. Webster, Mrs. Jacobs, Mrs. Kitch and Mr. Darcy being absent. Mr. Darcy continues to be hospitalized. His wife has informed the therapist that neurological surgery is imminent.

The hour began with references to the size of the group. The subject was changed. The therapist asked for group feelings about the absentees. The members spoke of group deterioration and wondered about the future. They felt Mrs. Webster and Mrs. Jacobs had never been in the group. There was concern about Mr. Darcy's being in the hospital. They felt that Foy was only there in name. His alcoholic behavior was frowned upon. He was not contributing to the meetings. They resented his coming when drinking. They resented his attitude and wished that he would quit the group if he planned to continue in this pattern. He was not even trying to work on his problems. At the same time they supported Foy by saying that they wanted him to be a member of the group and to contribute to its welfare. Once, Miss French spoke of going to California. Mr. Holt immediately asserted that the question was whether she wanted to run away from the group or to stay with it. The therapist explained that Mrs. Webster and Mrs. Jacobs had called prior to the meeting and relayed their reason for being absent. The members discussed the need for Mrs. Webster and Mrs. Jacobs to work on their problems. First, they had to recognize the need for help. The therapist asked what the members felt could be done about present group problems. Miss French spoke warmly of Mrs. Webster and wished that she would return to the group. Mr. Holt felt that they should exhibit more interest in the absent members in the future than in the past. He emphasized that this could be more important than a telephone call. Toward the end of the hour the therapist again asked for a discussion of the change in meeting date. All members agreed that the change would be satisfactory so far as attendance was concerned. No other feelings were expressed.

Theme and Dynamics

The theme of this hour concerned group dissolution. Was the group falling apart? If the group disintegrated no one would get any treatment. They were angry with the absent members and with Foy for not participating. At the same time, there was the recognition of their duties and responsibilities as a group to the absent members. Significant in this meeting was the group analysis of its major problem—dissolution.

There was active and direct mutual analysis of Miss French's remark about going to California, and Foy's role in the group.

Technique

During this meeting the members began recognizing problems that confronted them at the moment. They were aware that the therapist wanted them to look at group behavior. He had emphasized this feature to them from the onset of group therapy. With the increasing disappearance of the barriers created by hostility, the way was clearing for more constructive group work and analysis.

A barrier at this meeting arose over the members' feelings about absences. The members held the therapist responsible for absentees and became angry at him for not keeping the group together. The therapist could have focused on their feelings in this area by saying: "You have indicated interest and concern about the absent members. I wonder if you have any feelings toward me in relation to the absent ones."

Control of the group was becoming an easier task for the therapist. Pointing out group problems enlists group responses. This did not mean that hostility would be absent in future meetings. However, with the ability of the members to examine their feelings in an arena of acceptance and understanding, conflictual problems and issues would be resolved with greater ease. In this meeting the therapist easily guided the group into an evaluation of the current problems before them. Their analysis was complete and to the point.

Discussion

The members' resentment of Mr. Foy's alcoholic behavior is a common type of reaction in everyday groups. The relationship of alcoholism to mental illness, however, is now receiving more attention through educational media than at any previous time in our history. Industry has become more aware of the symptoms, causes, and effects of alcoholism. They are developing programs to combat alcoholism that are based on sound psychological grounds. There are national and international organizations interested in the field of alcoholism. State and municipal officials are developing educational programs and clinics for the dissemination of educational material about alcoholism and for the treatment of the alcoholic.

Alcoholism has several interesting racial and cultural features. For example, it occurs less frequently among Jews and Chinese, more frequently among people of Irish descent. In Europe, beer, wine, and alcohol are accepted beverages by the different religious organizations. In the United States the use of alcohol in any form is considered by some religious groups to be a sin, particularly among fundamentalists in the deep South. In thus attempting to eliminate alcohol completely, these groups disregard the fact that the incidence of alcoholism remains high even in those areas where alcohol is prohibited by law. One factor that may account for the wish to wipe out the sale of alcohol is their fear of anger. People get drunk and become violent and dangerous. Especially is this true with the Southern Negro. Under the influence of alcohol the Negro may exhibit very aggressive and savage behavior. One reason for the Negro's behavior may be the massive denial required of him in his relationship with the white man. (Similar behavior may occur in any race. The passive, nonassertive person who has to keep a rigid clamp on his aggressive feelings following a provocation may experience a sudden, uncontrollable explosive rage attack and exhibit destructive behavior.) Alcohol thus provides a release valve for aggressive feelings. These religious groups are also blind to the fact that emotional conflict and mental illness are causative factors in alcoholism. While religious experience and total abstinence may work for a few, the great majority of alcoholics are not reached by this approach.

Alcoholism, like juvenile delinquency, needs the total support and resources of a community. These resources should include psychological, religious, social, civic and municipal, industrial, educational, and other services working together as a team. No one group or agency has found a cure for alcoholism. In fact, the results of psychotherapy and group therapy for alcoholics have been disappointing. The group approach of Alcoholics Anonymous has been helpful to many alcoholics and suggests that future research in the utilization of specialized group methods may be of benefit in the problem of alcoholism (see Chap. 4).

THIRTY–FIRST MEETING

Seven members were present. Mr. Darcy continued to be hospitalized. An astrocytoma was discovered in the right temporal lobe of the brain. The members were aware of the surgical procedure, but not of the severity of the operation.

The hour began with references to Mr. Darcy's hospital status. The group questioned whether or not he would return. The therapist relayed a phone message from Mr. Darcy's wife in regard to his present condition and his return from the hospital in the near future. He focused on Mr. Darcy's illness and surgery, as well as its effect on the group. Mrs. Webster and Mr. Foy both expressed the wish that their own problems were physical rather than mental. Mr. Holt observed that since Mr. Darcy was physically ill, he would not have to return to the meetings.

Mr. Cain related an incident from the previous week when his daughter handed him his father's old watch. He became agitated and frightened at that time. The group's discussion with Cain revealed a poor relationship with his father. Mr. Foy felt that Cain was angry, and Cain agreed. Mr. Holt said Cain had discussed the matter with him previously and had demonstrated more emotional reactions then than in the group discussion. The therapist asked about Holt's remarks. The members agreed that group discussions were superficial. Mr. Holt brought out that the therapist's remarks left him blank and confused. The subject of fathers was introduced again. Mrs. Kitch related that statements from her father left her blank and feeling quite insignificant. The therapist then made the following statement: "Let me remind you of Mr. Cain's relationship with his father and the incident with the watch, Mrs. Kitch's feelings of being frozen with her father, and Mr. Holt's remarks that he goes blank and confused when I talk; do you see any comparison with this relationship to fathers and your feelings here?" Again, Mr. Holt did not understand. Mrs. Kitch immediately related her father to the therapist. She spoke of reacting to the therapist in the same way that she reacted to her father. Mr. Cain agreed with Mrs. Kitch.

Miss French, who was active in the discussion, attempted to draw Mrs. Jacobs and Mrs. Webster into the discussion by asking about their family relationships. Mrs. Jacobs discussed phobias her father had experienced. Mrs. Webster had been asking numerous questions of the other members, but had not discussed any of her own feelings. Miss French pointed out what Mrs. Webster was doing and asked about the relationship Mrs. Webster had with her father. Mrs. Webster did not discuss her father, but immediately began crying and admitted she had quit her job several weeks ago. Her financial problems were mounting, she said; and her depression and phobias had returned. She needed therapy, but might have to leave the state. The members supported her warmly. The therapist again brought to their attention the changes in the meeting day. He added: "I have also given some thought to discussing with you the possibility of lengthening the meetings from one hour to one and one-half hours and the period of group therapy for an additional six months. Frankly, I feel that an additional period of time will be profitable to you in understanding yourselves and others. Since we have already discussed changing the day of the meeting, I would like for you to consider these other proposals at the same time. What thoughts do you have about this?" The group members were extremely receptive to increasing the length of the meetings and extending the period of group therapy. Mrs. Jacobs questioned the advisability of the proposed plan and spoke of her uncomfortableness in the meetings. The other members admitted they were not exactly comfortable, but encouraged her to work on her problems and to agree to the changes.

Actually, the therapist had given considerable thought for a number of weeks to increasing the length of each meeting. He also felt that the members could benefit from extending the group from the original 12 months to 18 months.

Theme and Dynamics

There was concern regarding Mr. Darcy and his status. The members were not aware of the severity of his illness. This information was withheld from them since Mr. Darcy has not been informed of it by his surgeon or family.

The members have begun to identify actively with each other's problems and with the problems of the group. They are expressing feelings of inadequacy and inferiority, feelings that are related to their impounded anger and low self-esteem. There is the awareness that conflicts and problems with parental and authority figures outside of the group are similar to those with the therapist in the group. The defense used by Mrs. Webster of actively asking questions to avoid group involvement was recognized and pointed out to her. This defensive barrier was broken through by her expression of feelings, group interaction, and support.

The extensive contractual changes concerning the day of the meeting, length of the meeting, and extension of the life of the group were discussed and approved. The members of the group will experience a series of ambivalent reactions regarding these changes that will be revealed in future meetings.

The feelings of the therapist could have played a part in the additional changes of the group structure. Mr. Darcy's illness, as well as the failure of Mrs. Webster and Mrs. Jacobs to integrate into the group, may have created a necessity for the therapist to do more for them. There were probably conscious and unconscious factors playing a part in his actions. He was also aware that most of the members have just reached the stage in therapy where they were aware of their problems and were ready to work seriously on them.

Technique

The therapist explored the group's reactions in regard to Mr. Darcy's illness and surgery.

The comparison between parental figures and the therapist as an authority figure was identified. The therapist correctly pointed out group problems.

The therapist correctly consulted the members for approval or disapproval of contract modification. (See Chap. 4.)

THIRTY–SECOND MEETING

Six members were present; Mr. Foy and Mr. Darcy were absent.

The hour began with Mrs. Jacobs saying that she wanted to stop group therapy and have a baby. She made this request to the group. She felt that continuing group therapy and having a baby would be too expensive.

She was immediately challenged with such statements as "fighting the group," "a lack of group feeling," and "frequent absences in the past." Mr. Holt pointed out she was only coming to please her husband. Mrs. Jacobs admitted a lack of group feeling the others professed to have. For the initial time she spoke of irritation with her husband (although up until now she had frequently talked of her "perfect" marriage). Mr. Holt felt that Mrs. Jacobs was primarily angry with her husband, who wanted her to be in the group. The members encouraged her to stay and to attend regularly, as well as participate rather than to fight the group. The therapist reminded the members that they had been discussing irritations and asked about irritations in the meeting. There was superficial agreement, but the subject was quickly changed. Mr. Cain and Mr. Holt began discussing a conversation that had occurred between them outside a group meeting. Mr. Holt announced that Cain was living with him at the present time. The therapist immediately recognized this subgroup and asked how the members felt about Cain and Holt having conversations outside the group, as well as living together. Miss French was irritated and asked why they had not discussed this matter before. Mrs. Kitch said that such things as this would defeat the group. Mr. Cain and Mr. Holt recognized that the members did not approve of their behavior. Mrs. Webster had been very quiet during the meeting. The group began to draw her into the discussion. Mrs. Webster then began talking of returning to her former home in a distant state. The group felt that treatment for her emotional problems should come first. She was encouraged to stay in group therapy and get on her feet.

The therapist explored the group's feelings in regard to changes in the group structure before the end of the session. The various members continued to verbalize positive feelings. Mrs. Jacobs indicated that she would remain a member. Several members inquired about Mr. Darcy. The therapist informed them that Mr. Darcy had returned home and was improving.

Theme and Dynamics

The mood of the group was one of depression. The theme centered around whether or not the group was falling apart. If this happened group therapy would stop. The evidence was (1) Mr. Darcy's illness, (2) Mrs. Jacobs and her desire to stop therapy, (3) the subgroup of Mr. Cain and Mr. Holt, and (4) Mrs. Webster's statement of wanting to leave the state. The last three issues were dealt with by the group. Mrs. Jacobs' request was identified as a lack of group feeling and anger at her husband for coercing her into therapy. The subgroup was pointed out as group destructive. Mrs. Webster was reminded that leaving was an excuse on her part and was not realistic.

Another factor that must be considered was the effect of the changes in the group structure. Longer meetings and an extended period of therapy meant getting to know each other more closely. This would inevitably increase the members' anxiety level. The most anxious members were those who were talking of "getting out" while at the same time asking for support from the group. Their extreme ambivalence was evident. It was as if they were saying: "As long as I have to stay I want out." The side not visible or verbalized related to wanting to remain in therapy.

Hostility toward the therapist was not overt in this meeting but lay beneath the surface. The crucial matter of whether or not the group was disintegrating occupied the attention of the group.

Technique

The therapist was aware of the theme of the meeting and demonstrated control of the meeting by directing the group's attention to the issues at hand; namely, Mrs. Jacobs' request, the subgroup, and Mrs. Webster's situation. Again it was pointed out by the members and not by the therapist.

There have been a series of reality events affecting the group: the therapist's vacation and two cancelled meetings, a change in the day of the meeting, an increase in the length of group therapy from 12 to 18 months, an increase in the length of each group meeting from 1 to 1½ hours, the subgroup formed by two members living together, and Mr. Darcy's illness. The effect of these reality events of group therapy creates a mixture of emotional feelings among the members such as anger, guilt, and depression. The group members' responses to these reality events are distorted and immature. In each instance there is increased anger for the therapist, whom they hold responsible for anything that happens to the group—whether it be the absence of a group member or a change in the day of meeting. The importance of group reality events in the dynamics of group therapy cannot be overemphasized. The group therapist should be constantly aware of all reality events and encourage the group members to look at and examine their feelings about each particular event at the time of its occurrence. In this group the therapist has diligently pursued the group reality events with the group members. In time the group therapist hopes the group members will recognize their faulty emotional responses to group reality events and attempt measures to correct them.

After the meeting the therapist told Mr. Holt that the living arrangements with Mr. Cain were a violation of the group contract. He reminded Holt of the members' feeling that such behavior was destructive to the group. Mr. Holt assured the therapist that this arrangement would stop immediately; that it was done only as an emergency measure for Cain; and that his statements in the meeting were misleading. This subgroup did break up immediately. The therapist, however, was prepared to take even stronger measures if necessary, measures which included dropping Holt and Cain from the group if they continued to live together at the same house.

Holt's acting-out behavior with Cain is another example of his anger and defiance towards the therapist. Holt wants to twist and change the group contract to suit his own neurotic needs. The therapist should be alert for acting-out behavior by the members. He should be flexible in his handling of acting out and encourage the members to talk about their feelings rather than acting on them. If he is unable to control the acting out, then he must take firm action that may include dropping a member from the group.

THIRTY–THIRD MEETING

There were four members present. Mrs. Webster called in that she was leaving the state for several weeks but would return. Mrs. Kitch informed the therapist that she was going on a vacation. Mr. Darcy continued his convalescence at home. Mrs. Jacobs was absent with no prior communication.

The hour began with a discussion of the group's feelings about the absentees. They were disappointed, hurt, and angry at them. The subject of doctors and psychiatrists occupied their attention for several minutes. There were several hostile remarks that the therapist would not answer their questions. The therapist then made the observation: "You have been quite concerned about the absences and their effect on the meeting; you expressed feelings of disappointment and anger; and then you started talking about doctors and psychiatrists. I wonder if you have any ideas what really concerns you here." Miss French replied that it was like this at her office. She would get upset over something and then blame it on the manager. The subject was changed several times, the therapist kept focusing back on feelings about the group and the absent members. Several pertinent observations were made. Miss French added further that it was like getting your finger hurt as a kid and if daddy didn't do something, the finger kept hurting. Mr. Cain said that if they couldn't solve group problems, the therapist should do so. Mr. Holt added that the major problem was the absent members.

The therapist explored their feelings regarding the group structural changes. In their remarks an observation was made that this was a closed group and no new members should be added.

Theme and Dynamics

The theme of the meeting continued to relate to whether or not the group was disintegrating. There was anger toward the therapist for this turn of events. They were blaming him for not holding them together.

He should have been the omnipotent parent who solved any problem.

In actuality the group was not disintegrating. There was the possibility of losing one to three members in the immediate future. The fears of the members were distorted and imaginary to some degree, but understandable. Usually losses from groups occur much earlier (1 to 3 months). This group had been somewhat unique in retaining all of its original members for beyond thirty sessions. Thus, the threat of members leaving the group at this stage increased feelings of the group's dissolving.

Technique

The therapist correctly continued to direct the members' attention to an exploration of their feelings in regard to the absentees and the effect of absences on the group process. The members attempted a series of diversionary tactics by frequently changing the subject, but the therapist repeatedly brought them back to the group problem.

Again he asked for their reactions regarding group structural changes. He had done this at each meeting. He could also have asked the members of the group if the changes in group structure had any relationship to the increased absenteeism or to the wishes of the two members to leave the group.

Discussion

The group member who became angry at work and blamed her superior illustrated a common mechanism that is used over and over in our society. It is a much easier and more acceptable solution to place the blame on others rather than to admit to one's own weaknesses. Such feelings and attitudes are the basis for the mechanism of projection. To some extent projection is utilized by all people. In many instances, though, when the projected thought is recognized the individual can see his weakness and his use of projection to deny it. There is more paranoid thinking in society than people like to admit. An examination of the behavior in families indicates how some parents teach their children this mechanism rather than accept the fact that the children are not performing adequately. The child does poorly in his school studies and the parents blame the child's teacher. The child who does not win a competitive contest is told by his parents that others are to blame. The child who gets in a fight and receives a thrashing by a peer is not encouraged to try to care for himself—the blame is placed on the other child or his family. In athletic contests the referees, the playing field, or the weather are given as reasons for losing. The golfer shoots a poor score and places the blame on the clubs, balls, or the condition of the golf course. He does not want to admit that his own poor playing was probably the true cause of his high score. Children who live in a family atmosphere that always places the blame for reality events on others will continue to utilize such tactics as adults.

This type of behavior becomes learned behavior. The ability to face up to tasks and admit mistakes and weaknesses is a sign of healthy ego strength. The following example of the ways a college student can react to a poor grade exemplifies ego attitudes that can be applied to many different reality situations: (1) The student reacts to the poor grade by calling himself a weakling and a failure; he places all the blame on himself. (2) The student reacts to the poor grade by blaming the professor for giving an impossible examination and does not consider himself at fault. (3) The student reacts to the poor grade by admitting his mistakes. He realizes that he failed to study sufficiently. He sets his sights toward getting to work and bringing his grade up to normal.

THIRTY–FOURTH MEETING

There were five members present. Mrs. Kitch was on vacation. Mrs. Webster was still out of town. Miss French notified the therapist that she would be absent because of vacation. Mr. Darcy returned for the first time since his operation.

Initially, there was an interchange of conversation between the members of the group and Mr. Darcy in regard to his illness. Mr. Darcy told about the cobalt treatments he was now receiving. He exhibited a definite personality change from former meetings. He was somewhat childish and happy-go-lucky. His attention span appeared poor. The nonverbal attitudes of Mr. Cain and Mr. Holt indicated negative feelings toward Darcy's return. Mr. Cain thought Darcy would not have to return to the group any more. There was again concern about the absent members. Individual problems were discussed. The therapist focused on group problems. Mr. Holt became increasingly angry. He refused to recognize group issues and kept going back to individual problems. He was hostile towards all the members of the group and the therapist. He denied any group feeling and asked somewhat angrily, "What is a group?" Mr. Darcy felt the members were not concerned with each other. Mr. Foy changed the subject by relating a humorous story. The therapist brought the members back to group issues. Mr. Holt said the problem was not the absentees; it concerned the relationships of people in the meeting. The members who were aware of Holt's hostility pointed out his behavior. He agreed, but did not discuss his feelings, other than to admit that the antagonism and irritability was due to him (Holt) and not to the others.

Theme and Dynamics

The theme of the meeting concerned several factors: absent members, the return of Darcy, and the anger of Holt. The feelings being created by the group interaction were also apparent. There was a denial of group feeling along with an admission of problems in group relationships. The feelings toward Darcy were not identified. Holt's anger with all the others was identified and superficially discussed. Fear of the group's dissolving was present, as well as anger at the therapist for this imagined group problem. Then, too, there was the continuing fear that the therapist would bring the members of the group closer together at each meeting. They were also angry at him for suggesting longer meetings and a longer period of therapy.

Technique

The therapist correctly supported Darcy at the outset of the hour. He was aware that other feelings were present concerning Darcy, but steered toward other areas. Later meetings will clarify its etiology.

The therapist correctly dealt with group issues. He could have focused on himself more directly when problems in group relationships were verbalized. After Holt's hostility was discussed and identified, the therapist could have said: "You have been aware of Mr. Holt's irritability and antagonism to all of you. He has acknowledged its presence. Are there any thoughts as to where I fit into this picture?"

THIRTY–FIFTH MEETING

Six members were present. No communication had been received from Mrs. Webster. Mrs. Jacobs notified the therapist of a previous engagement which would prevent her attendance.

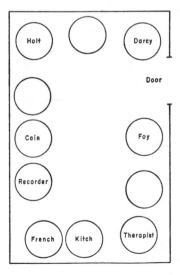

Mr. Cain: I have the seat of fortune today. (*He is sitting in the center of a sofa next to the recorder.*)

Mr. Holt: I don't think it's so good. I don't have to turn to look at her, you do!

> *Theme and Dynamics. Meeting begins with a reference to recorder.*
>
> *Therapist's Technique. The therapist is aware of the reality events affecting the group, such as Mrs. Webster's status and a modification of the group contract—i.e., longer meetings, a longer period of therapy, and a change in the day of the meeting. Therapist then asks about Mr. Cain's opening statement.*

Therapist: What's Mr. Cain talking about?

Mr. Holt: I agree with him.

Mr. Cain: I've been thinking of two things, neither of which is related to where I'm sitting. We've been coming here nine months. So far we have not made a friend of the doctor.

> *Theme and Dynamics. The theme of the meeting is suggested; it is the members relationship to the therapist.*

Miss French: I agree.

Mr. Holt: So do I.

Mrs. Kitch: Maybe it's because he's sane. We're not.

> *Theme and Dynamics. Longer meetings and a longer period of therapy may suggest to the members that they are sicker than originally thought.*

Mr. Cain: I wish the doctor would participate more. He always takes the Fifth Amendment.

Mr. Holt: We're supposed to work things out ourselves. If he answers them we don't work out these things ourselves.

Mr. Cain: I asked a question earlier about not being friends with the doctor. (He appeared angry with the others for not discussing this point.)

> *Theme and Dynamics. Now Mr. Cain states his problem in a different context. He is not friendly with the doctor.*

Mr. Holt (to Mr. Cain): What are you talking about?

Mr. Cain: If you don't know what I'm talking about we can discuss anything you like.

Mr. Darcy (to therapist): I have a question—why did you increase the length of the meeting one-half hour?

Mr. Cain (quickly and sarcastically): I did it.

> *Theme and Dynamics. Mr. Cain appears to be very angry. He began the meeting discussing his feelings about the therapist. Now he has angrily attacked Mr. Holt and Mr. Darcy.*
>
> *Therapist's Technique. The therapist should be aware at this time that Mr. Cain is angry with him. He should plan now to encourage the ventilation and etiology of his anger.*

Mr. Darcy (angrily): You did! I thought Holt did it.

Mr. Cain (angrily): No! I did it because we are not as happy as you!

Mr. Darcy: I still have problems. (He tells details of taking cobalt treatments.)

Mr. Cain: I think we should all have a tumor removed if it would make us as happy as you.

Therapist: What's Mr. Cain so angry about?

> ***Therapist's Technique.*** *The therapist focuses on Mr. Cain's anger.*

Mr. Cain (ignoring therapist): Unless I can get some help from some quarter I guess the discussion is ended.

Mr. Darcy (to therapist): You didn't answer my question about changing the length of the meeting.

Mr. Cain (still angry): I couldn't get going in one hour so they changed it for me. (Then in a less angry mood he explains to Mr. Darcy the reality of the change, adding that all of the members agreed, including the good doctor.)

> ***Theme and Dynamics.*** *Other themes of the meeting emerge: the changes in the length of meetings, period of group therapy, and day of the meeting.*
> *Mr. Cain's interaction with Mr. Darcy suggests displaced anger. He was initially angry with Mr. Darcy, but then he explained how the length of meeting was changed in a much less angry tone of voice.*

Therapist: I made an observation about Mr. Cain to you. What about it?

> ***Therapist's Technique.*** *Therapist refocuses on Mr. Cain's anger.*
> *The therapist should have attempted to get the members to see how they displace anger or scapegoat others. It is clear Mr. Cain is angry with the therapist. The therapist could say: "Mr. Cain began the hour today saying no one is a friend of mine. Then he gets angry at Mr. Holt and Mr. Darcy. I wonder if he is angry with me and taking it out on Mr. Holt and Mr. Darcy." He could also say: "Do you ever get angry at someone and take it out on others?" Therapist could also have said: "Mr. Cain asks for understanding from me and the others. Is he afraid that if he expresses his feelings he will be misunderstood or not accepted?"*

Mr. Cain: I don't have the vocabulary to express myself.

Mrs. Kitch: Your vocabulary is O.K.

Mr. Cain: Does anyone understand me?

> ***Theme and Dynamics.*** *Mr. Cain asks for understanding. If he verbalizes his anger to the therapist, then no one, especially the therapist, will like or approve of him. Thus Mr. Cain will not be understood in the group.*

Miss French: No!

Mr. Holt: No!

Mrs. Kitch: I read him!

Mr. Cain (to therapist): Do you understand me? You could at least say yes or no.

Mr. Holt: You don't make sense to me.

Miss French: I do know that the tempo of this group is changing.

Mr. Cain: It changed last week.

Mrs. Kitch (to Mr. Cain): You're mad at the doctor, and you're sarcastic. You're mad about something.

Mr. Cain (silently agreeing with Mrs. Kitch, then adding): I hope he understands me.

> *Theme and Dynamics. Mr. Cain's anger at the therapist is verbalized.*

Therapist: What's this all about? What's going on here? You talk about the tempo of the group changing. You say Mr. Cain is angry with me.

> *Therapist's Technique. Therapist continues to explore Mr. Cain's anger.*

Mr. Cain: I've been drained dry. I can't express myself as much as I used to.

Group: (Silence.)

> *Theme and Dynamics. The anxiety level of the group increases. The members become silent.*

Therapist: Let's go back a minute. Mr. Cain said he was concerned because no one had become friendly with me. Then he appeared to be angry with Mr. Darcy and also with me. What's he angry about?

> *Therapist's Technique. Therapist breaks the silence by refocusing on the main problem in this meeting.*

Mr. Cain: I think the doctor has misinterpreted me. I wasn't mad.

> *Theme and Dynamics. Mr. Cain, fearing disapproval from the therapist, denies his anger.*

Mr. Holt: Oh yes you were, and you're still mad.

Mr. Cain: I wish he (the therapist) would talk more. I want to know more about him.

> *Theme and Dynamics. Mr. Cain's denial is questioned by Mr. Holt.*

Mr. Holt: The doctor's personal life is not important to the group.

Mrs. Kitch (seemingly anxious): I'm bored. I'd like to talk about something else.

Mr. Darcy (to Mrs. Kitch): Tell us about your vacation.

Mr. Cain (attacks Mr. Darcy): What are your problems? You've never talked about them here.

> *Theme and Dynamics. An attempt is made to change the subject to a less threatening one. Again Mr. Cain attacks Mr. Darcy.*

Therapist: You say I'm not your friend. What are your ideas about me?

Mrs. Kitch: I don't feel that way.

Mr. Holt: Neither do I.

Therapist: Why would Mr. Cain be angry with me?

Mr. Cain (angrily): I'm not angry!

> **Theme and Dynamics.** *The members' denial is very evident.* **Therapist's Technique.** *The therapist brings the members back to exploring their feelings about him; however, he could have been more direct in his observation. He could say: "Now you say no one has become friendly with me. I wonder if you are experiencing unfriendly feelings about me which concern you.*

Mrs. Kitch: He (Mr. Cain) is mad at the doctor and us, too!

Mr. Cain: I'm not angry. I must admit I planned to get the doctor out in the open in this meeting, and to make him talk more.

Mr. Holt: But you (Mr. Cain) are angry with the doctor. What is there in your emotions that you have transferred to the doctor?

> **Theme and Dynamics.** *Mr. Holt again refuses to accept Mr. Cain's denial.*

Mr. Cain: Nothing I know of except he's not a friend of the group.

Mr. Foy: (He has remained quiet during the meeting, but his anxiety has gradually become more evident. He is shifting around in his chair and crossing and uncrossing his legs.) This group has certainly changed.

Mrs. Kitch: I'm going home in a minute.

Mr. Darcy (to Mrs. Kitch): Why don't we talk about your vacation?

Mrs. Kitch: (Describes her vacation. The other members join in this discussion, and seem glad that the subject has been changed.)

> **Theme and Dynamics.** *Mr. Darcy finally is successful in getting the subject changed. The anxiety level in the meeting is lower.*

Therapist: I notice that the subject has been changed.

> **Therapist's Technique.** *Therapist calls the group's attention to the change in the subject.*

Mr. Cain: Thank goodness!

Mr. Holt: It's an improvement.

Mr. Foy: I'm convinced we all need shock treatment.

Mr. Holt: (He asks Mrs. Kitch a series of questions about her vacation. The other group members join in.)

> **Theme and Dynamics.** *The members ignore the therapist and again discuss Mrs. Kitch's vacation.*

Therapist: Now hold up a minute. You were talking about how you feel here, then the subject was changed. I asked you about it. You ignored me and went back to the discussion of Mrs. Kitch's vacation. What's taking place here?

> *Therapist's Technique. Therapist tries to explore their group feelings.*

Mr. Holt (angrily): Nothing.

Mr. Cain: I don't like for people to miss meetings. (He specifically refers by name to the female members who have missed meetings but omits Mr. Darcy, who has missed more meetings than the others.)

> *Theme and Dynamics. Mr. Cain indicates anger about absences. However, his anger at the therapist is due to more than members' absences.*

Therapist: How do you feel about people who are absent?

Mr. Holt: Mr. Cain is mad with Mr. Darcy for missing meetings. I don't know why he named the women and not Mr. Darcy.

> *Theme and Dynamics. The members are angry about absentees; however, absenteeism is not the central issue at this meeting.*

Miss French: Mr. Cain feels that Mr. Darcy is not a part of the group because he has been absent a lot.

Therapist: I wonder if Mr. Cain or any of you react to me because of absences.

> *Therapist's Technique. Therapist attempts to explore their reactions to him for the members' absences. The members usually hold the therapist responsible for those who miss meetings.*

Mr. Holt: No, doctor. (Others join in with similar responses.)

Mrs. Kitch: I don't think I can last 'till the end of the meeting unless something interesting is brought up.

> *Theme and Dynamics. Mrs. Kitch is frightened and uncomfortable because of the group's anger. She has threatened twice to leave.*

Mr. Holt: I agree.

Therapist: Mrs. Kitch and Mr. Holt say they are bored. What do their feelings have to do with the group meeting?

Mr. Holt: Next week we'll play checkers. (The therapist has again been ignored.)

> *Theme and Dynamics. The members are so angry with the therapist that they completely refuse to deal with any of his remarks.*
>
> *Therapist's Technique. The extreme defiance of the members can be very trying for the therapist. Like angry children they ignore, deny, and refuse to cooperate. During such periods the therapist must be very patient and understanding.*

Mr. Holt: Maybe that's what's wrong. I'm getting too close to my problem. I wonder just where these feelings come from.

Therapist: What feelings is Mr. Holt talking about?

Mr. Holt: I'd like to talk about my problems during marriage. (He changes the subject and talks about his marital problems.)

> *Theme and Dynamics. Mr. Holt changes the subject and discusses problems outside of the group.*
> *Therapist's Technique. The therapist should have called Mr. Holt's avoidance of the question regarding feelings to the group's attention.*

Mrs. Kitch, Miss French, Mr. Cain, and Mr. Foy: (All join in with questions to Mr. Holt about his marriage.)

> *Theme and Dynamics. The anxiety level drops down.*

Therapist: I'm sure this is a real problem for Mr. Holt. However, I would like to bring you back to this meeting. What are your problems and feelings here?

> *Therapist's Technique. The therapist supports Mr. Holt in regard to outside problems and brings the group back to the theme of meeting.*

Mr. Holt: I don't know what you mean, doctor.

Mr. Cain: I have an emotional block. It may be due to various things. (A group silence followed of approximately 45–60 seconds.)

> *Theme and Dynamics. Anxiety level becomes high again.*

Therapist: You know, I get the feeling this is a group problem that is not being dealt with.

Miss French: I think the group is O.K., but we're not making any progress.

Mr. Holt: It's because of Mr. Cain. (At this time Mr. Cain and Mr. Holt make angry remarks to each other. Mr. Cain accuses Mr. Holt of knowing a secret. Mr. Holt angrily accuses Mr. Cain of the same thing.)

> *Theme and Dynamics. Again the members' hostility is ventilated toward each other rather than for whom it is primarily due—the therapist.*
> *Therapist's Technique. Here again the therapist could have asked about displacing anger on others.*

Therapist (interrupting Mr. Cain and Mr. Holt): Now hold up a minute. What's this all about? (Again they start arguing with each other.)

Mr. Cain: I must admit I am angry, very angry. I don't really know why.

> *Theme and Dynamics. Mr. Cain clearly verbalizes his anger.*

Therapist: I wonder if any of the rest of you feel the way Mr. Cain does? I would like to remind you of the group contract. You are here to look at the way you feel in the meetings. Any other thoughts now about your feelings in this meeting?

Mrs. Kitch: Maybe we're too close to our problems. It hurts; it makes me uncomfortable. I wonder if people get worse when they get too deep into their problems.

> ***Theme and Dynamics.*** *Another aspect of their anger to the therapist is verbalized. He is making them become closer to each other. They are fighting against closeness. The most common defense against closeness is hostility.*
>
> ***Therapist's Technique.*** *At this point the therapist could say: "Are you saying that you are fighting against becoming closer to everyone here? How does this make you feel?"*

Mr. Holt (to therapist): You may be right.

Miss French: I'm washed out. (At this point in the meeting Mr. Cain, Mr. Holt, Mr. Darcy and Mrs. Kitch get into a loud, angry argument about not helping each other. Mr. Foy was criticized strongly for not participating or contributing to this meeting.)

> ***Theme and Dynamics.*** *Anxiety level is high. The members begin attacking each other and finally attack Mr. Foy in unison.*

Therapist (quietly interrupting the argument): Now hold up a minute. Let's see if you understand what's going on here. You have spoken of looking deeper at problems. You admitted feelings but did not explore them when I asked you. In fact you ignored me then, and on several other occasions today. It seems to me the main feeling today is associated with anger. Is it true that you are angry with me?

> ***Therapist's Technique.*** *The therapist breaks into the argument and focuses on himself.*

Miss French: I think we are getting closer together. We're getting on each other's nerves.

> ***Therapist's Technique.*** *The therapist should have said: "Yes, I can see you are irritated with each other. But what about me? You have been more concerned about your reactions to me today than anything else. How do you really feel about me?"*

Mr. Holt: I doubt that.

Mrs. Kitch: We're beginning to see Mr. Cain's real self.

Miss French: I don't think anyone is coming clean with his feelings.

Mr. Cain (appears to be extremely angry, checks his watch and gets up from his seat): I've had enough. I'm leaving. (He leaves the room.)

Group: (The members become silent. They appear to be surprised that Mr. Cain left the meeting.)

Therapist: You seem surprised about Mr. Cain's leaving. What thoughts do you have?

> ***Therapist's Technique.*** *The therapist explores the members' feelings about Mr. Cain's leaving the meeting.*

Mr. Holt: I think he (Mr. Cain) was glad of an excuse to leave.

Mrs. Kitch: My, but he looked angry.

Mr. Foy: This group is getting just like a family. We're fighting and getting on each other's nerves.

> ***Theme and Dynamics.*** *The comment that the group is like a family is a good insight.*

Mrs. Kitch: I didn't think we would get to this. Mr. Foy is right. The group reminds me of my arguments with my husband and his mother.

Miss French: There's no doubt about the difference in the group from the time we started.

Mr. Holt (to Miss French): In what way have you improved?

Miss French: I didn't say I had improved. I do feel closer to the group. I think that most of us refuse to open up and say how we feel.

> ***Theme and Dynamics.*** *Miss French makes a reference to closeness.*

Therapist: You recognize that the group has changed. You refer to the group's being like a family and to getting on each other's nerves. Then, too, there have been comments about not talking about your real feelings. I wonder where you see me in all this?

Mrs. Kitch (to therapist): Maybe we're irritated with you.

Miss French: In a way I want to be close to the others here; in another way I fight it. I don't want to get hurt.

Therapist: Mrs. Kitch speaks of being irritated with me. I wonder if any of the rest of you feel this way.

> ***Theme and Dynamics.*** *The anxiety level drops after the verbalization of anger to the therapist.*

Miss French: (Nods affirmatively and smiles but does not comment. The other members also become silent.)

Therapist: I wonder if you are concerned over the fact that I encourage you to know each other better, to become closer to everyone here.

> ***Therapist's Technique.*** *The therapist could have been more direct in his statement. A major cause of their anger to the therapist is due to his role of promoting closeness among the members. He could say: "You have talked a lot today about closeness. Are you irritated with me for encouraging you to be closer to each other?"*

Mr. Foy: (He has detached himself from the group. Along with Mr. Darcy he remains silent.)

Therapist (recognizing that time is about up): This is our first meeting of one and a half hours. I wonder if the longer meetings and also the change in the day of the meeting have affected your feelings today.

> ***Therapist's Technique.*** *The therapist, as a general rule, should focus on reality events affecting the group at least thirty minutes prior to the end of the meeting. In this instance*

> *he did not allow sufficient time for the members to discuss their reactions to the changes in the structure of the group.*

Miss French: I don't know. I wanted the meetings to be longer; then I didn't. Maybe we are fighting getting to know each other.

Mrs. Kitch: I'm glad of the longer time.

Mr. Holt (boastingly): I have said before that we needed more time or more meetings.

Therapist: Well, time's up for today. See you next week.

SUMMARY

Theme and Dynamics

The anxiety level of the group is high. The intermember hostility, scapegoating, denial, and changing of topics of discussion to less threatening ones are methods the members utilized in this meeting to avoid looking at their relationship to the therapist. However, despite all the anger and rage at the therapist and each other, constructive interpretations and mutual analysis were achieved by the group. The members could express hostility toward themselves and toward the therapist, and feel accepted. Mrs. Kitch's observations that the members were there to look at themselves was very accurate. Mr. Foy's comments on the tempo changing and his comparison of the group to a family were accurate analyses. The members were becoming more and more aware of what group therapy is about and what they were supposed to do. The fact that Mr. Darcy can remain a member of the group and not reject it will be good for the others. Certainly, he will not benefit, but it would be devastating for him to stop coming.

The exact meaning of the hostility toward Mr. Darcy was not clearly established. Mr. Holt and Mr. Cain indicated irritability with him at the 34th meeting. At this meeting Cain began an attack on the therapist and then shifted to Darcy in somewhat of a scapegoating pattern. Actually, a number of factors were present: the members were angry at the therapist for poor attendances, for holding longer meetings, for increasing the period of therapy that meant getting closer to each other, and for allowing Darcy to return to the group.

Technique

It is during this period of group therapy that the therapist's awareness of group dynamics is so important. He should be aware of the meeting's theme. He should be able to assess the anxiety level of the group. The theme of this meeting was due primarily to the members' hostile feelings to the therapist. The members' anxiety level was high because they do not yet feel approved and accepted by the therapist. Therefore when the therapist attempted to explore the members' feelings about himself, they reacted with several defensive behavior patterns—intermember hostility, scapegoating, changing the topic of discussion, and denial. The therapist should be very supportive, patient, and understanding. In this meeting the therapist had to prevent arguments between members, watch out for scapegoating, understand the denial of the members, keep the discussion group-oriented, and encourage the members to explore their feelings and reactions to him. The successful group therapist will understand that the members' recognition and awareness of their feelings comes slowly, and will also understand that the members' awareness of his acceptance and approval comes just as slowly.

THIRTY–SIXTH MEETING

There were six members present. Mr. Holt called in to say that he was working and would be unable to attend. Mrs. Webster continued absent.

The meeting began with Mr. Cain's making hostile remarks to Mr. Darcy. The therapist immediately focused on Cain's behavior. The members dealt with Cain and supported Darcy. Mrs. Kitch felt that Cain had insulted the members of the group and the therapist at the last meeting. Mrs. Kitch was quite aggressive with Cain. Mr. Foy again referred to the group's going through a change. Mrs. Jacobs, who was active, asked the therapist a direct question. She admitted that the therapist irritated her by his indirect manner. Then she talked of group feelings and her earlier desire to please everyone and the therapist. Now, she was not so sensitive as formerly. At home when irritations occur with her husband she thinks of the group. Mr. Cain felt they were looking at everything that happened in the meeting and analyzing it. Vague references were made to the extension of group therapy for 7 more months. A television program concerning group therapy in a state hospital was discussed. Other references as to whether their own conditions were normal or abnormal, neurotic or psychotic, were touched on. Commitment of people to state hospitals was mentioned. At this point the therapist said: "Now, Mr. Foy speaks of the group changing; Miss French made a reference to the group being extended 7 months; you have talked of degrees of illness, what is normal or abnormal; and you have mentioned how group therapy functions, looking at yourself and analyzing motives. Can you tie these things together into your feelings at this meeting? Do you have any idea about these things you have discussed at this meeting?" The only direct comments were of a positive nature. Mrs. Kitch, however, discussed two recent dreams. In one, someone had been under her bed. In the other, there was a frightening face that initially resembled the devil and later a man. She had been frightened and experienced difficulty sleeping. At the meeting she was reminded of the dream and realized the face resembled Cain's. The therapist asked about Mrs. Kitch's dreams and on one member dreaming about another. He asked if there was any relationship to her dreams and the group meeting. Mr. Cain felt she had a fear of some kind. Mrs. Kitch felt the argument with Cain the previous week may have had something to do with her dream.

Theme and Dynamics

Following the initial period of hostility to the therapist, the members discussed their own feelings and the group problems. Mr. Cain and Mrs. Jacobs have become more involved in the group dynamics. The members have begun to feel the danger of getting closer together and the numerous fears of finding out about themselves. This was evident when the degree of illness was discussed. The members probably feared that if they exposed themselves, they would be committed to a state hospital. Mrs. Kitch's dreams indicated her fears and conflicts with men, and the group recognized this.

Technique

The therapist correctly supported Mr. Darcy by asking them to examine Mr. Cain's behavior. Regardless of the reasons for Cain's hostility toward Darcy, the therapist recognized that the latter needed support from the others. The therapist must be aware of all such factors. He will thus pursue, retreat, or support as the situation demands.

The therapist summarized the content of the group material in order to guide the members into exploring more basic feelings in the meeting.

By reflecting the dream material of Mrs. Kitch back to the members, the therapist helped them to identify her fears of men and its relationship to the hostility expressed at the previous meeting. The individual reporting of dreams in a group meeting is not encouraged by the therapist unless a dream is directly related to group issues, but in this case Mrs. Kitch's dream was related to group issues.

THIRTY–SEVENTH MEETING

Five members were present. Mr Cain, Mr. Holt, and Mrs. Webster were absent. There was no communication from the absentees.

The session began with the members discussing the state of their illness. Mr. Foy said he was a lunatic. Mrs. Kitch wondered if she was schizophrenic. The therapist then said: "There seems to be concern about your present state of health. You spoke of it at the last meeting. Do you have any thoughts about this and its relationship here?" Mrs. Kitch then related an incident concerning her husband's boss in which she had asserted herself. She spoke of being very proud of this achievement that would have been impossible a year ago. Mrs. Kitch added that she liked herself better than formerly. Mrs. Jacobs and Miss French agreed with

Mrs. Kitch regarding their own self-esteem. Miss French related a run-in with a supervisor where she had been assertive and spoke of the rewarding feeling afterwards. This supervisor had traits like Mrs. Jacobs. Miss French stated that she did not like Mrs. Jacobs for a long time until these similarities with her supervisor became clear. Now she likes both of them better. Mr. Foy was glad the other members could assert themselves, but felt he could not. He felt like a child. Miss French said there were likes and dislikes in the group as with people on the outside. The therapist pointed out her observation to the members, but no significant material was discussed. They discussed absentees, the therapist, and the recorder. They wanted a progress report, but knew the therapist would not tell them anything. Mrs. Jacobs asked permission to discuss an individual matter. She was afraid to bring it up because the therapist always focused on group matters when anything was discussed. The members encouraged her to go ahead. She related in detail a love affair with a football star during high school ten years ago. According to description, this athlete had a number of similarities to the therapist. The members were active in the discussion with Mrs. Jacobs. The therapist made the following statement: "Mrs. Jacobs is aware that I direct your attention to group matters. Let's look at this event she has been talking about. Do you see any relationship to it and relationships here in the group?" Mrs. Jacobs indicated she was still fond of this individual. Mrs. Kitch described a high school love affair as the hour ended.

Theme and Dynamics

The members were experiencing ambivalent feelings about this therapeutic program. On the one hand, they suffered discomfort and uneasiness from the anxiety of group relationships; on the other, they were able to assert themselves, and self-esteem has been raised. At this point they wanted a progress report. Mrs. Jacobs' revelation may indicate an increased concern for the group, and positive, tender feelings for the therapist. Mrs. Jacobs has been more comfortable and at ease during the last few meetings.

Now it has become clearer that the members are quite concerned about their behavior in the meetings. Their examination of their group feelings, as well as the therapist's suggesting more therapy and longer meetings, brought forth fears of severe mental illnesses.

Technique

The therapist asked the group members about their present state of being. The ambivalence was quickly demonstrated. He could have brought this mixture of feelings to their attention by saying, "You have discussed whether or not you are mentally ill, but make other statements that you have improved. What are your thoughts about experiencing both kinds of feelings?" He could have explored it further by statements relative to difference of feelings to others and to himself.

The therapist correctly related Mrs. Jacobs' story to their group feelings. Even though there were no pertinent observations from the members, he continued to ask them to look at any issue that was discussed during the therapy session from the standpoint of group dynamics.

THIRTY–EIGHTH MEETING

There were only two members present. Mr. Holt had been absent for three meetings. Mr. Foy notified the therapist that having to work would prevent his attendance. Mrs. Jacobs called in that she was out of the city. There was no communication from Mr. Darcy, Mrs. Webster, and Miss French.

The two members present (Mrs. Kitch and Mr. Cain) appeared uneasy and immediately began talking about the large number of people who were absent. Mrs. Kitch admitted being angry. Mr. Cain voiced concern about Mr. Holt but gave no details. The therapist explored their feelings regarding the absences and their effect on the meeting. From the statements made, there were no feelings of group disintegration and collapse that had been exhibited in former meetings. Mrs. Kitch discussed her husband and her father. Mr. Cain talked about his wife. The therapist dealt with their conversation about families and asked if they felt there was any comparison to their group feelings. Both agreed the group was like a family. Cain said he was like a child; that the group members were like children. He discussed his emotional immaturity. He wondered if they were rebelling against authority. Mrs. Kitch discussed another dream. The content concerned an explosion that might have occurred in the area where the Department of Psychiatry is located. She was frightened and unable to sleep for several nights. The therapist asked about her dream and its possible connection with their interpersonal relationships. Cain wondered if her dream could be interpreted as a desire to get rid of the department, since then she would not have to attend group therapy. The hour ended with Cain's discussing his need for the Psychiatry Clinic and group therapy.

Theme and Dynamics

Despite the low attendance, the group continued to function. There was increased recognition of its resemblance to family. The members compared themselves emotionally to children. There was the unconscious projection of the therapist as a parental authority figure. Absences could be rebellion and defiance against the authority figures who were symbolic of their parents. They were exhibiting child-parent relationships and behavior patterns utilized over the years. Mrs. Kitch's dream may exhibit her fear of retaliation from an authority figure (the therapist) if she asserts herself; a fear patterned after her early relationship with her father. Then, too, destroying the Department of Psychiatry means that she does not have to look at her angry and uncomfortable feelings.

Technique

The initial issue was the large number of absent members. The therapist explored their feelings in this area.

Recognition of the group as a family was verbalized after the therapist asked them to examine its relationship to group feelings.

The therapist reflected Mrs. Kitch's dream back to the group for analysis. Some of the dynamics mentioned above were recognized by the group members.

THIRTY–NINTH MEETING

There were four members present. Mrs. Jacobs and Mr. Cain notified the therapist of their inability to attend. There was no communication from Mr. Darcy. The therapist received a message from Mrs. Webster's daughter stating that her mother would not return to the state.

The hour began with references and inquiries as to the absences of the members. The therapist relayed the message concerning Mrs. Webster to the members. A sense of futility and disappointment related to group absences was voiced. The group had the feeling that the loss of Mrs. Webster was inevitable. Mr. Holt said the time of the year (vacations) was influential in attendance. He felt the group would be back in full swing. He discussed his own recent absences. Group feelings were focused by the therapist. Mrs. Kitch again spoke on asserting herself and of her inability to do so before the outset of group therapy. Families were discussed. The therapist asked about the comparison of the group to families by saying: "Several times in recent meetings you have referred to this group as a family. You have been speaking of families today. Are there any additional ideas about this group as a family?" Miss French initially disagreed with the therapist. Mr. Holt took issue with her by saying she had previously compared this group to her family. She had identified Mr. Holt with her father and Mr. Cain with her brother. Following this interchange, the members began asking Mr. Foy a series of questions about his family. He discussed a resentment to his brother, conflicts with his father, and nonassertiveness with his wife. He again appealed for a magical solution. The members encouraged him to become a part of the group, pointing out that he was reaching for help by coming to the meetings, but he would receive benefit only when he participated.

Theme and Dynamics

Absences continued to be a problem, but the fear of group dissolution and disintegration has been cleared away. Mrs. Webster becomes the first drop-out from the group. The members compared identifications within the group to their own family members. They began exploring the individual family conflicts of Mr. Foy. The dynamics of the group meeting at this point can be viewed from two positions: (1) the wish to draw Foy into the group by discussing his family relationships, or (2) the desire to avoid group feelings and interactions by leaving group problems and discussing Foy's individual situation.

The therapist has been notified that Cain's alcoholic behavior has recurred and that he has been arrested for driving an automobile while intoxicated (Mr. Holt announced this fact to the group at the next meeting). Cain's repetitive pattern of frustration, anger, and depression has again resulted in his use of alcohol for relief. Cain's behavior in the last few group meetings is significant. He has exhibited anger to the therapist and other members, particularly Darcy. Probably Cain was angry with the therapist and displaced much of it on Darcy and others. Even though Cain had become involved in the group interaction, he could not tolerate the accompanying anxiety and thus sought relief with alcohol. Cain's behavior patterns are common among alcoholics.

Technique

Early in the hour the therapist pointed out group behavior. There followed a discussion about families. Here he asked for a comparison of the group with a family.

There is a distinct possibility that the members utilized the latter part of the meeting to avoid group feelings by asking Foy a series of questions. The therapist could have interrupted this by-play by calling attention to their behavior. He could have said: "I had asked you to look at the group as compared to a family. You discuss it briefly and then begin asking Mr. Foy a number of questions. Do you have any thoughts about this?" If reticence to deal with the group problem should occur, the therapist could go back to his original observation concerning the group's comparison to a family and ask for further discussion of this aspect of the group. If necessary, he could do this at several subsequent meetings.

FORTIETH MEETING

There were four members present. Mrs. Kitch was absent due to a reality issue. There was no communication from Mrs. Jacobs or Mr. Cain.

At the outset Mr. Holt announced that Mr. Cain had got into trouble with the law over alcohol, resulting in a jail sentence of several months.

The members reacted with shock and astonishment at this turn of events. Group absenteeism was discussed. The therapist asked about problems of attendance by saying: "Attendance has concerned you here of late. Any thoughts about absences and the change of meeting days, as well as increased length of the meeting?" Miss French brought out that longer meetings made you look at yourself more closely. She did not enjoy this feature. Mr. Holt said it was a necessary ordeal. The group was again compared to a family. Mr. Foy spoke of his individual desires and his wishes for hypnosis and magic. The therapist then said: "Several times in recent meetings some of you have expressed some rather strong and angry feelings. Mr. Foy always avoids participating when they occur. He has also compared the group to a family." Mr. Holt said Foy has told him of losing his temper at work and having numerous angry conflicts with his family. Miss French felt Foy was hiding his real feelings, acting somewhat like a Dr. Jekyll and Mr. Hyde. Mr. Foy discussed his need for control. He was afraid of his anger because it brought out fears and guilt. He felt he would need a very large bottle of whiskey before he could show himself to the group. Foy made another demand for magic. Mr. Darcy felt he needed God and prayer. Miss French replied that God only helped those who helped themselves.

Theme and Dynamics

The members felt the loss of Mr. Cain very keenly. Absences continued to be a problem. The relationship to the change in group structure was superficially discussed. Mr. Foy's massive rage, with its accompanying fears and guilt, was identified. This explains his peripheral involvement. Getting close to other group members and the therapist is fraught with danger. Magic, miracles, or hypnosis would be an easy solution for him.

Technique

The therapist explored their feelings regarding the circumstances of Mr. Cain's alcoholic escapade.

The subject of absences and changes in the group structure was reflected to members for discussion.

The therapist utilized material from a previous session to illustrate Mr. Foy's behavior. The therapist's comments were followed by Mr. Foy's first ventilation of feelings.

Discussion

Mr. Darcy's request for a magical solution to his problems by religion and Miss French's observation that God only helps those who help themselves illustrate two prevalent religious concepts in our society. Religion is and has been a strong social and cultural force, having played an important role in the founding of the United States and its subsequent history. Today the large number of churches and denominations throughout the country attests to the pervasiveness of religion in our culture. Religious principles and values have permeated many walks of American life. Coins in use today bear the inscription, "In God We Trust." Presidential inaugurations and other public functions are opened with a prayer or invocation for God's help. The majority of Americans are members of one form of religious organization or another. Early experiences for most individuals include christenings, baptismal ceremonies, confirmations, or bar mitzvahs. During either early adulthood or later life, marriage vows are solemnized in a church. At death the funeral service is usually under the direction of a clergyman or deacon.

The most prominent religions in this country are the Protestant, Catholic, and Jewish faiths. They are not equally dispersed among the states. Some sections of the country have large Catholic populations, others are predominantly Protestant. In some areas religion has ethnic characteristics—i.e., most people of Irish and Italian extraction are Catholic. The religion in a city or state may influence political, educational, and other groups, while religious differences have produced conflicts regarding birth-control laws or federal aid to schools.

Religion has many meanings for people. Different denominations, sects, or organizations teach and practice different concepts. There may also be variations of concepts within the same religious body. For example, Protestant churches in the North and Northeastern sections of the country are more liberal in some religious principles than Southern Protestant churches with fundamentalist backgrounds. Then, too, there is a difference in the beliefs and practices of urban and rural congregations. In these areas religious principles have been influenced by existing social and cultural forces. In addition, there are evangelical groups who make use of radio, television, and other mass-communications media to promote faith healing, spontaneous conversions, and other mystical phenomena.

The most important religious experiences for a person begin in his family. A person's religion will more than likely be that of his family. All religions place extreme importance on the basic family group, and parents begin the child's religious instruction at an early age. Thus family attitudes reflect the attitudes that children have about religion. The child's religious concepts will be an embodiment of parental and family concepts. For example, parents may be cruel, restrictive, and severe disciplinarians to their children. In such cases children may feel the same toward church figures. Parents may also use religion as an ally in enforcing discipline and moral concepts in children. Parents and religious groups may teach that to express angry feelings is a sin and that a Christian never gets angry. Parents and religious groups may teach children that sexual drives should be repressed; that masturbation is a sin and leads to insanity; and that a wrong sexual thought is just as sinful as a wrong sexual act. Families and religious groups may use guilt as a weapon to correct misbehavior and to enforce "goodness and right." Children may be taught the Old Testament philosophy that God is a God of wrath who punishes man severely for his sins. Similarly, the child who feels loved, accepted, and secure in his family will regard the religion of his parents as a source of love, acceptance, and security.

Children may experience important and meaningful adult identifications and peer relationships from the social and recreational functions of church groups. During childhood and latency the ties to the church are very close. At puberty and during adolescence boys and girls begin to rebel about church attendance and other religious functions. Sports, social activities, and dating are more fun and enjoyable. Religious services sometimes seem to be boring. During late adolescence and early adulthood many doubts about religion are commonly experienced. In college, students often have difficulty in reconciling Biblical material with theories of evolution, history, and science. After marriage and the birth of children, however, the new family usually joins a church and begins to take a part in the religious activities of their community. For many adults, church membership is the accepted way of life. Although they may not be active in their religious group, they have a sense of inner security and community acceptance when they are identified with a church. Parents may also want their children to attend Sunday school during their formative years, just as they did themselves.

An individual's concept of religious values may be closely related to his emotional reactions. Because of different religious concepts and various interpretations placed on religious values by clergymen, emotional conflict over his angry and sexual feelings can occur in an individual. Such conflicts can lead to the development of anxiety, guilt, and depression. The very dependent person may hope to obtain through prayer a magical solution to his difficulties. Some people impart a mystical and magical quality to religion and constantly await the miracle that will solve their problems. Those people who are anxious, unhappy, and unable to form close relationships with others may seek a close relationship with God. When a religious experience does not help, they become angry at their religion and discard it. In this respect, some ministers, evangelists, and so-called faith healers who feel that people's problems can be solved through religion have done an injustice to religion. In the fundamentalist religious groups of the deep South and in other religious groups throughout other parts of the country, great emphasis is placed on a revival meeting once a year. A revival usually consists of twice-daily meetings of a religious group over a period of one to two weeks. Many revival ministers emphasize the sins of man and the ungodly state of the world. In the deep South, particularly in small communities and rural areas, the yearly revival is a strong cultural and social force. Revivals are characterized by the presence of intense dramatics, exhibitionism, and strong emotional behavior on the part of some members. In fact, many of the highly charged emotional states of the converted person have a hysterical quality to them.

An additional factor which is related to religion and contributes to the anxiety of the family group is intermarriage among Protestants, Catholics, and Jews. A mixed marriage presents several possible sources of anxiety. At the time of marriage the husband and wife do not usually consider their different religions as a large stumbling block; they are enmeshed in many other experiences. Religious differences are pushed aside as a secondary factor. After children are born, however, religious conflicts between the parents may occur as a separate issue or in combination with other conflicts. Additional anxiety in mixed marriages is caused by relatives. Such anxiety is more likely to occur if the interfaith family lives near the relatives. Relatives of one religious faith may take issue with the religious faith of the other. A common method used by relatives is to scapegoat the religious faith of a family member and blame all sorts of minor or major problems on the religion.

A serious religious problem that can contribute to high levels of anxiety in the family group is that created by the parent or parents whose patterns of behavior are those of the "religious fanatic." Such people have serious emotional conflicts and their primary difficulty is usually control of rage. Many religious fanatics have an obsessive-compulsive personality, characterized by a constellation of religious defenses that serve to prevent the overt expression of rage. The religious fanatic may be cold, aloof, dominating, controlling, and void of psychological aptitude in group relationships. He insists on such a strict religious code within the family that he has frequent conflicts with his spouse and children. The children of a fanatic are often denied many of the ordinary pleasures of childhood and adolescence, because the parent takes part in so many church activities that he has no time for his family. Constant conflict occurs even in his church group relationships. His fellow clergymen, who are duty-bound to associate with him, begin to find reasons for avoiding him and secretly rejoice if he leaves the congregation after an outburst of anger.

In the family group the religious fanatic may be very destructive to the other family members. The anxiety level of the family may be very high, and the patterns of behavior among the family members may be similar to those of a parent with a severe obsessive-compulsive personality disorder or neurosis.

FORTY–FIRST MEETING

There were five members present, Mr. Darcy and Mr. Cain being absent. Mrs. Jacobs called the therapist prior to the meeting, stating that she wished to stop group therapy. The therapist advised her to attend the meeting and talk it over with the other members of the group.

The hour began with a discussion of Mrs. Jacobs' desire to stop therapy. She spoke of having profited from the meetings and having improved considerably. She stated that she was again teaching school. Problems were still present, but they were less severe. Miss French questioned her motives, adding that the group was very important to her and every member was a part of her responsibility. Mr. Holt and Mrs. Kitch agreed. Mrs. Jacobs denied any group feelings for the other members. Mr. Holt and Mrs. Kitch both felt that Mrs. Jacobs should stop if there were no group feelings. Miss French said she felt fearful and guilty as a result of Mrs. Jacobs' request. The therapist asked about Miss French's statement. The members verbalized fears of others leaving, of group dissolution, and of the unknown. Miss French explored Mrs. Jacobs' situation in more detail, adding that she had not attended regularly and was less acquainted with the members. When Mrs. Jacobs did attend, the members were hostile to her. The therapist then made the following observation: "Mrs. Jacobs has not attended meetings regularly. Previously she has spoken of being more uncomfortable here than elsewhere. Miss French speaks of the members being hostile to Mrs. Jacobs when she attends. I wonder if you see any relationship to her request to stop coming and your acceptance of her." The group members admitted having concern about her absences, but wished her to remain. They hoped her cessation of therapy was temporary, suggesting that she would be welcome to return at a later date.

Approximately 30 minutes before the end of the meeting the therapist interjected the possibility of adding two new members to the group. He told the members that two men who lived in the immediate area had been in another group of the therapist's at a hospital a hundred miles distant for approximately the same length of time. The therapist related his plans to discuss this matter with them prior to Mrs. Jacobs' request. Group feelings were explored. Initially, Miss French voiced ambivalent feelings but agreed with the others, who greeted the proposal with very warm and positive statements. The therapist announced the new members would join the group at the next meeting.

Theme and Dynamics

Two important trends can be identified in the underlying theme of the meeting: (1) the emotional interaction of the group process is activating intense reactions between the members, and (2) three members have now left the group. Fears of group disintegration and guilt of the remaining members for their part in the loss of these members is present. The therapist has rescued them by providing replacements. The therapist's own anxiety about group dissolution can be seen in his rush to add new members to the group.

Mrs. Jacobs' decision to stop group therapy was felt by the therapist to be of psychological origin. Since the outset of group therapy she had experienced uncomfortable manifestations of anxiety in the group meetings. She was frequently tardy and absent. She was not pleased when the meetings were increased in length, nor when the duration of therapy was extended from 12 to 18 months.

Technique

The therapist handled Mrs. Jacobs' request by referring her to the group. The issue was a group problem. Regardless of Mrs. Jacobs' decision, the group members understood it better when she discussed it with them than when the therapist had merely announced that Mrs. Jacobs would not attend any future meetings.

The feelings of guilt and fears associated with group losses were explored in some detail. The fears of group dissolution were verbalized.

The therapist supported Mrs. Jacobs by pointing out her irregular attendance, uneasiness in the group meetings, and the attitude of the members to her in previous meetings.

The therapist correctly brought about a modification of the group contract by raising the issue of new members for approval. His technique would have been better, however, had he allowed the members several weeks to discuss their feelings about the change in the contract before he admitted the new members.

FORTY–SECOND MEETING

Seven members were present, including the two new members, Mr. Smith and Mr. Boler.

The therapist introduced Smith and Boler. The session began with references to the fact that a larger number of people made the group more like it was in the beginning. Very early the therapist asked for their reactions in the group with the new members. A number of questions were directed to the new members regarding their illness, hospitalization, and previous group experiences. The anxiety level of the members was noticeably increased. Smith and Boler were tense and defensive. Holt became overtalkative as a result of his extreme anxiety. Smith and Boler admitted defensiveness in this new situation. Holt said it was like a new group, as if they were starting over. Holt's anxiety continued to mount, reaching a peak with a burst of rapid-fire words that prevented others from participating. Several times Mrs. Kitch, in angry tones, asked Holt to shut up. The therapist dealt with Holt's behavior by saying: "Now, Mr. Holt speaks of being in a new group, like starting over, and his talking here in the meeting has concerned you. What ideas do you have about it?" Miss French said he was acting as he had in early meetings, adding, "The more he talks the louder he becomes." Smith felt it could be nervousness and tension, since he does the same thing himself at times. Miss French and Mr. Darcy agreed. Humor and laughter that occurred several times during the meeting was brought to the group's attention by the therapist. There was agreement as to its value in relieving anxiety and tension. The therapist refocused on their anxiety. With the exception of Holt, all the members verbalized their anxiety. Smith and Boler brought out fears of rejection and irritability toward the therapist for not continuing the other group. The meeting ended with a discussion of Cain's plight. The group asked the therapist to contact him for support and as an expression of their interest.

Theme and Dynamics

The theme of the meeting revolved around the "new group." This term is in essence correct. Defenses were again mobilized as in early meetings. Holt's anxietal manifestations were identified and related to his behavior in the past. Fears of rejection and irritation at the therapist for creating this "new group" were expressed. There were general expressions of the anxiety and tenseness present during the meeting.

Technique

The therapist was in control of the meeting. He was aware that the presence of Smith and Boler would mobilize anxiety among all. His remarks to the members were centered around the group interaction. Several times during the meeting he explored their feelings about anxiety. He recognized Holt's defense against anxiety, which the members identified. The employment of humor and laughter was identified as a tension-relieving maneuver.

It is extremely important for the therapist to be constantly aware of his role in the reality events affecting the members. In this instance he added two new members to the group on short notice. Much of the anxiety that was present was due to the members' reactions to the change in the group structure. They blame the therapist for the change and react with hostility. In this meeting the therapist dealt with their anxiety but he did not focus on himself. He could have said, "You recognize that the new group situation makes you anxious. Do you have any thoughts as to the source of this anxiety? How do you feel toward me for changing the group?"

The therapist should always support new members who are added to a group. The fears of new members are much more apparent than those of the regular members. In this meeting he should have supported Smith and Boler by asking the group how they thought these new members felt at their first meeting.

Discussion

The reactions of the group members to changes in the group structure are similar in many respects to many of the reactions people have to changes in everyday groups.

However, the amount of anxiety present will depend on the degree of closeness existing within the group. In large organizations people come and go with little effect on its members. In smaller groups, changes in the composition are more noticeable because the members know each other better and are closer to one another. In this group the members have been together for many months. They are much closer than they were at the outset of group therapy. Now two new members have been added. Immediately the group anxiety level increased. A "new group" behavior occurred because the emotional reactions of the group members are similar to those of the early group meetings. They are reacting to fears of closeness with the strangers. The new members also experience the same feelings as the other members.

A group in our society that has its parallel with the therapy group at this time is the new family group. The husband or wife who has lost a spouse by divorce or death creates a new family group by remarriage. If the new spouse also has children by a former marriage, the new family group will encounter anxiety and tension of moderately severe proportions. Children react to a new mother, father, or siblings with irritation and hostility. Children also become angry with their real parent for marrying and changing their family structure. Subgrouping in these new family groups is common. Children will tend to turn to their real parent and avoid the foster parent. If either parent has difficulty understanding the behavior of the new children and becomes angry with them, subgrouping may be further encouraged. The final result may be two separate families, angry at each other from both the parental and sibling level.

A parallel can be drawn from this therapy group and a new family group. In the therapy group new members create anxiety and tension. Group members become angry at the group therapist for bringing in new people. Before the therapy group can proceed with its function, the therapist must clear away the anxiety and tension produced by its new structure. Understandably, this will take a period of time. Failure of the therapist to recognize the anxiety created by additions to the group will interfere with its proper functioning. Understanding leadership from the parents is a necessity in new family groups. Children should be told about the problems they will have adjusting to a new parent and new brothers or sisters. Just as the therapist discusses new additions to the group prior to their entering, so should parents discuss a new marriage with their children before it takes place. Children should be advised that the new family group will produce anxiety and hostility and that it will take months for them to adjust to one another. The parents will have to support each other and the children from a unified position. Failure to do so encourages division in the family—the formation of subgroups. The success or failure of new family groups to integrate will depend on the understanding, support, and cooperativeness of its leaders, the parents.

FORTY–THIRD MEETING

Six members were present. Mr. Darcy and Mr. Cain were absent.

The meeting began with hostile remarks to the recorder. Mr. Boler began discussing conflicts with his mother, bringing out her hostility to psychiatrists. Family relationships were discussed by Miss French, Mrs. Kitch, and Mr. Holt. The therapist at this point focused on feelings in the group. The subject was changed. Mr. Smith reminded the group that the therapist's statement had been ignored, and then made a general observation that jealousy and competition were present between the members. He admitted antagonism toward Holt, who he felt was superior, dominating, and prone to usurp the therapist's role. There was immediate agreement from Miss French, who said she had felt the same way since the beginning of group therapy. Holt again brought out problems encountered in trying to correct his loud voice. There was a discussion of the group's resemblance to a family. Mr. Smith admitted that he had frequently been angry with the therapist in the past, and compared him to his parents. Boler said that he frequently displaces feelings about his mother on to the therapist because the therapist, like his mother, is an authority figure. Holt admitted irritation with the therapist. Mrs. Kitch spoke of getting to the meeting in a good humor and then becoming irritated with the therapist. The therapist pointed out the hostility and irritations expressed about him and asked them to explore their feelings. The group felt that he was an authority figure. Holt strongly emphasized that the therapist had not done anything for him; the group had helped, but the therapist did nothing. Foy remained uncommunicative throughout the meeting. Toward the end of the meeting the therapist read a letter addressed to them from Cain. He spoke of his earlier fears and guilt feelings in the group meetings. He apologized for the alcoholic behavior that resulted in his present predicament (being in jail), but felt encouraged that the members were interested in him. He was looking forward to returning to the group in several months.

The recorder pointed out to the therapist following the meeting that his questions and remarks to Holt were somewhat hostile. The therapist's behavior suggested an increased nonverbal anxiety toward Holt. The therapist had not been aware of these feelings. Consciously, he spoke of liking Mr. Holt.

Theme and Dynamics

The theme of the meeting was hostility toward the therapist as a result of the new group structure. The meeting began with hostile remarks about the recorder. Hostility toward parental figures followed. Group feelings were explored, but hostility was displaced away from the therapist to Holt. Admitted irritations with the therapist were later explored.

In all instances, the theme of the meeting was identical—anger at the therapist. The fact that these feelings were mobilized and expressed at this second meeting with the new member was a sign of group maturity. Countertransference feelings of the therapist prevented the recognition of the hostility expressed to Holt.

Technique

The therapist was aware of the hostility directed toward him and correctly focused on it except in one instance. The remarks directed to Holt were meant for the therapist. He was compared to a dominating, superior person who played the role of the therapist. The therapist, at this point, could have said to the members: "You began the hour with remarks about the recorder, then you talked angrily of mothers, fathers, and husbands. I asked you to look at your feelings here, following which you began attacking Mr. Holt. You said he was dominating, superior, and acted like me. Any thoughts as to what is going on in the meeting?" He could also have focused on the tension spoken of at the last meeting in relation to their present feelings of hostility, and asked them to explore its meaning. The therapist could be more direct by also pointing out the previous references to the group's resemblance to a family, their feelings expressed about him, what they have felt and said in the new group situation, and (although everyone had voiced pleasure) explored the possibility of other feelings being present.

FORTY–FOURTH MEETING

There were five members present. Mr. Darcy and Mr. Cain were absent. Mr. Foy called to report that he would be unable to attend. Mr. Holt had phoned the recorder during the past week seeking help for his daughter. He complimented the recorder, adding that the therapist was a person who would never understand. The recorder referred him to the therapist and advised the therapist of Holt's call. The therapist decided to await further developments.

The meeting began with Boler's discussing conflicts with his mother and his need for drugs. The group advised him to leave the drugs alone and to pull away from his mother. Mr. Holt asserted that he was also attending another group that meets daily at a nearby alcoholic clinic. (Holt had made passing reference to this clinic before.) The group advised him to participate here and not get confused. He would never profit in this way. The therapist focused on Holt's observation concerning the other group meeting and asked for the group's opinion of Holt's actions. The therapist also attempted to be supportive to Holt by saying: "Any thoughts as to why Mr. Holt feels he has to go to other meetings?" The members were very warm and supportive to Holt but, at the same time, quite directive in pointing out that running from one group to another meant avoiding this group. Holt discussed his feelings about the therapist in very angry tones. He refused to recognize the therapist as an authority figure. Smith spoke of getting angry with the therapist. He denied this. Holt continued to reiterate his refusal to accept the therapist as an authority figure. Smith spoke of getting angry with the therapist and wondered if his feelings toward Holt were the result of seeing him as an authority figure. Smith demanded more from the therapist and spoke very angrily of him and his method of directing the meetings. As the meeting ended, Holt admitted that he had called the recorder to ask for help with his daughter.

Theme and Dynamics

The hostility to the therapist had abated, except that of Holt. His hostile, dependent relationship with the therapist was apparent. The pressures of the group as well as the anxiety created by the new members was very threatening to him. (Reference is made to Holt's anxiety at the 42nd meeting, when Smith and Boler joined the group.) His acting out by contacting the recorder, attending other meetings, demanding the therapist to do more was truly his method of rebellion to authority.

Technique

The therapist, following a discussion with the recorder, became aware of his countertransference manifestations to Holt at the 43rd meeting. He pointed out Holt's attendance at other meetings and attempted to support him by asking the group to look at his need to do so. He encouraged Holt to ventilate his angry feelings at this meeting.

Holt's communication with the recorder was correctly referred to the therapist. The recorder also asked Holt to discuss his problems with the therapist. If Holt had not brought this matter to the attention of the group, the therapist should do so during the group meeting. In this instance Holt discussed his contact with the recorder during the meeting. Holt's behavior was directly related to the dynamics of the group. Here again we see the importance of discussing in the meetings any and all outside contacts between (1) group members, (2) group members and the recorder, and (3) group members and the therapist.

Holt's acting-out behavior is a major group problem. His anger and defiance to the therapist has been noted in many meetings. However, there is another factor that may be contributing to Holt's behavior—the therapist. The latter's hostility to Holt has been observed by the recorder on several occasions. This factor cannot be overlooked in assessing Holt's group behavior. For all groups the therapist's conscious and unconscious reactions affect the members and his reactions are an unknown factor in the losses that occur in groups. The recorder's observations during meetings, therapist-recorder discussions of the total group behavior, and group supervisory conferences (particularly for the therapist during his period of training) are helpful. However, in some instances the therapist, even though he consciously recognizes his negative responses to a member, may unconsciously continue to be hostile to the member. This area of the group therapist's influence and cause of group losses has not been studied sufficiently by group therapists.

Discussion

The group members' praise of the recorder and criticism of the group therapist illustrate another way in which people show their anger and defiance to others. Patients both in and out of hospitals who are unable to obtain magical, dependency wishes and a solution to their difficulties become angry and act out by praising their present doctor while criticizing previous doctors. Sociopathic personality disorders are characterized by attempts to create friction among staff physicians and nurses by criticizing and praising first one and then another. Their motivation seems to be to divide and conquer. Similar types of behavior occur in many everyday group relationships. In the family group, children may play one parent against the other in order to get their own way.

In highly competitive groups, situations may occur that are similar to the one in this group meeting. Anger at the leader of the group may be handled by heaping praise on another member of the group. The motivation is to seek revenge on the leader of the group and remove him from the position as leader. This type of motivation may occur in political organizations and many other groups in our society.

An examination of the dynamics of the group process up to this time reveals several interesting features. The anxiety of the group members had been gradually increasing since the initial meeting. One characteristic effect of anxiety is the forgetfulness which was exhibited in the group at the 9th meeting. Transference reactions were evident at the 11th meeting. The group members' references to the need to please others and to feelings of being coerced related to their feelings about the group therapist whom they viewed as an all-powerful, omnipotent person who can either magically love them or retaliate against them. The group member's fear of the group therapist from about the 15th to 25th group meeting suggested a group conformity. But actually it was a period of pseudoconformity, for underneath their conforming manner were very strong feelings of rage. During this period of pseudoconformity the group members' anxiety level was high. Minor provocations between the group members led to angry outbursts. Scapegoating was present (against Mr. Foy). At the 18th, 20th, and 28th meetings their manifestations of anxiety were again verbalized. Between the 25th and 40th meeting they began to recognize and ventilate their hostile feelings toward the group therapist. Their fears of the group therapist's omnipotence had diminished. They did not feel the intense need to please him and real feelings were more comfortably expressed.

The statement by one group member at the 41st meeting that every member was her responsibility indicated that group cohesiveness was nearer. Individual wishes and desires of the group members were being given up for those of the group.

This period of group therapy draws attention to a somewhat similar situation that exists in many everyday group relationships. There may be so much fear of the group leader that the members feel coerced to do his bidding. The premium is on "pleasing the boss." Ingratiating techniques are commonly used. The leader is placed upon a pedestal and revered as omnipotent. In such everyday groups a stage of pseudoconformity exists. Many different feelings may be experienced toward the leader. If the leader does not allow the expression of feelings, they are displaced on either fellow workers or family members. The anxiety level among them may be high, and acting-out behavior such as absenteeism, tardiness, and anger at one another may occur. In some, the increased anxiety may result in physical symptoms such as headache, gastrointestinal complaints, lassitude, etc.

This type of behavior may occur in occupational, professional, educational, and other groups. The interaction in any group will depend on the personality structure and patterns of behavior of the leader and its members. However, as in the dynamics of group therapy, the one person who can influence, modify, and affect the behavior of the members of the group is the leader. He is the most important figure in the group. The leaders in business, industrial, professional, and educational organizations whose members are not allowed to express their feelings and who must conform to the wishes of the leader at all times have a higher incidence of conflicts between members and more manifestations of group anxiety such as accident-proneness, less productivity, tardiness, and absenteeism. Those leaders who are more understanding of their members and allow the members to express their feelings will have less group anxiety. The result is a more homogeneous organization with greater productivity, less absenteeism, less illness, and better relationships with each other and the leader.

FORTY–FIFTH MEETING

There were five members present; Mr. Darcy, Mr. Cain, and Mr. Foy were absent. Mrs. Darcy reported that her husband's physical condition was gradually becoming worse. Mr. Foy called in to report that conflicts with his father and demands of his father and demands of his work would prevent his attendance.

The meeting began with Boler requesting drugs and describing conflicts with his mother. Boler had contacted the therapist prior to the meeting requesting drugs. The therapist referred him to the members of the group. They pointed out his dependence on drugs and its relationship to problems with his mother, suggesting that he move away from her at the first opportunity. Group feelings were focused on by the therapist. Holt stated he was going to start off by being nasty to the therapist. Smith felt he was being stared at by the therapist. Miss French commented that at times she trusted the therapist, at other times she did not. Smith said the pressure of authority was always present. Holt again refused to recognize the therapist as an authority figure and resented his method. He didn't understand the therapist's observations and became confused and blank when the therapist said anything. Miss French related that many times she didn't understand but would "catch on" at later meetings, adding that it was her own responsibility to learn in group therapy, not someone else's. She stated that Mr. Holt was just like Mr. Foy in wanting miracles. The members compared the therapist to their parents in relationship to authority figures. Holt described his parents. His mother must have been like Mr. Boler's mother. His father was a "good old Joe" with whom he had problems, but he never accepted his father as an authority figure. The therapist pointed out Mr. Holt's description of his father and his refusal to see him as an authority. The members told Holt that he was putting the therapist in the same role as his father. Absences were discussed. There was concern about Mr. Foy, who had missed a few meetings. The therapist relayed his telephone message after exploring group feelings.

During the meeting Mr. Smith talked about his conflicts with Holt. He recognized that hostility to Holt had been present since joining the group several weeks previously. Smith also recognized that he was competing with Holt and that he could now see in Holt's behavior some of his own personality characteristics.

Theme and Dynamics

Group relationships between each member and the pressure of authority (therapist) represented the theme of the meeting. It was interesting to see the various levels of interaction. Boler was angry because there are women in the group. His dependency on the therapist and his hostility towards women were evident. Smith, Miss French, and Mrs. Kitch recognized the pressure of authority problems along with fear and trust of each other and the therapist, but realized the solution is up to them, not someone else. Foy for many months has avoided group involvement and sought a cure by drugs, hypnosis, magic, etc. Now Holt's intellectual, pompous, and dictatorial façade has been broken through and his massive dependency strivings are on the surface. He has been identified with Foy as seeking a miracle. Mr. Darcy has remained a member whose participation is extremely limited.

Technique

The therapist correctly referred Boler's request for drugs to the group. Drugs have been a repeated problem with him and are closely allied to his anxiety both within and without the group. His use of drugs was a group issue. Group problems were dealt with throughout the meeting. After the therapist called it to the group's attention, the members recognized the similarity between Holt's relationship with his father and his relationship with the therapist.

Smith's recognition that his hostility to Holt is in part due to the fact that he sees his own patterns of behavior in Holt points out a behavior reaction that occurs frequently in group therapy. A group member may become hostile and antagonistic to the behavior patterns of another group member that are actually similar to his own. However, since this process occurs unconsciously, the behavior pattern is not recognized. However, in this group meeting Mr. Smith recognized his behavior with Holt. The therapist should be alert for this type of behavior among group members. When the therapist recognizes that competition and hostility are occurring between two group members, he should ask the group's opinion. Often the similarity of their behavior patterns is apparent to the therapist and the other group members. In order to uncover such behavior that has not been recognized, the therapist could say: "Mr. Smith and Mr. Holt have been angry at each other for several meetings. Do you have any ideas why they remain angry with each other?" The therapist could also say: "Do you think that Mr. Smith and Mr. Holt have similar reactions to each other?" "Could either one be recognizing traits of his own in the other and not be aware of it?" "Have any of you ever recognized traits of your own in other people?" "Maybe Mr. Smith gets angry at Mr. Holt because he recognizes traits in Mr. Holt that are like his, traits that he does not like in himself." Such questions and statements from the therapist will encourage group members to examine their own patterns of behavior with others.

FORTY–SIXTH MEETING

There were four members present; Mr. Boler, Mr. Darcy, Mr. Cain, and Mr. Holt were absent.

Considerable attention was focused on Mr. Foy, since he had been absent for two meetings. Foy began talking in his usual vein of self-derogatory remarks. He mentioned problems at home. The members pointed out his lack of involvement in group therapy. Foy agreed, adding fears of rejection were also present. Conflicts with his wife and disappointment in occupational endeavors were verbalized. The members encouraged and supported him, seemingly happy in seeing him participating in group conversation. Foy described periods of uncontrollable rage and of hating everybody. The therapist reminded them that Foy had commented previously that when an argument was occurring, the group was like a family. Foy replied that if he lost control an animal would emerge. He utilized alcohol in order to afford control during meetings. Smith was very supportive, pointing out to Foy that many of the same feelings occurred with him prior to hospitalization.

Concern about the absent members was voiced by Mrs. Kitch. The therapist announced that Mr. Boler had been readmitted to the State Hospital since the last meeting. (The therapist at that time had been advised by telephone of Boler's hospitalization. No details were available.) Group feelings were explored. This event was extremely depressing to the members. Mr. Smith and Miss French wondered whether or not his hospitalization was caused by them. Smith was concerned about whether or not any remarks he had made to Mr. Boler were contributing factors. He felt guilty for Boler's hospitalization.

Prior to the end of the meeting, Foy discussed briefly and with reservation his religious differences with the other group members (Foy is Jewish; the other group members are Protestant except Boler and Mrs. Kitch, who are Catholic). The therapist asked the group members about Foy's references to religious conflicts; however, there were only superficial comments from the group members.

Theme and Dynamics

The material verbalized by Foy indicated again the massive, murderous rage underneath the façade of humor, self-pity, and magical wishes. Revealing himself or becoming involved in the group is fraught with all kinds of dangers including rejection, retaliation, and destruction.

Group interest in Boler as well as guilt feelings for his predicament were expressed. Here again were highlighted many of their fears, guilts, and feelings of personal responsibility for Boler's hospitalization.

Technique

The therapist allowed the group to explore Foy's feelings and related them to the issues at hand. His need to stay on the periphery and not get involved became clearer.

The therapist should have explored the feelings of the group concerning Mr. Boler's hospitalization earlier. The impact on them was very noticeable, as such events usually are, with depression still evident at the close of the meeting. Allowance of more time for discussion and ventilation of feelings would probably have been helpful.

Time did not permit the therapist to explore the feelings of the group members regarding their religious differences. They are present. The therapist should explore them in more detail in future group meetings.

Discussion

Mr. Foy's remark about religious differences in the group has its parallel in many groups of our society. Religious and racial conflicts are present in this group, just as they are present in many groups. The Negro, the Jew, the Catholic, the Oriental, and the Protestant have all been subjected at times to scapegoating techniques, depending upon such factors as sectional prejudice, majority or minority status, and other stresses. The plight of the southern Negro is well known. During World War II loyal Japanese in this country were recipients of much hostility. The Protestant, especially in sections of the country that are overwhelmingly Protestant, often looks upon the Catholic with suspicion and reservation. Similarly, some Catholics under the same conditions treat the Protestant with suspicion. The Jews, being usually a minority group, have been a frequent scapegoat of other races.

Groups composed of members from mixed backgrounds may or may not be troublesome for the group therapist. Satisfactory group therapy can usually be accomplished in groups that contain a mixture of Catholic, Jewish, and Protestant members. Racial conflicts are more likely to interfere with group therapeutic procedures. For example, in the deep South, mixed therapy groups of Negroes and whites would not be possible. Personal communications by the author with group therapists in the New England area reveal that they, too, have difficulties in retaining Negro members in predominantly white groups. Vita Stein Sommers [4] has reported the success of a 2-year experience in group therapy with mixed minority groups on the West coast. Dr. Sommers' group membership (all male) was composed of two Chinese, two Negroes, three German Jews, one Englishman, and one Irishman. At first she noticed that each group member exhibited irrational hostility towards the other member of his own minority group. Later in group therapy the group members dealt with their cultural and social conflicts and finally their basic interpersonal conflicts with each other.

Social class conflicts are usually not severe problems in group therapy. The author has treated several groups whose membership has included patients from upper and lower levels of society. The patients from the lower-class levels initially are more fearful and suspicious of the others. Patients from higher social levels are generally quite supportive to those from lower social levels. Both types of patients find many common bonds of interest with each other during their experiences in group therapy.

FORTY–SEVENTH MEETING

There were six members present. Mr. Darcy and Mr. Cain were absent.

The meeting began with Mr. Boler discussing his recent five-day period of hospitalization precipitated by excessive use of alcohol and drugs. He talked of his anxiety and again referred to his other group experience. Boler also spoke of his dependency on his mother and on a newspaper editor when he was writing crime stories; now he could see that he was dependent on the therapist. On several occasions he was frankly irritated with the therapist. The therapist brought out the group's concern for Boler and their pleasure that he was back, but Miss French added that some people would go to any lengths to accomplish their goals.

Mr. Smith requested to discuss a group issue. At the previous meeting, during the conversation with Foy, Smith felt that he had exposed himself. He felt guilty and wondered what the others thought of him. The general conversation from the other members was very supportive to him.

Approximately 40 minutes before the end of the meeting the therapist announced he would have to terminate the session 20 minutes early. Group feelings were explored. They expressed feelings of irritability and anger. Holt wondered how the therapist would feel if the group members walked out on him. Boler was noticeably angry. He spoke of his dependency on the therapist and his resentment of it. He was sure the group was more important than anything the therapist had scheduled. Miss French didn't like any change in the group meetings.

Theme and Dynamics

Boler's problems that resulted in depression, with alcohol and drugs superimposed, appear to relate to his uncomfortable feelings in the group. His dependency needs were not being met. The therapist has placed him in a new threatening situation with strangers that include women.

Smith's fears of rejection from exposure were expressed. His feelings were distorted. However, this event was significant in that a common denominator in the group dynamics concerns fears of rejection, guilt, retaliation, etc., that are distortions in reality, but seem quite real and frightening to the patient.

Technique

The therapist was aware that Boler's hospitalization was related to group structure. He explored group feelings and pointed out Boler's hostility toward the therapist. There was only superficial discussion from the group members.

Smith's discussion was group-oriented and did not require intervention from the therapist.

The therapist correctly explored feelings concerning a change in the structure of the meeting (group reality event). The verbalizations indicated the members' reactions to reducing the length of the therapy session.

Discussion

Boler's hostile, dependent relationships to all authority figures is very evident. The person who has many dependency needs functions better in an occupational group where he can be dependent on others. He needs a superior who can help him share responsibility and decisions. Such people will often deny vehemently their dependency on others. Frequently they will try business ventures on their own, but they are not usually successful because they become overwhelmed with the responsibilities of their endeavors. Increased anxiety and depression are commonly seen. They may resort to the use of alcoholism to relieve anxiety. Then, too, the dependency relationship may be associated with so much hostility that repeated conflict occurs. A person who has a hostile dependent relationship with leaders or authority figures stays angry at his boss or leader, exhibits passive-aggressive techniques with him and may have a poor attendance record as well as less productivity in his occupation.

Boler's occupational patterns of behavior are related to his basic psychodynamics. The same situation is encountered in many people. Then, too, the patterns of behavior of a person may contribute to the type of occupation or profession that he chooses. In certain occupational roles, specific types of personalities tend to be more prevalent. The hypomanic person succeeds in salesmanship positions; such a person is happy, gay, humorous, friendly and makes a good impression in group relationships. The person who has many of the patterns of behavior of the obsessive-compulsive personality chooses such positions as a scientist, professor, or research worker. Meticulousness, perfectionism, and compulsiveness are advantageous to him. The person with an obsessive-compulsive personality may be very productive and work many hours seven days a week. He may find it necessary to engage in strenuous work with lengthy periods of activity to protect him against anxiety. The cold, aloof, rigid, and dictatorial person may be very difficult to work with in group relationships. Frequently such people isolate themselves in research duties or other types of work where they can be alone. Early childhood training of both men and women may place great emphasis on competitiveness. Self-esteem and personal security may be present only when these people are successful in competitive roles. They may become cold, ruthless, and destructive to others in their competitive group relationships. They are interested only in securing their goals and have no regard for the anxiety created among their group relationships.

The attractive female with a hysterical personality has charmed many a boss into hiring her as his secretary. She relies primarily on her good looks, exhibitionism, seductiveness, and flare for the dramatic. Even if her performance at work is below par she can frequently maintain herself in the occupational position by her patterns of behavior. Those people who are passive, withdrawn, or have difficulty in relating to others often seek out positions where they do not have to relate to people and can go quietly about their work without experiencing difficulty and anxiety. The farmer who is passive and nonassertive or who has schizoid patterns of behavior can go about his farming operations with a minimum of difficulty. He experiences little anxiety because he has few group relationships. The husband who has conflicts with his wife reduces his anxiety by securing a job that keeps him traveling and away from home most of the week. An example is a passive nonassertive male who has an angry and controlling wife. In family group relationships he becomes anxious and depressed. He may resort to alcoholism for the relief of anxiety. He finds that less anxiety occurs if he can avoid his wife. Accordingly, he takes up an occupational position that keeps him out of town and away from his wife as much as possible.

FORTY–EIGHTH MEETING

There were six members present. Mr. Darcy and Mr. Cain were absent.

The hour began with a discussion of guilt and fear feelings. Mr. Boler, Mr. Holt, Mr. Smith, and Miss French admitted that emotions of guilt and fear prevented closer group relationships. Mrs. Kitch said that this group is more comfortable than other groups because of the understanding here. Following an interplay between Miss French and Mr. Holt, with an interspersed observation by the therapist, Holt replied angrily that he could not understand the vagueness of the therapist. Miss French said she had to think for long periods about the therapist's statements. Miss French thought the therapist was trying to get the members to look at each other. She felt that Mr. Holt wanted magic. The therapist asked the group why they couldn't get down to business. Fears of disapproval by the therapist and an inability to trust one another were verbalized. Miss French said she used to see the therapist as one huge authority figure. Expectations from therapy and therapist were discussed. The therapist asked: "What are your expectations from me?" Boler wanted the therapist to take him over and run him. He needed individual treatment also. Holt angrily wondered what the therapist could do, since all he did was ask them questions and never did anything for him. Smith and Boler expected perfection from authority. Holt continued angrily to demand more from the therapist. Boler wondered what he wanted. Holt replied that actually he didn't know. Smith agreed with Miss French that

Holt wanted a magical solution. The therapist continued to deal with group feelings and expectations from group therapy. There was an interplay between Holt and Boler. Holt felt the group should expect something from the therapist and he shouldn't be criticized for wanting help. Holt was reminded that no one had criticized him; that he should expect direction, not solution. Miss French compared Mr. Holt's relationship with his father to his relationship with the therapist. Lack of relationship to his father seemed identical to his feelings toward the therapist. Smith agreed with Miss French's observation. Mr. Holt continued making comments about doctors and authority figures and became entangled in an argument over the definition of an authority figure. As far as he was concerned, the therapist was not even an authority figure. All he did was say "Hello," "What's going on?" and "Good-by." Boler felt that Holt ignored the group and the therapist. The therapist then made the following observation: "Let me remind you again of the group contract. For a number of meetings the actions of Mr. Holt and Mr. Foy have been this way. I wonder if you have any ideas why Mr. Holt continually reacts in this manner and Mr. Foy responds with humor?" Boler thought their reactions were an evasion of their emotional feelings. Mrs. Kitch said that all Mr. Foy wanted was pity. Smith asserted that their reactions were a mirror of the past. He also felt that even though Holt reacted in a hostile manner to criticism, he actually felt rejection. Holt continued his campaign against the therapist. Mrs. Kitch told Holt that the therapist must remind him of his father. Boler said the therapist reminded him of his mother. Holt silently agreed with Mrs. Kitch and added that his father was never capable of helping him. Smith reminded Holt again that he expected the therapist to react as an authority had in the past. Boler reacted by pointing out that Holt refused to look at himself. Foy reacted again with humor that created laughter. Miss French reminded him of the seriousness of their discussion of authority figures as the hour ended.

Theme and Dynamics

The members' feelings of fear and guilt, their inability to trust one another, and their fears of disapproval from the therapist are preventing closer group relationships. The dependency strivings of Boler and Holt were clearly demonstrated and analyzed. The relationship of Holt to his father and the therapist was again identified and interpreted to him. The members continued to point out to Foy his role. His use of humor to avoid emotional involvement continues as one of his defenses.

Technique

The therapist correctly focused on group relationships throughout the meeting. He recognized the pressure from the authority figure and its resulting feelings of disapproval, fear, and guilt. He continued to ask the group to look at their feelings toward him. He recognized that there is anger and hostility directed toward him for asking the members to bring themselves closer together, to cooperate and mutually help one another.

Boler's demand for both individual therapy and group therapy points out several features of these two types of psychotherapy of which the therapist should be constantly aware. Sometimes individual therapy and group therapy with different therapists may be recommended for a patient. Such recommendations may be made to the patient at the outset of group therapy, during the course of individual therapy, or during group therapy. The combination of group therapy and individual therapy has been rewarding to many patients. However, the group therapist and the individual therapist should be aware that complications may occur in the treatment of a patient who is receiving both individual therapy and group therapy. At the outset of group therapy, the patient's goals are not generally group-oriented. He usually enters the group hoping to secure from the group therapist individual attention which will cure him by some magical device. As his anxiety level rises in later group meetings, the patient may make demands for individual attention from the group therapist or request individual therapy from another therapist. In this instance the patient is avoiding the group. Such behavior should be pointed out to him and discussed in group meetings. He should remain in the group and not be allowed to manipulate the therapy at any stage of group therapy. Group members more often seek individual therapy during the first stage of group therapy. In other situations where the patient is in both individual therapy and group therapy, the patient may avoid group therapy and attempt to work out his difficulties with his individual therapist. He may attend group meetings regularly without becoming involved in the group interaction. This condition, which the author has observed in several patients, does pose the question of whether such combined therapy procedures are advantageous, particularly if both therapies are of long duration. In groups of psychotic patients the therapist occasionally has to arrange for an anxious patient to see another therapist for several interviews. As soon as the patient's anxiety has diminished, the individual interviews are terminated. This arrangement is usually free from any serious difficulties.

FORTY–NINTH MEETING

There were five members present, Mr. Foy, Mr. Darcy, and Mr. Cain being absent. The recorder was out of the city. A male resident who had recorded for this group at the 15th meeting served as substitute recorder.

At the beginning of the hour the therapist asked for the group's feelings concerning the absence of the regular recorder and the substitute recorder. Miss French replied angrily that she wanted to go home. Mr. Smith admitted anxiety. The substitute recorder was compared to a new member. The group verbalized that any change created anxiety and tension. They spoke of missing the regular recorder and stated that she was a part of the group. Mr. Boler made his usual request for drugs. Again the members discouraged his dependency on drugs. Mr. Boler felt himself to be more dependent on the therapist than on the drugs. Group feelings were focused on by the therapist. Miss French said the therapist made her think. At times she hated everyone, even those in the group. She had felt better ever since Smith had previously made a similar statement. Holt again discussed authority figures after Smith talked of seeking independence and resenting help from anyone. Holt replied that rebellion against authority plagued him. He felt that he had improved somewhat and that now he could accept help from others. Miss French agreed but added that the therapist didn't help at all. Holt wondered how the therapist felt about the members. The therapist then made the following statement: "Now Mr. Holt wonders how I feel toward you. What thoughts do you have of how I feel toward you?" There was a brief silence. Mr. Smith admitted he expected hostility from the therapist, adding, "If you have hostility toward someone, you expect hostility in return." He discussed the relationship with his parents when a youngster. He always reacted in this manner to his father and mother, as well as to other people. Miss French discussed how angry she always becomes after coming home from the group meeting. Frequently she will throw articles in her room. In the past she has blamed this on the maid who cleans her room, but now she wonders whether or not it related to her feelings in the meetings. Near the end of the meeting Mr. Boler discussed his feelings about the therapist. He spoke of wanting to be more friendly with him and had wondered what it would be like to have dinner with the therapist, to socialize with him, and to call him by his first name. Smith took issue with Boler, stating that the latter wanted the therapist to treat him on a social level rather than a professional one. The meeting ended with Smith discussing his hostility toward authority figures.

Theme and Dynamics

The anxiety and tension created by a stranger was verbalized. Their comments at this meeting should be compared to the statements made at the 15th meeting when the same person served as substitute recorder. Independent and dependent feelings were discussed. Holt identified the resentment of seeking help as rebellion against authority. Exploration of feelings toward the therapist produced the ventilation of the projected theme of hostility. If one has anger to another, such is expected in return. Smith identified its reality in the parent-child relationship and its extension to other people and the therapist. Miss French discussed her angry feelings toward people and brought her group feelings to the surface.

Technique

The therapist correctly focused on group feelings about the change of recorder for this meeting.

The therapist could have further identified Holt's rebellion against authority by making the following statement: "Now Mr. Holt admits anger to authority interferes with accepting help from authority. He agrees with Miss French that a function here is to help one another, but the doctor doesn't help at all. What do you make of this sequence of statements?"

The therapist explored their feelings toward him. He asked a direct question to the group members regarding how he (the therapist) feels toward them in such a manner that material was verbalized. The therapist did not answer their question. More importantly, they talked about their feelings for him. Feelings of hostility, its relationship to family surrogates and its extension to others as well as the therapist, were discussed for the first time.

The therapist could have related Miss French's statement of hating people at times to the members by saying: "Miss French speaks of hating people at times. I wonder if you have any ideas about her observation and your feelings here with one another?"

When Miss French spoke of getting angry at home after the meeting, the therapist could have said (if time permitted): "Miss French has related angry feelings to the meetings. What about getting angry here?" He might have also added: "You are here to look at and understand your feelings with one another. What causes you to get angry here?"

Some group therapists address their group members by their first names during group meetings.[5-7] The author does not feel that this practice is good technique. Therapy, regardless of whether it is on an individual or group basis, is a professional relationship between therapist and his patient. Many times patients with emotional illnesses wish to change the professional relationship to a social one or even one of a more intimate level. They may wish for the therapist to be a close personal friend and to love and care for them like a parent. On the other hand, many patients have a massive dread of closeness and become extremely frightened if the therapist's technique suggests increased closeness— for example, the use of first names. This is especially true in the schizophrenic patient. The therapeutic relationship between the therapist and the patient requires a proper structure. In this model of group therapy the structure is provided in the group contract. One important part of this structure is the group therapist's professional relationship with his group members. The manner in which the group therapist communicates with his group members is included in this structure. He should respect his patients, and address them as Miss Smith, Mr. Jones, or Mrs. Rogers. An exception occurs with teen-agers in our culture. Teen-agers are usually addressed by their first names. The same principle holds true in group therapy.

The author would also like to emphasize that the technique employed by the therapist in this group should not be strictly imitated by other group therapists. Every therapist should employ the technique that he can comfortably use with his group members. In this model of group therapy the therapist should remain committed to the suggested general format regarding technique and goals. However, it is just as important that the therapist feel free, flexible and comfortable in the group. He does not have to be stereotyped in his responses to the members. In this group the therapist frequently uses repetitive phrases in his observations to the members, such as, "What are your thoughts about this?" or "What ideas do you have?" Another therapist may word his remarks completely different and obtain adequate responses from the members.

During the training period of psychiatric residents in group therapy, the author has observed that some residents will try to copy the style and technique of the supervisor. In so doing they may become stereotyped and artificial in their role as therapist. Every group therapist should be encouraged to develop a technique with which he is comfortable. Such traits are necessary prerequisites for successful group therapy.

FIFTIETH MEETING

There were five members present. Miss French called to say that she was too depressed to attend the meeting. Mr. Darcy and Mr. Cain continued to be absent.

The hour began with statements of joy that the regular recorder was present. The substitute recorder was referred to as "that bird." Boler made his standard plea for drugs. Increased irritability toward him was apparent. When the therapist would focus on group issues, Boler would return to his need for medication. The therapist pointed out this behavior to the other members. Smith felt that Boler was bringing his home problems into the group meeting. He has a constant war at home with his mother about drugs, and now he wants to continue the same battle with the therapist. Boler and Holt thought that the therapist was always staring at them. Foy wanted the therapist to look straight through him and produce a magical cure. Following references to their relationships with one another, the therapist asked them to explore further their relationship to each other and to him. Smith admitted hostility toward Boler and Holt. They admitted competition for the therapist and desired his sympathy and attention. Holt felt the therapist was too impersonal and not human.

He would like to see the therapist get angry and would enjoy arguing with him. He accused the therapist of being like a Buddha. Mrs. Kitch replied the doctor's role did not concern her any more. Foy was exhibiting his usual role. When discussing Miss French's absence they said that Mr. Foy was absent too—only his body was present.

Approximately 20 minutes before the meeting was over the therapist interrupted the group and said: "You are discussing important aspects of your relationships here; if you wish, the subject can be brought up at a later meeting. I do have a matter to discuss with you now. I shall not be able to meet with you next week." Immediately Holt and Boler reacted with hostility. There were exclamations of "Why?" "What's going on?" "Where is the therapist going?" They felt that they were discussing emotional problems and needed regular meetings. Holt would like the group to meet the next day. As the hour ended there were questions as to the therapist's plans for the next week. He told them of a contemplated brief vacation.

Theme and Dynamics

The members continued to explore their relationships. Hostile feelings toward each other as well as a competitiveness for the therapist's attention were verbalized. There was increased irritability with Mr. Boler for his constant demand for drugs. The power struggle with his mother has now entered the group battleground in his relationship with the therapist. The members saw Mr. Foy as a lost cause. He continued to keep himself out of the group and made his periodic demands for a magical cure.

Technique

The members are gradually increasing the awareness of their interpersonal feelings in the group. The therapist has to be ever aware of the group anxiety and maintain it at a constructive level. In this meeting the anxiety level was never high enough to be called threatening or so low as to prevent group functioning. The therapist should be aware of the group problems—for example, (1) Holt, who needs careful, general, and supportive probing, and his hostile dependent relationship to the therapist; (2) Boler and his ever-demanding need for dependency as well as his fear of the female members of the group; (3) Smith, and (4) Miss French, both of whom have behavior patterns of a schizophrenic nature and are experiencing feelings of anger, guilt, and fear that can be very uncomfortable; (5) Foy, who is regular in attendance, but who has never integrated into the group, exhibiting his repeated demands for magic, drugs, and hypnosis; (6) Mrs. Kitch, whose improvement in aggressiveness, self-assertion and self-esteem is a constant reminder of the positive aspects of group therapy; (7) Darcy, with rapidly declining physical health, whose attendance is extremely sporadic, but who is still considered a member; (8) Cain, who has not attended since his confinement in a prison but who has had infrequent contacts by mail with the therapist, and will return within the next few weeks.

FIFTY–FIRST MEETING

All members were present except Mr. Holt, Mr. Darcy, and Mr. Cain.

At the outset of the meeting, the group members appeared to be functioning in their usual manner and mood. Miss French, however, was depressed and discussed her feelings openly. She did not like or trust anyone. She did not like herself. She had felt this way 4 years earlier. Her depression was contagious, and for the initial half of the meeting this mood prevailed. The therapist explored their feelings toward him and the cancelled meeting of the previous week. The members indicated that authority problems were not the concern at present. When they were asked for additional ideas about the depressed mood, Miss French finally observed that the season of the year (Christmas) might be responsible. She felt this way at every Christmas. The therapist asked about their feelings of the Christmas season. Miss French hated Christmas for any number of reasons. Mrs. Kitch said Christmas meant more unpaid bills to her. Smith talked of his deprivations when a boy; his family was poor, Christmas did not excite him, there were too many unpleasant memories. The depression of the group lifted considerably after the ventilation of feelings about the Christmas season. There was a decided change in Miss French. She began interacting with the other members. At a lull in the last half of the hour the therapist discussed with them the matter of unpaid bills. He said: "I have a matter to bring to your attention. In going over your accounts I find several of the members are negligent in payment. How do you feel about this?" Foy exhibited his usual role. He felt the fee was too high and should be reduced. Miss French admitted her laxity in payment was also her manner in handling everything. Mrs. Kitch admitted she was trying. With her husband in treatment too, the financial burden was severe. She stated that if you sacrificed to pay for something the reward was greater than when given to you. Smith, who pays his bills promptly, said that paying for group therapy was necessary to get anything out of it. As the hour ended, all the group members in arrears except Foy indicated that immediate attention would be forthcoming.

Theme and Dynamics

That Christmas is not a happy, gay time of the year for many people with emotional problems was clearly demonstrated in this meeting.

The finances of the group were in poor order. The passivity of the therapist and his unwillingness to discuss finances with them have been previously mentioned. A barrier has been created in the group that has interfered, to some extent, with the group's progress.

Technique

The therapist was aware early in the meeting that Miss French's depression seemed to permeate the members of the group. The therapist continued to pursue the cause until the relationship to the Christmas season was identified, ventilated, and resolved. The mood lifted considerably when their feelings about Christmas were brought out.

The therapist was correct in bringing up the unpaid accounts. Diligent attention to the fees for group therapy is necessary.

Discussion

The feelings expressed by the group members about Christmas are in sharp contrast to the merry, holiday spirit that the season represents. They do, however, represent the feelings and attitudes that many people now basically feel but never express about Christmas. The religious meaning of Christmas is being overshadowed by economic and advertising forces who are primarily interested in the next Christmas season's being bigger, splashier, and more expensive than the previous one. As a result the Christmas season means more debt and more borrowed money for families. Keeping up with the Joneses and maintaining the social status of the family is one motivating factor. Children, too, are caught up in the Christmas whirl. They tell parents explicitly the things they want for Christmas. The emphasis is on the material aspect of the gift rather than on the mutual sharing of love and esteem through gifts.

The financial stress placed on parents at Christmas time has its effect on their emotional health. Increased anxiety and tension occur to the family that has difficulty making financial ends meet. Many parents feel obligated to see that their children are treated on a par with their peers in school and in the neighborhood. There is no way of satisfactorily explaining to the child why Santa Claus "went next door but missed our house." The end result is a heavier debt each year and increasing anxiety and tension by the parents as they worry about the monthly payments that begin shortly after Christmas.

FIFTY–SECOND MEETING

There were four members present. Mr. Holt, Mr. Cain, and Mr. Foy were absent. There was no prior communication from the absent members. Mr. Smith was 20 minutes late. Mr. Darcy was present for the first time in several weeks.

The hour began with Darcy telling the others about his brain tumor, treatments, and difficulties in working. Boler wondered if group therapy helped any. Darcy replied that there was no solution, but that it helped to talk.

Boler again brought up the need for drugs, adding that the members did not "understand" him. The therapist focused on their relationships with each other. Boler spoke of being more comfortable. The therapist directed Boler's statement to the other members. Smith felt that Boler was not comfortable with the women. Boler became defensive, admitting there were feelings of importance not discussed in the meeting. Miss French said she could not trust anyone. The therapist focused on the lack of trust, evoking the following reasons: fear of betrayal through misplaced trust, fear of embarrassment, shame, and exposure, or fear of "getting hurt." The therapist related himself to this area of trust by saying: "What about me? How do you fit me into this situation?" Boler replied that the therapist was sitting in judgment. Miss French felt the therapist was angry. The therapist asked, "Why should I be angry with you?" Miss French couldn't answer. Smith said he always resented and distrusted authority figures. The therapist said: "What are you afraid of here?" Miss French said she was afraid that if she talked the others would laugh at her. Boler discussed fears of disclosure out of the group. Smith said his distrust began with his father. Miss French replied that her mother would always tell her neighbors about her daughter's shortcomings. Mr. Boler was afraid he would be sent back to the hospital.

Darcy again discussed his cancerous brain tumor. He was preparing for the end and expressed concern for his family. The therapist asked for group feelings regarding Mr. Darcy's statements. The members were very supportive, saying that he should talk about his situation and attend the meetings as often as possible.

Approximately 30 minutes before the end of the meeting the therapist made several announcements. There would be no meeting for 2 weeks during the holiday season. The regular recorder would be away for eight to ten meetings. Group feelings regarding each matter were explored. Concern about the cancelled meetings was voiced. Two weeks was too long to go without meeting. There were positive statements about the regular recorder. Negative statements were made about Dr. N., the recent substitute recorder. They did not want him to return.

Theme and Dynamics

The theme of the meeting concerned their relationship with one another and the therapist. Their fears and guilt of exposing themselves were expressed as: (1) people use things against you, (2) we fear exposure, (3) we fear embarrassment, (4) we fear shame, (5) people laugh at you, and (6) we are not able to trust ourselves or others.

Feelings about the therapist were expressed in the following statements: (1) he is sitting in judgment, (2) we are expecting punishment, (3) the therapist is angry, (4) the therapist is like mother and father, (5) we resent and distrust authority figures, (6) the therapist will expose us outside of the group, and (7) the therapist will send us back to the hospital.

Technique

The therapist was aware of the theme and was in control of the meeting. He explored the basic feelings the members are experiencing with each other and with him.

Initially, Darcy's plight was only superficially discussed. Later, when mentioned again, the therapist supported Darcy by asking for group feelings.

The therapist asked for their feelings regarding the change in the recorder and the cancelled meetings during the holidays. He will hear more about these changes at later meetings.

Discussion

Darcy's remarks about his difficulties in working illustrate an important area in the emotional health of people.

The culture of this country places particular emphasis on the head of the household, the male, to perform satisfactorily in an occupation so that the economic security of his family can be maintained. A man's occupation and earning capacity are closely related to his self-esteem. A combination of factors influences a person's concept of work and whether a successful occupation can be pursued. In this respect the parental relationships to a child are important. The assertive, competitive, and independent youngster will carry these traits into adult life. His chances of success in an occupation are much greater than the nonassertive, noncompetitive, and dependent one. Identification with a father who practices good work habits imparts similar feelings to his children. There are, however, exceptions, such as the father who works all the time, has no time for his children and indulges them with excessive material gifts. He may end up with children who are dependent and expect him to continue caring for them throughout life.

Children very early in life begin to think and talk about adult roles. Small boys enjoy pretending they are cowboys, detectives, or policemen. They wear cowboy suits and blaze away with their cap pistols. During latency, boys identify with their father and frequently express the desire to have the same occupation as his. Following puberty there is a period of uncertainty about their adult role that appears to be related to current dependency-independency conflicts. As the boy becomes more independent in thought and action, future adult roles are pursued with deliberation and care. During high school and college he is exposed to a variety of occupations and professions. To some extent his choice of occupation will be influenced by the economic condition of his family. In any event, good physical health and emotional maturity point the way to a successful occupation of one kind or another.

The female's role in past years was primarily confined to the family. However, her role in the United States has undergone changes in the past 20 to 30 years. She has become a more assertive, aggressive, competitive, and independent person. In fact, women now compose 35 per cent of this country's labor forces. Thus, the female's self-esteem may be related to success in both family and occupational roles.

Again it should be emphasized that the occupational role of a person, particularly the male, is one of the most important areas in which he can acquire self-esteem. The psychiatrist can accomplish the equivalent of many hours of therapy by using every tool at his command (occupational therapy, vocational counseling, vocational rehabilitation, etc.) to see the emotionally ill person gainfully employed.

FIFTY–THIRD MEETING

There were five members present. Mr. Holt, Mr. Cain, and Mr. Darcy were absent. There was no communication from any of them. The regular recorder was on a leave of absence for approximately eight to ten meetings. A substitute (female) recorder was present. Boler was 5 minutes late. Mrs. Kitch and Foy were approximately 15 minutes late.

The meeting began with references to absent members. When Boler arrived, he began his usual request for drugs. He had secured a tranquilizer from another physician. Boler's mother was accusing the therapist of giving him drugs. Mrs. Kitch felt his mother needed treatment. Boler admitted he had to make a break from home. Again he began talking about conflicts with his mother. The therapist focused on Boler's bringing up the problem of drugs and his mother at every meeting. Boler answered, quickly admitting that he felt guilty about taking drugs. Other members told him that drugs had an emotional meaning, not physical; that he talked about them to get attention from the therapist. The therapist asked about their relationship to each other and to him. Tenseness and indecisiveness were felt to be present. Boler again changed the subject to drugs and his mother. Group feelings were again focused upon and, for the third time Boler utilized the same maneuver. The therapist focused on his behavior by saying: "I notice that every time I mention relationships here with each other, Mr. Boler quickly changes the subject to his mother and his need for drugs. What thoughts do you have as to why he does this?" Mr. Boler answered that he felt accepted here, but not at home. Neither the therapist nor the other members condemned him. He described in more detail the relationship with his mother: He is bothered particularly by a physical attraction to her. He would like to embrace and kiss her. At the same time he has a morbid dread of being close to her. Rather than be close to her, he finds a reason to be angry and drive her away. He spoke of a general fear of all women, including those present. He has wished his mother would die and then felt very guilty afterwards. Mr. Smith, Mrs. Kitch, and Miss French indicated similar feelings in the past. Miss French related death wishes for her mother from the age of 8 years and then her mother died 4 years ago. She has felt guilty in the past but not now. Mr. Smith and Mrs. Kitch said that wishing something would happen didn't necessarily mean it would happen. The therapist kept focusing on group feelings. Boler, who was quite anxious, continued to interrupt and dominate the meeting. The therapist refocused on his behavior. Mr. Smith, Miss French, and Mrs. Kitch admitted being irritated at him for dominating the meeting and pointed out to him that he would not let them discuss any issue. At the same time he was supported by their expression of understanding that his behavior was due to anxiety and tension. The therapist focused on the use of anger to keep people from being close and related it to their feelings with one another. There was superficial agreement, but no significant discussion. Fifteen minutes before the hour was over the therapist made the following observation: "You knew we would have a new recorder for the next eight to ten meetings. The hour is well along and I notice you have made no reference to her as you did when Dr. N. was present." Immediately they launched into a tirade against Dr. N. Their objections to him was that he is a psychiatrist. The female recorder was not.

Theme and Dynamics

The theme of the meeting centered around Boler. The anxiety and tension exhibited by him was responsible for his controlling, dominating behavior through the session. The female members are very threatening to him. The sexual, aggressive, and guilty feelings expressed toward his mother are also present in the group. The use of anger to make people dislike and reject you was verbalized as well as utilized by Mr. Boler as a defense throughout the meeting. There was anger, too, at the therapist for attempting to increase the closeness of the group.

The issue of the substitute recorder was clarified. Their hostility was identified with the role of the psychiatrist primarily and not the individual. The hostility, too, means the therapist is responsible for the new recorder.

Technique

The therapist was aware of Boler's anxiety. By identifying his behavior, the therapist afforded the group a closer look at his dynamics.

The therapist made a general observation to the group regarding the use of anger to keep people from being close to others. He could have been more direct, since Boler verbalized and utilized this defense during the meeting. He could have said: "Now, Mr. Boler speaks of using anger to keep someone from being close to you. You have admitted being irritated at him at this meeting for his constant talking and frequent interruptions. What do you make of his statement and behavior? What is he doing to the group?"

The therapist devoted sufficient attention to the role of the recorder and substitute recorder so that the hostility was associated and understood to be related to the role and not the individual.

FIFTY–FOURTH MEETING

There were five members present; Mr. Holt, Mr. Cain, and Mr. Darcy were absent. There has been no communication from Mr. Holt in several weeks. Mr. Darcy's attendance will probably be sporadic, if he comes at all.

The hour began with the members quizzing Mr. Foy. They discussed his need for alcohol. Foy replied with his standard plea for hypnosis, magic, and miracles. He stated that he had been coming to group therapy for 14 months now and had received no help. He added that he had not put anything into the group. The therapist directed Foy's statement back to the group, pointing out that during all this period of time he had been regular in his attendance. Again the members encouraged him to be more active but emphasized that there were no miracles or magic here. He should put forward the desire to get help. Several members admitted the desire for miracles from the therapist at the outset of therapy. Foy said he could never reveal his deep-seated problems in mixed company. The therapist asked the other members about Foy's observation. Boler felt that he was referring to sexual difficulties. There followed a general discussion of sexual feelings. Foy admitted a marital problem. Smith spoke of sexual difficulties with his wife. Boler again spoke of the physical attraction to his mother that was repulsive. At times he wanted to strike her. He had a fear of all women that led him to sexual pursuits in other ways. He spoke of being bisexual, with a latent homosexuality. Foy said for the first time in fourteen months he felt the group was functioning. Mrs. Kitch discussed sexual difficulties with her husband and how she will refuse him in a defiant, angry manner. Miss French discussed her attraction to and enjoyment of association with older married men. She has never had sexual intercourse. She spoke of getting to the brink but being held back by something. Boler discussed his fears of homosexuality and his use of drugs and alcohol to relieve anxiety. He made reference to the previous meeting. They had made him aware that he talked about his mother too often. He referred to the value of group therapy in recognizing such behavior patterns. Foy seemed very enthusiastic and interested with the discussion and again referred to the new atmosphere present. The therapist said at this point, "You have been discussing your sexual feelings and fears. I wonder what sexual feelings you have experienced here?" Boler admitted feelings for both Miss French and Mrs. Kitch. Miss French spoke of her mother and the dirty feelings she had about sexual matters. She brought out that for many years she had wished to be a boy. Mrs. Kitch admitted the same feelings when a youngster. Additional discussion occurred with Foy. He again referred to the women in the group as a reason for not being frank with each other. Miss French said the relationship with her mother had pounded her into the ground; now she doesn't want people to know her. The others spoke of being censored. Foy felt that the women would censor him. Smith felt that the members would censor him more than the therapist.

Theme and Dynamics

The significant events in this session were: (1) the initial discussion of sexual feelings by the group members, (2) the disclosure by Boler of his homosexual problems and fears, and (3) the increased interest exhibited by Foy. There were still fears of exposure and censure if true feelings are expressed. The interaction of Foy was received with extremely warm and positive feelings by the members. The shift in his attitude at this meeting indicated an area of his conflicts and problems. It is important to note that the members required 54 meetings before the area of sexual feelings became a group issue. Foy, whose attendance at meetings has been excellent from the outset of group therapy, has remained at the periphery with repeated magical demands, self-abasement, and a constant refusal to join the group. His contribution at this meeting may be significant.

The fact that sexual feelings were not discussed until the 54th meeting of the group is indicative of the taboos existing in our society about sexual feelings. Even though a greater emphasis is now being placed on sexual education in schools, colleges, newspapers and magazines, the taboos against sex remain even greater than those related to aggressive (angry) feelings.

Technique

The therapist correctly asked the members to examine Foy's lack of contribution and help from the others. He correctly directed Foy's statement concerning his problems in mixed company back to the members. The verbalization of sexual feelings ensued, and all participated. The therapist continued to direct the members to look at their feelings.

Again notation should be made of the marked difference in the response of the members at this stage of group therapy compared to early meetings. They have become more comfortable with the therapist. There has been an increasing cohesiveness and bond between the members. They have become aware of the group therapy process. They have become alert to recognizing behavior patterns and defenses. The task of the therapist is a much easier one. Refocusing on group issues does not elicit anxiety to the extent of early meetings. Usually there is a group response. Individual desires have been sacrificed for the good of the group. The group now is willing and able to explore mutual conflicts and problems.

FIFTY–FIFTH MEETING

The therapist had cancelled the previous meeting. At this meeting, there were only two members present, Mr. Smith and Mrs. Kitch. Mrs. Kitch was approximately 30 minutes late. Miss French telephoned that she was ill. Mr. Boler was out of town. There was no communication from Mr. Holt, Mr. Foy, or Mr. Darcy. The recorder was approximately 15 minutes late.

For the initial one-third of the meeting only Smith was present. He spoke of feeling peculiar and lost because he was the only one present. The therapist was quite active. Mr. Smith's feelings about being the only member present as well as his speculative feelings about the absent members were focused on several times. Smith admitted hostility to the therapist for cancelling the meeting of the previous week, and said this might account for the others being absent at this meeting. He had missed meetings in the past for similar reasons. Any change for him produced an automatic reaction of hostility. When Mrs. Kitch entered the room, Smith soon began an argument with her. This was focused on by the therapist. Smith replied that the anger was there and he let it go on Mrs. Kitch. There followed a discussion of their feelings in therapy. Smith said his role had been crushed several meetings ago. The group had accused him of being a teacher's pet because he wanted approval from the therapist. In the interchange with Mrs. Kitch, he spoke of being extremely sensitive to critical remarks from anyone. He had reacted with anger to all the group members. Mrs. Kitch pointed out that the group meeting was the place to express feelings. She recalled the incident about Smith, agreed at the time, but had thought no more of it. She discussed her problem of talking in outside groups as compared to this group. The therapist focused on Smith's remarks regarding being teacher's pet and his inability to participate in meetings since that time. Mrs. Kitch reassured him that it was very helpful to be made aware of what you do in the meetings. Smith replied emphatically that approval was more important than any designation as a teacher's pet. Group feelings, the cancelled meeting, and present attendance were pursued by the therapist. Smith interjected the possibility that the sexual material that was discussed at the last meeting might also account for absences. Mrs. Kitch disagreed with him. She denied feelings of any kind. Smith finally told her she was like a vacuum at this meeting. Smith spoke of fears of getting too deep into sexual matters. A reference was made to the new recorder. Their feelings about her were explored. They denied any concern but couldn't recall her name or whether she was at the last meeting. Mrs. Kitch said she was like a lamp or fixture in the room and ignored her. Smith spoke warmly of the regular recorder. As the hour ended there were statements of concern as to whether or not the others will come to the next meeting.

Theme and Dynamics

A series of events during the past several weeks have influenced group feelings. Throughout this entire meeting there has been the theme of anger at the therapist. The members were angry about the status of the recorder because: (1) the regular recorder is absent, (2) a substitute recorder was used for one meeting, and (3) a second substitute recorder is now present. Their anger at the therapist for cancellation of the meeting was quite apparent. The fact that four meetings have been cancelled during the past two months has meaning to them. Smith's observations that any change in structure in this group or others produces an automatic reaction of anger were noted. Moreover, sexual feelings were explored for the first time at the previous meeting. Fears of rejection and disapproval by the therapist and other members cannot be dismissed if this area is pursued.

It should be pointed out that the members came much closer to each other at the 54th meeting when sexual feelings were discussed in considerable detail. There is the possibility that the feelings generated among the members were very frightening and accounted for the numerous absences at this meeting.

Their fears of closeness have been verbalized extensively a number of times. This fear of closeness certainly concerned Smith during the early part of the meeting. Smith is afraid of people. He has any number of fears associated with being close to people. He may have wanted the therapist for himself at one time, but now that he was alone with the therapist, in practically a one-to-one relationship, he was very uncomfortable. There is also the relationship between the authority figure and the "pet," a problem in many families. A child may want to be the favored sibling, but at the same time he may fear the hostility from his brothers and sisters. Mr. Smith has been in this position in the group.

The tardiness of the recorder was subconscious in origin. At first she felt the group met at a later time. Subsequent discussion between the therapist and the recorder revealed two sources of conflict. The recorder admitted being somewhat overwhelmed and uncomfortable at her initial meeting when sexual material was discussed in such detail. Also, she had become irritated when the therapist had given her extremely short notice that he wanted her to present the group at a supervisory session.

Technique

The group functions regardless of the number of members present. The therapist's technique when only one member was present centered around group function and feelings even though the structure is like that of an individual session. The therapist was correct in being more active so that the anxiety of the member could be allayed.

The therapist explored feelings concerning the absent members. He recognized that Smith was displacing to Mrs. Kitch his hostility for the therapist. After bringing it to the attention of the two members present, proper identification was made. Group feelings about the cancelled meeting, recorder, and sexual material from the 54th meeting were focused on. The therapist could have brought to their attention that a number of meetings had been cancelled in recent weeks.

Mrs. Kitch's denial of feelings concerning the new recorder could have been explored by saying: "Mrs. Kitch cannot recall the recorder's name, whether or not she was here last week, and considers her as a fixture like a lamp. In the past meetings you have demonstrated rather strong feelings about changes in the recorder. How do you account for this difference in feelings now?"

Discussion

"Teacher's pet" is a well-known phrase that children become acquainted with during their early years of school and remain aware of throughout school, college, and adulthood. In school there are several types of teacher's pet: (1) the child who only feels accepted by catering to the teacher with ingratiating techniques, (2) the child who is a favorite of the teacher, and (3) the studious child who always makes good grades and stands at the top of the class. The student who has the label of teacher's pet is not popular with other students and may be the recipient of many hostile remarks. In many public high schools the studious youth is relegated to this unpopular position because the main interests of the student body are in athletics, the opposite sex, and social activities. In this respect the students are reflecting the feelings of their parents. It is a sad fact in our society that parental interest in competitive athletic contests exceeds their interest in academic studies.

There is one other type of student who may be referred to as a teacher's pet by his fellow students. There are school teachers who do not communicate with their students. They build a hierarchy around themselves somewhat like that of a king and his subjects and remain aloof to all. There are high school coaches who handle their players in similar ways.

Since there is no communication between the students and their teachers, any student who attempts to talk and form a relationship with the teacher is referred to by the other students as a teacher's pet. In these types of group structure the anxiety of the students rises. The pent-up emotional tension is expressed in various ways: increased irritations among the students, less productive school work, etc. The coach who manages his players in this manner will have more contests in the lost column. The successful teacher and coach will encourage communication with his students and players and allow them to express their feelings in a constructive atmosphere. The need for outlets of aggressive feelings, so prevalent in high school students, will be managed in a firm, authoritative, and constructive atmosphere.

The teacher's pet label begins in school but is referred to in many everyday groups of adults. Many of the same principles apply in adult groups as in the school groups. In some instances it is due to ingratiating behavior. In others, a person's jealousy toward and rivalry with a successful peer may be the reason for accusing him falsely of being teacher's pet.

FIFTY–SIXTH MEETING

There were four members present; Mr. Boler, Mr. Cain, Mr. Darcy, and Mrs. Kitch were absent. Mr. Boler has been rehospitalized for a recurrence of alcoholic problems. There was no communication from Mr. Darcy or Mrs. Kitch.

The initial part of the meeting was taken up with verbal attacks on Foy for his role. After this group behavior had become clear, the therapist asked why they were attacking Mr. Foy. Holt replied that it could be a defense against feelings which were identical to those expressed by Mr. Foy. Smith said it turned attention away from themselves. Miss French agreed. The group members present agreed that they were avoiding feelings. At this point the therapist asked about their relationships to each other and to him. Smith and Miss French discussed the need to hide their angry feelings and keep them under control. Holt denied aggressive feelings, adding that it was depression, not anger, that concerned him. Smith reiterated his trouble with anger and discussed an angry outburst at work during the past week that made him ill and necessitated the use of tranquilizers. The therapist focused on Mr. Smith and Miss French's feelings of anger, Foy's previous remarks about his severe rage and his having instincts like an animal, and Holt's comments that he experiences depression rather than anger. Mr. Smith replied that he made Holt "damn mad" at one meeting. Holt equated anger with hating people. The therapist made the following observation: "Mr. Holt equates anger with hate. What thoughts do you have about this observation?" Mr. Smith replied that you could be angry without hating. Miss French said she got mad at people she liked and then got over it. The therapist then said: "Earlier you brought out the inability to express your feelings and then began discussing angry feelings." There were references to not liking each other and looking for dislikes in people. However, fears of rejection from the therapist and other group members were expressed. Foy was not participating in the meeting, and the therapist focused on his silence. Foy replied that he liked everyone. Miss French angrily replied that Mr. Foy's eyes indicated that he felt the other members are "sons-of-bitches." Mr. Smith said he was using a false front and covering up. Foy became anxious but did not participate in the discussion to any degree. Miss French remarked that Mr. Foy had participated in a recent meeting and that his participation was pleasing to everyone.

The therapist announced that Boler was back in the hospital. General concern was expressed about his difficulty with drugs and his relationship with his mother.

Cancelled meetings were brought up by Mr. Holt. After some discussion the therapist focused on their feelings concerning the four meetings that had been cancelled during the past few weeks, as well as the changes in the recorder. There was group denial, except for Smith, who stated that any change affected him. There were hostile remarks again by Miss French about Dr. N., the substitute recorder of several meetings back. Smith discussed this matter with her, finally saying that maybe the group was angry with the therapist, and when the other man was present their feelings toward the therapist were displaced onto the substitute. Mr. Smith talked again of his hostility to authority figures, saying that often he can't tell the therapist how he feels so he vents it on someone else.

Theme and Dynamics

The theme of the meeting concerned their relationships with one another. An attempt to scapegoat Mr. Foy was recognized as an avoidance of angry feelings by Smith and Miss French, denial by Smith, and inactivity by Foy. Boler's hospitalization was seen as a group loss, but was not as threatening as was his initial hospitalization. The hostility to the male recorder was recognized as displacement of hostility to the therapist.

Technique

The therapist recognized the familiar ruse of "ganging up" on Foy. After he had called this matter to their attention, the group immediately recognized that they were avoiding group feelings.

The therapist could have focused in more detail on their hostility to him so that an awareness of this maneuver could become more apparent to the members. He could have said: "Let me make an observation. I asked you to look at your feelings here. You became angry with me and said that I interrupted your conversation and wouldn't let you discuss what you wished. Any ideas why you get angry with me when I ask you to look at your feelings here with one another?"

Events affecting the group, such as Mr. Boler's hospitalization, cancelled meetings, and status of the recorder, were asked about during the meeting by the therapist.

The group therapist may also utilize another technique to advantage when he is unable to get the group members to examine their group relationships. If the group therapist recognizes that he becomes angry with the group members for repeatedly avoiding and denying their feelings about a group issue—e.g., their feelings toward the group therapist in this meeting for the four previously cancelled meetings, he can discuss his own feelings with the group members. He could say: "I wonder if any of you recognize how I have felt in the meeting today. I have asked you repeatedly about several things, but you deny any feelings, change the subject or ignore me." Many times group members will recognize the group therapist's feelings from his nonverbal behavior. They will state that he is bored or uninterested in the meeting. The group therapist might also say: "I wonder if you are aware that your refusal to talk about your feelings irritates me? This group has been meeting for many months. You have recognized feelings about such issues before. Today you deny them and you employ other maneuvers to keep from dealing with them." After some discussion he should ask for their feelings about his admitting irritation with them. He can say: "How does it make you feel to have heard me speak about being irritated with your behavior?" The group members may react to the group therapist with anger as they have reacted to their parents and other authority figures in the past. Statements may be made that the group therapist does not like them because he has become angry at them. Then the group therapist has the opportunity to deal with the emotion of anger and "hurting people's feelings" as well as feelings of disapproval and being disliked by an authority figure. The group therapist can say: "Does the fact that I get irritated with your behavior have anything to do with whether I like you or not? Are you reacting to my anger as you have to other authority figures who get angry with you?" He can continue to explore their feelings in this area. It will be very therapeutic for the group members to understand the give and take of emotional reactions between themselves and the group therapist. They will also better understand feelings of an authority figure.

This technique can be utilized to great advantage after the group members have established a working relationship (stage III) with the group therapist. It is not advisable during stage I of group therapy. During stage I, the group therapist should be more permissive, understanding, and accepting of the group members' feelings. Some problems that some group therapists have during group therapy, particularly in stage I, are the expectations that group members should deal with their conflicts and problems sooner than they are able, that anxiety and defensive patterns of behavior should be recognized quickly, and that tardiness and absenteeism are unnecessary. In these situations the therapist's irritations are not justified. He does not tell the group members his feelings, however—he reveals himself to them by his nonverbal behavior. With proper training and supervision, the therapist becomes more aware of these feelings toward his group members, whereupon his expectations of the group members can be approached on a more realistic level.

FIFTY–SEVENTH MEETING

There were six members present. Mr. Cain returned to the group for the first time in a number of months. He last attended the 38th meeting. Mr. Holt and Mr. Darcy were absent. There was no prior communication from them.

The meeting began with the members expressing pleasure and joy that Mr. Cain was back. Mr. Cain described his difficulties with alcohol that resulted in a prison sentence in a deliberately intellectual fashion. Miss French immediately remarked that Mr. Cain appeared calm now, compared with his previous attitude. The group members appeared somewhat anxious. The therapist focused on the feelings of the group regarding Mr. Cain's return, bringing out their previous remarks about changes in the group, new members being added, changes in the recorder, etc. Miss French admitted tension only for Mr. Cain. Mr. Smith and Mr. Boler denied any feelings about changes. Mr. Boler changed the subject and discussed his recent hospitalization. He had at first intended not to come to the meeting. He was not taking any drugs now whatsoever. He continued to belittle and attack his mother. The therapist focused on Boler's statement regarding attendance at the meeting. Boler immediately admitted his fear of rejection by the therapist. The members began to focus on Boler. They asked numerous questions regarding his recent hospitalization and his relationship with his mother. The anxiety level remained high. Smith and Miss French were laughing at intervals. Cain was intellectualizing in his old familiar role. Mrs. Kitch was quiet. Foy exhibited his usual uncommunicative role. The therapist focused on their relationships with each other. He was ignored. The members discussed how they blamed other people for their problems, picking up the cue from Boler's constantly blaming his mother for conflicts. The members wondered if Boler needed punishment to get love. Smith and Miss French admitted using this procedure in the past. Mrs. Kitch discussed one of her children whom she has not loved as much as the others. This child seems to seek out punishment to get attention. The therapist again focused on group feelings by saying, "You speak of blaming others for your own problems. Any thoughts of how you handle such feelings here with one another?" Boler complained of being "put on the spot." Smith said that it was easy to keep attention from yourself by getting one member to talk. The members agreed that relationships with each other were being avoided. Boler said he had been scapegoated. The therapist asked about the sporadic laughter that had been present. Mrs. Kitch replied that laughter indicated tenseness. Miss French agreed, adding she laughs to keep from crying. Smith stated that the therapist makes him feel that there was a law against laughter, but added that he covers up feelings with laughter. There followed a series of hostile remarks directed toward the therapist. They felt that the therapist refused to let them talk about what they wished. Miss French said that the therapist represented frustration to her. Smith asserted that the therapist represented authority, that it was "automatic" with him to feel hostile. The therapist then made the following observation: "Let's look at your feelings here. Smith observed that you pick out one member to talk with in order to avoid group feelings. You equate laughter with tenseness and as a cover-up. Previously Boler spoke of getting angry to keep someone from getting close to him. Any other ideas of the methods used to avoid seeing yourselves here?" Smith admitted he avoided issues due to fear of authority. Miss French feared rejection to get close to anyone. She didn't want people to know her. Boler replied he always gets angry with anyone who gets close to him. Miss French added that when the therapist asked for their feelings she has ten thousand thoughts. Mrs. Kitch said that a book she read tells you not to get attached to anyone. The therapist asked for additional feelings. Cain wondered if they were having trouble accepting him again. Smith added that rejection is a constant fear with him. Cain was reassured by the members, but his calmness, intellectualizations, and use of parables was questioned by Boler and Miss French. Boler said Mr. Cain protected himself in this manner. Miss French equated Mr. Cain's calm with her laughter. The therapist asked about Cain's use of these defenses. The discussion continued, and soon Cain stated that he had learned something that day (using parables, intellectualizing, etc. as protections against expressing feelings) which he hadn't been aware of previously. Mrs. Kitch's silence and Foy's role of bidding for sympathy was described as protective measures as the meeting ended.

Theme and Dynamics

Cain's return was greeted with ambivalent feelings from the other members. Smith and Boler denied any feelings and said neither of them had met Mr. Cain previously. His absence for approximately 20 meetings created a tension in the others. Exploration of their relationships to each other continued with the projection (blaming others) by Boler, laughter utilized by Smith and Miss French, intellectualizations by Cain, silence exhibited by Mrs. Kitch, hostility described by Boler, and ingratiation by Foy all being identified as protective measures to avoid group involvement. The wish to be punished to secure love and attention were recognized in Boler and Miss French. The members were aware that Boler was questioned extensively to avoid group interaction. Transient hostility to the therapist was evident when, having directed the members to an exploration of group relationships, he was ignored by them. The astute interpretations the members are making to one another are noteworthy. This is real mutual analysis. A series of defenses against closeness was verbalized and identified. The recognition of the wish to be punished to secure love and attention is a particularly significant accomplishment.

Technique

The therapist was in control of the meeting. He was cognizant of the feelings regarding Cain's return, although they were largely denied by the members. He was aware of Cain's need for support following a long absence and did not push into this area in any detail.

The members continued to explore their feelings with one another but only with the active direction of the therapist. They again demonstrated the wish to avoid closeness by quizzing one member. The therapist recognized their hostility to him for not allowing them to talk as they wished. When the members expressed hostility to the therapist for not allowing them to talk about other matters, he could have promoted an awareness of why they became angry when group issues are mentioned by saying: "Now you have spoken of group feelings being avoided. When I asked you to look at your feelings here, you became angry and complained about my interfering with your conversations. I wonder if you have any ideas why you get angry with me for asking you to examine your own relationships with each other and me?"

The therapist was active in focusing on their feelings. Identification of a number of defenses against anxiety were verbalized.

FIFTY–EIGHTH MEETING

There were six members present. Mr. Boler and Mr. Darcy were absent. There was no prior communication from Mr. Boler.

At the beginning of the meeting there was silence. When the meaning of the silence was explored, the members related that hostility was present. Cain observed that his return was interrupting the function of the group. The therapist focused on the group's feelings about Cain's return, pointing out previous feelings that had been expressed about group changes. Ambivalent feelings toward Cain were verbalized. The group was glad of his return but felt somewhat tense and anxious. A discussion of angry feelings followed, during which time Holt and Foy were inactive. Smith and Miss French verbalized their angry states in the group. Cain admitted boiling inwardly but not expressing it. The therapist focused on Cain's observation. Smith replied that even though you hide your anger, it shows itself in "sneaky and subtle ways." The therapist asked about their relationship to each other and to him. Miss French and Smith admitted hostility and antagonism toward the members. The subject was changed. The therapist brought the group back to the discussion of their feelings of anger by making the following comment: "I'd like to make an observation. You have heard Miss French and Mr. Smith speak of their anger. Mr. Cain spoke of boiling inside and hiding it. In previous meetings Mr. Holt denies anger, but admits depression. Mr. Foy has spoken of rage and of instincts like an animal; he has stated that his need for control of these feelings caused him to use alcohol. Now what about these feelings in relationship to the group meeting?" Cain replied that no one knew what to do with anger. Smith felt that hostility, anger, and depression were related. He spoke of getting angry, feeling guilty, and becoming depressed as a result of anger and guilt. Miss French said she gets mad with the other members, the doctor, and the recorder. She is either angry, frustrated, or depressed. Foy admitted anger and frustration, saying, "I can't do anything with it. I can't kill someone." Holt complained of boredom. They were not discussing anything of interest to him. Smith and Miss French attacked him for his disinterest. Mrs. Kitch remarked that he came to the group to find out why people didn't like him. If the group discussed any matter with him, she said he got quiet and felt that no one liked him. Smith admitted anger toward Holt for being intellectual and superior. Miss French spoke of repeated conflicts with Holt for reminding her of her father and mother. Cain began to intellectualize somewhat in the role of the therapist. Smith admitted irritations with Cain for trying to diagnose people. Mrs. Kitch felt that Holt and Smith saw a lot of themselves in the other person, adding that "we see things in others that don't click in ourselves." Miss French admitted that she was responsible for her own anger, but wished to find out about the cause of that anger. A ventilation of irritating and hostile feelings between the group members continued. The anxiety level was at a high, constructive pitch. Feelings toward the therapist were focused upon. The possibility of displacing feelings from the therapist onto others was brought out. There were several members who felt that the feelings being expressed were reflections of the way the individuals presented themselves to the others, rather than feelings toward the therapist.

Theme and Dynamics

The meeting involved two themes. One theme was concerned with the basic feelings of the members of the group toward each other. Feelings that have been kept hidden are being examined in more detail. Antagonism, hate, and anger toward others with the associated feelings of frustration, guilt, and depression were expressed.

Mr. Foy's murderous feelings require tight control. Mr. Holt denies anger but admits depression. Miss French observed that anger is her own problem and its cause is very important. Mr. Smith's guilt for verbally expressing feelings and his observation of the sequence of anger-guilt-depression were excellent interpretations.

The other theme was created by Mr. Cain's return to the group. Any reality change in the group creates anxiety and tension. Such feelings were verbalized to some extent early in the meeting.

Technique

The therapist was in control of the meeting and constructive group work was accomplished. Feelings relative to Mr. Cain's return were focused on and discussed early in the meeting. Throughout the meeting group issues were explored. The mechanisms of handling angry feelings were focused on, followed by Mr. Smith's interpretation of anger-guilt-depression. The anxiety level never reached a threatening or disintegrative state.

Discussion

Again the relationship between this group and a family group is borne out. A family is a group of people with the father as central or authority figure. If the brothers and the sisters in a family have an argument and get very angry, they may want to "throw out" one member of the family. Sometimes when the mother has too much trouble with some of them, she would like to "throw out" one of her own children. Similar situations occur in all family groups. At times the hostility between siblings is so great that they would certainly not stay together if they were completely free to act. But there is one cohesive force that is very strong. Because they all have needs toward the central figure of the family, they are not likely to leave. If this analogy is carried over into the therapy group it can be seen that what keeps the group together is the members' need for the therapist. For example, there is so much hostility in this particular group that the members would like to throw each other out at times. If you were to ask the members to meet without the therapist, they wouldn't be there very long; they would fly apart very quickly. But this need for the therapist—this constant need for one person that holds the group together and forces them, at the same time, to work out their own feelings—is what keeps the group going.

FIFTY–NINTH MEETING

Mr. Smith and Mr. Holt were the only members present. Three members had phoned in and said they were unable to attend. Mr. Boler and

Miss French were physically ill, and Mr. Foy had to work late. There was no communication from the others.

The initial part of the meeting was taken up with an expression of feelings about the absent members. Mr. Smith was quite disappointed over the small number present. He couldn't understand why the others were not there and felt that perhaps their feelings were responsible for their absence. Holt stated that people who were absent usually had good excuses. The therapist focused on how feelings cause absences. Holt answered that maybe there is resistance to changing their behavior. The therapist repeated Holt's statement. Smith felt the members wanted the others to change, not themselves. Holt added that in his difficulties with Smith there was the wish that Smith would change, not himself. Fears of being friendly with people were voiced by Smith. The therapist asked why the members were afraid to like someone. Smith feared domination and Holt feared dependency from others. Holt stated that he didn't like to be in a position where he needed someone and that he preferred to be aloof and alone. Smith also felt that such feelings were emotional in nature. Now he could accept realistic help; formerly he resented anyone wishing to help him. There followed an interplay about families and children. The conversational tones were low and both men appeared depressed. The therapist asked about this depressed mood. Holt stated he was constantly depressed and had to fight against it. Smith spoke of his morbid depression when in the hospital. The therapist again focused on depressed mood. Holt felt less animosity toward Smith than formerly and stated that neither was trying to be a "big shot" in front of a crowd. Smith disagreed and felt there was animosity present but not being expressed. He added, however, that the absence of members had quite an effect on him. Authority figures were mentioned, following which the therapist focused their feelings toward him. Smith spoke of his fear of authority, the need to act overcivilized around authority, and of wanting approval. Holt denied any feelings regarding the therapist and began a long-winded discussion about the capabilities of the therapist in other areas. (The recorder noted that Mr. Smith was becoming increasingly irritated by Holt's statements. The therapist was unaware of this non-verbal behavior.) Smith didn't see how Holt could be so impersonal to authority. Holt again went into a lengthy conversation which Smith countered by questioning his need and importance to get such a definition across. Holt continued his denial of authority relationships. The therapist again focused on the mood and commented that Holt and Smith had reacted to each other differently at this meeting than formerly. Smith felt that their desire to dominate each other created conflicts between them. He sensed a real or imagined pressure around Holt. At the end of the meeting the therapist informed them of prior telephone calls from other members and told of their reasons for not attending.

Theme and Dynamics

The theme of the meeting related to the absence of members and its associated feelings of group dissolution and destruction. Previous meetings had revealed a series of conflicts between the two members present. Having to face each other without the other members being present resulted in their retreating to their protective shells, although for the most part the remarks and exchanges between them were friendly and pleasant. The slightly depressed mood of the meeting was thus related to two factors: group absences and internalization of angry feelings, the latter being particularly evident in Mr. Smith.

Actually Mr. Smith and Mr. Holt were forced by the small attendance to be close to each other. The dynamics of their relationship was recognized as wanting to dominate each other. It was as if each was saying: "I want to dominate you. You want to dominate me. I don't like it." The relationship to their fears of expressing warmth or liking someone was also equated with domination and increased dependency.

There is the possibility that the free expression of hostile feelings at the 58th meeting contributed to the small attendance. Excessive hostility can result in depression, mutual withdrawal, silence, lateness, and absenteeism. In retrospect, the therapist may have allowed the hostility to reach too high a level at the last meeting. It may be remembered that only two members were present at the 55th meeting after sexual material was discussed at the 54th meeting.

Technique

The therapist felt that the absences would play an important role in the meeting. He was also aware of competitiveness and hostility between these two members that dated back for a number of meetings. The depression in the meeting was identified. The feelings between Holt and Smith were gently explored.

Discussion

Emotional growth and maturity go hand in hand with the ability for people to be dependent on each other and to help each other solve mutual problems. People have to be dependent on each other. However, it is necessary to qualify and distinguish between healthy, mature dependency and dependency that is pathological in nature. Examples of healthy dependency occur every day. A husband is dependent on his wife to keep the home in order, care for the children, prepare meals, etc. The wife is dependent on the husband to provide the financial support for the home and family. Doctors are dependent on nurses, aides, etc. to care for their hospital patients. People with automobiles are dependent on automobile mechanics and filling-station operators to keep them in operation. However, it is an indication of pathological dependency if an adult is completely dependent on others or reverts to a complete dependency status during a period of stress or emotional illness. If the dependency is pathological the individual wants someone to assume all responsibility for him and to care for his every need. Examples of pathological dependency are the adult who remains at home, refuses to work and wants his parents or wife to completely care for his every need; the student who refuses to pursue his intellectual studies and expects others to accomplish it for him; and the wife who expects her husband to perform her household duties as well as those of his own. In this group Foy's demands for magic or hypnosis demonstrate his pathological dependency demands. Boler and Holt have also shown strong dependency wishes.

SIXTIETH MEETING

There were five members present. Mr. Holt, Mr. Cain, and Mr. Darcy were absent. There was no prior communication from them.

Several extraneous subjects were discussed at the beginning of the hour. When the therapist asked about relationships in the group there was only superficial discussion with a change in the subject matter. Mrs. Kitch discussed a number of realistic problems that had occurred with her husband. These included his irresponsibility, childishness, financial difficulties, inability to hold a job, etc. (Mrs. Kitch's husband is in treatment. The diagnosis is chronic schizophrenic reaction, paranoid type.) Her anger and resentment were verbalized. Boler and Foy identified with her husband. Smith and Miss French disclosed that their early lives were spent in such a family as that described by Mrs. Kitch. Mrs. Kitch was against divorce, but Smith felt she could not rule it out completely. Miss French agreed with Smith. The therapist asked about their relationships to each other and to him, but the subject was again changed. The therapist pointed out that when he asked the members about relationships in the group the subject was changed. They again admitted fear and mistrust. Mr. Boler felt no one would like him if he revealed himself. Miss French admitted that she could not trust people because her mother and father taught her never to trust others. Smith stated he could never trust his family. The therapist reminded the members that they were discussing families, and that a number of times references had been made to him (the therapist) as an authority figure. He asked how they felt about him in relation to trust, fear, and rejection. Miss French admitted that sometimes she liked the therapist, but since he represented authority, she trusted him least of all. Boler asserted that he trusted the therapist. Foy, in a very ingratiating manner, spoke of liking the therapist and denied any conflicts with authority. Immediately Smith reacted with anger to Foy and his denial of authority relationships. He added that everyone has authority problems, particularly people who are emotionally or mentally ill. Mrs. Kitch said she would like the doctor to leave the room so she could bring up other matters; the doctor would not let her talk. The therapist focused on her statement. The members pointed out to her that the therapist wanted them to look at their feelings in the group. Smith felt that the meetings were 90 per cent hedging. The members did not want to look at their relationships in the group. Mrs. Kitch remarked that the therapist's statements left her confused, blank, and uncomfortable. The therapist said: "I recall that at an earlier meeting Mrs. Kitch spoke of becoming blank when I made an observation. She spoke of reacting to her father in a similar manner. Later she said she reacted to me as with her father. Do you see any relationship now with what she has said previously?" Smith, Boler, and Miss French pointed out her fear of the therapist and its relationship to authority. Mrs. Kitch said it must be authority because men, schoolteachers, and others who were in superior positions made her feel little, inferior, inadequate, and worthless. Miss French told Mrs. Kitch and Foy that she would feel closer to them if they would take part in the meeting in more detail. She spoke of knowing very little about Mrs. Kitch and hardly anything about Mr. Foy.

Theme and Dynamics

The theme of the meeting continued to center around their relationship with each other and the therapist. The anxiety level was not as high as at the 58th meeting. The recurrent problem of getting close to each other, with the feelings of authority reaction, fear, and rejection was still present. Mr. Smith's observation that everyone has authority problems, particularly people who are mentally or emotionally ill, was very significant.

Technique

The therapist was in control of the meeting. He allowed Mrs. Kitch to ventilate in detail reality problems with her husband, and then focused on group issues. Mrs. Kitch's relationship to authority was reidentified and accepted by her. The therapist continued to ask the members to explore in greater detail their relationship to him and to each other.

Discussion

The group members' observation that all people have problems with authority figures emphasizes an important factor in the social and cultural forces of our society. A group structure is composed of the leader or authority figure and the members of the group. The central group structure is the family group with the parents as the leaders or authority figures and the children the members of the group. As the child grows

older his social adjustment is influenced by many different groups. In
school he is a member of an educational group. The schoolteacher becomes the authority figure. In athletics the coach becomes the authority
figure. At church the Sunday School teacher can represent the authority
figure of the religious group. The boy scout or girl scout has as authority
figures the scoutmaster. The adult's occupational, professional, social and
other group relationships have a similar structure.

Throughout life the individual's adaptation to society is influenced by
these different group relationships. The most important group relationship is the family group. But other groups such as the school group, the
religious group, and the athletic group can help mold the personality of
the individual and in these groups the most influential person is the leader
or authority figure. For example, the child who doesn't feel accepted at
home may have a very rewarding and meaningful relationship with a
schoolteacher. The college professor may further clarify aims and ideals
of the college student. During adulthood the "boss" or authority figure
in occupational and professional groups can play a similar role. There are,
however, far too many authority figures who lack such psychological aptitude. They do not understand the relationship of psychological factors
to the social adjustment of people. In this respect the field of social psychiatry has recognized the important need for authority figures to be
aware of the effects of the emotional interaction of group behavior. The
dynamics of group therapy can point out one significant factor of all group
relationships: the group therapist, the authority figure to the group members, is the most important person in the group. The results obtained by
his technique of group therapy suggest that similar methods for all
leaders or authority figures, with modifications depending on the type of
group, could affect the emotional health of people. In all groups there
would be less anxiety and tension, improved interpersonal relationships
and more effective group function if the authority figure were aware of
the dynamics of group behavior.

SIXTY–FIRST MEETING

There were five members present. Mr. Cain, Mr. Darcy, and Miss
French were absent. There was no communication from Mr. Cain. Miss
French was confined at home with a throat infection.

Silence was quite pronounced during the early part of the meeting. The
therapist was active in attempting to break through this defense. The
subject was changed several times. Mr. Boler talked about his mother and
his occupational duties. Mrs. Kitch discussed her husband. The therapist
brought the members back to looking at their group relationships. Mrs.
Kitch and Mr. Smith finally admitted fears of exposure in discussing their
real problems. The therapist reviewed several incidences of previous

group behavior, pointing out the decreased attendance during the meeting after the members had discussed sexual feelings and a similar occurrence when the hostility was rather high with one another. Various defenses used by each one to avoid closeness, previously identified, were reemphasized. The members were again asked to examine reasons for their inability to be close to one another. Mrs. Kitch answered that a person reveals himself, then gets defensive and may not come to a meeting because of fears concerning what is thought of him. The subject was changed by Boler. Holt recognized this maneuver. There followed a discussion of sexual feelings. Smith stated that he has always been taught that sex was dirty and described a childhood incident when his mother washed out his mouth with soap. Mrs. Kitch remembered the embarrassment created by her mother when sex was mentioned in the home. Boler recalled seeing his father with another woman in an embrace and wanting to kill him. Foy spoke of being ashamed of sexual feelings. The subject was again changed. Authority figures were mentioned, following which the therapist reminded the members that he has often been referred to as an authority figure and compared to parents and others. He wondered how these previous feelings regarding sex compared to feelings in the group at the present time. Smith felt that the atmosphere at home was the same as in the meeting. Foy admitted thoughts of his childhood and wondered if others had similar thoughts. Smith added that anyone who had authority problems always had sexual problems. Mrs. Kitch said that she is as embarrassed around the therapist as she was with her father. Again the subject was changed. The therapist continued to be active in asking the members to examine group relationships. Mr. Smith spoke of fearing the therapist's feelings. Holt denied any sexual problems and discussed his sexual capabilities in a superior vein. Smith took issue with Mr. Holt, calling him a superman and again wondered why he was in group therapy since he never had any problems.

Approximately 30 minutes remained. The therapist interrupted the discussion by informing the group that the current subject was important and could be discussed at later meetings. He then told the members that the group would end one month earlier than previously announced. Approximately ten meetings remained. Group feelings were explored. Foy spoke of a feeling of panic which accompanied the realization that the group would soon stop. Mrs. Kitch wanted to keep in touch with everybody. Mr. Boler asked to be placed in another group. Smith was visibly shaken and held his face in his hands. Holt wondered if the members would graduate, receive a certificate of completion, and be told what the doctor thought was wrong with them. Boler replied angrily to Holt that he couldn't understand his worry since nothing is ever wrong with him. All of the group members became depressed. Foy wondered where to go from here. The therapist asked about the depressed mood. Holt asked if the therapist would publish his ideas so, at long last, the members would know how he feels. Foy, too, wondered if the therapist felt the group had been a success or failure and whether the members had failed. The silence of Smith and Mrs. Kitch was focused on by the therapist. Smith replied that he was trying to straighten out his feelings. In a way he considered the end of the group a step forward. He had made progress. The depression continued and the therapist brought this to their attention again. The remainder of the meeting was characterized by expressions of failure, inability to make progress, and a lack of clarification of their problems.

Theme and Dynamics

The theme of the meeting at the outset was related to the group's basic feelings that interfered with closeness. The anxietal manifestations and defenses against closeness as related to the therapist and each other continued to play a prominent part in the group's function. Their fears associated with sex and its relationship to their feelings were discussed in more detail. Sex was characterized as a dirty, embarrassing, shameful subject. The atmosphere in the group meeting was identified as similar to the atmosphere in the home. There was the fear the therapist would disapprove and reject them if sexual feelings were brought out in the open.

Examination of the contents during the first half of the meeting reveals the following subjects were discussed in this order: (1) fears of exposure, (2) inability to be close to one another, (3) sexual feelings, and (4) authority problems. The members must have sexual feelings toward one another and the therapist. In a mixed group sexual fantasies involving members and the therapist will be present. Statements have been made in the past that sexual feelings are related to authority problems. As members get closer together, sexual feelings interfere. Fear and fright associated with sexual feelings resulted in poor attendance following the initial disclosure of sexual feelings in the group. They felt the therapist would never approve of their feelings. The group members felt confused about the differences between sexual feelings and closeness. Ovesey[3] points out that the sexual mechanism may be used for dependency gratifications; the patient mistakenly interprets his motives as truly sexual in nature. There is the possibility of similar feelings in this group. The wishes to be cared for and the attempts to get closer are interfered with by frightening sexual feelings which tend to push the members apart.

The theme of the latter part of the session was set by the therapist's remarks relative to termination of the group. Separation anxiety with its many real and imagined feelings will be a focal point of the group dynamics from now until the end. At this point in the meeting depression became very evident.

Technique

The persistent, recurrent problem of closeness and the various defenses utilized for avoidance necessitate constant attention from the therapist. Patterns are repeated over and over again by the members. The therapist was aware of this situation and asked about the silence, extraneous subject matter, and absences in this context. He utilized group material from previous meetings in a comparison of group attendance. He continued to explore their feelings concerning himself. Their fears of discussing sexual material were discussed.

The therapist correctly brought to their attention the forthcoming termination of the group. Sufficient time will be needed to ventilate their feelings regarding separation. He is announcing termination of the group more than two months beforehand. He was correct in allowing sufficient time during this meeting for an initial exploration of feelings. The depressed mood was very evident, as well as the pleading atmosphere to give them more.

The recorder was quite concerned about the depression in the group. She identified with the members and asked the therapist later what future plans he had for them regarding treatment or transfer to another group. She felt the therapist also became somewhat depressed during this interval. The therapist is quite aware of his investment in the group and has spoken of discussing with the members additional plans for treatment if desired.

There are two very important features illustrated in this meeting regarding technique.

1. A group reality issue, such as termination of the group, should be brought to the attention of the members sufficiently early for adequate exploration and understanding.

2. When the therapist brings such an issue to the members he should allow adequate time during the meeting for discussion. By no means should such matters be handled by an announcement from the therapist at the end of the meeting.

SIXTY–SECOND MEETING

Only four members were present, Mrs. Kitch, Mr. Foy, Mr. Darcy, and Miss French being absent. Prior communication had been received from Mr. Foy and Miss French.

The recorder was on vacation. Dr. N., who was the recorder on two occasions in the past, served as substitute recorder.

At the outset there was increased tension and anxiety. Silence alternated with laughter and restlessness. The therapist explored the meaning of the silence. Immediate references were made to the group's breaking up. Boler and Smith admitted being angry. Holt said he felt resentment but not anger. Boler was concerned about ending the group one month earlier than originally planned and stated that the members should sue the therapist for breaking the contract. A number of sarcastic, hostile remarks were directed to the therapist. This behavior was pointed out to the members by the therapist who asked why they were angry with him. Boler wanted to continue in another group. Smith admitted he was "mad as hell." Holt was anxious to find out what the doctor thought about their progress. Boler felt the therapist was angry with them. This feeling was explored. Boler said that one of his major problems was getting angry with people and expecting them to be angry in return. The subject was changed by Cain. Holt appeared to be asleep and the therapist asked about this behavior. The members admitted being irritated at him. Holt spoke of being bored and not interested in the meeting. The therapist recalled that Holt initially came to the group to find out why people didn't like him and at this meeting he goes to sleep. His behavior was called hostile, impolite, and self-centered. The therapist explored with the group Holt's need to exhibit this pattern of behavior. Boler spoke of a baby who can sleep at will and shifts responsibility, adding that Holt wanted the therapist to tell him his problems rather than to dig them out himself. There was a change in the subject material, interspersed with several silences. The therapist at this point said: "I'd like you to look at the meeting now. Any thoughts as to what is going on here?" Holt replied somewhat angrily, "Silences, boredom, and antagonism." Boredom was equated with tension by Smith. Holt admitted that he used sleep and alcohol as an escape. The therapist related their feelings of tension to earlier remarks about the group ending and asked for additional feelings. Holt wanted to go ahead and quit now. Boler said everyone wanted to reject the therapist before he rejected them. The therapist focused on their feelings of rejection. A few comments were made and a change in the subject material followed. Again the therapist focused on their feelings in regard to the group ending. Cain discussed his need for more understanding of himself and his loss in being absent for 6 months. Boler wanted additional advice from the therapist in regard to future treatment. Smith suggested making his own decision. Holt denied any help from group therapy since its outset, adding that housewives and salesmen couldn't help him in a group setting. There followed an interplay with Holt regarding his definition of an authority figure. The therapist again asked for feelings regarding the group ending. Insecurity was voiced by Smith and Boler. The substitute recorder was mentioned. They denied any feelings regarding his presence. Toward the end of the hour the therapist made the following statement: "I've been impressed by the denial of feelings here today. What thoughts do you have about this?" Cain stated that this has always been a problem with him. Holt said it didn't apply in his case. Smith spoke of not wanting to accept problems. The denial might be due to the members not wanting to admit that the group was ending. He added that when hostility was present, feelings were denied. The therapist pointed out the use of denial by Holt in statements about the recorder. The hour ended with Holt elaborating on the positive feelings of the original recorder.

Theme and Dynamics

The theme of the meeting was clear from the outset. The members were very angry with the therapist for terminating the group. There was also considerable anxiety about stopping one month sooner than originally planned. The substitute recorder created a certain amount of tension which was overshadowed by the other factors. Tension and anxiety were markedly increased. Silences, laughter, and other manifestations of non-verbal behavior were more pronounced. The ambivalence has now been tipped over to the negative side. Group function will be interfered with until these feelings of separation can be aired. Anger, resentment, and antagonism for the therapist was voiced. Anger and hostility from the therapist was expected in return for their feelings. Then, too, the sentiment seemed to be "why not reject the therapist before he rejects them?" Denial of feelings was equated with hostility that has been brought about by the ending of the group.

Technique

The therapist was aware of the theme of the session and directed attention toward exploring their feelings regarding the group termination. The increased tension, anxiety level, and use of denial prevented a more clarified understanding of why the members were angry with the therapist. Earlier in this session he could have focused more on this feeling of why they were irritated with him, but later meetings will give him ample opportunity to explore this important matter in detail.

The therapist was correct in pointing out Holt's defense of withdrawal and appearance of going to sleep. The members identified it as a childlike pattern, and the behavior was finally spoken of by Holt as a means of escape.

The effect hostility created in the group by the use of denial was discussed. Segments of anger, anxiety, and the defenses against anxiety, of which denial is a part, were identified.

The author has observed on many occasions that when the members are very angry with the therapist, denial of their feelings and defiant behavior may occur. This type of behavior may be present even if the members have reached stage III of group therapy. Sometimes the therapist will become frustrated by the members' constant denial of group reactions if they have identified and understood such group feelings and reactions in previous meetings. In many ways the members act like angry and defiant children and teen-agers who refuse to deal with conflicts with their parents until their anger has subsided. Moreover, group members react in a similar manner; only when their anger subsides can they deal effectively with group conflicts and problems. In such situations the therapist should recognize that several meetings may be necessary for the members to work through their reactions to a disturbing group issue.

SIXTY–THIRD MEETING

There were five members present. Mr. Holt, Mr. Darcy, and Mr. Cain were absent. There was no communication from the absentees.

The meeting began with the discussion of extraneous topics. The therapist asked about relationships in the group. Within a few minutes Mrs. Kitch mentioned the group was ending soon. There was general discussion about the termination of the group in a superficial and somewhat humorous vein. The therapist remarked that the subject was now being treated differently as compared with its earlier handling. Mr. Foy replied that he was panicky. Miss French didn't know how she felt. Mr. Smith spoke of trying to push the ending out of his mind, accepting it, but not liking the change. Miss French then admitted anxiety but that she was making an effort to think of what she has learned from group therapy. Mr. Boler admitted that he was aware of problems not previously recognized. He hated the thought of the group breaking up and recognized the need for more therapy. Miss French wanted to try some kind of therapy on her own. She spoke of becoming aware of previous personality traits. Now when she gets angry at people she tries to take a second look at them and herself. She spoke of fears of anyone getting close to her and using a cover-up of laughter. She admitted hating some people. Many of her feelings that were not clear before the group began were clear now. Smith agreed, and spoke of his fears and hostility. The therapist recalled the anger expressed toward him at the previous meeting. Miss French and Smith again admitted being angry at the therapist. Mrs. Kitch expressed the feeling as one of resentment. The therapist asked about their feelings toward him in relation to the termination of the group. They said they felt angry and defeated because it seemed to them that the group had not really helped them. Miss French felt they were informed in sufficient time to prepare for the group's stopping. The therapist then asked again about their feelings toward him. Miss French wondered why the therapist was stopping the group. Foy made another plea for hypnosis. Several hostile statements were then directed at the therapist. The therapist again asked about their feelings of anger, guilt, resentment, and panic which were directed at him for the group's ending and where such feelings come from. Smith felt it was the members' attitude toward authority. Foy said that when he initially came to group therapy he was looking for a miracle. There followed an interplay between Miss French and Foy. The therapist pointed out that group issues were being explored and the conversation was sidelined in an old, familiar pattern. The members agreed. The therapist made the following statement: "You have recognized certain feelings toward me. Let's look at what your expectations were from me and the effect produced by the group." Boler said his conception of group therapy had changed. At the outset he had expected to be remade into a new individual with a new personality and now he was disappointed because he and the others were not cured. Mr. Foy expected the therapist to cure everyone and put a feather in his cap. The therapist again asked about the group's feelings toward him. He pointed out their prior recognition of anger toward him for bringing them closer together in the group, for absences, cancelled meetings, and recorder changes, and stating that the same feelings were experienced about terminating the group. He asked where such feeling came from and what the members planned to do with these feelings. Smith felt that the group equated the therapist with God and expected a miracle. They would not recognize that the therapist was only human. Mr. Boler added that perhaps fear of punishment was involved, since that is the reason people fear God. Miss French also hoped the therapist would express opinions that she found impossible to do herself. Boler felt the important thing was what to do about these reactions to people. He spoke of trying to break a cycle of anticipating certain feelings toward people by recognition and control. Foy wondered what to do when you recognized faults but had no will to change. Smith felt it was better to know faults than to be blind, adding that his biggest problem is his feeling toward authority. Miss French felt she was more relaxed around authority now. Boler discussed his pattern of ingratiation with the therapist which he was trying to change and, by so doing, express his real feelings.

Theme and Dynamics

The theme of the meeting remained the same: separation. The anxiety level, however, was pitched to a different key than at the 62nd meeting, and more constructive group work was accomplished. The anger and hostility to the therapist had dissipated to some extent through ventilation and recognition of its source. Expectations from group therapy were discussed. The members' original goals were verbalized as being quite different from their present ones. They expected the therapist to be like God and perform miracles. He was supposed to make the group all well. This was the members' expectation from group therapy. Later they realized the therapist was a human being like anyone else. Then came the awareness to the group members to look at and work on their own problems.

Previous references have been made to the initial goals of the group members as being quite different from those of the therapist (Chap. 3). A clear illustration of this important factor is pointed out from this meeting.

Technique

The therapist was in control of the meeting. He encouraged the members to explore their feelings about him regarding separation. That this was being accomplished was reflected in the lowering of the tension and anxiety during this session. This factor becomes an important issue at any stage of group therapy. Changes in the reality of the group increase the hostility of the group members and tip the identification with the therapist over on the negative side. The therapist introduced separation to the group at the 61st meeting. There was depression. At the 62nd meeting the anxiety level was quite high, with very pronounced anger and irritability directed toward the therapist. At this meeting (63rd) the negative identification with the therapist was still present but less evident. Group anxiety is now at a constructive level and several areas of group feelings were explored. The therapist should be aware of these features of group dynamics and use every cue available to clear away the hostility directed toward him as the authority figure.

SIXTY–FOURTH MEETING

There were only three members present, Mr. Foy, Mr. Holt, Mr. Cain, Mr. Darcy, and Mrs. Kitch being absent. There was no prior communication from any of these.

The session began with critical reference directed at the absent members. The therapist pointed out their criticism and asked for feelings regarding those present. Mr. Boler discussed his difficulty in being close to people. The therapist reminded the members of the therapeutic contract and asked them to explore feelings encountered in relating to others. Mr. Smith spoke of his hostility to authority, a recurrent pattern with him, and stated that he reacted with fear to hostility. He said that the members have to put on a false front in the group because of their fear. He wanted to know the source of this fear. Miss French replied that she builds up things in her mind and becomes afraid. She spoke of often wondering where this feeling comes from, and revealed that on every occasion when she examines her feelings, thoughts of her mother enter her mind. Mr. Smith stated that he didn't fear his own reaction, but did fear the reaction of authority. He felt this fear was a result of his dependency relationship with his father, who browbeat him in childhood and used his dependency as a weapon against him. He spoke of a fear of dependency and not wishing to depend on authority even when it was needed. He wondered if the members were not trying to seek out a relationship with the therapist similar to the one they had with their parents. Mr. Boler said that he still reacted with fear in almost every situation. Miss French spoke of combined feelings of insecurity, low self-esteem, fear, anger, and guilt, adding that her ability to understand some of these feelings was very helpful. The therapist asked if the ending of the group had any relationship to their feelings of fear. They agreed that their fear was magnified several meetings ago when the therapist announced the termination of the group. At this point the therapist made the following statement: "Let me take a minute or two and review several facts with you. You have talked about the various ways and means utilized to handle tension and uncomfortable feelings. You have identified many of these feelings in yourselves and in others. For example, you are aware of getting angry at me for a number of things, such as the times when others are absent, when meetings are cancelled, when the recorder is changed, and the like. You have recognized that venting hostility on each other is easier than venting it toward me. You are aware of becoming angry in order to avoid being close to each other. Now you became angry at me about the group disbanding, which anger you demonstrated rather clearly two meetings ago. You have recognized and identified these feelings. What do you plan to do about them in the future?" Miss French replied that the members have acted childish and immature. She had let little things bother her. She admitted that all the items spoken of by the therapist had made her angry, and that such behavior was immature and should be corrected. Smith and Boler agreed. The subject shifted again to their feelings of fear and hostility and its relationship to authority. Boler discussed feeling ill and uncomfortable around authority, but, at the same time, needing to be dependent on authority. He mentioned wanting individual interviews when the group concluded. Smith felt that Boler should try to overcome his being so dependent on authority. The therapist was discussed again by the members. Their thoughts of the therapist's feelings about the members were explored. Miss French felt that the therapist liked the group. She had formed her opinion by his attitudes, not by what he expressed.

Theme and Dynamics

The theme of the meeting continued to revolve around the members' reactions to the termination of the group. This event has increased their feelings of fear and hostility. At the same time, constructive group work is being accomplished concerning the origin of these feelings of fear, anger, etc. and what each member plans to do to control these feelings in the future. The recognition of their reaction to group reality issues (absences, cancelled meetings) as being childish and immature was an important insight.

The anxiety level has decreased since the 62nd meeting. As the group approaches the end, positive feelings for individual members and the therapist will be more in evidence. Patients have positive feelings in therapy for long periods of time, but the extent is not seen clearly until the time approaches to discontinue treatment. The identical situation occurs in a family. Positive feelings are not particularly evident until a sibling goes off to school, members separate for one reason or another from the family, or illnesses or accidents occur. In this group their positive feelings are being expressed in more detail.

Technique

The therapist was in control of the meeting. Group relationships were explored throughout the session. He was aware that the authority relationship of the members continued to be one of paramount importance.

The summary given by the therapist followed by the question regarding the origin of certain feelings and future plans concerning them can be considered correct technique. Early in group therapy this form of technique would have been inappropriate. Now he is helping them to identify clearly these feelings and to look to the future.

SIXTY–FIFTH MEETING

There were five members present. Mr. Holt and Mr. Cain were absent. There was no prior communication from Mr. Cain.

The first part of the meeting was taken up with a discussion of the values of group therapy versus those of individual therapy. Boler again talked about his fears of closeness in the group and his need to see one doctor rather than a group of people. He discussed his homosexual fears and the taboo society places upon homosexuality. Smith pointed out to Boler that he would always have to associate with groups of people, that the group to him didn't mean that you had to completely tell all and be so close to each other; to look at your feelings and reactions was just as important as discussing problems. The members discussed their reaction to group therapy. Miss French spoke of being less confused and having a clearer look at her relationship with other people. Because she was aware that other people had problems she could better tolerate her own. Mrs. Kitch agreed. Smith felt his biggest problems involved his reactions to others. He had become more aware of how he reacted since being in the group. Boler felt that his reactions were a major problem. Foy said group therapy had made him aware of being scared and afraid. He admitted using sarcasm and humor as a cover-up when he had not felt like laughing for eight years. A discussion of pleasing people followed. The therapist asked about the group's feelings with each other and with him. There was rather general agreement that it was not as necessary to please the therapist now as it had been in the early months of group therapy. Positive feelings regarding therapy were expressed. Miss French talked of her initial confusion, sensitivity, and inability to get along with others. Now she could separate her feelings and use her mind better. Foy discussed his marital problem and numerous conflicts with his father and brother.

Mrs. Kitch felt she could handle problems and conflicts with her husband on a more constructive level than formerly. They agreed that their problems were not solved and that people with whom they live and work have problems which will continue. Miss French felt they should be more objective with others. Smith said that to remain clear-headed was important. Miss French said that she had isolated one feeling: the therapist was an authority figure. She did not like him as much as in the early days of the group. She added that maybe she could return home and understand her relationship with her father better. She might get angry but hoped to maintain control.

At a lull the therapist explored with the members the possibility of reporting the results of the group experiences in a professional journal. There was agreement by all the members with such statements as: "It will be a credit to us," "I'm all for it if someone else can be helped," and "It's a good idea; lots of people have problems." A reference was made to the recorder and the notes that have been made during the meetings. The therapist focused on their feelings regarding the recorder. Miss French admitted former resentment of the recorder and a continuous wondering of what the recorder would write. Smith said he was still conscious of notes being taken but was not uncomfortable. Miss French admitted being quite irritated with the therapist at one meeting when a tape recorder was used; she "froze" that night and wanted to go home. The therapist focused again on feelings about the group ending. Foy spoke of a hopeless, frustrated, panicky state. The remainder of the session was spent in constructive, supportive statements from the other members to Foy. During recent meetings his degree of participation in group discussion has shown a marked increase. He has discussed problems. Mr. Boler felt he should try to continue in another group if at all possible.

At intervals throughout the meeting, Smith reacted with prolonged laughter. Several times Miss French asked him the meaning of so much laughter. His response was that he used laughter as a means of relieving tension.

Theme and Dynamics

The hostility to the therapist had somewhat dissipated and the members continued to examine the results of the group therapy experience. There was general agreement that difficulties in getting close to people remained but should not necessarily be a stumbling block in their relationships with others. The members were more aware of their own feelings and could identify patterns of reaction. There was insight, too, that problems are not just confined to the group but are present in other people. The need to be objective and clear-headed in interpersonal relationships was voiced. There were many expressions of warm feelings for one another. Separation is now being viewed on one level as a more pleasant experience than formerly.

Technique

The therapist was in control of the meeting. Clarification of the dynamics of separation was dealt with. This subject should be continued at future meetings.

The therapist correctly brought to the group's attention the possibility of the publication of material concerning the group. This matter is a group issue and needs its attention and approval.

The therapist notified the group that an individual interview would be held with each member prior to the end of the group. With the end of this treatment in view, the therapist should begin to ascertain the members' psychological status and help them decide on future plans.

Discussion

Mrs. Kitch's discussion of how group therapy has helped her to understand herself and the conflicts with her husband illustrates one of the great values of group therapy. People learn to talk about their problems. They recognize defense mechanisms and patterns of behavior used by themselves and others. A major problem with husbands and wives is their inability to communicate with each other. Because they do not talk to each other there is no understanding. Marital conflict results in silence, defiance, absences from home, excessive spending of money, sexual conflicts, conflicts with relatives and siblings, occupational difficulties, and other types of acting-out behavior. Many of these difficulties had occurred with Mrs. Kitch. Now she can more clearly recognize the marital behavior between her husband and herself.

SIXTY–SIXTH MEETING

There were four members present. Mr. Boler, Mr. Holt, Mr. Darcy, and Mr. Cain were absent. Mr. Holt called to inform the therapist that he would not attend any future meetings. Mr. Cain had secured a job that required working in the evenings. It is interesting that he has not attended a meeting since the therapist announced termination of the group. There was no communication from Mr. Boler. Mrs. Foy called the therapist and informed him of her husband's improvement. She wanted to discuss certain matters about Mr. Foy with the therapist. The therapist advised her that this would have to be taken up with Mr. Foy and the group members. This was agreeable to her.

The meeting began with a reference to the absent members. Mr. Holt's phone call and Mr. Cain's conflicting schedule were discussed. Concern was voiced for Mr. Boler, whose past absences indicated a recurrence of drug or alcohol problems.

Mr. Smith's laughter in the previous meeting was discussed by Miss French. Smith agreed that his laughter was a mechanism used to cover up tension and hostility directed toward the therapist. He mentioned the presence of fear and related it to the ending of the group. Smith felt the members were on friendlier terms and that the ending of this friendship concerned him. Miss French and Mrs. Kitch agreed. The therapist referred to their associations over the entire period of group therapy and asked how they felt about ending the group and separating from one another. Smith stated that, in the past, separation had been a very traumatic experience for him and occurred on unfriendly terms. He did feel this group was ending under different circumstances. Miss French related an incident in which she went on a binge because of a friend's leaving. She said it upset her to think that friends will not be seen again. She compared separation with death. The therapist asked about Mr. Foy's quiet but attentive behavior in the meeting. Foy immediately began participating. The other members entered into a lengthy discussion with Foy about his problems. They felt he was better, even though he denied improvement. Foy discussed conflicts at home and at work. He admitted being angry and resentful. He described being bitter toward people for long periods of time and of fearing reaction from his family. The therapist asked about his role in the group and if there was any possibility that Foy feared reaction from the group. Miss French felt that this fear prevented his talking. Smith asked Mr. Foy if he ever became angry, and also wanted to know why Foy couldn't express himself. Miss French thought that Mr. Foy was angry at the therapist. Mrs. Kitch told him that everyone else had been angry at times and it was strange that he was the only one who hadn't shown anger. Miss French said that he did not trust anyone and that he was angry at the therapist for not curing him. Foy stated that his wife felt he had improved. The group agreed that he showed improvement. The therapist informed them of Mrs. Foy's phone call and the content of the conversation. Foy and the others agreed that the therapist should talk with her. The therapist asked about the time taken up with Mr. Foy during the meeting. The members indicated that they wanted to help him and were aware that they were not avoiding other feelings. Miss French said that Mr. Foy had made more progress than Mr. Holt or Mr. Cain. (She had also made this statement in previous meetings.)

The therapist announced that the group would not meet for two sessions after the next meeting. Group feelings were explored. Foy stated that the future absences added to his panic. Miss French said that she didn't depend on the therapist as much now as formerly. Again the discussion focused on Foy for the remainder of the meeting.

Theme and Dynamics

Ambivalent feelings regarding separation are being expressed. On the one hand they recognize certain areas of improvement in their relationship with others; on the other, they have the fear of loss of dependency from the therapist. Miss French's expression that a friend's leaving was like someone dying has symbolic meaning to the group.

Positive feelings for group therapy continued to be expressed. Considerable attention is being focused on Mr. Foy. It is as if they wish to help him as much as possible during the remaining sessions. Another meaning, however, may be present, as explained below.

Foy has become more active in the last few sessions. His reaction to the ending of the group has been more realistic than that of Holt or Cain, and supports the statement made by Miss French that Mr. Foy has made more gains than Holt or Cain.

Technique

The therapist correctly brought to the group's attention Mr. Holt's telephone call, Mr. Cain's occupational conflicts, and Mrs. Foy's request concerning her husband.

Additional feelings regarding separation and the group's ending were explored.

The therapist was aware that on numerous occasions in the past the members had utilized Foy as a scapegoat to avoid interaction. There is the remote possibility that at this meeting uncomfortable feelings regarding separation were avoided by focusing on Foy, but the interaction with him was group-oriented and quite supportive. The therapist allowed it to continue, and focused in this area on one occasion. Later, when the therapist announced the cancellation of two meetings, positive feelings were expressed, and again the conversation centered on Foy. The therapist could explore this with the members at a future meeting.

SIXTY-SEVENTH MEETING

There were four members present. Mr. Boler, Mr. Holt, Mr. Cain and Mr. Darcy were absent. Mr. Boler notified the therapist of a physical illness.

The session began with Miss French's discussing her joy in seeing Dr. N. (substitute recorder on three occasions) in the hallway with a cast on his leg. Examination of her reaction was interpreted as displacement of feelings she actually meant for the therapist. Mr. Smith said his initial reaction to her remarks was that she wished the therapist's leg was broken. The regular recorder and former recorder were discussed. They admitted that they were still not completely comfortable and associated this with distrust of authority. Becoming aware of their reaction to others was discussed. Miss French spoke of leaving many meetings feeling angry. She said that when she got home and began thinking about her feelings, somehow by a slow process of osmosis she would realize what she was doing. Foy lamented his inability to grasp from the group what the others had gained. Smith said he had given thought for several weeks to a question asked by the therapist: "Where do feelings come from?" He again spoke of his fear and hostility to authority and talked in more detail of his anger at the therapist when he initially entered group therapy. He brought up the subject of sexual feelings and their relationship to authority. The members superficially agreed with Smith. The therapist suggested that a clearer picture might be forthcoming if they would examine their sexual feelings with each other, the therapist, and the recorder. Foy said he was embarrassed. Miss French said she immediately thought of her mother and recalled an incident in childhood. She admitted being tomboyish and identifying with her father. One day she was whittling a piece of wood. Her mother angrily said to her: "Why not make that a penis and use it?" Mr. Smith felt the women present had made him more comfortable with women on the outside. Mrs. Kitch discussed her fear of Mr. Holt, that he might be oversexed and make a pass at her some night after a meeting. The therapist asked about sexual feelings and authority and where they fitted him into this picture. The subject was not dealt with at all. The therapist asked about himself again. There was superficial conversation and a change of subject material. The therapist asked if they recalled discussing this matter in a previous meeting. They couldn't recall until the therapist reviewed previous statements made. The therapist also asked about their inability to recall feelings about sex and authority. Smith admitted it was a "touchy" subject. He wanted to understand but was glad to get on another subject. Mrs. Kitch spoke of feeling guilty. Smith stated that one objection to ending the group was the lack of closeness to each other.

The therapist focused on feelings in regard to ending of the group and made reference to the previous meeting (see page 341). Miss French said she had been reading about the French Revolution. She compared people being sent to the guillotine with the group ending, adding, "The group ends, the group dies." Foy felt he should have used his head more during the length of therapy and maybe he would have gotten more out of the group. He spoke of failing the therapist miserably by not helping himself to help the therapist and the group. He talked of his cruel, dominating, and mean father. At one time he considered him a god. He still considers him a god but "a damned tyrant, too." The therapist focused

on Foy's inability to express feelings and referred to several previous incidences in past meetings including Foy's statement that the therapist
was "God." Mrs. Kitch felt he had been afraid so long that he could not
overcome it. Smith felt that Foy was reacting to the therapist as he did
to his father. Foy denied any anger to the therapist but admitted irritations with the initial psychiatrist seen in the department before beginning
group therapy. The other members told Foy that he did have hostile
feelings toward the therapist whether he would admit it or not.

Theme and Dynamics

The relationship of sexuality to closeness and dependency had been previously discussed and was now again identified. The role played by authority in sexuality was approached superficially. Their real sexual feelings have not been discussed in any detail.

The role of the recorder was more fully explored and its relationship
identified as mistrust of authority.

Miss French's comparison of the group ending and death of the group
was a significant point.

Foy's activity and participation continues to be very noticeable since
the therapist announced the group was terminating.

Technique

The therapist was in control of the meeting. He explored further their
feelings regarding the recorder. He attempted to promote a discussion of
sexual feelings. It appears to be necessary that the therapist help the
members identify the presence of sexual feelings toward him and its relationship to dependency and closeness. He could say: "Several times you
have attempted to discuss sexual feelings. You have related them to
closeness, fears of exposure, and authority relationships. I wonder if you
are experiencing sexual feelings toward me and the others here which
you find frightening. What thoughts do you have about this matter?"

The therapist continued to explore their feelings regarding the end
of the group.

The therapist had completed an individual interview with a majority
of the group members. Boler and Foy wished to continue in another
group. Boler admitted being much more aware of conflicts and reactions
with people in authority. He wanted more help and asked the therapist to
place him in another group if at all possible. Foy, in a pleading tone,
begged not to be left stranded without any crutch at all. The therapist
suggested additional group therapy which Foy had requested in a previous meeting. This pleased Foy immensely. Mrs. Kitch discussed her
progress and asked for individual interviews on a monthly basis primarily
for support with her husband who functions on a marginal level with
periodic outbursts of psychotic behavior. Smith and Miss French did
not want any additional treatment at this time. Smith felt he was doing

quite well at work and spoke of receiving a salary increase recently. Miss French is performing well in her duties as a library technician and has started college at night. Mr. Holt stopped coming after the 62nd meeting. He had married and was working sporadically. There has been no change in his alcoholic behavior. Cain attended only a few meetings after his release from an institution. He had secured a job which interfered with the meetings. Superficially he expressed interest in being placed in another group. Darcy's physical condition was gradually deteriorating. He was unable to work and was confined to his home.

Discussion

Miss French's statement about her leaving the group meetings angry, thinking about her feelings, and then slowly recognizing these feelings as being related to her relationships with the group therapist and other group members points out several important features of group therapy. The recognition of the cause of anxiety cannot be obtained in an easy course of several lessons. Many meetings of the group over months of group therapy have gone into Miss French's observation. She has become aware of her relationship to the group therapist. She has learned how to talk more freely and express her feelings. She has recognized that other relationships within the group (with the therapist and members) are similar to those of her previous life experiences, and that her reactions were distortions of her own emotional responses. Miss French has recognized her hostile reactions to authority figures in everyday life from her understanding of her hostile reactions to the group therapist. Through the development of self-assertion in the group she has become more self-assertive in other groups. A rise in her self-esteem has occurred. She aired her sexual and aggressive feelings in the group, and her guilt was lessened by the knowledge that other people have similar problems and that they, too, have distorted and misunderstood them.

Miss French can now talk about her feelings rather than acting them out. The socialization from group therapy has resulted in more socialization in other groups. She can test reality better. She has developed psychological aptitude. If future difficulties occur in later life Miss French would probably not hesitate to seek aid from a psychiatrist.

SIXTY–EIGHTH MEETING

There were four members present. Mr. Boler, Mr. Cain, Mr. Holt, and Mr. Darcy were absent. The therapist had received information that Mr. Boler had been hospitalized for a stomach disorder, but details were not known.

Miss French: Where's Mr. Boler?

Mr. Foy: I wonder if he has had more trouble. I hope he is not back in the hospital.

Mrs. Kitch: He can't let drugs alone and he has so many problems with his mother.

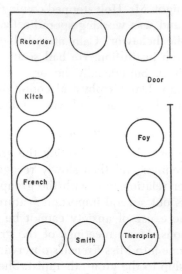

Theme and Dynamics. *They are expressing concern over absent members, especially Mr. Boler.*

Therapist's Technique. *The reality events of the group are: (1) the ending of the group, (2) the two cancelled meetings of the group by the therapist, and (3) the absent members. The therapist should be aware of the reality events and their effect on the members. He should discuss with the members their reactions to these reality events.*

Mr. Smith (to therapist): Have you heard from him? I wonder if he is back in the state hospital.

Therapist: His mother called me yesterday. He's in a local hospital for some kind of stomach trouble. I don't know any details.

Theme and Dynamics. *The mood of the members is subdued and depressed.*

Therapist's Technique. *The therapist informs the members of Mr. Boler's illness.*

Mr. Smith: Well, thank goodness it's not the state hospital.

Miss French: I miss him. I wish he was here.

Therapist: You have recognized many feelings and reactions about absences since starting the group. Any other thoughts about Mr. Boler's absence as well as those of Mr. Holt and Mr. Cain?

Therapist's Technique. *The therapist explores the members' reactions to absences.*

Miss French: I used to get real angry at you (therapist) and the ones who were not at meetings. I would be disappointed also.

Mr. Smith: I think emotions are associated with missing meetings. I used to get mad with the doctor and then pay him back by not coming the next time.

Miss French: I still get anxious and concerned when people miss meetings but I'm better about it. I find myself concerned over what may have happened to them. Now I'm really worried about Mr. Boler. I've given up on Mr. Holt and Mr. Cain.

Therapist: Well, you know I've been away for two weeks and the group did not meet. How did you feel toward me for my absences?

> *Theme and Dynamics. The members can express their feelings about absences comfortably. They are more objective in their feelings and reactions to absences. Even though they are depressed, the group anxiety is at a constructive level. The members' response to the therapist's observations and questions are group-centered and group-oriented. Noticeably absent are the anxietal responses and defensive patterns of behavior characteristic of the meetings of the group during stage I.*
>
> *Therapist's Technique. The therapist explores their reactions to his absence of two weeks.*

Miss French: The last two weeks with the group not meeting is like a test of the final end. I wonder if he (therapist) did this just to try us out.

Mr. Foy: I didn't have anybody to talk with so last Tuesday (day of the group meeting) I got drunk and poured out all my troubles to a minister.

> *Theme and Dynamics. The members continue to be depressed.*

Miss French: I've been depressed and angry.

Mr. Smith: I've been down in the dumps too.

Mr. Foy: I became panic-stricken. I couldn't sleep well. I'm not over it yet.

Mrs. Kitch (appears depressed): I missed the meetings. I've had all kinds of trouble with my neighbors. They've been talking about me. They don't like me.

> *Theme and Dynamics. The members' reactions to the cancelled meetings are clearly verbalized—i.e., depression, anger, panic, and difficulty with others.*

Therapist: You have recognized in previous meetings that you get angry when people do not attend meetings. You have also recognized how angry you get at me for cancelling meetings. But you are depressed now.

> *Therapist's Technique. The therapist explores the depression of the members.*

Miss French: Anger can drift off into depression.

Mrs. Kitch: (Again discusses her conflicts with neighbors.)

Therapist: Do you have any other ideas about your depression the past two weeks and today?

Mr. Smith: I'm not happy about the group's ending. At times I get afraid.

Miss French: So do I.

Mr. Smith: I have also felt guilty as if I have done something wrong.

Miss French: Yeah, I get to feeling guilty and I don't know why.

> *Theme and Dynamics. The members have now recognized the emotions of anger, depression, and guilt. Their responses throughout this meeting indicate how comfortable they are with the therapist and each other. An observation by the therapist is followed by a group response. The members do not fear disapproval, rejection and retaliation from the therapist as they did during stage I of group therapy. Then, too, the members' dependency needs and magical expectations are now on a more realistic level than they were during the early meetings of the group.*

Therapist: You have been able to understand that anger, depression and guilt are associated.

> *Therapist's Technique. The therapist recalls to the members their association of anger, depression and guilt that they have discussed in previous meetings.*

Mr. Smith: We could be angry with you (therapist) and get guilty for being angry. My parents always tried to impress on me to never get angry.

Miss French: I've been angry many times here. I understand myself better but I still get awfully mad at home and at work. I get mad here. Sometimes I just stay mad with the doctor all the time. I don't like him as much as I did when the group started.

> *Theme and Dynamics. The members' anger toward the therapist and the guilt for their anger is verbalized.*

Mr. Smith: I used to get awfully mad with him at the hospital. I'd be so mad I'd have to leave meetings. Sometimes I wouldn't even come to the meetings.

> *Theme and Dynamics. Mr. Smith points out that anger toward the therapist can be the cause of absences from meetings.*

Mr. Foy: (Remained quiet but was following the conversation very intently.)

Therapist: Apparently you've been pretty angry with me. Looks like this may have been the cause of your depressed feelings.

Mr. Smith: There's something else. We talked about sex at the last meeting. It made me uncomfortable. I got angry talking about it.

> *Theme and Dynamics. The subject of sexual feelings that was discussed at the previous meeting is reintroduced.*

Group: (There was a superficial discussion of sexual feelings by all the members except Mr. Foy.)

Therapist: Well, you've been angry because of two cancelled meetings, the group ending and the discussion of sexual feelings.

> *Therapist's Technique. The therapist encourages the members to pursue their sexual feelings.*

Mr. Smith: You can't eliminate part of your personality from the meetings. I've had sexual feelings about people here for a long time. I can't separate my sexual feelings from other feelings.

> *Theme and Dynamics. Mr. Smith verbalizes his inability to separate sexual feelings from other feelings.*

Miss French: I've wanted to talk about sex, then I didn't want to. I would get frightened. It's taken me a long time to admit how I feel. I always associate anger with sex. I've never had any understanding about sex.

> *Theme and Dynamics. The association between sexual feelings and angry feelings is expressed.*

Mr. Foy: I wish I had sexual feelings. That's one of my troubles. I don't feel like a man.
Therapist: How do sexual thoughts and feelings here make you feel?
Mrs. Kitch: It's not easy. I've always been taught not to discuss sex with anyone.

> *Theme and Dynamics. The theme of the meeting is clear: The members' reactions to the ending of the group, the meetings cancelled by the therapist, and the discussion of sexual feelings. Therapist's Technique. Therapist explores the sexual feelings within the group.*

Miss French: I've found myself liking the older men in the group. I like them better than men my own age.
Mrs. Kitch: I was always afraid of Mr. Holt. I use to wonder whether he would try to make a pass at me after meetings.

> *Theme and Dynamics. Mrs. Kitch verbalizes fears of heterosexual attack.*

Therapist: What has been the relationship of sex to your feelings about each other here? How does sex enter into forming relationships with others?

> *Therapist's Technique. The therapist focuses on sexual feelings and close relationships.*

Mr. Smith: I said a while ago that I can't get sex separated from my other feelings. They're all mixed up.
Mr. Foy (to Mr. Smith): What do you mean?
Mr. Smith: I always wonder about shaking hands with a man and placing my hand on someone else's shoulder. I'm afraid they'll think I'm a homosexual. Once a man placed his hand on my leg. I got very angry. I hit him. I thought he was making a pass at me.
Mrs. Kitch: When I was back in high school I used to want to hug another girl, put my arm around her; but I was afraid to. I was afraid other people would think I was a homosexual.

> *Theme and Dynamics. Close relationships, they say, suggest homosexuality.*

Group: (The members discussed at length negative parental attitude toward sex.)

Therapist: You mention parents and sex. You have often referred to me as an authority figure, as a parent. I wonder where you fit me in regarding your sexual feelings here?

> *Therapist's Technique. The therapist focuses on their sexual feelings toward him.*

Mr. Smith: I have been afraid of you (therapist). I have not wanted to discuss sex.

Mrs. Kitch: I'm more comfortable here talking about sex than I am at home. I wouldn't think of talking about sex to my parents. I can remember getting my mouth washed out with soap when I was young.

Mr. Smith: I get uneasy. I'm uneasy now. I usually get angry and blame someone else.

> *Theme and Dynamics. The members have fears and reservations about discussing sexual feelings toward the therapist.*

Therapist: What was my question?

Mrs. Kitch: I don't remember.

> *Theme and Dynamics. The anxiety level of the group rises.*
> *Therapist's Technique. Since the members' statements do not directly deal with the therapist's observation he refocuses on it by asking them what he said.*

Mr. Smith: About sex.

Group: (Becomes silent but not overly anxious.)

Therapist: My question made you anxious, eh?

Mr. Smith: Yes, I've been afraid to like you. I've had homosexual feelings about you. I didn't want you to know it. It's easier not to like you.

> *Theme and Dynamics. To like the therapist, Mr. Smith feels, also suggests homosexuality.*
> *Therapist's Technique. Therapist recognizes that his question has made the members anxious. He calls it to their attention and encourages them to discuss their sexual feelings about him.*

Miss French: I don't know how I feel about you (therapist). I get angry talking about this. I'm angry now.

Mr. Foy: I wish I had interest in women; I don't. That's one reason I come out here for help. I'm just not a man.

> *Theme and Dynamics. The depressed mood of the group is now lifted.*

Therapist: So getting to know everybody here, getting closer to each other and to me is uncomfortable.

Miss French: I'm always afraid I'll get hurt.

Mr. Smith: It's my hostility that bothers me.

Therapist: Well, you know much more about your relationships to each other and to me. You can now recognize much of your anger and the various ways you hide it. Your relationship to authority figures is better understood. Now you are becoming more aware of sexual feelings and its relationship to closeness and to anger.

> *Therapist's Technique. The therapist ties in previous insights of the members with their present discussion of sexual feelings. At this stage (stage III) of group therapy, he can explore with the members their feelings and reactions in much more detail than he would be able to do in stage I.*

Miss French: I've talked more about sex here than I ever have before.

Mrs. Kitch: I have too. I don't ever talk to my husband. It's sort of an understanding. One of those that you don't talk about. You know what I mean.

Therapist: As you have discussed many times, the feelings and reactions in this group are just the same as in other groups. Today you have talked about having sexual feelings here as you have in other groups. Would you agree that talking about these feelings and understanding them help you in your relationships with other people?

> *Therapist's Technique. Therapist makes a general statement encouraging the group members to talk about their feelings and reactions in all group relationships.*

Miss French: When he talked to me the other day about whether I wanted to continue in another group (the therapist has had individual interviews with each member regarding future plans) I decided I wanted to try by myself. I know I'm better. I get along with people at work now. I still get mad. I get mad here. I can see that it isn't always the other person. I've got my own problems.

> *Theme and Dynamics. Miss French's observations point out the rewards as well as the limitations of group therapy.*
> *Therapist's Technique. Toward the end of group therapy it is advisable for the therapist to consult with each member individually regarding future plans.*

Mr. Smith: I don't know what I want to do. I believe it would be better for me to keep seeing somebody. I don't like the idea of seeing someone else. I still get awfully mad at times. I've been to the hospital so many times. This is a constant fear. Will I have to go back?

Miss French (to Mr. Foy): What are you going to do?

Mr. Foy: That's a good question. I don't know. My bottle will still be around, I hope.

Miss French (to therapist): Didn't his wife tell you he was better and that she wanted treatment too?

Mr. Smith: That's what he (therapist) told us. Mr. Foy would never admit it.

Therapist: Well, I notice that although all of you were depressed during the first part of the meeting, the depression is now gone.

Mr. Smith: Yes.

Miss French: I was depressed.

Therapist: Let's look again at the meeting today. You were depressed initially. There was a discussion of two cancelled meetings and the ending of the group. Your feelings regarding sex occupied the latter part of the meeting. After you talked about sexual feelings the mood lifted here, and the depression was gone. What are your thoughts about this change in the group mood?

Mr. Smith: I think everyone wanted to talk about sex. It's been bothering me. It's a relief when these things are out in the open. Sex makes me guilty. Guilt may have something to do with hiding the way I feel.

Miss French: It makes me guilty too.

Mr. Foy: Guilt and fear go hand in hand. One overshadows the other.

Therapist: Let me make this observation to you. You can now recognize and understand many of your feelings and reactions. When you first started group therapy this was not clear to you. You did not actually know your feelings. In this meeting you were depressed, then after talking about your feelings the depression went away. Would you agree that recognizing how you feel and talking about it is helpful?

> *Therapist's Technique. The hour is up; however, the therapist continues the meeting in order to get across several important points regarding their group relationships in the therapy group and in outside group relationships.*

Group: (Verbally and nonverbally agreed with the therapist.)

Therapist: Well, if this is true don't you think it would be helpful for you to look at and examine your feelings and reactions in all of your relationships on the outside? For example, if you are depressed and down in the dumps, why not try to find out what's behind the depression? This is what you did today. You were depressed. After we discussed all of the things affecting the group it became clear that you were angry at me for cancelling the meetings and stopping the group after two more meetings; and then, too, you were angry about having to talk about sexual feelings. Once you talked about these things the depression went away.

> *Therapist's Technique. Therapist suggests to the members that exploring and recognizing their feelings and reactions in all groups can be helpful to them as it has in this particular meeting.*

Mr. Foy (pleading): That's the very reason I hate to see the group stop. We're just getting started!

Miss French (angrily): You (Mr. Foy) have had plenty of opportunities. You've had the same chance we've had.

Therapist: We're past stopping time. That's all for today. See you next week.

SUMMARY

Theme and Dynamics

Sexual feelings and their relationship to closeness had been a recurrent theme in the last few meetings. At this meeting there were the issues of the cancelled meeting, termination of the group, and sexual feelings associated with closeness. The depression in the meeting was felt to be related to all three of these issues. It was interesting that the depressed mood lifted rather dramatically when sexual feelings were verbalized.

Parental attitude toward sex was equated with similar attitudes toward the therapist. Its relationship to closeness with homosexual fears for liking and being friendly with others was discussed. Fear of homosexual feelings toward the therapist was brought out by Smith. Hostility as a defense against closeness had been discussed in previous meetings. Now sex enters into the same picture. To be close to others has a sexual connotation. As Mr. Smith said, this uncomfortable area can be avoided by getting angry or by blaming others.

It is generally true in emotions that a feeling is not impounded by itself. Sexual feelings, angry feelings, and tender feelings are often impounded altogether. This particular group meeting emphasizes this point. The group members, being closer to each other, are beginning to free all kinds of feelings: hostility, closeness, tenderness, and sexual feelings.

The two cancelled meetings were compared as a test of the group's ending. Feelings of rejection from the therapist may have contributed to the guilt expressed by Smith and Miss French who spoke of depression, irritation, and guilt. By a like token the defense used by Mrs. Kitch was increased paranoid trends, while Foy drowned his panicky, depressed state in alcohol and found a minister to listen to his woes.

Technique

The therapist was in control of the meeting. The members' feelings regarding the cancellations of the meetings and termination of group therapy were explored. The depressed mood was continually brought to their attention. The therapist again utilized material from previous meetings by pointing out the sequence of anger, depression, and guilt and asking what relationship it had to the present meeting.

Sexual feelings were verbalized at greater length. Attention to this area from the therapist contributed to their discussion.

As the group approaches termination the therapist is making more detailed observations to the members. The therapist is also calling attention to the similarity of their relationships in the therapy group and those in their everyday group relationships.

There is a great deal of difference in the members' responses to the therapist's technique in this meeting as compared to their responses in meetings during stage I; e.g., the 12th and 35th meetings. Now that the members feel more accepted and approved of by the therapist, they do not react with all the numerous manifestations of anxiety so characteristic of meetings during stage I.

Discussion

This group discussed sexual feelings for the first time at the 54th meeting. The next reference to sexual feelings occurred nearly 2 months later at the 61st meeting. At that meeting, group members said that sex was a dirty and embarrassing subject. One and one-half months (67th meeting) later, sexual feelings as related to authority figures received some attention. Statements were made that their parents had taught the group members that sex was dirty and embarrassing. At the 68th meeting the group members discussed sexual feelings more freely than at any previous time. Sexual feelings, they said, were actually a barrier against closeness, for fears of homosexuality or heterosexual attack were equated with being close and friendly with others and with the therapist. They recognized that they used anger and hostility as protective measures to ward off closeness and sexual feelings.

Sexual conflict in this group has, of course, been present since the early meetings. However, the guilt which results from sexual taboos has inhibited the discussion of sexual feelings. These sexual taboos, which originated with parental figures, have prevented any earlier discussion of sexual feelings. In some people sexual feelings, feelings of closeness and tenderness, and angry feelings may be associated. When these people have feelings of closeness, they may exhibit defensive and hostile behavior. They may become angry, frightened, or withdrawn. Sometimes people will break away completely from others because of uncomfortable feelings and repeat the same behavior pattern in other groups. In these instances people are not able to separate sexual feelings from close and tender feelings or from angry feelings. This fact was clearly stated by the members of this group. A lesson can be learned here that applies to all groups in our culture. Sexual feelings and conflicts should be solved by talking it out as these group members have done, not by the acting-out behavior that occurs in many other groups.

The taboo against the discussion of sexual feelings is not confined to people who have emotional illnesses but is somewhat characteristic of our society. In the family group, sex is not considered an appropriate topic for free discussion. Parents are either secretive, noncommunicative, or critical of their children if they discuss sex. Masturbation is referred to as a harmful practice or the forerunner of insanity. Children are often frightened with punishment for examining or looking at their own bodies or those of their peers. In other groups (social, professional, religious, occupational, etc.) sex is treated in the same manner as in the family group—it is taboo.

The relationship of sexual feelings to closeness also has its origin within the family group. Other aspects of behavior occurring in the child-parent relationship are self-assertion and one of its special forms—aggression. The child uses self-assertion and aggression to obtain dependency gratifications. Thus the child experiences a mixture of feelings: warmth and tenderness, sexual feelings and feelings related to self-assertion and aggression (angry feelings). The healthy child should be able to separate these feelings. However, family conflict may interfere with the healthy emotional development of the child. Parents who are sexually frustrated may either consciously or unconsciously seek love, closeness, and (indirectly) sexual pleasure from a child. Thus the child may associate love and closeness with sexual feelings. Parental behavior such as hostility between the father and mother, hostility to children, ambivalent discipline, sibling favoritism, and the like may result in the child's being confused about feelings of love, anger, and sex. In addition, the many taboos and sexual restrictions present in the family may induce fear and guilt in the child. The child may become inhibited, and these inhibitions may spread over a wide area of behavior. The child may develop a mixture of feelings that cannot be separated one from another. Warm and tender feelings, sexual feelings, feelings related to self-assertion and aggressiveness, or angry feelings may be all associated with each other. The teen-ager and adult who cannot separate these feelings may experience similar situations as those described so accurately by the members of our group.

SIXTY–NINTH MEETING

There were four members present. Mr. Holt, Mr. Darcy, and Mr. Cain continued to be absent. The therapist was informed on the morning of this meeting that Mr. Boler died at a local hospital during the previous night. After talking with relatives and physicians, the following information was obtained: Several weeks prior to this meeting he began taking Mellaril (a phenothiazine) in excessive amounts. A.P.C. tablets were also consumed in large doses. He developed a hepatitis and had been hospitalized approximately 10 days ago. Death was sudden and unexpected since Mr. Boler had shown improvement in the hospital. An autopsy was being performed. Results were not available at this time.

The session began with references to the size of the group and the whereabouts of Mr. Boler. At this point the therapist told them of his death, adding the details stated in the above paragraph. The expression on the members' faces was one of immediate and profound shock. Mr.

Foy remained standing as if in a trance. Miss French had a weird look on her face. Mr. Smith became depressed. Mrs. Kitch's reaction was not so striking. Smith said that Boler had confided and trusted in him. Now he felt helpless and wished he could have helped him more. Miss French said she was sorry, yet glad in a way that made her feel guilty. The therapist focused on their feelings with the realization that a member of the group had died. Miss French replied that in the past depression would overcome her when people died. Now she did not feel so downcast and helpless. She admitted frustration and anger, as though someone were imposing on her to die. She talked of her mixed feelings. In a way she was glad for him to escape from his mother. She was afraid the drugs contributed to his death; he didn't have the strength to stay away from medication. Mrs. Kitch agreed with Miss French, adding that Mr. Boler was unhappy and didn't want to live. She recalled that he had made suicidal attempts before. Mr. Foy felt the morale of the group was destroyed. Miss French asked Mr. Foy how he was affected emotionally. Foy identified with Boler, saying that the same fate awaited him. Mrs. Kitch stated Mr. Boler was better off. Smith took issue with her saying he would rather live with problems and troubles than to be dead. He felt you should always have hope. He recalled that during his illness at the hospital, when his existence was on another level, the hope to get well never left him. Smith was sorry Boler didn't get to finish the group. The therapist pointed out that several feelings had been expressed: depression, anger, and frustration. Miss French admitted feeling guilty and expressed several ambivalent thoughts. She was glad that he had died, but felt quite guilty about this feeling. At other times she had wished his mother had died instead of him. Mrs. Kitch spoke of being resentful, adding she is only angry when it affects her life. The therapist said: "In the past you have made numerous statements about death. Now death has occurred in the group. How does this affect you in relationship to your experiences here with one another?" Miss French stated she used to have a violent reaction. Now she does not get so upset and feels that she can sort out her feelings. Smith spoke of death as a depressing subject which he tried to avoid thinking and talking about. Mrs. Kitch said she worried about getting old and being placed in a home with nothing to do. Foy appeared to be asleep and was not participating in the meeting. The therapist asked for their feelings about Boler's death occurring near the termination of the group. Smith replied that he could see no connection. Miss French wondered if the therapist "made up" the death of Boler to test out the group. She discussed her doubt about reality matters, stating that she always had to see to believe. Smith immediately took issue with her. The therapist asked about Foy's drowsiness and nonparticipation in the meeting. Foy admitted being sleepy, adding that he was not drinking and had never been this way before at a meeting. Smith felt he was using sleep as an escape, and recalled his own use of sleep in the past when under emotional strain. Miss French spoke of Foy's building a mental block and becoming immersed in himself. The subject returned to the group's feelings about Mr. Boler's death. Mr. Smith stated that when someone you like dies, it is as though part of yourself had gone; the relationship is ended and you experience a loss. Miss French said that formerly she had experienced the same feelings when someone moved away. The therapist asked if any of these feelings had been experienced in the past few weeks, or since they first learned that the group would end. There was agreement that ending the relationship with each other was a loss because they would not be seeing each other any more. Toward the end of the meeting the therapist asked about their relationship with people in the future. He asked if they could view the group therapy experience as a pleasant one. They have met new people and formed new friendships that included likes and dislikes. He then asked what could the termination of these friendships mean in their later group relationships. Time did not permit a discussion of the therapist's observations. Immediately Foy began asserting in an apologetic manner that he could talk in this group but nowhere else. He reiterated his problem with his family and others. He couldn't face people; when he encounters someone from the group it is like seeing a brother or sister. He can talk to them. Miss French said the group was like a family. Smith agreed. The time was up. The therapist ended the session by pointing out the last observation was not discussed but could be so done at the next meeting.

Theme and Dynamics

The theme of the meeting was directly related to the death of Mr. Boler. A mixture of feelings was expressed, the predominant mood being depression. Boler's death was related to the end of the group in that friendships will cease and relationships will terminate. These factors constitute a loss.

The individual psychodynamics of each member are interesting. Mr. Smith became depressed. Even though he was quite verbal in his comments, death was a subject he wished to avoid discussing. He equated Boler's death as though a part of himself were dying. Similarly, the end of group therapy could be compared to losing something from each group member. Miss French became slightly depressed. She expressed mixed feelings that included frustration, anger and guilt, as well as doubt of the reality of Mr. Boler's death. Mrs. Kitch revealed less emotion than any of the other members. She felt Mr. Boler did not want to live and was better off dead. Mr. Foy became quite depressed and utilized sleep as a means of escaping the reality of the group meeting. He identified with Boler and wondered if the same fate was in store for him.

The ability of the group members to express various feelings about Boler's death again indicates their closeness. Certainly the feelings expressed were quite different from the eulogizing that takes place at the usual funeral of an individual.

Miss French's feelings as to whether or not Boler had actually died could be variously termed a paranoid trend, schizophrenic doubt, or the initial stage of a grief reaction where denial of the event occurs.

Technique

The therapist, admittedly, was quite shocked to learn of Boler's death. The depression of both the therapist and the recorder carried over into the meeting. Immediately after being informed of Boler's death, the therapist made plans to bring this matter to the group's attention as soon as possible. He wanted to explore: (1) their feelings regarding the death of a group member; (2) its relationship to group therapy; and (3) their feelings toward the therapist for this tragic event in the group. Another immediate thought of the therapist was the possibility of several additional group meetings beyond the termination date. The therapist expressed ambivalent feelings about additional sessions and decided to "play it by ear," depending on the reaction at the meeting. After the meeting was over the therapist was pleased with the manner in which Boler's death was handled by the members. The matter of the extra meetings was only discussed with the recorder and was never broached in the actual meeting.

Discussion

Funeral and memorial services for people who have died have several different meanings. They are influenced to some extent by racial, cultural, and geographic factors. The funeral service may be a small, private one with only the immediate family and close friends in attendance. In smaller cities the funeral service is usually conducted in the deceased's church. If the person is well known in the community people are expected to pay their respects by attending the funeral. The southern Negro expends considerable effort and time honoring the deceased person. The funeral may not occur until 5 to 7 days after death. In contrast to the usual brief funeral service of most people, the Negro funeral service may be very long (2 to 4 hours) with many eulogies.

Food is closely associated with the funeral. The deceased's family is the recipient of food from the church membership, friends and neighbors. The Irish wake is an example of how food is brought in for the deceased's family. References have been made of the use of the wake in cities with a large Irish population by politicians to cement and protect political strength. In the South, mammoth amounts of food are prepared and brought to the family.

Funerals are conducted in a religious atmosphere by all the different racial and religious groups. The specific ritual employed will vary with different religious and cultural customs.

The death of a close friend or of a person in a younger age bracket may induce many fears of death in people. For example, the death of an active business man from a sudden heart attack may bring a number of other men to the doctor's office for thorough physical examinations.

There are people who are phobic of viewing the body of a dead person or attending funerals. They become uncomfortably anxious in such situations. In some cases fear of their unconscious angry impulses accounts for this type of fear and anxiety.

Funerals have many characteristics of superficial communication between people. Regardless of what feelings were experienced towards the deceased person, only positive feelings are mentioned at the funeral. Their true feelings, such as the ones spoken at this group meeting about Mr. Boler, are not expressed.

SEVENTIETH MEETING

Only four members were present—Mrs. Kitch, Mr. Smith, Mr. Foy, and Miss French. Mr. Cain's wife informed the therapist that Mr. Cain has been hospitalized for alcoholism. Mr. Darcy remained incapacitated at home. No communication had been received from Mr. Holt. The autopsy report on Mr. Boler revealed a toxic hepatitis with the immediate cause of death attributed to congestive heart failure.

All four members were on time. As the therapist entered the room the members were writing addresses and phone numbers for each other. They were laughing and talking but became silent when the therapist took his seat. Miss French and Mrs. Kitch had brought cookies; Mr. Smith and Mr. Foy, coffee. The recorder prepared the coffee. Several meetings previously, the therapist had given permission for refreshments at this final meeting.

The initial part of the meeting was taken up by Mr. Foy, who spoke of feeling guilty and worthless and made his usual statements of self-pity. He asked the group and the therapist why they had not helped him. He admitted drinking before the meeting and that he would continue to do so in the future in order to escape reality. The therapist pointed out that Mr. Foy knew that arrangements were being made for him to continue group therapy and that his wife had called, reporting a substantial improvement in Foy since beginning group therapy. Mr. Smith felt that Mr. Foy was better. He added that another person can gauge how much better you are than you yourself. He described how improved his family relationships were at this time. The therapist asked if Mr. Foy's statements had anything to do with the group's ending. Miss French replied that Mr. Foy felt the group was like a family, and the family had let him down.

Mr. Foy replied in a pleading tone: "I'll ask you as a child, why haven't you helped me?" A general discussion followed, with the members agreeing that Mr. Foy needed to express his feelings; when he got in the other group he should try to help himself and not expect miracles from the therapist or other group members. The therapist explored the reactions and impressions of the other members about the ending of the group. Mr. Smith stated he felt more confident and sure of himself than he did a few weeks ago when the therapist first announced that the group was terminating. He added that he was conscious of being more accepted on his job and that his employer now valued his work—feelings that he has never experienced before. Miss French stated that she had been depressed, angry, and confused about the group ending but feels better now. Mrs. Kitch denied any strong feelings but said she would like to see everyone again. The therapist said: "I would like to repeat the observation I made at the end of the last meeting. We were talking about separation and the end of group therapy. I wonder if you can see that separation can be a pleasant experience. You have been here together for many months, formed friendships, observed likes and dislikes in each other and in me. As you pull away now, can you see this experience as a pleasant one?" Smith said the members were parting on friendlier terms. Miss French said: "I'll go my own way. I'm glad I've known everybody and that everybody has gotten something from the group." Smith added that the group's ending was like death and other things, a necessity and a reality. He spoke of rejecting separation in the past. Foy in a hostile, humorous vein said: "Shakespeare said: 'Parting is such sweet sorrow.' I think he's a damned liar." Mrs. Kitch said the ending was not pleasant. The therapist focused on how they saw the relationship with him at this last meeting. Smith said he did not see the therapist as "one of the group," and still considers him as an authority figure. He spoke again of his hostility and conflicts with authority figures, and talked of his father. Miss French agreed with Smith, adding that she now felt more comfortable in the therapist's presence but still didn't trust him. Mrs. Kitch denied any strong feelings about the therapist and referred to him as a statue. She became somewhat restless and agitated. Mr. Smith accused Mrs. Kitch of rejecting and resenting the therapist. He didn't see how she could be void of feelings. Mrs. Kitch, displaying more emotion than at any time previously, continued to deny any feelings, finally saying, with good affect: "What difference does it make? The group is breaking up and it will not help any!" Smith felt Mrs. Kitch was angry with the therapist. Mrs. Kitch admitted the therapist stirred her up. Smith spoke of his wish to have a close relationship with the therapist, like a father and child; maybe, he thought, Mrs. Kitch wanted the same thing from the therapist and was resentful for not having it. The therapist asked if Mrs. Kitch was sensitive to his remarks and referred to previous observations from her of being blank and confused when the therapist made observations in meetings. Smith felt sensitivity was a hostile feeling. He discussed feelings of wanting to be the therapist's pet at the outset of group therapy and of childish feelings that were embarrassing for an adult to experience. Mrs. Kitch admitted when the group started she wished for extra attention from the therapist but soon found out differently.

Boler's death was mentioned. They expressed guilt and admitted concern as to whether he could have been helped more. They saw his death at the end of the group as an ironic event. Mrs. Kitch wondered if it was suicide and if it was the group's fault. Miss French replied no, that he had made suicide attempts before joining the group. If such happened it would be a result of his feelings, not theirs. The therapist explained the cause of Boler's death. An interplay followed between Smith, Miss French, and Mrs. Kitch in regard to their behavior in previous meetings.

Mrs. Kitch charged that Mr. Smith ignored her. Smith claimed she was denying feelings. At this point the end of the hour was near. The therapist interrupted the members and said: "I feel that interrupting you now at the end of the hour points out what I want to say to you. You are aware of still having problems with each other in the group. You have spoken of understanding that other people also have problems and the need to be objective in your relationships. You have recognized that group therapy has no magic or miracles to offer. It is not a cure-all. You have been able to understand yourselves better. Mr. Smith has pointed out how letting off steam and understanding his feelings has helped. Miss French has said that being able to identify her feelings and to separate them has been very valuable in her relationships with others. Mrs. Kitch has spoken of understanding the relationship of her husband, and this has not been an easy task with his illness. She can now use tact and understanding rather than anger and defiance in her relationship to him. Mr. Foy denied improvement, but you feel that he has improved and his wife reports substantial gains. You have suggested other ways that he can benefit from a new group experience. I want you to know that having been here has been a pleasant experience for me. I have enjoyed knowing you and working with you for nearly 19 months. I have your addresses. I will be interested in your progress. If at any time I can be of help to you, do not hesitate to get in touch with me." The therapist then shook hands with each member and bade them good-by.

Theme and Dynamics

Serving refreshments has a psychodynamic relationship to separation and the end of the group. To take in food and drink, oral gratifications, helps to relieve the anxiety of separation. The therapist, with his own personal investment in the group, shared these feelings with the group members.

The mood of the group has changed considerably from the 69th meeting. The anxiety level was considerably higher. The theme of the meeting was clear from the beginning; the members were angry about the group breaking up. The death of Mr. Boler was generally discussed realistically, even though they felt they should have helped him more.

The individual psychodynamics of the members revealed that separation had been worked through relatively well with Mr. Smith and Miss French. Their statements of feeling more at ease now than when the termination was initially announced points out this factor. Mr. Foy denied any improvement and made a passionate plea for the group to continue. His statements pointed out his dependency on the group and his fears now that it was being taken away. Mrs. Kitch exhibited more emotion during the meeting than at any time previously. She angrily denied any feelings about the therapist but spoke warmly of the group. Her feelings about separation were vividly expressed in her reference to the group ending.

Separation was compared to death and other reality events—i.e., it was an event that was a necessity.

Technique

The therapist had a valuable cue as to the theme of the meeting from the initial silence. The anxiety level was high. Separation was now going to be a reality. The therapist at that point planned to support the members as much as possible during the meeting.

Mr. Foy was allowed to ventilate his dependency feelings but was supported by the therapist by statements of improvement from the group and from his wife, as well as by pointing out future plans for him. In the interchange the other members attempted to support Foy. Mrs. Kitch's reaction was not expected by the therapist. Her anger and resentment to the therapist was pointed out by the other members.

The feelings at this last meeting were again explored in relationship to separation as it affected each other and the therapist.

Boler's death was discussed and feelings about this loss were again explored, with a comparison made to the ending of the meeting.

The therapist ended the meeting at an appropriate time. An argument and differences of opinion was taking place among the members. He indicated to the group their awareness that problems are still present and referred to those brought out in the present meeting. He reminded them that they had discussed on several occasions that problems will still be present with themselves and with others; that group therapy was not a magical procedure. He spoke of his own interest in the group and demonstrated this interest by wanting to know how they fared in the future and expressed further interest in also wanting to help the members in any way possible that was needed.

The death of a group member raises the question of whether the therapist should have extended the group meetings beyond the termination date. Prior to Boler's death, the group members had spoken several times of separation in terms of death—e.g., "the death of our relationships with each other" and "death of the group." There is no question that the group members, faced with the actual death of Boler at the end of group therapy, were greatly disturbed by this tragic happening. Even though the members discussed at length many of their feelings and reactions about Boler's death, one might question whether it would have been possible for them to work through all of their reactions to this real death of a group member in two meetings. Possibly the tragic death of a group member forced the members to deny, disguise, cover up and repress the entire termination process of group therapy. Personal reality events more than likely influenced the therapist's handling of the group. He was completing his psychiatric residency on the same date as the previously agreed-upon termination of the group. The therapist may have also denied and repressed his own reactions to the termination process of group therapy. In this particular situation, the therapist's personal reality situation may have aided the process of denial and repression.

In such situations as this it might have been more feasible had the therapist managed to extend the group for a period of from one to two months. In four to eight additional meetings the members should have been able to clarify many of their feelings and reactions to the separation from the group and Mr. Boler's death. Here again the need for the therapist to be most flexible in his technique is emphasized. Just as he should allow a group meeting to go over the allotted time if disturbing group conflicts have not been resolved, so should he modify the length of group therapy in such emergency situations as the one that occurred in this group. If reality events prevent his attendance beyond a prescribed date, other arrangements should be considered. Possibly it would have been better for this group to have met for additional meetings even if the recorder had to take the role of the therapist.

On the other hand, the one-year postgroup therapy follow-up interviews and evaluations of the group members did not reveal any information or reality difficulties to suggest that the members fared worse by not having additional meetings after Boler's death. In fact, the gains made from group therapy had been utilized to advantage in their everyday group relationships. Although the members may have been more comfortable had the therapist extended the group, the lack of extension apparently left no long-run complications.

Discussion

In our culture there is a long list of family "farewell" parties associated with separation. There are farewell parties when a son or daughter leaves home to go to college. Parties of one kind or another frequently are given to people who leave one community and go to another. The bon voyage parties for ship cruises are well known. Wedding dinners and parties are extremely common. Wakes and funerals are often associated with large amounts of food. In the deep South the death of a family member mobilizes a group of people (usually members of a church) who prepare food for the family and relatives until after the funeral.

Family parties tend to occur on such special occasions and at the transitional periods of crucial stages in life. In this group the therapist reacted to the loss of the group members. He was leaving people for whom he had grown quite fond. Symbolically they were part of his family. In effect, he had a farewell party for them.

INDEX TO GROUP MEETINGS
(Numbers refer to meeting numbers)

SEATING ARRANGEMENT OF GROUP MEMBERS

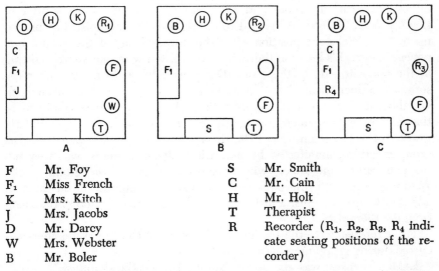

F	Mr. Foy	S	Mr. Smith
F₁	Miss French	C	Mr. Cain
K	Mrs. Kitch	H	Mr. Holt
J	Mrs. Jacobs	T	Therapist
D	Mr. Darcy	R	Recorder (R₁, R₂, R₃, R₄ indi-
W	Mrs. Webster		cate seating positions of the re-
B	Mr. Boler		corder)

F Mr. Foy
F₁ Miss French
K Mrs. Kitch
J Mrs. Jacobs
D Mr. Darcy
W Mrs. Webster
B Mr. Boler

S Mr. Smith
C Mr. Cain
H Mr. Holt
T Therapist
R Recorder (R_1, R_2, R_3, R_4 indicate seating positions of the recorder)

The seating arrangement of the group members is depicted in the three diagrams. Diagram A represents the average seating arrangement during the initial 35 meetings. Diagram B covers the period from the 36th to the 55th meeting, and diagram C the remaining fifteen (56th–70th) meetings.

The room was 16 by 20 feet in size and was located in the Department of Psychiatry. The group therapy room also served as a library and conference room. Ceiling-high book shelves lined two of the walls. The furnishings had a modern décor and consisted of two sofas, seven chairs, a center table, end tables with lamps, and a wall-to-wall carpet.

A number of observations can be made from the seating arrangements of the group members, the therapist, and the recorder. The therapist sat in the same location throughout the entire period of group therapy. No group member ever questioned his seating position and his chair was always vacant when he entered the room to begin the meetings. The recorder had no specific seating place.* She usually positioned herself apart from the therapist.

* The therapist and recorder discussed seating arrangements prior to the beginning of group therapy. The therapist suggested that she could better observe both him

From the first to the 36th meeting (Diagram A) there were more variation and differences in the seating positions of the group members than at any other time. What is interesting, though, is the general consistency of the group members in retaining the same seating positions in the room from the onset of group therapy until the termination—70 meetings over a period of nearly 19 months.

During the initial group meetings Holt sat on the sofa next to the therapist and was quite competitive with him. After the station wagon incident of the outside group meeting (see page 195), he moved to the opposite side of the room and sat there throughout the remainder of therapy. Mrs. Webster always sat to the right of the therapist. Foy moved up to Mrs. Webster's position after she dropped out of the group, and never changed his location thereafter. Mrs. Kitch was consistent in sitting at the opposite side of the room. Darcy usually sat in a chair near the sofa or the door. Cain's position was on the distant sofa. Miss French invariably sat on the sofa at every meeting. Mrs. Jacobs moved about more than any other group member, and at one time or another occupied nearly every seat in the room except the therapist's. Mrs. Jacobs' anxiety in the group meetings, manifested by extrinsic body movements, was very noticeable. Smith and Boler, who became members of the group at the 42nd meeting, sat in the same seats at every meeting; Smith on the sofa adjacent to the therapist and Boler in a chair diagonally across the room from the therapist.

Three references to the seating arrangement of the group members occurred during group meetings:

1. Mrs. Webster was accused of "hiding behind the therapist."
2. Foy sat near the therapist so he could "get cured."
3. Smith, seeking the approval of the therapist, sat adjacent to him.

An Analysis of Group Members' Attendance at Meetings

The average attendance (Fig. 1) of the group members for the 70 meetings was 75.4 per cent. The key explains the method of arriving at the attendance percentage for each meeting.

A comparison of the attendance graph with the meetings reveals several interesting factors that contributed to group absences and illustrates the relationship of absences to group dynamics.

During the initial 20 meetings the attendance never fell below 75 per cent. On seven occasions the attendance was 100 per cent. Beginning with the 21st meeting the attendance graph shows wider swings of variations from 100 to 25 per cent. At eight meetings (meetings 21, 29, 30, 33, 38, 55, 59, 64) the attendance percentage was at or below 50 per cent.

---

and the group members if she sat away from him. The recorder made a practice of entering the room for the meeting with the therapist and decided on her seating position at that moment.

In meetings 21, 29, 30, and 33 the group attendance was affected by Mrs. Webster and Mrs. Jacobs. In all four of these meetings Mrs. Webster and Mrs. Jacobs were absent. In general their absences were emotional in origin and related to the dynamics of group therapy. Reality factors (physical illness, vacations) contributed to the absences of other group members.

At the 38th meeting the attendance dropped to 25 per cent. The theme of several previous group meetings was increasing hostility to the therapist and fears of mental illness if the group members' true feelings were revealed. The group contract had been modified (increased length of group meetings and a longer period of group therapy) at the 35th meeting. These factors may have contributed to the lack of attendance at the 38th meeting.

The 54th meeting was characterized by the initial discussion of sexual feelings by the group members. At the 55th meeting attendance dropped

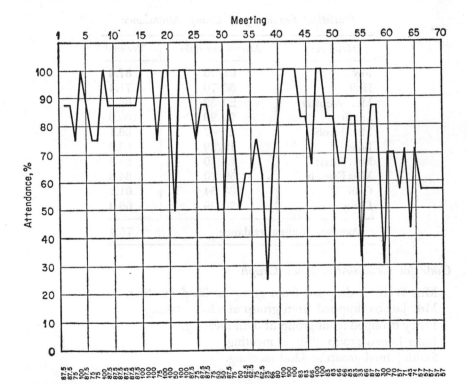

Figure 1. Group attendance graph.

NOTE:
1–38. Percentage based on eight members.
39. Based on six members; Mr. Darcy and Mrs. Webster absent.
40–41. Based on five members; Mr. Cain absent until session 56.
42–56. Based on six members; Mrs. Jacobs absent; Mr. Boler and Mr. Smith added.
57–70. Based on seven members; Mr. Cain returned.

to 33 per cent. Later statements by group members indicated that fears associated with discussing sexual feelings contributed to the poor attendance at the 55th meeting.

At the 59th meeting the attendance was 30 per cent. Physical illnesses of several group members were reported as the causes of the absences. A significant reality event affecting the group at that time was the return of Cain (57th meeting) after a lengthy absence. Increased group anxiety was evident in the 57th and 58th meetings.

The 64th meeting saw a drop in attendance to 43 per cent. Termination of group therapy had been announced by the therapist at the 61st meeting. Group depression occurred at the 61st meeting but was followed by a rise in the group anxiety level at the 62nd meeting, diminishing somewhat at the 63rd and 64th meetings but still elevated. The emotional feelings created by separation anxiety may have played a part in the low attendance at the 64th meeting.

Statistical Summary of Group Attendance

Member	Attendance ratio	Per cent
Foy	61/70	87.6
Holt	50/70	71.4
Mrs. Webster	20/32	62.5
Smith	29/29	100.0
Mrs. Jacobs	27/42	66.1
Boler	19/29	65.5
Mrs. Kitch	62/70	88.5
Miss French	59/70	84.3
Cain	33/54	61.1
Darcy	26/39	66.6
Average group attendance		75.4

Code for Group-Attendance Graph

Mrs. Webster dropped from group at 32nd meeting.
Mrs. Jacobs dropped from group at 42nd meeting.
Darcy dropped from group at 39th meeting.
Boler joined group at 42nd meeting.
Smith joined group at 42nd meeting.
Cain's attendance not reported for 16 meetings.

The Anxiety Level of the Group

Figure 2, schematic in design, indicates the anxiety level of the group from the standpoint of the members' verbal and nonverbal behavior. It has been prepared from the therapist's and recorder's evaluation of the group anxiety at each meeting and utilizes a base line that represents an in-between level of each type of group behavior.

By "anxiety level" the author means the extent to which the members manifest their verbal and nonverbal anxiety during meetings. The manifestations of high anxiety were exhibited by denial, projection, silence, restlessness, laughter, humor, scapegoating, intermember hostility, member-to-therapist hostility, competitiveness, tardiness, and absences. The author is aware that anxiety is present during periods of group depression as well

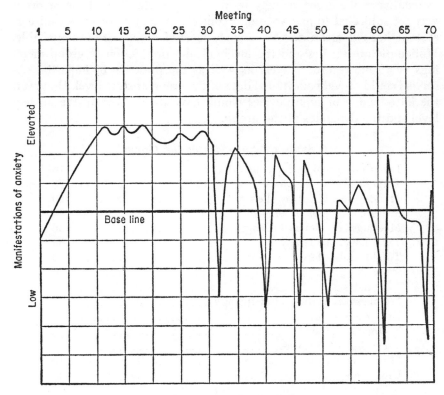

Figure 2. The anxiety level of the group.

Reality events affecting the group

32	Fear of group dissolution	12	Open expression of hostility toward therapist
40	Loss of Mr. Cain		
46	Hospitalization of Mr. Boler	19	Two members repeatedly tardy and absent
51	Christmas holidays		
61	Announcement of termination	29	Two meetings cancelled
69	Death of Mr. Boler	35	Meetings increased in length, 6-month extension of group therapy
		41	Two new members added
		47	Meeting cut by 20 minutes
		54	New recorder, 2 cancelled meetings
		57	Mr. Cain returns to group
		62	Reaction to termination

as during periods of group hostility. On the graph (Fig. 2) these periods of depression (less manifest anxiety) are shown by the points below the base line. When members were depressed their overt manifestations of anxiety and the emotions associated with the anxiety were hidden by more denial and repression. Generally, there was much more evidence of verbal and nonverbal anxiety during the periods when members recognized and discussed their feelings of fear, anger, guilt, and sex.

The author is aware that the graph's accuracy can be questioned. The evaluation of the group anxiety by the group therapist and the recorder was not subjected to any adequate controls. Actually adequate and correct methods of measuring the anxiety level of groups are not available. Motion-picture studies and the mechanical reproduction of group meetings (via tape recorders, etc.) as well as the presence of impartial observers could provide additional data of the group anxiety level. However, the introduction of such devices would have their effect on the anxiety level and the dynamics of the group.

A Statistical Summary of the Group

Length of group therapy, months	18¾
Total number of meetings	70
Meetings cancelled by therapist	10
Meetings, 1 hour in length	34
Meetings, 1½ hours in length	36
Total hours of therapy	88
Total membership of the group	10
Males	6
Females	4
Membership at the end of therapy	4
Group losses	6
Organic causes	2
Psychological causes	4
*Improved members, per cent	40
Unimproved members, per cent,	60
Unimproved—organic causes, per cent	20
Unimproved—psychological causes, per cent	40
Development or increased development of psychological aptitude, per cent	80

* Improvement is based on group function and adaptive changes in family, social, and occupational roles.

The graph reveals a gradual increase of anxiety and tension from the first to the 12th meeting, when hostility to the therapist was initially verbalized. Its level remained high with minor fluctuations until the 32nd meeting, when depression occurred as a result of the members' fears of group dissolution.

The group members' denial of their feelings (fear, anger, guilt), accompanied by their defenses against exposure of these feelings, contributed significantly to the high anxiety level during the first 32 meetings.

From the 32nd meeting to the end of group therapy (70th meeting) there are fluctuating swings of the group mood between depression and hostility that are very closely associated with reality events affecting the group members, the therapist, and the recorder.

The ability to express feelings of depression and hostility in reaction to group reality events was a positive sign of group maturity. Also noteworthy in this latter period was the absence of the sustained high anxiety levels that were present during the first 32 meetings. Peaks of anxiety were short-lived and reflected the results of the group members' ability to express feelings.

Moreover, the graph illustrates the negative identification with the aggressor (therapist) and its relationship to group reality events. Finally, the graph shows the relationship of group depression to group hostility. Note that the depressive periods occurred prior to the periods of increased anxiety and hostility.

SUMMARY OF INDIVIDUAL GROUP MEMBERS

Mr. Foy

Foy's group attendance was excellent. He avoided group interaction for many months, always considering himself unworthy of any help, and made innumerable pleas for magic or hypnosis. Because of the role that he played in the group he was frequently the scapegoat for the other members. He avoided any show of aggressive behavior, commenting several times that unless he exercised strict control over his feelings the instincts of an animal would emerge. During the last three months of group therapy, particularly after the termination of the group was announced by the therapist, Foy made a more concentrated effort toward group interaction. He expressed interest in additional group therapy.

Mrs. Foy reported that her husband had shown remarkable improvement in his social, occupational, and family roles. The marriage, which two years ago was shaky, had become more stable. Angry outbursts from Mr. Foy were considerably less. His occupational record had improved. Mrs. Foy was particularly impressed that her husband had not been given various types of drugs and pills. She expressed interest in also joining a group, feeling that maybe she, too, could receive benefit.

A one-year follow-up evaluation reveals no significant change in Foy since the end of group therapy. He again pleaded for drugs and magic but admitted that group therapy had helped him. He felt that additional therapy was needed but has neglected to obtain further therapy.

Miss French

Miss French's group attendance was excellent. She was very perceptive to group dynamics. As she became aware of her relationship to the therapist and the other group members, she improved in self-esteem and self-assertion within and without the group. The ability to identify her emotions and defense mechanisms resulted in improved interpersonal relationships. The confusion, suspiciousness, repressed anger and difficulties in concentration that were so apparent at the outset of therapy grew noticeably less. During the last six months of group therapy she began attending a night college. Her grades were in the A and B range. Miss French's progress in group therapy was considered excellent.

One year after the completion of group therapy Miss French reported increased self-confidence and greater ease in making decisions. She still has hostility to authority figures but realizes that most of these feelings originate within herself. She is performing well in social, occupational, and educational roles. Through dieting Miss French has lost over 40 pounds, has discarded heavy-rim eyeglasses for contact lenses, and now looks neat and pretty.

Mr. Holt

Holt's group attendance was excellent. His attitude in the group was pompous and dictatorial. At times he would seem to become involved in the group, but would withdraw immediately. His behavior was analyzed on numerous occasions by the other members. He exhibited a repetitive pattern of denial-acceptance-denial. He particularly used denial when he was angry or demanding of the therapist. He refused to look at the transference relationship, constantly maintaining the therapist was not an authority figure. He made repeated dependency requests from the therapist. His acting-out behavior was a constant problem. For example, he (1) got the group together without the therapist, (2) reverted to alcoholism, (3) encouraged another member of the group to live with him, (4) attended other group meetings at a clinic for alcoholism, and (5) quit the group when termination was announced. Holt did not improve as a result of his group therapy experience, but he did become more aware of emotional reactions and acquired a certain degree of psychological aptitude.

At the end of one year indirect reports from other group members concerning Holt reveal recurrent alcoholic problems. He could not be located for an interview.

Mrs. Webster

Mrs. Webster's group attendance was only fair. She only remained in the group for 32 sessions. She could not tolerate the anxiety of the group and her manifestations of acting out were (1) tardiness, (2) absenteeism, (3) securing a job that interfered with attendance, and (4) leaving the state after arrangements had been made for her to remain and participate in group therapy. Mrs. Webster was unimproved when she stopped attending the group. She could not be located for a one-year follow-up evaluation, having left the state without a forwarding address.

Mrs. Jacobs

Mrs. Jacobs' group attendance was only fair. This passive, dependent, phobic female experienced recurrent anxietal manifestations during her stay in the group. Tardiness and absenteeism were frequently used to avoid the group anxiety. She was extremely frightened of group relationships and constantly utilized denial as a defense. On several occasions she made attempts to leave the group but returned when she received support and understanding. She was unable to look at the transference relationship with the therapist and eventually left the group after plans were made to increase the length of the meetings and the period of group therapy.

Mrs. Jacobs developed a certain amount of psychological aptitude. Prior to group therapy she felt her phobic difficulties were caused by various physical illnesses. She consulted physicians on a number of occasions for drugs, surgery, etc. She became aware of the import of emotional interaction and its influence on her symptoms, although there was no amelioration of the latter when she stopped attending the group.

At one-year follow-up evaluation Mrs. Jacobs reported fewer phobic problems. She was teaching school without any apparent difficulty. She spoke of being more assertive with her husband. Mrs. Jacobs felt her greatest gain from group therapy was recognizing and accepting the fact that her difficulties were emotional in origin.

Mr. Cain

Cain's group attendance was only fair. During the early months of therapy he remained somewhat aloof from the other members, intellectualized and was quite adept in the use of parables. He often utilized denial and when confronted with anxiety, resorted to his habitual pattern of alcoholism. He was unable to hold down a regular job. Repeated alcoholic behavior resulted in a prison sentence for six months. He was absent from the group during this period of time. He returned for a few meetings, only to stop again when termination of the group was announced. At the end of therapy Cain reverted to his former pattern of alcoholism. Although he did not profit from the group therapy experience, he became somewhat more aware of the influence of emotional reactions on his behavior.

A one-year follow-up reveals that Mr. Cain has been continuously hospitalized at an alcoholic treatment center since prior to the ending of group therapy. He remains chronically depressed. Weight loss was obvious. There was no apparent improvement in his condition.

Mr. Boler

Boler's group attendance was excellent. This passive, nonassertive, homosexual male with a history of barbituric addiction and alcoholism began group therapy at the state hospital. There he developed an intellectual awareness of his relationships with the peers and the therapist but used the group primarily for dependency needs. He joined this group at the 42nd meeting. He had a history of a hostile dependent relationship with his mother. He talked of this problem often in the group but could never pull away from her. Often he demanded individual interviews and drugs from the therapist. When the group pointed out that his use of drugs was a plea for magic, he would act out by obtaining drugs from other doctors and druggists. A readmission to the state hospital occurred following a depression complicated by alcoholism. For a short time during group therapy he was able to work part-time but was on drugs during this interval. His relationship with the therapist was a hostile and dependent one. He constantly needed reassurance from the therapist and would try to get in a few words with him either before or after meetings. He was perceptive to group dynamics and became more comfortable in his relationships to others, particularly women. He expressed a desire to continue group therapy when termination of this group was announced. Boler had been taking excessive amounts of tranquilizers and died of complications from toxic hepatitis at a local hospital. Whether or not separation factors played any part in his drug intake is not known.

Mr. Smith

Smith's group attendance was excellent. During group therapy he progressed from a severely ill, psychotic individual hospitalized in the state hospital to a position as an engineer (his former occupation) at a construction plant. He has received two salary increases. Smith was extremely perceptive to group dynamics and in the group he often played the important role of a catalyst. At the end of group therapy he admitted that conflicts still remained, particularly with authority figures, and that the control of hostility was an ever-present problem. Interpersonal relationships at home and at work were, however, less threatening to him. Smith showed marked improvement from group therapy.

A one-year follow-up interview reveals that Smith continues to perform well in occupational, social, and family roles. A measure of his improvement can be seen from the manner in which Smith handled two severe stressful situations during this interval. A younger brother was committed to the state hospital and within a few weeks committed suicide. Two months later Smith's father was committed to the state hospital. In each instance Smith was able to call the therapist and benefit from talking with him. Smith stated that the greatest gain from group therapy was the recognition of his hostility to authority figures.

Mrs. Kitch

Mrs. Kitch's group attendance was excellent. Her perception of group dynamics did not reach the same level as did that of Smith or Miss French, and at times she appeared to be somewhat hazy and foggy during group discussions. A prominent paranoid trend would occur with Mrs. Kitch as a defense against anxiety. The reality situation of a psychotic husband who exhibited frequent irresponsible, immature, and infantile behavior kept her immersed in numerous family problems. The group therapy experience, however, did make her more aware of the need to exercise tolerance and understanding rather than to display anger or defiance with her husband. Mrs. Kitch's progress in group therapy was considered satisfactory. As she became aware of the authority figure problem with the therapist, she began to understand similar problems with her father and others. She improved in self-esteem and self-assertion.

When interviewed one year later, Mrs. Kitch was doing well except during periods of stress with her husband. She is more comfortable in group relationships. Mrs. Kitch felt her greatest gain from group therapy was the development of psychological aptitude. She is more aware of how she handles anger with her husband and mother-in-law. Mrs. Kitch also spoke of being more assertive with them. She asked for additional group therapy at the follow-up interview.

Mr. Darcy

Mr. Darcy's group attendance was fair. Neurological surgery was performed during the seventh month of group therapy. His attendance and participation was practically nil afterwards. Presently he is confined at home with a very poor medical prognosis. He did not receive any material benefit from his group therapy experience.

One year after the end of group therapy there is no essential change in Mr. Darcy. Mrs. Darcy is working and supporting the family.

SUMMARY—GROUP DYNAMICS

Meetings 1–10, Stage I

Individual testing procedures were evident and dependency wishes were expressed. The group members became aware that meeting with the therapist was different from meeting without him. The anxiety of the group gradually increased. Mutual analysis began at the 6th meeting. During this period the goals of the members were for magical cures, individual attention, and dependency fulfillment, and were different from the therapist's goal to encourage patients to help each other, give up their wishes for a magical cure, and develop independence and assertiveness.

Meetings 10–20, Stage I

The group anxiety level remained high. Group members began showing an increasing awareness of group problems. Mutual analysis continued. Open hostility was expressed to the therapist beginning at the 12th meeting. The need to please the therapist was evident, as if by coercion the therapist promoted group interaction. The goals of the members appeared to be changing.

Meetings 20–30, Stage I

The relationship of the members to the therapist was the central theme during this period. The therapist was recognized as an authority figure at the 22nd meeting. Group spirit and cohesiveness were apparent. Group problems received more attention and mutual analysis reached a high level. Hostility to the therapist was more comfortably voiced.

Meetings 30–40—Transition from Stage I to Stage II

The average attendance of the group members decreased during this interval. The loss of three members (Darcy, Holt, and Mrs. Webster) brought about fears of group dissolution. The group was identified as a family, the therapist was identified as a parental figure and other members of the group were compared to siblings. The group contract was modified (longer meetings and an increased period of therapy). There was an open expression of angry feelings, and problems with control of feelings were ventilated. The group anxiety fluctuated with group reality issues. An improvement in self-assertion and self-esteem was evident in several members. Mutual analysis continued at a high, constructive level.

Meetings 40–50—Transition from Stage II to Stage III

The loss of one member and the addition of two new members occurred. The members solidified into a well-functioning group. Mutual analysis continued at a high, constructive level. Angry feelings related to group reality issues were more freely ventilated. The theme of projected hostility was recognized: "If we are angry at him, he should be angry with us." An inability to trust the therapist and a fear of the therapist's disapproval was voiced. Group anxiety fluctuated with group reality issues.

Meetings 50–60, Stage III

The problems associated with getting close to other members and the therapist was the general theme during this period. Competition from the therapist as well as resentment and distrust of him and other authority figures (parents) were brought out by the members. Mutual analysis continued at a constructive level. Various mechanisms of defense were identified. Getting angry to prevent closeness and the use of laughter, silence, overtalkativeness, intellectualization, and denial by members in the group were identified as means of avoiding tenseness and anxiety in the group situation. The relationship of anger and guilt to depression was discussed. The initial disclosure of sexual feelings occurred. Group anxiety continued to fluctuate, depending on reality issues within the group.

Meetings 60–70, Stage III

The central theme of the meetings during this period was termination of the group. Three members were lost from the group. Holt and Cain stopped coming to meetings after the termination date was announced by the therapist. Boler died from organic causes on the day of the 69th meeting. Feelings expressed as being related to separation were initially depression, then anger, followed by numerous expressions of positive feelings for group therapy. Ambivalent reactions were expressed regarding the end of the group. Sexual feelings within the group received more attention and analysis. The members verbalized their fears that increasing closeness would excite homosexual and heterosexual feelings. An assessment of the gains made during the life of the group was made. Previous reactions to group reality issues were seen as a major gain by the members, particularly in their relationship to the therapist as an authority figure. The awareness that they (the group members) continued to have problems and that also other people have problems pointed out the need to be objective and understanding in future interpersonal relationships.

The death of Boler, although a severe shock to the group, was not a disruptive force. The initial group depression was followed by a realistic appraisal of his death as related to the group.

The final meeting (70th) was characterized by increased group anxiety. Individual psychodynamics revealed that Smith and Miss French had worked through separation anxiety. Mrs. Kitch, exhibiting more emotional feeling than at any previous time in the group, reacted with anger and defiance to the therapist but denied the presence of these feelings. Similarly, Foy, threatened by his loss of dependency from the group and the therapist, made his standard plea for help, for a magical solution, and denied any improvement in any respect.

A GENERAL SUMMARY OF THE GROUP

There are a number of features about this particular group that are worthy of additional comment. In general, the therapeutic results with this group were consistent with the average results obtained in group therapy. However, several problems (recorder, fees, length of meetings, duration of group therapy and selection of group members) were present which, could they have been avoided, would probably have improved the group. These were group reality events, and as such were closely related to the dynamics of group therapy. Over the course of any group therapy program reality events will, at times, occur that will affect the entire group. However, careful planning of the group contract prior to the outset of group therapy will help to curtail such problems.

The majority of these problems were not severe and did not disrupt the group. In fact, the group contract made it possible for these problems to be clarified with the members. Good group therapy is dependent on a group contract that integrates the physical factors and arrangements of group therapy into the dynamics of the group process. The value and importance of the group contract is clearly illustrated by the following aspects of this group.

The therapist would have been wise to have started group therapy with a recorder who could have remained with the group throughout its entirety. Of course, there are always reality factors that interfere and cannot be determined at the time group therapy begins. However, the therapist should carefully consider obtaining a recorder who can remain with the group from its start to its finish.

Group-therapy fees should have been handled differently in this group. The group therapist's initial policy regarding fees was lax. Even though the fees for each group meeting were very reasonable ($1 to $3), difficulties were encountered with the group members. They tended to let their accounts ride, and so did the group therapist. The lesson to be learned here is that group members pay their fees proportional to the attitude of the group therapist about fees. He should be very firm. Bills should be sent out monthly. Failure to pay fees should be brought to the attention of the group within 15 days. Reality hardships encountered by group members should be treated flexibly, but group members who do not pay their bills within a reasonable period of time should be dropped from the group. These arrangements about fees should be clarified with each member before the onset of group therapy and become a part of the group contract. There should be a clear understanding at the beginning of group therapy that the therapist will not retain members in the group who do not pay their fees.

There was another aspect about fees in this group that should have been handled differently. The therapist only charged the weekly fee to those group members who attended the meeting. In group therapy the therapist's and the recorder's time and the physical conditions (room, lights, seating arrangements) remain the same regardless of whether one member or all members attend. Group-therapy fees are less than fees for individual therapy and are usually based on total attendance of the group members. Therefore, group members should be charged for meetings even if they are absent. For reality factors, such as prolonged physical illnesses that require a series of absences, the payment of fees might be adjusted by the therapist. In fact, the group itself should be made aware of reality situations that affect group members. Their advice is usually in line with group policies. Group members with exaggerated dependency needs are looking for a magical solution to their problems. They want the therapist to care for them completely. A frequent desire is for free treatment from the therapist. They may plead or complain about fees in an effort to make the therapist feel guilty. If the therapist will clarify all features of fees with the group members prior to beginning group therapy and remain firm during the early months of group therapy, problems about fees will not be worrisome. In the final analysis the manner in which group members handle fees of group therapy is a reflection of the group therapist's attitude about fees.

The group therapist became aware during the first year of the group that meetings of one hour length were too short. The therapist also realized that one year of group therapy was insufficient. The group would have profited if the original group contract had specified meetings of $1\frac{1}{2}$ hours and the length of group therapy 18 months. The author feels that neurotic groups should be of a minimum length of 18 months when meetings are held on a once a week basis.

The results obtained at the end of group therapy suggest that the therapist should have been more careful in the selection of group members for group therapy. Three members of this group (Cain, Holt and Boler) were addicted to alcohol and drugs. Throughout group therapy all three of the group members had recurrent addiction problems. Cain was in prison several months. He returned to the group for only a few meetings before he was rehospitalized in an alcoholic treatment center. Holt attended group meetings quite regularly even though several episodes of alcoholism occurred. He was not, however, able to become involved in the dynamics of the group process. He became angry and quit the group when termination of group therapy was announced. Boler had repeated problems with drug and alcohol addiction during the time he was in the group. Hospitalization was necessary on several occasions. Drugs may have been an indirect factor in his death.

Patients with drug and alcohol addictions do not seem to be able to tolerate the anxiety of this model of group therapy. These people notoriously react to anxiety and tension by securing drugs or alcohol. Probably another type of group therapy or group activity that is less anxiety-provoking should be considered for these patients.

Two events occurred in this group that do not ordinarily take place in the average group: the malignant brain tumor of Darcy and the death of Boler.

Mr. Darcy's illness points out the need for group therapists to require a thorough physical examination of group members prior to the outset of group therapy and at regular intervals (yearly) during group therapy. In this instance Darcy was examined by an internist a few weeks before beginning group therapy. No physical disease was found. Emotional problems had been present for a number of years. No doubt the emotional component of his illness was influenced by the brain tumor.

Boler's death was significant in that the group members discussed many feelings about death that differs sharply from the general eulogizing that occurs at the usual funeral.

The group was composed of ten members—eight original members and two replacement members. At the end of group therapy four of the members had shown improvement. Two members were lost from the group because of organic disease and four members dropped out of the group for causes felt to be psychological in origin. Here again the three group members with alcohol and drug problems played a major role in the percentage of group losses or unimproved cases. Group losses or drop-outs are a constant problem in all models of group therapy. Estimates of group losses average 40 per cent of the original membership. Excluding the two members (Darcy and Boler) the losses from this group fall within the range of average group losses.

The improvement made by four group members (Miss French, Mrs. Kitch, Smith and Foy) has been discussed in individual summaries. Several observations can be made. Foy should have had additional therapy. Evaluation at the end of group therapy and at the one-year follow-up indicates the need for long-term treatment if he is to receive any lasting benefit. Group therapy for Mrs. Foy also would enhance the chances of successful treatment. The difficulties and stress encountered by Mrs. Kitch with her husband point out the influence of family members on any form of psychotherapy. Mr. Kitch is a chronic, paranoid schizophrenic who has suffered from repeated job losses, financial stress, etc. There are three small children. Mrs. Kitch seems to move from one crisis to another. Additional therapy for both Mrs. Kitch and her husband is definitely indicated.

The two patients with the diagnosis of schizophrenic reaction (Miss French and Smith) were the most perceptive members of the group. They made greater gains from group therapy than the other members. Their involvement in the dynamics of the group process was very evident. At the end of group therapy and at one-year follow-up interviews continued progress was reported. Their improvement emphasizes that group therapy can be an excellent type of treatment for people with schizophrenia. This is particularly true for the ambulatory schizophrenic who has not suffered psychotic or episodic psychotic attacks.

This group was made up of members who fall mainly in the lower and middle class of society. Group members selected from upper and middle-class cultured levels generally have higher intellectual and motivational levels. Training groups, which are usually composed of professional personnel, have very high intellectual and motivational levels. In such groups with superior intellectual and motivational levels the gains from group therapy will be greater and group losses will be less. However, the fact remains that the majority of people with emotional illnesses fall in the lower and middle classes of our society. For this reason most group-therapy patients will come from this large segment of the population.

The results of this group point out that group therapy is not a panacea for people with emotional illnesses. Deep-seated conflicts are not resolved. Characterological structures are not modified. However, for four members of the group changes occurred over the length of group therapy that resulted in improved reality testing, increased socialization and increasing awareness of the effects of anxiety in their interpersonal relationships. Improvement in self-assertion, self-confidence and self-esteem was evident. Release of repressed anger and the recognition of the origin of hostility to authority figures occurred. Changes in the conscience led to more freedom in group relationships and less reactions of guilt. The relationship of sexual feelings to closeness was identified. The emotional reactions to group reality events and separation were recognized and understood.

It may be that other members of the group who cannot be classified as improved at this time have a better awareness of their emotional difficulties and will take advantage of future opportunities for psychotherapy. One of the other improved members of this group, Mrs. Kitch, asked for additional group therapy at the one-year follow-up interview, and still another member, Mrs. Jacobs, who was considered unimproved when she stopped group therapy after approximately one year, has improved and is much more aware of the emotional component of her illness.

Finally, a discussion of this group would not be complete without an assessment of the working relationship between the therapist and the recorder, an assessment of their own feelings about the group members during therapy.

In this group the therapist was fortunate in having two recorders who were psychologically sophisticated. Reality events made it necessary for the original recorder to relinquish her role 4½ months before the group ended. A second recorder was used for the remainder of the meetings. At weekly therapist-recorder discussions the recorders would constructively criticize the therapist's technique and behavior in group meetings. Both recorders were fond of group therapy, of the therapist, and of this group. The working relationship between the therapist and each recorder was one of mutual respect and understanding. The recorder's mood and demeanor were often a reflection of group function—joy and pleasure when the group was working well, an individual member improving, or the group attendance good; or concern and depression when the group moved slowly, when there was poor attendance, when the group encountered reality-event difficulties, or when there was loss of a group member. Both recorders tended to identify with the members during those periods when reality events created group anxiety—i.e., cancelled meetings or therapist's vacations. At the end of group therapy the recorder asked several times for an extension of the group.

The therapist's feelings about the group members can be assessed from a series of factors: his interest in group therapy, attendance at meetings, contacts with absent members, increasing the length of the group meetings or length of group therapy, the plans he helped make for members near the end of group therapy, and the interest he showed in the welfare of the members in the postgroup therapy period. During the course of group therapy, a general idea can be obtained of the therapist's feelings for the individual members from a survey of the weekly therapist-recorder discussions and group supervisory conferences. At the outset of group therapy the therapist's feelings about the individual members were generally similar. He displayed optimism about the group, stating on several occasions, "This should be a good group to work with."

During the first 25 meetings the therapist made several comments to the recorder that indicated positive comments about Miss French, Mrs. Kitch, Foy, Mrs. Jacobs and Holt. The recorder noted the therapist was anxious at times when there were group issues involving Holt.

From the 25th to the 50th meeting the recorder felt that the therapist had reservations about Foy and Cain. The therapist was very fond of Smith and Boler, both of whom joined the group at the 42nd meeting. On several occasions during therapist-recorder discussions the therapist made slips of the tongue and referred to these two members by their first names. He was much more disappointed over Mrs. Jacobs' loss from the group than over the other losses—Mrs. Webster and Cain. An unconscious conflict between the therapist and Holt became more apparent. The recorder remarked to the therapist on several occasions that he was anxious and hostile to Holt. The recorder also recognized that the therapist consciously liked Holt. The recorder felt that the therapist modified his behavior with Holt in later meetings; however, she wasn't sure the therapist resolved his unconscious hostility to Holt.

During the last 20 meetings of the group the therapist often spoke warmly of Smith, Boler, Holt, Miss French, and Mrs. Kitch. However, he spoke most often of Smith, Boler and Miss French. The therapist was dubious of Cain's return to the group and prophesied that his alcoholism would recur. The therapist became irritated with Foy for his failure to pay a very reasonable fee ($1 per meeting) for group therapy. However, the therapist did recognize his own failure in not being assertive and directive with Foy about fees. The new recorder also recognized the therapist's anxiety and unconscious hostility to Holt. This issue was never resolved and may have played a part in Holt's rejection of the group after the therapist announced the termination date.

The therapist's technique and the manner in which termination of the group was generally handled is subject to debate. This period was marred by the unexpected death of Boler, which was a depressing event for the therapist, recorder, and members. At the final meeting the therapist and recorder shared with the members in a going-away party.

An idea of what the group identity or group atmosphere meant to the therapist and recorder came in their frequent comments to each other during the latter part of therapy about the group as a unit rather than specific individuals in the group. The group atmosphere was quite apparent to the therapist and recorder as well as the group members.

We have made reference in Chap. 4 to the effect of the therapist's feelings for patients, and the influence of his feelings on the patient's progress in therapy. In this group the positive feelings of the therapist and the recorder for most of the members, and for the group itself, were very apparent. However, the therapist's unconscious conflict with one member, Holt, cannot be dismissed lightly. We are not able to draw any definite conclusions other than to speculate that this unresolved conflict may have played a part in Holt's withdrawal from the group. Many patients are just as fearful of warm and tender feelings as they are of hostile feelings. Possibly a therapist who exhibits positive feelings to such a patient may frighten him to such a degree that he leaves treatment. Then, too, a therapist may be consciously or unconsciously hostile in his responses, and, accordingly, influence the members' reactions to group therapy. Thus there are many unanswered questions in this particular area of the therapist's feelings about patients. Generally speaking, a group of patients profit from the therapist's and recorder's interest, acceptance, and respect as exemplified in this group.

REFERENCES

1. Rado, Sandor: *Psychoanalysis of Behavior*, Grune & Stratton, Inc., New York, 1956, p. 354.
2. Kardiner, Abram: *The Individual and His Society*, Columbia University Press, New York, 1955, pp. 319–320.
3. Ovesey, Lionel: "The Homosexual Conflict," *Psychiatry*, 17:215–243, 1954.
4. Sommers, Vita Stein: "An Experiment in Group Psychotherapy with Members of Mixed Minority Groups," *Internat. J. Group Psychotherapy*, 3: 254–269, 1953.
5. Mullan, Hugh, and Max Rosenbaum: *Group Psychotherapy*, The Free Press of Glencoe, New York, 1962.
6. Locke, Norman: *Group Psychoanalysis*, New York University Press, New York, 1961.
7. Spotnitz, Hyman: *The Couch and the Circle*, Alfred A. Knopf, Inc., New York, 1961.

8

Group Therapy in Schizophrenia, Manic Depressive and Chronic Psychotic Depressive Reactions

Group therapy has become a helpful adjunct in the treatment program for people who fall into the diagnostic categories of schizophrenia, manic-depressive psychosis, and chronic psychotic depressive reactions. No effort will be made to delineate the illnesses of these patients into clear-cut entities. Such factors as regionalism and the orientation of the psychiatrist strongly influence diagnosis. For example, in the southern part of the United States the diagnosis of manic-depressive psychosis is made more frequently than in the North or Northeast. Many chronic depressive states may be labeled chronic schizophrenic reactions, again depending on the location and orientation of the psychiatrist. Other types of patients with psychoses such as involutional psychotic reactions and psychotic reactions of obscure etiology are included in this grouping. Regardless of the diagnostic label used, people who fall into these diagnostic categories exhibit certain fundamental characteristics related to their psychodynamics that influence the treatment program in group therapy.

CLASSIFICATION OF PATIENTS FOR GROUP THERAPY

For purposes of simplicity, the diagnostic categories have been divided into two general types. They are classified in this manner so as to clarify the goals of treatment, the structure of the group, and the technique of the group therapist. Type I includes ambulatory patients who have not experienced recurrent, overt psychoses with regressive behavior, hallucinations, and delusions. Many are in adequate reality contact but encounter conflicts in one or more areas of their behavior. Difficulties in interpersonal relationships are usually present. Perceptual difficulties, withdrawal, autism, suspiciousness, various other aspects of paranoid behavior, sexual conflicts, depression, hypomania, inappropriate affect, disturbed thought processes, ambivalence, periods of confusion, hyperactivity, and aggressive outbursts may occur in varying degrees. Very often schizoid personality traits are present—in fact, many psychiatrists feel that most of these people are basically schizophrenic. Their defenses against anxieties being at times quite rigid, environmental stress may often see a breakthrough of unconscious material that increases their difficulties in relationships with other people.

Patients who are classified in type I can be treated in the same way as neurotic patients and they function well in outpatient groups of neurotic patients. The reader is referred to Chap. 4.

Type II includes those patients with severe ego psychopathology resulting in chronic psychotic and episodic behavior. Their marginal adaptive capabilities usually result in prolonged hospitalization, frequent readmissions, or immobilization at home. Their anxiety tolerance is very tenuous. There may be varying degrees of psychotic behavior with loose and distorted thought associations, confusion, difficulties in concentration and perception, delusions, hallucinations, and bizarre, irrational behavior. Either depressed or manic behavior may be present. Regardless of the clinical picture put forward, there is severe ego psychopathology present which poses certain problems in their management in group therapy.

GROUP ANXIETY IN PSYCHOTIC PATIENTS

There are no essential differences in the group dynamics of patients with severe ego psychopathology and patients with neurosis. What is present, though, is a different degree of anxiety that is more massive, threatening, and frightening in content than in other types of emotional disorders. It is most important to understand what the psychotic patient feels and experiences. Feelings that are unconscious in the neurotic patient may be in conscious awareness in the psychotic patient. For example, the passive, nonassertive person who has a neurotic depression is fearful of authority figures and reacts to them with ingratiation, denial, and fear. He maintains this role as a defense against unconscious (rage) impulses and the subsequent expectation of retaliation from others. His passive, nonassertive personality assures him he will not express his rage and thus he avoids the fear of retaliation that would be aroused. The patient with a psychosis may experience these feelings of rage and the subsequent expectation of retaliation from others in conscious awareness. The patient's defensive behavior patterns that held these unconscious impulses in check have disintegrated. The unconscious impulses have bubbled over into consciousness. The psychotic patient's feelings of massive rage, guilt for the rage and fear of retaliation from others accounts for much of his anxiety in group relationships. Homosexual impulses may be extremely uncomfortable and a strong need for control has to be exerted. A guilt-ridden conscience usually plagues the psychotic patient. He is extremely sensitive to the feelings of others and exhibits labile emotions, shifting very rapidly from one extreme to another. He fears relationships with others. He cannot trust them and his sensitive feelings misinterpret any number of minor nuances to mean rejection and separation. There is an acute and overwhelming need for dependency, love, security, and help.

When these people are brought together for group therapy, anxiety occurs very quickly. There is more silence, withdrawal, depression, over-talkativeness, competition, tardiness, and absenteeism than in outpatient groups of neurotic patients. The particular response to anxiety by each person will reflect his psychodynamics and his habitual patterns of behavior. During group therapy the psychotic patient's defense mechanisms or defensive behavior patterns may or may not be sufficiently reestablished or reintegrated to withstand the anxiety that occurs in group meetings. Thus there is always the possibility that increased anxiety during group therapy may precipitate overt psychotic behavior. Patterns of behavior vary. Some defenses may remain intact, others may give way. There may be a transient state of psychotic behavior which lasts only minutes or hours and clears up when the patient's anxiety has diminished. The psychotic process may also continue day after day, week after week, or month after month. Again, at this point, we would like to reemphasize that regardless of the diagnosis or the behavior picture presented, anxiety and its manifestations are the crux of the illness.

MODIFICATIONS OF THE GROUP CONTRACT

Except for certain modifications, the framework of group therapy set forth in Chap. 4 is recommended for patients in type II. The group contract embraces 12 sections: (1) Purpose of group therapy, (2) composition of the group, (3) role of the group therapist, (4) recorder, substitute recorder, and mechanical reproduction of meetings, (5) physical arrangements, (6) period of group therapy, (7) loss and addition of members, (8) attendance of members, (9) fees, (10) drugs, physical illnesses, hospitalization and other therapies, (11) conversations, telephone calls, personal contacts and meetings by group members outside of the regular structured group therapy session, and (12) modifications of the group contract.

Due to the nature of the illness of patients whom we have classified in type II, certain suggestions and modifications of the contract are deemed advisable. Chapter 4 should be consulted as the key to the group-therapy structure and applies *in toto* to severely ill patients (type II) except as modified below.

Purpose of Group Therapy

It is imperative to understand that we are now dealing with people who have shattered ego structures, poor reality testing, perceptual difficulties, disintegrated defensive patterns of behavior, and intense anxiety arising from their feelings of fear, rage, and guilt. Therefore, any form of treatment should be directed toward strengthening the ego structure, improving reality testing, and reintegrating the defensive patterns of behavior. When patients of this type are brought together into the atmosphere of a group, a forum is provided to increase socialization. Being together in group therapy provides new identifications with peers and with the group therapist. Finding other people with similar feelings and problems diminishes one's own feelings of isolation, encourages the ventilation of material, and promotes a spirit of mutual cooperation in attempting to solve one's problems. Extremely important is the interest and acceptance from the group therapist and members of the group. Probably in no other form of therapy is the human interest, acceptance, and devotion of the therapist more significant than with a group of severely ill, psychotic people. The dilution of transference feelings among a group of people, as compared to the one-to-one relationship of the patient in individual therapy, diminishes some of their anxiety and promotes interaction in the group.

Group therapy can provide a series of ameliorative procedures for such people, the effects of which may be minimal in some cases, moderate in others, and dramatic in a few. Generally speaking, group therapy has limited goals and does not always have a high percentage of recoveries. Group therapy has accomplished a tremendous amount for the individual whenever it can bring about: (1) increased repression, (2) new, positive identifications, (3) sociability, (4) expiation of guilt, (5) strengthening of old defenses and addition of new defenses, and (6) lessening of inner tensions. Just the awareness of difficulties encountered in interpersonal relationships may help the patients in their own problems. Group therapy may provide benefit and help in the following ways:

1. Resolution of psychoses and the prevention of future episodic psychotic attacks.

2. Support within the hospital with other patients and the staff.

3. Support within the home, family, and other areas (social and occupational).

4. Relief of inner tension and guilt feelings.

5. Provision of a forum (group) whereby reality issues and problems in interpersonal relationships can be aired with other people and the group therapist.

6. Encouragement for patients to leave the hospital, and a security

valve between the hospital and outside world after discharge from the hospital.

7. Service as a dependency measure whereby the patient can feel secure, accepted, and understood by others in the group and the therapist.

8. Possible point toward the way to additional psychotherapy either in a group or on an individual basis through the development of psychologic aptitude and insight.

Composition of the Group

No modifications of the group contract are recommended for the age and intelligence quota of patients or the size of the group. However, special consideration is necessary regarding the sex of the group members and the types of group therapy.

Sex of Groups. Segregation of the sexes in hospitals naturally results in groups of the same sex. In general, type II patients, regardless of the physical setting, function better when the groups are segregated by sex. The anxiety created in mixed groups reaches levels too high for satisfactory group therapy.

Types of Groups. A wide variety of group programs that include both group therapy and therapeutic group activities can be utilized in the hospital setting. All are helpful to some degree from a standpoint of the current hospital admission of the patient. Ward meetings are particularly valuable. Some short-term group therapy patients are members of a group only during their hospital stay. These groups are open-ended and add new members as others leave the hospital. Group therapy is also being utilized with patients who have lengthy periods of hospitalization in the "back" wards of state hospitals. One of the most successful forms of group therapy is the inpatient-outpatient model. The group membership remains stable whether the patient is on inpatient or outpatient status. New members are added only by the loss of regular members. Many state and private institutions are now located sufficiently close to the homes of patients so that weekly group meetings can be attended without undue hardship. The group is originally formed from recently admitted hospital patients. After a patient's discharge from the hospital, arrangements are made for the patient to return weekly for group therapy. Psychiatrists in private practice find this method of treatment very rewarding for the severely psychotic patient who needs support and guidance after leaving the hospital. At the time of discharge, the hospitalized patient is often apprehensive or terrified of the world outside. He fears that he will be rejected or stigmatized. The group provides a place where these feelings can be ventilated, and thus forms a beneficial bond between the hospital and the world of reality.

Indications and Contraindications of Type II Patients for Group Therapy. Patients should not be placed in groups during the acute psychotic manifestations of their illness. Hallucinations, delusions and other manifestations of acute psychotic behavior should have subsided before the patient is placed in group therapy.

Episodic attacks of psychotic behavior often occur during group therapy with type II patients. The sick group member should be encouraged to attend group meetings if reality factors (hospitalization) do not interfere. The author does not feel that an acutely ill group member should be dropped from the group during the period of the illness. However, hospitalization and other therapies take precedence in the treatment and should be arranged immediately by the group therapist. For example, a patient who becomes depressed and suicidal should be hospitalized immediately and treated for the depression. The patient can return to the group when the depression has lifted.

Probably the most difficult patient to handle in group therapy is the paranoid schizophrenic whose delusional system is fixed and rigid. Once these patients become involved in the group process their paranoid projections within the group are quite disturbing and disrupting to the other members. Group therapy is often of little benefit to the paranoid schizophrenic himself. However, the patient whose paranoid behavior is acute, recent, and not characterized by rigid and fixed delusions can be treated more successfully in group therapy. In most cases this type of illness is not a paranoid schizophrenic reaction. The patient merely shows paranoid behavior during the period of the acute psychosis.

The intelligent, shrewd, and manipulative paranoid schizophrenic patient who has been committed to a state institution may take advantage of group therapy programs and others in order to ingratiate himself with staff personnel. He develops "hospital insight" into all of his problems, admits his difficulties prior to hospital commitment, and then professes that he is well. In group therapy he enters into the meetings with vigor and leaves the impression that he is actively involved in treatment. Actually the patient's illness has not changed since he entered the hospital. This type of paranoid schizophrenic patient uses every manipulating measure within his repertory to gain his discharge from the hospital. Once he is successful, group therapy or any other form of therapy is cast aside.

Hyperactive, manic patients can also create problems but can be treated in group therapy in the hospital setting. Their behavior, though difficult and trying for the group members and the group therapist, can be controlled successfully in some cases. This type of patient is discussed in detail in the present chapter.

Generally, group therapy with chronic schizophrenic patients who have been hospitalized from 3 to 5 five years or longer has not been very successful. The anxiety level of the group members has constituted a major problem. These patients move extremely slowly in a group and the therapist's attempts to promote group activity are usually too anxiety-provoking. Often the therapist cannot cope with the massive silence and inactivity of the group members when it continues week after week. Loose associations and bizarre verbal productions also frequently occur. An example of this type of problem took place in a group of chronic psychotic women with an average hospitalization of 6 years. The group met once a week for a period of one hour. At the 18th meeting the therapist was having recurrent attendance problems. He had personally to go to the wards and bring the patients to the group therapy room. Five of the patients were silent and withdrawn, never participating in any group discussion. One patient spoke in a guttural tongue that was not understandable. Two patients were quite verbal and for a number of meetings were the only participants. Attempts to deal with the silent members or with the overtalkativeness of two members were mostly fruitless. The group therapist was interested in his group but felt that his progress was nil. One reason for his concern may have been related to group supervision of his group and the groups of neurotic patients that were being managed by other residents. The groups of neurotic patients were more verbal and their group therapists were interested and excited. The dynamics of the group moved at a faster pace. The resident who was working with the group of psychotic patients felt competitive and jealous, and expressed the desire to work with a group that created more interest. It would probably be advisable for a group therapist to have prior experience treating outpatient groups of neurotic patients before he attempts group therapy with chronic psychotic patients who have been hospitalized over long periods. Groups of psychotic patients have been successfully treated by therapists who had had previous training in group therapy and who were experienced in this particular type of therapy.

Of great importance in determining the indications and contraindications of patients for group therapy, particularly for severely psychotic (type II) patients, is the interest and enthusiasm of the group therapist in wanting to help his patients. The group therapist's attitude that he wants to help the group members; that he is personally interested in their welfare; that he will accept them as they are; that he will meet with them week after week and month after month, provides extra benefits that cut across diagnostic categories. Probably these factors account for such dramatic improvements in some cases of severely psychotic patients. Regardless of the type of therapy, the therapist's relationship to his patients is a most important tool in the psychotherapeutic process.

Loss and Addition of Members. The same problems in group losses occur with severely psychotic patients as with neurotic patients. Attention is again called to fact that the anxiety of the group process can contribute to increased absenteeism and losses from groups of this type. Similar problems also occur when new members are added to a group. Chapter 4 should be consulted for more detailed information.

Role of the Group Therapist

The requirements and qualifications of the group therapist have been discussed in detail in Chap. 4. For psychotic patients, an additional recommendation is suggested: a group therapist should not attempt group therapy with severely psychotic (type II) patients until he has had adequate training and supervision with a group of neurotic patients. An awareness of group dynamics both from the standpoint of the group members and of his own role will greatly facilitate the group therapist's transition from groups of neurotic patients to groups of psychotic patients.

Anxiety Tolerance. We have pointed out previously that anxiety takes a different form in groups of psychotic patients. Their tolerance for anxiety is minimal. Loose associations and disturbed thought processes are more prevalent. At times there may be bizarre and irrational behavior. Patients are prone to use metaphors and symbolic language in their verbal productions. Distortions of statements made by the therapist as well as by other group members frequently occur. Fears of closeness within the group are extremely intense and anxiety-provoking. Transference feelings develop very quickly, the ambivalent, highly charged identification with the aggressor (therapist) weighing heavily on the negative side. Extreme sensitivity to the feelings and reactions of others in the group, particularly the therapist, is evident. One might imagine these people as having a highly developed radar that can detect the unconscious feelings of other people. For an undetermined period of time in group therapy—perhaps months—they discuss reality situations of the hospital, home, social activities, and occupational roles of the present and past years. Conflicts and problems with parents, brothers and sisters, authority figures and peers are discussed. Their dependency strivings are extremely strong. They need love, security, support and help from the group, and the therapist tends to delay an examination of their feelings within the group for an indefinite period of time.

Group Approach. The various factors discussed in the preceding pages of this chapter about type II patients—severe ego psychopathology, minimum tolerance for anxiety and goals of the therapist—necessitate modification of the therapist's technique for groups of type II patients. The remainder of this section illustrates many of the common problems in technique that confront the therapist in groups of psychotic patients. The therapist should be aware that the basic principles for groups of neurotic patients are generally applicable to groups of psychotic patients. These are an accurate assessment of the anxiety level of the group members, an awareness of the theme of the group meeting, and the maintenance of control of the group meeting.

Symbolic and Metaphorical Communication. From the onset of group therapy the therapist should be more liberal, supporting, and giving to the group members. He allows the group members more freedom in discussing issues not particularly relevant to the group at the moment. Actually their conversations do concern the group interaction but they are couched in symbolic and metaphorical terms relating to past figures in their lives. They may express hostility in terms of general complaints about a hospital, its food and staff, families, peers, bosses, etc. For example, a group of hospitalized schizophrenic patients utilized a number of meetings to talk about dominating, cruel, and angry parents. The group therapist allowed them free rein in this ventilation of feelings, well aware that symbolically he (the therapist) was the dominating and cruel figure who was bringing them together week after week at the group meeting. In the early months of group therapy the therapist does not make every issue a group issue. He may make attempts to explore intragroup relationships and proceeds according to the anxiety created within the group members. Generally speaking, when the therapist asks about the relationships within the group, increased anxiety occurs.

The therapist should be able to recognize the symbolic and metaphorical productions of the group members. By reading between the lines he can recognize the theme of the meeting and so control his group. This form of communication may go on for many months. Actually it is a necessary and safe means of expressing hostility to the group therapist. There is no threat to the members of looking at their own feeling with fantasied possibilities of retaliation, rejection and loss of dependency. The following example illustrates how a group dealt symbolically with a reality issue. The group was composed of psychotic and postpsychotic women. Meetings were held weekly for 1½ hours. At the 40th meeting the session began with hostility being expressed toward husbands who (1) took vacations, (2) frequently stay away from home, and (3) neglect wives. The therapist had cancelled the immediately preceding meeting. He recognized the theme of the meeting. At an appropriate time he referred to the prior cancellation of the group meeting and asked for their feelings of the doctor taking a vacation from therapy. There was immediate denial by the members, followed by ingratiating statements of his need to be away from the office.

The group therapist refocused on their denial only to see an increase in the anxiety level of the group. His remarks at supervision were: "They seem to be tangential and never get the point." In all possibility the group members "got the point," but fear of the transference prevented them from dealing with their relationships to the group therapist.

Another example of the use of symbolic language occurred in the fourth meeting of an inpatient-outpatient male group of psychotic patients. The meeting began with statements of opposition to the regimentation of the hospital. Locked doors, lack of freedom, and orders to attend activities were discussed. The subject shifted to difficulties in talking before other people. Several members mentioned that problems could not be discussed in front of a lady (the recorder). The next two subjects discussed were dancing and playing bridge. Mental illness, insanity, and the definition of psychotic terms (depression, manic depressive reaction, and paranoia) were talked about. The effect of depression and problems of talking before others when depressed were verbalized by two group members. The theme of the meeting concerned their regimentation in the group and the requirement of talking to each other. The group therapist was making them come closer to each other. Dancing and bridge playing also means closeness between people. There is the fear of being tagged with insanity or mental illness if their true feelings are expressed in the group. Thus this meeting centered around their feelings of group therapy and the hazards involved in relating to the others and the group therapist. Symbolic terms were used to express these feelings.

Symbolic language is illustrated in the 8th meeting of a group of psychotic patients. The 5th, 6th, and 7th meetings of a group of chronic schizophrenic patients were characterized by repeated silences and other manifestations of anxiety. The recurrent theme involved difficulties in talking before people. At the 8th meeting of this group the therapist asked about their difficulties in talking during the meeting. The members immediately began to complain about the recorder and their inability to talk in the woman's presence. The therapist asked again about their difficulties within the group. At this point two patients began to discuss problems with their ward physicians. Loss of confidence and numerous fears related to other men were discussed. Men were spoken of as being rough and crude. The therapist asked about their feelings regarding confidence and fears. One patient spoke of a fear that his arm and leg would be amputated, as well as a fear of going blind. Another patient spoke of being placed in a lion's cage. The theme of this meeting related to the "here and now" of the group. Hostility to the group therapist was displaced to the recorder and to other doctors. For these patients talking in the group is somehow associated with violence; they seem to picture themselves as caged animals under the control of a "keeper" who may cause them physical impairment if they do not "behave."

A recurrent theme related to religious feelings has been noted in meetings with psychotic patients. Often when hostility has been expressed to family figures or even in a very subtle manner to the hospital and its staff, the subject will change to religious values—God or the Bible. Their feelings of guilt for expressing hostility appear to be rectified by shifting to a religious subject. Symbolically, God can also be equated with a parent and the therapist.

On several occasions when new members have been added to groups of psychotic patients the subject of the integration of the races comes up. The patients were from the South where integration problems have recurred for the past several years. The subject seems to come up in groups, though, when a new member is added. In a symbolic way they are telling the group therapist of the anxiety created by bringing in a new person—integrating a new individual into the group.

Interpersonal Relationships. Current reality issues that patients face within the hospital with other patients and the staff, at home with relatives, and at work with associates, bring out into the open their difficulties in interpersonal relationships. As these matters are discussed within the group, other patients speak of encountering similar difficulties. Constructive advice and mutual analysis are often given by other members of the group. The therapist should explore reality difficulties with the patients by reflecting to the group pertinent comments and observations about the reality conflicts his group members are experiencing. He does not necessarily focus on the group interaction at this time. The following group meeting illustrates the proper technique. At the 9th meeting of a male, inpatient-outpatient hospital group of psychotic and postpsychotic schizophrenic patients, the content of the meeting concerned conflicts and difficulties with wives. Wives were said to be controlling, dominating, and lacking in understanding. The group therapist asked the group members about such behavior and its relationship to their illnesses. He also asked whether difficulties were encountered only with wives. Once he cautiously asked the group about their reaction within the group itself. There was immediate denial with the verbalization of positive feelings, followed by silence and increased anxiety. The therapist detected this increase in anxiety and immediately focused back on their earlier comments about wives.

Avoidance of Individual Therapy. The therapist needs to exert extreme care in handling all issues, questions and observations from a standpoint of the group and not of the individual. The identical technique applies here as with outpatient groups of neurotic patients. Individual therapy within a group of people must be avoided. An example of the feelings group members have about this important aspect of technique occurred in the 52nd meeting of an inpatient-outpatient group of psychotic women, who were discussing the fact that the group therapist did not answer their questions. Several members stated that if the therapist had shown partiality or answered individual rather than group questions, the group would have disintegrated. They admitted irritations during the initial weeks of the group when the therapist did not answer questions, but could see now the importance of working together to help one another.

Scapegoating. A very pressing problem in all group therapy, and particularly in groups composed of patients in type II, is the directing of hostility to one another within the group rather than to the therapist, to whom it is primarily meant. Scapegoating of all forms, from the mild jabs at one another to overt hostility between members, can be a troublesome problem for the therapist. When it does occur, he should use every method at his disposal to clear the hostility away. Acting-out behavior falls in the same category and should be handled in a similar fashion. Here the techniques are identical to those suggested for outpatient groups of neurotic patients.

The Psychotically Depressed Patient. Several forms of illness may occur during the course of therapy that need the immediate attention of the therapist. We refer to the member who goes into a psychotic depressive state with suicidal wishes, the member who loses control of his impulses and becomes overtly aggressive and assaultive, the paranoid schizophrenic, the member who goes into a state of hypomania or manic behavior, and the one who is silent, frightened and withdrawn. A group member with a psychotic depression should be immediately hospitalized and proper treatment instituted. Hospitalization is by far the safest procedure. The patient may or may not be turned over to another psychiatrist. If a transfer is not possible, the therapist has to be responsible for treatment. In any event the treatment of the patient becomes a group issue and should be discussed within the group. Events that may have contributed to the depression should be clarified if at all possible. As soon as permissible the patient should return to the group. Proper planning with the hospital staff will usually get the patient to all meetings of the group unless time and distance interfere.

The Assaultive Patient. The problem of assaultive behavior poses another emergency situation for the group therapist. It is imperative that the therapist exert every effort to keep motor activity within limits, to encourage *talking* about feelings and impulses rather than *acting out*. The group members may have several ideas about this form of behavior. Will the group therapist exert control over the group? Will he prevent us from losing control? Can we count on him to be strong and authoritative in this respect? Does he know that we have identical feelings, and that to see another member become upset makes us fear that we may do the same? The following example illustrates the problem. A group was composed of psychotic and postpsychotic male inpatients and outpatients that met for one hour once a week. Between the 35th and 45th sessions, increasing hostility between the group members was evident. One large, heavy-set male patient became so enraged that he had to leave the session on several occasions. He had been discharged from the hospital but returned during this interval for several weeks. The therapist used every cue possible to work through this hostility. A tranquilizer was prescribed and several individual interviews were held, both being reported to the group. He improved for several sessions and then returned to his former pattern. He was very abusive to two other members. The abuse was primarily verbal in nature, but on one occasion he rose from his chair, clenched his fists, and strode menacingly toward the other two members. He had said they reminded him of "other people." The group therapist got up from his seat, walked over to him and asked him to sit down. The therapist, in exploring this behavior, asked if getting angry was ever due to having angry feelings toward someone other than the one to whom it is expressed. One member talked of getting mad with his father, following which he experienced trouble with his brother. The therapist asked if there was anyone in this particular group who could be playing a similar role. He reviewed the group contract, pointing out their need to look at how they felt toward everyone in the group. Another member suggested that maybe this man was angry with the therapist and was "taking it out" on the other members. The member in question answered that perhaps this was true. In the following ten meetings a closer awareness of their feelings toward the therapist was verbalized. There continued to be moderately severe verbal hostility toward each other. They approached feelings toward the therapist with trepidation and fear. Important, however, was the control of motor activity—which was not a serious problem thereafter.

The Paranoid Schizophrenic Patient. The paranoid schizophrenic patient can, at times, be very disruptive to group meetings. Delusional material expressed to the other members and to the therapist can be attacked by the therapist in several ways. He can focus on the feelings of the paranoid schizophrenic patient by asking the group for their thoughts concerning the way this patient feels during the meetings. Often paranoid schizophrenic patients are filled with low self-esteem and have received insults in this area from reality events that bring about delusional productions. The therapist can ask what the other members think of the statements made by the patient. The other members will usually recognize that the patient is upset and will point out that the delusional material is a manifestation of his illness. In time the members become accustomed to such behavior, and with the active direction of the therapist will work on reality events and group events that influence paranoid outbreaks.

The Hyperactive or Manic Patient. The hyperactive, flighty, and circumstantial person creates a tremendous amount of anxiety within a group. Such a person speaks of feeling fine, acts grandiose, and utilizes denial constantly. He keeps up a continual barrage of words during the meeting, changing the subject at frequent intervals, interrupting other members and the group therapist, and taking over the meeting if given the opportunity. He becomes competitive with the therapist and assumes the role of a substitute leader. There is a theme of hostility in the manic patient's humorous remarks. Many of these remarks are directed to the therapist. Such patients create a tremendous amount of hostility within the group. This defense against anxiety (denial of depression) has its element of origin in the transference and the negative identification to the aggressor. The therapist should recognize the dynamics of the hypomanic or manic patient. From a standpoint of technique he can make several moves. If the behavior cannot be controlled within the group, drugs can be prescribed by either the group therapist or a colleague. In some instances with outpatients, rehospitalization and electroconvulsive treatments are necessary. Within the group the various manifestations of the patient's behavior should be pointed out to the members. If he is competing with the therapist, this fact should be pointed out. If he interrupts everyone and allows no one to talk, the group's opinion and feelings should be sought. There is a large element of rage associated with this condition. When the patient is constantly interrupting the group and the therapist, his rage can be focused on by referring to these interruptions, and asking the group to explore the reasons for his anger. The therapist can also support the patient by asking the group to examine the need and cause of this form of behavior. These measures are not always successful and are very trying as well as anxiety-provoking to the therapist. The therapist may be tempted to get him away from the group immediately and to hospitalize him until the manic state subsides. However, every effort should be made to resolve the situation from a viewpoint of group dynamics before considering other measures.

The following example illustrates the problem encountered with the manic type of patient. A group was composed of psychotic and postpsychotic male patients between the ages of 22 and 48 years. Meetings were held weekly for one hour. The patient in question, Mr. Edwards, was a 45-year-old married male who was admitted to the hospital with a severe depression. He was given eight electroconvulsive treatments prior to becoming a member of the group. During the first 6 months of therapy he remained depressed and withdrawn, utilizing denial at every opportunity. Efforts to draw him into the group were not successful. At the 38th meeting he began to exhibit hypomanic behavior that went rapidly into a manic state. He was flighty, circumstantial, extremely overtalkative, and competitive with everyone. The hostility in the group reached a very high level. Other members would angrily attack him. The therapist focused on every aspect of his behavior and supported him by focusing on his need to behave this way. The members recognized that he was ill and voiced hostility to the therapist for not controlling his behavior. The therapist had prescribed drugs (phenothiazine). A rather large dosage over a period of several weeks was necessary to control him.

The use of drugs was discussed with other members of the group. While Mr. Edwards was in his manic state he ventilated a series of conflicts with his mother, wife, and the group therapist. At times he became quite hostile in his remarks. He leveled off within a few weeks and became more active in the group only to become depressed again. He had been discharged from the hospital but readmission was necessary during this second episode of depression. He followed the depressed episode with a second attack of hypomanic behavior. In this instance he was handled more constructively and understandingly by the group members. This second attack was of much shorter duration than the first. It was interesting that during the second phase the group members attempted to analyze his behavior in terms of reality issues and supported him at every opportunity.

The hypomanic and manic patient is very difficult to treat in group therapy on an outpatient basis because he usually tries to leave the group. During his periods of depression, however, he will often return to the group meetings and exhibit interest in group therapy.

The Silent, Withdrawn Patient. The silent, withdrawn patient is frequently encountered in groups composed of patients with severe psychopathology. Fear and inhibitions cover all areas of group interaction. A patient may go for weeks in the group without communicating verbally to the other members. There is, however, nonverbal communication—and herein lies a significant feature of group therapy for these people: their investment in the group is greatly enhanced by nonverbal communication. They will attend meetings regularly and promptly. Brief verbal statements may be made to other members in response to questions, but spontaneous conversation is usually absent. The therapist should call attention to the silence at every meeting in a supportive manner; he should focus on the silent member at every meeting and explore with the group the reasons for the silence, as well as its effect on the other group members.

At first, other group members become angry at the silent member for failing to carry his load in the group. After a period of time, however, the group members become very supportive to the silent member. Important here is the therapist's technique in pointing out for analysis the meaning and need for silence. Other group members become warm and understanding and gradually encourage the silent member to participate in the group discussions. How long a member remains silent is subject to individual variation. In most instances the initially silent group member begins to participate in group meetings by the second to third month of group therapy. Although rare, some group members may remain relatively silent for three or more months.

Sexual Feelings of Group Members. The discussion of sexual feelings in groups of psychotic patients requires extremely careful management. The intense anxiety experienced by type II patients in the sexual area contributes to the separation of the sexes in these groups. Homosexual and heterosexual fantasies may be quite disturbing and uncomfortable for type II patients. In general, the members will not discuss sexual feelings in group meetings except on a superficial level.

An analysis of four groups of psychotic patients reveals that sexual feelings have been discussed briefly at sporadic periods. In every instance the sexual discussions were very guarded and superficial. The groups averaged 30–35 meetings before sexual feelings were first mentioned. In one group of psychotic women with a male therapist the initial discussion of sexual feelings occurred at the 61st meeting. In another group of psychotic women with a female therapist, three references to sexual feelings had been made in 55 meetings. Here again the content of the sexual discussion was superficial, being verbalized in terms of difficulties with their husbands. A group of psychotic men with a male therapist discussed sexual feelings superficially at the 34th, 49th, and 60th meetings. One member admitted homosexuality. At no time were intragroup sexual feelings mentioned.

Groups composed of psychotic patients require a much longer period of time than groups of neurotic patients before sexual feelings can be talked about. The therapist should avoid the sexual area for at least 30–40 meetings, if not longer. As the members become more comfortable with each other and with the therapist, sexual difficulties in marriage and other day-to-day group relationships will be brought out. The therapist can gauge the difficulties created with sexual material by the anxiety level of the members. If their anxiety becomes very high he can change the subject and steer the group members away from sexual topics. If the members can comfortably discuss sexual conflicts and problems, the therapist should phrase his observations toward day-to-day group relationships and avoid any discussion of sexual feelings within the group. It is possible, but more than likely improbable, that a group of psychotic patients can reach the stage where sexual feelings within the group can be discussed. Groups of several years' duration can approach such problems more comfortably. However, the therapist should be constantly aware of the anxiety existing in the sexual area in psychotic patients. He should observe very strict caution in his technique of handling sexual material in group meetings.

Recorder, Substitute Recorder, and Mechanical Reproduction of Meetings

Three stages of group therapy are described in Chap. 3. Stage I is prolonged for an indefinite period of time with patients in type II. There are several factors involved: the dependency needs of the patient, anxiety created by the transference, intragroup member anxiety, and countertransference feelings of the therapist. From the standpoint of the therapist's role, an understanding of countertransference feelings is most important. These patients are extremely sensitive to the verbal statements and nonverbal attitudes and reactions of the group therapist. As we have emphasized many times, the therapist is by far the most important person in the group. His verbal and nonverbal statements and reactions during group meetings always need careful observation and analysis, and he should be especially attentive in groups of psychotics because of the extraordinary perception of these patients. The services of a recorder or an observer fulfill a most important role in this respect. Therapist-recorder discussions and supervisory conferences assume the same importance as with other types of group therapy. The therapist will be afforded a closer awareness of what is taking place in the group. Absenteeism, group losses, and all the general problems that occur with group members will be curtailed when the therapist utilizes a recorder properly and participates in supervisory or control conferences.

Modifications of the therapist-recorder technique are usually unnecessary. However, the use of tape recorders and the admission of observers or visitors should not be undertaken without full consideration for the anxiety level of the group.

The mechanical reproductions of meetings as well as infrequent visitors (other staff personnel) increase the anxiety level in any group, but particularly so in severely ill people. For this reason many therapists do not allow their sessions to be recorded, nor do they allow visitors. At the outset of group therapy the group contract should include plans to allow changes in the group structure. The need to discuss such events with the group has been stressed in Chap. 4.

Physical Arrangements: Time, Place and Length of Meetings

No modifications are suggested over those previously outlined for groups of neurotic patients. Special attention, however, should be given to the length of meetings. It is not unusual for the therapist treating individual patients to limit the length of the interviews in order to curtail patient anxiety. In groups of this type, one-hour sessions may be advisable at the beginning of group therapy. Group meetings of 1½ hours' duration may be too anxiety-provoking for the patients. Later they can be lengthened to 1½ hours if desired.

Period of Group Therapy

There is no rule of thumb for establishing the period of group therapy. The location of the group therapy program—i.e., intensive treatment sections of state hospitals, chronic wards of state hospitals, private hospitals, outpatient clinics or those for private practice—influences the amount of therapy needed. Some groups are designed for short periods—e.g., the period of actual hospitalization. Other groups may be of several years' duration. Many therapists in private practice and in outpatient clinics employ an open-end group for psychotic patients. These groups do not have specific termination dates. New members are added as others drop out.

The therapist should pay particular attention to cancelled meetings. In groups of psychotic patients, a cancelled meeting early in group therapy may have a disastrous effect on the members (Chap. 4).

Loss and Addition of Members

No modifications to the general program are recommended. A special point about open-end groups of psychotic patients should be emphasized. Since these groups are adding new members as others drop out, the therapist should explore carefully and thoroughly the members' feelings and reactions to the addition of all new group members or the loss of any group member.

Attendance of Members

Here again it should be emphasized that type II patients have much more anxiety, rage, fears, guilt, and dependency needs than the neurotic patient. The type II patient is very fearful of rejection by the therapist and the members, and for this reason may stay away from meetings. The therapist should diligently follow the same procedure suggested in Chap. 4.

Fees

Fees are not usually charged to patients who are hospitalized in state institutions. Outpatient clinics associated with institutions may charge a small fee depending upon the regulation of the clinic. Private practice groups are subject to the same consideration regarding fees as in other groups.

Drugs, Physical Illnesses, Hospitalization and Other Therapies

It is of great importance for the therapist to be outgoing, supportive, and understanding. Drugs must often be prescribed. These patients have to be rehospitalized more frequently than those of other groups. Individual interviews should be granted, but the content of these should be brought to the group meeting. When another therapist is available, the member can be referred to him for the necessary private attention. In this instance there is no need to divulge material to the group. However, whenever the group therapist is involved, all matters involving the members become group material. In the group, the therapist must always be aware that he is doing *group* therapy, not *individual* therapy.

Conversations, Telephone Calls, Personal Contacts and Meetings by Group Members Outside of the Regular Structured Group Therapy Session

The therapist will receive more telephone calls and personal requests from patients classified in type II. At times he may have to offer advice, support, and direction outside the regular group meeting. On other occasions he can refer the request to the group for discussion by asking the member to bring the request to the next meeting. In any event, the material should be brought to the group for discussion.

Modification of the Group Contract

Modification of the group contract should be handled in the same manner as those suggested in Chap. 4.

AN ANALYSIS OF A GROUP OF PSYCHOTIC PATIENTS

An analysis of a state hospital inpatient-outpatient group that met once a week for 16 months (60 meetings) illustrates the rewards as well as the limitations of group therapy. The group was composed of eight male patients, a male group therapist and a male recorder. Those patients who stopped treatment were replaced by others, making a total of 11 patients in the group. The group members were patients on the same ward at the hospital; nine had been committed to the hospital through court procedures and two were admitted by voluntary request. The diagnoses of the members were eight schizophrenic reactions, one chronic alcoholic of 12 years' duration with four previous hospital admissions, one drug and alcohol addiction and on psychotic depression. The age range was 22 to 48 years.

The group contract initially specified weekly sessions of one hour for 18 months. Emphasis was placed on returning to the meetings after discharge or furlough from the hospital. A Vocational Rehabilitation Counselor arranged to pay transportation to and from the hospital for those in need of travel funds. Interestingly, when seven of the eight group members were on an outpatient status, together they traveled over 900 miles per week to and from their homes to attend group meetings. Although no fees were to be charged for group therapy, plans had been made to charge a small fee to those patients on an outpatient status. However, the group therapy program was new in the hospital and no hospital policy had been established about fees. At the tenth month the group contract was modified; the meetings were increased to 1½ hours in duration and the length of group therapy was curtailed 2 months.

The meetings were held in a conference room on the floor of the hospital ward. Attendance was voluntary. Absences from meetings were pursued diligently by the therapist by personal contact, telephone, or letter.

Two members did not return for group therapy after discharge from the hospital. One member, who felt threatened by group relationships, asked to be removed from the group.

A brief synopsis of each member, including two-year follow-ups, is presented below.

Mr. Jackson, a 22-year-old schizophrenic male, received approximately 50 electroconvulsive treatments in a private hospital before he was committed to the state hospital. Repeated parental conflicts and the death of a favorite aunt were felt to be the precipitating stress of the psychosis. He became an active group member and was discharged from the hospital after 6 months of group therapy. He returned to the hospital regularly for group meetings until the end of group therapy. Two-year follow-up reveals that he has left home and entered college. He has been seen infrequently for supportive therapy at his own request. He has requested additional group therapy.

Mr. Morris, a 48-year-old obsessive-compulsive carpenter, had been depressed for three years. Conflicts with his mother and an alcoholic brother resulted in a psychosis. After he was committed to the hospital a series of electroconvulsive treatments was administered. He expressed interest in group therapy initially but soon became very ambivalent about it. His group attendance was only fair. He was furloughed from the hospital after 3 months of group therapy. Morris was readmitted to the hospital on one occasion during group therapy. His rage was so severe that its expression in a group meeting was followed by his absence for several weeks. Two-year follow-up reveals two brief readmissions to hospital during the first year and one readmission during the second year. He improved and began part-time work at his former trade for the first time in 3½ years during the first year. However, Morris has now reverted to his pregroup-therapy status of moderately severe depression. He has stopped work and requested long-term hospitalization.

Mr. Daniels, a 46-year-old accountant, had for 4 years experienced episodic psychotic attacks characterized by withdrawal, autism, regressive behavior, and depression. Repeated conflicts with an aggressive, dominating wife occurred before and after hospital admission. His group attendance was good while he was in the hospital but only fair when he was on a furlough status. He was the silent member of the group and spoke only when questions were directed at him. Two readmissions to the hospital occurred during group therapy. Two-year follow-up reveals two additional episodes of psychotic behavior of brief duration that were resolved satisfactorily by supportive therapy and drugs. Hospitalization was not necessary. In between these attacks he has functioned well in his work. During the second year Daniels functioned even better. He has returned to a full-time work status. Difficulties with his wife continue to be present, which he has partially resolved by taking an occupational position that keeps him out of town on weekdays. Daniels' most important gain has been the development of psychological aptitude.

Mr. Edwards, a 45-year-old electronics worker, was psychotically depressed on admission to the hospital. The precipitating stress was conflicts with his mother and wife. He began group therapy after a series of electroconvulsive treatments. During group therapy he vacillated between depression and hypomanic behavior. One readmission to the hospital was necessary. The following year after completion of group therapy he was readmitted to the hospital on three occasions. During the second year he has been on a continuous hospital status. Even though he was an active group member with regular attendance no improvement in his mental condition can be seen.

Mr. Roberts, a 38-year-old schizophrenic male, was committed to the hospital with erratic, bizarre behavior, delusions and hallucinations. The precipitating stress was the death of his father. He joined the group at the 26th meeting. Two-year follow-up reveals two readmissions to the hospital with recurrences of psychotic behavior.

Mr. Harrison, a 36-year-old former bank cashier, had a 12-year history of chronic alcoholism, repeated occupational failures, family conflicts, and recurrent difficulties with law-enforcement officials. On admission, Harrison was confused, irrational, and hallucinatory. The toxic delirium had subsided when he began group therapy. He was an active group member. Harrison was discharged from the hospital after 6 months of therapy and returned regularly to the meetings until the end of group therapy. Two-year follow-up reveals that Harrison has been granted a driver's license, has secured a job as a state milk inspector and has been reunited with his wife and children. He has maintained complete abstinence from alcohol.

Mr. Cole, a 28-year-old schizophrenic, was admitted to the hospital in a confused condition. Hallucinations and delusions were present. An occupational stress influenced his illness. He improved rapidly on drugs. Cole attended only eight group meetings and did not return after discharge. No follow-up information is available.

Mr. Webb, a 32-year-old truck driver, was committed to the hospital for psychotic behavior. He was autistic, confused, withdrawn, delusional, and hallucinatory. The illness was of 6 weeks' duration. The precipitating stress was felt to be due to conflicts with his wife and mother. In the hospital, Webb improved rapidly on drugs and supportive therapy. He appeared to be quite interested in group therapy and attended meetings regularly while on a patient status. After discharge from the hospital, he ceased coming to meetings. He was readmitted to the hospital 2 months after discharge for a recurrence of psychotic behavior. He soon left the hospital against medical advice but was later hospitalized in a neighboring state. Two-year follow-up reveals a continuation of illness to such a degree that he has not been able to function adequately outside of a hospital for any satisfactory period of time.

Mr. Yates, a 36-year-old clerk, had experienced episodic psychotic behavior for 10 years. Several lengthy periods of hospitalization have occurred. Yates was very dependent and seemed content to stay in the hospital. He attended meetings regularly but was quiet, ingratiating and remained at the periphery of group discussions. He was on patient status throughout group therapy. Two-year follow-up reveals that he is still a patient in the hospital. There is no essential change in his mental condition.

Mr. Boler, a passive dependent 37-year-old newspaper writer, was admitted to the hospital chronically depressed. Alcohol and drug problems were also present. Homosexual conflicts had been present for many years. During the year prior to admission, two suicidal attempts had been made. He had not worked for 3 years. Boler joined the group as a replacement member. He was very verbal in the meetings but was also quite dependent on the group and on the therapist. Two readmissions to the hospital occurred during therapy. Along with Smith he was transferred to an outpatient clinic group in another city following termination of the state hospital group. He continued his same role in the second group. Both groups—the hospital and the outpatient clinic group—had the same therapist. The outpatient clinic group is the same one discussed in Chap. 7. A third readmission to the state hospital was necessary. Boler died of complications from a toxic hepatitis immediately prior to termination of the group to which he was transferred.

Mr. Smith, a 30-year-old machinist, had been beset for ten years with emotional conflicts that culminated in an acute psychosis characterized by violent and assaultive behavior, auditory hallucinations and delusions. Initially he was treated in a private hospital where he received a lengthy series of electroconvulsive treatments before being committed to the state hospital. He began group therapy soon after admission to the hospital. Smith became a very active group member and was quite perceptive of group dynamics. He improved rapidly and was furloughed home after three months of group therapy. He attended meetings regularly as an outpatient. One brief readmission to the hospital was necessary. At the termination of the state hospital group he entered a group with Boler in a neighboring city. Smith continued to progress satisfactorily in the second group. Two-year follow-up reveals that he had completed therapy in the second group. He is successfully employed in his former occupation and has received two promotions. Smith reports that he is more comfortable in family, occupational, and social relationships than at any time previously.

This inpatient-outpatient group was composed of a mixture of type I and type II patients. Edwards was initially classified as a type I patient but was reclassified as a type II patient. Daniels, Morris and Yates are classified as type II patients. Two patients, Harrison and Boler, had illnesses that were complicated by addictions to alcohol and drugs. Both patients had passive-dependent and nonassertive personalities.

The results of group are tabulated in Table 8.1. Included the three patients (Roberts, Cole, and Webb) who dropped out of group therapy, there was a 36 per cent improvement in all the group members at the end of the 2-year follow-up period. The dramatic improvement in Jackson, Harrison, and Smith cannot be overlooked. At the same time, however, the failures with Edwards, Roberts, Cole, Webb, Morris, Yates and Boler indicate the limitations of group therapy. The case of Yates, a chronic schizophrenic of 10 years' duration, points out the problems and difficulties in group therapy with patients of long-standing psychotic illnesses. An additional observation from Table 8.1 is significant. A majority of the patients showing improvement at the termination of group therapy maintained or improved their status during the next 2 years. Similarly, those considered failures remained in the same category.

Table 8.1   *Results of Group Therapy* *

Patient	Excellent	Moderate	Minimal	None
Jackson	1, 2, 3			
Morris			1, 2, 3	
Daniels	3	2	1	
Edwards				1, 2, 3
Roberts				1, 2, 3
Harrison	1, 2, 3			
Cole				1, 2, 4
Webb				1, 2, 4
Yates				1, 2, 3
Boler †			1	2
Smith	1, 2, 3			

1. Status at termination of group therapy.
2. Status one year after termination of group therapy.
3. Status two years after termination of group therapy.
4. No second year follow-up available.

* Results of group therapy were based on group function, need for rehospitalization, and adaptive changes in family, social and occupational roles.
† Deceased.

The follow-up studies, accomplished by individual interviews with the therapist, emphasize another significant factor about group therapy—the group spirit and mutual interest that continued to be present among the members after the termination of group therapy. In every follow-up interview there were questions about the status of the other members. Further inquiry revealed that letters had been exchanged among the group members. On occasions, rehospitalized members received cards of encouragement from others. Three members contacted Boler's family after his death. During the interviews warm expressions of former group therapy meetings were recalled to the therapist.

The therapist also shared in their contacts. In the two years following completion of group therapy he was frequently called on for advice and counsel. Harrison periodically telephoned him every 2 to 3 months from a neighboring city. Daniels and Morris have been seen by the group therapist during periods of stress. Jackson kept the group therapist informed of his plans for college, which have now been accomplished. The therapist was instrumental in arranging for the college psychiatrist to see Jackson. Boler's and Smith's progress were followed in the other group. Edwards has consulted the therapist on several occasions when depressed. In recent months (as of the time of writing) Edwards had not fared well, having been hospitalized for an entire year. Yates seemed content in the hospital. He was very dependent on the hospital and worked there as a part-time patient employee as of the present writing.

Table 8.2 *Number of Readmissions to the Hospital*

Patient	During group therapy	One-year follow-up period	Two-year follow-up period
Jackson	None	None	None
Morris	1	2	1
Daniels	2	None	None
Edwards	1	3	Continuous patient status
Roberts *			
Harrison	None	None	None
Cole *			
Webb *			
Yates	Continuous patient status	Continuous patient status	Continuous patient status
Boler	2	1	
Smith	1	None	None

NOTE: Excluding the three patients who dropped out of the group, there was a total of seven hospital readmissions of five patients during the active period of group therapy, six hospital readmissions of three patients during the next year, and one extended readmission (Edwards) during the second year. Morris was also readmitted to the hospital during the second year. Only one patient (Yates) remained on a patient status during all periods.

* Drop-outs.

In the final analysis, the results with this group of psychotic patients can be considered satisfactory. The development of psychological aptitude, improved reality testing, and socialization occurred in four of the group members. The group drop-outs, three in number, were no greater than in groups of neurotic patients. Group attendance was excellent (70 per cent), considering the distance the group members had to travel each week. Possibly two of the members (Cole and Webb), who attended meetings only while in the hospital, might have been able to continue if group therapy had been near their homes. The four group members who improved continue to have emotional problems. However, their development of psychological aptitude has been beneficial because they are much more aware of their emotional reactions to other people in their everyday group relationships. Their requests for help and advice from the therapist during the 2 years since the completion of group therapy emphasize a significant point: when difficulties beyond their capabilities are encountered, these patients now have enough confidence in the group therapist and in psychiatry to seek professional advice.

9

Hospital Ward Meetings:
A Therapeutic Group Activity

Hospital ward meetings that bring all of the patients of a ward together in a structured group activity have been found to be beneficial in their overall treatment program. The dynamics of group relationships in hospital ward meetings are identical to the dynamics of group relationships in group therapy. The hospital ward meeting, however, is composed of a much larger group of people and has different goals and purposes. Therefore, for the purposes of this study, the hospital ward meeting is considered a group activity and not group therapy.

A psychiatric hospital ward usually contains a high percentage of psychotic patients. The specific make-up will vary depending upon the particular type of facility. Many private hospital units admit only voluntary patients. State hospitals have more of a variety of illnesses, since they are a legal facility of the state and strict screening procedures are not possible. Patients are usually committed to the hospital through court action, although many states provide for voluntary admissions.

The purpose and structure of a hospital ward meeting can be better understood if one has an awareness of the feelings and reactions of the hospitalized patient. All patients, regardless of their diagnosis and psychodynamics, bring to the ward the same behavior patterns that are present prior to their admission. Naturally, these patterns vary, depending on the psychodynamics of the individual and the nature of their defense mechanisms. The patient may be angry, depressed, hallucinatory, confused, preoccupied, overtalkative, overactive, delusional, passive, or ingratiating. Feelings of isolation from the world are very apparent. Often the patient has no idea that other people can have feelings such as he is experiencing. He drowns himself in self-abasement, guilt, worthlessness, and other forms of self-castigation that contribute to his already low self-esteem. The patient experiences resentment and a further blow to his self-esteem when he faces the stigma of being in a mental institution. Some patients deny any illness and blame others for their hospitalization. Most have experienced difficulties in day-to-day living within their family, social, and occupational roles. Authority problems they have had with their superiors are now transferred to the ward staff. Their relationships to men and women of the staff depend on their habitual reactions to the particular sex in the past. Some relate easier to men, others to women. Some may be overly aggressive and assaultive, then fear retaliation from authority; others may be passive and nonassertive, while still others may be ingratiating and intellectual. Their relationships to other patients will reveal competitiveness, jealousy, suspiciousness, aggressive outbursts, and other patterns characteristic of their behavior with their peers prior to hospitalization. Some patients may be aware of their emotional interaction, but many have no clear idea of how they react with others or where their feelings come from.

Another feature of the psychiatric ward that contributes to the feelings and actions of the patient is his relationship to the staff. Many problems that occur on the wards are the result of staff attitudes and reactions to patients. This situation is not peculiar to psychiatric wards; it accounts for difficulties encountered in the operation and management of wards in general hospitals.

Thus the feelings and reaction of the patient to the staff and to other patients, together with the feelings and reaction of the staff in return, contribute significantly to the tone of the ward. The patterns of behavior exhibited on the ward will relate to the psychodynamics of the patients and the staff. It is into this formulation of ward dynamics that the hospital ward meeting helps the patients understand their relationships with the other patients and with the staff, and helps the staff to understand their role with the patients.

From the standpoint of group dynamics there are many similarities between ward meetings and group therapy. Since a much larger group of people is involved for an indefinite period of time (length of hospital admission), the purpose and structure of ward meetings and the technique of the ward leader must be somewhat different from that of group therapy.

GOALS AND PURPOSE OF HOSPITAL WARD MEETINGS

The chief purpose of hospital ward meetings is to encourage the free expression of feelings. To many patients this is an experience perhaps hitherto deemed impossible. From the ventilation of feelings comes acceptance and understanding from other patients and the leader. The recognition that other people have similar problems diminishes feelings of isolation and encourages patients to look at themselves. Withdrawn, silent patients may not be able to participate in the ward meetings but profit when others express their feelings. Ward meetings encourage patients to help one another through a mutual interchange of feelings and thoughts, an interchange that is not confined to the actual meeting but continues day and night at other activities on the ward. New patients coming to the ward with overtly psychotic behavior are often understood and supported at meetings or even before attending meetings. In this respect ward behavior and management become a matter of concern not merely for the staff but for other patients as well. Ward meetings afford an opportunity for the patients to examine individual conflicts with other patients. Many such instances are a form of scapegoating and occur as a result of hostility displaced from authority figures to other patients. The opportunity for examining this type of behavior can occur in a ward meeting. Ward meetings can be very beneficial in giving patients an opportunity to express their feelings about current ward problems and ward management. Patients will use opportunities at ward meetings to express hostility about food, censorship of mail, locked doors, ward discipline and rules, lack of activities, and difficulties with other patients, attendants, nurses, or doctors. In state hospitals, complaints about food or treatment are often well-founded. Interestingly, these complaints usually greet a new ward leader and cease after several meetings even though the quality of the meals remains unchanged. New patients frequently reintroduce the subject. In certain instances patients can help the staff in making decisions for privileged activities such as social and recreational events that are not a regularly scheduled ward activity.

The ward meeting offers a valuable experience to patients in socializing with others. For example, a patient in individual interviews reveals low self-esteem, inhibitions, and shyness with others. The therapist interprets this behavior to the patient time and again in individual interviews. However, in a ward meeting the patient has an opportunity to experiment with being among people, talking before others and expressing feelings. Thus, in the ward meeting the patient has the opportunity to observe his feelings and behavior patterns in a group.

An important feature emphasized in any dynamic intensive treatment program is the total behavior of the patient throughout every hour of the day. Patients actually live together during their period of hospitalization. They play, work, and socialize together in all the ward activities. Being this close to each other brings into play patterns of behavior associated with their faulty emergency responses to fear, rage, and guilt. They encounter difficulties in the day-to-day atmosphere of the ward. They get angry, fearful, and guilty in their relationships with each other. Since the meeting is held in the ward setting, these feelings cannot always be hidden. They ultimately come up in the ward meeting. Conflicts that occur between patients and the staff offer the patients a true picture of an active reliving of emotional experiences. Patients will verbalize that having to live with each other throughout the entire day creates difficulty. They dislike incurring the anger of others. Needless to say, the ward meeting provides a social setting or a frame of reference for observing and analyzing feelings. This, in itself, is a stimulus for other types of psychotherapy.

A very important goal of the ward meeting is accomplished by helping patients overcome the acute manifestations of illnesses. The expression of feelings and the understanding and support obtained from such a ward atmosphere, along with the other therapeutic procedures (individual therapy, other group activities, drugs, and electroconvulsive treatments), help bring about a resolution of psychoses by increasing repression, diminishing guilt, providing temporary new identifications, and reestablishing defense mechanisms or defensive behavior patterns.

As a part of an overall intensive treatment program, ward meetings may also contribute significantly to a better understanding of the patients by the staff. At staff conferences of attendants, aides, nurses, and doctors, information from ward meetings can promote staff understanding of patient behavior and lead to improved management. Doctors can learn how their patients react in a group activity and receive cues about their relationship with other patients and the staff—a relationship which may be very different from their relationship with him, as seen in the following cases.

1. An extremely psychotic female was quite delusional and bizarre in her individual interviews. She repeatedly talked of having given birth to everybody in the world and declared that she had now been made pregnant by God. In the ward meetings she exhibited an entirely different type of behavior. She was quite receptive to the ward meeting discussions and made a number of brilliant interpretations. Usually she maintained a very good social front in the ward meeting.

2. A depressed female seemed to be making considerable progress in individual interviews. The therapist was of the opinion that she was near time for discharge. At ward meetings, however, she was always depressed. She spoke of her difficulties in talking to people in a group, her inability to talk without crying, and her constant feeling of depression.

The ward meeting was very helpful in aiding the staff to understand the total behavior of these patients. These factors become extremely important when plans are being made for treatment.

If the staff utilizes what it can learn from ward meetings, these meetings can play a beneficial part in feedback operations with other forms of therapy on a ward that utilize the expression, acceptance, and understanding of a patient's feelings. Occupational therapy, recreational activities, social events, staff relationships, group therapy, individual therapy, and ward meetings feed in and back to each other. Behavior in a ward meeting can be examined and looked at in an individual interview. The patient may become aware that he exhibits identical behavior patterns in several forms of group activities. He may talk about his problem in a ward meeting, another group activity, or with his therapist. Various problems encountered by the patient might be initially discussed in a ward meeting before a large group of people. The patient might be too timid or frightened to speak before a smaller group. Later, after talking over a matter with a large group and seeing that nothing disastrous resulted, the patient receives support to speak up in a smaller group or with his therapist. In another instance the patient may discuss with his doctor certain problems or conflicts with other patients and the staff. The therapist may advise him to discuss this matter in a ward meeting in order to obtain a clearer understanding of his role.

Finally, the ward meeting may serve as a stimulus to the patient for obtaining treatment after discharge from the hospital. In many instances hospitalization can be considered successful if the patient develops psychological aptitude and is motivated for treatment after leaving the hospital. Having the opportunity to look at their feelings and behavior in the ward meetings encourages patients to seek treatment on an outpatient basis.

STRUCTURE OF THE WARD MEETING

The ward meetings should be structured around the entire therapeutic program of the ward. Meetings may be held on a daily, biweekly, or weekly basis. The usual length of ward meetings is one hour. They should be held at a regular time on the same day of each week at a central area on the ward. The day room or lounge of the ward can provide an excellent place for the meetings.

The ward meeting leader should be a member of the professional staff of the ward. Experiences with leaders in various roles (ward administrator, residents assigned to the ward) have been satisfactory. Difficulties have not been encountered by the ward leader who is also seeing several of the patients on an individual basis.

A recorder or observer serves the same valuable function in the ward meeting as in group therapy. Written notes are taken. Observation of the leader's technique, perception of the anxiety of the patients and the leader, and an assessment of nonverbal attitudes and communication are all afforded by the use of a recorder. The recorder is a nonparticipating member of the ward meeting and should be selected from the ward staff; a nurse, aide, attendant, secretary, or other staff member may also be used as recorder.

Several members from the ward staff should be in attendance at the ward meeting, including a nurse and attendant. However, the staff attendance should be curtailed so that the ward meeting remains primarily a patient meeting. Staff members can rotate in their attendance so that everyone may observe patient interaction and behavior at some time during their hospital admission. Staff personnel who attend the meeting should do so on a nonparticipating basis, unless certain issues come up in the ward meeting that the leader feels should be handled by the nurse or another responsible person.

The patient population of psychiatric wards varies, depending on its physical structure. Private facilities tend to be smaller than those in state hospitals. Ward meetings with private units of 20 patients and state hospital wards of 40 patients have been satisfactory. In the smaller private unit of 20 patients there is more interaction during ward meetings than in the larger group. All patients should be encouraged to attend the meetings. A certain amount of coercion may be necessary to encourage patients to attend, even to the point of bringing them to the meeting on a compulsory basis. No one will question the need to structure the ward activities of the acutely psychotic patient. Their confusion, disorganized thought processes, bizarreness, and emotional actions stress this need.

TECHNIQUE OF THE WARD MEETING LEADER

The dynamics of a large group are similar to those of a small one, except that the size of the group limits the degree of group interaction. In order to facilitate the ventilation of feelings by patients as well as to encourage the self-examination of behavior (patient-to-patient and patient-to-staff relationships), the behavior, emotions, and reactions that occur should be evaluated during the meeting. As in group therapy, the leader does not prepare a lecture, show a movie, or structure the meeting in any way. He does not necessarily answer questions from patients. It is the interaction between the patients (verbal and nonverbal) that forms the basis of the leader's technique. Every attempt is made to foster group interaction by referring verbal statements, questions, and observations from one patient to the rest of the group for discussion. Nonverbal manifestations of anxiety are handled similarly. Every opportunity is utilized to encourage the patient to express hostility to the leader. In the psychotic patient whose unconscious feelings are on the surface, a chance to ventilate rage feelings may be very helpful. The leader gauges the meeting by the anxiety level of the patients. In a ward meeting with a large group of people of whom many may be psychotic, the leader's task is not an easy one. The anxiety may easily reach an extremely high level. There is a tendency for anxiety in ward meetings to fluctuate between high and low levels. The leader has to keep a careful eye on the anxiety level. When it becomes too high the subject can be changed or the leader can talk for a few minutes. When the anxiety is too low the leader can focus on previously discussed material that is relevant to the purpose of the ward meeting.

The leader's assessment of the anxiety level is the key to an effective control of the ward meeting. Of extreme importance also are the conscious and unconscious reactions of the leader. Can the leader accept hostility or does he allow it to be diverted to a patient? Is the leader aware of the way in which his behavior influences the patients and sets the mood for the meeting? Leader-recorder discussions and supervisory conferences are very helpful to the leader in developing an awareness of effective leadership. They carry the same import that therapist-recorder discussions and group supervisory conferences do for the therapist.

The structure of a hospital ward meeting emphasizes the need for the leader to be understanding, supportive, and outgoing with the patients. The hospital ward leader has to be much more active in meetings when compared to the activity of the therapist in group therapy. With the patient population always changing, the leader has to keep new patients informed of the purpose and structure of the meeting. Frequent attempts to spell out the meaning of the meetings have to be made in an effort to foster interaction between the patients.

At the outset of a ward meeting the leader should orient the patients to its general purpose and structure. The time, place, and date of the meeting are repeated at each meeting. The purpose of the meeting can be explained as follows:

"These meetings are for you. All of you are here for some reason, some difficulty on the outside that made it necessary for you to be admitted to the hospital. This difficulty may have involved getting along with other people—your wives, husbands, families, or the people that you worked with. Many people find that they have the same problems here on the ward with other patients, nurses, attendants, doctors, or with the doctor who runs these meetings—me—as they do with people outside the hospital. Sometimes it is helpful to understand how you feel about one another here and about me so that you can get a better understanding of the feelings you have for people you know outside the hospital.

"Now the purpose of these meetings is simply for you to talk about the way you feel. It doesn't matter who or what these feelings are about. They may concern problems you had before coming here, problems you have here with one another on the ward, or feelings you may have about your doctors or about me here in this meeting. Many of you have feelings that are difficult for you to understand or express, and some of you have feelings that you may not even be aware of. What we want to do in these meetings is to understand them. I want to say again how important it is for you to be able to express your feelings as well as understand them, particularly as they concern you here in this meeting—your feelings toward one another and toward me.

"Since the meetings are for all of you, no attempts will be made to discuss medications, drugs, or other matters that should be discussed with your doctor. You will notice that notes will be made during the meeting. I will review the notes between meetings so that I can have a clearer idea of some of your feelings and problems. This may help me and the other doctors on this ward in your treatment while here in the hospital. I would like to emphasize that what you say here and the notes that are taken are treated confidentially within the staff of this ward."

The structure and purpose of the ward meeting has to be repeated by the leader at the beginning of each meeting. On frequent occasions during a meeting the leader can repeat the purpose of the meeting or any parts he feels are applicable so as to encourage patient interaction.

After the structure and purpose of the meeting has been stated, the leader should remain quiet and await developments from the meeting itself. If silence occurs the leader can focus on it by saying: "You greet me with silence. Any ideas as to why the silence occurred?" At other times the purpose of the meeting or any parts of it can be restated in order to focus on the meaning of silence. Another statement the leader can make is, "Does silence have anything to do with my being here at the meeting?" At all times the leader must try to get an expression of feelings. Silence during the meeting can be focused on in the same manner. Silence can be a very troublesome problem in ward meetings and needs constant attention by the leader.

It is common for patients to start a meeting by expressing hostile remarks about food, clothing, regulations, the radio or television set, recreation, or the regimentation of the ward. These subjects provide convenient ways of expressing hostility to the staff. There are two methods of technique the leader can employ. Sometimes there are ward problems that need staff attention. The leader can turn to the staff member who is present at the meeting and suggest that the problem in question be checked on. If necessary this can be repeated with other complaints. Soon the leader will recognize that many complaints are unrealistic. At this point the following observation can be made: "You have really complained today. Do you have any idea why you are making so many complaints?" Other follow-up remarks are helpful: "Let's look again at the purpose of this meeting. Does the way you feel have anything to do with your complaints?" Or, "Did you make complaints like this before you came to the hospital?" Very often patients will recognize the line of questioning and will discuss feelings of depression and irritations that they experience when everything seems to be wrong. Sometimes irritations and complaints are interpreted as being subtle ways of expressing resentment against authority.

A common subject during ward meetings is the difficulty and fear of talking before other people. The leader should pursue the relation of their fears to illness and to the hospital admission. An example of how feelings may be expressed occurred in a ward meeting with a female leader. The patient was a man with a long history of social withdrawal and difficulty in identifying, exploring, and expressing his feelings. When the leader focused on the apparent difficulty in self-expression in the group, this patient rose to his feet, glared at the leader and said: "It's hard for any of us to speak here because we all have problems with authority and we have all been dominated by women. You, being both an authority and a woman, represent both problems; but if you want me to blast off in the face of your authority, I will." He then turned to the group and delivered a long tirade against women and authority. "I have been dominated by my wife, family, and business associates all my life," he said, and proceeded to blast women for not being able to understand and manage their sons, for spending all the money a man made, and for creating "sexual problems." At the end he stated: "You may think I've talked a long time, but my wife would have talked much longer." This patient had a receptive audience in the patients and received unanimous support from them. Following this meeting, he was noted to be more relaxed not only on the ward itself, but also during therapeutic sessions with his therapist.

Very early the problem of not answering direct questions from patients will confront the leader. When direct questions are asked they should be reflected to the entire group. For example, during a meeting a patient asked the leader, "What does depression mean?" The leader referred the question to the entire group by saying: "Mr. A. wants to know what depression means. What does depression mean to the rest of you?" The patient again asked the leader to answer his question. A period of silence followed and the patient repeated his request for the third time. At this point the leader restated the purpose of the ward meetings and asked about the feelings among the patients when questions are not answered. The leader finally focused on the individual patient who had made the three requests that a direct question be answered, and asked the others how they felt about not having their questions answered. Several members responded by saying that apparently he was somewhat irritated with the leader for not answering the question. It is in this area that patients in ward meetings initially express resentment and hostility to the leader—very guarded at first but, with encouragement from the leader, gradually in a more open manner. Later, after attending several meetings, a few patients will recognize and state that the leader wants them to answer the questions themselves. In this way the answers to problems that come up in ward meetings are given by patients and not by the leader.

The most prevalent feelings present in a ward meeting are anger and rage. The patients' behavior patterns, seen in ward meetings and elsewhere, are protections against this anger and rage. With psychotic patients, feelings of anger and rage bubble over into conscious awareness.

Maintaining control of these feelings is very difficult at times. On the ward itself this particular problem demands constant vigilance from the staff. Explosive outbursts may occur in some form of acting out, such as assaulting another patient or staff member, destruction of property, or running away from the hospital. The ward leader must recognize these feelings in a patient, encourage their expression in the meetings, and promote an atmosphere of understanding and support for the patients. At times patients become intensely hostile and give way to an outburst of rage. The acceptance and understanding of the leader is valuable in two respects: (1) the angry patients are able to see that nothing happens after a violent tirade—no one was destroyed and no one attempted to retaliate or hurt them; (2) other patients, frequently astounded to see such hostility expressed, also recognize that nothing happens and are encouraged themselves to speak up at later times. Many patients have repressed anger for long periods. They have been subjected to condemnation and reprisals from families and others when any anger was shown. To be accepted and understood when these feelings are shown certainly constitutes a new experience for them.

Patients may also show their hostility in other, more subtle ways— such as being late for meetings, holding side conversations, walking around the room, changing seats, leaving the room and returning at sporadic intervals, leaving the room and not returning, expressing inappropriate remarks, or indulging in sarcastic laughter. In every instance the leader should focus on this behavior with the patient. If a patient leaves the room and returns, the leader can point out that this patient had to leave the meeting for a few minutes and ask the others what their ideas are on this type of behavior. If there is inappropriate laughter and a side conversation going on, the leader can stop the discussion and say to the patients: "Mr. Jones seems quite amused in another discussion. What are your thoughts about this other conversation now going on?" If necessary, the leader can spell out the purpose of the meeting and explore why people wish to obstruct the regular discussion. The leader can focus on the feelings associated with the regular discussion, or on their relation to illness and to hospitalization.

Patients with mental illness are very sensitive to any type of reality change. They feel rejection at the slightest change in ward structure. Cancelled interviews, cancelled ward meetings, and staff vacations are frequently interpreted as rejection and loss of dependency; as a result, the anxiety level rises. The ward leader should pay close attention to these reality ward events and attempt to explore the patients' reactions to changes. Cancelled ward meetings should be dealt with prior to the actual cancellation if planned, or in later meetings if cancellation has been unpremeditated. It is not an easy matter to get patients to discuss these feelings openly in a ward meeting. They will refer to absences in symbolic and metaphorical terms. Becoming aware of feelings regarding changes, though, is helpful to patients whether openly expressed or not.

Reference has been made previously to silence that occurs at the beginning of meetings. At any point during the meeting silence may occur. Additional suggestions for handling silence of the entire group are given in Chap. 6. There are always a number of patients who do not verbally participate in the ward meetings. The leader should attempt to bring the silent members into active participation during the meeting. Recognizing their silence as well as supporting them is beneficial whether or not participation on a verbal level occurs, and accounts for the support, encouragement, and understanding some silent patients can receive from group activities. The leader can focus on silence in the following ways: "Today we have a number of people who are not participating in the meeting. What about their inability to talk today?" The leader can also make other statements, such as "What does being quiet have to do with the way you feel?" or "What suggestions do you have for helping them take part in the meeting?" Two interesting comments have been made that indicate the feelings patients have about silence. One severely ill schizophrenic patient said: "Silence is like a cancer, it grows and grows and grows." Another patient equated silence with hostility when he said, in a humorous tone, "Silence is better than violence."

Silence, as well as talking, may have many meanings to patients with mental illness. Often talkative patients feel guilty for being overly active during the meeting but then become angry at the silent patient for not participating in the discussions. The following incident illustrates feelings patients have about silence and silent members. One meeting began with a comparison of other meetings on the ward when the ward leader was not present. The patients recognized that the leader made a distinct difference. Statements were made about their reacting to the leader in the same way that they did to people who had previously "pushed them around." One patient remarked that the leader was "leading them down the path," and that he had prevented them from using ordinary techniques of avoiding personal feelings. Following several irritable comments from talkative patients directed to the silent patients, they spoke of fright or fear. The ward leader focused on their feelings of fear in the meeting. A young, 21-year-old male made an interesting comment: "Talking in a meeting like this is just like jumping into cold water for the first time. After you once do it, the next time it's not so bad." He spoke of the difficulties he had encountered when he had talked in a previous meeting, but then others seemed to understand and now it was easier to talk at this meeting. In the discussion that followed most of the patients felt that they had to have the approval of everybody in the room. One male patient stated that if one or two people in the room disapproved of him, he could not bring himself to say anything. Others admitted this feeling was silly and unrealistic, but nevertheless they feared disapproval. The silent members were discussed again and one man said that the silent patients indicated disapproval of the others by their silence. The discussion continued with three-fourths of the patients agreeing with the observation that silence means disapproval. At this point, an elderly lady, previously silent, spoke up in a cracked, tremulous voice denying that silence meant disapproval. She admitted being one of the silent ones, adding that she had never been able to talk in a group, and that she couldn't even talk to her brothers. She wanted everyone to know that she did get something out of the meeting and reiterated that certainly she didn't disapprove of anything they said by her silence. The theme of this ward meeting related to their feelings of fear, disapproval, and fear of each other and particularly the ward leader. On one level silence was uncomfortable because it meant disapproval. On another level (not verbalized), silence was a protection, for to talk and show their real feelings would result in disapproval.

Patients often recognize that meetings without the leader are definitely different from those with the leader. They voice concern and irritation about the lack of ward meeting structure, the inactivity of the ward leader, and the refusal of the ward leader to answer questions. In one ward meeting the patients spoke of wanting to put the leader "on the spot" and back her into a corner for not answering questions. When the leader focused on this behavior the patients felt that it was much easier to put the leader "on the spot" than themselves. They felt the leader's purpose was to put them on the spot; now they wanted to turn the tables on her. The patients received an awareness of the authority relationship of the ward leader. When encouraged and fostered by the ward leader's technique this relationship can be looked at in more detail during the meeting.

There are reality factors that influence the content and progress of ward meetings. Hospital wards that have a rapid turnover of patients exhibit more anxiety. If the ward census remains rather stable for a period of weeks, patients will attend sufficient meetings to feel more accepted and understood. When encouraged to examine their feelings toward the leader, hostility may be forthcoming. The following incidence occurred in a series of hospital ward meetings: The ward population of forty males was fairly stable. Many of the patients had attended ten or more meetings. The leader, a female, was referred to as "professionally incompetent," "cold," "impersonal and indifferent," and "stupid" as well as being a "liar and a quack." The patients stated that "she should be replaced by a psychologist," "she cannot help patients," "she runs the meetings like a prison warden or policeman," and "being a woman, she represents a gross imbalance of nature."

The inability of the ward leader to accept hostility from a large group of patients carries important weight and has a definite influence on patient interaction and behavior during the meeting. If the ward leader can recognize the theme of the meeting and effectively exert control of the meeting, the therapeutic work of the patients will be enhanced.

The importance of the leader in a ward meeting cannot be overestimated. The leader is an authority figure who is seen by the patients as omnipotent and all-powerful. The leader is the one person in the meeting who plays the most significant part in setting the tone of the meeting. If the leader is depressed there is a good possibility that the meeting will reveal the same feeling. If the leader is uninterested or preoccupied with other matters, the patients will detect it immediately. The sensitivity and perception of patients to the mood and feeling of the authority figure or leader is phenomenal. The nonverbal communication between the leader and the patients, and vice versa, is most significant. It is for this reason that the use of a recorder or observer, leader-recorder discussions and supervisory conferences assume the same importance in a hospital ward meeting as in the more formal types of group therapy.

The overactive, manic patient creates the same problems in a ward meeting as in group therapy. He talks rapidly, changes the subject often, interrupts other patients as well as the leader, moves about in the room from one seat to another and attempts to usurp the role of the leader. This type of behavior creates hostility among the other patients. The ward leader has to be very active in attempting to identify this problem in a patient as well as promoting understanding and support for the patient among the other patients. The behavior of the patient must be focused on by asking the others their feelings about being constantly interrupted and having the subject changed. Patients will frequently verbalize their irritations to the one involved. The leader should also explore the manic patient's need to be overactive. The leader might say: "You admit irritations with Mr. Brown; do you have any idea why he does this?" "How do you think he feels?" "Does his action have anything to do with his coming here to the hospital?" On occasion, a ward meeting or other forms of group activity will increase the manic behavior of a patient. Having to be close to people and to participate in group relationships increases the patient's anxiety. His defense against this anxiety is an increase in hypomanic and manic behavior. Often other patients will recognize that overactivity and overtalkativeness are more prominent in group relationships than at other times and will constructively point out this fact to the patient. The manic patient can be very troublesome to the ward leader. At times nothing seems to help, and the entire meeting may be disrupted by this type of behavior, with no improvement noted until drugs or electroconvulsive treatments are given.

Changing the subject frequently is another form of hostility encountered in ward meetings. With a large group of patients, this matter can be troublesome. In psychotic patients with blocking and loose thought associations, support should be given by focusing on why they make inappropriate statements and have difficulty talking or following the conversation of the meeting. Other patients will recognize their degree of illness and give them support. In other instances, patients change the subject in order to avoid looking at their behavior during a meeting. They may accomplish it by a bland statement or by sarcastic, hostile remarks. In either event the leader can focus on the particular behavior exhibited. An example of this problem is given in the following account.

Patients were discussing their difficulties in talking before others. The subject was changed to a physical complaint about the ward. The leader returned the meeting to the original discussion. The subject was changed a second and then a third time. At this point the leader spelled out again the purpose of the meeting, adding that the subject being discussed was one that had to do with their feelings, but that on three occasions the subject had been changed. The reasons for the subject's being changed were explored with the patients. Several patients claimed that having to talk in the meetings was not easy and that to talk about other matters was much more comfortable. One patient expressed the fear that he would be killed if he talked out in the meeting. The leader at this point said: "Who would hurt anyone who talks in this meeting?" The other patients supported the fearful patient with a number of positive and encouraging statements.

The fear of being killed for talking in a meeting clearly expressed how a patient can equate verbal assertion with lethal retaliation. Lionel Ovesey [1] has described how some people inhibit assertion as a life-saving device, because, as this patient stated, assertion is an invitation to suicide. Ovesey defines assertion as behavior which may or may not have hostile meaning that is designed to gratify a need. Aggression is a special form of assertion that has a hostile meaning toward an object and seeks to hurt or destroy it. Some people unconsciously perceive all forms of aggression in terms of extreme violence, destruction, or murder, for which retaliation is inevitable. Thus they inhibit their own aggression in order to protect themselves against such retaliation. Usually, however, the inhibition does not stop at forms of aggression, but includes all forms of self-assertion that may or may not have a hostile component. The end result is a person who, because of the fear of retaliation, is completely blocked in all forms of assertion and aggression.

The patient with a passive, nonassertive personality maintains his role so that he will not have to fear retaliation from an authority figure. He is not consciously aware of why he is passive and nonassertive, and reacts to the remarks or action of an authority figure with fear and anxiety. He "freezes up" or "becomes blank." There is, however, a difference between this patient in the ward meeting and the ordinary person with a passive, nonassertive personality. Because the patient in the ward meeting is psychotic, the meaning of retaliation is no longer repressed and held in check by defensive patterns of behavior. The prior unconscious feelings are in consciousness. Thus he actually feels that he will be killed if he talks in the meeting.

When a patient exhibits anger in his remarks and actions to the leader, the emotion should be identified. The leader can say: "Mr. Black appears to be upset with me. I wonder if any of you have any idea why he feels this way?" The leader should encourage the ventilation of his feelings. In other statements, the leader might say: "Do any of you get irritated with me?" "What about being upset with me? Let's look again at the purpose of the meeting and see what this is all about. Are you irritated with me, with others here, with people at home?" From such statements the patients feel encouraged, supported, and understood, and will frequently talk about their problems with anger. The emphasis is on the expression of their feelings and not on a dynamic insight into the cause of their anger. It should be emphasized, however, that getting patients to look at their feelings in a ward meeting is not easy. There will be frequent silences as well as other manifestations of increased anxiety. At times patients completely refuse to deal with their feelings in a meeting. If the anxiety level becomes too high, the leader must immediately recognize that further examination of their behavior should be delayed until a later time. This retreat, however, does not preclude the necessity of going back to this area at later times during the meeting or at following meetings.

The ward meeting can be very supportive to the new patient, particularly if he is quite ill. Delusional patients will have the irrational aspects of their demands and actions pointed out to them by other patients. On occasion, other patients will say to them: "Why are you blaming all your problems on someone else?" "You can't hide how you feel forever." "Why do you think you are here?" "He's too sick right now to understand, but later on he will." "You will get better, don't get discouraged." Support from other patients can be more meaningful than from the leader.

Many psychotic patients enter hospitals or are committed to state institutions denying their illness and blaming their relatives for their present predicament. Over a period of several meetings, patients will recognize their difficulties and gain insight into an awareness of mental illness. The leader's task here is to reflect pertinent observations from patients to the others for discussion. With the delusional patient, the behavior and statements of the patient can be reflected to the group for discussion, as follows: "Mr. S. says that everyone here is against him, that his food is poisoned, and his cigarettes taste funny. What do you make of these statements?" Later the leader can explore the relationship of illness to such statements. In another situation with an acutely psychotic male, the leader said: "Mr. R. says that he is Jesus and that he hears God and the prophets talking to him. He feels he is here to save the world. What do you think of these statements from Mr. R.?" Experience has shown that pointing out reality to a psychotic patient is a proper technique. When encouraged, patients in a ward meeting will very effectively point out reality over and over to a particular person.

It is to be expected that acutely ill people will develop a number of conflicts and animosities with each other. Angry, paranoid schizophrenic patients can create a tremendous amount of hostility with other patients and with the staff. On a ward where patients are living together rather closely, such problems quickly erupt out into the open. The following example illustrates this situation. Mr. B., a very large individual, made excessive demands on everyone. He started arguments and fights with other patients and the staff. He constantly uttered profane epithets about the doctors. He accused everyone of being against him. He disrupted recreational and social events at every opportunity. He had incurred the wrath of nearly all the patients, particularly two other males, Mr. C. and Mr. S. Conflicts with Mr. B. had been discussed in individual interviews. It was suggested that the problem should be aired in the ward meeting. Before Mr. C. and Mr. S. could do this, however, Mr. B. disclosed in a meeting his hostile feelings to Mr. S. and to Mr. C. Nearly the entire meeting was taken up with this conflict, which was characterized by numerous outbursts of anger. Mr. B., Mr. C., and Mr. S. were the main participants, but Mr. B. became aware of having incurred the wrath of many of the patients. Mr. B. was told a number of times that his behavior was part of his illness. An older patient on the ward pointed out the personality conflicts on both sides and the involvement of all three of the participants. The conflict between these patients was resolved in this ward meeting. They talked out their angry feelings rather than acting them out. They were accepted by the leader, who remained impartial and noncritical, and at the same time controlled the situation. Again there was no emphasis placed on obtaining insight. The expression of feelings did occur.

Feelings of guilt for some real and many imaginary thoughts are present in patients with mental illness. In hospital ward meetings the leader will note the presence of patient's guilty feelings by various remarks that are made. Patients may make such statements as: "I'm afraid to talk here, I might be transferred to another ward," "I will be punished if I talk here," "I'm afraid to talk, I might be placed in seclusion," "I'm afraid to talk in front of a group of people," "It's not easy to talk here," "I don't want to hurt anybody's feelings," "I'd rather get along with people," "The attendants will get back at me," etc. The ward leader can be supportive to the patients by recognizing their fears and guilt. The ward leader can say: "Some of the observations made here suggest that if you express how you feel others will not like you or will punish you." Other statements can be made to the patients, such as: "Do your thoughts and feelings make you fearful and guilty?" "Have you had such thoughts and feelings before coming to the hospital?" "Do these thoughts and feelings have anything to do with your illness and admission to the hospital?" The ward leader thus encourages the patients to express their feelings. Recognizing that other patients have similar feelings along with encouragement from the ward leader to discuss these feelings is very supportive to the patients.

The patient with organic brain disease may pose certain problems for the ward leader. When there is severe memory impairment, confusion, and poor attention span, behavior during a ward meeting may be repeated over and over. At times it is difficult to know the proper management. Many patients with organic syndromes have an overlay of emotional trauma that precipitates hospitalization. This is particularly true in the depressed elderly patient with minimal to moderate organic disease. Understanding, support, and encouragement in ward meetings may be very rewarding. Attempts should be made to include the patients in ward meetings. If, however, the patient's memory impairment is too severe and management is a problem, there seems to be no real value in having the patient attend the meeting.

Ward meetings for elderly patients in geriatric wards have proven very helpful. Their purpose and structure may be somewhat different from the ward meetings described in the present chapter. The author's experience with weekly ward meetings on a state hospital reception ward for elderly patients (age 65 and above) was very rewarding. There was no formal structure to the meeting. The atmosphere was more social than that of usual ward meetings; parties were held, refreshments served, and short subjects offered for discussion. The patients' interest in the meeting was demonstrated by their wishing to return weekly after discharge from the hospital. This factor proved to be very significant to new admissions on the ward. They observed that patients were discharged from the hospital and that admission to a state hospital did not mean you were forgotten. The interest taken in the patients by the staff and the ward leader played an important role in ward behavior.

A clearer idea of the content of a ward meeting, the interaction of the patients, and the technique of the ward leader is illustrated in the ward meeting reported in detail below. The ward was composed of forty male patients who had been screened from recent admissions to a state hospital for intensive treatment. The turnover rate was two to three admissions per week. The leader, a female resident in psychiatry, had been conducting ward meetings for 2 months on a twice-weekly basis. Reality events prior to this meeting were: (1) three successive ward meetings had been cancelled by the ward leader, and (2) a very angry, paranoid schizophrenic (Mr. G.) had been admitted to the ward exhibiting assaultive behavior to the staff and other patients that had necessitated his isolation from others.

The meeting began with the leader explaining the structure and purpose of the ward meeting. A silence followed. The leader suspected this most likely represented hostility toward her for the cancelled meetings.

MR. A.: Why is everyone so quiet? When I first came here, Mr. B. and several others talked a good deal, but no one is saying anything now.

LEADER: Mention has been made that there was more talking in past meetings than now. I wonder what some of your feelings are about that.

MR. B.: Some patients have gone. The old ones have already given their opinions once and the new ones are timid.

LEADER: Do any of the rest of you have any ideas about everyone's being quiet today?

MR. C.: We are a bunch of introverts—we don't talk much. I guess we bring that (nontalkativeness) here from outside the hospital.

MR. D.: Some of us have conflicting personalities.

MR. A.: (*interrupting*) That's why we are in here—I guess I should shut up now.

MR. B.: (*somewhat belligerently*) Those who do talk have said the same things once already and get tired of repeating themselves. We've said all these same things with Dr. W. and with the student nurses.

MR. E.: Talking here and in the nurses' groups is for the doctors to understand us. Some people just don't seem to want help.

LEADER: I wonder if others of you have feelings about being tired of repeating the same things over in here.

MR. F.: Well, I agree with him (Mr. E.).

MR. E.: If we repeat ourselves, it will give the new patients some idea of how we got sick. We can help break the ice for the new people.

MR. G.: (*the new patient*) What's the right way to get home after you get well? I'm well now and I know it. There is no point in my being here—it's like a jail! Milledgeville State Hospital! Milledgeville State Prison! (*Mr. G. laughs derisively.*)

LEADER: Mention was made as to how you leave here, and also that it is like a prison here. What are some of your feelings?

MR. G.: (*interrupting, quite angry*) You wake up and see bars on your window! It makes you wonder.

MR. C.: (*to Mr. G., trying to be helpful*) Walk-out privileges make it better.

MR. D.: (*to Mr. G.*) The situation is the same for all of us. You and I are in a fairly poor position to be a judge of all this. If we had been able to analyze the situation before, we wouldn't be here now. Your opinion of your case may be true, but after you gain mental balance, you have to go through a period of observation to make sure no deviations from that balance occur.

MR. G.: (*to Mr. D.*) Outside the hospital is normal; inside isn't. So how are you going to learn to be well in here?

MR. D.: (*to Mr. G.*) Tensions here are *less* than on the outside.

MR. G.: (*becoming quite angry and moving restlessly in his chair*) Tensions are *more* in here. If I only had a chance to start over. This place is a damned prison!

MR. D.: (*reflectively*) I'd rather give it a good trial here. I don't want to risk breaking up again. When people learn I have been here, my chances of making more than the average living in my field (airline pilot) are nil. If I run into a problem I can't cope with, I'll be glad to come back. An observation period is like insurance, so we can control our emotions and feelings about others and about situations.

MR. G.: (*shouting*) No! I want to get out! (*None of the other group members have agreed with Mr. G., and by now he is having marked difficulty in controlling his rage. His hands tremble and his general appearance is that of someone who is about to become violent. He stands up from where he has been sitting. Although Mr. G.'s anxiety level seems almost intolerably high, the leader and the rest of the group are not anxious. Mr. G. moves to the back of his chair and grips it with both hands. He continues emphatically.*) I might as well stand up and get started saying what is on my mind. I fail to see the point in keeping a man here if he is well. If he knows he's well, he shouldn't be here. This isn't a mental institution if people are kept here who are well.

MR. H.: (*mildly*) Maybe you need more treatment.

MR. G.: (*angrily*) What kind?

MR. H.: The kind you are getting now.

MR. G.: (*somewhat incoherently*) Who's the judge here anyway? I'm kept here like an animal. I told everyone before I came here that I was going crazy, but I can't get crazy. If I need shock treatment why don't they give it to me?

MR. E.: (*quietly*) I'd like to say a word about what G. has just said. We don't know how we *do* feel. I've been sick a year. I thought before that I was well. The doctor said I wasn't, but I went back to work anyway. I wound up here, sick like *you* (*to Mr. G.*). A man has got to cooperate with himself and with the doctors.

MR. G.: (*somewhat calmer*) I believe what you say, but *you* don't seem sick to me.

MR. E.: We can't tell if we are well. This time I am accepting what the doctor said. Why go home when you are not well? If you go home and blow, you'll be worse off than you are now.

MR. G.: (*belligerent again*) So you mean that I am expected to stay here and take it and not show any emotion at all?

MR. E.: (*calmly*) No, a man is human and must show his emotions—but in a sensible way.

MR. D.: (*to Mr. G.*) There are certain advantages to being in a state hospital rather than a private one. We're on the top of the heap here (*referring to the intensive-treatment ward*), and as far as the facilities go, the state is improving.

MR. G.: (*sullenly*) I don't care. I just want to get out.

MR. E.: You need time to realize you're sick.

MR. G.: I've been here three and a half weeks, and I want to go home.

MR. H.: (*slowly and emphatically*) Well, I've been here three and a half years.

MR. E.: And I've been sick on and off for *four* years.

MR. G.: Well, I don't want to get happy here. If I did that, then I would want to stay.

MR. E.: (*somewhat impatient and quite earnest*) Look, everyone wants to go home, not just you.

MR. G.: (*questioningly*) How long will it be then for me here?

MR. H.: That all depends on *you*.

MR. G.: (*now in good control of himself*) The way it is—here I go talking again—but people have got to know how you feel. It's like this: All the insane people are outside, and all the sane ones are inside.

MR. E.: Well, compare yourself to others here.

MR. G.: They all seem better than me. Guess there is nothing to do but go along with it. (*Mr. G. then becomes ill at ease because of all the talking he has done and turns to another patient.*) Mr. J., I've been talking too much. How do you feel about being here?

MR. J.: Well, I don't like getting shock treatment. I appreciate what they are trying to do, but shock will hinder me more than it will help me.

MR. G.: Well, the only thing *I* have against it (hospitalization at Milledgeville) is *being* here.

MR. H.: Well, we're all here.

MR. G.: (*quips in reply, laughing anxiously*) I'm not all here. (*He then becomes serious.*) I try to be happy and not worry; maybe that means I'm unbalanced. *But* who's to say who's unbalanced and who isn't?

MR. H.: (*slowly*) There's an old saying about people who are disturbed and don't know it. We know it; you don't.

MR. G.: (*angrily*) Look, I'm not mad, I'm happy. I don't want to be a prisoner here. I can't fight it all alone. (*Pauses.*) It seems you are all trying to convince me that I'm insane.

MR. H.: We all have problems.

MR. G.: (*vacillating*) Well, I've got many. The fact that I can't get out is the only thing that worries me though. But, I'm afraid of many things. I'm afraid of God. I'm afraid of the wrath of God.

MR. H.: Show me one person here in this room who doesn't want to get out. You should see some of the other wards to really know what it means to want to get out. This (ward) is heaven in comparison.

MR. G.: I'm emotionally disturbed, I suppose. But, I'm locked up and I want the quickest way out.

MR. H.: (*emphatically*) We have accepted the fact that there is something wrong with us and that therefore we can't leave yet.

MR. G.: But, I feel helpless here. If I could go home I could get treatment there—I could take medicine.

MR. H.: (*mockingly*) I suppose you think all you have to do is pop a pill in your mouth to get well!

MR. G.: (*agitatedly*) I have to get some water. (*He rises and walks out of the room, shouting to the group on his way.*) Go ahead and laugh at me while I'm out of the room if it will do you some good! (*The group remains quiet and silent until Mr. G. returns and takes his seat a few minutes later. The leader chooses this opportunity to elicit group support for Mr. G. She focuses on their reaction to the feelings he has expressed.)*

LEADER: Now, we're all here to express our feelings. Mr. G. has been doing that and has expressed feelings about various things. What are some of your thoughts about this?

MR. H.: In my opinion, Mr. G. has got a problem and is disturbed. His is not the best or worst problem from what else I've seen, but I don't think he wants to be helped right now.

MR. G.: I'm being helped right now.

MR. H.: *(to Mr. G.)* Say you go home, be with your family, get a job, and then get worse. You'll have to say that you had your chance and you lost it. Your life is in your hands and you are fiddling with it.

MR. G.: *(becoming uncomfortable, both from the subject under discussion [his sanity] and from the feeling that he should not be talking so much during the meeting, i.e., that his feelings are not worthy of receiving so much time and attention from the group and from the leader.)* I'm still talking too much—let's change the subject to something else.

MR. H.: *(supporting Mr. G.)* I don't see why we should do that. We've got a good thing going here, why change it?

MR. G.: *(clearly relieved and reassured by Mr. H.'s comment which indicates to him that his feelings are well worth continued consideration by the group; for the first time during the hour he appears composed; pauses for a moment and then begins with evident self-confidence)* I have feelings of persecution. . . . I'm afraid of many things. . . .

MR. H.: You mean about what you think people may feel about you here during this meeting?

MR. G.: *(gloomily)* Well, yes, and I'm talking so much and seem to be talking out of my mind . . . I suppose I could do this forever.

MR. H.: You could, but the purpose of the doctors here is to help you with whatever problem you've got. After all, there's something bothering all of us.

MR. G.: *(quietly)* Talking is good for the heart. The fact that it is out in the open has done me more good than anything else. I've always tried to escape from my problems before.

MR. H.: Well, I've even escaped from the hospital several times, but it was wrong.

MR. G.: I'm not trying to escape. I want treatment.

MR. H.: Your attitude has changed. Before, you were saying that you weren't sick; now you are saying you are.

MR. G.: I'd still rather be at home.

MR. H.: But, you're here, not at home, and you can't get treatment at home.

MR. G.: I'm sick. I'm also sick of Milledgeville Hospital. But, then, who isn't, I suppose. *(Mr. G. having openly accepted his emotional illness, the leader chooses this time to elicit group support for this man once more, this time in regard to the simple fact that he has expressed his feelings.)*

LEADER: Mr. G. has expressed many of his feelings during this hour. I wonder what some of your thoughts are regarding that. (*Mr. G. then receives warm support from the other group members.*)

MR. D.:   He has helped himself today.

MR. B.:   I think Mr. G. is to be commended.

MR. D.:   (*to Mr. G.*) You've taken a big step today; and, the quicker each of us can put our story forth as you have here, the quicker we'll be helped, too.

MR. B.:   Mr. G. is cooperative and friendly on the ward. He does more than his share of the work. (*By his facial expression, Mr. G. is obviously pleased and surprised by these comments. However, he wishes to conceal his warm response to the group and attempts to do this in his usual manner—either by making the support illogical or unimportant or by dismissing it with a quip, which is, incidentally, almost always quite clever. Interestingly, as will be seen, the group does not let him escape with these defenses. In reply to the supportive comments given him, a member says challengingly.*)

MR. G.:   But, I'm sick. Therefore, so what? My being friendly isn't important in regard to my being sick.

MR. B.:   (*refusing to accept this statement as evidence that support is irrelevant*) That doesn't matter—you're still taking the right approach to getting well.

MR. G.:   (*lightly*) Well, all I'm looking for is the right way to get out.

MR. D.:   (*retorts*) Well, you're taking it. (*By expressing feelings, accepting his illness, etc. Several patients then discuss the response of people outside the hospital to a person who has been to Milledgeville.*)

MR. G.:   It's going to be rough meeting people who knew us before we came here.

MR. E.:   I've had that problem come up for me, and I don't see that it is something to worry about.

MR. J.:   I don't see how it's possible to face people you knew before.

MR. B.:   Mr. J. is wrong. I've been in Milledgeville before. When I went home, I didn't find this to be a problem.

MR. J.:   But, I'm self-conscious.

MR. B.:   People will help you. You'll get over these feelings. Things will be quite different from what you expect.

MR. K.:   (*a young man with depression who had been silent the entire hour*) I feel better than I did when I came here. I still worry, but not as much as I used to. (*The meeting ends with an outburst from one patient, Mr. E., who speaks briefly about his anger concerning recent stealing on the ward. It would appear that he would like to have brought the subject up before, but could not do so due to the concentration of the group on Mr. G.*)

The understanding and support that Mr. G. received from the other patients was very instrumental in his recovery from the psychosis. He was not a management problem from that time on. Four weeks later he gave an excellent performance as Santa Claus at the annual Christmas party on the ward.

At supervision, two questions regarding technique were raised: (1) no reference was made to the cancelled meetings, and (2) the silent members were not encouraged to participate in the meeting. The ward leader was aware that cancelled meetings, as well as the problem of the silent members, should have been brought to their attention, but she correctly felt that the support for Mr. G. was more important and allowed the discussion to continue rather than introduce another subject. Thus the technique of the ward leader should be flexible. Significant issues as they relate to the overall treatment program of the patients should take precedence over others. The issues of cancelled meetings and silent patients were not dealt with in this meeting. More important, a potential management problem to the ward was looked at and resolved.

In Chap. 4 three stages of group therapy are described. In this respect, if we compare the dynamics of a ward meeting to group therapy, the ward meeting stays in stage I. The patients are not expected, nor is it the goal of the ward leader, to reach stage II and stage III. The emphasis is placed on the expression of feelings. As with the more formal types of group therapy, mutual analyses and interpretations of behavior occur very early in ward meetings. When encouraged by the ward leader, patients begin to help one another and to point out their patterns of reaction and behavior.

Hospital ward meetings are particularly valuable to those patients, who, after discharge from the hospital, begin group therapy in outpatient groups. We have repeatedly observed that the members of outpatient groups, who previously had attended hospital ward meetings, are less fearful and more at ease in the early meetings of group therapy than those members who have had no contact with hospital ward meetings. Then, too, drop-outs from group therapy have occurred less frequently among group members who have attended hospital ward meetings. Among the most rewarding advantages of hospital ward meetings is the stimulus they give the patient to continue with professional therapy after leaving the hospital.

REFERENCE

1. Ovesey, Lionel: "The Pseudo-Homosexual Anxiety," *Psychiatry,* 18:19–20, 1955.

Index

437

Anger, equated, with resentment, 251
expressed by verbal acting out, 236–237
group therapist's exploration of, 214, 263–270, 301–305
impounded, 21, 36
projection of, 301–302
in group therapy, 301–302
in parent-child relationships, 301–302
recognition of, 345–354
related to depression and guilt, 316–317, 322–325, 345–354
subtle manifestation of, 422
(*See also* Hostility; Rage)
Angry feelings associated, with sexual feelings, 345–354
with sexual and tender feelings, 353–355
Animal rage, 294, 316–317, 322
Antisocial behavior, 20
(*See also* Sociopathic personality)
Anxiety, in addictions, 33, 99–101
in adolescents, 33
alcohol relieves, 297, 298
concepts of, 10–11
constructive, 11
defense mechanisms and, 3
definition of, 10
destructive, 11
development of, in childhood, 13–14
etiology of, 3
in group relationships, 2, 11–16, 45–50, 228, 247–298, 316
everyday, 28, 203–204, 290–291, 316
family, 2, 282
therapeutic (*see* in group therapy, *below*)
in group therapy, 3, 12, 62, 67–69, 100, 110–114, 388–412
addition of new members causes, 145–146, 284–286
blocking, confusion, distortion, vagueness from, 208–209, 214–221, 231–232
change in group structure results in, 130, 135–145, 167–171, 301–302
defense against, competitiveness, 194
conversation, rapid, 182–190
superficial, 182–191
forgetfulness as, 290
frozen attitude as, 250
headache as, 192–193
humor as, 299
intellectualization as, 319–325
laughter as, 338–339
sarcasm as, 338–340
silence as, 167–171
sleep as, 332, 356–357

Anxiety, in group therapy, defense against, structure as, 206
subgroups as, 195–196, 288–290
emotional closeness, influences losses, 135–145
necessity for resolution of, 34
in neurotic groups, 87–92
in psychotic groups, 388–412
sexual discussion causes, 114–117, 403
subgrouping from, 258–260
termination causes, 161–166, 329–364
therapist influences, 112–114, 229, 287–289
in hospital ward meetings, 418–435
importance of, in dynamic psychiatry, 11–12
in juvenile delinquents, 33
necessity of, 34
nonverbal, 235–236, 418–419
origins of, 2, 12, 22
in patients, neurotic, 87–92
psychotic, 92–94, 388–412
in personality disorders, 96–101
types, 87–92
in psychophysiological disorders, 94–96
in schizophrenia, 19–20, 153–154
separation (*see* Separation anxiety)
social and cultural influences on, 30–32
symptoms of, 178–234
theory of, 13–16
of therapist (*see* Group therapist, anxiety)
Anxiety reactions, 90–91
results in group therapy for, 90–91
symptoms in, 90–91
Anxiety tolerance of patients, 87
Approval, 30
meaning in group behavior, 29–30
members' wish for, 69, 199
Aptitude, psychological, definition of, 3
Aronod, B. M., 56
Arrangement, seating (*see* Seating arrangement)
Arthritic patients, group therapy for, 94–96
Arthritis, 94–96
Assertion, 244
definition of, 157, 426
during therapy, 2, 242
psychotic patients, 426, 427
(*See also* Self-assertion)
Association, thought, looseness of, 388–395, 418, 426
Asthma, 94–96
Asthmatic patients, 94–96
group therapy for, 94–96

Conversation, superficial, in everyday
groups, 26–27, 190–191
in group meetings, 180–190
Conversion hysteria, 91
Cooper, M., 94
Corrective emotional experiences, 71
Corsini, R., 101
Cotherapists in group therapy, 54–56
Countertransference reactions, 5, 52, 76,
132, 288–289, 403–404
Crime, 31
Crises in family groups, 384
Cultural characteristics of alcoholism,
254–255
Cultural groups (*see* Everyday groups)
Cyclothymic personality, 18–19, 21, 96–98
results in group therapy for, 97–98

Day, M., 121
Daydreams, 20
Death, associated with separations, 340–
342
death wishes and associated guilt, 309–
310
denial of feelings at time of, 358–359,
364
of group member, 355–364, 378–381,
409
doubts of, 356–357
reactions of other members to, 355–
364
Defense mechanisms, 67, 96, 389–390,
413–414
definition of, 15
during group therapy, 15–16, 364–369
mode of action, 15
mode of development, 13–14
need to strengthen, 391–393
in psychotic patients, 388–390
relationship to personality type, 15
types of, 14
Defiant behavior, 262–263, 333–334
Deity (*see* God)
Delinquency, 31, 255
Delinquent behavior, 20
Delinquents, juvenile (*see* Juvenile delinquents)
Delirium, acute, 408
Delusions, 393, 400–401, 407–409, 413,
428–429
Denial, 15, 67, 174–175, 185, 188, 204,
255, 262–263, 272, 273, 388–390,
396–398
of death, 358–359, 364
of group's termination, by members,
362–364
by therapist, 362–364

Dependency, 62
definition of, 325–326
gratifications by sexual means, 330
healthy, 27, 325–326
needs of group members, 35, 67, 152,
201–202, 246, 250, 388–412
pathological, 326
unhealthy, 27
Dependency-independency conflicts, 308
Dependent feelings in group therapy, discussion of, 71
Depression, during Christmas season, 305–
306
contagion of, in group meetings, 305–
306
in meetings, internalized anger causes,
325
psychotic, 92–94
treatment of, 399
related to anger and guilt, 316–317,
322–325, 345–354
Depressive personality, results in group
therapy for, 88–89
(*See also* Passive-nonassertive personality)
Depressive psychotic reactions, 388–412
group therapy for, 388–389
classifications of, 388–389
Depressive reaction, 177–178, 180
common behavioral patterns of, 88–89
results in group therapy for, 88–89
Diagnosis, 36, 40, 388–389
*Diagnostic and Statistical Manual of the
American Psychiatric Association*, 16
classification of personality disorders,
96
Diagram, of anxiety level in group therapy, 373
explanation of, 372–375
suggested psychodynamics of, 373–
375
of seating arrangements of group members, 182, 214, 263, 346, 369
Didactic group therapy, 206
description of, 9
Didactic groups, 111
(*See also* Training groups)
Disapproval, 30
group members' fears of, 67, 72, 148,
243, 248–249, 263–270, 296, 299,
345–354
hospital patients' fears of, 423–424
meaning of, in group behavior, 29–30
and rejection, 243
Discussions, group therapist-recorder (*see*
Group therapist, discussions)
Disorders, personality (*see* Personality
disorders; Personality types)
Displacement, 15